PMP® Exam Study Guide

Belinda's Program for Exam Success

Aligns with the *PMBOK® Guide, 6th Edition*

By Belinda S. Goodrich
PMP, PMI-SP, PMI-RMP, PgMP, CAPM, PMI-ACP

www.BelindaGoodrich.com

www.PMLearningSolutions.com

ISBN: 978-1-7323928-3-0

Goodrich Fremaux Publishing

First Printing: 2018

VCN 060-18-09-24-01

Author: Belinda Goodrich
Illustrator: Ana Ranko
Editor: Lisa O'Donnell

PM Learning Solutions, LLC
Phoenix, AZ 85027
www.PMLearningSolutions.com
888-871-7657
Info@PMLearningSolutions.com

This book is not a product of one author at one point in time. It is a culmination of knowledge and feedback from hundreds of PMP students and instructors over several years. It is continuously evaluated and updated based on the most recent information and contributions of those instructors, and students who have taken the most recent version of the PMP exam. We would love to hear your feedback. Please contact us at PMLearningSolutions.com/contact

Ordering Information:
Special discounts are available on quantity purchases by corporations, associations, educators, and others. For details, contact the publisher at the above-listed address.

Although the authors and publisher have made every effort to ensure accuracy and completeness of the information in this book, we assume no responsibility for errors, inaccuracies, omissions, or inconsistencies included herein.

Dedication

You are the company you keep….

To my tribe -
You have inspired me, encouraged me, challenged me, and kept me focused on the important things. I cannot begin to express my gratitude for your support and empowerment. Together, we make this world a better place by using our words, written and spoken, to help others. Thank you for reminding to stay true to who I am and to honor what I can offer.
K.H., B.B., B.B., B.B., L.O., H.K., K.B., E.S., A.V., A.M., N.L., J.F., J.D., M.S., C.Y., and my angel, S.A.L.

Table of Contents

About the Author

Globally recognized as a project and change management expert, Belinda Goodrich is the founder and CEO of The Goodrich Institute and PM Learning Solutions. PM Learning Solutions is focused on delivering world-class project management exam preparation programs and materials. Under The Goodrich Institute, Belinda serves as a consultant to a number of Fortune 500 companies with a focus on improving the project management processes and practices in order to drive business growth.

After over 20 years of corporate project management and executive leadership experience, Belinda "retired" to serve the project management community. The first woman in the world to achieve five of the PMI credentials, Belinda now holds the following: PMP®, CAPM®, PMI-SP®, PMI-ACP®, PMI-RMP®, PgMP®. In addition, Belinda is a Certified Scrum Master.

With a focus on industrial and organizational psychology, Belinda is fascinated with the mind, emotions, and behaviors of project managers and stakeholders and she leverages that fascination to bring practical application to project management techniques. The author of multiple books and courseware on project management and PMI exam topics, Belinda is an in-demand facilitator, speaker, and consultant. As an instructor, Belinda has helped thousands of project managers achieve their project management credentials. Her passion is creating the connection between theoretical project management concepts and real-world business needs through energetic and engaging sessions.

Belinda is the treasurer of the Arizona Chapter of the National Speakers Association.

Follow Belinda!

Facebook: www.facebook.com/PMBelindaSpeaks/

Twitter: @PMBelindaSpeaks

LinkedIn: www.linkedin.com/in/belindagoodrich/

Belinda's Publications:
- Kick Ass Project Manager
- The Will to Win, with Brian Tracy and Jim Cathcart
- You@Work, anthology with HR and OD experts
- PMP / CAPM Exam Prep – Courseware Bundles
- PMP Flashcards
- PMP Pocket Guide, Ultimate Cheat Sheets
- CAPM Flashcards
- PMI-RMP Exam Prep Study Guide
- PMI-RMP Flashcards
- PMI-ACP Flashcards
- PMI-ACP Quick Reference Guide

Engage Belinda for Your Audience!

Are you interested in increasing the engagement and translating that engagement to actual results? Belinda offers a number of keynote presentations and workshops on project management, change management, innovation, disruption, and agility. For more information on her most popular topics, vist her speaker site: www.BelindaGoodrich.com

About PM Learning Solutions, LLC

PM Learning Solutions, LLC is a professional development firm focused on project and change management concepts and certifications. PMLS is founded on the belief of doing the right thing for our students. Unlike other training providers, we take a personal interest in our students, focusing on the highest quality programs and resources with small, personal class experiences. Based out of Phoenix, Arizona, PMLS (formerly Passionate Project Management) was launched in 2008 after Belinda Goodrich recognized a need for more student-first training options. Unlike other providers, we are constantly evaluating and updating our materials based on actual student outcomes on the certification exams, using that data to validate the content aligns with the test exerience.

In 2017, PM Learning Solutions launched PM University (PMU). PMU offers online mock exams and training programs.

With a global reach, the PMLS PMP, CAPM, PMI-ACP, and PMI-RMP courseware is utilized by numerous training companies. PM Learning Solutions, LLC is a PMI Registered Education Provider (R.E.P.) #2973.

www.PMLearningSolutions.com

Foreward

So you purchased this book and are prepared to launch yourself into the world of Project Management Institute for the Project Management Professional (PMP) certification. Well before you get started you might want to consider this a new project that you have been assigned to.

Think about what things do I need to get into place to run this project successfully and how will this new project results change my life? This is a new venture and will require commitment today and for as long as you want to remain a PMP.

The most important step is to get off on the right foot, develop a study plan – in that plan you will list out the when and where you will be working on this project. This book provides valuable resources for assisting with building that plan, what resources you will use and when, and develops your understanding of all the concepts needed to pass this certification exam. However, this plan will also require your expertise in understanding these concepts and when to apply them. The "how to" take a garden rake and use it to be a successful gardener, not just a person with a rake. Most individuals approach this exam lightly, thinking they will memorize the content and be able to answer the questions. Although there is some of that available on this exam, it is more than just a memory effort. It is helpful to visualize the situation or understand the key words in a concept and take action on that particular question.

I have used these materials to teach the PMP Exam Prep to many groups over some 6 years and have found that to be successful you must absorb the content, translate the concepts into stories that you assist you in remembering how to apply a technique and then see the vision into how that technique results in an improved project and communication effort to accomplish more. This is what the PMP Exam Prep is all about, not just the exam but the future lifestyle that you will be creating for yourself and your team.

Note that with this certification you can change the world as you know it and achieve great successes. Using this content, you will have everything that you need to know to prepare for the exam, practice several exams before going to sit for the real test, and continue to review your plan to determine how you are preforming against plan. Belinda Goodrich and PM Learning Solutions is the best partner to take your goals to reality.

John Riopel, PMP, MCP, MCTS

Chapter 1

The PMP Exam

What's in This Chapter

- Introduction
- The Project Management Institute (PMI)®
- The PMP Credential
- The Application Process
- The PMP Exam

Introduction

Congratulations on your decision to pursue Project Management Institute's (PMI) Project Management Professional (PMP)® credential! Being a credentialed (and possibly multi-credentialed) project manager can greatly enhance your career opportunities and salary. While no certification, credential, or degree can guarantee your success nor your skill as a project manager, the PMP is the most widely recognized achievement. Many organizations are using the PMP credential as criteria for employment.

This book is intended to give you a robust study and preparation program to ensure your success on the exam, and to do so, it includes comprehensive yet straightforward information on project management as it aligns with PMI's standards. PMI's credentialing exams are notoriously difficult, and the PMP exam is no different. However, with the appropriate focus and study, I have found that many professional project managers are able to pass on their first attempt.

An important step toward completing your PMP exam is committing to and following through with a dedicated study plan and approach. I recommend pinpointing a date by which you want to complete the exam and building your study plan accordingly. Commit to your date below:

I, _____, commit to completing my PMP exam by

_____.

Using This Book

Aside from the current chapter, each of the chapters in this book includes review questions covering the material. Ideally, you should be scoring at least 80-85% on the review questions. If you are scoring less than that, be sure to identify your gaps and go back to the related sections.

You will also find that each chapter includes a vocabulary review exercise. One of the goals of PMI is to formalize a common project management vernacular, so it is important that you are very strong in your knowledge of these terms and definitions. It is possible that you will find a difference between a term you have used in practice and PMI's definition of that term. Always align with the PMI definition!

This self-study program is broken into four distinct sections. After each section, there is a 75-question practice test in order to give you another informative metric as to your readiness. If you are scoring below 80% on those tests, do not move into the next section until you have remediated your gaps. Finally, this book includes a full-length PMP practice exam, which aligns with the PMI exam blueprint, its allocation of questions, and its timing. Approach this practice exam as though it were the actual exam. Ideally, you should score at least 75 -80% on the practice test to indicate readiness for the actual exam.

Access to PM University – Online Exams

With your purchase of this book, you receive 90-day access to PM Learning Solutions' PM University, our online learning portal with the practice tests. All of the tests in this book are available to you online at PM University. This will allow you to take the tests multiple times in order to track your progress and your readiness! To activate your subscription, go to the following link and enter your tracking number:

https://lp.pmlearningsolutions.com/pmp-self-study/

Project Management Institute (PMI)®

Founded in 1969, the Project Management Institute (PMI) has a primary focus on advancing the practice of project management. A not-for-profit organization, PMI develops and publishes project management standards, manages an extensive research program, and offers professional development opportunities to project managers working in all industries. PMI has more than 250 chapters around the world and 30 industry- or interest-based communities of practice.

As of August 2018, PMI's annual membership fees are:

- Individual – $139 to join, $129 to renew
- Student – $32 to join, $32 to renew
- Retiree – $65 to renew

Benefits of membership include:

- Access to members-only information and resources on PMI.org
- Discounts on the PMI credential exams
- Access to PMI's career framework
- A digital copy of all of the PMI practice standards, including the *PMBOK® Guide*, 5th Edition
- Leadership and volunteer opportunities
- Publications including *PM Network®*, *PMI Today®*, and *Project Management Journal®*
- Up to a 20% discount on PMI store purchases

The PMP® Credential

Created and administered by PMI, the first PMP certification exam was held on 6 October 1984 and of the 56 individuals that participated, 43 passed. As of June 30, 2018, there are more than 859,000 PMP credential holders globally. The PMP credential recognizes professional project managers with demonstrated experience and knowledge of leading and directing project management teams.

PMP Credential Snapshot

	PMP®
Credential Name	Project Management Professional®
Project Role	Experienced project manager responsible for all aspects of project delivery, leading and directing cross-functional project teams.
Eligibility	**HS Diploma or Associates Degree or Global Equivalent:** 7,500 hours leading and directing projects and 35 hours of project management education **OR** **Bachelor's Degree or Higher:** 4,500 hours leading and directing projects and 35 hours of project management education
Exam Information	4 hours 200 questions
Fees	Member $405 Non-Member $555
Credential Maintenance	3 years; 60 PDUs

PMP Requirements

To qualify to apply for the PMP credential, you must meet the following criteria:

- With a high school diploma or global equivalent:
  - Minimum of five years / 60 months non-overlapping professional project management experience with at least 7,500 hours leading and directing the project within the last eight consecutive years *and*
  - 35 contact hours of formal education in project management
- With a bachelor's degree or global equivalent:
  - Minimum of three years / 36 months non-overlapping professional project management experience with at least 7,500 hours leading and directing the project within the last eight consecutive years *and*
  - 35 contact hours of formal education in project management

PMP Application

To complete your PMP application:

1. Create a profile on www.PMI.org.

2. From the PMI home page: Home > Certifications > Project Management Professional (PMP).

3. Select "Apply Now"

4. You will be guided through the application process and asked to provide your educational history and your project management experience.

   - Project management experience must be within eight years from the date of submission.
   - Project management experience is required in each of the five domains: initiating, planning, executing, monitoring and controlling, and closing, although you do not need experience in all domains for all projects.

5. Once you submit your application to PMI, it will take approximately five business days to be reviewed and approved.

   - Approximately 25% of PMP applications are randomly selected for audit. If you are selected, you will need to comply with the audit requirements prior to receiving your eligibility ID.

6. You will receive a notification that your application has been approved, and you will be directed to pay your credential fees.

- If you are a PMI member, the exam fees are $405. For non-members, the fees are $550.
- Upon payment of the exam fees, you will be provided with a payment receipt containing your eligibility ID, which will be used to schedule your exam

Audit

The word *audit* strikes fear into the heart of most people. I assure you, however, if you are truthful and have access to your verification sources, the audit is not that bad! PMI randomly selects approximately 25% of applications for audit to ensure integrity of the credential. If you are audited, verification of your experience and education must be provided to PMI before they will issue your eligibility ID, which you will need to schedule your exam.

You will complete your experience verification using forms that are pre-printed with your submitted experience. You will need to have these forms physically, not electronically, signed by the contact person for the organization you identified on your application. The signed forms need to be placed into an envelope and sealed with the contact's signature across the flap.

These experience forms, your training transcripts, and proof of your education (a photocopy of a diploma or an unofficial transcript) should be sent to PMI in one envelope. It typically takes less than a week from the receipt of the materials for PMI to clear a candidate from audit.

I advise my students to assume that they are going to get audited. It's better to have a good surprise than a bad surprise from PMI. Be certain that the information you are submitting is factual. I also recommend giving the organization contact you list (manager, supervisor, etc.) a heads-up as to what you will be submitting on the application and advise them that you may need them to sign off on the work. There is no need to get proactive signatures, nor is there a need to submit any type of work products or deliverables.

The PMP Exam

Once you have your Eligibility ID, you will be able to schedule your PMP exam online at www.Prometric.com/PMI. PMP exams are offered year-round at designated Prometric sites, and in most U.S. regions, candidates can secure a seat within a few weeks. For other global areas, it can be more challenging to schedule the test.

If you need to reschedule or cancel your exam, do so more than 30 days prior for no cost. If you must cancel or reschedule within 30 days prior to your exam, there will be a $70 fee. If you cancel or reschedule within 48 hours prior to your exam, you will forfeit your entire exam fee.

There are 200 questions on the PMP exam, and you will have four hours to complete the test. Of the 200 questions, 175 are scored and 25 are considered "pre-test" or unscored questions. These are questions that PMI is evaluating for future inclusion in their testing bank. There will be no indication of whether a question will be scored or unscored, so assume that every question counts and never leave a question blank.

The Exam Experience

There are Prometric locations globally, and many of them are located in educational centers such as Sylvan Learning Centers. These test centers provide exams on a multitude of topics, not just the PMI credentials.

You will be asked to provide your government-issued ID, and the name on your ID must match the name on your PMI application. Each testing candidate is provided with a locker, and everything you bring must go into that locker, including your phone, wallet, purse, jacket, etc. Given the introduction of smart watches, do not be surprised if they ask you to leave your watch, and possibly other jewelry, in your locker as well.

If you cannot go through the exam without a drink or a snack, be sure to leave those items outside of your locker on the designated shelf. Food, drinks, and gum are not allowed inside the testing room, and you will not be able to open your locker once the exam has started.

Before you are escorted to your testing seat, it is very likely that you will be searched, asked to turn your pockets inside-out, and/or checked with a security wand. There is no need to be offended by these actions, as they are in-place to protect the integrity of the testing site, the various exams, and the test-takers.

Additional security measures include cameras in the testing room and a camera over your test station. The proctor will also walk through the room periodically. The testing centers are used to administer a number of different exams, and their seating times may vary. Because of this, you may notice that there are people coming in and leaving throughout your exam. If you are worried that this may be distracting to you, the test centers do offer headphones that you can use.

According to the PMI testing guidelines, candidates must use the calculator that is built into the testing module on the computer. However, when asked, some test centers will provide candidates with a single-function calculator. If you prefer the hand-held calculator to the system calculator, it does not hurt to ask for it. The worst that they can say is "no."

The testing system is relatively straightforward. Once seated at your test station, you will be allowed 15 minutes to complete a system tutorial. This tutorial will show you the features of the exam system, and it typically does not take more than a few minutes to complete.

Once you are done with the tutorial, you can choose either to wait for the remaining time to expire or to start the actual exam, starting your four-hour clock. You will be provided with either scratch paper and pencils or a dry-erase board with markers. Many of the test centers are moving to the dry-erase boards.

Some candidates choose to start by doing a memorization "dump sheet," including formulas, key concepts, etc. I would recommend assuming you are going to be provided with a dry-erase board rather than a packet of paper and being cognizant of the amount of space required for your dump sheet. Ensure that you leave room for any notes and equations that you will need to work through during the exam.

In 2017, there was a change instituted at the Prometric locations. Previously, candidates could write their "dump sheet" during the 15-minute time allocation to complete the system tutorial. Now, however, candidates will be instructed to wait until their actual exam time begins. As such, be sure that you are able to complete your "dump sheet" quickly. I will discuss the "dump sheet" in more detail in Chapter 14.

On the testing screen, you will be shown one question at a time, with a clock in one corner and a question counter in the other. For each question presented, you will have the opportunity to answer it, answer it and mark it, or leave it blank. In addition, there are now options to strike through answers that you believe are incorrect and highlight pieces of information that you believe are important within the content of the question.

Exam Anxiety

Exam anxiety is one of the most concerning aspects of these tests and can be particularly harmful. It is important to recognize the symptoms of our "fight-or-flight" response to testing. When we are nervous, our body is getting ready to either fight the threat or run from the threat, which means that our blood flow is redirected from the logical processing part of our brain to our large muscles. Unfortunately, those large muscles are not very helpful for reading complex questions.

My recommendation is to cycle through the questions, answering short or easy ones first. Grab the low-hanging fruit first! This will help you burn down your adrenaline to a more helpful level while also dispelling your fear of the unknown. You can cycle through the questions as many times as you need to within the four hours. Do not sit on one question for an extended period of time. It will not only waste time, but it can potentially increase your anxiety.

Once you finish a pass of the 200 questions, you will have the option to review all the questions or just the questions you left blank and/or marked. Go to the questions you left blank and/or marked, answering as many as you can easily, and repeat.

Exam Strategy

I strongly discourage reviewing questions you have already answered. Your first gut instinct is usually correct, even if you do not know why your gut is leaning towards a particular answer. The exception to this is math questions involving some calculations. It is never a bad idea to run through the calculations again to be sure you answered correctly. I suggest marking any math questions to be sure you double-check your math. Another exception would be if another question prompted you to remember something applicable to a previous question.

It is very possible that you will have questions on the exam that contain typographical, punctuation, or grammatical errors. It happens. Do not allow that to distract or discourage you as you work through the questions.

For example, on my exam, I had a question that referenced my "high rise" project, so I envisioned building a high-rise building. After reading it through a few times, I realized that it was actually a "high-risk" project, not a "high rise" project.

Submitting Your Exam

Once you complete all 200 questions, you can submit your exam. Be sure that you have not left any questions blank, as they will count against you. It is more likely than not that you will feel a bit unsure when you submit your exam. This is due to the fact that, for many of the questions, you have answered from PMI's perspective rather than your own. Do not use that as an excuse to go back through the exam and change your answers. Usually your first response to a question is the correct one.

Upon submission, you will be prompted to complete a brief survey that will ask questions about your exam preparation and experience. After you submit the survey, you will be shown your pass or fail result on the screen. Acknowledge your result on the computer and collect your printed score report from the front desk.

Your score report will show your results and proficiency ratings (Needs Improvement, Below Target, Target, Above Target) in the following domains:

- Initiation – 13% of the exam questions
- Planning – 24% of the exam questions
- Execution – 31% of the exam questions
- Monitoring and Controlling – 25% of the exam questions
- Closing – 7% of the exam questions

Passing the PMP Exam

"What is the passing score?" is the most common question I receive related to the PMI exams. And the unwelcome response is "it's not that easy." A number of years ago, PMI stopped publishing the passing score for the exams and changed the approach to scoring. PMI employs a robust psychometric analysis model. Each exam question is evaluated and scored by a test population of project managers, and an appropriate weighting is applied. Depending on your particular pull of questions and their associated weights, the score to pass can vary. If you have an "easy" pull of questions, your passing score will be higher than someone that has a "difficult" pull of questions. Each exam experience is unique.

Candidates can pass the exam without being "above target" in any one domain but must have multiple domains in which they are at "target." A frustration associated with PMI exams is its inability to identify and address gaps beyond a simple proficiency rating in a domain. You will not receive a copy of your exam, nor will you know how many questions you answered correctly. However, in August 2017, PMI did enhance the score report to provide additional information and guidance.

If you do not pass your exam, you have the option to repeat the exam up to two more times during your eligibility year. Your eligibility year begins the day your application is approved by PMI. To repeat the exam, you will be responsible for paying the re-examination fee. The fee is $275 for PMI members and $375 for non-PMI members.

As I mentioned previously, I suggest that you score at least a 75% on the practice test given in this book to indicate readiness for the actual exam. If you are able to score 75% or higher within the time allocation, you are in a very strong position to pass your actual PMP exam.

Maintain Your PMP Credential

Once you pass your exam, your PMP credential will be valid for a period of three years from the exam date. During those three years, you must achieve no less than 60 professional development units (PDUs) of continuing education in order to maintain your credential.

PMI recently launched the Talent Triangle®, requiring credential holders to earn PDUs in the following categories: Technical, Leadership, and Strategic and Business. PMP credential maintenance requires a minimum of 35 education PDUs:

- Technical education – a minimum of 8 PDUs
- Leadership education – a minimum of 8 PDUs
- Strategic and business education – a minimum of 8 PDUs

In addition to education, PDUs can be earned through your experience and activities, up to a maximum of 25 PDUs.

- Working as a practitioner – a maximum of 8 PDUs.
- Other giving back, such as creating content, giving presentations, sharing knowledge, and volunteering – a maximum of 25 PDUs (including those you have earned working as a practitioner)

All PDUs you earn are reported through PMI's Continuing Certification Requirements (CCR) system.

Study Guide Introduction

This certification exam preparation program is based upon the information contained within *A Guide to the Project Management Body of Knowledge (PMBOK® Guide),* 6th Edition. The *PMBOK® Guide* is the Project Management Institute's (PMI)® sum of knowledge and identified best practices for project management.

After completing each chapter in this study guide, test your retention of the concepts with the chapter review questions. Questions should be completed as a closed-book exercise. If you will want to complete the chapter review questions multiple times, I suggest writing your answers on a separate sheet of paper. Each chapter review includes 15 questions and the time limit to complete the questions is 18 minutes. The answer key and explanations are provided for all questions.

For chapters two through fifteen, there are also vocabulary reviews. Vocabulary is an integral part of the PMP exam, so be sure to complete all of the vocabulary review exercises. I recommend also purchasing or making flashcards to test yourself on the terms and definitions.

This study guide is split into four sections:

- Section 1: Chapters 1 - 5
- Section 2: Chapters 6 - 8
- Section 3: Chapters 9 - 11
- Section 4: Chapters 12 - 15

There is a 75-question practice test at the end of each section. These should be completed closed-book and within the time allocation assigned. Target score for the 75-question practice tests is 80% or higher. I recommend tracking your review question and practice exam results on the next page. This will help you target any gaps for further review.

Score Tracking Sheet

Section 1

Chapter 2 Review: _____	/	15	=	_____ %
Chapter 3 Review: _____	/	15	=	_____ %
Chapter 4 Review: _____	/	15	=	_____ %
Chapter 5 Review: _____	/	15	=	_____ %
Practice Test 1: _____	/	**75**	=	_____ %

Section 2

Chapter 6 Review: _____	/	15	=	_____ %
Chapter 7 Review: _____	/	15	=	_____ %
Chapter 8 Review: _____		15		_____ %
Practice Test 2: _____	/	**75**	=	_____ %

Section 3

Chapter 9 Review: _____	/	15	=	_____ %
Chapter 10 Review: _____	/	15	=	_____ %
Chapter 11 Review: _____	/	15	=	_____ %
Practice Test 3: _____	/	**75**	=	_____ %

Section 4

Chapter 12 Review: _____	/	15	=	_____ %
Chapter 13 Review: _____	/	15	=	_____ %
Chapter 14 Review: _____	/	15	=	_____ %
Chapter 15 Review: _____	/	15		_____ %
Practice Test 4: _____	/	**75**	=	_____ %
PMP Final Exam: _____	/	**200**	=	_____ %

Proficient	=	**85% - 100%**
Moderately Proficient	=	**75% - 85%**
Below Proficient	=	**< 75%**

Chapter 2

Project Management

What's in This Chapter

- Introduction to Project Management
- Project Environment

Introduction to Project Management

What is a Project?

According to the *PMBOK® Guide*, a project is defined as "a temporary endeavor undertaken to create a unique product, service, or result" (Project Management Institute, 2017, p. 4). All projects are conducted to attain an objective and then terminate. Even in the earliest civilizations, people utilized projects to create, develop, and enhance their surroundings, their products, and their cities. Looking back at history it is easy to find evidence of projects and project management long before the industrial or technical revolutions. Consider the Pyramids of Giza or the Great Wall of China as examples of project marvels.

In today's modern businesses, projects are used to propel organizations forward by adding to or enhancing their existing product lines, creating a service or capability to perform a service, improving the existing product or service lines, researching a topic or strategy, or a combination of any of these. For businesses to grow, thrive, succeed, and compete, they must innovate and adapt. Innovation and adaptation require change. And the purposeful management of change is the concept of project management.

Projects should provide a benefit. Those benefits may be tangible or intangible. Tangible benefits may be profits, equity, tools or market share whereas intangible benefits may be brand recognition, strategic alignment, reputation, or goodwill. Projects may result in intended or unintended positive and negative impacts.

Projects create a unique result, although there may be some repetitive elements. A developer has purchased land and is subdividing the land into individual home lots. The construction of each home is a project. While each home that is built in the subdivision will leverage similar floor plans, landscaping, and contractors, each home has its own individual attributes, and as such, would be considered a unique output.

While all projects are temporary, the actual duration of projects can vary, from a few weeks to years. Projects can terminate for many reasons, but ideally when the objectives are met or for convenience. However, many projects terminate under less than desired situations, such as when funding is exhausted, the objectives cannot be met, or the resources are not available to do the project work.

Example: Projects

A local chamber of commerce is putting together a large recognition event for its members.

A financial services firm is launching a new website with on-line account capabilities.

An engineering firm is implementing a new software system.

A training company is developing a new instructor-led training course.

Belinda's Hint

The PMP® exam is a "generalist" exam. Although many of the questions are structured with an information technology or construction set-up, that information is immaterial to what PMI® is really asking. Be careful that you do not fall into the trap of thinking they are testing you on something industry-specific.

For example, I had a student who worked in the construction field. Upon completing his exam, he was frustrated that one of the questions did not state the correct time for concrete to cure. I explained that they were most likely asking a question about lag time or about a dependency, not a question on concrete curing. Do not go down the rabbit hole because a question happens to be staged in your area of subject matter knowledge. Look for the project management concept!

Project Drivers

Leaders initiate projects based on factors that impact their organizations. Typically, those factors are categorized as regulatory, legal or social, stakeholder requests, business or technological strategy change or implementation, or product, service, or process creation, improvement, or fix.

Projects are conducted to achieve or contribute to an organization's strategic plan. Each project is authorized in reaction to a driver. As the project manager, it is important to understand the driver behind your project. Based on the driver, your management, structure, oversight, and tasks may vary. Project management is never a one-size-fits-all approach.

Common project drivers include:

- Business process improvements
- Competitive forces
- Customer requests
- Economic changes
- Environmental considerations
- Legal requirement
- Market demand
- Material issues
- New technology
- Political changes
- Social need
- Stakeholder demands
- Strategic opportunity or business need

Strategic Alignment

The alignment of the project to the organization's strategic plan should be understood by the project manager. By understanding that link, the ability to successfully lead and complete the project is increased. The project manager is responsible for ensuring that their assigned project contributes to the organization's strategic goals and plan.

Belinda's Hint

On the PMP exam you may experience questions related to the appropriate escalation of issues. While "escalate" is not a common response to a question on this exam, if your project does not align with, or conflicts with, the organization's strategic goals, the project manager is expected to escalate that information to the sponsor.

If the sponsor chooses to pursue the project regardless, the project manager may have to escalate further. I jokingly call this a "career limiting move" (CLM!) that in practice you may not necessarily think to do, but on the exam, it is imperative you answer from PMI's recommended handling.

The Role of the Project Manager

Project managers have the responsibility to satisfy the needs of the project, which can include task needs, team needs, and individual needs. The role of the project manager has moved from being strictly a subject matter or technical expert to being a leader. The project manager's role is increasingly strategic. Effective project management involves not only having specific technical skills and general management knowledge, but also the ability to apply effective project management concepts and best practices.

As a project manager, you should possess knowledge of project management practices and theories and the ability to accomplish assigned tasks while applying your project management knowledge. In addition, you should have personal effectiveness (soft skills!), such as attitudes, core personality characteristics, and leadership, so that you are able to guide the project team while achieving project objectives and balancing project constraints.

PMI classifies project management skills and competencies into three categories, known as the PMI Talent Triangle®: technical project management, strategic and business management, and leadership. As mentioned in Chapter One, upon earning your PMP® credential, there are continuing education requirements related to the PMI Talent Triangle. PMP holders must complete 60 professional development units (PDUs) every three years via PMI's Continuing Certification Requirements System (CCRS).

Technical project management. Technical project management includes the skills and knowledge related to performing the job of a project manager. Technical project management involves understanding personal expertise and being skilled at securing additional expertise as necessary. Managing the technical aspects of a project involves managing the critical success factors, the project schedule, the resources, the project budget and financial reporting, and the issue log, as some key artifacts. It also involves understanding different approaches to project management, such as traditional, waterfall, iterative and agile, and applying the most appropriate approach based on the environment and project constraints.

Strategic and business management. Strategic and business management skills speak to the increasingly strategic role of the project manager as a key party in enabling the organization to achieve its strategic goals. The project manager must be able to work with various levels of leadership within the organization and implement the work of the project that enables the business value to be captured.

Leadership. Leadership includes the knowledge and skills that are necessary to guide, motivate and direct the project team and project stakeholders. An often-times overlooked competency of project management, effective leadership is critical to project success. Leadership encompasses the soft skills, such as communication, active listening, problem solving, facilitation, and cultural sensitivity and diversity. A skilled leader can assess a situation and apply the most appropriate leadership style. Leadership styles include:

- Servant leader – puts others first, focusing on their growth, learning, development and well-being
- Transformational – empowers others through sharing ideals, encourages innovation and creativity
- Transactional – focuses on goals, feedback, and accomplishment to determine rewards, management by exception (only intervening when necessary)
- Laissez-faire – allows the team to make their own decisions, hands-off style
- Charismatic – inspires others, high-energy, and enthusiastic
- Interactional – combination of transactional, transformational, and charismatic leadership styles

Leadership Versus Management

While the terms leadership and management are often used interchangeably, they are distinct behaviors and skill sets. When a project manager perceives their self as simply a task-manager or "glorified babysitter," they are describing management, not leadership. In today's complex environment, it is necessary for project managers to transcend just managing the project and must provide leadership to the team and the organization.

Management may involve using positional power, relying on control, focusing on near-term goals, accepting the status quo, and focusing on operational issues. This reflects the old-school style of command-and-control management. Leadership, in contrast, is more about guiding, influencing, and collaborating. Leadership inspires trust, creates a compelling long-range vision, challenges the status quo, and focuses on vision, alignment, motivation and inspiration.

Politics and Power

One of the key aspects of leadership is understanding the impact of organizational politics and power on the project, the project objectives, and the project team. Regardless of the type of organization, politics abound when multiple parties are brought together in an organization. Internal politics must be recognized and considered as they will impact the project and the project management approach. External politics associated with any vendors, customers, government regulators or sources, must also be considered.

There are numerous forms of power that the project manager may have or can use. It is up to the project manager to understand the forms of power and when it is appropriate to use it; if it's an option. There is not one source of power that is right or wrong, it is about understanding the different sources of power and influence and applying them based on the needs of the project, the organization, and the team.

Power	Description
Positional	Power that is designated within the project charter allowing the project manager to act on behalf of the sponsor, also known as formal, authoritative, and legitimate power
Referent	The ability to influence because individuals respect the project manager
Reward	The ability to influence by incenting the project team and stakeholders with something that they value
Expert	The ability to influence the project team and stakeholders because they respect the project manager's skills or subject matter expertise
Coercive / punitive	The ability to influence the project team and stakeholders based on the fear of punishment (such as losing their jobs or bonuses), also called penalty authority
Informational	The power and authority to gather and distribute information
Situational	Power that is gained due to a situation or circumstance
Personal / charismatic	Similar to referent, influence based on the project manager's personality
Relational	Power that comes through the development of networks and connections
Ingratiating	Power that comes through flattery or actions to win favor
Pressure-based	Control originating from limiting choices or options to gain compliance
Guilt-based	The ability to influence by using an obligation or sense of duty
Persuasive	Influence that originates from being persuasive in arguments or case-building
Avoiding	Power derived from refusing to participate

Project Management

According to the *PMBOK® Guide*, project management is defined as "the application of knowledge, skills, tools and techniques to project activities to meet project requirements" (Project Management Institute, 2017, p. 5). The project manager's primary role is to successfully achieve the project's objectives while minimizing change, especially in predictive or waterfall project approaches. Adaptive or agile projects are able to incorporate changes by way of their approach. According to the Project Management Institute, poorly managed projects can result in rework, poor quality, unmet schedule or budget requirements, reputational damage, stakeholder dissatisfaction, and an inability to achieve the project objectives.

Constraints

The project manager has the primary responsibility of managing the project constraints. Project constraints are limitations placed upon the project that the project manager must consider, manage, and balance throughout the project life cycle. Project constraints commonly include:

- Scope
- Schedule
- Cost
- Quality (project and product)
- Resources
- Risk (uncertainty)

The constraints are related in that if one changes, there will likely be an impact on the other constraints (likely, but not always!). For example, to build a two-bedroom house, we determine it will cost $200,000 and take four months. If the customer changes the scope and is requesting a five-bedroom house, it is likely that the cost will increase. The timeline may change, as well. There are some situations, however, when a constraint may be adjusted without impacting the others, such as when we fast-track the schedule: the delivery date has been accelerated, without impacting the scope or the cost.

The management of the constraints and the ability to deliver the project within the constraints dictates the perceived quality of the project. If the project is delivered within the schedule and budget requirements, typically this would be considered high project quality. It is possible to have high project quality with low product quality and vice versa. Product quality is determined by the customer or end-user based on how well the result meets their expectations. The project could be late or over-budget, thus low project quality, yet the final product meets expectations and is considered high product quality.

Belinda's Hint

In Chapter 3, you will be introduced to the PMBOK® Guide Framework. The left-hand column of the Framework references the project management knowledge areas. You will notice, not coincidentally, that the constraints align with most of the knowledge areas.

The most commonly referred to constraints are scope, time (or schedule), and cost. In the past, this was known as the "triple constraint" or the "iron triangle." It evolved to also encompass quality. You may see this still referred to as the triple constraint, iron triangle, or triple constraint plus quality on the exam. However, it is important to understand that constraints can come from multiple areas, as described above.

Project Life Cycle

Project management involves managing the project life cycle. The project life cycle consists of the defined project phases for each project, from initiation through to completion. Allowing for increased control, the project life cycle is defined by the organization and is documented within the project management methodology. If an organization does not have a methodology in place with dictated project phases, the project manager may break the work down into manageable phases, intuitively.

The project life cycle will vary based on the industry, project, and organization, and may have sequential, iterative or overlapping phases. Typically, the project life cycle has relatively low cost and staffing levels at the beginning that peak during the middle phases and taper off near completion. However, the typical cost and staffing curve may be different for some projects, specifically those that require a large up-front expenditure. Project risk is the opposite: at the beginning of the project there is increased risk, or uncertainty, that gradually decreases as project decisions are made and deliverables are accepted. The project life cycle produces one project.

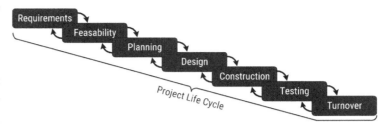

The ability to influence the final characteristics of the product, without significantly impacting cost, is highest at the beginning of the project, and decreases as the project proceeds and more work has been completed on the design and development of the products to be delivered. Introducing change late in the project can be very costly from a re-work perspective. This is especially true in waterfall or predictive environments.

There are various types of project life-cycles, typically driven by the organization, the industry, and the type of product the project is creating.

Predictive life cycles. In a predictive life cycle, the project scope, time, and cost are determined as early in the life cycle as possible. These are also known as fully plan-driven life cycles. Predictive life cycles are typically used for projects that are repetitive and predictable, such as building track housing.

Iterative / incremental life cycles. Iterative and incremental life cycles have project phases, or iterations, that intentionally repeat as the project team's understanding of the product increases and the scope is elaborated one iteration at a time. This is known as *progressive elaboration*, adding detail as the project progresses. Progressive elaboration recognizes the fact that "we don't know what we don't know". Given the volatility and pace of change of the environment, many organizations are moving more towards these types of life cycles.

Adaptive life cycles. Adaptive life cycles are utilized to respond to high levels of change and increased stakeholder involvement. These life cycles are also known as agile or change-driven approaches, such as Scrum, XP, and Lean. Adaptive life cycles tend to be used primarily in IT and software development projects, but there are expanding applications in other industries.

Within the project life cycle, some phases are involved in developing the product, service, or result the project was chartered to deliver. These phases are known as the development life cycle. Development life cycles may be predictive, iterative, incremental, adaptive, or a hybrid of the various types.

Project Phases and Phase Gates

The project and development life cycle consist of multiple phases. A phase is a "collection of logically related project activities that culminates in the completion of one or more deliverables" (Project Management Institute, 2017, p. 20). Phases may be defined by a name, a number, a duration, resource requirements, or entrance/exit criteria to start or complete the phase. The naming of phases is generally dictated by the organization's project management methodology, industry standard, best practice, or the project manager's experience.

Phase gates represent the stopping or completion point or the starting point of a phase and are used to determine what will happen next for the project based on the progress against the plan or expectations. In the go/no-go decisioning process, the project may continue to the next phase as-is or with modifications, the project may end, it may stay in the phase, or it may repeat the phase or components of the phase. Phase gates are also known as phase reviews, stage gates, kill points, and phase entrances/exits.

Product Life Cycle

As compared to the *project life* cycle, the product life cycle reflects the phases involved in any type of product, regardless of product type or industry. The product life cycle has sequential but non-overlapping phases and does not differ by industry or product. The product life cycle will include multiple project life cycles, in a one-to-many relationship: one product life cycle encompasses multiple project life cycles. On the exam, read the question carefully and be cautious not to confuse the *product life cycle* with the *project life cycle*. Your exam is focused on project life cycles which are frequently a component of the product life cycle.

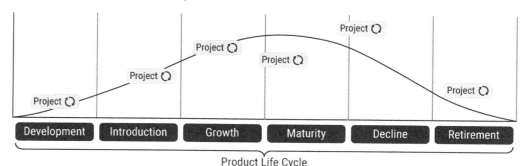

Product Life Cycle

Project Management Office

Depending on the organizational structure, there may be a project or program management office (PMO). A PMO functions as a centralized coordinator of projects or programs and may have roles and responsibilities that vary by organization. Some of the key features of a PMO:

- Share and coordinate resources across projects
- Develop and manage project policies, procedures, templates, and other standard documentation. These policies, procedures, and templates are considered organizational process assets (OPA). OPA will be discussed in more detail in an upcoming section.
- Coordinate communication across projects
- Conduct and coordinate project manager education and mentoring
- Identify and develop standards
- Centrally monitor the status of all projects

PMOs can have varying roles and responsibilities based on the organizational need and structure. PMOs may be supportive, controlling or directive.

Supportive PMO. A supportive PMO is a PMO with low control, serving in a consultative role to the project. The PMO provides templates, lessons learned, and training to the projects and mainly serves as a project repository. Consider it a one-way street: providing support and tools.

Controlling PMO. A controlling PMO is a PMO with moderate control, offering support but also measuring compliance. The PMO provides support and implements controls and procedures and monitors the projects' compliance with the defined framework. Typically, the PMO validates compliance with the project management frameworks or methodologies, standardized templates and tools, and conformance to any type of organizational governance. Consider it a two-way street: we will provide the tools, but we are going to check for compliance with those tools, standards, and procedures (AKA the "project police!).

Directive PMO. A directive PMO is a PMO with high control that directly manages the projects. The project managers report directly into the PMO versus the PMO being a separate party or organization.

Project Stakeholders

One of the most important aspects of project management is identifying and managing the project stakeholders. It is so important, in fact, that PMI added the Stakeholder Management Knowledge Area in the 5th edition of the *PMBOK®Guide*.

Stakeholders are individuals or organizations that are either involved in the project or are affected by the project's result. Stakeholders may be resistors or supporters. While ideally there are multiple supporters on a project, the reality is that there will always be resistors. Those resistors will need to be managed very closely. Remember the old adage "keep your friends close, keep your enemies closer!": this is especially true in project management. This is one of the reasons that high emotional intelligence is important for project managers: you need to purposely seek out those that can cause problems for your project. This is very much against our natural instinct to surround ourselves with people who support and value our work and contributions.

Stakeholders will have varying levels of interest and authority and may have a positive or negative influence on the project. Stakeholders are considered *key* stakeholders if they have decision-making authority or can make changes to the project. Because we are typically seeking to minimize changes on the projects, it is critical to determine the *key* stakeholders, so we are aware of the potential change-makers.

It is the responsibility of the project management team to identify the stakeholders (early and proactively). It is not up to the stakeholders to raise their hand or step-forward proactively: *you* need to seek them out. It is important to understand and document their requirements, expectations, and concerns as it relates to the project and manage those expectations and concerns throughout the project. In doing so, you will need to manage their influence as it relates to the requirements, based upon their power, interest, and influence. Stakeholders should be classified as internal or external in order to full assess their impact and role.

Stakeholders include:

The project sponsor. The sponsor is the individual who authorizes the project and the project funding. The sponsor may be external or internal to the project manager's organization and is responsible for promoting the project, from initiation through to completion. The sponsor leads the project through the initiating processes until the project is formally authorized and plays a significant role in the development of the initial scope and charter. In most organizations, the sponsor serves as an escalation path for the project manager. They may be involved in go/no-go decisions, phase-end reviews, and scope changes. The sponsor also ensures smooth transition after project closure.

Belinda's Hint

As the sponsor is the ultimate decision-maker on the project, whenever possible you only want to have one sponsor. More than one sponsor can cause conflicts and delays in decision-making, thus increasing the risk to the project. (Think: too many cooks in the kitchen!).

You are the project manager, implying that whenever possible, you should be attempting to resolve issues and problems with your project team prior to escalating to the sponsor. The primary exception to this would be a question of scope where only the sponsor can confirm the requirement. If you get a question with the potential answer of "escalate", read the question carefully! Is this something that you and your team can work through first, prior to escalating?

Customer or end-user. The customer or end-user may be internal or external to the project manager's organization. They will be the recipient of the final product, service, or result delivered by the project. On the exam, they will give various scenarios in the questions – in some you are working on an internal project, others you are delivering for an external customer.

Sellers. Also known as vendors, suppliers, or contractors, sellers are parties external to the organization that provide products or services based on an agreement or contract. I will be discussing sellers and the procurement processes in more detail later in this book.

Business partners. Business partners are organizations that have a relationship with the enterprise, providing specialized expertise or fill a specified role such as installation, customization, training, or support.

Organizational groups. There are multiple organizational groups that may be involved in the project. They are internal stakeholders who are affected by the activities of the project team (sales and marketing, human resources, legal, finance, operations, etc.).

Functional managers. Functional managers have the responsibility for a specific functional area and may provide resources, such as subject matter experts (SMEs) for the project.

Other stakeholders. Anyone involved in or affected by the project are considered stakeholders. They could be subject matter experts, consultants, financial institutions, or government regulators. It is important to recognize that from a PMI-perspective, the work *stakeholder* is a very generic term!

Project Team

Members of the project team are also considered stakeholders. The project team includes the project manager and the group of individuals who will be performing the work of the project. Typically, the team is comprised of individuals from different groups with varying subject matter expertise. The structure and characteristics of the project team can vary widely, but the project manager is the leader of the team regardless of the authority the project manager may have over its members.

Project teams may be dedicated to the project full-time or they may be assigned to the project on a part-time basis. In dedicated teams, all or a majority of the project team members are assigned to work full-time on the project and may be co-located or virtual. This represents the simplest structure for the project manager as the lines of authority are clear. In part-time teams, the project manager and the team members work on the project while remaining in their existing organizations and continuing to carry out their normal functions. The functional managers maintain control over the resources.

The project team includes:

Project manager. The project manager is the individual assigned by the performing organization to achieve the project objectives.
Project management staff. The project management staff are the members who perform project management activities such as scheduling, budgeting, reporting and control, communications, risk management, etc. This role may be performed or supported by a PMO.
Project staff. The project staff are the members of the team who carry out the work of creating the project deliverables.
Supporting experts. Supporting experts perform activities required to develop or execute the project management plan, such as contracting, financial management, quality control, etc. and may have a full-time or ad-hoc role.
User or customer representatives. User or customer representatives are members of the organization who will accept the deliverables or products of the project.
Business partner members. Business partner members are members of business partners' organizations assigned primarily for coordination aspects.

Project Environment

In organizations, projects do not exist alone but are a component of a much broader context. The project manager needs to understand the relationship between projects, programs, portfolios, and operations.

Programs

A program is a collection of related projects managed in a consistent method to achieve a shared objective. Programs are managed by a program manager who has the responsibility for obtaining the program objectives through oversight of the project managers that own the individual, component projects. Project managers that are managing projects that are part of a program need to be aware of any schedule dependencies or required sharing of data, information, or outputs that are related to the program. Program management focuses on those interdependencies between the projects and the program level, ensuring the optimal approach for managing them. Although your exam is focused on project management, it is very possible that you will receive a question or questions regarding the implications of managing a project that is a component of a program. Program management in and of itself, however, is not a component of the PMP exam.

Portfolios

A portfolio is a collection of projects or programs that may or may not be related. An organization's portfolio of projects and programs should align with the company's strategic goals and direction. Portfolios may be organized at the enterprise or the organizational level. Portfolio management focuses on aligning the projects and programs to achieve strategic objectives.

Operations

Operations are the ongoing production of goods and services and the core business functions of the organization. Unlike projects, operations are ongoing and sustain the business. Although operations are not within the scope of projects and project management, there is a relationship between projects and operations that needs to be understood and managed. As products are developed, processes are improved, products are retired, and phases are closed, there will be interactions between the projects and the organization's operations.

Organizational Structures

Based on the organizational structure of the parent organization, a project manager may have varying levels of authority and responsibility. There are many diverse types of organizational structures:

Organic or simple. In an organic or simple structure, the project work is flexible, and the resources work side-by-side. The project manager has a part-time role and little to no authority.

Multi-divisional. In a multi-divisional structure, the work is grouped by the product, process, program, region or customer type. The project manager has a part-time role and little to no authority.

Virtual. In a virtual structure, work is conducted in a network with various points of connection. The project manager may be full time or part time with low to moderate authority.

Hybrid. In a hybrid structure, there is a mix of the various types of organizational structures. The project manager's role and their authority, therefore, are mixed.

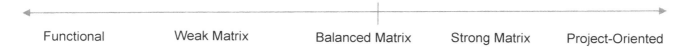

| Functional | Weak Matrix | Balanced Matrix | Strong Matrix | Project-Oriented |

Functional. In a functional structure, the project work is done within the functional area. The project manager has a part-time role and little to no authority. This structure best leverages the depth and breadth of subject matter expertise as projects reside in the respective functional area.

Weak matrix. In a weak matrix structure, the work is grouped by job function and resembles a functional structure. The project manager has a part-time role and minimal authority, and functions more as a coordinator or expeditor of project activities. Coordinators typically have no authority, whereas expeditors may have some authority.

Balanced matrix. In a balanced matrix structure, the work is grouped by job function, and the project manager is embedded in the functions, with low to moderate authority. A balanced matrix organization may also be referred to as a matrix organization.

Strong matrix. In a strong matrix structure, the work is grouped by job function with the project manager having a full-time, designated project management job role. The project manager has moderate to high authority.

Project-oriented. In a project-oriented structure, work is grouped by the projects. The project manager has a full-time designated job role and high to almost total authority. Typically, project-oriented organizations deliver products, services, or solutions to external customers as their primary business, such as consulting firms, construction companies, etc. The project manager will have resources available to them, such as project schedulers, business analysts, etc. This is also known as a projectized organization or structure.

Belinda's Hint

On the exam, you can assume you are in a balanced matrix environment unless given reason to believe otherwise. In a balanced matrix (or simply "matrix") environment, the team members report administratively to their functional manager and dotted-line to the project manager. As such, the functional manager retains the control of the individuals. Because communication is both horizontal (to the team members) and vertical (to the functional managers), it can be more complex. Essentially the team members have two managers which can lead to potential conflicts.

Chapter 2 - Review Questions

Time Limit: 18 Minutes

1. **Based on the PMI definition, which of the following would not be considered a project?**
   A. Running an election campaign for a political candidate
   B. Building a bridge over a river to add a new transportation route
   C. Piloting aircraft for a commercial airline with global reach
   D. Writing a book on project management

2. **The product life cycle differs from the project life cycle in that a project life cycle:**
   A. Produce multiple projects within it
   B. Will differ by industry
   C. Does not use a methodology
   D. Dictates the project management activities to be used

3. **A project is:**
   A. A set of sequential activities performed in a process or system
   B. A revenue-generating activity that needs to be accomplished while achieving customer satisfaction
   C. An ongoing endeavor undertaken to meet customer or market requirements
   D. A temporary endeavor undertaken to create a unique product, service, or result

4. **Project management is:**
   A. The integration of the critical path method and the earned value management system
   B. The application of knowledge, skills, tools, and techniques to project activities to meet project requirements
   C. The application of knowledge, skills, wisdom, science, and art to organizational activities to achieve operational excellence
   D. A subset of most engineering and other technical disciplines

5. **Managing a project includes:**
   A. Balancing the competing demands for quality, scope, time, and cost
   B. Integrating requirements of profitability, low cost, and legal responsibility
   C. Implementation of software, hardware, and other systems to enhance organizational efficiency
   D. Supporting human factors, communications, discipline, and performance management

6. **A program is a:**
   A. Group of related tasks lasting one year or less
   B. Group of related projects managed in a coordinated way
   C. Project with a cost over $1 million
   D. Sequence of steps constituting a project

7. **Organizations perform work to achieve a set of objectives. All of the following are true about projects and operations work except:**
   A. Both projects and operations are constrained by limited resources
   B. Operations are ongoing and repetitive, while projects are temporary and unique
   C. Both projects and operations are planned, executed, and controlled
   D. All activities in the organization can be addressed within the organization's normal operational limits. Therefore, projects are rarely utilized as a means of achieving an organization's strategic plan.

8. **Project managers or the organization can divide projects into phases. Collectively, these phases are known as the:**
   A. Project waterfall
   B. Project life cycle
   C. Project life stages
   D. Project life quality circle

9. **In understanding the project environment, all of the following are true except:**
   A. Projects are planned and implemented in a social, economic, and environmental context
   B. Projects may have intended positive and/or negative impacts
   C. Projects may have unintended positive and/or negative impacts
   D. The project team rarely should consider the political and physical environmental contexts of the project

10. **In considering project stakeholders, the project management team must do all of the following except:**
    A. As much as possible, create conflicts among stakeholders to allow the project team to get its work done
    B. Identify the stakeholders
    C. Determine the stakeholders' requirements and expectations
    D. To the extent possible, manage stakeholders' influence in relation to the requirements to ensure a successful project

11. **The project manager is more likely to have a full-time role in what type of an organization?**
    A. Functional
    B. Weak matrix
    C. Strong matrix
    D. Small capitalization

12. **Your friend has been hired as a project manager at a new company. She has very little project experience but has been assigned a new project. The organization she will be working in is a matrix organization. She can expect communications to be:**
    A. Complex
    B. Non-automated
    C. Open
    D. Easy

13. **The term "progressive elaboration" refers to:**
    A. Constantly changing project scope
    B. Adding detail to project deliverables as the project moves from phase to phase
    C. Letting team members make scope changes without customer approval
    D. None of the above

14. **You have been assigned a project with a very tight timeline and limited resources. When assigned the project and the team, you are concerned about delivering on-time. What is the first thing you do?**
    A. Document your concerns and submit those concerns to your manager and the sponsor
    B. Evaluate the potential schedule implications and concerns with your project team
    C. Refuse the project as the defined timeline makes the project impossible
    D. Escalate to the sponsor immediately to identify flexibility with the schedule

15. **Janelle Wright has approached you with a project opportunity. She explains that you will be responsible for delivering one component of the organization's new product. The other components will be developed by other project managers within the group. What is your primary concern?**
    A. You are concerned that you may not have enough knowledge of the particular component
    B. You are concerned that you are friends with Janelle and it may not be appropriate to work with her
    C. You are concerned that you will not have enough resources given that there are other project managers involved
    D. You are concerned that there are dependencies between the projects, rolling up to Janelle's program

Review Question Answers

1. **Answer: C**

   While the flight itself may have attributes of a project (it is temporary, etc.) it is an ongoing part and attribute of the business operations and therefore, it would not be considered a project.

2. **Answer: B**

   The question is asking specifically about the project life cycle. The project life cycle will vary between organizations, industries, different types of projects. The project life cycle produces one project, does use a methodology and the project management methodology will dictate the project management activities to be used, not the project life cycle.

3. **Answer: D**

   The definition of a project is a temporary endeavor undertaken to create a unique product, service, or result. It is not a set of sequential activities performed in a process or system, a revenue-generating activity that needs to be accomplished while achieving customer satisfaction, nor an ongoing endeavor undertaken to meet customer or market requirements.

4. **Answer: B**

   Project management is the application of knowledge, skills, tools, and techniques to project activities to meet project requirements. It is not the integration of the critical path method and the earned value management system, the application of knowledge, skills, wisdom, science, and art to organizational activities to achieve operational excellence, nor a subset of most engineering and other technical disciplines.

5. **Answer: A**

   Managing a project includes balancing the competing demands for quality, scope, time, and cost. The other answers were much too specific and could not be considered a general definition. Oftentimes, the mention of the triple constraint plus quality will be a great hint, as that is typically the basis for project management.

6. **Answer: B**

   A program is a group of related projects managed in a coordinated way. Answers A and C are too specific and answer D is not referring to a project

7. **Answer: D**

   Of the four answers, D is the only false answer. All activities cannot be addressed within the organization's normal operational limits. As such, projects are utilized as a means to achieving an organization's strategic plan.

8. **Answer: B**

   The project lifecycle allows the project to be broken down into phases.

9. **Answer: D**

   Answers A, B, and C are all true statements. However, the project team should consider the political and physical environmental contexts of the project, as these will have an impact on the management of, and approach to, the project.

10. **Answer: A**

    The project team must identify the stakeholders, determine their requirements, and manage their influence as it relates to the project requirements. The project team should not create conflicts among stakeholders

11. **Answer: C**

    The project manager is more likely to have a full-time role in a strong matrix environment. If project-based environment had been there as an option, that would have been the best response.

12. **Answer: A**

    Communications in a matrix environment can be very complex as the communication must flow horizontally (from the PM to their dotted-line reports) and vertically (from the PM to the administrative managers of the team members.)

13. **Answer: B**

    Progressive elaboration means starting with a high-level and adding details, further defining and refining the project as the team learns more about what will be needed.

14. Answer: B

The first thing you will do as a project manager is to evaluate those schedule implications with your team. It is possible that your team has the knowledge, experience, and availability to get the project done within the constraints. There is no mention of cost, so there may be the potential to outsource work, etc. so refusing the project is not appropriate. Escalation should only be made once a problem gets to a point where no solution can be identified or if there is a legal or ethical issue.

15. Answer: D

As there are other projects that will all be contributing components to the overall product, Janelle is managing a program. As the project manager of a project within a program, you are concerned that there are dependencies between the projects that roll up to the program. If you do not have enough knowledge of the component, you can disclose that to Janelle and seek out expertise for your team. Although you and Janelle have a friendship, you can still manage a project within her component if you have the appropriate authority and skills. There is no mention of resource constraints within the context of the question.

Chapter 2 - Vocabulary Review

* Adaptive life cycle	Laissez-faire leadership	* Project management
Avoiding power	Multi-divisional structure	* Project management office
Balanced matrix structure	Operations	* Project manager
Business partner	Organic structure	* Project-oriented structure
Charismatic leadership	Organizational groups	* Project sponsor
Coercive power	Personal power	Referent power
* Constraint	Persuasive power	Relational power
Controlling PMO	* Phase	Reward power
Customer	* Phase gate	* Seller
Directive PMO	*PMBOK® Guide*	Servant leader leadership
Expert power	* Portfolio	Situational power
Functional manager	Positional power	* Stakeholder
* Functional structure	* Predictive life cycle	Strong matrix structure
Guilt-based power	Pressure-based power	Supportive PMO
Hybrid structure	* Product life cycle	Transactional leadership
Informational power	* Program	Transformational leadership
Ingratiating power	* Progressive elaboration	Triple constraint
Interactional leadership	* Project	Virtual structure
* Iterative life cycle	* Project life cycle	Weak matrix structure

1.	A collection of projects or programs and other work that are grouped together to facilitate effective management of that work to meet strategic business objectives
2.	The application of knowledge, skills, tools, and techniques to project activities to meet the project requirements
3.	A group of related projects managed in a coordinated way to obtain benefits and control not available from managing them individually
4.	Sequential and non-overlapping phases of a product
5.	Continuously improving and detailing a plan as more detailed and specific information and more accurate estimates become available
6.	The state, quality, or sense of being restricted to a given course of action or inaction
7.	A collection of generally sequential project phases whose name and number are determined by the control needs of the organization or organizations involved in the project
8.	Person or organization that is actively involved in the project, or whose interests may be positively or negatively affected by execution or completion of the project

9.	A collection of logically related project activities that culminates in the completion of one or more deliverables
10.	An organization where the project work is done within a functional area, the project manager has a part-time role and little to no authority
11.	A temporary endeavor undertaken to create a unique product, service or result
12.	An organizational structure where the work is grouped by the projects and in which the project manager has full authority and a designated job role
13.	A project life cycle, also known as change-drive or agile methods, that is intended to facilitate change and requires a high degree of ongoing stakeholder involvement
14.	A PMO that provides support and implements controls and procedures and monitors the projects' compliance with the defined framework
15.	A PMO that directly manages projects
16.	A project life cycle where the project scope is generally determined early in the project life cycle, but time and cost estimates are routinely modified as the project team's understanding of the product increases
17.	A form of project life cycle in which the project scope, and the time and cost required to deliver that scope, are determined as early in the life cycle as possible
18.	A PMO that provides templates, lessons learned, and training to the projects and mainly serves as a project repository
19.	A provider or supplier of products, services, or results to an organization.
20.	Organizational structure where the project work is flexible, resources work side-by-side and the project manager has a part-time role with little to no authority
21.	The power and authority to gather and distribute information
22.	Power that is designated within the project charter allowing the project manager to act on behalf of the sponsor, also known as formal, authoritative, or legitimate power
23.	Leadership style that puts others first, focusing on their growth, learning, development and well-being
24.	The ability to influence by incenting the project team and stakeholders with something that they value
25.	PMI's standard for the practice of project management
26.	The defined project limitations of scope, time, and cost or resources
27.	A management structure that standardizes the project-related governance processes and facilitates the sharing of resources, methodologies, tools, and techniques

28.		Power that is gained due to a situation or circumstance
29.		Leadership that focuses on goals, feedback, and accomplishment to determine rewards, management by exception
30.		The ability to influence because individuals respect the project manager
31.		Defined point at the end or beginning of a project phase during which a go/no-go decision is made
32.		The ability to influence the project team and stakeholders based on the fear of punishment (such as losing their jobs or bonuses), also called penalty authority
33.		Influence that originates from being persuasive in arguments or case-building
34.		An organizational structure where the work is grouped by the product, process, program, region or customer type. The project manager has a part-time role and little to no authority.
35.		Power that comes through flattery or actions to win favor
36.		Leadership that empowers others through sharing ideals, encourages innovation and creativity
37.		The person assigned by the performing organization to lead the team that is responsible for achieving the project objectives
38.		Internal stakeholders who are affected by the activities of the project team (sales and marketing, human resources, legal, finance, operations, etc.)
39.		An organizational structure where the work is grouped by job function with the project manager having a full-time, designated project management job role, with moderate to high authority.
40.		The ongoing work of the organization
41.		The ability to influence the project team and stakeholders because they respect the project manager's skills or subject matter expertise
42.		Individuals with responsibility over a specific functional area and may provide resources, such as subject matter experts (SMEs) for the project
43.		An organizational structure where the work is grouped by job and resembles a functional structure. The project manager has a part-time role and minimal authority.
44.		Recipient of the final product, service, or result delivered by the project, external to the project manager's organization
45.		Similar to referent, influence based on the project manager's personality
46.		Organizations that have a special relationship with the enterprise, providing specialized expertise or filling a specified role such as installation, customization, training, or support

47.	A person or group who provides resources and support for the project, program, or portfolio and is accountable for enabling success
48.	Leadership that is a combination of transactional, transformational, and charismatic
49.	The ability to influence by using an obligation or sense of duty
50.	An organizational structure where the work is conducted in a network with various points of connection. The project manager may be full time or part time with low to moderate authority.
51.	Leadership that inspires others, is high-energy and enthusiastic
52.	An organizational structure that is a mix of various types of organizational structure. The project manager's role and their authority, as such, is mixed.
53.	Control originating from limiting choices or options to gain compliance
54.	Power derived from refusing to participate
55.	An organizational structure where the work is grouped by job function and the project manager is embedded in the functions, with low to moderate authority
56.	Leadership that allows the team to make their own decisions, hands-off style
57.	Power that comes through the development of networks and connection

* These definitions are taken from the Glossary of Project Management Institute, A Guide to the Project Management Body of Knowledge, (PMBOK® Guide) - Sixth Edition, Project Management Institute Inc., 2017.

Vocabulary Review Answers

1. Portfolio
2. Project management
3. Program
4. Product life cycle
5. Progressive elaboration
6. Constraint
7. Project life cycle
8. Stakeholder
9. Phase
10. Functional structure
11. Project
12. Project-oriented structure
13. Adaptive life cycle
14. Controlling PMO
15. Directive PMO
16. Iterative life cycle
17. Predictive life cycle
18. Supportive PMO
19. Seller
20. Organic structure
21. Informational power
22. Positional power
23. Servant leader leadership
24. Reward power
25. PMBOK® Guide
26. Triple constraint
27. Project management office
28. Situational power
29. Transactional leadership
30. Referent power
31. Phase gate
32. Coercive power
33. Persuasive power
34. Multi-divisional structure
35. Ingratiating power
36. Transformational leadership
37. Project manager
38. Organizational groups
39. Strong matrix structure
40. Operations
41. Expert power
42. Functional manager
43. Weak matrix structure
44. Customer
45. Personal power
46. Business partner
47. Project sponsor
48. Interactional leadership
49. Guilt-based power
50. Virtual structure
51. Charismatic leadership
52. Hybrid structure
53. Pressure-based power
54. Avoiding power
55. Balanced matrix structure
56. Laissez-faire leadership
57. Relational power

Chapter 3

The *PMBOK* Guide

What's in This Chapter

- Project Management Framework
- Project Management Knowledge Areas
- Project Management Process Groups
- Commonly Applied Inputs, Tools & Techniques, and Outputs

Project Management Framework

The *PMBOK® Guide*

This course is based upon *A Guide to the Project Management Body of Knowledge (PMBOK® Guide), Sixth Edition*, published by the Project Management Institute (PMI) in 2017. The *PMBOK® Guide* encompasses project management processes that are generally recognized as good practice. It is meant to be a guide, not an absolute nor a methodology. It is intended for organizations and project managers to apply the practices as appropriate within their organizations and on their projects to achieve the best results.

There are two common frustrations often expressed regarding the *PMBOK® Guide*: it is not practical to implement everything in it and it is very dry. I cannot do anything about the dryness of the material, however, I do want to point out that PMI's expectation is not that you should be doing each and every process in the *PMBOK® Guide*, but rather you should select those processes and techniques that make sense within your environment. Do not confuse the *PMBOK® Guide* with a project management methodology. While that can be great news for most people, it does make the preparation for the exam more challenging. Studying a step-by-step methodology is easier to learn than a collection of processes, practices, tools and techniques that are oftentimes iterative and frequently interpreted differently in different environments.

Belinda's Hint

As you learn the processes and tools and techniques, consider your own environment and experience. Many of the topics and techniques are practiced in organizations, although they may be practiced intuitively versus formally or they are named something different. Challenge yourself as you work through this material to consider if you do perform some of these processes within your projects, perhaps not recognizing it by a certain name.

If you have trouble sleeping while preparing for your exam simply pull out the *PMBOK® Guide* and start reading. You will be asleep before you know it!

Framework

One of the most significant components of the *PMBOK® Guide* is the project management framework. Throughout the remainder of the book, I will be reviewing the framework and all the components within that framework. The project management framework consists of ten project management knowledge areas, five process groups (or domains), and forty-nine processes. As you can see from the framework each process is associated with a project management knowledge area and a process group.

Knowledge Areas	Process Groups				
	Initiating	Planning	Executing	Monitoring and Controlling	Closing
Integration	▪ Develop Project Charter	▪ Develop Project Management Plan	▪ Direct and Manage Project Work ▪ Manage Project Knowledge	▪ Monitor and Control Project Work ▪ Perform Integrated Change Control	▪ Close Project or Phase
Scope		▪ Plan Scope Management ▪ Collect Requirements ▪ Define Scope ▪ Create WBS		▪ Validate Scope ▪ Control Scope	
Schedule		▪ Plan Schedule Management ▪ Define Activities ▪ Sequence Activities ▪ Estimate Activity Durations ▪ Develop Schedule		▪ Control Schedule	
Cost		▪ Plan Cost Management ▪ Estimate Costs ▪ Determine Budget		▪ Control Costs	
Quality		▪ Plan Quality Management	▪ Manage Quality	▪ Control Quality	
Resource		▪ Plan Resource Management ▪ Estimate Activity Resources	▪ Acquire Resources ▪ Develop Team ▪ Manage Team	▪ Control Resources	
Communication		▪ Plan Communications Management	▪ Manage Communications	▪ Monitor Communications	
Risk		▪ Plan Risk Management ▪ Identify Risks ▪ Perform Qualitative Risk Analysis ▪ Perform Quantitative Risk Analysis ▪ Plan Risk Responses	▪ Implement Risk Responses	▪ Monitor Risks	
Procurement		▪ Plan Procurement Management	▪ Conduct Procurements	▪ Control Procurements	
Stakeholder	▪ Identify Stakeholders	▪ Plan Stakeholder Engagement	▪ Manage Stakeholder Engagement	▪ Monitor Stakeholder Engagement	

Project Management Institute, *A Guide to the Project Management Body of Knowledge, (PMBOK® Guide) – 6th Edition, Project Management Institute Inc., 2017.* Page 25.

Project Management Knowledge Areas

There are ten knowledge areas that form the left-hand column of the framework, representing areas of interest or consideration for projects.

1. **Integration.** The integration processes provide some of the most important project outputs and could be considered "umbrella" processes as they bring together, or integrate, all the processes within that process group. While other team members or stakeholders may execute other framework processes, the integration processes are typically the responsibility of the project manager. The word *integrate* implies bringing things together, and that is exactly what these processes do. These processes tend to be relatively light on tools and techniques and are redundant in detail to some of the other processes within that process group – again demonstrating that they are integrating the work of that process group. You will notice that the integration knowledge area is the only area that has processes across all five process groups.

2. **Scope.** Scope is the work of the project and the scope processes ensure that the project includes all the work required, and only the work required to complete the project successfully. The work of the project is based on the requirements and includes the work involved in producing the product, service, or result as well as the work involved in the administration and management of the project. As one of the three primary constraints, the scope planning processes will result in the scope management baseline, a component of the project management plan.

3. **Schedule**. The schedule processes are required to manage the timely completion of the project through the creation, management, and control of a realistic project schedule. The schedule planning processes will result in the schedule management baseline.

4. **Cost.** The cost processes are used to estimate, manage, and control the project costs so that the project can be completed within the approved budget. The cost management baseline will be an output of the cost planning processes. In controlling costs, there are several analysis techniques that may be used including earned value management and forecasting. The formulas involved in controlling costs will be a majority of your PMP exam dump sheet!

5. **Quality.** There are three quality processes in the quality management knowledge area. The quality processes incorporate the organization's quality policy regarding planning, managing, and controlling project and product quality requirements, in order to meet stakeholder expectations. Anticipate a number of questions on quality topics, including terms and definitions.

6. **Resource**. The resource processes identify, acquire, manage, and control both the human and physical resources needed for the successful completion of the project.

7. **Communications.** The communication processes ensure timely and appropriate planning, collection, creation, distribution, storage, retrieval, management, control, monitoring, and the ultimate disposition of information.

8. **Risk.** Risk is considered uncertainty that may result in a positive or negative impact. The risk processes conduct risk management planning, identification, analysis, response planning, response implementation and monitoring risk on a project. As with quality, there are a number of terms and definitions that will be a part of the PMP exam.

9. **Procurement.** The procurement processes are necessary to purchase or acquire products, services, or results needed from outside the project team. The procurement processes determine the make-or-buy decisions, define the contract types that will be used, select sellers, and awards the contracts. You want to be familiar with the contract types as PMI defines them, recognizing that there are many variations in practice.

10. **Stakeholder.** The stakeholder processes are required to identify the people, groups, or organizations that could impact or be impacted by the project, to analyze stakeholder expectations and their impact on the project, and to develop appropriate management strategies for effectively engaging stakeholders in project decisions and execution.

You will notice significant overlap and redundancy between the stakeholder, communication, and resource processes.

PMBOK® Guide - Sixth Edition. Pages 23-24

As the project is being planned and executed, or changes are requested or needed, it is important to consider the implications to each of these areas or aspects of the project.

Belinda's Hint

It is often helpful to consider these knowledge areas as a "checklist" for the project. In evaluating a project, I will consider each of these areas as they apply to my project. For example, a regulatory project may have a very strict schedule but will not be using any vendors. As such I will focus on the schedule knowledge area but can disregard the procurement processes.

Project Management Process Groups

While the knowledge areas are relatively straight forward, I find many people stumble on the process groups. The process groups (or domains) represent groups of related processes that may be occurring concurrently and repeatedly throughout the project. While they may resemble them, the process groups are *not* project phases. This is important to understand and acknowledge, because if you think of them as phases, you will soon get confused when a control process precedes an executing process, for example.

The processes within the process groups may be repeated or iterated throughout multiple project phases. The project management framework consists of five process groups:

- Initiating
- Planning
- Executing
- Monitoring and controlling
- Closing

Because a project is a temporary endeavor, the work of the project will generally begin with the initiating processes and end with the closing process. However, the planning, executing, and monitoring and controlling processes will be conducted iteratively throughout all the project phases.

The Initiating Process Group

The initiating process group encompasses those processes that begin to define the project and objectives. The initiating processes secure authorization for the project to begin and identify the project stakeholders. While the initiating processes generally occur at the beginning of the project, they may be revisited throughout the project as necessary, such as at the start of a new phase. There are two initiating processes: **develop project charter** and **identify stakeholders** and 13% of the PMP® exam questions will be from those processes.

The Planning Process Group

The planning process group encompasses those processes that define and refine the project objectives. The planning processes plan the project approach to achieve the objectives and scope of the project. There are planning processes within all ten knowledge areas, reflecting the fact that we need to plan for all aspects of our project.

With 24 processes, there are almost half of the framework processes within this process group. This does not illustrate the proportional time spent on these processes in practice, but rather reflects the need to ensure we have planned appropriately for all aspects of the project. The planning process group represents 24% of the questions on the PMP® exam: almost half of the processes, but less than a quarter of the questions.

These planning processes will be performed iteratively throughout the project and do not represent a "planning phase." As changes occur on the project and/or the project objectives are updated, the planning processes will be revisited as part of the feedback loop in all phases of the project. Critical outputs from the planning process group include the project management plan and all the associated subsidiary plans and project baselines.

Look at the framework on page 33 and you will notice that for every knowledge area after integration there is a "**plan xxxx management**" process. Those processes are focused on creating the subsidiary plans to the project management plan, providing details and context about that particular aspect of the project. For example, **plan scope management** will give us the *scope management plan* and the *requirements management plan*. The **plan schedule management** process will give us the *schedule management plan*. The **plan communications management** process will give us the *communication management plan*, etc. Subsidiary plans may or may not be used on your project. I will discuss the subsidiary plans in further detail later in this chapter. You will be planning and re-planning throughout the project life cycle.

The Executing Process Group

The actual work of the project is conducted through the executing processes. The executing process group encompasses those processes that integrate the project resources to carry out the project management plan. The ten executing processes represent 31% of the questions on the PMP exam, reflecting the fact that although there are less than a quarter of the processes, they represent those that are the most time-consuming in practice. A large portion of the project's budget is spent during the executing process group processes, and this is where much of the time and effort of the project team are expended. You are executing the project work from the beginning until the end. Again, this is not a phase.

The Monitoring and Controlling Process Group

The monitoring and controlling process group are those processes that measure and monitor progress against the project management plan and the performance measurement baselines in order to identify variances and actions that need to be taken to address any of those variances in order regulate and review the progress and performance of the project. There are 12 monitoring and controlling processes and they represent 25% of the PMP exam questions. As with the planning and executing process groups, as a project manager you are monitoring and controlling your project from start to finish.

The Closing Process Group

The closing process group includes the one process that formalizes acceptance of the product, service or result. The closing process brings the project or phase to a close and completes the administrative closure of the project. On the PMP exam, 7% of the questions will be from the one closing process: **close project or phase**.

Plan-Do-Check-Act Cycle

As mentioned previously, although they may resemble them, the process groups are not project phases, but rather iterative groups of related processes. The interactions of the process groups are based on the Plan-Do-Check-Act (PDCA) cycle as defined by Shewhart in the ASQ Handbook (American Society for Quality, 1999), later modified by Deming.

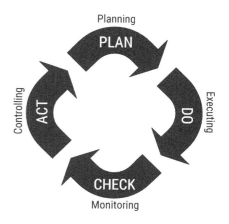

- "Plan" represents the planning process group
- "Do" represents the executing process group
- "Check" and "Act" represent the monitoring and controlling process group

Note the iterative nature of the relationship indicating that as work progresses, the results will be continuously monitored, controlled, and potentially re-planned based on the work results.

Belinda's Hint

Be sure to relate Shewhart (pronounced "shoe-heart") to the Plan-Do-Check-Act cycle.

As part of this self-study program you will be learning multiple theorists – both in the quality knowledge area and the resource knowledge area. Typically, candidates only experience one or two questions on the theorists, however, it is impossible to determine what theorists you may receive on your exam.

To adequately prepare for any questions you receive, a high-level understanding is all that is needed: theorist name, quality or HR/organizational theorist, theory, and the basic premise of the theory.

Project Management Framework Processes

There are 49 processes contained within the project management framework. The processes may be used once or at pre-defined points (such as **develop project charter** or **close project or phase**), performed periodically as needed (such as **acquire resources** or **conduct procurements**), or performed continuously (such as **direct and manage project work**).

Progressive Elaboration

The reality of project management is that there will be change and there will be risk or uncertainties. Earlier, I mentioned the concept of progressive elaboration. As you learn the *PMBOK® Guide* processes contained within this book, keep in mind that many of these processes will be progressively elaborated: the project information is defined broadly at the beginning of the project and then continually defined and refined in more detail as the project progresses, recognizing that "we do not know what we do not know". Progressive elaboration will be applied to multiple project management processes such as those within the scope, schedule, cost, and quality areas. As we learn more, discover more, we elaborate our original definition.

It is important that you do not confuse progressive elaboration with scope creep. Progressive elaboration refines the preliminary definition without adding extra features whereas scope creep adds additional expectations and requirements to the project outside of the defined change control process.

Example: Progressive Elaboration

At the beginning of the training course project, it was defined as: "An instructor-led course teaching basic customer service skills" with an approximate cost of $30,000 and a development time-line of three months."

As the project progresses, more details will be refined such as: the course will be an 8-hour course with six role-play scenarios, set up in such a way as to accommodate 20 students per class. The cost estimates for the project will become more definitive as information is gathered: development hours, cost of materials and supplies, classroom rental, etc. And possibly the timeline will be adjusted as the project progresses.

If there were an expectation that all students would receive laptops for the class, although that was never in the preliminary definition, this would represent possible scope creep.

For each of the 49 project management processes, there are:

- Inputs to the process
- Tools and techniques that are used during the process
- Outputs from the process (which may become inputs to other processes)

We will refer to these as the "ITTOs" throughout this course. There are hundreds of ITTOs across the 49 processes. And no, you do not need to memorize them all! The majority of the ITTOs are used for many of the processes. To provide a strong foundation of understanding for each process, I will first introduce you to these common ITTOs. In this manner, I will dig into specific ITTOs as I present each individual process.

Belinda's Hint

There are 100s of ITTOs associated with the project management processes. In previous versions of the PMP exam, many candidates felt inclined to attempt to memorize the ITTOs. The 6th edition is different, and PMI has applied the ITTOs in a common fashion – meaning that memorizing them will not contribute to passing the exam. Success comes from understanding the 49 processes, their objectives and use, and how they all relate! When you understand the process, the ITTOs will make more sense. You will experience very few ITTO questions on the exam.

Common Inputs

There are six common inputs to the project management processes. You do not need to know which processes have them, which do not, why the ones that do do, and why the ones that don't don't. Nor do you have to memorize this list. However, you should understand what each of the common inputs are and how they are used in the different processes.

1. Project charter
2. Project management plan
3. Project documents
4. Enterprise environmental factors
5. Organizational process assets
6. Work performance data

1. Project Charter

The project charter is the official authorization of the project that is created based on the project business case and the project benefits management plan. The project charter is created by the project initiator or sponsor of the project, and it provides the project manager with authority to apply organizational resources to the project work. The project charter is a common input as it provides a high-level overview of the project objectives, risks, constraints and assumptions, schedule milestones, and funding estimates. According to PMI, the project charter (written authorization) is considered mandatory for all projects. Note that in your environment, you may call it something other than a charter. The project charter is an output of the **develop project charter** process that will be discussed in the next chapter in further detail.

2. Project Management Plan

One of the most critical aspects of project management according to PMI, is the project management plan, which PMI considers as mandatory for all projects. The project management plan is created throughout all the planning processes and it may be summary level or detailed, based on the project environment and the complexity of the project. The project management plan (or "project plan") provides the foundation for the entire project and instruction/direction to the project team. It is developed iteratively throughout the project, being updated when circumstances or the environment changes.

The objective of the project management plan is to aide in managing team member and stakeholder expectations, while reducing the risk to the organization: should the project manager or key team members leave the project or the organization, the project management plan will allow new team members to get up-to-speed quickly on the project.

Belinda's Hint

Think of the project management plan and any subsidiary plans as the ultimate "how-to" guide or instruction manual, for your project. It may be referred to simply as the "project plan," dropping the word "management." In practice, many PMs refer to their project schedule as their "plan." Do not confuse the project management plan with your project schedule.

On the PMP exam, many of the questions asked will be "what is the best thing/next thing you should do?". Typically, the best thing that the project manager should do is check the plan before taking any action.

The project management plan includes the project baselines (scope, schedule, and cost) and the subsidiary plans.

The project baselines are "frozen" versions of the scope, schedule, and budget that will be used to measure and monitor progress of the project. The baselines can be typically only modified when there is an approved, significant change in scope. Baselines may also be called "performance baselines" or "performance measurement baselines." Think of the baselines as your measuring sticks!

The subsidiary plans are developed based on the environment, complexity, and organizational needs and are detailed plans pertaining to specific areas of focus within the project. The subsidiary plans are created throughout the planning processes – for example, the **plan communication management** process will produce the "communication management plan" as an output; the **plan risk management** process will produce the "risk management plan" as an output. These plans may be simple bulleted lists of items related to that area or more comprehensive and detailed. You may or may not create all the subsidiary plans that will be presented, as it is based on the needs of your project.

Examples of subsidiary plans include:

- Scope management plan
- Cost management plan
- Communications management plan
- Procurement management plan

- Schedule management plan
- Quality management plan
- Risk management plan
- Requirements management plan

Belinda's Hint

If it ends in the word "plan," regardless of what precedes that word, it is a subsidiary plan – meaning that it is part of the project management plan. All "plans" explain how we are going to manage that aspect of the project. For example, the Purple Dinosaur Management Plan will describe how we are managing purple dinosaurs on our project.

3. Project Documents

Project documents are a generic input, simply referring to any type of project documentation that may be applicable to or used during the process. Project documents encompass all associated project documentation, including, but not limited to:

- Project schedule
- Stakeholder register
- Issue log

- Change log
- Project memos and correspondence
- Risk register

4. Enterprise Environmental Factors (EEF)

Enterprise environmental factors (EEF) are internal and external environmental factors that can influence a project's success. (For the purposes of this book, I will use the acronym EEF, however, it will be spelled out on the exam!) As the project manager, you will need to be aware of these factors and take them into consideration throughout the project. Enterprise environmental factors may include:

- Organizational culture
- Organizational structure
- Internal and external political climate
- Existing human resources

- Available capital resources
- Regulatory environment
- Financial and market conditions

5. Organizational Process Assets (OPA)

Organizational process assets include any of the organization's assets that may be used to enable project success. (For the purposes of this book, I will use the acronym OPA, however, it will be spelled out on the exam!) Leveraging OPA typically increases your efficiency as a project manager. In project management, it is very important to use the past to predict the future, improve processes, and continue to grow our project management maturity.

OPA generally falls into two categories:

1. Processes, guidelines, and procedures, such as:
   - Organizational standard processes
   - Standardized guidelines
   - Templates

2. The corporate knowledge base, such as:
   - Lessons learned
   - Historical information
   - Past project files

Belinda's Hint

On the exam, you can assume you have access to, and use, the organizational process assets, including the corporate knowledge base. Many of the techniques used in project planning leverage historical data from past projects and lessons learned. So even if you do not have such a thing within your organization, you need to assume you do on the exam.

PMI loves to give correlation and comparative questions, such as comparing EEF to OPA. To help you differ between the two, consider that factors are things that we "consider" and assess as to how they will impact the project. OPA, on the other hand, are things that we use to make our project more efficient. Contrast EEF to OPA: factors = things we consider; assets = things we use.

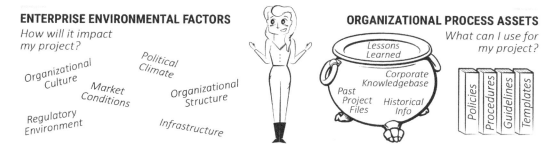

6. Work Performance Data

Work performance data is the raw information coming from the project activities, including what percentage of the work is completed, any performance measurements, start and finish dates of activities, etc. Work performance data is an output of the **direct and manage project work** process, a key integration / executing process.

This work performance data will be an input to the monitoring and controlling processes, making it a common input. Throughout the monitoring and controlling processes, this "raw" data will be analyzed and compared to the planned progress of the project. Upon being analyzed, work performance data becomes work performance information (a common output). That work performance information is used to create the work performance reports – written status reports. This is a sequence you will want to know for the exam.

Easy way to remember: they are in alphabetical order – data – information – reports.

WORK PERFORMANCE DATA — "Raw" → WORK PERFORMANCE INFORMATION — "Analyzed" → WORK PERFORMANCE REPORTS — "Communicated"

Common Tools and Techniques

The first three common tools and techniques are just that. The last five are actually categories or buckets of various techniques. I will present the specific tools and techniques within the categories here at just a high-level. As you go through the lists, highlight those that are not familiar to you. Later in the book, when I present the individual processes, I provide more detail around the specific tools and techniques used for the processes within those categories. The common tools and techniques are:

1. Expert judgment
2. Meetings
3. Project management information system
4. Decision making
5. Data gathering techniques
6. Data analysis techniques
7. Data representation
8. Interpersonal and team skills

1. Expert Judgment

Expert judgment encompasses expertise provided by any group or individual with specialized knowledge or training.

This could include:

- Consultants
- Stakeholders
- Professional association
- Industry groups
- The project management office (PMO)
- Subject matter experts

The project manager does not necessarily need to be the technical expert on the project but should have enough knowledge as to be able to address project issues and know how to leverage the expertise within and external to the team.

Belinda's Hint

PMI wants to ensure that you recognize that you most likely do not "know everything" and must leverage other individuals to most effectively manage your project.

In the earlier days of project management, it was not unusual for the subject matter expert to be the "project manager" for any changes to that area. Project management has since grown to be a designated profession spanning multiple industries and you may not be the most technical expert on your project.

2. Meetings

Meetings are a fundamental communication tool utilized throughout the project. Meetings allow for interactive communication and exchange of project information.

3. Project Management Information System (PMIS)

The project management information system (PMIS) is any collection of tools or systems used to manage project information. Examples include software such as Microsoft Project, network directories, change management tools and databases, web interfaces, and interactive online and collaboration tools. On the exam, PMI will likely use the PMIS acronym.

4. Decision-Making Techniques

There are two decision-making techniques that may be used for the processes.

Technique	Description
* Multicriteria decision analysis	Utilizes a decision matrix to provide a systematic analytical approach for establishing criteria, such as risk levels, uncertainty, and valuation, to evaluate and rank many ideas
Voting	Allowing the members of the group to vote on the decision or action. May include technique such as fist-to-five, unanimity, majority, or plurality.

These definitions are taken from the Glossary of the PMBOK® Guide – Sixth Edition

5. Data Gathering Techniques

There are several data gathering techniques that may be used during the processes.

Technique	Description
* Benchmarking	The comparison of actual or planned products, processes, and practices to those of comparable organizations to identify best practices, generate ideas for improvement, and provide a basis for measuring performance
Brainstorming	Gathering ideas freely from several different parties
* Checksheets	Tally sheets that can be used as a checklist when gathering data
Checklists	A series of steps or questions that have been developed based on lessons learned and/or historical data
* Focus groups	Brings together prequalified stakeholders and subject matter experts to learn about their expectations and attitudes about a proposed product, service or result
* Interviews	Formal or informal approach to elicit information from stakeholders by talking to them directly
Market research	Evaluation and consideration of market trends, approaches, and breakthroughs to use as a basis of comparison
* Questionnaires/ surveys	Written sets of questions designed to quickly accumulate information from many respondents
* Statistical sampling	Choosing part of a population of interest for inspection

These definitions are taken from the Glossary of the PMBOK® Guide – Sixth Edition

6. Data Analysis Techniques

There are several data analysis techniques that may be used during the processes.

Technique	Description
* Alternatives analysis	Used to evaluate identified options in order to select the options or approaches to use to execute and perform the work of the project
Assessment of other risk parameters	Evaluation of risk parameters, other than probability and impact; such as, urgency, etc.
Assumption and constraint analysis	Evaluation of the assumptions and constraints of the project to determine quality, consistency, and validity
* Cost of quality (CoQ)	All costs incurred over the life of the product by investment in preventing nonconformance to requirements, appraisal of the product or service for conformance to requirements, and failure to meet requirements
* Cost-benefit analysis	Used to determine the benefits provided by a project against its cost
* Decision tree analysis	Diagramming and calculation technique for evaluating the implications of a chain of multiple options in the presence of uncertainty
Document analysis	Review and evaluation of existing project documentation to provide insight to the project data
Earned value analysis	Assessment of the scope, schedule, and resource measurements to determine project progress. Considers value earned in the project as compared to actual costs and planned value.
* Influence diagrams	A graphical representation of situations showing causal influences, time ordering of events, and other relationships among variables and outcomes
Iteration burndown chart	A graph that shows how much work the team has left in their current iteration in order to meet their iteration goal, displayed in a downward trend
* Make-or-buy analysis	Gathering and organizing data about product requirements and analyzing against available alternatives including the purchase or internal manufacture of the product
* Performance reviews	Used to measure, compare, and analyze actual performance of work in progress on the project against the baseline
Process analysis	Evaluation and assessment of current and proposed processes to determine quality and efficiency
Proposal evaluation	The process of reviewing proposal provided by suppliers to support contract award decisions

These definitions are taken from the Glossary of the PMBOK® Guide – Sixth Edition

7. Data Representation Techniques

There are a number of data representation techniques that may be used during the processes.

Technique	Description
* Affinity diagrams	Allows large numbers of ideas to be classified into groups for review and analysis
* Cause-and-effect diagrams	Traces an undesirable effect back to its root cause
* Control charts	Display process data over time and against established control limits, which has a centerline that assists in detecting a trend of plotted values toward either control limit
* Flowcharts	The depiction in a diagram format of the inputs, process actions, and outputs of one or more processes within a system
Hierarchical charts	Depicts parent-child relationships either vertically or horizontally
* Histograms	Bar charts that show the graphical representation of numerical data
Logical data model	A visual representation of an organization's data, described in business language and independent of any specific technology. Used to identify where data integrity or other quality issues can arise.
* Matrix diagrams	Show the strength of relationships between factors, causes, and objectives that exist between the rows and columns that form the matrix
* Mind mapping	Used to consolidate ideas created through individual brainstorming sessions into a single map to reflect commonality and differences in understanding and to generate new ideas
* Probability and impact matrix	A grid for mapping the probability of occurrence of each risk and its impact on project objectives if that risk occurs
Scatter diagrams	Depict a relationship between two variables, using a regression line to explain or to predict how the change in an independent variable will change a dependent variable
* Stakeholder engagement assessment matrix	Compares current and desired stakeholder engagement levels
Stakeholder mapping/ representation	An evaluation of the stakeholders and the stakeholder relationships
Text-oriented formats	A listing of data in a spreadsheet or word processing application

These definitions are taken from the Glossary of the PMBOK® Guide – Sixth Edition

8. Interpersonal and Team Skills

There are a number of interpersonal and team skills that will be used in the processes.

Technique	Description
Active listening	Listening with the intent to understand and empathize with the speaker
* Communication styles assessment	Identifies the preferred communication method, format, and content for stakeholders for planned communication activities
Conflict management	Actions related to effectively resolving conflict and differences of opinions
Cultural awareness	Understanding the implications and considerations associated with different cultural affiliations within the project
* Decision making	Used to select a course of action from different alternatives
* Emotional intelligence	The ability to identify, assess, and manage the personal emotions of oneself and other people, as well as the collective emotions of groups of people
Facilitation	Effective coordination and management of meetings and events
Influencing	Ability to persuade a person or group of people towards a certain course of action
Leadership	Motivating a group of people towards the accomplishment of a goal
Meeting management	Effective coordination of meetings including developing an agenda, time-keeping, summarizing actions, and distribution of minutes
Motivation	The general desire or willingness of someone to do something
Negotiation	Discussion aimed at reaching an agreement
* Networking	Establishing connections and relationships with other people from the same or other organizations
* Nominal group technique	Enhances brainstorming with a voting process used to rank the most useful ideas for further brainstorming or for prioritization
Observation/conversation	Watching someone perform their job duties or interact with a system and/or having an interactive dialogue
Political awareness	An understanding of the internal and external political influences, processes, and culture
Team building	Activities intended to enhance and develop the relationships within the team

These definitions are taken from the Glossary of the PMBOK® Guide – Sixth Edition

Common Outputs

The six most common outputs produced by the project management processes are:

1. Project document updates
2. Project management plan updates
3. Change requests
4. Organizational process assets updates
5. Work performance information
6. Enterprise environmental factors updates

Belinda's Hint

If it ends in the word "updates," it is an output from a process.

1. Project Document Updates

Document updates reflect the need to continuously keep project information current and as accurate as possible per the current project conditions.

2. Project Management Plan Updates

As the project progresses, the project management plan is progressively elaborated to include project updates and reflect a changing environment. If a change is required to the baselines due to a change in scope, the project management plan and baselines would be modified, as necessary, through the **perform integrated change control** process.

3. Change Requests

While one of the key responsibilities of the project manager is to achieve project objectives while minimizing change, change is inevitable and needs to be managed. All change requests will become an input to the **perform integrated change control** process where they will be evaluated and reviewed for approval.

Any project stakeholder can request a change, and that change may or may not impact the project baselines. Some changes that do not impact the project baselines may be handled by the project manager without going through formal change control. Change requests can originate internally or externally and may be optional or mandatory (such as contractually-driven changes). Change requests include:

Scope changes. Scope changes are those requests originating from the sponsor, customer, or end-user for different functionality or other changes to the project scope. Scope changes most likely will necessitate an update to the project baselines, as they represent a change in the work of the project. Typically, if work is being added or removed from the project it will have an impact on the cost and schedule.

Corrective actions. Corrective actions are those requests that are reactive in nature, with the intent of bringing the project back into alignment with the performance baselines, typically related to the project being over-budget or behind schedule. Because measurement of the impact of the corrective action is key, the baselines are not updated for a corrective action. The team will need to validate, by using the baseline comparison that the corrective action did serve to correct the negative impact.

Preventive actions. Preventive actions are those requests that are proactive in nature with the intent of reversing a negative trend, such as trending over-budget or behind schedule. As with corrective actions, preventive actions would not involve a change to the project baselines, as the comparison of the baseline with the progress of the project will validate that the preventive action was successful.

Defect repairs. Defect repairs are those requests that are due to an error in the quality of a deliverable or non-compliance with a defined requirement. There is no baseline update when a defect repair is implemented as the progress and impact against the baselines needs to be captured as it relates to the defect repair. The defect may be identified by the team or may be found by the customer or end-user (an escaped defect).

Updates. Updates can include changes to any formally controlled project document or project plan, reflecting the modified or updated ideas, information or content. Typically, updates do not involve a baseline update.

Belinda's Hint

A great way to remember the differences in these change requests is to align them with the triple constraint:

Corrective and preventive actions are related to either the schedule or the budget. Defect repairs are related to a problem with quality (regardless of whether the customer/end-user has the seen the quality issue). Scope changes impact the scope of the project. Do not confuse a "corrective action" with a "defect repair." If you are correcting an error in a deliverable, it is a defect repair, not a corrective action. Always remember that corrective actions are typically related to cost or schedule issues.

4. Organizational Process Assets Updates

Organizational process assets updates include updates and modifications to policies, procedures, guidelines, templates, lessons learned and historical project information. As the project progresses, the project manager should ensure that OPAs are being updated to reflect the most current information.

5. Work Performance Information

When work performance data is analyzed and compared to the project baselines, the result is work performance information. Work performance information helps the project manager and the project team understand the health of the project, identify variances, and determine the need for any type of changes. Work performance information is a common output from the monitoring and controlling processes and will be an input to the **monitor and control project work** process where it will feed the work performance reports (also known as status reports).

6. Enterprise Environmental Factors Updates

As the project progresses, the enterprise environmental factors will be updated to reflect the changing influences on the project.

Chapter 3 - Review Questions

1. **The project management process groups are:**
   A. Planning, checking, directing, monitoring, and recording
   B. Initiating, planning, executing, monitoring and controlling, and closing
   C. Planning, executing, directing, closing, and delivering
   D. Initiating, executing, monitoring, evaluating, and closing

2. **All of the following are characteristics of the project management process groups except:**
   A. The process groups are linked by the objectives they produce
   B. The output of one process generally becomes an input to another process or is a deliverable of the project
   C. All of the processes will be needed on all projects, and all of the interactions will apply to all projects or project phases
   D. When a project is divided into phases, the process groups are normally repeated within each phase throughout the project's life to effectively drive the project to completion

3. **Which statement is most accurate?**
   A. Since management of a project is a finite effort, the initiating process group begins the project and the closing process group ends it
   B. If a project is divided into phases, the process groups will only be utilized once during the project
   C. Risk management is considered a process group
   D. The project management framework consists of nine process groups

4. **The following statements are true about the *PMBOK® Guide*, except:**
   A. The *PMBOK® Guide* provides and promotes a common vocabulary within the project management profession
   B. The *PMBOK® Guide* is the mandatory methodology for projects
   C. The *PMBOK® Guide* is a guide rather than a methodology
   D. The *PMBOK® Guide* identifies the subset of the project management body of knowledge generally recognized as good practice

5. **Common inputs to the project management processes include:**
   A. Organizational process assets, enterprise environmental factors, work performance information and project management plan updates
   B. Organizational process assets, change requests, project management plan, and enterprise environmental factors
   C. Project management plan, project documents, and change requests
   D. Project management plan, project charter, organizational process assets, project documents, work performance data, and enterprise environmental factors

6. **You have assumed the responsibility for a high-risk project that is instrumental to your company's growth. As you begin to evaluate the project, you take into consideration the availability of skilled resources that will be needed for the project. You are considering:**
   A. The organizational process assets
   B. The enterprise environmental factors
   C. The project management plan
   D. The organizational methodology

7. **You are new to the project organization within your company. You have been asked to develop a project management plan and you have sent an inquiry to the PMO asking for any type of templates or sample plans that may exist. The templates and sample plans:**
   A. Would be considered enterprise environmental factors
   B. Would constitute the need for a scope change request
   C. Are not the most efficient manner of establishing the project documentation
   D. Are both components of the organization's process assets

8. **Which of the following is not a data analysis technique?**
   A. Cost of quality
   B. Mind mapping
   C. Iteration burndown chart
   D. Proposal evaluation

9. **A key role of the project manager is to manage the project knowledge. Which sequence is most accurate regarding project knowledge management:**
   A. Once work performance information is analyzed it becomes work performance data. The work performance data is used to create the work performance reports.
   B. The work performance report provides the work performance information and data.
   C. Work performance information is used to create the work performance reports. Work performance data is analyzed to become work performance information.
   D. The work performance information is raw, and it is analyzed to create work performance data. The work performance data is used in the work performance report.

10. **Which of the following is not a common tool / technique for the *PMBOK® Guide* processes?**
    A. Data representation techniques
    B. Data analysis techniques
    C. Data gathering techniques
    D. Data interpretation techniques

11. **The difference between the project management plan and the project charter can best be described as:**
    A. The project management plan is optional whereas the project charter is mandatory
    B. The project charter provides guidance to the leadership of the organization regarding the project whereas the project management plan provides guidance to the stakeholders.
    C. The project manager determines whether the project charter or the project management plan are needed on the project
    D. The project charter provides the project manager with authorization to complete the work of the project whereas the project management plan describes how the work will be defined, managed, and controlled.

12. **Your team has submitted three change requests: Request #1 is to change the status report due date from Friday to Thursday. Request #2 is to add an extra page to the new website that is under development. Request #3 is to replace the more expensive resource with a less expensive resource as the project is trending over budget. Which statement is most accurate?**
    A. Only change request #2 would change the project baselines
    B. All three change requests would require a change to the project baselines as they are changing the project
    C. Change request #2 and #3 would require a change to the project baselines as they reflect material changes
    D. None of the change requests would require a change to the baselines, as the baselines are frozen and should not be updated

13. **Your customer unexpectedly the job-site and found a number of problems with the interior work in the building. Upon evaluating the identified problems, you agree that they need to be addressed. You:**
    A. Submit defect repair change requests to the change control board without updating the project baselines
    B. Create corrective action change requests and determine the impacts to the project baselines
    C. You have your team fix the problems without involving formal change control
    D. With your foreman, you re-baseline the project to incorporate the problems being resolved

14. **The bridge between project management processes are best described by the following:**
    A. The processes are in order of importance
    B. One process must finish before the other process begins
    C. There is no bridge or correlation
    D. Processes are linked by the outputs that are produced

15. **The *PMBOK® Guide* is**
    A. The guide for managing all projects consistently
    B. The standard for managing most projects most of the time
    C. Used only in the IT industry
    D. None of the above

Review Question Answers

1. **Answer: B**

   There are five process groups (groups of related processes): initiating, planning, executing, monitoring and controlling, and closing

2. **Answer: C**

   Not all of the *PMBOK® Guide* processes will be needed on every project and not all of the interactions will apply to all projects or phases. For example, if the internal project you are managing does not have a cost tracking component, none of the cost processes will apply to your project.

3. **Answer: A**

   Generally speaking, the initiating processes begin the project while the closing processes end it. The process groups may be used iteratively throughout the project. Risk management is a knowledge area. There are five process groups.

4. **Answer: B**

   The *PMBOK® Guide* is not a mandatory methodology for projects. It is a "guide" to the project management body of knowledge and is intended to be applied as appropriate in various situations.

5. **Answer: D**

   The most common inputs to the processes are: project management plan, organizational process assets, project documents, work performance data, and enterprise environmental factors.

6. **Answer: B**

   The clue in this question is the word "considering". We consider the enterprise environmental factors, understanding the implication to our project. Enterprise environmental factors are things we "consider".

7. **Answer: D**

   Organizational process assets include policies, procedure, guidelines and templates and the corporate knowledge base including past project files, sample plans, lessons learned, etc.

8. **Answer: B**

   Mind mapping is a data representation technique, not a data analysis technique. The cost of quality, an iteration burndown charter, and project evaluations are all data analysis techniques.

9. **Answer: C**

   Work performance data is the raw data that is analyzed during the monitoring and control processes. Once analyzed, the data becomes work performance information. Work performance information is then used to create the work performance reports. Data → Information → Reports

10. **Answer: D**

    There is no "data interpretation techniques", however there are data analysis techniques.

11. **Answer: D**

    Per PMI, both the project management plan and the project charter are considered mandatory. The charter is the authorization to conduct the project, whereas the project management plan provides instruction and direction as to how the work will be conducted.

12. **Answer: A**

    Because change request #2 involves changing the scope of the project, a baseline change would be appropriate from that point forward. Change request #1 does not have an impact on the project constraints, so it would not be appropriate to change the baselines. Change request #3 is a corrective action.

13. **Answer: A**

    Because there is an error in the quality of the work, this would be addressed with a defect repair. The project does not get re-baselined for a defect repair. It is not a corrective action as there is no indication that it is a budget or schedule problem.

14. **Answer: D**

    The processes are linked by the outputs they produce: key outputs may become inputs to other processes.

15. **Answer: B**

The *PMBOK® Guide* is the standard for managing most projects. There will be some projects in which the *PMBOK® Guide* will not be appropriate or leveraged.

Chapter 3 - Vocabulary Review

Active listening

* Affinity diagrams

* Alternatives analysis

Assessment of other risk parameters

Assumption and constraint analysis

* Baseline

* Benchmarking

Brainstorming

* Cause-and-effect-diagrams

* Change request

* Checksheets

Checklists

* Communication styles assessment

Conflict management

* Control charts

* Corrective actions

* Cost-benefit analysis

* Cost of quality

Cultural awareness

* Data analysis techniques

* Data gathering techniques

* Data representation techniques

* Decision making

* Decision tree analysis

* Defect repair

Document analysis

Earned value analysis

* Emotional intelligence

* Enterprise environmental factors

* Expert judgment

Facilitation

* Flowcharts

* Focus groups

Hierarchical charts

* Histograms

* Influence diagrams

Influencing

* Interpersonal and team skills

* Interviews

Iteration burndown chart

Leadership

Logical data model

* Make-or-buy analysis

Market research

* Matrix diagrams

Meeting management

Meetings

* Mind mapping

Motivation

* Multicriteria decision analysis

Negotiation

* Networking

* Nominal group technique

Observation / conversation

Organizational process assets

Performance reviews

Plan-Do-Check-Act Cycle

Political awareness

Preventive action

Probability and impact matrix

Process analysis

Progressive elaboration

Project charter

Project documents

Project management plan

Proposal evaluation

Questionnaires and surveys

Scatter diagrams

Scope change

Stakeholder engagement assessment matrix

Stakeholder mapping / representation

Statistical sampling

Subsidiary plan

Team building

Text-oriented formats

Updates

Voting

Work performance data

Work performance information

1.	Enhances brainstorming with a voting process used to rank the most useful ideas for further brainstorming or for prioritization
2.	Utilizes a decision matrix to provide a systematic analytical approach for establishing criteria, such as risk levels, uncertainty, and valuation, to evaluate and rank many ideas
3.	Discussion aimed at reaching an agreement
4.	Allowing the members of the group to vote on the decision or action. May include techniques such as fist-to-five, unanimity, majority, or plurality.

5.	Diagramming and calculation technique for evaluating the implications of a chain of multiple options in the presence of uncertainty
6.	An evaluation of the stakeholders and the stakeholder relationships
7.	Used to determine the benefits provided by a project against its cost
8.	A listing of data in a spreadsheet or word processing application
9.	Listening with the intent to understand and empathize with the speaker
10.	A formal proposal to modify a document, deliverable, or baseline
11.	Brings together prequalified stakeholders and subject matter experts to learn about their expectations and attitudes about a proposed product, service or result
12.	Knowledge provided based upon expertise in an application area, knowledge area, discipline, industry, etc., as appropriate for the activity being performed
13.	The process of reviewing proposals provided by suppliers to support contract award decisions
14.	Establishing connections and relationships with other people from the same or other organizations
15.	Organized and interactive sessions for project communication
16.	Choosing part of a population of interest for inspection
17.	Plans, processes, policies, procedures, and knowledge bases that are specific to and used by the performing organization
18.	The general desire or willingness of someone to do something
19.	Compares current and desired stakeholder engagement levels
20.	Continuous improvement model developed by Shewhart
21.	Formal or informal approach to elicit information from stakeholders by talking to them directly
22.	An intentional activity that ensures the future performance of the project work is aligned with the project management plan
23.	Techniques used to organize, assess, and evaluate data and information
24.	Watching someone perform their job duties or interact with a system while having an interactive dialogue
25.	The iterative process of increasing the level of detail in a project management plan as greater amounts of information and more accurate estimates become available

26.	Used to measure, compare, and analyze actual performance of work in progress on the project against the baseline
27.	All costs incurred over the life of the product by investment in preventing nonconformance to requirements, appraisal of the product or service for conformance to requirements, and failure to meet requirements
28.	A document issued by the project initiator or sponsor that formally authorizes the existence of a project and provides the project manager with the authority to apply organizational resources to project activities
29.	Used to select a course of action from different alternatives
30.	An intentional action to add to, or remove work or scope from, the project
31.	Evaluation and consideration of market trends, approaches, and breakthroughs to use as a basis of comparison
32.	Depict a relationship between two variables, using a regression line to explain or to predict how the change in an independent variable will change a dependent variable
33.	Identifies the preferred communication method, format, and content for stakeholders for planned communication activities
34.	A component of the project management plan that provides additional details and direction regarding a specific area or aspect of the project
35.	The comparison of actual or planned products, processes, and practices to those of comparable organizations to identify best practices, generate ideas for improvement, and provide a basis for measuring performance
36.	An intentional action to modify the project documentation or project management plan to align with the current status or conditions
37.	Evaluation and assessment of current and proposed processes to determine quality and efficiency
38.	Effective coordination and management of meetings and events
39.	The document that describes how the project will be executed, monitor and controlled, and closed
40.	Gathering and organizing data about product requirements and analyzing against available alternatives including the purchase or internal manufacture of the product
41.	Activities intended to enhance and develop the relationships within the team
42.	A grid for mapping the probability of occurrence of each risk ad its impact on project objectives if that risk occurs
43.	Used to evaluate identified options in order to select the options or approaches to use to execute and perform the work of the project
44.	The raw observations and measurements identified during activities being performed to carry out the project work

45.	Gathering ideas freely from a number of different parties
46.	The approved version of a work product that can be changed only through formal change control procedure and is used as a basis for comparison to actual results
47.	Review and evaluation of existing project documentation to provide insight to the project data
48.	Actions related to effectively resolving conflict and differences of opinions
49.	The performance data collected from controlling processes, analyzed in comparison with project management plan components, project documents, and other work performance information
50.	Assessment of the scope, schedule, and resource measurements to determine project progress. Considers value earned in the project as compared to actual costs and planned value.
51.	Used to consolidate ideas created through individual brainstorming sessions into a single map to reflect commonality and differences in understanding and to generate new ideas
52.	Effective coordination of meetings including developing an agenda, time-keeping, summarizing actions, and distribution of minutes
53.	Graphic representations or other methods used to convey data and information
54.	Evaluation of the assumptions and constraints of the project to determine quality, consistency, and validity
55.	Any and all documentation created by, and updated throughout, the project
56.	Tally sheets that can be used as a checklist when gathering data
57.	Skills used to effectively lead and interact with team members and other stakeholders
58.	Evaluation of risk parameters, other than probability and impact; such as, urgency, etc.
59.	Conditions, not under the immediate control of the team, that influence, constrain, or direct the project, program, or portfolio
60.	The ability to identify, assess, and manage the personal emotions of oneself and other people, as well as the collective emotions of groups of people
61.	An intentional activity to modify a nonconforming product or product component
62.	Techniques used to collect data and information from a variety of sources
63.	Written sets of questions designed to quickly accumulate information from a large number of respondents

64.	An intentional activity that realigns the performance of the project work with the project management plan
65.	A graphical representation of situations showing causal influences, time ordering of events, and other relationships among variables and outcomes
66.	Show the strength of relationships between factors, causes and objectives that exist between the rows and columns that form the matrix
67.	Understanding the implications and considerations associated with different cultural affiliations within the project
68.	A visual representation of an organization's data described in business language and independent of any specific technology. Used to identify where data integrity or other quality issues can arise.
69.	Bar charts that show the graphical representation of numerical data
70.	Motivating a group of people towards the accomplishment of a goal
71.	Depicts parent-child relationships either vertically or horizontally
72.	The depiction in a diagram format of the inputs, process actions, and outputs of one or more processes within a system
73.	A series of steps or questions that have been developed based on lessons learned and/or historical data
74.	Display process data over time and against established control limits, which has a centerline that assists in detecting a trend of plotted values toward either control limit
75.	Traces an undesirable effect back to its root cause
76.	Ability to persuade a person or group of people towards a certain course of action
77.	Allows large numbers of ideas to be classified into groups for review and analysis
78.	A graph that shows how much work the team has left in their current iteration in order to meet their iteration goal, displayed in a downward trend
79.	An understanding of the internal and external political influences, processes, and culture

* These definitions are taken from the Glossary of *PMBOK® Guide – Sixth Edition*

Vocabulary Review Answers

1. Nominal group technique
2. Multicriteria decision analysis
3. Negotiation
4. Voting
5. Decision tree analysis
6. Stakeholder mapping / representation
7. Cost-benefit analysis
8. Text-oriented formats
9. Active listening
10. Change request
11. Focus groups
12. Expert judgment
13. Proposal evaluation
14. Networking
15. Meetings
16. Statistical sampling
17. Organizational process assets
18. Motivation
19. Stakeholder engagement assessment matrix
20. Plan-Do-Check-Act Cycle
21. Interviews
22. Preventive action
23. Data analysis techniques
24. Observation / conversation
25. Progressive elaboration
26. Performance reviews
27. Cost of quality
28. Project charter
29. Decision making
30. Scope change
31. Market research
32. Scatter diagrams
33. Communication styles assessment
34. Subsidiary plan
35. Benchmarking
36. Updates
37. Process analysis
38. Facilitation
39. Project management plan
40. Make-or-buy analysis
41. Team building
42. Probability and impact matrix
43. Alternatives analysis
44. Work performance data
45. Brainstorming
46. Baseline
47. Document analysis
48. Conflict management
49. Work performance information
50. Earned value analysis
51. Mind mapping
52. Meeting management
53. Data representation techniques
54. Assumption and constraint analysis
55. Project documents
56. Checksheets
57. Interpersonal and team skills
58. Assessment of other risk parameters
59. Enterprise environmental factors
60. Emotional intelligence
61. Defect repair
62. Data gathering techniques
63. Questionnaires and surveys
64. Corrective actions
65. Influence diagrams
66. Matrix diagrams
67. Cultural awareness
68. Logical data model
69. Histograms
70. Leadership
71. Hierarchical charts
72. Flowcharts
73. Checklists
74. Control charts
75. Cause-and-effect diagrams
76. Influencing
77. Affinity diagrams
78. Iteration burndown chart
79. Political awareness

Chapter 4

Establishing the Project

What's in This Chapter

- Develop Project Charter
- Develop Project Management Plan
- Identify Stakeholders
- Plan Stakeholder Engagement

Depending on the organization, the project manager's role in initiating and establishing the project can vary. In some situations, the project manager is assigned prior to the project being officially chartered. In other situations, the project manager may not become involved until after the project has authorized.

Regardless of when the project manager becomes involved, there are processes and procedures that will most likely occur to initiate any project. These include a request to do the project, either from inside or outside of the organization, some type of business and financial justification, a high-level risk assessment, identification of key stakeholders, and an official authorization to fund and begin the project.

Generally speaking, projects can be categorized as:

- Creating, developing, or enhancing a product, a service or a process
- Satisfying the needs of our stakeholders
- Responding to legal, regulatory or social requirements
- Strategically adding or updating business or technology approaches

In this chapter I will be presenting four of the *PMBOK® Guide* processes that are involved in getting the project established. While you may or may not be directly responsible for these processes, it is up to the project manager to ensure the key aspects have been completed and are in-place. You will notice that two of the processes are in the initiating process group and two are in the planning process group.

In establishing the project, activities from four processes may be used. The four processes included in this Chapter are:

Develop Project Charter. This process is in the initiating process group and the integration knowledge area and secures the authorization for the project.

Develop Project Management Plan. This process is in the planning process group and the integration knowledge area and develops the plan and approach for managing, executing, controlling, and closing the project.

Identify Stakeholders. This process is in the initiating process group and the stakeholder knowledge area and identifies and prioritizes the project stakeholders.

Plan Stakeholder Engagement. This process is in the planning process group and the stakeholder knowledge area and details the approach for engaging the stakeholders throughout the project.

As I move through the processes, I will be providing examples of some of the processes and tools and techniques, using the following scenario:

Our Project

Sandy Hendrix, the Bingham Hospital CEO, looks at the proposal that has been submitted for her consideration. Brooke Little, the Chief Nursing Officer (CNO), is proposing that the hospital create a new holistic health center that would serve both in-patients and the community. The proposed center and its programs would not only improve the service and care for patients, it would also add a new source of revenue to the hospital. Sandy remembers that one of the hospital's newer project managers, Kim Lane, had expressed interest in holistic modalities, so she requests a meeting with her.

Kim is excited when she hears Sandy's proposal and the details of the new project. "Sign me up!" she exclaims. She has been looking for an opportunity to leverage her project management skills in a challenging project. This looks like the perfect opportunity!

Develop Project Charter

integration knowledge area | initiating process group

The **develop project charter** process formally authorizes the project by the project sponsor and verifies that the initiative is in alignment with, and will contribute to, the strategic direction of the organization. This process may occur at the beginning of the project, or throughout the project at designated points if re-authorization is required.

For internal projects, the charter demonstrates that there is commitment from both sides to complete the requested initiative. If the project is being performed for an external customer, there would need to be a formal, legal agreement in-place with the customer. In that case, a charter may still be developed internally to authorize the project with the internal resources.

While the project charter may be developed without input from the project manager, as in when the project manager has not yet been assigned, the preferred approach is that the project manager participates in charter development. This allows for a better understanding of the project scope, approach, needs, and resource allocations.

The charter authorizing the project is initiated by the sponsor, governing body chairperson, PMO leadership or some type of authorized representative. The party authorizing the project is in a position to validate the project's contribution to the strategic objectives of the organization and can authorize resource and funding allocations. From an organizational perspective, typically the higher "ranking" the sponsor, the more weight the charter will carry.

As mentioned previously, PMI considers the charter mandatory for all project initiatives. This means that you need written authorization to begin the project. In your environment, what does that authorization look like? Is it called a project charter?

Develop Project Charter: ITTOs

Inputs	Tools & Techniques	Outputs

1. Business Documents
  • Business case
  • Benefits management plan
2. Agreements
3. Enterprise Environmental Factors
4. Organizational Process Assets
	1. Expert judgment
	2. Data Gathering
	  • Brainstorming
	  • Focus groups
	  • Interviews
	3. Interpersonal and Team Skills
	  • Conflict management
	  • Facilitation
	  • Meeting management
	4. Meetings
		1. Project Charter
		2. Assumptions Log

PMBOK® Guide – Sixth Edition. Page 75

Develop Project Charter: Inputs

Business Documents

To evaluate and the project and determine the feasibility, the sponsor or authorizing individual will analyze various business documents related to the project costs, benefits, and strategic alignment. This can include developing a business case and a benefits management plan prior to the charter being developed and the project being authorized.

Business case - The business case is generally completed by the project sponsor and will confirm the business need and drivers for the project. The business case will most likely include information on a cost-benefit analysis, to justify the funding of the project, such as net present value (NPV), internal rate of return (IRR), and/or return on investment (ROI). In previous versions of the PMP exam, there were occasional questions on calculating the various measurements. However, there is an understanding that sponsor is responsible for the calculations. However, while you will not need to calculate the values, you do need to understand the implications of them as it relates to your project. It is possible that you will get a question on the exam that involves the interpretation of these measurements.

NPV compares the value of a dollar today to the value of that same dollar in the future, taking inflation and returns into account. A positive NPV indicates the project will have a positive cash flow, while a negative NPV indicates the project will not. Negative NPV projects may still be required, however, specifically for regulatory and legal initiatives.

Using the data in the following table, the best investment would be Project A as it has the highest NPV. The term of the project is already factored into the NPV so that information can be disregarded. Notice that Project D has a negative NPV. While based on the NPV, it will not make a profit, the project may still be pursued if it is required from a legal or regulatory perspective.

Project	Term	NPV
Project A	3 years	$75,000
Project B	2 years	$38,000
Project C	5 years	$50,000
Project D	1 year	($25,000)

Belinda's Hint

While evaluating NPV, note that the term of the project is irrelevant. PMI often adds extra data or "noise" to questions to ensure that you fully understand the concept. In this example, the term needs to be disregarded as the NPV already factors the term into the value.

Internal rate of return (IRR) is the rate of growth a project is expected to generate. Generally, a higher IRR value than other available options would provide an increased chance of strong growth.

Return on investment (ROI) – may be calculated differently depending on the organization but it is generally the amount of net profit made as a result of an investment

Benefits management plan - Using the business case and a needs assessment, the benefits management plan describes how the project will fulfill business needs related to the strategic direction of the organization. The benefits management plan will include when and how the benefits will be accomplished and how those benefits will be measured.

In addition, the benefits management plan will identify the accountable person to monitor and report on the benefits (the benefits owner), any assumptions, and any risks associated with the achievement of the benefits. As the project progresses, the benefits management plan will be updated to reflect the project accomplishments, while aligning with the project charter and the project management plan.

Agreements

If, and only if, the project is being conducted for an external customer, there will be an agreement (a contract, memo of understanding (MOU), service level of agreement, email, etc.) between that customer and the organization completing the project work. Work cannot begin internally until an agreement is received from the external customer.

Belinda's Hint

If the project is being done internally and there is no external customer involved, you will not have an agreement or contractual relationship. For example, if marketing has requested that IT provide enhancements to the customer relationship management (CRM) system, an agreement would not be necessary as the project is internal.

However, if you are working on a project for an external customer, an agreement needs to be in-place before work can begin. Read these questions carefully – are you doing the work for an external customer or an internal party?

Common Inputs:

- **Enterprise environmental factors** - In developing the project charter, internal and external influences should be considered, including, but not limited to the type of organization where the work will be performed, any type of standards that are in place, legal or regulatory considerations, the stakeholders' expectations, and the governance framework of the organization.
- **Organizational process assets** - Policies and procedures will provide information on how the project charter should be formatted, developed, and managed. Leveraging the use of a project charter template will ensure consistency and will also increase efficiency. If you are new to the organization, historical information or past project files may provide insight into the chartering process for previous projects.

Develop Project Charter: Tools & Techniques

Common Tools and Techniques:

Expert Judgment

As the project charter is developed, various parties may be involved to provide feedback, insight, and approval as to the format and content of the project charter. Expert judgment may come from the sponsor, key stakeholders, the project manager, and/or the PMO.

Data Gathering Techniques

As the sponsor or authorizing party and the team evaluate and develop the project charter, they may leverage multiple data gathering techniques: brainstorming, focus groups, and interviews.

Brainstorming involves having the participating parties contribute ideas as to the development of the charter.

Focus groups are action-based meetings of pre-qualified stakeholders or representatives, guided by a facilitator. This enables the project team to gather representative feedback in an efficient manner while developing the project charter.

Interviews may be conducted one-on-one or with a group. This interactive communication approach allows for active exchange of information and ideas. Interviews may be appropriate with the key stakeholders when creating the charter.

Interpersonal and Team Skills

There are multiple interpersonal and team skills that will be leveraged while developing the project charter: conflict management, facilitation, and meeting management.

Conflict management is used to help guide stakeholders into alignment when there are differences of opinions regarding the project and the project charter.

Facilitation is the ability to effectively guide a group event to a successful decision, solution, or conclusion.

Meeting management is the active and effective management and coordination of meetings, such as preparing the agenda, sending follow-up notes and action items.

Meetings

Depending on the complexity of the project, meetings may be very brief or extensive and numerous. The goal of the meetings is successful execution of the project charter.

Develop Project Charter: Outputs

Project Charter

The project charter formally authorizes a project and details the business needs that the new product, service, or result will satisfy. The charter is signed by the sponsor and provides the project manager with the authority to use organizational resources for project activities. The charter links the project to the ongoing work and strategic plan of the organization. Unlike the other project documents, the project charter is typically <u>not</u> continually updated throughout the project or iteratively developed, as it represents the up-front authorization of the project.

The project charter may include information such as:

- Project purpose and justification, measurable objectives and success criteria
- High-level requirements, project description and risks
- Summary milestone schedule and high-level budget

- The key stakeholders that will be involved in the project
- Project approval requirements including what constitutes success, who would decide if the project is a success, and who is on-point to sign-off on the project once it is completed
- Project manager assignment, responsibility, and authority level (if the project manager has been assigned)
- Project sponsor name and authority level

Assumption Log

The assumption log documents the project assumptions and constraints, beyond the high-level project assumptions that were documented within the benefits management plan and the project charter. Assumptions are those conditions believed to be true, real, and factual and need to be documented, monitored, and updated throughout the project to ensure accuracy and applicability.

*The **develop project charter** process information is adapted from: PMBOK® Guide – Sixth Edition. Page 75-81*

Project Authorization

Kim is anxious to get started on the high-profile project of adding a holistic health center to the hospital. As a relatively new project management at Bingham Hospital, she decides to meet with Lisa O'Donnell, one of the senior managers in the PMO to ensure she gets started on her project properly.

Lisa is very helpful and provides Kim with the Bingham Hospital project charter template to get her started. Lisa asks Kim if Sandy Hendrix, the sponsor, has created a business case. The PMO has a requirement that a business case is developed for all projects over $50,000. Kim does not remember seeing a business case, so she realizes that she is going to need more information from Sandy and Brooke Little, one of the key stakeholders, before moving forward with developing the charter.

Kim is able to schedule a quick meeting with both Sandy and Brooke and they are able to work through the development of the business case. Armed with that information, Kim develops the draft project charter and gives it to Sandy for her signature.

Develop Project Management Plan

integration knowledge area | planning process group

The **develop project management plan** process documents the approach for the project and defines how the project will be executed, monitored and controlled, and closed within the project management plan. The project management plan may include a definition of the project phases, the change control process and will incorporate all the subsidiary plans and the project baselines.

Subsidiary plans provide additional details and approaches for areas of focus within a project. These subsidiary plans will be developed throughout many of the planning processes that are discussed further in this book. The depth and context of the project management plan and the subsidiary plans will depend on the type and complexity of the project. If a project is a longer-term, complex, or high-risk project, the expectation would be that the project management plan is more robust. However, if the project is brief, well-defined, or lower risk, then the project management plan may be no more than some key points or bulleted items.

The project management plan will be baselined once the scope, schedule, and budget have been defined. Prior to that baselining, the project management plan may be updated as necessary. Once it has been baselined, any changes would need to go through the defined change control process. The project management plan is considered mandatory for all projects.

Belinda's Hint

The best way to think of the project management plan is to picture it as the "how-to" guide for your project. You can envision it as a notebook, with the knowledge areas as the tab dividers, followed by the respective subsidiary plans.

Just keep in mind that in practice the project management plan may be made up of various documents created with different software, and not necessarily all "housed" together. For example, your project schedule baseline may be developed in Microsoft Project and your change control process and your subsidiary plans are created with Microsoft Word.

Develop Project Management Plan: ITTOs

Inputs	Tools & Techniques	Outputs
1. Project charter	1. Expert judgment	1. Project management plan
2. Outputs from other processes	2. Data gathering	
3. Enterprise environmental factors	• Brainstorming	
4. Organizational process assets	• Checklists	
	• Focus groups	
	• Interviews	
	3. Interpersonal and team skills	
	• Conflict management	
	• Facilitation	
	• Meeting management	
	4. Meetings	

PMBOK® Guide – Sixth Edition. Page 82

Develop Project Management Plan: Inputs

Outputs from Other Processes

The outputs from other processes that will be added to the project management plan include the project baselines (scope, schedule, and cost) and the subsidiary plans that are, and will be, created through the planning processes. As you can see by this input, the planning processes are concurrent and iterative in nature. This concept can certainly make it a challenge when studying or preparing for the exam! It would be much easier if the processes were linear, versus concurrent and iterative.

Common Inputs:

- **Project charter** - Containing the overview and description of the project, the project charter will provide the foundation for the project management plan.
- **Enterprise environmental factors** - In developing the project management plan, internal and external influences should be considered, including, but not limited to the type of organization where the work will be performed, any type of standards that are in place, legal or regulatory considerations, the stakeholders' expectations, and the governance framework of the organization. I always take into consideration the maturity of the project management within the organization. For example, if the project is being conducted in an organization that have very in-depth

methodologies and project processes, my project management plan is likely to be more detailed. However, if the organization is more intuitive versus formal with their project management, my project management plan may be more high-level to align with the culture of that organization.

- **Organizational process assets** - Policies and procedures will provide information on how the project management plan should be formatted, developed, and managed. Leveraging the use of a project management plan template will ensure consistency and will also increase efficiency. If you are new to the organization, historical information or past project files may provide insight into the planning process for previous projects.

Develop Project Management Plan: Tools & Techniques

Common Tools and Techniques:

Expert Judgment

As the project management plan is developed, various parties may be involved to provide feedback, insight, and approval as to the format and content of the plan. Expert judgment may come from the sponsor, key stakeholders, the project manager, the PMO, and the key project team members. It is essential that the project management plan is developed with insight and input from the project team, as they will be the individuals leveraging the plan to guide their work on the project.

Data Gathering Techniques

To ensure that the project management plan is comprehensive, appropriate, and applicable to the project work, various data gathering techniques may be leveraged.

Brainstorming involves having the participating parties contribute ideas as to the development of the project management plan.

Checklists are standardized documents with information based on personal or industry experience. They can be used to guide the development of the project management plan, ensuring that everything is included appropriately.

Focus groups are action-based meetings of pre-qualified stakeholders or representatives, guided by a facilitator. This enables the project team to gather representative feedback in an efficient manner.

Interviews may be conducted one-on-one or with a group. This interactive communication may be formal or informal and ensures that all key parties have provided insight and input into the development of the project management plan.

Interpersonal and Team Skills

The interpersonal and team skills leveraged while developing the project management plan include:

Conflict management may be necessary because participants will have varying opinions and positions on how to accomplish the project work.

Facilitation ensures that all participants are engaged in the processes of developing the project management plan and that buy-in has been accomplished.

Meeting management is active and effective management and coordination of meetings.

Meetings

The goal of the meetings is successful development, ongoing maintenance, and the updating of the project management plan.

Develop Project Management Plan: Outputs

Project Management Plan

The project management plan is the ultimate "how-to" guide for the project and includes the project baselines (schedule, cost, and scope), the project management processes selected by the project management team and the level of implementation of each process, a description of the tools and techniques to be used (such as any software, systems, or web interfaces), how the work will be executed, how the changes will be managed, monitored and controlled, how the integrity of the baselines will be maintained and under what circumstances the baselines may be modified, the selected project life cycle/phases, and the timeline for key management reviews to ensure the project management plan remains relevant.

*The **develop project management plan** process information is adapted from: PMBOK® Guide – Sixth Edition. Page 82-89*

Identify Stakeholders

stakeholder knowledge area | initiating process group

Throughout the project, the project manager and the project team will identify the project stakeholders, while determining their level of power over, and involvement with, the project. This process enables the team to document the stakeholder needs, wants, and expectations from the project. In doing so, the project manager is best able to prioritize their time and effort with multiple stakeholders.

Stakeholder identification must be comprehensive and performed early in the project, although it should be considered an ongoing process if there are any project changes or discoveries that would involve other parties. Stakeholder identification has also been conducted prior to project chartering to identify the key stakeholders for the project.

Given the very generic nature of the term 'stakeholder', you and your project team could conceivably identify thousands of stakeholders. All stakeholders are not treated equally, however! It is essential to clarify and categorize the stakeholders and their involvement in the project to prioritize your time and your team's time with them. As project manager, you need to know who has the power to make changes to your project, who are your resistors (you will always have some!) and who are your supporters.

Identify Stakeholders: ITTOs

Inputs	Tools & Techniques	Outputs
1. Project charter	1. Expert judgment	1. Stakeholder register
2. Business documents	2. Data Gathering	2. Change requests
• Business case	• Questionnaires and surveys	3. Project management plan updates
• Benefits management plan	• Brainstorming	• Requirements management plan updates
3. Project management plan	3. Data analysis	• Communications management plan
• Communications management plan	• Stakeholder analysis	• Risk management plan
• Stakeholder engagement plan	• Document analysis	• Stakeholder engagement plan
4. Project documents	4. Data representation	4. Project documents updates
• Change log	• Stakeholder mapping/ representation	• Assumption log
• Issue log	5. Meetings	• Issue log
• Requirements documentation		• Risk register
5. Agreements		
6. Enterprise Environmental Factors		
7. Organizational Process Assets		

PMBOK® Guide – Sixth Edition. Page 507

Identify Stakeholders: Inputs

Business Documents

The business case and the benefits management plan may be used to identify the stakeholders who will benefit from the project. This will be a likely source of "supporters" for your project.

Agreements

All individuals that are identified on any project contracts or agreements would be considered stakeholders for your project. The agreements will provide their information.

Common Inputs:

- **Project charter** - The project charter will identify the key stakeholders for the project and may also include information as to their roles and responsibilities on the project. The charter gives the overview of the project and, as such, can be valuable in identifying people, groups, or organizations that will need to be involved.

- **Project management plan** - Although you may not have the project management plan and subsidiary plans at the beginning of your project, stakeholder identification is ongoing throughout the project. As the project progresses, you can leverage the project management plan, including the communications management plan and the stakeholder engagement plan to evaluate impacted stakeholders.

- **Project documents** - Like the project management plan, there will be documents developed throughout the project that may be leveraged to identify stakeholders, including the change log, the issue log, and requirements documentation

- **Enterprise environmental factors** - In identifying stakeholders, internal and external influences should be considered, including, but not limited to the reach and impact of the project, groups that need to be involved, and the sensitivity of the project.

- **Organizational process assets** - Policies and procedures will provide information on how the stakeholder register should be developed and maintained. Leveraging the use of a stakeholder register template will ensure consistency and will also increase efficiency. If you are new to the organization, historical information or past project files may provide insight into the stakeholders and the stakeholder identification process on previous projects.

Identify Stakeholders: Tools and Techniques

Common Tools and Techniques

Expert Judgment

As the project begins, and ongoing throughout the project, various parties may be involved to provide feedback and insight as to how different stakeholders may be impacted by the project. Expert judgment may come from the sponsor, key stakeholders, the project manager, the PMO, and the key project team members.

Data Gathering Techniques

There are two data gathering techniques that may be used to identify and assess the project stakeholders:

Questionnaires and surveys are mechanisms used to collect feedback from various parties, groups, and organizations for the purposes of identifying stakeholders. This could be a simple survey describing the project and asking for feedback as to impact or requested involvement.

Brainstorming involves having the participating parties contribute ideas as to who may be impacted by, or need to be involved with, the project.

Data Analysis Techniques

There are two data analysis techniques used to identify and assess the project stakeholders:

A *stakeholder analysis* will determine whose interests should be taken into consideration throughout the project, identify the stakeholder's expectations and influence as it relates to the project, identify relationships that can be leveraged to benefit the project through coalitions and partnerships and those relationships that may need to be managed closely due to resistance or lack of support. This will prioritize the project manager's time, interactions and communications with the various stakeholders. Stakeholders should be evaluated in terms of:

- Their interest in the project or outcomes
- Their legal and/or moral rights as it relates to the work of the project
- Their ownership of any property or asset used or impacted by the project
- Any specialized knowledge they possess
- Any contributions they may be making to the project

In a *document analysis*, any pertinent documentation is assessed to determine stakeholder identification, role, and impact.

Data Representation Techniques

As the stakeholders are identified and assessed, there are several techniques that can be used to display or classify the stakeholders.

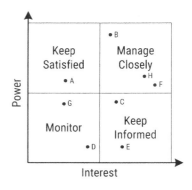

Stakeholder classification grids

- Power/interest grid – groups stakeholders based on their level of authority (power) and their level of concern (interest)
- Power/influence grid – groups stakeholders on their level of authority (power) and their active involvement (influence)
- Influence/impact grid – groups the stakeholders based on their active involvement (influence) and their ability to effect changes to the project (impact)
- Salience model – classifies stakeholders based on their power (ability to impose their will), urgency (need for immediate attention), and legitimacy (their involvement is appropriate)

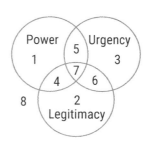

Stakeholder cube

Like the grids mentioned, the stakeholder cube combines the various classifications into a 3-dimensional model.

Directions of influence

Another classification of stakeholders is related to the impact of their influence on the project and project team.

- Upward: senior management or leadership, such as the sponsor or steering committee
- Downward: the team or specialists involved in the project
- Outward: groups or representatives outside of the team, such as suppliers or end-users
- Sideward: peers of the project manager, such as functional or operational managers

Meetings

The goal of the meetings is the ongoing identification and evaluation of the project stakeholders.

Identify Stakeholders: Outputs

Stakeholder Register

The key output of stakeholder identification is the stakeholder register. The stakeholder register contains pertinent information on the stakeholders, such as:

- Their identification information
- An assessment of their major requirements
- Main expectations
- Potential influence
- A classification of the stakeholders such as internal/external or supporter/neutral/resistor
- Typically, does not include financial information

The stakeholder register should not be confused with the detailed roles and responsibilities of the stakeholders. This will be detailed and documented within the **Plan Resource Management** process.

Belinda's Hint

If the stakeholder is involved in the project due to a sensitive issue, their involvement should be documented as appropriate, however the dissemination of, and access to this information, should be carefully controlled.

There are two processes that begin with the word IDENTIFY – **Identify Stakeholders** and **Identify Risks**. Both processes produce REGISTERS as an output: **Identify Stakeholders** produces the Stakeholder Register, and **Identify Risks** produces the Risk Register.

Common Outputs:

- **Change requests** - As stakeholder identification is revisited throughout the project, updated information on the project stakeholders may necessitate change requests for the project, the product, or the project plan.
- **Project management plan updates** - As stakeholder identification is revisited throughout the project, the project management plan may be updated; specifically, the following subsidiary plans: requirements management, communications management, risk management, and stakeholder engagement plans.
- **Project document updates** - As stakeholder identification is revisited throughout the project, the project documents may be updated, such as the assumption and issue logs and the risk register.

*The **identify stakeholders** process information is adapted from: PMBOK® Guide – Sixth Edition. Page 507-515*

Plan Stakeholder Engagement

stakeholder knowledge area | planning process group

The **plan stakeholder engagement** process develops strategies to engage stakeholders throughout the project, based on the analysis of their needs, expectations, and impact on the project and will define how the project will impact the stakeholders. The intention of this process is to create an approach that will actively engage the stakeholders throughout the project.

Keeping the stakeholders engaged in the project is critical to managing their expectations. Failing to manage expectations can lead to project failure. As with all subsidiary plans, the stakeholder engagement plan should be kept updated, reflecting the current conditions and challenges on the project, new or obsolete stakeholders or stakeholder groups, and the completion of project activities that may impact the stakeholder engagement.

Plan Stakeholder Engagement: ITTOs

Inputs	Tools & Techniques	Outputs
1. Project charter	1. Expert judgment	1. Stakeholder engagement plan
2. Project management plan	2. Data gathering	
• Resource management plan	• Benchmarking	
• Communications management plan	3. Data analysis	
• Risk management plan	• Assumption and constraint analysis	
3. Project documents	• Root cause analysis	
• Assumption log	4. Decision making	
• Change log	• Prioritization / ranking	
• Issue log	5. Data representation	
• Project schedule	• Mind mapping	
• Risk register	• Stakeholder engagement assessment matrix	
• Stakeholder register	6. Meetings	
• Requirements documentation		
4. Agreements		
5. Enterprise Environmental Factors		
6. Organizational Process Assets		

PMBOK® Guide – Sixth Edition. Page 516

Plan Stakeholder Engagement: Inputs

Agreements

Agreements may exist with contractors, vendors, and suppliers. The agreements will be used for analysis and review to ensure that they stay appropriately engaged in the project.

Common Inputs:

- **Project charter** - The project charter provides an overview of the project scope, objectives, and goals. This information can be used to assess engagement needs and levels.
- **Project management plan** - The project management plan and select subsidiary plans may be leveraged to determine engagement. Subsidiary plans that may be used include the resource management, communications management, and risk management plans.
- **Project documents** - After initial planning, the following project documents may be leveraged: assumption, issue, and change logs, the project schedule, and the risk and stakeholder registers.
- **Enterprise environmental factors** - In developing the stakeholder engagement plan, internal and external influences should be considered. Because this process is about engagement, the factors that could lead to the stakeholders not being engaged should be investigated, such as the length of the project, part-time team members, or maybe the project is just exciting!
- **Organizational process assets** - Leveraging the use of a stakeholder engagement plan template will ensure consistency and will also increase efficiency. If you are new to the organization, historical information or past project files may provide insight into stakeholder engagement activities.

Plan Stakeholder Engagement: Tools and Techniques

Common Tools and Techniques:

Expert Judgment

As the stakeholder engagement plan is developed, various parties may be involved to provide feedback, insight, and approval as to the format and content of the plan. Expert judgment may come from the sponsor, key stakeholders, the project manager, the PMO, and the key project team members.

Data Gathering Techniques

Benchmarking is a data gathering technique that is used to compare actual performance to planned or target performance to identify areas for improvement. It can be used in stakeholder engagement planning to validate approaches based on past projects, for example.

Data Analysis Techniques

An *assumptions and constraints analysis* is a data analysis technique that considers the assumptions and constraints associated with the project in order to identify or adjust stakeholder engagement activities.

A *root cause analysis* is a data analysis technique that looks at the underlying causes or reasons for a stakeholder's engagement and level of support in order to identify strategies to improve their engagement.

Decision-Making Techniques

As stakeholder engagement approaches and activities are evaluated, there will be a prioritization and ranking of the stakeholders based on their role on the project, their level of power and authority, etc.

Data Representation Techniques

During stakeholder engagement planning, several tools may be used to represent and visualize the data and information surrounding that engagement.

Mind mapping may be used to create a visual representation of the stakeholders and their relationships to each other and to the organization.

A *stakeholder engagement assessment matrix* displays the current engagement levels as compared to the needed or desired engagement levels to result in a successful project. Engagement levels can be defined as:

- Unaware – unaware of project and potential impacts
- Resistant – resistant of project and potential impacts and resistant to change
- Neutral – aware of project yet neither supportive nor resistant
- Supportive – aware of project and potential impacts and supportive to change
- Leading – aware of project and potential impacts and actively engaged in ensuring the project is a success

Stakeholder Engagement Matrix

	C = Current	D = Desired			
	Unaware	Resistant	Neutral	Supportive	Leading
Lisa Jones	C			D	
Tim Martin		C		D	
Shelby Day				C, D	

PMBOK® Guide – Sixth Edition. Page 522.

Meetings

Meetings with appropriate members of the project team and key stakeholders are used to evaluate stakeholder engagement and to develop the stakeholder engagement plan.

Plan Stakeholder Engagement: Outputs

Stakeholder Engagement Plan

The key output from this process is the stakeholder engagement plan. The plan documents the approach for actively engaging the stakeholders in the project and the decision-making. As with any subsidiary plan, the stakeholder engagement plan may be high-level or detailed, depending on the project and the environment.

While this may not be a commonly developed plan, there are certainly some situations where it may be more appropriate. For example, if your project is a long-term project where it is more likely that stakeholders may disengage over time, efforts should be in place to keep them engaged. This is also a concern for projects that may not be as exciting or glamorous as other projects: compliance, regulatory, decommissioning, etc. The project manager and the project team may need to be creative with ways to keep the folks involved and engaged!

As project manager, it is important that you exercise discretion and caution with the information contained within the stakeholder engagement plan, protecting sensitive information as appropriate.

*The **plan stakeholder engagement** process information is adapted from: PMBOK® Guide – Sixth Edition. Page 516-522*

Chapter 4 - Review Questions

Time Limit: 18 Minutes

1. All of the following may be included in the project management plan except:

    A. Subsidiary plans
    B. Performance baselines
    C. Project status reports
    D. The definition of project phases

2. As you develop the project management plan for the system renovation project, you are determining the need for any subsidiary plans. Which statement is least accurate regarding subsidiary plans?

    A. For a small project, it would be most appropriate to only use a subsidiary plan
    B. The need for subsidiary plans is based upon the type of project and the organizational requirements and control needs
    C. The subsidiary plans are all a component of the project management plan
    D. The subsidiary plan details specific actions surrounding a particular aspect of the project, such as cost, schedule, and communications

3. As PM, you are evaluating the various stakeholders that will be involved in the project. You have identified the key players and are now considering their role and impact on the project. What tool would be most beneficial to develop next?

    A. A risk register
    B. A stakeholder register
    C. A control chart
    D. A stakeholder engagement matrix

4. You have recently assumed the management of a high-profile, but confidential, project for your organization that has been underway for more than six months. Unfortunately, the previous project manager left the company abruptly and there was no opportunity for training, transition, or handover. In order to get up-to-speed as quickly as possible:

    A. You notify the sponsor of the risk associated with the previous project manager's exit to ensure they are aware of the implications.
    B. You request a copy of the project charter from the procurement lead to understand the benefits of the project.
    C. You leverage the project management plan to get an understanding of the management approach for the project.
    D. You request a meeting with each team member to understand their role on the project.

5. The performance measurement baselines that are included in the project management plan are:

    A. Change, quality, budget
    B. Scope, configuration, technical
    C. Quality, time, budget
    D. Scope, schedule, cost

6. In a stakeholder engagement matrix, stakeholders can be classified as all of the following except:

    A. Unaware
    B. Directing
    C. Neutral
    D. Leading

7. You have been assigned a new project with your consulting agency. You will be working with a number of internal teams to develop an intranet to provide easy access to company information. Which statement is most accurate?

    A. Because it is an internal project, you will not need a project charter but should have an agreement in place.
    B. Because you work in a consulting agency, you must have an agreement in place.
    C. A project charter would be required but the agreement is not required
    D. To ensure the project has properly authorized, you will need to ensure there is both a project charter and an agreement in place in order to begin.

8. **To initiate a project properly, business documents should be created and/or evaluated to ensure that the project is worth the investment and should be pursued. Those business documents may include:**
   A. A business case and a benefits management plan
   B. A charter and an agreement
   C. A charter and a business case
   D. A stakeholder agreement and a risk register

9. **One of your stakeholders has approached you with concerns about your current project. She was reviewing the business case and saw that the net present value (NPV) was only $280,000. However, the project is going to take four years to complete. Because the project is going to take four years, she is concerned that it is only going to have a $70,000 benefit. What statement is most accurate?**
   A. If the organizational threshold for project profitability is more than $70,000 than the stakeholder is justified in being concerned
   B. Because the NPV is below the stakeholder's comfort level, the project should be cancelled
   C. The NPV is already discounted for the duration, indicating a $280,000 value, well above the level of concern for the stakeholder
   D. As project manager, you are responsible for escalating the stakeholder's concern to the project sponsor

10. **The _____ process creates the _____ as an output, which documents the project conditions that are believed to be true and the project constraints.**
    A. Develop project charter, assumption log
    B. Develop project management plan, subsidiary plan
    C. Identify stakeholders, stakeholder register
    D. Develop project charter, project charter

11. **These are action-based meetings attended by pre-qualified stakeholders or representatives to gather feedback:**
    A. Facilitated workshops
    B. Chartering sessions
    C. Meetings
    D. Focus groups

12. **Directions of stakeholder influence include all of the following, except:**
    A. Sideward
    B. Inward
    C. Outward
    D. Downward

13. **This stakeholder classification grid evaluates stakeholders based on their active involvement and their ability to effect changes to the project:**
    A. Stakeholder cube
    B. Influence / impact grid
    C. Power / interest grid
    D. Power / influence grid

14. **How is mind mapping used in planning stakeholder engagement?**
    A. It is used to create a visual representation of the stakeholders and their relationships to each other and to the organization.
    B. It is used to create an understanding of the root causes of the issues anticipated to occur with the stakeholders.
    C. It is used to understand the minds, thoughts, feelings, and emotions of the project stakeholders.
    D. It is used to illustrate the current state of the organization and the future state of the organization once the project is complete.

15. **Which of the following would not be considered to be an input to evaluating and planning stakeholder engagement?**
    A. Project charter
    B. Agreements
    C. Benchmark study
    D. Project management plan

Review Question Answers

1. **Answer: C**

   Think of the project management plan as the how-to guide for your project. Within that how-to guide, you would include your subsidiary plans, your performance baselines, and perhaps the definition of your project phases. Project status reports are stand-alone documents detailing the progress of the project. These are separate from the project management plan.

2. **Answer: A**

   There is no such thing as just a subsidiary plan – the word subsidiary implies that it is a component of something. In this case, a subsidiary plan is a component of the project management plan.

3. **Answer: D**

   Because you have already identified the stakeholders, the next thing to develop would be the stakeholder engagement matrix. This will allow you to assess their level of engagement in the project, both current and desired.

4. **Answer: C**

   The project management plan will provide information as to how the project is being managed, including the approaches documented in any subsidiary plans and the cost, schedule, and scope baselines.

5. **Answer: D**

   The three project baselines are the scope baseline, schedule baseline, and cost baseline.

6. **Answer: B**

   Stakeholders may be unaware, resistant, neutral, supportive, or leading. Directive is not a classification in the stakeholder engagement matrix.

7. **Answer: C**

   The project described is for an internal project and is not for an external customer. A project charter is necessary for all projects, but as there is not an external customer, an agreement is not necessary.

8. **Answer: A**

   The business documents that are involved in project investment analysis include the business case and the benefits management plan.

9. **Answer: C**

   The net present value (NPV) already discounts the value over the life or term of the project. As such, the project has a $280,000 value not a $70,000 value.

10. **Answer: A**

    It is the **develop project charter** process that creates the assumptions log as an output, along with the project charter.

11. **Answer: D**

    Focus groups bring together pre-qualified stakeholders or representatives, guided by a facilitator to capture their opinions, feelings, and feedback on the proposed change or impact of the project.

12. **Answer: B**

    The impact of the stakeholders' influence on the project and project team can be classified as upward, downward, outward, or sideward. Inward is not a classification.

13. **Answer: B**

    A stakeholder's active involvement is considered their "influence" and the stakeholder's ability to effect change to the project is considered their "impact". This is describing the influence / impact grid.

14. **Answer: A**

    Mind mapping is used in stakeholder engagement planning to create a visual representation of the stakeholders and their relationships to each other and to the organization.

15. **Answer: C**

The benchmark study is not an input to the plan stakeholder engagement process. However, the project charter, the project management plan, and agreements are all inputs to the process.

Chapter 4 - Vocabulary Review

* Agreements
  Assumption and constraint analysis
* Assumption log
* Benchmarking
* Benefits management plan
  Brainstorming
* Business case
  Checklists
  Conflict management
  Directions of influence

  Document analysis
  Facilitation
* Focus groups
  Influence / impact grid
* Interviews
  Prioritization / ranking
  Power / interest grid
  Power / influence grid
* Project charter
* Project management plan

* Questionnaires
* Root cause analysis
  Salience model
* Stakeholder analysis
  Stakeholder cube
* Stakeholder engagement assessment matrix
* Stakeholder engagement plan
* Stakeholder register

1.	A documented economic feasibility study used to establish validity of the benefits of a selected component lacking sufficient definition and that is used as a basis for the authorization of further project management activities
2.	Evaluation of the project's assumptions and limitations to determine accuracy
3.	A data representation tool that categorizes stakeholders by their level of power on the project and their level of influence on the project
4.	A component of the project management plan that identifies the strategies and actions required to promote productive involvement of stakeholders in project or program decision making and execution
5.	An organizational standard document providing a listing of considerations or steps that may be used to create the project management plan
6.	Any document or communication that defines the initial intentions of a project. May be a contract, memorandum of understanding, letters of agreement, etc.
7.	A stakeholder analysis technique that evaluates stakeholders based on their power, urgency, and legitimacy
8.	A decision-making technique that prioritizes the stakeholders based on their role on the project, etc.
9.	The management and coordination of effective meetings
10.	An analytical technique used to determine the basic underlying reason that causes a variance or a defect or a risk.
11.	A data representation tool that categorizes stakeholders by their level of influence on the project and their level of impact on the project
12.	A project document that includes the identification, assessment, and classification of project stakeholders
13.	A formal or informal approach to elicit information from stakeholders by talking to them directly

14.	Comparison of actual or planned products, processes, and practices to those of comparable organizations to identify best practices, generate ideas for improvement, and provide a basis for measuring performance
15.	An evaluation of project documents to assess and determine stakeholder identification, role and impact
16.	A document issued by the project initiator or sponsor that formally authorizes the existence of a project and provides the project manager with the authority to apply organizational resources to project activities
17.	The documented explanation defining the processes for creating, maximizing, and sustaining the benefits provided by a project or program
18.	An elicitation technique that brings together prequalified stakeholders and subject matter experts to learn about their expectations and attitudes about a proposed product, service, or result
19.	A data analysis tool that combines the various stakeholder classifications into a 3-dimension model
20.	Classification of stakeholders related to the impact of their influence on the project and project team and may include: upward, downward, outward, and sideward
21.	A data representation tool that categorizes stakeholders by their level of power on the project and their level of interest or concern for the project
22.	A matrix that compares current and desired stakeholder engagement levels
23.	A project document used to record all assumptions and constraints throughout the project life cycle
24.	Written sets of questions designed to quickly accumulate information from a large number of respondents
25.	The document that describes how the project will be executed, monitored and controlled, and closed
26.	A technique of systematically gathering and analyzing quantitative and qualitative information to determine whose interests should be taken into account throughout the project
27.	A leadership skill leveraged when working with individuals and organizations with differences in opinions that need to be resolved
28.	Used with a group as a method for capturing a number of different ideas

* These definitions are taken from the Glossary of *PMBOK® Guide – Sixth Edition*

Vocabulary Review Answers

1. Business case
2. Assumption and constraint analysis
3. Power / influence grid
4. Stakeholder engagement plan
5. Checklists
6. Agreements
7. Salience model
8. Prioritization / ranking
9. Facilitation
10. Root cause analysis
11. Influence / impact grid
12. Stakeholder register
13. Interviews
14. Benchmarking
15. Document analysis
16. Project charter
17. Benefits management plan
18. Focus groups
19. Stakeholder cube
20. Directions of influence
21. Power / interest grid
22. Stakeholder engagement assessment matrix
23. Assumption log
24. Questionnaires
25. Project management plan
26. Stakeholder analysis
27. Conflict management
28. Brainstorming

Chapter 5

Project Scope Planning

What's in This Chapter

- Plan Scope Management
- Collect Requirements
- Define Scope
- Create WBS

Project "scope" is the work of the project, nothing more and nothing less. Scope is what we are delivering by way of the project, and it is addressed in terms of both product scope and project scope. Product scope is specific to what the project team is delivering: product, service, or result; whereas project scope is all the work of the project, including the product scope. The completed project scope is measured against the project management plan, and the product scope is measured against the product requirements.

Of the triple constraint, scope is the foundation and the most critical. If you are unable to deliver on the project scope, having or not having enough time or budget is irrelevant. Certainly, however, if there are limitations to the schedule or to the budget, the scope is most oftentimes affected. The project manager will need to assess their project environment to determine the best approach to managing the project scope and the requirements. This includes understanding and defining how requirements are reused on future projects, the type of governance and validation procedures and processes that are in place, how development is going to occur (predictive versus adaptive), and the stability of the environment and the requirements.

Scope Management – Predictive Versus Adaptive

There are various approaches to project management, as discussed previously in this book. Scope management is performed differently in a plan-driven or predictive project environment versus an agile or adaptive project environment. For any environment, it is essential that the key stakeholders are involved early on defining the product and project requirements and identifying success criteria. During the **control quality** (QC) process, the products will be validated against that criteria to ensure conformance to requirements.

Predictive projects have the scope defined at the beginning of the project, and the project manager manages to the scope baseline. Any changes to that scope baseline would need to be handled progressively, through a formal change control process.

Adaptive projects, or agile approaches, are utilized in environments where a high level of change is expected. Requirements are prioritized via the use of a product backlog. Scope is approved, built, tested, and delivered one

. The product backlog is frequently reviewed, and scope is controlled and validated during each

ng Processes

ing the project, activities from four processes may be used. The four processes included in this lesson are all
nning process group and the project scope management knowledge area:

cope Management. This process creates the scope management and requirements management plans.

llect Requirements. This process results in the requirements documentation and the requirements traceability matrix.

Define Scope. This process produces the project scope statement, a detailed description of the project and product scope.

Create WBS. This process breaks the work of the project down into smaller, more manageable components, resulting
in the work breakdown structure (WBS). The key output from this process will be the scope baseline which will include
the scope statement, WBS, and WBS dictionary.

Plan Scope Management

scope knowledge area | planning process group

The scope management and requirements management plans are developed based on the current information on the
project, including from the project charter. Both subsidiary plans provide instruction and direction to the project team
related to the management of the project scope and collection, prioritization, and development of the project
requirements. While these plans are typically developed early in the project progress, they should also be revisited and
updated periodically to reflect the current status of the project and any changes that have been approved.

Plan Scope Management: ITTOs

Inputs	Tools & Techniques	Outputs
1. Project charter	1. Expert judgment	1. Scope management plan
2. Project management plan	2. Data analysis	2. Requirements management plan
• Quality management plan	• Alternatives analysis	
• Project life cycle description	3. Meetings	
• Development approach		
3. Enterprise Environmental Factors		
4. Organizational Process Assets		

PMBOK® Guide — Sixth Edition. Page 134

Plan Scope Management: Inputs

Common Inputs

- **Project charter** - The project charter provides the foundation for the project, including the high-level requirements,
  assumptions and constraints, the project description, and the overall project purpose. This information will be used
  to determine the scope and requirements management approach.

- **Project management plan** - As the scope and requirements management plans are revisited periodically throughout the project, the project manager may consult the project management plan (documenting the project life cycle and development approach) and subsidiary plans such as the quality management plan.
- **Enterprise environmental factors** - In developing these subsidiary plans, internal and external influences should be considered, including, but not limited to the type of organization where the work will be performed, any type of standards that are in place, legal or regulatory considerations, the stakeholders' expectations, and the governance framework of the organization.
- **Organizational process assets** - Policies and procedures will provide information on how the project scope and the project requirements will be documented, validated, prioritized and delivered. Leveraging a subsidiary plan template will ensure consistency and will also increase efficiency.

Plan Scope Management: Tools & Techniques

Common Tools and Techniques:

Expert Judgment

As these subsidiary plans are developed, various parties may be involved to provide feedback, insight, and approval as to the format and content of the plan. Expert judgment may come from the sponsor, key stakeholders, the project manager, the PMO, and the key project team members. It is essential that the subsidiary plans are developed with insight and input from the project team, as they will be the individuals leveraging the plan to guide their work on the project.

Data Analysis Techniques

The project manager, business analysts and/or the project team will analyze project data to determine the most appropriate approach. Data analysis can include conducting an *alternatives analysis* as it relates to the scope and requirements management approach, seeking out various means or methods for accomplishing the project scope objectives.

Meetings

Meetings may be held with various project team members, stakeholders, and business analysts to determine the best approach for scope and requirements management.

Plan Scope Management: Outputs

There are two key outputs from **plan scope management**, both of which are subsidiary plans. These subsidiary plans may be high-level or detailed, depending on the complexity of the environment and the project.

Scope Management Plan

The scope management plan may include information such as how the project scope statement will be documented, how the WBS will be created and maintained, how formal acceptance of the deliverables will be obtained, and how to handle changes to the project scope statement.

Requirements Management Plan

The requirements management plan, which may be included in the scope management plan, documents how requirements will be analyzed, documented and managed throughout the project. The requirements management plan may include how requirements activities will be planned, tracked and reported, configuration management activities, the process to prioritize requirements, which product metrics will be used and why, and the traceability structure.

An aspect of requirements management that may be included in the plan is related to configuration management. Configuration management encompasses changes to the technical specifications of what is being delivered. For example, if the product was originally going to be blue and now it is going to be green, that is a change to the technical specifications and therefore falls under configuration management. The configuration management approach is documented in the requirements management plan and may include: how the impacts of the changes will be assessed, how the changes will be monitored, traced, and reported, what is the authorization process for the changes, and how will the changes be initiated.

*The **plan scope management** process information is adapted from: PMBOK® Guide – Sixth Edition. Page 134-137*

Collect Requirements

scope knowledge area | planning process group

Collecting the project requirements is one of the most important, foundational processes, as it is the requirements that feed the WBS and in turn, feed the cost, schedule, quality, and procurement plans and approaches.

One of the most common challenges to project success is adequately and accurately collecting comprehensive, detailed, and realistic requirements. This is especially true as we find our environments becoming increasingly complex and the pace of change even faster. The reality of requirement challenges has influenced the growth of the business analyst role.

Business analysts are individuals with sufficient business analysis skills and expertise, and it is during this process that they are most leveraged. If a business analyst is assigned to the project, they will be responsible, at least in part, for collecting the project and product requirements. As such, the project manager and the business analyst need to work closely and collaboratively.

Collecting Requirements

Kim is anxious to get started on the Holistic Health Center project. Now that the project has officially been chartered and she has identified her stakeholders, she begins to drill down into the specific requirements.

To collect the requirements, Kim first considers the stakeholders' roles on the project. For her key stakeholders, such as Sandy Hendrix, CEO, Brooke Little, CNO, and Dr. Don Teagan, the physician representative, she wants to be exceptionally diligent with the capture of the requirements. As such, she chooses to conduct interviews with each of them, expanding on the preliminary requirements that were in the project charter.

With her nursing unit representatives, Kim conducts focus groups to capture representative feedback from their perspective on enhancing the in-patient experience. Kim also conducts focus groups with individuals from the local community that have been an in-patient within the last three years.

Kim has found two other hospitals in the United States that have created a holistic health program. She uses the information from them as the basis to benchmark their goals and requirements for the project. Lastly, Kim sends out surveys to all the hospital employees to get a sense of their perspectives on holistic approaches as well as learning what services they may be interested in using.

Collect Requirements: ITTOs

Inputs	Tools & Techniques	Outputs

1. Project charter
2. Project management plan
  • Scope management plan
  • Requirements management plan
  • Stakeholder engagement plan
3. Project documents
  • Assumption log
  • Lessons learned register
  • Stakeholder register
4. Business documents
  • Business case
5. Agreements
6. Enterprise Environmental Factors
7. Organizational Process Assets
	1. Expert judgment
	2. Data Gathering
	  • Brainstorming
	  • Interviews
	  • Focus groups
	  • Questionnaires and surveys
	  • Benchmarking
	3. Data analysis
	  • Document analysis
	4. Decision making
	  • Voting
	  • Multicriteria decision analysis
	  • Autocratic decision making
	5. Data representation
	  • Affinity diagrams
	  • Mind mapping
	6. Interpersonal and team skills
	  • Nominal group technique
	  • Observation / conversation
	  • Facilitation
	7. Context diagram
	8. Prototypes
		1. Requirements documentation
		2. Requirements traceability matrix

PMBOK® Guide – Sixth Edition. Page 138

Collect Requirements: Inputs

Business Documents

The business case contains information regarding the criteria for meeting the business needs. This is used to capture the requirements related to successful alignment with that business case.

Agreements

Existing agreements will most likely contain project and product requirements related to the portion of the work that is being done for the benefit of an external customer or for the work being done by any vendors or suppliers.

Common Inputs:

- **Project charter** - The project charter provides the high-level requirements for the project and the product. Those high-level requirements will be elaborated through collecting the detailed and specific requirements.
- **Project management plan** – As the requirements are collected and re-visited throughout the project, various aspects of the project management plan may be considered. This includes, but is not limited to, the scope management, requirements management, and stakeholder engagement plan.
- **Project documents** - Project documents that may be evaluated or analyzed to collect or revisit the requirements include the assumption log, the lessons learned register, and the stakeholder register.
- **Enterprise environmental factors** - In collecting requirements, internal and external influences should be considered, including, but not limited to the organizational culture and infrastructure, the administration of personnel, and marketplace conditions.

- **Organizational process assets** - Policies and procedures will provide information on how the project requirements should be captured, documented, prioritized, and managed. Leveraging historical information or past project files may provide insight into the requirements for the project or the methods for collecting requirements.

Collect Requirements: Tools and Techniques

There are many techniques for collecting the requirements from your stakeholders. In collecting requirements, you always want to take into consideration the individuals and/or groups that will be submitting the requirements. Requirement collection is not a one-size-fits-all, and ideally several techniques will be used based on that stakeholder's role in the project, their level of power and influence, and the impact of their requirements on the overall scope of the project.

Context Diagram

The context diagram is a scope model that visually depicts the product scope by showing a business system and how people or users interact with it.

Prototypes

Prototypes create a working model of the expected product, allowing the stakeholders to experiment with a tangible product rather than interpreting abstract requirements. Creating prototypes aligns with progressive elaboration because there are iterative cycles of development and enhancements.

Prototyping allows for early feedback on the requirements before delivering the final product. Prototypes may be small-scale products, mock-ups, simulations, or computer-generated models.

Common Tools and Techniques:

Expert Judgment

Requirements are gathered from any number of parties. Expert judgment may come from the sponsor, stakeholders, the project manager, the PMO, regulators, partner organizations and the project team members.

Data Gathering Techniques

Collecting the requirements involves multiple data gathering techniques.

Brainstorming involves having the participating parties contribute ideas freely as to the project and product requirements.

Interviews may be conducted one-on-one or with a group. This interactive communication approach allows for active exchange of information and ideas as to the project and product requirements.

Focus groups are action-based meetings of pre-qualified stakeholders or representatives, guided by a facilitator. This enables the project team to gather representative feedback in an efficient manner as to the requirements.

Questionnaires and surveys are electronic or paper-based means of collecting feedback and information from a large number of participants. Low-response rate, however, needs to be considered, and as such, would not be appropriate for key stakeholders.

Benchmarking allows the project team to compare the project and product requirements to an existing project, best practice, or industry-standard.

Data Analysis Techniques

Data analysis for requirements collection involves analysis of several project and industry documents. This can include analyzing use cases, issue logs, process flows, process documentation, agreements and business plans, regulatory documentation, and policies and procedures.

Decision-Making Techniques

The process of collecting requirements will involve making decisions within the team and with the stakeholders as to what requirements will be included for the project and the product.

Voting is a collective technique where the opinions of the members are gathered, and a decision is made based on a pre-defined technique: unanimity implies that all members must agree, majority implies that more than half of the members must agree, and plurality implies that the largest subset of the group must agree even if it is not majority.

Multicriteria decision analysis uses a decision matrix with identified criteria. The criteria may be related to risk, valuation, or other factors. The team or the sponsor may place higher weighting on particular aspects the project or product and that weighting can then be used to determine which requirements are the highest priority for inclusion.

Autocratic decision-making implies that one person is making the decision for the group. May also be referred to as a dictatorship.

Data Representation Techniques

There are two data representation techniques that may be used to display the information collected regarding the project requirements.

Affinity diagrams classify a large number of ideas into groups for review and analysis. These are often called a sticky-note diagram or process.

Mind mapping takes ideas that are generated through brainstorming or other techniques and creates a visual mapping of similarities and differences in understanding. When collecting requirements, mind mapping allows the visualization of the relatedness of the requirements.

Interpersonal and Team Skills

Collecting requirements involves working with multiple parties, stakeholders, and team members. Interpersonal and team skills will be leveraged to solicit information and manage the relationships and interactions appropriately.

Nominal group technique enhances brainstorming with a voting process to rank or prioritize the ideas. To conduct the technique:

- The scenario, question or problem is presented to the group
- The participants write down their ideas
- A facilitator typically writes the ideas on a flip chart
- The ideas are shared and discussed to ensure understanding
- Votes are submitted privately, typically on a 1 to 5 scale and there may be multiple rounds to re-vote and select the top scoring ideas

Observation and conversation is a way of viewing and interacting with individuals to see how they perform their work or interact with systems. This is especially helpful when people are involved in complex tasks and have difficulty articulating what it is they do. May be called job-shadowing or ghosting. Not only can this be beneficial in gleaning requirements from the user community, it also serves to build relationships with those users.

Facilitation involves the skills associated with the effective leadership and management of group interactions and activities. Those skills may be applied to multiple situations and scenarios. Specifically, when collecting requirements, these skills are used in the following processes:

- Joint application design or development (JAD) sessions – used in software development, JAD sessions are facilitated workshops that bring business user experts and the development team together to gather requirements and improve software. Facilitated workshops may be conducted in-person or virtually and are attended by key cross-functional stakeholders, allowing quick reconciliation of stakeholder differences.
- Quality function deployment (QFD) – also facilitated workshops, QFD sessions determine characteristics for new product development, using the voice of the customer (VOC).

- User stories – short descriptions of functionality developed within a requirements workshop. User stories describe the stakeholder role, the role(s) that benefit from the feature, what the user needs to accomplish, and the benefit to the user or stakeholder.

Collect Requirements: Outputs

There are two key outputs from collecting requirements:

Requirements Documentation

The requirements documentation describes how the individual requirements will meet the business need for the project. Once the requirements are measurable, testable, traceable, complete, consistent and acceptable to key stakeholders, they can be baselined.

Requirements documentation may include:

- Business need or opportunity and why the project has been undertaken
- Business and project objectives
- Functional requirements, which may be in the form of a requirements list, model, or both
- Non-functional requirements, such as performance, safety, security, level of service
- Quality requirements and acceptance criteria
- Impacts to other organizational areas and to other entities inside or outside the performing organization
- Support and training requirements

The requirements themselves can include:

- Business requirements – the higher-level needs of the organization as a whole (business issues, opportunities, reasons for the project)
- Stakeholder requirements – the needs of a stakeholder or a stakeholder group
- Solution requirements – features, functions, and characteristics of the product, service, or result
- Transition requirements – temporary capabilities to transition from the current "as-is" state to the future "to-be" state, such as training, data conversion, etc.
- Project requirements – actions, processes, or other conditions the project needs to meet
- Quality requirements – conditions or criteria needed to validate the successful completion of deliverables and other project requirements

For adaptive or agile projects, the requirements are documented in the product backlog. One of the most significant changes between the 5th and 6th editions of the *PMBOK® Guide*, is the introduction of more agile approaches, terminology, and practices. For the exam, you need to know that the product backlog is the requirements document for adaptive projects. The backlog typically contains the features for the product in a generally prioritized format. Between each sprint or iteration, the agile team selects the work for the next sprint, allowing for re-prioritization and changes as needed.

Requirements Traceability Matrix

The requirements traceability matrix links requirements from their origin through to the completion of the deliverables. This matrix helps ensure that each requirement adds business value by linking it to the business and project objectives and ensures that requirements that are approved are actually delivered at the conclusion of the project.

Requirements may be traced to:

- Business needs, opportunities, goals and objectives
- Project objectives
- Project scope/WBS deliverables
- Product design
- Product development
- Test strategy and scenarios (one of the most common in practice)

Requirements Traceability Matrix									
Project Name:									
Cost Center:									
Project Description:									
ID	Sub ID	Requirement	Business Need/Goal	Project Objective	WBS Deliverables	Product Design	Product Development	Test Cases
001	1.0							
	1.1							
	1.2							
	1.3							
002	2.0							
	2.1							
	2.2							
003	3.0							
	3.1							
	3.2							
004	4.0							

PMBOK® Guide – Sixth Edition. Page 149

*The **collect requirements** process information is adapted from: PMBOK® Guide – Sixth Edition. Page 138-149*

Define Scope

scope knowledge area | planning process group

With the requirements collected, the next process will be to define the scope and create the project scope statement, based on the requirements that will be included in the project. Just because a requirement was identified, it does not mean it will be included in the project. This process will develop the detailed written description of the project and the product within the scope statement, reflecting those requirements that will be included. The scope may be continuously defined in more detail and updated as the project evolves (progressively elaborated). Information from the project charter will serve as the basis for the scope statement. This includes information on the major deliverables, assumptions, and constraints.

While there may be multiple iterations to comprehensively define the scope, the goal is to accurately define the project scope in as much detail up front, to minimize scope creep. Scope creep is considered any unmanaged changes to the project scope. The project scope statement documents both "in-scope" and "out-of-scope" requirements, as it is just as important to reflect what is *not* being done as what *is* being done within the constraints of the project. If a requirement was submitted to the team, the owner may assume that the requirement will be part of the scope of the project unless explicitly advised otherwise.

Define Scope: ITTOs

Inputs	Tools & Techniques	Outputs
1. Project charter	1. Expert judgment	1. Project scope statement
2. Project management plan	2. Data analysis	2. Project documents updates
• Scope management plan	• Alternatives analysis	• Assumption log
3. Project documents	3. Decision making	• Requirements documentation
• Assumption log	• Multicriteria decision analysis	• Requirements traceability matrix
• Requirements documentation	4. Interpersonal and team skills	• Stakeholder register
• Risk register	• Facilitation	
4. Enterprise Environmental Factors	5. Product analysis	
5. Organizational Process Assets		

PMBOK® Guide – Sixth Edition. Page 150

Define Scope: Inputs

Common Inputs:

- **Project charter** - The project charter provides the high-level project description, risks, assumptions and constraints.
- **Project management plan** - The project management plan will be consulted as the scope is defined, specifically leveraging the scope management plan.
- **Project documents** - Project documents that may be evaluated to define the scope include the assumption log, requirements documentation, and the risk register.
- **Enterprise environmental factors** - In creating the scope statement, internal and external influences should be considered, including, but not limited to the organizational culture and infrastructure, the administration of personnel, and marketplace conditions.
- **Organizational process assets** - Policies and procedures will provide information on how the project scope statement should be formatted, developed, and managed. Leveraging the use of a scope statement template will ensure consistency and will also increase efficiency.

Define Scope: Tools and Techniques

Scope definition and the creation of the project scope statement involves the use of multiple tools and techniques.

Product Analysis

A product analysis may be conducted if the project is producing a product as a deliverable. Product analysis techniques include product breakdowns, systems and/or requirements analyses, systems engineering, value engineering and value analyses.

Common Tools and Techniques:

Expert Judgment

Creating the scope statement will involve leveraging feedback, participation and expertise from multiple project participants, team members, stakeholders, customer representatives, and others with knowledge that may be pertinent to the project scope.

Data Analysis Techniques

To create the scope statement, data analysis may include an *alternatives analysis* where various ways to meet the requirements and the project objectives are considered and evaluated.

Decision-Making Techniques

Decision making on what will and what will not be included in the project scope may include using a *multicriteria decision analysis* with a decision matrix that provides an analytical approach for establishing criteria to refine the project or product scope. The criteria may include considerations of schedule, budget, resources, etc.

Interpersonal and Team Skills

As with collecting requirements, interpersonal and team skills used to define the scope include effective *facilitation* such as for workshops and working sessions with stakeholders. The goal is to reach a common understanding of the project deliverables and the project boundaries.

Define Scope: Outputs

Project Scope Statement

The project scope statement describes in detail the project's deliverables, the work required to create those deliverables with the goal of providing a common understanding of the project scope among all project stakeholders. The project scope statement is one of the critical documents, along with the charter and the project management plan. The charter gives the approval for the project, the project scope statement describes what we are doing on the project, and the project management plan tells us how we are doing it.

The detailed project scope statement includes:

- Product scope description – product details
- Product acceptance criteria – quality standards, acceptance process, acceptance responsibilities
- Project deliverables – tangibles created by the project
- Project exclusions – the "out-of-scope" requirements
- Project constraints and assumptions – limitations on the project and information that is believed to be true

Common Output:

- **Project document updates** - Project document updates may include updating the assumption log, the requirements documentation, the requirements traceability matrix and the stakeholder register.

*The **define scope** process information is adapted from: PMBOK® Guide – Sixth Edition. Page 150-155*

Create WBS

scope knowledge area | planning process group

The scope statement details in writing what will be included and not included in the project. Using that as a base, the next process would be to create a visual representation of the work of the project. When creating the work breakdown structure (WBS), the major deliverables will be broken down into smaller, more manageable pieces.

The WBS is a deliverable-oriented (set up by deliverables), hierarchical (each descending layer of the WBS rolls up to the higher level), commonly graphical, decomposition of the work to be completed on the project and it is a representation of all the work that is being done on the project.

The lowest level of a WBS is called a work package: a group of related work activities. You know that you have decomposed to the work package level when one person (the work package owner) can easily estimate, schedule, and monitor and control the work within the work package.

Belinda's Hint

Remember that the lowest level of a WBS is a work package, not an activity. We do not break the work packages down into activities until we move into the schedule knowledge area and create our activity list.

In the scope knowledge area, we break the work down only as far as the work package.

As the final scope planning process, the key output will be the scope baseline. The scope baseline includes the WBS, the WBS dictionary and the scope statement that was an output of the **define scope** process.

DEFINE SCOPE

With all of the requirements gathered, Kim works through the prioritization and selection process with the key stakeholders. Based on the authorized budget and preliminary analysis, the team creates the scope statement, drafting specifically what is going to be included in the project and what is not.

CREATE WBS

With the scope defined, Kim creates the work breakdown structure, giving the team members the visual representation of all the project work. Along with the WBS, Kim develops the WBS dictionary. Once these are acceptable to the key stakeholders, Kim creates the scope baseline and adds it to the project management plan.

Create WBS: ITTOs

Inputs	Tools & Techniques	Outputs
1. Project management plan • Scope management plan 2. Project documents • Project scope statement • Requirements documentation 3. Enterprise Environmental Factors 4. Organizational Process Assets	1. Expert judgment 2. Decomposition	1. Scope baseline 2. Project documents updates • Assumption log • Requirements documentation

PMBOK® Guide — Sixth Edition. Page 156

Create WBS: Inputs

Common Inputs:

- **Project management plan** - The project management plan will be consulted, including the scope management plan. The scope management plan documents how the WBS will be created using the scope statement.
- **Project documents** - Project documents will be reviewed while creating the WBS and the scope baseline. Documents can include the project scope statement and the requirements documentation.
- **Enterprise environmental factors** - Internal and external factors will be considered when developing the WBS. This can include considering industry specific WBS standards that are relevant to the project.
- **Organizational process assets** - Policies, procedures, guidelines, and templates will be leveraged in creating the WBS and the WBS dictionary. Many organizations have WBS templates that can be modified with the unique aspects of the particular project.

Create WBS: Tools and Techniques

Decomposition

Decomposition is the process of subdividing project deliverables into smaller, more manageable components. The level of decomposition will vary in detail from project to project, depending on the complexity. To decompose the project into work packages:

1. Identify and analyze the deliverables and the work required to produce those deliverables

2. Structure and organize the WBS

3. Decompose the WBS into lower level details

4. Assign identification codes (typically from the code of accounts/chart of accounts) to each component

5. Verify that the level of decomposition is appropriate

The WBS may be structured by deliverable, phase, location or a structure that best meets the needs of the project and the project team. The WBS represents all the project work, including any project management or administrative work. The WBS follows the 100% rule where the total of the lower level work rolls up to the higher levels; nothing is left out, and no extra work is completed.

Example WBS

Vision of End Product		**1 Bicycle**				Project Management WBS Element at Level 2

1.1 Frame Set — 1.1.1 Frame (Hierarchical Code Scheme), 1.1.2 Handlebar, 1.1.3 Fork (Specific Tangible Deliverables), 1.1.4 Seat

1.2 Crank Set

1.3 Wheels — 1.3.1 Front Wheel, 1.3.2 Rear Wheel

1.4 Braking System — Child Elements Include 100% of Parent Element; Sufficient Level of Decomposition

1.5 Shifting System — Need More Decomposition

1.6 Integration — 1.6.1 Concept, 1.6.2 Design, 1.6.3 Assembly, 1.6.4 Testing (Rollup or Collapse): 1.6.4.1 Component Test, 1.6.4.2 Product Test, 1.6.4.3 Customer Test

1.7 Project Management

Each Subordinate Element Belongs to Only One Superior (Parent) Element

Branches are Decomposed to Different Levels of Detail for Different Control Needs

Legend

Level 1 | Level 2 | Level 3 | Level 4

Project Management Institute, *Practice Standard for Work Breakdown Structures – Second Edition*, Project Management Institute Inc., 2006, Page 9

Control accounts. Control accounts are established for the work packages and are assigned a unique identifier typically from the code of accounts (also known as a chart of accounts). Control accounts make it easy to produce summaries of costs, schedule and resource information. A control account may include one or more work packages, but each work package must be associated with only one control account, as the WBS is hierarchical in nature.

WBS dictionary. A companion document to the WBS, the WBS dictionary provides detailed information on the WBS, such as:

- Code of account identifier
- Description of the work
- Responsible organization
- Associated schedule activities
- Cost estimates
- Contract information

The WBS dictionary is necessary because the WBS itself only includes the name of the work package and possibly the code of accounts identifier. All the back-end details are contained within the WBS dictionary.

Belinda's Hint

Keep in mind that this process of creating the WBS is iterative throughout the project. At the beginning of the project, as you start to define your work packages, you may not have all these attributes for the WBS dictionary identified. As we move through the remaining planning processes, we will add more of these details.

Common Tools and Techniques:

Expert Judgment

Expert judgment may come from multiple sources, but specifically from those individuals involved in the work and the work package owners.

Create WBS: Outputs

The key output from the **create WBS** process is the scope baseline.

Scope Baseline

The scope baseline, a component of the project management plan, includes the project scope statement, the WBS, and the WBS dictionary. Once the final scope baseline is approved, any further or future updates or changes will need to go through the formal change control process.

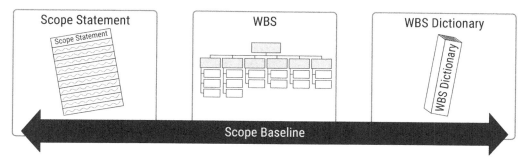

In addition to the scope statement, the WBS, and the WBS dictionary, the scope baseline may also include one or more planning packages. Planning packages are below the control account but above the work package. The planning packages are essentially placeholders containing known and identified work that has yet to be broken down into activities within a work package.

If you get a question on the exam that is asking about updating the scope baseline, remember that means the scope statement, the WBS, and the WBS dictionary are being updated. They should always align.

Common Output:

- **Project document updates** - Project document updates because of the WBS creation process may include updating the assumption log and the requirements documentation.

The create WBS process information is adapted from: PMBOK® Guide – Sixth Edition. Page 156-162

Congratulations on Completing Section 1!

To evaluate your learning and retention of the Section 1 concepts. After you have completed the review questions and the vocabulary, complete Practice Exam 1 in Appendix A as a closed-book, 90-minute timed exam. Upon completion, record your score and your time-to-complete on your Performance Evaluation sheet on Page 9.

Chapter 5 - Review Questions

1. **Your PMO has indicated that a WBS is recommended for all projects that are longer than three months in duration or are estimated to cost more than $100,000. The following is true about the WBS:**
   A. The WBS is another term for the Gantt chart
   B. Each descending level of the WBS represents an increasingly detailed definition of the project work
   C. Work not in the WBS is usually defined in the scope statement of the project
   D. The WBS shows only the critical path activities

2. **As project manager, you are defining the project scope in association with your stakeholders and team members. As such, you are decreasing the probability of scope creep. Scope creep is:**
   A. A type of residual risk
   B. An activity that needs to be included in the project schedule
   C. Unmanaged changes to the project scope
   D. None of the above

3. **As project manager, you are careful to follow the recommended guidelines for developing the WBS for your project. In the WBS, the total of the work at the lowest levels must roll up to the higher levels so that nothing is left out and no extra work is completed. This is called:**
   A. The 80/20 Rule
   B. The WBS Rule
   C. The Hierarchy Rule
   D. The 100% Rule

4. **Which of the following statements is true about the WBS?**
   A. The WBS is a deliverable-oriented hierarchical decomposition of the work to be executed by the project team, to accomplish the project objectives and create the required deliverables
   B. The WBS is an unstructured list of activities in chart form
   C. The WBS is the same as the organizational breakdown structure
   D. The WBS refers to the bill of materials

5. **You have just been made the Project Manager of the ABC project. You are trying to read the WBS and are unable to understand some of the WBS components. What would be your first step to understand this?**
   A. Refer to the WBS dictionary
   B. Refer to the scope statement
   C. Refer to the project charter
   D. Contact the previous project manager

6. **All of the following are true about the project scope statement except:**
   A. It describes the project's major objectives
   B. It provides a common understanding of the project scope among all project stakeholders
   C. It describes, in detail, the project's deliverables and the work required to create those deliverables
   D. It is an output of the validate scope process

7. **What is the WBS typically used for?**
   A. To organize and define the total scope of the project
   B. To identify the logical person to be project sponsor
   C. To define the level of reporting the seller provides the buyer
   D. As a record of when work elements are assigned to individuals

8. **Which of the following is not true of the project scope management plan?**
   A. It provides guidance on how project scope will be defined and documented
   B. It provides guidance on how project scope will be verified
   C. It provides guidance on how project scope will be managed and controlled
   D. It is separate from the project management plan

9. Upon evaluating the work breakdown structure (WBS), you observe that work package 6.2.3 is included in the 6.2 and 6.3 control accounts. What is the next thing you should do?
   A. Break it down into two work packages, one for each control account
   B. Do nothing as work packages can be related to multiple accounts
   C. Submit a scope change with an associated baseline update
   D. Evaluate the work packages in a QFD session

10. The scope baseline includes all of the following except:
    A. WBS dictionary
    B. Project charter
    C. Scope statement
    D. WBS

11. The lowest level of a WBS is known as a(n):
    A. Activity
    B. Task
    C. Control account
    D. Work package

12. You have worked with the assigned business analyst to capture and document the requirements from the stakeholders. What is the next thing you do?
    A. Seek sponsor approval on the requirements
    B. Decompose the work into work packages to create the WBS
    C. Submit the changes to the steering committee to ensure alignment
    D. Analyze the requirements to determine what will be included in the project and create the project scope statement.

13. ABC Corp has recently expanded its project management team as the company has been experiencing significant growth and acquiring many new clients for their software offerings. Upon being assigned your first project, the PMO contact has requested that you provide her with the requirements documentation once it is complete. Your project will be using the Scrum approach to product development. Which statement is most accurate?
    A. Because your project is an iterative life cycle, you will only have incremental requirements
    B. The requirements documentation for your project will be in the form of a product backlog
    C. There are no requirements documents in agile projects
    D. Given the approach that you are using, your project will have a requirements traceability matrix along with the requirements documentation

14. The scope statement differs from the project charter, in that the scope statement:
    A. May be progressively elaborated as more information becomes known
    B. Details the milestone schedule
    C. Is typically created by the project sponsor
    D. Will include the sponsor name, authority level, and the project manager assigned to the project

15. An output of the define scope process is the:
    A. Work breakdown structure (WBS)
    B. Resource breakdown structure (RBS)
    C. Project scope statement
    D. Schedule delays control plan

Review Question Answers

1. **Answer: B**

    Each descending level of the WBS represents an increasingly detailed definition of the work. A Gantt chart is a schedule bar chart and is not related to the WBS. All the work in the scope statement must be represented on the WBS (100% rule). The WBS does not represent activities, as the work is only decomposed to the work package level.

2. **Answer: C**

    Scope creep is considered any unmanaged changes to the project scope.

3. **Answer: D**

    Including all of the work of your project in the WBS follows the 100% rule – the lower levels add up to the higher levels, nothing is left out and no extra work is completed.

4. **Answer: A**

    The WBS is a graphical hierarchical decomposition of the work of the project. Work is decomposed to the work package level.

5. **Answer: A**

    The WBS dictionary will contain all of the detailed information related to each of the WBS work packages. This would be the most likely and most efficient source of information for the project manager.

6. **Answer: D**

    The project scope statement is an output of the define scope process, not the validate scope process. The validate scope process is in the monitoring and controlling process group. Validate scope is securing customer acceptance on the completed deliverables.

7. **Answer: A**

    The WBS is typically used to organize and define the total scope of the project, following the 100% rule – lower levels roll up to the higher levels. All work is included. The WBS would not be used to identify the project sponsor or to define reporting for the buyer. The WBS dictionary may include information on the work package owners.

8. **Answer: D**

    A subsidiary plan is always part of the project management plan and will always document how that particular aspect of the project is being managed, defined, and verified.

9. **Answer: A**

    A control account can have multiple work packages, but a work package can only roll-up to one control account (representing a one-to-many relationship). As such, you will need to break the work package into two distinct work packages, one to roll up to control account 6.2 and one to roll up to control account 6.3. This would not be considered a scope change, as the work was there, it is simply being realigned appropriately. A QFD session is a facilitated workshop and would not apply to this situation.

10. **Answer: B**

    The scope baseline includes the scope statement, the WBS, and the WBS dictionary. The project charter is not part of the scope baseline.

11. **Answer: D**

    The lowest level of a WBS is a work package. The work packages will be decomposed into activities during the define activities process, leading to the development of the project schedule.

12. **Answer: D**

    After collecting the requirements through the **collect requirements** process, the next step would be to analyze those requirements to determine what will be included in the project and create the project scope statement. This is the **define scope** process. Approval is an implied component of the processes. Decomposing into the work packages will come after the scope statement is created.

13. Answer: B

Scrum is an adaptive / agile project lifecycle. As such, the requirements will be documented in the product backlog.

14. Answer: A

While the project charter is a static document, the project scope statement may be progressively elaborated as more information becomes known about the project. The milestone schedule and sponsor name, authority level, and the project manager assignment would be in the charter. Typically, the project scope statement is developed by the project manager.

15. Answer: C

The project scope statement is an output of the define scope process. The WBS is created during the create WBS process. The RBS is an output of the estimate activity resources process. There is no such document as the "schedule delays control plan".

Chapter 5 - Vocabulary Review

* Affinity diagram	Majority	* Questionnaires
* Alternatives analysis	* Mind mapping	* Requirements documentation
* Benchmarking	* Multicriteria decision analysis	* Requirements management plan
Brainstorming	* Nominal group technique	* Requirements traceability matrix
* Code of accounts	Observation/conversation	* Scope baseline
* Context diagram	* Planning package	* Scope creep
* Control account	* Plurality	* Scope management plan
* Decomposition	* Product analysis	* Unanimity
Facilitation	Product backlog	* Work breakdown structure
* Focus groups	* Project scope statement	* WBS dictionary
* Interviews	* Prototype	* Work package
JAD session	Quality function deployment	

1. _____ A working model of the expected product

2. _____ Adding features and functionality (project scope) without addressing the effects on time, costs, and resources, or without customer approval

3. _____ A planning technique that subdivides the project scope and project deliverables into smaller, more manageable components

4. _____ A management control point where scope, budget, and possibly the schedule are integrated to manage and track project progress and costs

5. _____ A document that describes each component in the work breakdown structure

6. _____ A general data gathering and creativity technique that can be used to determine requirements and the project approach

7. _____ A deliverable-oriented hierarchical decomposition of the work to be executed by the project team

8. _____ A grid that links product requirements from their origin to the deliverables that satisfy them

9. _____ Enhances brainstorming with a voting process to rank the ideas

10. _____ A work breakdown structure component below the control account with known work content but without detailed schedule activities

11. _____ Any numbering system used to uniquely identify each component of the work breakdown structure

12. _____ A group creativity technique that allows large numbers of ideas to be classified into groups for review and analysis

13. _____ A technique used to develop as many potential options as possible in order to identify different approaches to execute and perform the work of the project

14.	Determines characteristics for new product development, using the voice of the customer
	A visual depiction of the product scope showing a business system and how people and other systems (actors) interact with it
15.	
16.	An elicitation technique that brings together prequalified stakeholders and subject matter experts to learn about their expectations and attitudes about a proposed product, service, or result
17.	Technique used to consolidate ideas created through individual brainstorming sessions into a single map to reflect commonality and differences in understanding and to generate new ideas
18.	Support from more than 50 percent of the members of the group
19.	Decisions made by the largest block in a group, even if a majority is not achieved
20.	A description of how individual requirements meet the business need for the project
21.	The approved version of a scope statement, work breakdown structure, and its associated WBS dictionary, that can be changed only through formal change control procedures and is used as a basis for comparison
22.	Agreement by everyone in the group on a single course of action
23.	The work defined at the lowest level of the work breakdown structure for which cost and duration can be estimated and managed
24.	A component of the project management plan that describes how requirements will be analyzed, documented, and managed
25.	A formal or informal approach to elicit information from stakeholders by talking to them directly
26.	Engaging with users or subject matter experts to evaluate how they perform their work or interact with systems
27.	Used in adaptive project management, a prioritized list of requirements
28.	Comparison of actual or planned products, processes, and practices to those of comparable organizations to identify best practices, generate ideas for improvement, and provide a basis for measuring performance
29.	The management and coordination of effective meetings
30.	A component of the project management plan that describes how the scope will be defined, developed, monitored, controlled, and validated.
31.	Used in software development, these sessions bring business user experts and the development team together to gather requirements and improve software
32.	Utilizes a decision matrix to provide a systematic analytical approach for establishing criteria, such as risk levels, uncertainty, and valuation, to evaluate and rank many ideas

33.	A tool used in scope definition to ask questions about a product and form answers to describe the use, characteristics, and other relevant aspects of what is going to be manufactured
34.	The description of the project scope, major deliverables, assumptions, and constraints
35.	Written sets of questions designed to quickly accumulate information from a large number of respondents

* These definitions are taken from the Glossary of *PMBOK® Guide – Sixth Edition*

Vocabulary Review Answers

1. Prototype
2. Scope creep
3. Decomposition
4. Control account
5. WBS dictionary
6. Brainstorming
7. WBS
8. Requirements traceability matrix
9. Nominal group technique
10. Planning package
11. Code of accounts
12. Affinity diagram
13. Alternatives analysis
14. Quality function deployment
15. Context diagram
16. Focus groups
17. Mind mapping
18. Majority
19. Plurality
20. Requirements documentation
21. Scope baseline
22. Unanimity
23. Work package
24. Requirements management plan
25. Interviews
26. Observation/conversation
27. Product backlog
28. Benchmarking
29. Facilitation
30. Scope management plan
31. JAD session
32. Multicriteria decision analysis
33. Product analysis
34. Project scope statement
35. Questionnaires

Section 1 - Process/Output Match

Match each process to its key output(s). Please note that some processes may have more than one key output, and some may have no key outputs.

Develop project charter   Plan stakeholder engagement   Define scope

Identify stakeholders   Plan scope management   Create WBS

Develop project management plan   Collect requirements

Process	Key Output
1.	Assumptions log
2.	Project charter
3.	Project management plan
4.	Project scope statement
5.	Requirements documentation
6.	Requirements management plan
7.	Requirements traceability matrix
8.	Scope baseline
9.	Scope management plan
10.	Stakeholder engagement plan
11.	Stakeholder register

Process/Output Match Answers

1. Develop project charter
2. Develop project charter
3. Develop project management plan
4. Define scope
5. Collect requirements
6. Plan scope management

7. Collect requirements
8. Create WBS
9. Plan scope management
10. Plan stakeholder engagement
11. Identify stakeholders

Chapter 6

Project Schedule Planning

What's in This Chapter

- Plan Schedule Management
- Define Activities
- Sequence Activities
- Estimate Activity Durations
- Develop Schedule

The project schedule represents one of the primary project constraints. How much time do we have to design, develop, test, and launch the product? Is there a forced deadline for delivery? The project schedule details when the products, services, or results that were defined in the scope statement will be delivered. As such, the schedule is a necessary communication tool for setting and managing the stakeholder expectations. The schedule baseline will serve as the basis for performance reporting as compared to actual schedule progress.

The level of complexity of the project will dictate how in-depth and detailed the schedule processes will be handled. For small projects, the scheduling processes may occur quickly and seamlessly by one or just a few team members. Larger projects may employ more robust scheduling approaches and leverage multiple resources and experts. Regardless of the size of the project, the schedule should be somewhat flexible as necessary to account for risk and the incorporation of value-added activities.

Schedule Management – Predictive Versus Adaptive

In traditional, stable, and repetitive project environments, a predictive approach to scheduling would include building the schedule out, with activities and milestones, encompassing all of the project work and predicting the completion date. However, in many environments, the ability to predict the exact launch or delivery dates is nearly impossible. This is especially true in projects that anticipate a high-level of change, have poorly defined requirements, or are innovative in nature.

In adaptive environments, new approaches to scheduling are emerging. Requirements that are documented in user stories are prioritized and refined, the resulting features are time-boxed. The team and the client can then assess how many features can be delivered per increment or iteration. This is known as iterative scheduling with the product backlog. Another approach is on-demand scheduling which leverages a Kanban system to limit work-in-progress. Versus using a pre-defined schedule, team members pull their work from the queue as they become available.

Schedule Planning Processes

All the processes presented in this Chapter are in the planning process group and the project schedule management knowledge area:

Plan Schedule Management. This process establishes the policies and procedures for the development, management, and control of the project schedule through the development of the schedule management plan.

Define Activities. This process identifies the activities that will be needed to complete the project work and documents those activities in the activity list.

Sequence Activities. This process creates the schedule network diagrams by identifying and documenting the relationships and dependencies between the activities.

Estimate Activity Durations. This process determines the activity durations by leveraging several different estimating techniques.

Develop Schedule. This process consolidates all the activity information into the project schedule, identifies the critical path, and creates the schedule baseline.

Plan Schedule Management

schedule knowledge area | planning process group

The schedule management plan is developed as a subsidiary plan to provide information, instruction, and direction to the project team regarding the project schedule. This may include information on policies and procedures related to schedule development and control, estimating approaches, and accuracy levels.

Plan Schedule Management: ITTOs

Inputs	Tools & Techniques	Outputs
1. Project charter	1. Expert judgment	1. Schedule management plan
2. Project management plan	2. Data analysis	
• Scope management plan	• Alternatives analysis	
• Development approach	3. Meetings	
3. Enterprise environmental factors		
4. Organizational process assets		

PMBOK® Guide Sixth Edition. Page 179

Plan Schedule Management: Inputs

Common Inputs:

- **Project charter** - The project charter provides a summary milestone schedule that will influence schedule management

- **Project management plan** - As this process is revisited throughout the project, components of the project management plan may be leveraged such as the scope management plan and the development approach.

- **Enterprise environmental factors** - Internal and external considerations that may impact the management of the project schedule include: the organizational culture, organizational structure, the software that is used, scheduling policies and procedures, and commercial databases.
- **Organizational process assets** - Templates, policies and procedures, and historical information can be leveraged to plan the approach to schedule management.

Plan Schedule Management: Tools and Techniques

Common Tools and Techniques:

Expert Judgment

Expert judgment may come through any individuals with specialized training or knowledge in schedule development, scheduling methodologies or software, and industry or project-specific considerations.

Data Analysis Techniques

Data analysis can include conducting an *alternatives analysis* where various approaches are evaluated and considered to determine the most appropriate scheduling approach for the project.

Meetings

The project team may hold meetings to determine the approach for schedule management, with various stakeholders being involved as is appropriate.

Plan Schedule Management: Outputs

Schedule Management Plan

The schedule management plan is a subsidiary plan that provides information to the project team as to how the schedule will be developed, managed, and controlled. Depending on the complexity of the project and the scheduling, the schedule management plan may be high-level bullet points or something more detailed and robust.

Information that may be included:

- The tools and methodology for developing the project schedule model
- The units of measure being used in the schedule and the expected level of accuracy (i.e., hours, days, weeks)
- Control thresholds are the variance thresholds that would dictate that an action is required (i.e., more than a five-day delay requires notification to key stakeholders)
- The formats for reporting on schedule progress and updates
- Methods for evaluating and measuring the schedule performance such as using earned value management techniques, how percent complete is determined, and any other calculations

If the project is being conducted using an adaptive approach, the schedule management plan should define the time periods or time-boxes for the releases, waves, and iterations.

*The **plan schedule management** process information is adapted from: PMBOK® Guide – Sixth Edition. Page 179-182*

Define Activities

schedule knowledge area | planning process group

To create the activity list, the work packages are decomposed into their component schedule activities. This is an iterative process that will occur throughout the project as the work becomes defined.

Define Activities: ITTOs

Inputs	Tools & Techniques	Outputs

1. Project management plan
  • Schedule management plan
  • Scope baseline
2. Enterprise Environmental Factors
3. Organizational Process Assets
	1. Expert judgment
	2. Decomposition
	3. Rolling wave planning
	4. Meetings
		1. Activity list
		2. Activity attributes
		3. Milestone list
		4. Change requests
		5. Project management updates
		  • Schedule baseline
		  • Cost baseline

PMBOK® Guide – Sixth Edition. Page 183

Define Activities: Inputs

Common Inputs:

- **Project management plan** - The project management plan will provide guidance information, iteratively, on the activity definition, including guidance contained within the schedule management plan and the scope baseline.
- **Enterprise environmental factors** - Internal and external factors to be considered when defining the project activities include: the organizational structure, the organizational culture, commercial estimating information, and the organization's project management information system (PMIS).
- **Organizational process assets** - Lessons learned information, historical information, project templates, and activity planning processes and procedures may be leveraged during activity definition.

Define Activities: Tools and Techniques

Decomposition

Decomposition, just as we saw in the **create WBS** process, is breaking something down. In this process, it is the breaking down of the work packages into smaller, more manageable components called activities or schedule activities. While in-practice, you may use the term 'task', PMI uses activity. That is not to say, however, that you will not see the word 'task' on the exam. Just know that 'task' is synonymous with activity.

We often use the 8/80 rule for developing and decomposing work into the activities. If an activity is going to take less than 8 hours, consider combining it with other activities as it will be too granular to manage effectively. However, if the activity is going to take more than 80 hours to complete, consider breaking it down into multiple activities as it will be too abstract to manage effectively.

Belinda's Hint

Although it is called the 8/80 rule, it is better to consider it a guideline versus a hard-and-fast rule. There are certainly situations and circumstances that may dictate falling outside of the 8/80 parameters. For example, for activities that are not yet clearly understood or fully decomposed, we may add them as placeholders with a duration of greater than 80 hours.

Vice versa, there may be situations when you want to call out a very short activity that is less than eight hours: the activity is using a specialized resource and the work cannot be combined with other activities or perhaps the activity is especially important, and you want to call it out to the stakeholders. Adding granular activities that are less than eight hours because you want better control is not acceptable: that's called micromanaging. And no one likes a micromanager!

Rolling Wave Planning — on test — House

For longer-term projects, rolling wave planning is an iterative planning technique where the near-term work is planned in detail, and future work is indicated with placeholders. Rolling wave planning is a form of progressive elaboration, where work becomes defined as more information on the project becomes known. This is also considered "moving window" planning.

Common Tools and Techniques:

Expert Judgment

Project team members, PMO representatives, work package owners, and other individuals may provide expertise on the project activities. Ideally, we want the people that are going to be either doing the work or managing the work to define the activities.

Meetings

Depending on the complexity of the project, meetings may be very brief or extensive and numerous. The goal of the meetings is comprehensive activity definition.

Define Activities: Outputs

There are three key outputs from activity definition:

Activity list

The activity list is a comprehensive list of all the schedule activities and includes the activity identifier and a description of the activity. The activity identifier should be a derivative of the code of account numbering on the WBS. For example, if the work package is 1.1, the activities for the work package would be 1.1.1, 1.1.2, 1.1.3., etc. Activity descriptions should be clear and concise so that the team members are able to understand and interpret the information appropriately. Activities have an expected duration, consume budget and/or resources, and are named in a verb-noun format.

Activity attributes

Along with the description of the activities, activity attributes are also documented. Activity attributes may include predecessor and successor activities, leads and lags (these will be discussed in the next process), resource requirements, constraints and assumptions, the person responsible for executing the work, and the location of where the work will be performed.

Belinda's Hint

Keep in mind that this process is iterative throughout the project. At the beginning of the project, as you start to define your activities, you may not have all these activity attributes identified. As we move through the remaining time planning processes and as this process is revisited iteratively, we will add more of these details, such as leads and lags, resources, etc.

Milestone list

The milestone list identifies the project milestones. Milestones are considered any significant point or event in the project and typically describe an end-state with no duration (i.e. "final contract executed"). The milestone should be indicated as either mandatory or optional for the team to understand where there is flexibility within the schedule. Mandatory milestones may be those required by contract or other factors that must be completed before any further work is completed. Optional milestones may be those based on historical information, best practice, or preference and as such, work may be able to progress even if the milestone has not been accomplished.

Common Outputs:

- **Change requests** - As the activity list, activity attributes, and milestone list are revisited throughout the project there may be changes required. Change requests are evaluated through the **perform integrated change control** process.
- **Project management plan updates** - As the project progresses, the project management plan will be updated, including any changes to the schedule or cost baselines. Changes to the project baselines must be approved through the **perform integrated change control** process, as well.

Belinda's Hint

It will be important to understand the difference between all of the scheduling terms. To help you remember the differences between "activity," "milestone," and "lag," think in terms of duration and budget and/or resources consumed:

Activity – has a duration and consumes budget and/or resources

Milestone – does not have a duration and does not consume budget or resources

Lag – has a duration but does not consume budget or resources as it is simply a delay in the start of the successor activity (such as waiting for the primer to dry before painting the wall). We will learn more about lag in the next process.

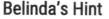

	Duration	$/ 人
Activity	⊠	⊠
Milestone	---	---
Lag	⊠	---

*The **define activities** process information is adapted from: PMBOK® Guide – Sixth Edition. Page 183-186*

Sequence Activities

schedule knowledge area | planning process group

To sequence the schedule activities, the relationships and dependencies between the activities will be identified and defined. Using the activity list and the activity relationships, a schedule network diagram can be developed. Network diagrams can be created manually or automated with project scheduling software, such as Microsoft Project.

Every activity, apart from the first activity and the last activity will have at least one predecessor activity and one successor activity. Predecessor activities are those that come before the activity and successor activities are those that come after the activity. The objective of this process is to create a realistic schedule while also determining the shortest schedule possible by understanding the relationships between the activities and which activities can be done in parallel.

Sequence Activities: ITTOs

Inputs	Tools & Techniques	Outputs

1. Project management plan
  • Schedule management plan
  • Scope baseline
2. Project documents
  • Activity attributes
  • Activity list
  • Assumption log
  • Milestone list
3. Enterprise Environmental Factors
4. Organizational Process Assets
	1. Precedence diagramming method
	2. Dependency determination
	3. Leads and lags
	4. Project management information system
		1. Project schedule network diagrams
		2. Project documents updates
		  • Activity attributes
		  • Activity list
		  • Assumption log
		  • Milestone list

PMBOK® Guide – Sixth Edition. Page 187

Belinda's Hint

On the exam, it is likely that you will need to sketch out a network diagram to answer a question. The diagram itself will not be the answer but will lead to the answer. It is important that you can effectively represent the dependency relationships between the activities in order to get to the correct answer.

Sequence Activities: Inputs

Common Inputs:

- **Project management plan** - In the project management plan, the schedule management plan and the scope baseline may be used to provide information necessary for sequencing the project activities.
- **Project documents** - Project documents leveraged may include the activity attributes, the activity list, the assumption log, and the milestone list.
- **Enterprise environmental factors** - Environmental factors to be considered include, but are not limited to, any government or industry standards, the project management information system (PMIS), the scheduling tools that will be used, and any type of organizational work authorization system.
- **Organizational process assets** - Policies, procedures, guidelines, and templates may be used to determine activity relationships and dependencies. In addition, past project files and lessons learned documentation could lend information to those dependencies.

Sequence Activities: Tools and Techniques

Precedence Diagramming Method (PDM)

PDM is a method of constructing a project schedule network diagram where the nodes or boxes represent activities, and the arrows depict the dependencies between those activities. The four dependencies are finish-to-start, start-to-start, finish-to-finish, and start-to-finish. They will be discussed in more detail shortly.

The resulting diagram may be called a PDM, or it may also be called an activity-on-node (AON) diagram. For the exam, you need to know it by either name and possibly the acronyms.

Depending on the complexity of the project and the number of project activities, it may be appropriate to use hammock or summary activities. A hammock or summary activity includes a group of related schedule activities that, for reporting purposes, are shown as a single aggregate activity.

Notice on the following diagram, the positioning of the arrows to indicate the relationship. For example, between activities B and C, you will see the arrow goes from the start of B to the start of C, indicating a start-to-start relationship. The numbers on this diagram represent lag (to be discussed shortly).

Example: Project Schedule Network Diagram

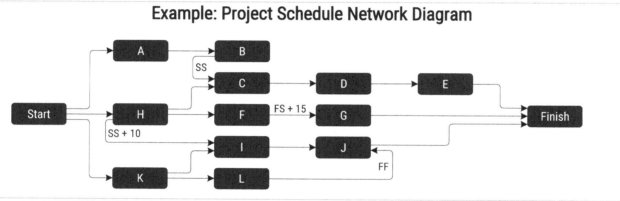

PMBOK® Guide – Sixth Edition. Page 193

Dependency Relationships

As mentioned previously, there are four types of dependency relationships that may be depicted in a PDM.

Each dependency relationship is read as: "A" must (_____) before "B" can (_____) with "A" being the predecessor activity and "B" being the successor activity.

Finish-to-Start. Activity "A" must finish before activity "B" can start. This is the most common type of dependency relationship. If not specifically stated on the exam, you can assume they are referring to a finish-to-start relationship. The arrow is indicating the relationship going from the finish of the predecessor to the start of the successor. Duration would be A + B.

Example: Finish-to-Start

The books must be printed before they can be shipped

Start-to-Start. Activity "A" must start before activity "B" can start. The dependency is on the first activity starting and once it starts, the second activity can start any time thereafter, resulting in a best case (concurrent) or worst-case (sequential) result. The arrow is indicating the relationship, going from the start of the predecessor to the start of the successor. Best case duration would be the duration of whichever activity duration is longer and worst-case would be A + B.

Example: Start-to-Start

The concrete for the new building will be poured. Once the concrete has started to be poured, the team can begin testing it. Best case, the concrete is poured and tested concurrently and worst case the concrete is poured completely before the testing begins.

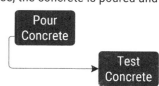

Finish-to-Finish. Activity "A" must finish before activity "B" can finish. Both activities can happen concurrently, but the successor activity cannot finish until the predecessor has finished. Once it finishes, the second activity can finish any time thereafter, resulting in a best case (concurrent) or worst-case (sequential) result. Best case duration would be the duration of whichever activity duration is longer and worst-case would be A + B.

Example: Finish-to-Finish

The website must be fully designed and developed before the website quality review can be completed. Best case, the website design and development and the quality review end on the same day. Worst case, the activities happen sequentially.

Start-to-Finish. In a start-to-finish relationship, activity "A" must start before activity "B" can finish. This dependency relationship is the least common and very rarely used and unlikely to be on the exam.

Example: Start-to-Finish

The new nurses' shift must start at the hospital before the previous nurses' shift can finish.

Let's check your understanding of the dependency relationships! The answers to Exercise 6.1 are on page 150.

Exercise 6.1 Dependencies and Durations

1. Activities A, B and C have finish-to-start relationships. A has a duration of 6 days, B has a duration of 4 days, and C has a duration of 5 days. What is the total duration?

   A. 23 days
   B. 15 days
   C. 6 days
   D. 10 days

2. Activity X is 9 days and Activity Y is 14 days. The activities have a start-to-start relationship. What is the best-case duration?

   A. 14 days
   B. 9 days
   C. 23 days
   D. 21 days

3. Activities L and M have a finish-to-finish relationship. L is 10 days and M is 8 days. What is the worst-case duration?

   A. 2 days
   B. 8 days
   C. 10 days
   D. 18 days

4. Activity J is 13 days and Activity K is 9 days. What is the difference between the best and worst-case duration if they have a start-to-start relationship?

   A. 9 days
   B. 4 days
   C. 22 days
   D. 13 days

5. Activities N, O, and P have finish-to-start relationships. P and Q have a start-to-start relationship. Activity N is 4 days, Activity O is 7 days, Activity P is 6 days, and Activity Q is 9 days. What is the best case and the worst-case duration?

   A. Best case is 23 days and the worst case is 26 days
   B. Best case is 20 days and the worst case is 20 days
   C. Best case is 17 days and the worst case is 23 days
   D. Best case is 20 days and the worst case is 26 days

Dependency Determination and Integration

There are four types of dependencies that may be used in the sequencing of activities:

- Mandatory
- Discretionary
- External
- Internal

Mandatory dependencies. These dependencies are inherent to the work being done and often involve physical limitations. Because there is a physical limitation or restriction, mandatory dependencies cannot be changed or manipulated. As such, the more mandatory dependencies in the schedule, the higher the risk. Mandatory dependencies may be known as hard logic or hard dependencies.

Example: Mandatory Dependency

The books cannot be shipped until they are printed.

Discretionary dependencies. These dependencies are usually established based on the discretion of the project team, based on best practices or experience, policies, or procedures. The discretionary dependencies may come from outside sources or industry experts. Because they are discretionary, these dependencies may be overwritten if necessary to fast-track the project schedule. While there is risk associated with removing the dependency, there is not a physical limitation. Discretionary dependencies are also referred to as preferred logic, preferential logic or soft logic.

Example: Discretionary Dependency

The screen shots of the new system are to be approved prior to beginning the development of the user guides.

Belinda's Hint

Be careful on the exam not to confuse questions on the dependencies with ethical questions. These activity dependencies are not "moral" judgments, but rather physical or non-physical dependencies. For example, if they state that there is a company policy that requires products to be signed off by a VP prior to shipping to the customer – that is a discretionary dependency. It does not mean we would violate it, but that we physically could, if necessary.

External dependencies. These dependencies are those that involve a relationship between project activities and non-project activities. External dependencies are usually outside of the project team's control, and as such, are difficult if not impossible to change.

Example: External Dependency

The city must issue the permits before construction can begin.

Internal dependencies. These dependencies involve a precedence relationship between project activities that are within the team's control. Because the dependency is within the team or the project, it may be possible to adjust the dependency if necessary to accelerate the schedule.

Example: Internal Dependency

The team cannot test a software program until it is designed and built.

Let's check your understanding of the dependency types! The answers to Exercise 6.2 are on page 150.

Exercise 6.2 Dependency Types

For each of the following scenarios, identify the type of dependency or dependencies (mandatory, discretionary, external, internal)

1. ___Discretionary___ The team requires authorization from the PMO to begin the project

2. ___Discretionary___ The web designer is creating the mock-ups of the new site so the team can create marketing collateral

3. ___Mandatory___ The drilling equipment is needed in order to begin the next phase of construction on the large project.

4. ___External___ Because the project is being conducted on protected land, permits must be received from the federal government

5. ___Man + Internal___ To begin designing the prototype, the team is waiting for the business analyst to complete the requirements

6. ___Mandatory___ The shipping team will ship the final products to the clients

Leads and Lags

Some activity dependencies allow a lead (an acceleration of a successor activity) or require a lag (a delay of the successor activity).

Lead. A lead is an acceleration of the successor activity. Leads can only exist in finish-to-start relationships. The finish-to-start relationship must be a discretionary dependency if we are able to accelerate the successor with a lead. On a network diagram, a lead is indicated as a negative number above the arrow. It is a negative number because it represents the time that is being saved.

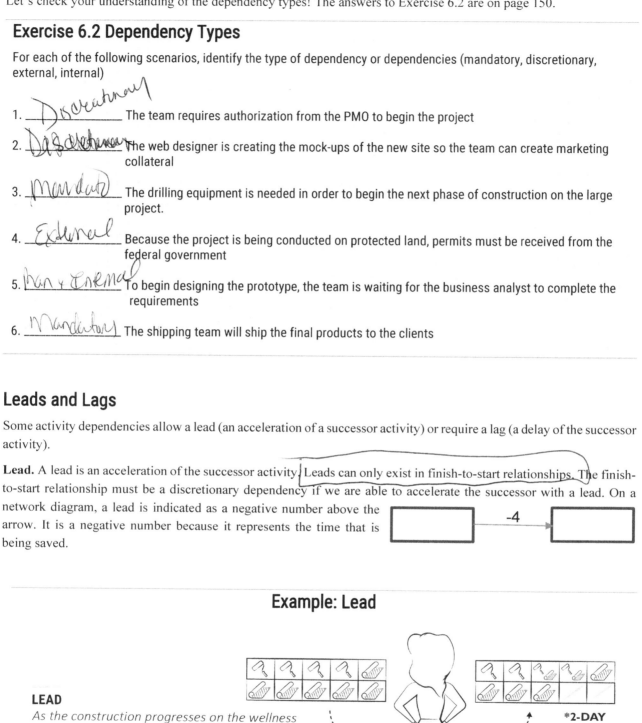

Example: Lead

LEAD

As the construction progresses on the wellness center, Kim reviews the schedule. She sees that the painting is scheduled for next week and will take four days. The flooring install is scheduled after the painting and is estimated to take six days. Kim knows that she can accelerate the flooring install by using a 2-day lead. The total duration will decrease from 10 days to eight days.

*2-DAY LEAD

Belinda's Hint

An easy way to remember that "lead" is an acceleration of a successor activity is to think of baseball. When a player leads off base, they are starting their next activity early, with the intent of saving time. This is the same concept! One thing to be wary of is that in manufacturing, we often refer to "lead time" as the amount of time before the product will complete or delivered. In PMI language, that is technically a lag (a delay) and not a lead. Think baseball!

Let's check your understanding of lead! The answers to Exercise 6.3 are on page 150.

Exercise 6.3: Lead

1. Activity A is 10 days, and Activity B is 12 days. If you were to apply a 5-day lead between A and B, what is the revised duration?

2. Activity X is 22 days and there is a 3-day lead. The total time to complete Activity X and Activity Y is 40 days. What is the duration of Y?

3. Activity M and Activity N have a start-to-start relationship. Activity M is 8 days and Activity N is 10 days. With a 4-day lead, what is the best-case duration?

Lag. A lag is a delay in the successor activity. There are no resources associated with the lag as it is just time that must pass before the second activity can begin. All four dependency relationships can have lag: F-S, S-S, F-F, and S-F. On a network diagram, lag is indicated as a positive number above the arrow as lag is the time that is being added.

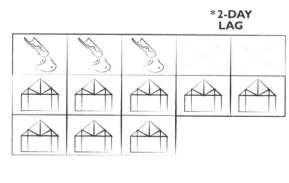

Example: Lag

LAG

To accommodate the space needed for the wellness center, the hospital is putting on an addition. As Kim evaluates the job site, she sees that the concrete foundation has been poured and it took three days. Framing can begin two days after the pouring of the concrete and is estimated to take eight days. The two days between the concrete and the framing is considered lag time.

Let's check your understanding of lag! The answers to Exercise 6.4 are on page 150.

Exercise 6.4: Lag

1. Activity A is 9 days, and Activity B is 17 days. If you were to apply a 4-day lag between A and B, what is the revised duration, assuming a finish-to-start relationship?

2. Activity X is 14 days and there is a 13-day lag. The best-case time to complete Activity X and Activity Y is 30 days. What is the duration of Y if there is a finish-to-finish relationship?

3. Activity M and Activity N have a start-to-start relationship. Activity M is 18 days and Activity N is 12 days. With a 4-day lag, what is the difference between the best-case duration and the worst-case duration?

Common Tools and Techniques:

Project Management Information System (PMIS)

The PMIS is any collection of systems and/or software that is used to manage the project information. For sequencing the activities, the project manager, and the project team may use scheduling software that will allow sequencing, dependencies, and relationships between activities.

Sequence Activities: Outputs

The key output from sequencing the activities is the schedule network diagram.

Project Schedule Network Diagrams

The project schedule network diagrams may be produced either with scheduling software or done manually. In software, as the relationships and dependencies are added to the activities, typically one of the views will be a network diagram. The most common schedule network diagram is the activity-on-node (AON) / precedence diagramming method (PDM), where the nodes or boxes represent the activities, and the arrows indicate the relationships. An AON can depict all four relationship types: F-S, S-S, F-F, and S-F.

Another less common type of schedule network diagram is an activity-on-arrow (AOA)/arrow diagramming method (ADM). In an AOA diagram, the activities are represented by the arrows, versus the nodes. The other difference is that an AOA can only depict finish-to-start relationships.

ACTIVITY ON NODE   ACTIVITY ON ARROW

Common Outputs:

- **Project document updates** - Documents that may be updated as the process is conducted and revisited include: activity attributes, activity list, the assumption log, and the milestone list.

*The **sequence activities** process information is adapted from: PMBOK® Guide – Sixth Edition. Page 187-194*

Exercise 6.5: Sequence Activities

Using the information in the table below, create a PDM. The answer is on page 150.

Activity ID	Activity	Predecessor
1.1	Evaluate product requirements	
1.2	Identify key subject matter experts	1.1
1.3	Determine prototype team lead	1.1
1.4	Conduct brainstorming sessions	1.3
1.5	Design prototype	1.2 1.4
1.6	Build prototype	1.5
1.7	Create user documentation	1.5
1.8	Draft prototype result report	1.6 1.7

Estimate Activity Durations

schedule knowledge area | planning process group

The **estimate activity durations** process assesses and estimates the durations of the project activities. In addition to documenting the durations, it is important to always include the assumptions that were used when making the estimate. If there is uncertainty associated with the duration estimate, that range of variance should be captured, as well. Depending on the type of project and the environment, the project manager may not be able to fully estimate the durations at the beginning of the project and, as such, the estimates may be progressively elaborated over the life of the project.

To estimate the amount of time required for the work, the project manager and team will first want to consider how much effort is going to be required. Effort would be the number of work units, such as staff-hours or staff-days, to complete the work. Once the available resources are applied to the effort, the team can estimate the duration of the work. Generally, duration is considered the number of work days and does not include holidays and non-working days. Elapsed time would be the calendar span or calendar time to get the work completed.

Effort vs Duration vs Elapsed Time

In talking with her work package owners, Kim is starting to put together her project estimates for the schedule. According to the facilities manager, the outside landscaping including adding a serenity fountain and seating will take approximately 120 hours. Kim has been evaluating landscaping vendors and has narrowed it down to two local companies.

PrettyLand, Inc. can offer two laborers, Monday through Friday, for eight hours per day. That represents a total of 16 hours per day x five days per week = 80 hours per week. With 80 hours of effort, it will take seven and a half days in duration to complete the work, which would be considered two weeks of elapsed time.

Teagan & Co. can provide three laborers for 8 hours per day on the weekends. That represents a total 24 hours per day x two weekend days = 48 hours per week. With 48 hours of effort, it will take five days in duration, but will be three weeks of elapsed time as the work is only on the weekends.

With that information, Kim estimates:

PrettyLand, Inc. will take 7.5 days in duration and two weeks of elapsed time

Teagan & Co., will take 5 days in duration but three weeks of elapsed time

Because the pricing and recommendations are the same, Kim chooses PrettyLand, Inc. as the elapsed time is quicker.

Let's check your understanding of effort, duration, and elapsed time! The answers to Exercise 6.6 are on page 151.

Exercise 6.6: Effort, Duration, and Elapsed Time

1. The work is expected to take 390 hours of effort. You can use two resources, three days per week, five hours per day. What is the elapsed time of the work? What is the duration?

2. Your team has five resources, working five days per week, and four hours per day. The elapsed time of the project is six weeks and there will be one holiday during that six-week period. What is the effort?

3. Vendor A has proposed providing a three-person team, eight hours per day, four days per week. Vendor B has proposed a four-person team, 12 hours per day, two days per week. With a total estimated effort of 480 hours, which vendor can complete the work in the shortest duration? Which vendor can complete the work in the shortest elapsed time?

While in some cases, the number of resources you apply to the effort dictates the relationship, it is not necessarily a straight-line relationship, and other factors should be considered:

The law of diminishing returns states that if one factor of production increases but the other factors remain the same, eventually adding more of that factor will diminish the increases in output. For example, just adding more people to the project team does not guarantee an increase in productivity and to continue to add people will eventually decrease the output. Not only does the law of diminishing returns apply, but the risk to your project may increase as you add more people: increased chance of misunderstanding, communication challenges, learning curves, etc.

Human behavior significantly impacts the duration of your project. Do you know which day of the week is most productive for project teams in traditional project environments? According to research, the most productive day of the week is Thursday. Why? Because status reports are typically due on Friday. This is known as "student syndrome," in other words, people procrastinate. Just because you are halfway through your project from a calendar perspective, does not mean you are 50% complete with the work of the project. In fact, that is very unlikely. Parkinson's Law states that "work expands so as to fill the time available for its completion." Consider this in project work as you are evaluating your project schedule. If you give your team two weeks to do the work, it will take two weeks.

On the positive side, however, there are factors that can decrease duration. For example, technological advances that serve to automate processes, provide faster access to information, or streamline workflow can significantly decrease the amount of effort needed for the project. Another key factor that is often overlooked is employee and team member motivation. How motivated is your team to achieve the project goals? Understanding human behavior is a component of emotional intelligence. As a project manager, understand emotional intelligence and how you can improve it! Keeping your team motivated and excited will only benefit your project and the project outcomes. We will discuss emotional intelligence further in this course.

Estimate Activity Durations: ITTOs

Inputs	Tools & Techniques	Outputs
1. Project management plan • Schedule management plan • Scope baseline 2. Project documents • Activity attributes • Activity list • Assumption log • Lessons learned register • Milestone list • Project team assignments • Resource breakdown structure • Resource calendars • Resource requirements • Risk register 3. Enterprise Environmental Factors 4. Organizational Process Assets	1. Expert judgment 2. Analogous estimating 3. Parametric estimating 4. Three-point estimating 5. Bottom-up estimating 6. Data analysis • Alternatives analysis • Reserve analysis 7. Decision making 8. Meetings	1. Duration estimates 2. Basis of estimates 3. Project documents updates • Activity attributes • Assumption log • Lessons learned register

PMBOK® Guide – Sixth Edition. Page 195

Estimate Activity Durations: Inputs

Common Inputs:

- **Project management plan** - While estimating the activity durations, initially and throughout the project, the project management plan is considered, specifically the schedule management plan and the scope baseline.

- **Project documents** - A number of project documents may lend to duration estimating, including but not limited to: the activity list, activity attributes, and milestone list; the assumption log, lessons learned register, and risk register. To consider the resources that will be applied to the activities, the project manager will leverage the project team assignments, the resource breakdown structure (RBS), the resource calendars, and the resource requirements.

- **Enterprise environmental factors** - In estimating the activity durations, internal and external influences should be considered, including, but not limited to any type of estimating databases, productivity metrics, published commercial information and the location of the team members.

- **Organizational process assets** - Duration estimating is performed more efficiently and accurately by leveraging several organizational process assets. This includes using historical project information, lessons learned repository, scheduling templates and methodologies, and project calendars. Many of the estimating techniques leverage historical information as the basis for the estimate.

Estimate Activity Durations: Tools and Techniques

Analogous Estimating

Analogous estimating uses a previous similar project as the basis for the estimate by taking the similarities into consideration to determine project duration. Because this is done based on the project duration, not individual activity durations, it is also known as top-down estimating. Analogous (analogy) estimating is frequently used when there is a lack of detailed information about the current project, specifically early in the project. It is considered a combination of historical information and expert judgment.

While analogous estimating is less costly and time-consuming than other types of estimating, it is generally not as accurate as other estimating techniques. The team wants the historical project to be as similar as possible to the current project to ensure accuracy in the resulting estimate.

Example: Analogous Estimating

ANALOGOUS ESTIMATING

Kim is planning a job fair to secure employees for the wellness center.

Using historical records, Kim sees that a previous job fair of approximately the same size took about three weeks to plan and execute. As such, she estimates this year's job fair will take three weeks.

Parametric Estimating

Parametric estimating involves using a statistical relationship between two variables to determine a unit duration. The productivity rate may be gleaned from historical information from prior projects, published estimating data, commercial databases, or the lessons learned register. Parametric (think math!) estimating is more accurate when underlying data is accurate and scalable. Keep in mind, however, the law of diminishing returns that was mentioned earlier. Doubling the number of resources assigned to a task does not necessarily cut the delivery time in half.

Example: Parametric Estimating

PARAMETRIC ESTIMATING

A relaxing mural will be painted in each of the six treatment rooms.

Each mural takes three days to complete and as such, the total duration will be 18 days to get the murals completed.

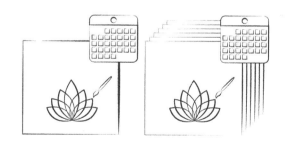

Three-Point Estimating

Three-point estimating factors in uncertainty related to the duration estimates by using three duration points: optimistic, most likely, and pessimistic. Three-point estimating is also known as the program evaluation and review technique (PERT). In presenting three-point duration estimating in the *PMBOK® Guide, 6th Edition*, PMI references only what is considered a triangular distribution. However, in practice, and quite possibly on the exam, a three-point estimate can either be a triangular distribution or a beta distribution.

Beta distribution. In a beta distribution, the PERT is calculated by weighting the most likely duration estimate by four, thus dividing by six for the six variables:

Beta PERT = (O +4M + P) ÷ 6   You may also see the formula written: $t_e = \dfrac{t_o + 4t_m + t_p}{6}$

Notice that the most likely duration was weighted with a factor of four and then the weighted average was calculated by dividing by six, reflecting one optimistic and one pessimistic estimate, and four most-likely estimates.

Triangular distribution. In a triangular distribution, the most likely is not weighted, and the sum of the optimistic, most likely and pessimistic estimates are divided by three.

Triangular PERT = (O +M + P) ÷ 3   You may also see the formula written: $t_e = \dfrac{t_o + t_m + t_p}{3}$

Example: Three-Point Estimating (Triangular)

THREE-POINT ESTIMATING

Kim meets with IT to firm up the duration estimates for installing all of the workstations. The team lead explains that if the work is done completely in-house, it could take as long as 14 days. If they are able to secure their IT partner organization, it will only take five days. Based on resource availability from the partner organization, it will most likely take eight days.

IN-HOUSE ⑭

+
IT PARTNER (+5)

RESOURCE
AVAILIBILITY (+8) / 3 = 9

Using a triangular three-point calculation, Kim estimates that it will take nine days:
(14 days + 5 days + 8 days) / 3 = 9 days

Belinda's Hint

For the three-point estimating questions, always verify what the question is asking you to find. For example, they may give you the PERT estimate and the optimistic and most-likely estimates, and they want you to solve for the pessimistic estimate.

Even if you hate math, you will wish that there were more math questions on the PMP® exam. They can be so much easier than the subjective, scenario-based questions! For the math questions that you do get on the exam, I offer three hints:

1. Always double-check your math 2. Use your calculator and 3. If time allows, go back and run your numbers again to be sure you answered correctly.

Bottom-Up Estimating

When the work is decomposed into lower-level details, it may be possible to use a bottom-up estimate for each component of the project and then aggregate those estimates to come up with a duration. The biggest consideration in bottom-up estimating is that the team must recognize and document the relationships and dependencies between the activities. For example, if I sum up all the individual durations, it would not account for activities that are happening in parallel with no existing dependencies.

Example: Bottom-Up Estimating

BOTTOM-UP ESTIMATING

Kim is estimating the total duration to complete the landscaping portion of the work. Because each component of the work will be completed sequentially, Kim recognizes that she can do a bottom-up estimate to determine the total time it will take to complete the work.

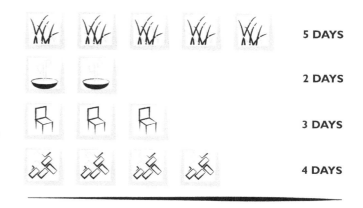

	5 DAYS
	2 DAYS
	3 DAYS
	4 DAYS
	14 DAYS

Let's check your understanding of duration estimating techniques. The answers to Exercise 6.7 are on page 151.

Exercise 6.7: Estimate Activity Durations

You are the project manager for the Chamber of Commerce Annual Banquet and Recognition Event. This is your first time managing a project of this size and you need to estimate how long the project will take. There are three separate components of the project that will occur sequentially: event logistics, venue selection, and room set-up. Consider the following:

Event logistics: Last year's event was held on-site at the Chamber, and it took approximately three months to complete the project. This included the time to develop the guest list, arrange the food, and order the food.

Venue selection: In a review of previous projects that utilized an off-site venue, you see that the time to locate, select, and book a venue has ranged from three weeks, best case, to nine weeks worst case. You expect that it will most likely take your team approximately five weeks to identify, select, and book the location.

Room set-up: Last year's event hosted 100 guests, and it took approximately four hours to set up the room and prepare the food. This year, however, you are expecting 300 guests.

1. What is the best estimate for the venue selection?
   A. 23 days
   B. 15 days
   C. 6 weeks
   D. 5.3 weeks

2. What technique is best used to estimate the venue selection?
   A. Parametric
   B. Analogous
   C. Reserve analysis
   D. Three-point

3. What is the best estimate for the event logistics?
   A. 3 months
   B. 6 months
   C. 10 weeks
   D. 12 weeks

4. What technique is best used to estimate the event logistics?
   A. Parametric
   B. Analogous
   C. Reserve analysis
   D. Three-point

5. What is the best estimate for the room set-up?
   A. 2 days
   B. 12 hours
   C. 1 week
   D. 4 hours

6. What technique is best used to estimate the room set-up?
   A. Parametric
   B. Analogous
   C. Reserve analysis
   D. Three-point

Common Tools and Techniques:

Expert Judgment

Expert judgment can be applied to duration estimating from individuals with experience and knowledge of the specific activities, the estimating approach, or schedule development. The preference is to have the individuals responsible for the work to provide the estimates on duration.

Data Analysis Techniques

There are two data analysis techniques that may be used while estimating or re-estimating activity durations:

An *alternatives analysis* is used to consider different types of resources, capabilities, or skills to apply to the project activities. May also evaluate various schedule compression techniques, different tools or techniques, and possibly make-or-buy decisions.

A *reserve analysis* is used to evaluate the amount of contingency time (also known as time buffers or schedule reserve) as compared to the amount of risk or uncertainty on the project. Contingency reserve is determined based on known-unknowns: risks that have been identified and are known, it is just unknown if the risk event is going to happen (thus it being a risk). As the project progresses and the work is defined with increasing confidence, the contingency reserve should be reduced or perhaps eliminated. Schedule contingency reserve is included in the schedule baseline.

The assumption on the exam is that as a project manager, a reserve analysis is part of your professional responsibilities. As the project progresses, the estimates should become more and more accurate, minimizing the use of the buffers. In addition, it is assumed that you, as project manager, control the identification and the use of the contingency buffers.

Decision-Making Techniques

When determining the duration estimates within the team, a decision-making tool that can be used as a voting method is fist-to-five, also known as the fist-of-five. In a fist-to-five process, all parties involved in the decision are asked to cast their vote by a show of fingers to indicate their level of support: a closed fist is no support, and five fingers represent full support. If a participant holds up fewer than three fingers, there should be a discussion regarding their position and their objections.

Meetings

Meetings are used to discuss duration estimates. For agile projects, sprint or iteration planning meetings will be used to estimate the duration of the portion of the product backlog that will be targeted during the upcoming sprint. Typically, these sprint planning sessions occur on the first day of the sprint and are attended by the scrum master or agile project manager, the product owner, and the scrum team.

Estimate Activity Durations: Outputs

There are two key outputs from estimating the activity durations:

Duration Estimates

The duration estimates will document the number of work periods required to complete an activity and may include a range of possible results. For example, one week ± three days to indicate that the activity will take at least two days and no more than eight days. It is important as the project manager to always document the assumptions and the sources used to determine the estimates. This protects you as the project manager, but also creates a record that can be used as a reference for future projects.

Basis of Estimates

With the duration estimates, the basis of the estimates should be documented. The basis of the estimates may include how the estimate was developed, what technique was used, the range of estimates, the confidence level of the estimate, and any risks that are known with the estimate.

Common Output:

- **Project document updates** - Documents that will be updated as this process is conducted and iterated may include the activity attributes, the assumption log, and the lessons learned register.

*The **estimate activity durations** process information is adapted from: PMBOK® Guide – Sixth Edition. Page 195-204*

Develop Schedule

schedule knowledge area | planning process group

Schedule development incorporates the outputs from the other time planning processes into the project schedule. The project schedule will include the start and finish dates for all the project activities, the planned dates for meeting project milestones, and will be used to track schedule performance and to coordinate all activities in a master plan. The project schedule is continually analyzed and updated throughout the life of the project. This process will produce both the schedule baseline (the frozen version of the schedule) and the project schedule (the living/updated version of the schedule).

Develop Schedule: ITTOs

Inputs	Tools & Techniques	Outputs
1. Project management plan	1. Schedule network analysis	1. Schedule baseline
• Schedule management plan	2. Critical path method	2. Project schedule
• Scope baseline	3. Resource optimization	3. Schedule data
2. Project documents	4. Data analysis	4. Project calendars
• Activity attributes	• What–if scenario analysis	5. Change requests
• Activity list	• Simulation	6. Project management plan updates
• Assumption log	5. Leads and lags	• Schedule management plan
• Basis of estimates	6. Schedule compression	• Cost baseline
• Duration estimates	7. Project management information system	7. Project documents updates
• Lessons learned register	8. Agile release planning	• Assumption log
• Milestone list		• Requirements documentation
• Project schedule network diagrams		• Requirements traceability matrix
• Project team assignments		• Stakeholder register
• Resource calendars		
• Resource requirements		
• Risk register		
3. Agreements		
4. Enterprise Environmental Factors		
5. Organizational Process Assets		

PMBOK® Guide – Sixth Edition. Page 205

Develop Schedule: Inputs

Agreements

Any work that is being conducted and delivered, in whole or in part, by vendors needs to be included in the project schedule. The agreements will provide information as to the delivery schedule that can be incorporated into the overall project schedule.

Common Inputs:

- **Project management plan** - The project management plan may be consulted, including information contained within the scheduling management plan and the scope baseline.

- **Project documents** - Multiple project documents may be leveraged, including the activity list, activity attributes, and the milestone list; the duration estimates and the basis of those estimates; the lessons learned register, assumption log, and risk register; the project schedule network diagrams; and to validate resources the project team assignments, resource calendars, and the resource requirements.
- **Enterprise environmental factors** - In developing the project schedule, internal and external influences should be considered, including, but not limited to any type of government or industry standards and the communication processes and channels within the organization.
- **Organizational process assets** - The scheduling methodology, the project calendars, and past project files may be leveraged to develop and update the project schedule.

Develop Schedule: Tools and Techniques

Schedule Network Analysis

The schedule network analysis is an ongoing analysis of the project schedule using various analytical techniques that will be reviewed later in this process. These analysis techniques include but are not limited to critical path method (CPM), what-if analysis, modeling and simulation, and resource leveling. These techniques will be discussed further in the remaining tools and techniques.

Critical Path Method (CPM)

Critical path concept. The critical path is the longest path through the schedule network with zero or negative total float. Total float is the amount of time an activity or sequence of activities can be delayed before it delays the overall project duration.

Float occurs when there are more than one concurrent activities of different durations. The duration difference between the concurrent activities represents the amount of float the shorter path or paths will have.

Example: Float

5 Days Float	6 Days
3 Days Float	8 Days
0 Days Float *(Critical Activity)*	11 Days

For example, prior to planting the flowers, the irrigation system is to be installed and the rock wall is to be built. The irrigation installation and the construction of the rock wall are occurring concurrently, as there is no dependency between them. The irrigation system is going to take two days to install and the rock wall is going to take five days to construct. The irrigation system installation can "float" up to three days without having an impact on the planting of the flowers. The irrigation may start anytime between day one and day four. The irrigation installation has three days of total float, whereas the rock wall construction has no float as it is the longest activity.

If the rock wall construction is delayed, the overall project would be delayed by that amount, delaying the start of the flower planting. Because there are no other activities happening concurrently with the flower planting, we know that it is a critical activity, having zero float.

Using the information in the diagram below, Activity A and Activity F will be on the critical path, having zero float, as they do not have concurrent activities. The combined duration of Activities B and C is 7 days. The combined duration of the concurrent path of Activities D and E is 11 days. As such, D and E have no float and are on the critical path. Activities B and C can "float" by as much as four days without affecting the overall project duration.

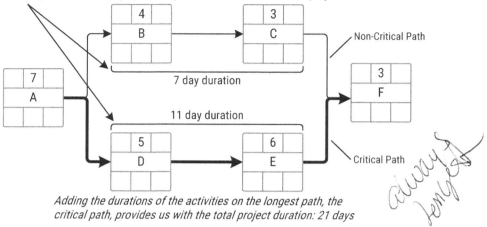

The 4 day difference between the two sequences indicates that activity B and C can be delayed, combined, by up to 4 days before it would affect the project duration

Adding the durations of the activities on the longest path, the critical path, provides us with the total project duration: 21 days

Let's check your understanding of the concept of critical path. The answers to Exercise 6.8 are on page 151.

Exercise 6:8: Critical Path Calculation

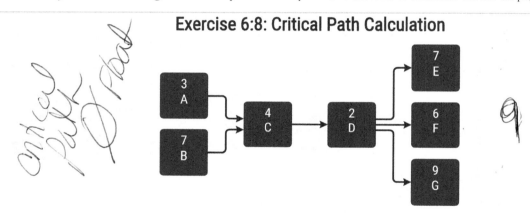

1. Which activity has the greatest amount of float

   A. Activity E
   B. Activity F
   C. Activity A
   D. Activity D

2. Which activities are on the critical path?

   A. A – C – D – G
   B. C – D
   C. B – C – D – E
   D. B – C – D – G

3. Activity B has ___ days of float

   A. 0
   B. 6
   C. 4
   D. (4)

4. Activity A has ___ days of float

   A. 4
   B. 3
   C. (4)
   D. 0

5. Activity F has ___ days of float

   A. 0
   B. 3
   C. (1)
   D. 1

6. If Activity A is delayed by 9 days, what is the impact on the project?

   A. There is no impact
   B. The project is delayed 3 days
   C. The project is delayed 5 days
   D. The project is delayed 9 days

Critical path method (CPM). The more challenging process of calculating critical path is actually using the critical path method (CPM). Because of the potential for error in using the full CPM, only use this when necessary on the exam.

CPM calculates the early start and early finish dates and late start and late finish dates for all schedule activities by:

- Performing a forward pass analysis and a backward pass analysis through the project schedule network paths
- The forward pass determines the early start (ES) and early finish (EF) dates: ES + duration (DU) – 1 = EF
- All early starts (ES) and early finishes (EF) must be calculated before beginning the backward pass
- The backward pass determines the late start (LS) and late finish (LF): LF – DU + 1 = LS

In standard diagramming notation, the early dates are on the top and the late dates are on the bottom; starts are on the left and finishes are on the right. You may see duration listed in the top center box or sometimes it is documented under the activity name or ID. Total float may be in the bottom center box or it may be documented under the bottom right of the box.

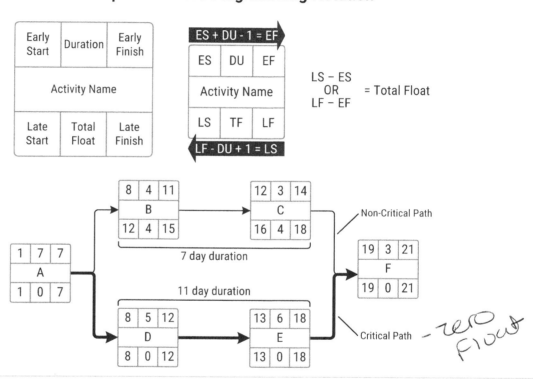

In the 4th Edition of the *PMBOK® Guide*, PMI used a "day zero" method which starts the first early start on day zero versus day one. When manually calculating critical path, the math is much simpler and more intuitive than in a "day one" method. PMI changed to referencing a day one method in the *PMBOK® Guide, 5th Edition*. This change is to reflect consistency with most project scheduling tools, which start the first day of the project on day one, not day zero.

To calculate critical path:

1. Start the forward pass with the first activity; the ES is one.
2. Add the duration to the ES and subtract one to calculate the EF.
3. The ES of any successor activities would be the next day.
4. Add the duration to the ES and subtract one to calculate EF and repeat for remaining activities.
5. For activities with more than one predecessor activity, use the highest predecessor EF plus one as the ES.

6. Once all activities have ES and EF, begin the backward pass on the last activity by using the highest last EF as the last LF.

7. Working backward through the activities, subtract duration from LF and add one to calculate LS.

8. The LS of the successor activity minus one becomes the LF of the predecessor activity.

9. For activities with more than one successor activity, use the lowest successor LS as the LF.

10. Remember to include any lag or lead time in the calculations.

11. When the backward pass is complete, the first activity's LS should be one.

12. To calculate total float, subtract EF from LF or ES from LS for each activity.

13. To calculate free float, on the last activities in a sequence, subtract their EF from the ES of the successor and minus one.

14. Identify the critical path as the longest path through the network with no float.

Example: Critical Path Method

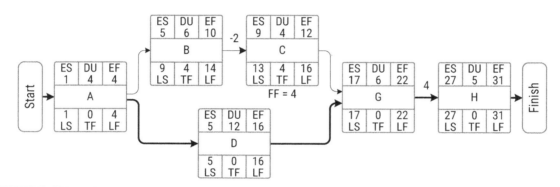

In this example, you will see that free float is only calculated on activity C. Free float is only calculated on the last activity in a sequence before a point of path convergence. Whereas total float tells how much time an activity can be delayed before delaying the project, free float tells us how much time that last activity can be delayed before it delays the early start of the successor activity. You will notice in the example above that the free float and the total float for activity C are both four. In network diagrams with multiple paths and sub-paths, you may find that the free float differs from the total float.

Although calculating free float is not a common practice on many projects, I would recommend having a high-level understanding for the exam. Certainly, it is much more likely that you will get questions on total float on the exam, you may have a free float question, as well.

Let's try a few easy diagrams and check your understanding of critical path method. The answers to Exercise 6.9 are on page 151.

Exercise 6.9: Critical Path Method

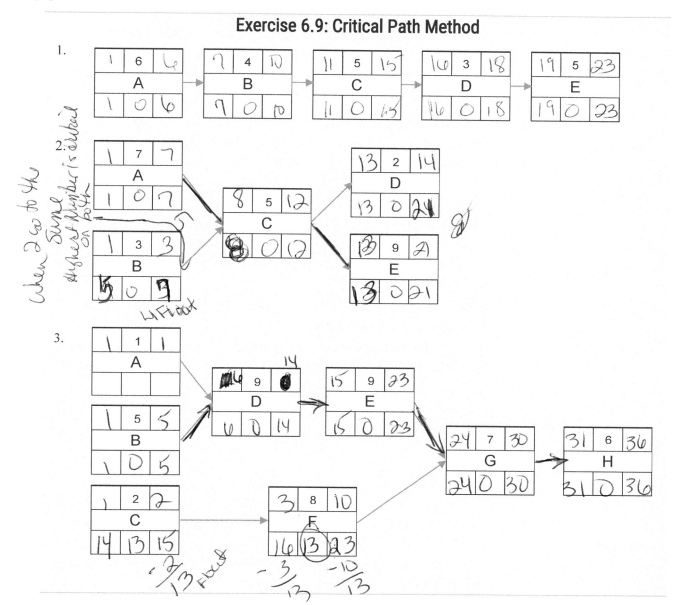

Belinda's Hint

I do not want you to stress too much about critical path. Yes, it is a concept you need to understand for the exam but be cautious of making critical path method your nemesis and putting too much focus and time on it.

I had a young lady who attended one of my PMP® boot camps with her manager. Her manager completed his exam prior to her and he offered her well-meaning advice: study, study, study critical path. The young lady devoted the rest of her preparation time to practicing critical path. You can imagine her frustration and disappointment when she only had a few critical path questions on her exam. That does not give you a free pass, however! Still do your best to practice CPM and most importantly, understand the concept of critical path.

Term	Definition
Path Divergence	Any point in a schedule network diagram where a single predecessor activity has more than one unrelated successor activity, forming multiple "paths". At a point of path divergence, the early finish (EF) becomes the early start (ES) of the successor activities. When there is a path divergence, setting up multiple concurrent paths, there will be float associated with the shorter path.
Path Convergence	Any point in a schedule network diagram where more than one path has a shared successor activity with another path or paths. It is immediately prior to the point of path convergence that you will calculate free float.
Critical Path	The longest path through the network with zero or negative total float
Total Float	The amount of time an activity can be delayed before it delays the project. Total float occurs when there is more than one activity happening concurrently with different durations. The difference in the durations represents the amount of float available for the shorter activity.
	Total float is shared between activities in a sequence (between a point of path divergence and path convergence).
	Using CPM, float is determined by the difference between the late start (LS) and early start (ES) or the difference between the late finish (LF) and early finish (EF).
	Negative total float indicates that the activity delay has exceeded the float available. As such, negative float indicates the project is delayed by that amount. For example, if the schedule has three days of negative float, the project is delayed three days.
	Total float is also known as float or slack.
Free Float	The amount of time an activity can be delayed before it delays the early start (ES) of the successor activity. Free float is only calculated on the last activity in a sequence before the point of path convergence.
	Free float is the difference between the ES of the successor and the early finish of the last activity in a sequence (minus one for the day one CPM).
Critical Activity	An activity with zero or negative total float.
Near Critical Activity	An activity with very little float. What is considered near-critical would be subjective based on the situation and the schedule.

Let's try a more challenging example of critical path method. The answer to Exercise 6.10 is on page 152.

Exercise 6.10: Critical Path Method #2

Use the PDM diagram below to conduct the CPM. Determine ES, EF, LS, LF, float, the critical path, and the total project duration.

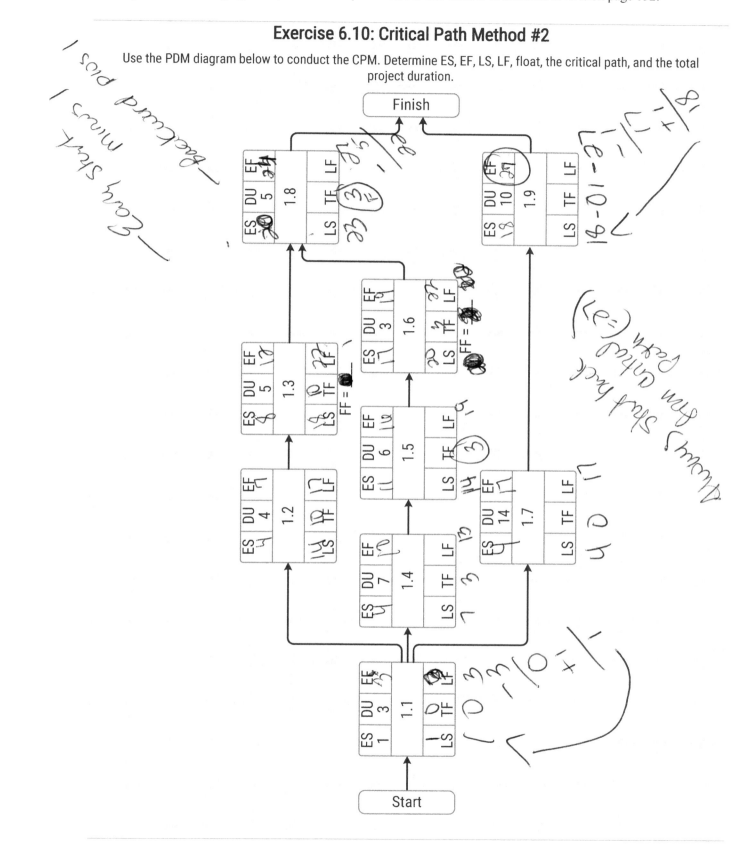

Resource Optimization Techniques

Consider that you have built out your project schedule and your critical path, simply based on the durations of the project activities. The next step would be to factor in your resources that you can apply to those activities. The reality of pretty much every project environment is that resources are scarce! They are not just sitting there at your beck and call.

Resource optimization techniques evaluate the critical path while considering the availability of those resources. Resource leveling always occurs first, and then potentially the schedule is smoothed by leveraging the schedule flexibility (float).

While there is typically an auto-resource level option in scheduling software, both resource leveling, and resource smoothing should be done manually. As the project manager, you will be best suited to know the human factors of your team versus relying on the software to make resource allocation decisions. Believe it or not, this may be a question on the exam!

Resource leveling. Resource leveling is done after developing the critical path in the schedule model. Leveling is used when there are shared or critical, required resources that are only available at certain times or in limited quantity and is often employed when resources have been over-allocated. The result of resource leveling is a resource-limited schedule or resource-constrained schedule. Resource leveling will most likely lead to a change in, or shifting out, of the critical path.

For example, based on simply activity durations and dependencies, it is going to take three weeks to complete this portion of the project. However, upon reviewing the activities, I discover that my key resources are over-allocated and cannot possibly complete all the work assigned to them within the designated work hours. Because of this, some of the activities will need to be pushed out, altering my critical path.

Resource smoothing. After leveling my resources, I may notice that I have peaks and valleys in my daily or weekly resource utilization. One week we may have 100 hours of work while the next week we have 300 hours of work and the following week we have 200 hours of work. Resource smoothing is performed after resource leveling, adjusting the activities so that the effort is more evenly allocated. Unlike resource leveling, the critical path is not changed, and the completion date may not be delayed. Activities may only be adjusted within their free and total float and, as such, it may not be possible to optimize all resources. The goal is just to smooth the work out as much as possible without impacting the completion date.

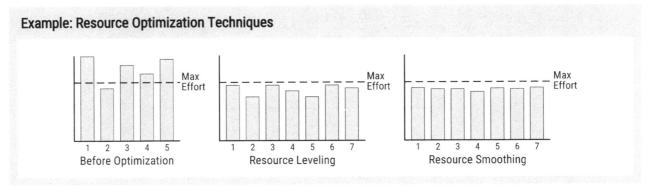

Example: Resource Optimization Techniques

Before Optimization | Resource Leveling | Resource Smoothing

Leads and Lags

As discussed previously, a lead is an acceleration of a successor activity, only used in finish-to-start discretionary relationships. Lead represents time being saved and as such, is indicated as a negative number on a network diagram.

A lag is a delay in the start of the successor activity and may be found in all four types of activity relationships (F-S, S-S, F-F, and S-F). Lag represents time being added and as such, is indicated as a positive number on a network diagram.

Schedule Compression

If the project schedule does not meet the time constraint of the project, the project management team may pursue schedule compression techniques. Both schedule compression techniques will preserve the scope of the project while shortening the schedule. In reality, as project managers, we use these techniques all the time, although we may not formally label them as "fast-tracking" and "crashing".

Fast-tracking is the first option considered as it does not add costs to the project. If enough compression is not realized with fast-tracking, however, crashing is the second option as it does add costs to the project.

Fast–tracking. Fast-tracking is a technique in which phases or activities that normally would be done sequentially are performed in full or partial parallel (the same concept as a lead). Fast-tracking does not result in increased cost, but it does increase the risk as there was a reason why the activities were originally going to be conducted sequentially. To fast-track activities, they must have a finish-to-start discretionary relationship. Activities on the critical path are always the primary target, as non-critical activities that are fast-tracked will only gain additional float with no impact to the overall schedule duration.

Example: Fast-Tracking

The marketing team will be developing a brochure, a print advertisement, and a video for the new holistic health center. The brochure is estimated to take 10 days, the print advertisement is estimated to take six days, and the video is estimated to take 11 days. The total duration is estimated to be 27 days.

However, Kim needs to shorten that timeframe in order to launch the publicity campaign on time. Working with the marketing team she finds that they can fast-track the print advertisement by two days and the video by five days. There is some risk in overlapping the activities, but the team will monitor the work closely.

By fast-tracking the marketing efforts, the duration decreases from 27 days to 20 days.

Let's check your understanding of fast-tracking. The answers to Exercise 6.11 are on page 152.

Exercise 6.11: Fast-Tracking

Activities A, B, C, and D all have sequential finish-to-start relationships. Activity A has a duration of six days, and Activity B has a duration of nine days. You can fast-track Activity B by three days. Activity C has a duration of twelve days and can be fast-tracked by one day. Activity D has a duration of five days and can be fast-tracked by four days.

What was the original duration and what is the fast-tracked duration?

Crashing. Crashing is used if fast-tracking did not save enough time on the schedule. Crashing is a technique in which cost and schedule tradeoffs are analyzed to determine how to obtain the greatest amount of compression for the least incremental cost. Do you remember the days before Amazon Prime? If we wanted to get our delivery faster than a week or 10 days, we had to pay for it. And it was expensive! That is the exact concept of crashing – paying to get it done faster.

To crash the project schedule, the critical activities are analyzed and prioritized based on the lowest crash cost per time unit. This will allow the team to identify those candidate activities that would produce the greatest value at the least incremental cost. As with fast-tracking, we always focus on critical path activities first, as that is where we will experience a reduction to our overall project schedule. To fast-track or crash activities that have float will only add more float and not serve to give us a reduction in time.

Belinda's Hint

If the question mentions that you are "adding resources" to your project or to the critical path, consider that crashing. Resources = Money. An easy way to think of an evaluation for crashing is the following. You have three teams that all make a different hourly wage:

Team A makes $10/hour

Team B makes $20/hour

Team C makes $30/hour

If their quality and availability were all considered equal, what team would you pick first? Second? Third? Team A, followed by Team B, and lastly Team C. That is the concept of evaluating for the lowest incremental crash cost!

Example: Crashing

The current project schedule will not meet the timelines required for the project even after fast-tracking. You are provided with the following information:

Activity	Normal Duration	Crash Duration	Normal Cost	Crash Cost	Float
A	15	11	$800	$1,200	11
B	8	5	$1,000	$1,600	0
C	12	8	$1,400	$2,000	0
D	6	5	$600	$900	0
E	10	8	$500	$1,000	10
F	20	15	$1,200	$1,700	0

Because activities A and E are not on the critical path (as indicated by the fact that they have float), you will not crash them as it will not impact the schedule. Leaving activities B, C, D, and F. You determine the lowest incremental crash cost in order to prioritize the order of crashing:

- Activity F will be crashed first, with an incremental cost of $100/day
- Activity C will be crashed second, with an incremental cost of $150/day
- Activity B will be crashed third, with an incremental cost of $200/day
- Activity D will be crashed fourth, with an incremental cost of $300/day

Incremental cost is calculated: (crash cost – normal cost) / (normal duration – crash duration)

The crash activities can then be plotted in a crash graph:

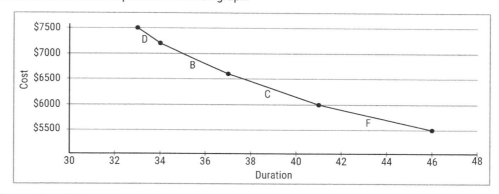

Reading from right to left:

- F's first graph point is 46 / $5500. 2nd graph point is 41 / $6,000
- C's first graph point is F's 2nd point. 2nd graph point is 37 / $6,600
- B's first graph point is C's 2nd point. 2nd graph point is 34 / $7,200
- D's first graph point is B's 2nd point. 2nd graph point is 33 / $7,500

The total project duration is 46 days (the total duration of the activities without float – the critical path activities). However, total project cost is the cost associated with all activities: $5,500.

The original cost of the project was $5,500 with a duration of 46 days. If all the activities are crashed, the new duration is 33 days and a cost of $7,500.

Let's check your understanding of crashing. The answers to Exercise 6.12 are on page 152.

Exercise 6.12: Crashing

Based on the information in the following table, answer the questions below:

Activity	Normal Duration	Crash Duration	Normal Cost	Crash Cost	Float
1.1	10 days	8 days	$300	$700	0
1.2	15 days	11 days	$800	$1,200	0
1.3	6 days	2 days	$500	$700	0
1.4	18 days	10 days	$1,000	$1,400	6 days
1.5	6 days	4 days	$500	$1,000	0
1.6	5 days	4 days	$600	$750	0
1.7	8 days	7 days	$1,200	$1,500	5 days

What was the original project duration?

What was the original project cost?

What activities would you crash and in what order?

Agile Release Planning

For adaptive projects, agile release planning will result in a high-level visual mapping of the product vision and the product roadmap. During release planning, the team determines the number of iterations that will be needed and/or conducted during the project and when increments of functionality will be released. Unlike a traditional project schedule, the release schedule defines what features will be complete and released at the end of each iteration or sprint. This is a planning hierarchy that will be beneficial to understand for the exam.

Relationship Between Product Vision, Release Planning, and Iteration Planning

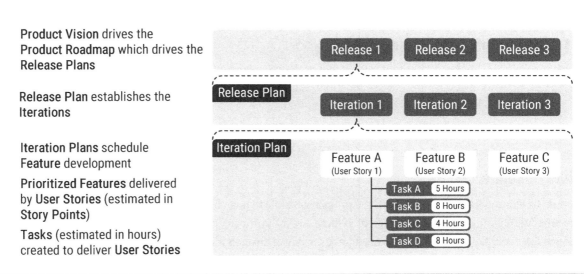

Product Vision drives the **Product Roadmap** which drives the **Release Plans**

Release Plan establishes the **Iterations**

Iteration Plans schedule **Feature** development

Prioritized Features delivered by **User Stories** (estimated in **Story Points**)

Tasks (estimated in hours) created to deliver **User Stories**

PMBOK® Guide – Sixth Edition. Page 216

The *product vision* is the engaging, emotional and compelling view of the future of the product that is under development by the agile project team. According to ScrumAlliance.org, the "product vision should be clear and stable; broad and engaging; and short and sweet".

The *product roadmap* is a visual representation of how the product is expected to grow and how the product will change over time. The product roadmap is used to manage stakeholder expectations.

A *release plan* describes approximately how many iterations will be contained within one release (typically three to twelve iterations) and what type of functions or features may be released at that time.

An *iteration* is a defined, time-boxed cycle of project work and product development. In Scrum, iterations are known as sprints. Iterations are typically two to four weeks in length, with a preference toward the shorter time. In order to capture team productivity (known as velocity) accurately, the iteration should be set a consistent timebox throughout the project.

A *feature* is a chunk or piece of functionality that delivers value. A feature is made up of one or sometimes more user stories.

A *user story* is a description of how the deliverable, feature, or function benefits a specific user. For example: As a registered user of the XYZ site, when I log-in with my correct user name and password, my account history will be displayed.

Story points are used as a relative estimation technique as an alternative to hours or days or another time measure. The agile team defines story points based on the relative effort size of the tasks. For example, a task worth five story points will take slightly more than double the time of a task worth two story points.

A *task* is the lowest level of work that is completed by the agile project team during their iteration or sprint.

Common Tools and Techniques:

Data Analysis Techniques

Schedule development data analysis may leverage two techniques:

A *what-if scenario analysis* is an evaluation of different options, scenarios and possibilities that are analyzed to assess the feasibility of the project schedule under adverse conditions.

A *simulation* calculates multiple project durations with different sets of assumptions and typically uses probability distributions constructed from three-point estimates to assess the schedule implications. The most common technique is a Monte Carlo evaluation, which will be discussed in more detail in the **perform quantitative risk analysis** process.

Project Management Information System (PMIS)

There are a number of automated scheduling tools that are components of the PMIS that can be used to generate start and finish dates, network diagrams, resource allocations, etc.

Develop Schedule: Outputs

Schedule Baseline

The schedule baseline is a specific version of the project schedule that is "frozen" and added to the project management plan. The schedule should only be "re-baselined" if there was a significant, authorized change to the scope of the project. Any changes that would affect the baseline need to be approved through the integrated change control process.

Project Schedule

The project schedule includes at least a planned start date and planned finish date for each schedule activity. This is the "living" project schedule that will be updated throughout the project and compared to the project schedule baseline. Depending on the audience, the project schedule may be presented in summary form, such as a milestone schedule, or in more detail.

There are several presentation formats:

Schedule Format	Description
Milestone chart	Similar to bar charts but it only identifies the scheduled start or completion of a major deliverable or event
Bar/Gantt chart	With bars representing activities, the bar chart shows activity start and end dates and activity durations
Schedule network diagram	Shows both the network sequencing and the critical path activities. Network diagrams can be in a PDM format or a time-scaled diagram (logic bar chart) or an ADM.

Schedule Data

Schedule data includes the schedule milestones, schedule activities, activity attributes, and the assumptions and constraints.

Project Calendars

The project calendars identify working days and shifts that are available for scheduled activities.

Common Outputs:

- **Change requests** - Change requests may be generated because of developing or updating the project schedule. The change requests will be evaluated through the **perform integrated change control** process.
- **Project management plan updates** - Updates to the project management plan could include updating the schedule management plan and the cost baseline.
- **Project document updates** - Updated project documents include, but are not limited to activity attributes, the assumption log, the duration estimates, the lessons learned register, the resource requirements, and the risk register.

*The **develop schedule** process information is adapted from: PMBOK® Guide – Sixth Edition. Page 205-221*

Chapter 6 – Answer Key

Exercise 6.1

1. B
2. A
3. D
4. A
5. D

Exercise 6.2

1. Discretionary
2. Discretionary
3. Mandatory
4. Discretionary / external
5. Mandatory / internal
6. Mandatory

Exercise 6.3

1. The original duration was 22 days and the new duration is 17 days. 10 days + 12 days = 22 days; 22 days – 5 days = 17 days

2. The duration of Y is 21 days. 40 days = 22 days – 3 days + x days; 40 days = 19 days + x days; 21 days = x days

3. The best-case duration is 10 days. Leads are only used in finish-to-start relationships. In a start-to-start relationship, there would be no use for a lead, as both activities can start on the same day. In this situation, the best-case duration is always that the activities happen concurrently.

Exercise 6.4

1. The revised duration is 30 days: 9 + 4 (lag) + 17 = 30 days

2. The duration of Y is 17 days: Y = 30 – 13, Y= 17 days

3. The difference between the best-case duration and the worst-case duration is 16 days. Best-case is that the activities are happening concurrently and worst-case is that the activities are happening sequentially. The lag is always applied before the start of the successor activity. Best-case: 18 days; worst-case: 18 days + 4 days + 12 days = 34 days; difference: 34 days – 18 days = 16 days

Exercise 6.5

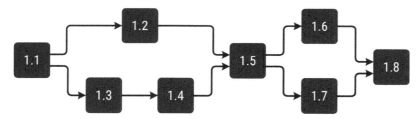

Exercise 6.6

1. Elapsed time is 13 weeks, duration is 39 days
2. 580 hours (5 weeks at 100 hours and 1 week at 80 hours)
3. Vendor A: 24 hours/day x 4 days/week. Elapsed time is 5 weeks, duration is 20 days. Vendor B: 48 hours/day x 2 days/week. Same elapsed time of 5 weeks, but duration is only 10 days.

Exercise 6.7

1. D
2. D
3. A
4. B
5. B
6. A

Exercise 6.8

1. C
2. D
3. A
4. A
5. B
6. C

Exercise 6.9

1.

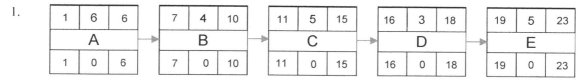

2.

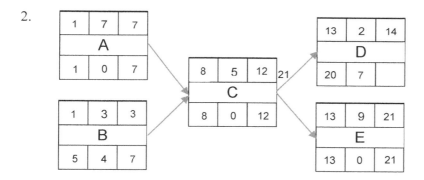

3.

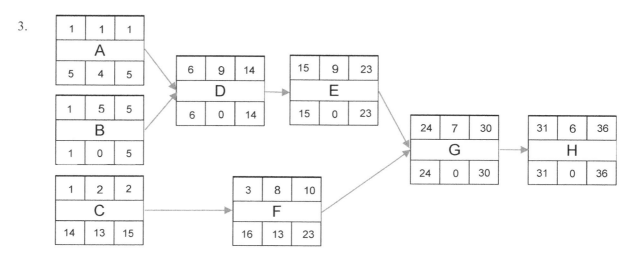

Exercise 6.10

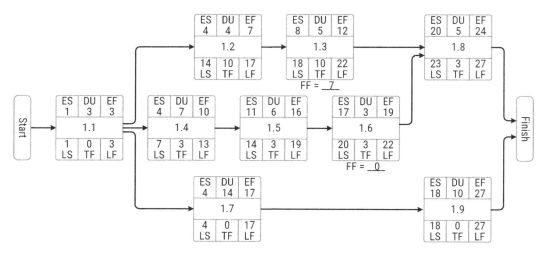

Exercise 6.11

Original duration was 32 days and the fast-tracked duration is 24 days.

Exercise 6.12

Original duration: 42 days

Original cost: $4,900

Crashing order: 1.3, 1.2, 1.6, 1.1, and 1.5

Chapter 6 - Review Questions

Time Limit: 18 Minutes

1. **You are in the process of developing your project schedule. You determine that you are able to leverage a one-day lead for activity 7.2.9. Which statement is least accurate?**
   A. The successor activity can start one day before the predecessor activity is completed
   B. The precedent activity can start one day before the subsequent activity
   C. The predecessor/successor activities have a finish-to-start relationship
   D. There is a preferred relationship between the predecessor/successor activities

2. **Which statement is most accurate regarding agile release planning?**
   A. The roadmap drives the release plans which establish the iterations
   B. The features drive the product vision which establishes the tasks
   C. The iterations drive the tasks which establish the release plan
   D. The tasks drive the iterations which establish the product vision

3. **The PERT estimate is nine hours. The best-case estimate is four hours and the worst-case estimate is 18 hours. What is the most-likely duration estimate for a beta distribution?**
   A. 11 hours
   B. 9 hours
   C. 8 hours
   D. 5 hours

4. **As PM, you are working with your team leads and you realize that you have a scheduling problem that will result in a delay of the project. What is the first thing you should do?**
   A. Crash activities on your critical path
   B. Reduce project scope in order to bring the project in on time
   C. Fast-track activities on your critical path
   D. Out-source to a more appropriate team that can deliver the project in a timely manner

5. **When crashing a task, the project team needs to focus on:**
   A. Non-critical tasks
   B. As many tasks as possible
   C. Accelerating performance of those tasks on the critical path
   D. Accelerating performance by minimizing costs

6. **The "fast-tracking" method of schedule compression involves:**
   A. The use of industrial engineering techniques to improve productivity, thereby finishing the project earlier than originally planned
   B. Performing activities in parallel, thereby increasing risk
   C. Going on a "mandatory overtime schedule" in order to complete the project earlier
   D. Assigning "dedicated teams" to the critical path activities

7. **The critical path is established by calculating the following dates:**
   A. Start-to-start, start-to-finish, finish-to-finish, finish-to-start
   B. Early start, early finish, late start, late finish
   C. Predecessor-to-successor, predecessor-to-predecessor, successor-to-successor
   D. Primary-to-secondary, primary-to-finish, secondary-to-secondary, finish-to-finish

8. **The precedence diagramming method provides project managers with knowledge of:**
   A. All levels of the work breakdown structure
   B. Activities likely to be involved in the project integration and resource allocation functions
   C. A graphical representation of interdependencies of activities
   D. The project completion date

9. **A schedule compression technique to determine how to obtain the greatest amount of compression for the least incremental cost is called:**
   A. Crashing
   B. PERT
   C. Precedence diagramming method
   D. Fast tracking

10. **Analogous duration estimating is:**
    A. Bottom-up estimating
    B. Frequently used to estimate project duration when there is a limited amount of detailed information
    C. Similar to multiple duration estimating
    D. Deductive estimating

11. **What is the total duration of the project?**

Activity	Duration	Float
1	4	0
2	7	0
3	3	0
4	9	1
5	16	0
6	8	8
7	5	2
8	6	0

    A. Unable to determine
    B. 36 days
    C. 25 days
    D. 58 days

12. **The ES of the activity is day seven and the duration is six days. If the LF of the activity is day 15, what statement is most accurate:**
    A. The activity is on critical path
    B. If the activity gets delayed by two days, the project will be delayed by one day
    C. The activity is not on critical path
    D. If the activity gets delayed, there will be an impact on the project

13. **Activity 9.2.1 has 7 days of free float. The early start of the successor activity, 9.2.2 is day 29. If activity 9.2.1 is delayed by 12 days, what is the adjusted early start of activity 9.2.2?**
    A. 42
    B. 22
    C. 29
    D. 34

14. **Based on the following information, which statement is most accurate?**

Activity	Duration	Float	Cost
1	10	0	$125
2	8	0	$75
3	15	0	$200
4	12	3	$150
5	16	0	$110
6	4	2	$50
7	10	2	$90
8	9	0	$175

A. The total duration is 85 days and the cost is $975
B. The total duration is 58 days and the cost is $685
C. The total duration is 58 days and the cost is $975
D. The total duration is 84 days and the cost is $685

15. **Activity 7.1 is 5 days, Activity 7.2 is 9 days, Activity 7.3 is 4 days, Activity 7.4 is 11 days, and Activity 7.5 is 6 days. The predecessor for Activity 7.2 is Activity 7.1. The predecessor for Activity 7.3 is Activity 7.2. The predecessor for Activity 7.4 and 7.5 is Activity 7.3. What statement is the most accurate?**

A. The total duration is 35 days
B. Activity 7.5 is a critical activity
C. The total duration is 29 days
D. If activity 7.2 gets delayed 3 days, there will be 5-day delay on the project

Review Question Answers

1. **Answer: B**

   Only finish-to-start discretionary (AKA preferred, preferential, or soft logic) relationships can leverage lead. Using a lead, the successor activity can begin one day before the predecessor activity has been completed. This will "overlap" the activities by one day, saving one day on the total duration.

2. **Answer: A**

   The product roadmap drives the release plans which establish the iterations. The iteration plans schedule the feature development which is then broken down into user stories.

3. **Answer: C**

   The question provides the PERT (3-point) estimate and the optimistic and pessimistic estimates. You need to solve for the most likely using the PERT formula $(O + 4M + P) / 6$.

   $9 = (4 + 4M + 18)/6$

   $54 = 4 + 4M + 18$

   $54 = 22 + 4M$

   $32 = 4M$

   $8 = M$

4. **Answer: C**

   The first option is to fast-track activities (take activities that were going to be done sequentially and do them in parallel). This allows the project to be shortened without increasing the costs or limiting the scope. De-scoping and outsourcing would only be considered if fast-tracking and crashing did not result in the needed compression.

5. **Answer: C**

   Crashing accelerates the performance of activities/tasks on the critical path by increasing costs. Crashing would focus on critical activities first as crashing non-critical activities would simply result in more float and would not offer any true compression.

6. **Answer: B**

   Fast-tracking takes activities that were going to be done sequentially and instead performs them in parallel. In order to fast-track, the activities must have a discretionary dependency. Violating the dependency does imply that there is increased risk. Overtime or dedicated teams would be examples of crashing.

7. **Answer: B**

   The critical path method (CPM) determines the critical path of the schedule network by determining the early start (ES) and early finish (EF) of activities via a forward pass and the late start (LS) and late finish (LF) via a backward pass.

8. **Answer: C**

   The precedence diagramming method (PDM) diagrams the activity relationships, with nodes representing the activities and the arrows indicating the types of relationships. The diagram itself will not provide the project completion date.

9. **Answer: A**

   The two scheduling compression techniques are fast-tracking and crashing. Crashing evaluates potential candidate activities for acceleration based on the lowest incremental crashing cost. Fast-tracking incurs no additional cost.

10. **Answer: B**

    Analogous estimating, also known as top-down estimating, is frequently used when there is not a lot of detailed information about the current project. As such, the PM will leverage a past similar project as the basis of the estimate.

11. Answer: B

As there are no predecessor relationships defined in the table, the duration cannot be determined by a CPM diagram. As such, you can assume a singular critical path. To determine total duration, you would not include any activities with float, as float indicates that the particular activity is happening concurrently with another activity. Including the duration of those activities with float would be "double" counting.

12. Answer: C

Using CPM: ES of 7 + 6 duration – 1 = EF of 12. If the EF is 12 and the LF is 15, the activity has three days of float. As such, the activity is not a critical activity. If it gets delayed by two days, there would be no impact as the activity has three days of float.

13. Answer: D

Free float indicates the amount of time an activity can be delayed before it delays the early start (ES) of the successor activity. If the activity only has seven days of free float and it's delayed by 12 days, it is a difference of five days. The successor activity will be delayed by five days, changing the ES of the successor to day 34.

14. Answer: C

To determine duration, only those activities that are critical would be included (zero float). The activities with float are occurring concurrently with other activities and as such, the duration would be double-counted if included. That would bring the duration to 58 days. However, all activities, critical or not, will cost money, so all activity costs will be summed to $975.

15. Answer: C

Activities 7.1, 7.2, and 7.3 are occurring sequentially. Activities 7.4 and 7.5 are happening concurrently. Critical path is 7.1, 7.2, 7.3, and 7.4. Activity 7.5 has five days of float. The total duration is 29 days. Activity 7.2 is critical, so if it were to be delayed by three days, the project would be delayed by three days.

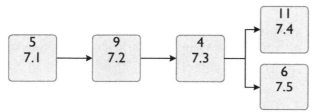

Chapter 6 - Vocabulary Review

* Activity
* Activity attributes
* Activity list
* Alternatives analysis
* Analogous estimating
* Backward pass
* Crashing
* Critical activity
* Critical path
* Critical path method
* Decomposition
* Discretionary dependency
* Duration
* Early finish date
* Early start date
* Effort
  Elapsed time
  External Dependency
* Fast-tracking
* Finish-to-finish

* Finish-to-start
  Fist-to-five
* Forward pass
* Free float
  Hammock activity
  Internal dependency
  Kanban
* Lag
* Late finish date
* Late start date
  Law of diminishing returns
* Lead
* Mandatory dependency
* Milestone
  Near critical activity
* Parametric estimating
  Parkinson's Law
* Path convergence
* Path divergence
* Precedence diagramming method

* Predecessor activity
* Project management information system
* Project schedule network diagram
  PERT
  Release planning
* Reserve analysis
* Resource leveling
* Resource smoothing
* Rolling wave planning
* Schedule compression
* Schedule management plan
* Schedule network analysis
* Simulation
* Start-to-finish
* Start-to-start
  Student syndrome
* Successor activity
* Three-point estimating
* Total float
* What-if scenario analysis

1.	A technique used to evaluate identified options in order to select the options or approaches to use to execute and perform the work of the project
2.	A delay of the successor activity
3.	An acceleration of the successor activity
4.	The amount of time that an activity can be delayed without delaying the early start date of any immediately following schedule activities
5.	A group of related schedule activities aggregated at some summary level, and displayed/reported as a single activity at that summary level
6.	An ongoing process that establishes a reserve for the budget or schedule of a project based upon the remaining level of project uncertainty
7.	The number of labor units required to complete a schedule activity or work breakdown structure component
8.	A component of work performed during the course of a project
9.	Any schedule activity on a critical path in a project schedule

10.		A significant point or event in the project
11.		The amount of calendar time it will take to complete an activity or component
12.		The point in a schedule network diagram where more than one path has a shared successor activity with another path or paths
13.		A list of schedule activities that shows the activity description, activity identifier, and a description of the activity
14.		A specific project schedule compression technique that changes network logic to overlap activities that would normally be done in sequence
15.		An analytical technique that uses three estimates to represent the optimistic, most likely, and pessimistic scenarios to calculate a weighted average
16.		A diagram the shows the sequencing of the project activities
17.		A method of constructing a project schedule network diagram where the nodes or boxes represent activities and the arrows depict the dependencies
18.		A form of progressive elaboration planning where the work to be accomplished in the near term is planned in detail while the work further in the future is planned at a relatively high level
19.		An estimating technique that uses a statistical relationship between historical data and other variables to calculate an estimate for the cost or duration of an activity
20.		The longest path through the schedule with zero or negative total float
21.		The amount of time that a schedule activity may be delayed without delaying the project finish date
22.		Any form of schedule network analysis in which scheduling decisions (start and finish dates) are driven by resource constraints
23.		A specific type of project schedule compression technique performed by taking action to decrease the total project schedule duration using those activities that provide the most compression at the least incremental cost
24.		Various descriptions or requirements associated with each schedule activity that can be included within the activity list
25.		An estimating technique that uses values from a previous, similar project as the basis for estimating the current project
26.		The total number of work periods to complete an activity, such as work days or work weeks
27.		The point in a schedule network diagram where a single predecessor activity has more than one successor activity
28.		An activity that logically comes before a dependent activity in a schedule
29.		A critical path method technique for calculating the early start and early finish dates by working forward through the schedule model from the project start date or a given point in time

30.	In the critical path method, the earliest possible point in time when the uncompleted portions of a schedule activity can finish based on the schedule network logic, the data date, and any schedule constraints
31.	A component of the project management plan that establishes the criteria and the activities for developing, monitoring, and controlling the schedule
32.	A schedule activity that has low total float
33.	A logical relationship in which a successor activity cannot finish until a predecessor activity has finished
34.	In the critical path method, the earliest possible point in time when the uncompleted portions of a schedule activity can start based on the schedule network logic, the data date, and any schedule constraints
35.	In the critical path method, the latest possible point in time when the uncompleted portions of a schedule activity can finish based on the schedule network logic, the project completion date, and any schedule constraints
36.	A logical relationship in which a successor activity cannot start until a predecessor activity has started
37.	A dependent activity that logically comes after another activity in a schedule
38.	In the critical path method, the latest possible point in time when the uncompleted portions of a schedule activity can start based on the schedule network logic, the project completion date, and any schedule constraints
39.	Ongoing use of a number of techniques to analyze the current status of the project schedule and likelihood of achieving the schedule objectives
40.	A logical relationship in which a successor activity cannot start until a predecessor activity has finished
41.	A critical path method technique for calculating the late start and late finish dates by working backward through the schedule model from the project end date
42.	A logical relationship in which a successor activity cannot finish until a predecessor activity has started
43.	A method used to estimate the minimum project duration and determine the amount of scheduling flexibility on the logical network paths within the schedule model
44.	Techniques used to shorten the schedule duration without reducing the project scope
45.	A technique used for dividing and subdividing the project scope and project deliverables into smaller more manageable pieces, down to the activity level
46.	A relationship that is established based on knowledge of best practices within a particular application area or an aspect of the project where a specific sequence is desired

47.	A voting technique where members vote using their hand and a number of fingers to signify support for the topic
48.	A relationship between activities within the project team's work responsibilities
49.	An adaptive project management technique that leverages a visual board to identify and limit the work-in-progress
50.	A relationship between project activities and non-project activities
51.	A principle that states that when a single factor in a process is increased, but other factors are not increased, there will be a point where productivity or output will decrease
52.	A relationship that is contractually required or inherent in the nature of the work
53.	The principle that work expands so as to fill the time available for its completion
54.	An acronym that represents a method of estimating that factors in uncertainty in the process by using optimistic, most likely, and pessimistic estimates
55.	Consists of the tools and techniques used to gather, integrate, and disseminate the outputs of the project management processes
56.	An agile approach to scheduling that determines iteration lengths and frequencies and defines the features to be delivered
57.	A resource optimization technique in which free and total float are used without affecting the critical path
58.	An analytical technique that models the combined effect of uncertainties to evaluate their potential impact on objectives
59.	A theory that individuals will procrastinate on doing their work until the deadline is imminent
60.	The process of evaluating scenarios in order to predict their effect on project objectives

* These definitions are taken from the Glossary of *PMBOK*® *Guide   Sixth Edition*

Vocabulary Review Answers

1.	Alternatives analysis	31.	Schedule management plan
2.	Lag	32.	Near-critical activity
3.	Lead	33.	Finish-to-finish
4.	Free float	34.	Early start date
5.	Hammock activity	35.	Late finish date
6.	Reserve analysis	36.	Start-to-start
7.	Effort	37.	Successor activity
8.	Activity	38.	Late start date
9.	Critical activity	39.	Schedule network analysis
10.	Milestone	40.	Finish-to-start
11.	Elapsed time	41.	Backward pass
12.	Path convergence	42.	Start-to-finish
13.	Activity list	43.	Critical path method
14.	Fast-tracking	44.	Schedule compression
15.	Three-point estimating	45.	Decomposition
16.	Project schedule network diagram	46.	Discretionary dependency
17.	Precedence diagramming method	47.	Fist-to-five
18.	Rolling wave planning	48.	Internal dependency
19.	Parametric estimating	49.	Kanban
20.	Critical path	50.	External dependency
21.	Total float	51.	Law of diminishing returns
22.	Resource leveling	52.	Mandatory dependency
23.	Crashing	53.	Parkinson's Law
24.	Activity attributes	54.	PERT
25.	Analogous estimating	55.	Project management information system
26.	Duration	56.	Release planning
27.	Path divergence	57.	Resource smoothing
28.	Predecessor activity	58.	Simulation
29.	Forward pass	59.	Student syndrome
30.	Early finish date	60.	What-if scenario analysis

Chapter 7

Project Cost Planning

What's in This Chapter

- Project Cost Management
- Plan Cost Management
- Estimate Costs
- Determine Budget

Project Cost Management

On any project, the costs of the project and the project work are a primary consideration. As projects are conducted to attain an objective and then terminate, one major constraint is the cost that can be, or needs to be, spent on the project activities. Even in project environments where costs are not tracked in-depth, the organization must consider the opportunity costs associated with resources applying effort to a project and compare that effort and cost to the anticipated return. As part of project initiation and chartering, a business case is typically developed to validate that the project is a worthwhile investment. In order to assess various business case measurements, such as net present value (NPV), internal rate of return (IRR), or return on investment (ROI), the costs of the project must be quantified.

I worked for a company that did not have the project management team or leads track their hours nor their costs. I was presented with an opportunity to manage two distinct projects. Project A had the potential to generate significant income while Project B had the potential to generate modest income. While Project A seemed to be the best option, when I factored in the amount of time that the team and I would need to spend on the project, the story began to look different. Using a loaded resource rate, I was able to do a cost-benefit analysis to show that Project B was the better option. While it took some convincing with the leadership, the numbers gave the full story. So even if you do not "track" costs, it needs to be a consideration for every project.

While resource costs are typically the largest expenditure, there are other costs to be considered, as well. This can include travel, materials, equipment, product-related expenses (such as maintenance), and overhead or indirect expenses. How the costs are tracked, paid, and reported on can vary not only from organization to organization, but also there are possible differences within the stakeholder group for the project.

Hot Topics in Project Cost Management

While earned value management (EVM) has been practiced in some industries in the past, the application is continuing to grow as companies seek methods for tracking progress on their projects. One of the newer concepts in earned value management is earned schedule (ES). Classically, schedule variance was determined by the difference between earned value (EV) and planned value (PV). ES is an alternate approach to schedule variance that compares earned schedule (ES) to actual time (AT). Earned schedule theory (EST) also provides methods for forecasting the project completion date using earned schedule, actual time, and estimated duration. (Does this topic seem misplaced in the project cost management section of the book? Consider that time is money and in earned value and earned schedule techniques, we are placing a dollar value on time!). At this time, EST will not be on the PMP exam in the form of scored questions, but I would not be surprised if you had a question on EST that was a pre-test question.

The following processes are used in creating the project budget and the cost baseline. All three processes are within the planning process group and the cost knowledge area.

Plan Cost Management. In creating the cost management plan, a subsidiary plan, this process involves identifying and documenting the approach for estimating, managing, and controlling costs on the project.

Estimate Costs. This process determines the cost estimates for the activities, work packages, and the overall project.

Determine Budget. This process will create the cost baseline and the project funding requirements for the project by aggregating the costs to determine the overall project budget.

Plan Cost Management

cost knowledge area | planning process group

The **plan cost management** process documents how the costs will be defined, validated, and controlled throughout the project, leading to the creation of the cost management plan. This process may be performed throughout the project at appropriate points when there are changes to the project or in the environment.

In practice, you may or may not develop subsidiary plans. If you do create these plans, they may be nothing more than a bulleted list. From an exam perspective, understand the types of information that may be included in a cost management plan but do not spend time memorizing specific components.

Plan Cost Management: ITTOs

Inputs	Tools & Techniques	Outputs
1. Project charter	1. Expert judgment	1. Cost management plan
2. Project management plan	2. Data analysis	
• Schedule management plan	3. Meetings	
• Risk management plan		
3. Enterprise environmental factors		
4. Organizational process assets		

PMBOK® Guide – Sixth Edition. Page 235

Plan Cost Management: Inputs

Common Inputs:

- **Project charter** - The project charter details the approved financial resources for the project and the project approval requirements.
- **Project management plan** - The project management plan components that may be leveraged during iterations of this process include the schedule management plan and the risk management plan.
- **Enterprise environmental factors** - In developing the cost management plan, the internal and external influences should be considered. These factors may include, but are not limited to, the type of organization where the work will be performed, any type of standards that are in place, legal or regulatory considerations, the stakeholders' expectations, and the governance framework of the organization as it relates to cost management.
- **Organizational process assets** - Policies and procedures will provide information on how the project costs should be estimated, documented, managed and controlled. Leveraging the use of a cost management plan template will ensure consistency and will also increase efficiency. If you are new to the organization, historical information or past project files may provide insight into the cost management process for previous projects.

Plan Cost Management: Tools & Techniques

Common Tools and Techniques:

Expert judgment

Expert judgment may come through the team members, PMO representatives, stakeholders, finance organization representatives, etc.

Data analysis techniques

Data analysis techniques for planning cost management may include leveraging an *alternatives analysis* to evaluate different funding options, how to acquire resources, make-or-buy considerations, etc.

Meetings

Planning meetings may be held with the team members, PMO representatives, and key stakeholders that have cost management expertise, insight, or responsibilities.

Plan Cost Management: Outputs

Cost Management Plan

The cost management plan may include:

- The units of measure that will be used on the project, such as $1, $10, $100, $1,000, etc.
- The level of accuracy and precision: the degree of precision, how the estimates may be rounded and the accuracy of the estimates (for example, ±10%).
- Organizational procedures links which may include instruction and direction related to the organizational procedures that are used for cost accounting, how control accounts may be used, etc. It is important that project costs are tracked and managed in accordance with the organization's policies and procedures. Identifying and segmenting direct versus indirect costs may be appropriate.
- Control thresholds, including what are the variance thresholds that are in place, indicating when action needs to be taken, or an escalation pursued.

- Rules of performance management such as how earned value or other measurements will be calculated including the earned value management (EVM) techniques and processes to be employed on the project and to track progress.
- Reporting formats including how information regarding the project cost and budget management will be communicated to the stakeholders.

*The **plan cost management** process information is adapted from: PMBOK® Guide – Sixth Edition. Page 235-239*

Estimate Costs

cost knowledge area | planning process group

The cost estimating process develops the cost estimates for the project and the project activities. Cost estimating is closely linked to the activity resource and duration estimating and will use many of the same techniques as activity duration estimating. This process will be revisited throughout the project as more information becomes known and progress is made on the project. When estimating project activity and resource costs, consideration may be made as to make-or-buy, make-or-lease, or resource sharing decisions.

The accuracy of the cost estimates can vary depending on the known information of the project. Early in the project, it is common to use a rough order of magnitude (ROM) estimate, which is essentially an educated guess: -25% to + 75%. As more information becomes known about the project, the estimates should become increasingly more accurate, with a range of -5% to +10%. If you are able to estimate to within 10% accuracy, this could be considered a definitive estimate as there is always some level of inherent risk and uncertainty in projects.

Belinda's Hint

One thing you may notice in the range of variance of estimates provided above is that we are more likely to come in over our estimate than under our estimate. Very rarely have I ever heard someone say "Boy, we estimated poorly. It was actually cheaper than we thought to get the work done!". Exceeding our estimates is a common planning fallacy, where typically estimates are very optimistic. As a project manager, to counterbalance this, get used to asking, "what is the worst-case scenario?". This allows the individual providing the estimate to consider the factors that may cause the costs to be increased. FYI, a ROM in slang terms is called a "S.W.A.G." As I am sure you understand, S.W.A.G. is not a PMI-approved term! 😊

Estimate Costs: ITTOs

Inputs	Tools & Techniques	Outputs

1. Project management plan
  • Cost management plan
  • Quality management plan
  • Scope baseline
2. Project documents
  • Lessons learned register
  • Project schedule
  • Resource requirements
  • Risk register
3. Enterprise Environmental Factors
4. Organizational Process Assets
	1. Expert judgment
	2. Analogous estimating
	3. Parametric estimating
	4. Bottom-up estimating
	5. Three-point estimating
	6. Data analysis
	  • Alternatives analysis
	  • Reserve analysis
	  • Cost of quality
	7. Project management information system
	8. Decision making
	  • Voting
		1. Cost estimates
		2. Basis of estimates
		3. Project documents updates
		  • Assumption log
		  • Lessons learned register
		  • Risk register

PMBOK® Guide – Sixth Edition. Page 240

Estimate Costs: Inputs

Common Inputs:

- **Project management plan** - As the process is conducted and iterated, the project management plan and various subsidiary plans may be leveraged. This includes the cost management and quality management plans and the scope baseline.

- **Project documents** - Project documents that may be leveraged to estimate costs include the lessons learned register, project schedule, resource requirements, and the risk register.

- **Enterprise environmental factors** - Market conditions, published commercial information, and exchange rates and inflation are among the environmental factors that may be considered for estimating the project costs.

- **Organizational process assets** - Cost estimating policies and templates, and the historical information and lessons learned files are typically leveraged to develop cost estimates for the project.

Estimate Costs: Tools & Techniques

Analogous Estimating

Analogous estimating, as we learned in duration estimating, is considered top-down estimating and is frequently used when there is a limited amount of information about the project. Analogous estimating, like an analogy, uses the actual cost of a previous, similar project, work package or schedule activity as the basis, partnered with expert judgment. This estimating technique is most reliable when the two projects or components are very similar.

Example: Analogous Cost Estimating

ANALOGOUS COST ESTIMATING

A component of the wellness center project is the design and launch of a custom-branded website. The vendor that developed the website for the birthing center charged $4,500.

Given that this website will be similar, Kim estimates that it will also cost approximately $4,500.

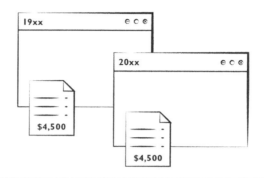

Parametric Estimating

Parametric estimating is calculated by multiplying or dividing the quantity of work to be performed by the cost rate. Parametric estimating leverages historical information and expert judgment. It is important that the underlying data is scalable and accurate.

Example: Parametric Cost Estimating

PARAMETRIC COST ESTIMATING

Kim will be purchasing six water features for the various meditation, massage and treatment rooms. Each water feature is estimated to be $75. To purchase all six water features, Kim budgets $450.

Bottom-Up Estimating

Bottom-up estimating uses the cost of individual work packages or individual schedule activities and aggregates or "rolls up" those costs to the higher levels for reporting and tracking purposes. This is the most time-consuming method of estimating, but it is the most accurate estimating technique.

Example: Bottom-Up Cost Estimating

BOTTOM-UP COST ESTIMATING

The employee orientation for the new wellness center employees will include three-days of training. To determine the cost estimate, Kim reviews each of the following components:

Employee handbooks $300
Hospital badges $125
Lunches $180
Breakfast $95
Classroom Rental $450
Total: $1,150

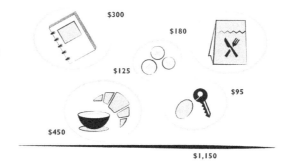

Three-Point Estimating

As with the other estimating techniques, three-point cost estimating is the same technique that was learned in duration estimating. Also known as program evaluation and review technique (PERT), a three-point estimate may be calculated using a beta distribution or triangular distribution.

Beta distribution. In a beta PERT, the most likely estimate is weighted by four and the sum of the optimistic, pessimistic and four times the most likely estimate is divided by six.

Expected = (O + 4M + P) ÷ 6

Triangular distribution. In a triangular PERT, the most likely is not weighted. The calculation is the sum of the optimistic, pessimistic, and most likely estimates divided by three.

Expected = (O + M + P) ÷ 3

Example: Three-Point Cost Estimating

THREE-POINT COST ESTIMATING

The landscapers have offered a most likely estimate of $15,000. However, if there is a late frost in the spring and extra excavating equipment is needed, the cost will increase to $18,000. If the hospital agrees to install the walkway as part of the campus maintenance, the cost will decrease to $7,000.

($7,000 + 4($15,000) + $18,000) / 6 = $14,167

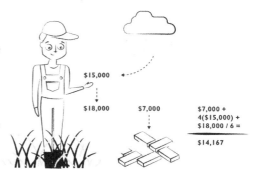

Belinda's Hint

On the exam, they will typically be using the beta distribution formula. If you are unsure which formula to use, always assume beta.

Ultimately these are a math question, so remember: use a calculator, double-check your math, and read the question carefully! You may not be solving for the 'expected' but for the optimistic, pessimistic or most likely. If you have extra time on the exam, review any math questions

The quickest way to solve the problem may be to plug in the four answers!

Let's check your understanding of the cost estimating techniques. The answers to Exercise 7.1 are on page 180.

Exercise 7.1: Cost Estimating Techniques

1. In order to fulfill the client's requirements, the team will need to provide three trainers. Each trainer is compensated at $750 per day. Which statement is most accurate?

    A. Because you have not worked with these trainers in the past, an analogous approach would be most appropriate
    B. Because there is a price per unit, parametric estimating would be most appropriate
    C. Because you have detailed information, a bottom-up estimate would be most appropriate
    D. Because the base is variable, a parametric estimate would not be reflective of actual costs

2. On previous projects, renting a war room cost the project approximately $1,500 for six months. You estimate your current project is going to take approximately six months to complete.

    A. Using the $1,500 would be an analogous estimate
    B. The $1,500 is a good foundation for a parametric estimate
    C. You are only renting one war room, so this is a bottom-up estimate
    D. You would need to factor in additional costs and conduct a PERT estimate

3. You are reviewing previous projects using files provided by the PMO. You are discovering a significant variance for this type of project. For projects of the same size and similar scope, the best case is $75,000 and the worst case is $110,000. You determine that the PERT estimate is $87,500.

    A. A triangular estimate would be $90,833
    B. A 3-point estimate would be $89,167
    C. The most likely estimate is $85,000
    D. A beta estimate would be $89,167

Common Tools and Techniques:

Expert Judgment

Individuals or groups may provide expertise and guidance on developing or modifying the cost estimates. Specialized knowledge can come from previous similar projects, industry experience, and various cost estimating methods.

Data Analysis Techniques

In estimating or re-estimating project and resource costs, there are a number of data analysis techniques that may be used:

An *alternatives analysis* evaluates various options to select which option or approach to use, such as conducting a make-or-buy analysis.

A *reserve analysis* evaluates the amount of contingency and management reserve that is allocated as compared to the amount of risk associated with the project constraints. This is an ongoing analysis and is used to determine if the contingency will be reduced, eliminated, or potentially increased, as additional information becomes available. If the contingency can be reduced, that funding would be returned to the organization as there would be an associated opportunity cost to hold onto it.

The *cost of quality* includes the cost of conformance – money spent to avoid failures, such as training, process documentation, inspections and the cost of non-conformance – money spent because of failures such as re-work, scrap, warranties, damage to reputation. The cost of quality will be discussed in more detail in the **plan quality management** process.

Decision-Making Techniques

Voting allows each member to submit their opinion or select the estimate that they feel is most realistic. It is often helpful in cost estimating to gather various opinions and have discussions to uncover risks associated with the estimating. Again, people are typically optimistic, so playing devil's advocate and asking for worst-case may encourage more realistic estimates.

Project Management Information System (PMIS)

There are multiple cost estimating software applications available, including computerized spreadsheets, simulation, and statistical tools.

Estimate Costs: Outputs

Cost Estimates

The cost estimates can include facilities, materials, equipment, services, resources, information technology, and contingency allocation and risk responses. Other cost considerations may involve interest rates, inflation, exchange rates. Indirect costs may also be included, depending on the organizational policy.

Basis of Estimates

Information regarding the basis of the cost estimates should be documented. Supporting detail may include how the estimate was developed, the assumptions that were made, the identified constraints, the range of possible estimates, and the confidence level of the final estimate.

Common Output:

- **Project document updates** - The project documents that will be updated from this process include the assumption log, the lessons learned register, and the risk register.

The **estimate costs** *process information is adapted from: PMBOK® Guide – Sixth Edition. Page 240-247*

Determine Budget

cost knowledge area | planning process group

Using the cost estimates and the project schedule, the project costs will be budgeted across individual work packages or activities to establish the cost baseline. This process will determine when the project costs will be charged to the organization, allowing the project manager to communicate anticipated costs and the dates those costs will be incurred. This will provide the finance organization with information so that funding availability can be confirmed.

Essentially, the cost estimating and budgeting processes are similar to what we all do at home for our household expenses and budget. We determine how much our bills are and how much our income is. After which, we determine when those bills are due as compared to when we get paid. If we are living check-to-check, we recognize that there needs to be money in the account to cover the expenses when they're due. Consider a project as a check-to-check endeavor! We have to make sure there is money in the account before we write the check.

One of the key outputs of this process is the cost baseline, a component of the project management plan. The cost baseline is going to include the cost estimates plus any contingency funding. Above and beyond the cost baseline, management reserve may be allocated. Management reserve is not included in the cost baseline, but it is considered part of the overall project budget.

Term	Definition
Budget contingency reserve	A risk funding allocation that is established for each activity, work package, or phase based upon the known risk or uncertainty associated with the project or project work.
	Budget contingency reserve is typically managed and controlled by the project manager for "known-unknowns": risks that are known (identified), it is just unknown if they will occur.
	Budget contingency reserve is also called contingency, budget contingency, or contingency reserves. Contingency is included as part of the cost baseline and factored into earned value calculations.
Contingency buffers	Contingency buffers are time allocations that are assigned at the activity, work package or phase level based upon the known risk or uncertainty associated. This is the same concept as budget contingency reserve, but instead of money, it is time that is allocated.
	Contingency buffers are typically managed and controlled by the project manager for "known-unknowns": risks that are known (identified), it is just unknown if they will occur.
	Contingency buffers are also called buffers or time buffers.
Management reserve	Management reserve is a risk funding allocation established for the overall project, above and beyond contingency reserves. Management reserve is typically managed by the sponsor and is allocated for "unknown-unknowns": risks that are not identified, major scope changes, etc.
	Management reserve is not included in the cost baseline, but it is considered part of the overall project budget. Not all organizations use "management reserve."

Determine Budget: ITTOs

Inputs	Tools & Techniques	Outputs

1. Project management plan
  • Cost management plan
  • Resource management plan
  • Scope baseline
2. Project documents
  • Basis of estimates
  • Cost estimates
  • Project schedule
  • Risk register
3. Business documents
  • Business case
  • Benefits management plan
4. Agreements
5. Enterprise environmental factors
6. Organizational process assets
	1. Expert judgment
	2. Cost aggregation
	3. Data analysis
	  • Reserve analysis
	4. Historical information review
	5. Funding limit reconciliation
	6. Financing
		1. Cost baseline
		2. Project funding requirements
		3. Project documents updates
		  • Cost estimates
		  • Project schedule
		  • Risk register

PMBOK® Guide – Sixth Edition. Page 248

Determine Budget: Inputs

Business Documents

Business documents considered while determining the budget include the business case and the benefits management plan. The business case provides information as to the financial success criteria for the project. The benefits management plan provides a benefits analysis related to the project costs and the anticipated return.

Agreements

Agreements with vendors or suppliers will detail the costs and the payment terms which will be needed for the project budget.

Common Inputs:

- **Project management plan** - As the budget is calculated and iterated throughout the project, the project management plan will be leveraged as a resource. This may include using the cost management plan, the resource management plan, and the scope baseline.

- **Project documents** - Project documents that may be used to determine the budget include the cost estimates and the basis of the estimates, the project schedule, and the risk register.

- **Enterprise environmental factors** - If the project is a multi-year project, environmental factors to consider may include currency fluctuations, interest rates, etc.

- **Organizational process assets** - Cost budgeting policies and procedures, historical information and lessons learned documentation, budgeting tools, and other procedures may be leveraged to determine the project budget.

Determine Budget: Tools and Techniques

Cost Aggregation

Using the WBS, costs are aggregated by work packages, which are then aggregated for the higher component levels of the WBS. All component levels will be aggregated for the entire project cost budget.

Historical Information Review

Estimating techniques such as parametric and analogous estimating leverage historical information. That historical information may also be used to predict total project costs and when those costs will affect the project.

Funding Limit Reconciliation

Some organizations may have established periodic funding limits for project spending. In the event there is a variance between the funding limits and the planned project spending, work may need to be re-planned or rescheduled. In this situation, the project manager and the team may need to place imposed date constraints on the work to ensure that all work currently underway is funded.

Financing

If the project is a very large, long-term project, financing external to the organization may need to be secured. The external source of the funding may have budgeting and tracking requirements that will need to be met.

Common Tools and Techniques:

Expert Judgment

Expertise may be provided by team members, stakeholders, PMO representatives, and other individuals with project budgeting knowledge and experience.

Data Analysis Techniques

The primary data analysis technique for determining the project budget is a *reserve analysis*. During this analysis, the amount of contingency is aligned to the amount of risk or uncertainty on the project. It is ongoing throughout the project.

Contingency reserve is for risk that is known-unknown (identified but uncertain to occur), to cover unplanned but required changes that can result from realized risks. Contingency is managed by the project manager. Management reserves are budgets that are reserved for unknown-unknown risks, such as major events, changes to project scope, etc. Under most circumstances, management reserves require that the project manager obtain approval before spending. Management reserve should not be included in the cost baseline but may be in the total project budget.

Example: Reserve Analysis

The website development project has estimated costs of $25,000. A 10% contingency was added in alignment with the level of risk for the project. In addition, there is $5,000 in management reserve.

Project cost estimate:	$25,000
Contingency:	$2,500
Cost baseline:	$27,500
Management reserve:	$5,000
Total project budget:	$32,500

Determine Budget: Outputs

There are two key outputs from the **determine budget** process: the cost baseline and the project funding requirements.

Cost Baseline

The cost performance baseline is the time-phased budget that is used as a basis against which to measure, monitor, and control overall cost performance on the project. Typically, it is displayed in an S-curve graph. The cost baseline is a component of the project management plan. The project budget may include the following components:

- Activity cost estimates + activity contingency reserve = work package cost estimates
- Work package cost estimates + contingency reserve = control accounts / cost baseline
- Cost baseline + management reserve = project budget

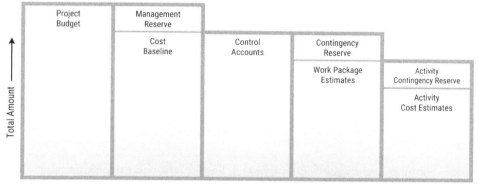

PMBOK® Guide – Sixth Edition. Page 255

Example: S-Curve Graph

Activity	Estimate	1	2	3	4	5
1.1.1	$1,000	$100	$200	$400	$0	$300
1.1.2	$500	$0	$0	$300	$200	$0
1.1.3	$1,300	$300	$300	$500	$100	$100
1.1.4	$700	$0	$100	$200	$200	$200
1.1.5	$1,700	$300	$200	$500	$400	$300
Total	$5,200	$700	$800	$1,900	$900	$900
Cumulative		$700	$1,500	$3,400	$4,300	$5,200

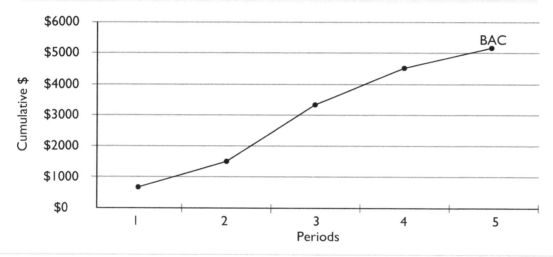

Belinda's Hint

When we begin discussing the earned value technique in the **control schedule** and **control costs** processes, we will be using this information for some of our calculations. The total estimate of $5,200 reflects the budget at completion (BAC). The cumulative planned spend represents the planned value (PV) of the work to be completed:

BAC: $5,200

Period 1 PV: $700

Period 2 PV: $1,500

Period 3 PV: $3,400

Period 4 PV: $4,300

Period 5 PV: $5,200 ← notice that PV at the end of our project is equal to our BAC.

Let's check your understanding of planned value. The answers to Exercise 7.2 are on page 180.

Exercise 7.2: Planned Value

1. Your project is estimated to take 10 months and cost $50,000. After five months, what is the PV?

    A. $5,000
    B. Unable to determine
    C. $2,500
    D. $25,000

2. The budget for your project has been estimated as follows: $32,000 for the first quarter, $48,000 for the second quarter, $54,000 for the third quarter, and $40,000 for the fourth quarter. After six months, the project is 40% complete and you have spent $40,000. What is the PV?

    A. $32,000
    B. $69,600
    C. $80,000
    D. $40,000

3. The PV of your project is $35,000 and the BAC is $175,000. If the budget has been applied estimate equally across five months, how many months of work have you completed?

    A. Unable to determine
    B. 1
    C. 3
    D. 5

Project Funding Requirements

The project funding requirements include both the total and periodic funding requirements, as derived from the cost baseline. Quite often, funding will occur incrementally, especially in larger and longer-term projects. Total funds required are those included in the cost baseline plus the management reserve amount.

Common Output:

*   **Project document updates** - Project documents updated through this process include the cost estimates, the project schedule, and the risk register.

*The **determine budget** process information is adapted from: PMBOK® Guide – Sixth Edition. Page 248-256*

Chapter 7 – Answer Key

Exercise 7.1

1. B
2. A
3. C

Exercise 7.2

1. B – unable to determine as the budget allocation is not provided
2. C - $80,000 ($32,000 + $48,000)
3. B – 1 month at $35,000 per month

Chapter 7 - Review Questions

Time Limit: 18 Minutes

1. **You are working with your work package owners to determine the activity cost estimates. An activity cost estimate includes all of the following resource categories except:**

    A. Labor
    B. Materials
    C. Equipment
    D. Time shortages

2. **Your team lead has suggested that you evaluate various estimating techniques in order to provide the most comprehensive estimate possible. You decide to use parametric estimating. Parametric cost estimating involves:**

    A. Defining the parameters of the project life cycle
    B. Calculating individual cost estimates for each work package
    C. Using a statistical relationship between historical data and other variables to calculate a cost estimate
    D. Using the actual cost of a similar project to estimate total project costs

3. **The previous project manager of your newly assigned project leveraged analogous estimating to determine the project costs. Analogous estimating:**

    A. Uses bottom-up estimating techniques
    B. Uses the actual cost of previous, similar projects as the basis for estimating the cost of the current project
    C. Is used most frequently in the later stages of a project
    D. Summarizes estimates for individual work items

4. **Your project is getting ready to kick-off and your sponsor has requested updated cost estimates. Which of the following is not true about cost estimates?**

    A. Are generally expressed in units of currency (dollars, euro, etc)
    B. The costs for schedule activities are estimated for all resources that will be charged to the project
    C. They do not generally consider information on risk responses
    D. Involve developing an approximation of the costs of the resources needed to complete each schedule activity

5. **You have been assigned a project that you have minimal experience with in the past. Unfortunately, the organization has also not pursued this type of initiative previously. The leadership team is asking for an estimate of costs. Based on your limited knowledge, what type of estimate would you most likely provide?**

    A. Parametric
    B. Phased
    C. Analogous
    D. Rough order of magnitude

6. **You are gathering the cost estimates for the renovation project. Upon reviewing cost data on previous projects, you find that for 20-member teams, the average equipment cost was $3,800. You anticipate a 15-person team. Which statement is most accurate?**

    A. A parametric estimate would be $2,850
    B. An analogous estimate would be $2,850
    C. The estimate would not be able to be determined due to pricing increases
    D. A budgetary estimate would be $2850

7. **The difference between the cost baseline and the total project budget can be best described as:**

    A. They are synonymous
    B. The total project budget includes management reserve and the cost baseline does not
    C. The cost baseline includes management reserve and the total project budget does not
    D. The total project budget is managed by the project manager and the cost baseline is managed by the team

8. Given the launch of the new system, you need to take into consideration the cost of associated hardware and software. Your IT team lead anticipates the costs to be approximately $18,000. However, if an upgrade is necessary, it could cost as much as $30,000. There is a chance that existing hardware can be used, which would bring the costs as low as $7,000. What is the best estimate?

   A. $17,167
   B. $18,170
   C. $18,330
   D. $13,750

9. Successful adoption of the CIS project is going to be dependent upon a thorough training program for the service representatives. In order to develop your sizing, you review the documentation from the financial system roll-out last year. To provide the same population with classroom training for that project cost $37,500. In addition, IT recently provided all users with trouble-shooting manuals for a similar system, at a cost of $12,000. Troubleshooting manuals will be used for this project as well. Which statement is most accurate?

   A. The parametric estimate would be $49,500
   B. The analogous estimate would be $49,500
   C. The budgetary estimate would be $49,500
   D. The three-point estimate would be $49,500

10. During the pilot of the CIS project, 1,000 customer records were updated and added to the new system. The cost from the vendor was $500. You know that for the full launch you will need to update and transfer 500,000 additional customer records. What will be the best estimate for the full launch?

    A. $250,000
    B. $250,500
    C. $500,000
    D. $200,000

11. Your client requires a major scope change due to a change in the market conditions. The scope change would add costs to the project. You currently have funding in your budget contingency reserve. What is the best thing you should do?

    A. Escalate to the sponsor to inquire about the application of management reserve funds
    B. Utilize the contingency reserve until it is exhausted and then escalate if necessary
    C. Deny the change
    D. Ask the client for additional funding to cover the scope change.

12. Your $85,000 project is estimated to take 12 weeks and you are 30% complete. What will the planned value (PV) be at the end of the project?

    A. Unable to determine until the project is 100% complete
    B. $59,500
    C. The budget at completion (BAC)
    D. $7,083

13. You have been assigned the management of a $750,000 infrastructure renovation project. The work is anticipated to take two years to complete and the budget has been allocated as below. What is the planned value (PV) of the work upon completion of period six?

Period	Estimate
1	25,000
2	35,000
3	95,000
4	135,000
5	175,000
6	195,000
7	50,000
8	40,000

   A. $195,000
   B. $660,000
   C. Unable to determine
   D. $465,000

14. The work package owners and other team members have provided the cost estimates for their components of the project. You have evaluated the estimates provided and assessed the contingency requirements. What should you do next?

   A. Seek approval on the cost estimates
   B. Estimate the need for management reserve
   C. Review the cost estimates with the sponsor and key stakeholders
   D. Using the scheduling of the work packages and the activities, determine the project budget

15. On a particular component, the work package owner leveraged a triangular 3-point estimate, calculated at $128,333. If the optimistic estimate was $98,000 and the most likely estimate was $112,000, what was the pessimistic estimate?

   A. $112,778
   B. $175,000
   C. $223,998
   D. $112,389

Review Question Answers

1. **Answer: D**

   Resource cost estimates will include labor, materials, and equipment. Time shortages would not be a resource cost estimate.

2. **Answer: C**

   Parametric estimating uses a statistical relationship between variables to calculate a unit cost, which can then be applied to the number of units that will be consumed/used for the project. Individual cost estimates would be bottom-up estimating. Using the actual cost of a similar project would be analogous estimating.

3. **Answer: B**

   Analogous estimating uses the costs from a previous similar project as the basis for the estimate. It is considered top-down and is not done on individual work items. Analogous estimating is most commonly used early in the project life cycle.

4. **Answer: C**

   Cost estimates should include information on risk responses – including the cost to invoke risk responses and costs associated with contingency reserve.

5. **Answer: D**

   Because the organization has not done this type of project previously, that minimizes the opportunity to use an analogous estimate. There is not enough known, scalable data to do a parametric estimate. A phased estimate would require knowing the near-term work in detail. Thus, a ROM would be the most appropriate estimate.

6. **Answer: A**

   Using a unit cost of $190 per team member, the estimate would be accomplished through parametric estimating : $190 x 15 = $2,850. Analogous would be top-down and a budgetary estimate would be based on a periodic allocation.

7. **Answer: B**

   The total project budget includes both the cost baseline (which includes the cost estimates plus contingency) and the management reserve. The project manager is responsible for managing the cost baseline, but the sponsor is typically responsible for the management reserve.

8. **Answer: B**

   The best technique to determine the cost estimate would be a three-point estimate: $(O+4M+P)/6$

   ($7,000 + 4($18,000) + 30,000) / 6

   $109,000 / 6

   $18,166.67

9. **Answer: B**

   Because you are using costs from a past similar project, this would be considered analogous estimating.
   $37,500 + $12,000 = $49,500

10. **Answer: A**

    For the full launch, you can use a parametric estimate based on the pilot date: $500 / 1,000 records = $0.50 per record. For $500,000 records, the cost would be $500,000 x 0.50 = $250,000.

11. **Answer: A**

    Contingency would not be used for major scope changes as it reserved for known-unknowns (risks that are known, just uncertain if they will occur). Simply denying the change is not appropriate without taking the appropriate steps first. Before asking the client for the additional funding, it would be appropriate to escalate to the sponsor to confirm the existence of any management reserve, as that may be the most appropriate source of funding for the major change given that it was due to a change in market conditions and apparently outside of the control of the client.

12. **Answer: C**

The planned value (PV) at the end of any project is equal to the budget at completion (BAC). The PV is the cumulative planned value of the work to be completed by that point. At the end of the project, all work is planned to be complete, thus equaling the budget at completion.

13. **Answer: B**

Planned value (PV) is the cumulative planned value of the work. To determine the PV by the end of period six, sum all periodic estimates up through period six. This would equal $660,000.

14. **Answer: D**

Once the costs are estimated, the next step will be to apply those costs across the schedule to aggregate the costs into the periodic and overall budget, creating the cost baseline. As a project manager, you would typically not secure approval on the estimates nor review those estimates with the sponsor and key stakeholders until the overall project budget is estimated. The PM does not estimate the need for management reserve, as it is set by the sponsor and is for "unknown-unknowns" and as such, is not able to be estimated.

15. **Answer: B**

Using the triangular 3-point formula:

$(O + M + P) / 3$

$128,333 = (\$98,000 + \$112,000 + P) / 3$

$384,999 = \$98,000 + \$112,000 + P$

$384,999 = \$210,000 + P$

$174,999 = P$

Chapter 7 - Vocabulary Review

* Analogous estimating

* Bottom-up estimating

  Budgetary estimate

* Contingency reserve

* Cost management plan

* Cost of quality

  Definitive estimate

* Funding limit reconciliation

* Management reserve

* Parametric estimating

  Phased estimate

  Rough order of magnitude estimate

* Three-point estimating

  Vendor bid analysis

1.	An estimating technique that uses a statistical relationship between historical data and other variables to calculate an estimate, such as a unit cost
2.	The amount of funds or budget needed above the estimate to reduce the risk of overruns of project objectives to a level acceptable to the organization. For known-unknowns.
3.	Estimating technique that uses the values from a previous, similar project as the basis for estimating
4.	An evaluation of submitted seller bids to determine which vendor would be most appropriate for the budget restrictions of the project.
5.	A method of determining the costs incurred to ensure quality. Includes the cost of conformance and the cost of non-conformance.
6.	An analytical technique that uses three cost estimates to represent the optimistic, most likely, and pessimistic scenarios.
7.	The document that sets out the format and establishes the activities and criteria for planning, structuring, and controlling the project costs
8.	An evaluation of the projected costs of the project and when those costs will be incurred to ensure that the costs will fall within the funding limit.
9.	A method of estimating where cost estimates are placed on each component of work and the estimates are then aggregated for an overall estimate
10.	The amount of funds or budget set-aside to cover major unknown risks or changes. For unknown-unknowns.
11.	Used to appropriate funds on a periodic basis
12.	A high-level educated guess
13.	Used for longer term projects where the near-term work is estimated in detail and future term work has place-holders
14.	An extremely accurate estimate of costs

* These definitions are taken from the Glossary of *PMBOK® Guide - Sixth Edition*

Vocabulary Review Answers

1. Parametric estimating
2. Contingency reserve
3. Analogous estimating
4. Vendor bid analysis
5. Cost of quality
6. Three-point estimating
7. Cost management plan

8. Funding limit reconciliation
9. Bottom-up estimating
10. Management reserve
11. Budgetary estimate
12. Rough order of magnitude estimate
13. Phased estimate
14. Definitive estimate

Chapter 8

Project Quality Management

What's in This Chapter

- Project Quality Management
- Quality Approaches, Definitions, and Theorists
- Plan Quality Management
- Control Quality
- Manage Quality

Project Quality Management

In project management, managing quality involves both quality of the product and quality of the project. Depending on the industry and the type of product being developed, quality practices and measurements may be very different, as quality measures are specific to the types of deliverables being produced.

There are four key aspects related to modern quality management:

Customer satisfaction. Customer satisfaction comes from understanding, evaluating, defining, and managing customer expectations. Customer expectations are met when there is conformance to requirements, and the product meets their needs or fitness for use. In agile/adaptive environments, stakeholder engagement throughout the project ensures that these expectations are frequently managed.

Supplier partnership. In organizations and environments where vendors or suppliers are being used to augment the delivery of the project's product, service, or results, the supplier partnership must be mutually beneficial. Ideally, the relationships with vendors focus on long-term relationships, allowing both parties to create value for each other.

Management responsibility. While project success relies on the focus and participation of all team members, management has a responsibility to provide the resources needed to fulfill quality requirements. If team members are not provided with the tools, resources, and support to deliver a quality product, they cannot be expected to uphold the required quality standards.

Continuous improvement approach. The team and the leadership must be focused on continuous process improvement, constantly seeking out avenues for improvement in their products and processes. The plan-do-check-act (PDCA) cycle is an example of a continuous improvement model. There are a number of other practices that may be leveraged depending on the organization and the industry. These include Six Sigma, Lean Six Sigma, total quality management (TQM), etc.

Effective Quality Management

Effective project quality management can be viewed as progressive levels, with the lowest level being the customer finding the defects and the highest, most effective level being a corporate culture that is aware and committed to quality in processes and products.

In agile and adaptive environments, quality is built-in to the approach throughout frequent and consistent involvement with the stakeholders and end-users. Retrospectives are conducted during each iteration or sprint, where the effectiveness of the process is evaluated, and changes are made if there are any concerns or issues. In addition, product demos are delivered at the conclusion of each iteration or sprint in which that component of functionality is reviewed with the end-users to ensure compliance with requirements.

Quality Management Vocabulary

Vocabulary is very prevalent on the PMP® exam. This is especially true for the quality knowledge area. Questions will often be phrased in a comparative format – comparing two quality terms that are frequently used synonymously even though there are differences.

Accuracy vs Precision

Term	Definition
Accuracy	The measured value is very close to the true value
Precision	The values of repeated measurements are consistent. Precision does not imply accuracy.

PMBOK® Guide – Sixth Edition, Glossary

Example: Accuracy vs Precision

ACCURACY VS PRECISION

The wellness center will have a weight-management program, and there are electronic scales being added to each of the treatment rooms. Kim and her team are testing each scale to ensure they are operating properly. In all but one treatment room, the scales are providing accurate results – a 20-pound weight is registering as 20 pounds. However, in treatment room 7, the scale consistently returns a weight of 18 pounds when tested with various 20-pound weights. That scale is giving a precise result (consistent), but it is not accurate (should be 20 pounds).

Quality vs Grade

Term	Definition
Quality	The degree to which characteristics fulfill requirements. Can be considered subjective, based on the needs, perspectives, and requirements of the recipient.
Grade	A category assigned to products having the same functional use but different technical characteristics. Grade is measurable and therefore objective. High grade does not ensure high quality.

PMBOK® Guide – Sixth Edition, Glossary

Example: Quality vs Grade

QUALITY VS GRADE

Kim is purchasing the equipment for the exercise area of the wellness center, including the yoga mats. There are a number of types of mats, including basic sticky mats, natural rubber mats, and cotton and hemp mats. Because the mats will be used by many people and therefore need to stand up to repeated use, Kim chooses to go with the natural rubber mats. Even though the cotton and hemp mats are made of higher grade materials, they do not meet the quality requirements for the wellness center.

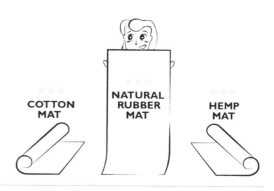

Attribute Sampling vs Variable Sampling

Term	Definition
Attribute sampling	The result conforms, or it does not (pass/fail, accept/reject)
Variable sampling	The result is rated on a scale the measures the degree of conformity

PMBOK® Guide – Sixth Edition, Glossary

Example: Attribute Sampling vs Variable Sampling

ATTRIBUTE SAMPLING VS VARIABLE SAMPLING

The comfort of patients is of utmost consideration in the wellness center. The HVAC team is installing the heating and air conditioning units and will test the system in each of the treatment rooms. Checking to see if the unit turns on is an example of attribute sampling: the unit either turns on or it does not. In addition to verifying that the units are operational, each treatment room is monitored for temperature maintenance. The ideal temperature range is from 70° to 73°. The temperature is measured for a 24-hour period to validate that the room is in the acceptable range. This is considered variable sampling.

Common Causes of Variance vs Special Causes of Variance

Term	Definition
Common causes of variance	Normal process variation, also called random causes
Special causes of variance	Unusual events, difficult to predict

PMBOK® Guide – Sixth Edition, Glossary

Example: Common Variance vs Special Variance

COMMON VARIANCE VS SPECIAL VARIANCE

Kim and her team are evaluating the pipeline for the wellness center employment candidates. Every candidate must be screened through an external vendor. The background check and employment verification take between five to seven business days. The two-day variance is considered common or random variance. However, Kim notices that for one candidate, the verification took over two weeks. Upon investigation, she learns it is because the candidate was from out of the country and it too a significantly longer period of time to complete the verification. This additional delay is a special variance.

EMPLOYMENT CANDIDATES

Tolerances vs Control Limits

Term	Definition
Tolerances	The result is acceptable if it falls within the range specified by the tolerance
Control limits	The process is in control if the result falls within the control limits

PMBOK® Guide – Sixth Edition, Glossary

Example: Tolerances vs Control Limits

TOLERANCES VS CONTROL LIMITS

Kim is evaluating the schedule progress for the project, including calculating the schedule performance index (SPI). As per the PMO, schedule variances of 20% or less are considered stable. As such, the control limits for SPI are 1.2 and 0.8. However, because the wellness center has a very aggressive timeline, Kim's tolerance is no more than 10% behind schedule. If the SPI represents more than a 10% delay, Kim will need to submit a special action report.

Quality Approaches

The *PMBOK® Guide* approach is also compatible with various approaches to quality management such as those recommended by Deming, Juran, Crosby, and Shewhart.

Quality Theorists

W. Edwards Deming
(1900 – 1993)

W. Edwards Deming. American statistician, professor, author, lecturer, and consultant. He believed that organizations could increase quality and reduce costs by practicing continuous process improvement and by thinking of manufacturing as a system, not as bits and pieces.

Joseph M. Juran
(1904 – 2008)

Joseph M. Juran. 20th-century management consultant and evangelist for quality and quality management. He applied the Pareto principle to quality issues (80% of the problems are caused by 20% of the causes) and developed "Juran's Trilogy": quality planning, quality control, and quality improvement.

Philip B. Crosby
(1926 – 2001)

Philip B. Crosby. American businessman and author. Crosby's response to the quality crisis was the principle of Doing It Right the First Time (DIRFT). He applied four major principles:

- The definition of quality is conformance to requirements
- The system of quality is prevention
- The performance standard is zero defects
- The measurement of quality is the price of non-conformance

Walter Shewhart
(1891 – 1967)

Walter Shewhart. American physicist, engineer, and statistician, sometimes known as the father of statistical quality control. Developed the plan-do-check-act (PDCA) cycle.

Belinda's Hint

Sometimes hints are great to help you remember concepts. Here are my silly hints for the quality theorists:

Deming – he doesn't really need a hint because he is the most well-known of the four theorists

Juran – 1) Juran and Pareto are both foreign/Italian sounding and 2) Juran's trilogy reminds me of Jurassic Park Trilogy

Crosby – for DIRFT, I think Bing Crosby singing White Christmas (snow DRIFT)

Shewhart – Shew rhymes with Do (plan-do-check-act)

There are three processes within the project quality management knowledge area that interface, overlap, and interact with each other on a continual basis throughout the project:

Plan Quality Management. During the **plan quality management** process, the quality standards that need to be achieved are determined and documented. In addition, the team will document how compliance with the quality requirements and standards will be measured and monitored. **Plan quality management** is in the project quality management knowledge area and the planning process group.

Control Quality. The **control quality** process may be referred to as "quality control (QC)." During **control quality**, the team will verify the correctness of the deliverables and changes that have been implemented. The goal is to ensure that the deliverables and the outputs of the project are complete, correct, and meet expectations. **Control quality** is in the project quality management knowledge area and the monitoring and controlling process group.

Manage Quality. In previous versions of the *PMBOK® Guide,* this process was known as "quality assurance (QA)," and it is possible that you may see references to QA under the umbrella of the **manage quality** process. During this process, the quality activities defined within the quality management plan will be executed. Quality assurance, a component of **manage quality**, is focused on quality and process improvement based on the results of the **control quality** process.

Belinda's Hint

The relationship between the three quality management processes illustrates the process group relationships. If you were to consider the process groups to be linear and/or phase-like, **manage quality** (in the executing process group) would precede **control quality** (in the monitoring and controlling process group).

However, the quality assurance aspect of the **manage quality** process cannot be performed until after **control quality** as there is a dependency on using the quality control measurements to improve the quality of the project. Think of a portion of quality management as "quality improvement." We wouldn't know what to improve if we did not have the measurements!

Plan Quality Management

quality knowledge area | planning process group

The **plan quality management** process is performed in parallel with the other project planning processes, and it identifies the quality requirements and standards for the project and the product. The quality management plan will document how the project will demonstrate compliance with those requirements and standards. While some of the most common techniques are described within this process, there are a wide variety of other techniques leveraged within specific industries.

Plan Quality Management: ITTOs

Inputs	Tools & Techniques	Outputs
1. Project charter	1. Expert judgment	1. Quality management plan
2. Project management plan	2. Data gathering techniques	2. Quality metrics
• Requirements management plan	• Benchmarking	3. Project management updates
• Risk management plan	• Brainstorming	• Risk management plan
• Stakeholder engagement plan	• Interviews	• Scope baseline
• Scope baseline	3. Data analysis	4. Project documents updates
3. Project documents	• Cost-benefit analysis	• Lessons learned register
• Assumption log	• Cost of quality	• Requirements traceability matrix
• Requirements documentation	4. Decision making	• Risk register
• Requirements traceability matrix	• Multicriteria decision analysis	• Stakeholder register
• Risk register	5. Data representation	
• Stakeholder register	• Flowcharts	
4. Enterprise Environmental Factors	• Logical data model	
5. Organizational Process Assets	• Matrix diagrams	
	• Mind mapping	
	6. Test and inspection planning	
	7. Meetings	

PMBOK® Guide - Sixth Edition. Page 277

Plan Quality Management: Inputs

Common Inputs:

- **Project charter** - The project charter provides a high-level description of the project and the products, as well as success criteria, approval requirements, and measurable project objectives that will be useful in planning the approach to quality for the product and the project.

- **Project management plan** - As this process is conducted and revisited throughout the project, components of the project management plan may be leveraged such as the requirements management plan, the risk management plan, the stakeholder engagement plan, and the scope baseline.

- **Project documents** - Project documents leveraged for this process include the requirements documentation and traceability matrix, the assumption log, the risk register, and the stakeholder register.

- **Enterprise environmental factors** - Internal and external considerations that should be considered while planning quality management include the organizational culture, marketplace conditions, cultural perceptions, rules, standards, and guidelines, company policies, and governmental regulations.

- **Organizational process assets** - Templates, policies and procedures, and historical information can be leveraged to plan the approach to quality management.

Plan Quality Management: Tools and Techniques

Test and Inspection Planning

An aspect of quality management planning is determining the approach for testing and inspecting the product, deliverable or service that will be developed by the project. This will ensure that the final products meet the customers' or stakeholders' requirements and expectations. Oftentimes, the tests that are utilized are industry- or product-specific.

Common Tools and Techniques:

Expert Judgment

Expertise will be provided from individuals with specialized knowledge of project quality management approaches, tools, and techniques.

Data Gathering Techniques

Benchmarking compares actual or planned project practices or the project's quality standards to those of comparable projects to identify best practices and ideas for improvement. These comparable projects may be within the organization or external.

Brainstorming is used to gather ideas freely from a group of participants who may have feedback or insight into the quality approach.

Interviews may be conducted one-on-one or with a group to determine the best approach to implementing the quality policy.

Data Analysis Techniques

Data analysis for planning quality management may include validating the costs associated with the quality activities and the quality results.

A *cost-benefit analysis* considers the cost-benefit tradeoffs of quality activities and documents the primary benefit of meeting quality requirements. These tradeoffs can include less rework, higher productivity, lower costs, and increased stakeholder satisfaction. Conducting this analysis may also include a business case to compare the cost of the quality to the expected benefit for the quality activities proposed.

The *cost of quality* encompasses evaluating all costs incurred by preventing non-conformance to quality requirements as well as appraising conformance to requirements.

Cost of Conformance	VS	Cost of Non-conformance
Prevention Costs (Build a quality product) <ul><li>Training</li><li>Process documentation</li><li>Quality activities</li></ul> **Appraisal Costs** (Assess the quality) <ul><li>Testing</li><li>Audits</li><li>Inspections</li></ul>		**Internal Failure Costs** (Failures found by the project) <ul><li>Inconsistent results</li><li>Rework</li><li>Scrap</li></ul> **External Failure Costs** (Failures found by the customer) <ul><li>Send-backs</li><li>Warranties</li><li>Damage to reputation</li></ul>
Money spent during the project to <u>avoid failures</u>		Money spent during and after the project <u>because of failures</u>

PMBOK® Guide Sixth Edition. Page 283

Decision-Making Techniques

A common decision-making technique leveraged to plan quality management is a *multi-criteria decision analysis* in which a prioritization matrix is leveraged to identify the key issues and suitable alternatives to be prioritized. The criteria can be prioritized and weighted and then alternatives are evaluated and scored against that criteria.

Data Representation Techniques

There are four data representation techniques that may be used for this process:

Flowcharts display the sequencing of steps, branching possibilities and decision points in a graphical representation of the process. These may also be called process maps, process flows, or process flow diagrams. When used as a value chain, a common approach is the SIPOC model: suppliers, inputs, process, outputs, and customers.

Example: SIPOC Model

A logical data model is a visual representation of an organization's data, described in business language versus specific technical jargon. These are used to identify where quality issues or data integrity issues can arise.

Matrix diagrams find relationships among different factors, causes, and objectives that exist between the rows and the columns. Depending on what is being compared, the diagram may have different shapes: L, T, Y, X, C, or roof-shaped.

Mind mapping is a method used to visually organize information, showing relationships and groupings of ideas.

Meetings

The project manager, project sponsor, selected stakeholders and team members, and PMO representatives may meet to discuss the approach to quality management for the project.

Plan Quality Management: Outputs

There are two key outputs from planning quality management:

Quality Management Plan

The quality management plan describes how the project management team will implement the organization's quality policy. It is a subsidiary plan to the project management plan, and will include quality control, quality assurance, and continuous process improvement plans for the project. It is important that the quality management plan is thoroughly reviewed and evaluated early in the project to ensure it represents the quality needs of the project accurately to ensure compliance with expectations. Information within the quality management plan may include, but is not limited to:

- Quality standards, objectives, and roles and responsibilities
- Project deliverables and processes that will undergo a quality review
- Quality control and quality management activities that are planned
- Quality tools that will be used
- Procedures for dealing with nonconformance, corrective actions, and continuous improvement

Quality Metrics

Quality metrics provide an operational definition that describes what something is and how the quality control process measures it. These quality metrics will be used in the **control quality** and **manage quality** processes. Examples of quality metrics include: defect density, failure rate, availability, reliability, and test coverage.

Common Outputs:

- **Project management plan updates** - The project management plan may be updated, including the risk management plan and the scope baseline.
- **Project document updates** - Project document updates include updating the lessons learned register, the requirements traceability matrix, the risk register, and possible the stakeholder register.

*The **plan quality management** process information is adapted from: PMBOK® Guide — Sixth Edition. Page 277-287*

Control Quality

quality knowledge area | monitoring and controlling process group

The **control quality** (also known as quality control or QC) process evaluates project results (outputs, deliverables) to ensure they comply with quality standards and also validates that approved change requests have been implemented as approved. This process ensures that the deliverables and the work meet the requirements that were specified for the stakeholders for final acceptance.

Control quality must be conducted prior to the **validate scope** process, where the product is delivered to the customer or end-user for acceptance. In addition, there is an iterative relationship between **control quality** and **manage quality**. To perform the quality assurance aspect of managing quality, the results of **control quality**, the quality control measurements, are needed.

Depending on the environment, complexity of the project, and the industry, the degree and level of effort put forth on QC will vary. In agile or adaptive project environments, all team members participate in controlling quality through frequent checks and inspection. In waterfall project environments, quality control is performed at set intervals, such as during or before each phase gate.

Belinda's Hint

The **control quality** (QC) process precedes both the **validate scope** process and the QA aspect of the **manage quality** process.

Before we can **validate scope** (secure customer acceptance), we need to ensure the deliverables have been verified through QC.

Before we can perform quality assurance, we need the QC measurements to perform the quality audit, where we will compare the QC measurements to the quality metrics. Note that there is no relationship or dependency between **validate scope** and **manage quality**.

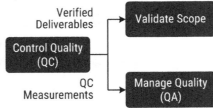

Control Quality: ITTOs

Inputs	Tools & Techniques	Outputs

1. Project management plan
  • Quality management plan
2. Project documents
  • Lessons learned register
  • Quality metrics
  • Test and evaluation documents
3. Approved change requests
4. Deliverables
5. Work performance data
6. Enterprise environmental factors
7. Organizational process assets
	1. Data gathering
	  • Checklists
	  • Check sheets
	  • Statistical sampling
	  • Questionnaires and surveys
	2. Data analysis
	  • Performance reviews
	  • Root cause analysis
	3. Inspection
	4. Testing/product evaluations
	5. Data representation
	  • Cause-and-effect diagrams
	  • Control charts
	  • Histogram
	  • Scatter diagrams
	6. Meetings
		1. Quality control measurements
		2. Verified deliverables
		3. Work performance information
		4. Change requests
		5. Project management plan updates
		  • Quality management plan
		6. Project documents updates
		  • Issue log
		  • Lessons learned register
		  • Risk register
		  • Test and evaluation documents

PMBOK® Guide – Sixth Edition. Page 298

Control Quality: Inputs

Approved Change Requests

Approved change requests, an output from the **perform integrated change control** process, are considered in **control quality**. Those approved change requests may include modifications such as defect repairs that will impact the project quality. When these approved change requests are implemented, they will be evaluated through **control quality** to verify that they were implemented as approved and validate that the change was effective.

Deliverables

The deliverables are any type of unique, verifiable output from the project. The deliverables are an output of the **direct and manage project work** process. During **control quality**, the deliverables are inspected for correctness and conformance to the acceptance criteria that was defined in the project scope statement.

Common Inputs:

- **Project management plan** - As this process is conducted and revisited throughout the project, components of the project management plan may be leveraged such as the quality management plan.
- **Project documents** - Project documents leveraged for this process include the lessons learned register, the quality metrics, and the test and evaluation documents.
- **Work performance data** - Work performance data is the raw measurements and information coming from the execution of the project activities. This data will be used to validate the project quality, such as performance against our performance measurement baselines. (Note: this is the first monitor and control process presented in this book. You will see for all but two of the monitor and control processes, work performance data is an input and work performance information is an output. This is the project knowledge sequence that was discussed earlier).

- **Enterprise environmental factors** - Internal and external considerations that may be considered include governmental regulations, application area rules and guidelines, and the project management information system and associated software that may be used.
- **Organizational process assets** - Templates, policies and procedures, and historical information can be leveraged to control the project and product quality.

Control Quality: Tools and Techniques

Inspection

Inspection is an examination of a work product to determine whether it conforms to standards and the validation of defect repairs. These inspections can occur as a single activity or at the final project level. Inspections are also known as reviews, peer reviews, audits, or walkthroughs.

Testing/Product Evaluations

Testing is conducted to identify errors, defects, bugs, or any other nonconformance in the product or service. The extent and depth of the testing that is conducted are dependent upon the situation, the industry, and the environment. These tests may be conducted throughout the project and at the end of the project on the final deliverables. Early and ongoing testing can identify nonconformance problems early, helping to reduce the cost of fixing future issues.

Common Tools and Techniques:

Data Gathering Techniques

Four common data gathering techniques leveraged to control quality include:

Checklists help in managing quality activities in a structured manner by providing a list of points to evaluate or steps to take.

Check sheets are used to organize details or results in a manner to facilitate effective collection of data. Once the information is collected, it can then be displayed in other quality charts for analysis. They are also known as tally sheets.

Statistical sampling chooses a representative population for inspection, representing a statistically significant population from which to draw conclusions. It can help reduce the cost of quality by limiting the number of outputs that are checked for correctness.

Questionnaires and surveys are leveraged to gather data from various parties and could include customer satisfaction inquiries. This may lead to the discovery of data regarding quality issues discovered by the customer, representing the cost of non-conformance.

Data Analysis Techniques

Data analysis for controlling the project and product quality includes two techniques:

A *performance review* measures and compares the quality metrics to the actual results from the project activities.

A *root cause analysis* is used to identify the source of defects that are being discovered throughout the quality control processes.

Data Representation Techniques

There are four data representation techniques that may be used during QC:

A *cause and effect diagram* is a brainstorming tool that starts with the quality problem and works backwards to identify all the root causes for that quality problem or risk. Also known as a fishbone or Ishikawa diagram.

A *control chart* shows stability or predictability in any type of output over time. Upper control limits (UCL) and lower control limits (LCL) are typically calculated as three σ from the mean. A process is out of control when one of the following is present:

- Results fall outside the control limits

Or results are within the control limits but:

- Seven results in a row fall above the mean
- Seven results in a row fall below the mean
- Seven results in a row trend up or trend down

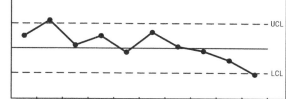

A *histogram* is a bar chart that shows the distribution of variables, where the height of the bar represents the frequency of the attribute or characteristic occurring. A Pareto chart is a special type of histogram that ranks causes of poor quality in order by frequency of occurring. A prioritization tool, the Pareto chart will typically have a cumulative percentage arc.

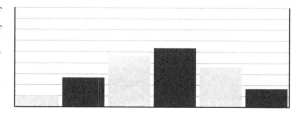

A *scatter diagram* shows the pattern of relationship between two variables. The graph uses a regression line to explain or to predict how the change in an independent variable will change a dependent variable. These are also known as correlation charts.

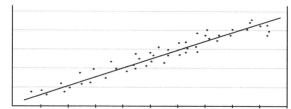

Meetings

Meetings for quality control may include approved change requests review meetings to verify that the changes were implemented as approved. In addition, retrospectives and lessons learned meetings occur within the project team to consider what has been accomplished, what went well, what needs improvements, and what should be added to the organization's process assets.

Control Quality: Outputs

Quality Control Measurements

The quality control measurements are the results of the quality control activities that are fed back to the **manage quality** process for use in re-evaluating and analyzing the quality standards and processes of the performing organization.

Verified Deliverables

Verified deliverables have been verified as correct and conforming to the documented and accepted requirements and will be an input to the **validate scope** process for customer acceptance.

Common Outputs:

- **Work performance information** - Work performance information is the analyzed results from comparing the work performance data to the performance measurement baselines. Information may include recommendations for corrective actions, lists of verified deliverables, the status of the quality metrics, causes for rejection, etc. The work performance information will be used to create the work performance reports.
- **Change requests** - Change requests may be generated based on the quality control activities. These changes will become an input to the **perform integrated change control** process.
- **Project management plan updates** - The project management plan may be updated, including the quality management plan.
- **Project document updates** - Project documents that are updated through control quality may include the issue log, the lessons learned register, the risk register, and the test and evaluation documents.

*The **control quality** process information is adapted from: PMBOK® Guide – Sixth Edition. Page 298-306*

Manage Quality

quality knowledge area | executing process group

The **manage quality** process involves executing the quality activities defined with the quality management plan, implementing the quality policies for the project. An important aspect of the **manage quality** process is quality assurance (QA). Quality assurance audits the quality requirements defined in the quality management plan and the measurements from **control quality** (QC) to ensure the appropriate standards and processes are in place. This continuous process improvement (CPI) is the ongoing improvement of all processes with a goal of reducing waste and eliminating activities that do not add value. In Juran's trilogy, QA is represented as 'Quality Improvement.'

The work of quality assurance falls under the cost of conformance: the costs associated with building quality into a product. Ideally, everyone on the project team, including the customer, is involved with managing the quality of the project. In adaptive or agile environments, quality management is performed by all team members. In traditional or waterfall environments, quality management may be the responsibility of specific team members or even a quality assurance team or department.

Manage Quality: ITTOs

Inputs	Tools & Techniques	Outputs

1. Project management plan
  • Quality management plan
2. Project documents
  • Lessons learned register
  • Quality control measurements
  • Quality metrics
  • Risk report
3. Organizational process assets
	1. Data gathering
	  • Checklists
	2. Data analysis
	  • Alternatives analysis
	  • Document analysis
	  • Process analysis
	  • Root cause analysis
	3. Decision making
	  • Multicriteria decision analysis
	4. Data representation
	  • Affinity diagrams
	  • Cause-and-effect diagrams
	  • Flowcharts
	  • Histograms
	  • Matrix diagrams
	  • Scatter diagrams
	5. Audits
	6. Design for X
	7. Problem-solving
	8. Quality improvement methods
		1. Quality reports
		2. Test and evaluation documents
		3. Change requests
		4. Project management plan updates
		  • Quality management plan
		  • Scope baseline
		  • Schedule baseline
		  • Cost baseline
		5. Project documents updates
		  • Issue log
		  • Lessons learned register
		  • Risk register

PMBOK® Guide Sixth Edition. Page 288

Manage Quality: Inputs

Common Inputs:

- **Project management plan** - As this process is conducted and revisited throughout the project, components of the project management plan may be leveraged such as the quality management plan.
- **Project documents** - Project documents leveraged for this process include the lessons learned register, the quality metrics, quality control measurements, and the risk report.
- **Organizational process assets** - Templates, policies and procedures, and historical information can be leveraged to control the project and product quality.

Manage Quality: Tools and Techniques

Audits

Quality audits are structured, independent reviews to determine whether project activities comply with organizational and project policies, processes, and procedures. Quality audit objectives may include identifying inefficient and ineffective policies, processes, and procedures that are in use, identifying best practices and sharing best practices used in similar projects, and offering assistance to improve implementation and increase team productivity. Quality audits may be scheduled or random and conducted in-house or with a third-party auditor. Results of these audits are used in the lessons learned repository for the organization.

Design for X (DfX)

Design for X is a technical guideline that may be applied during the product design to optimize a specific aspect, such as assembly, manufacturing, cost, usability, safety, quality, customer satisfaction, etc. Design for X is also known as design for excellence in that particular attribute. DfX methodologies may be applied in one or more phases of the product life-cycle, but most commonly from a project perspective, DfX is used during the development of a product.

Problem-Solving

The **manage quality** process is performed to execute the quality policy while also seeking out quality improvement activities. A structured problem-solving approach should be used to assess issues identified through quality control and quality assurance. Effective problem-solving involves identifying the problem and the root cause or causes, generating solutions and selecting the most appropriate solution, implementing the solution, and validating the solution effectiveness.

Quality Improvement Methods

There is a wide-expanse of quality improvement methods, as discussed earlier in this lesson. Quality improvement methods and approaches include the plan-do-check-act (PDCA) cycle, total quality management (TQM), and Six Sigma.

Common Tools and Techniques:

Data Gathering Techniques

A *checklist* is a structured tool, used to verify that a set of steps has been performed or to validate that a list of requirements has been met. It may be simple or complex depending on the environment or the use. Oftentimes, professional associations or service providers will offer these to organizations.

Data Analysis Techniques

Data analysis for managing the project and product quality includes four techniques:

An *alternatives analysis* evaluates options in order to select the most appropriate quality option or approach to use.

A *document analysis* is used to analyze various documents such as quality reports, test reports, performance reports and a variance analysis to evaluate where there may be indications of concern.

A *process analysis* is used to identify opportunities for process improvements by evaluating problems, constraints, and non-value-added activities that occur during a process.

A *root cause analysis* is an analytical technique to find the underlying reason for a problem or issue.

Decision-Making Techniques

A decision-making technique that may be used during the **manage quality** process is a *multi-criteria decision analysis*. Used to evaluate several criteria, this technique can be used to evaluate both project and product quality decisions.

Data Representation Techniques

There are six data representation techniques that may be used during quality management:

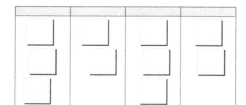

An *affinity diagram* organizes potential causes of defects into groups. In practice, these are often considered a "sticky note process".

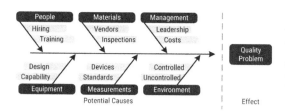

A *cause-and-effect diagram* is a brainstorming tool that starts with the quality problem and works backwards to identify all of the root causes for that quality problem or risk. Also known as a fishbone or Ishikawa diagram.

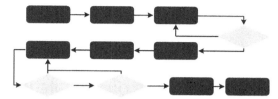

A *flowchart* graphically displays the steps, relationships, decision points, and/or checkpoints in a process.

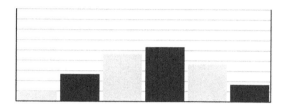

A *histogram* is a bar chart that shows the distribution of variables, where the height of the bar represents the frequency of the attribute or characteristic occurring.

A *matrix diagram* demonstrates the strength of relationships among factors, causes, and objectives that exist as displayed via rows and columns.

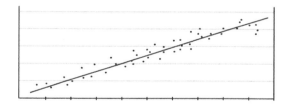

A *scatter diagram* shows the pattern of relationship between two variables. The graph uses a regression line to explain or to predict how the change in an independent variable will change a dependent variable. These are also known as correlation charts.

Manage Quality: Outputs

There are two key outputs from the **manage quality** process:

Quality Reports

Quality reports from quality management and quality assurance may document the quality management issues that were escalated by the team; recommendations for improvement of the product, process, or project; corrective actions recommended, and any additional findings. The form and format of the quality reports can vary and may be graphical, numerical, or qualitative.

Test and Evaluation Documents

Test and evaluation documents are created based on the industry needs and the organization's templates. These test and evaluation documents will be an input to the **control quality** process and are used to evaluate the achievement of the quality objectives.

Common Outputs:

- **Change requests** - Change requests may be generated based on the quality management activities. These changes will become an input to the **perform integrated change control** process.
- **Project management plan updates** -The project management plan may be updated, including the quality management plan and the scope, schedule, and cost baselines.
- **Project document updates** - Project documents that are updated through **control quality** may include the issue log, the lessons learned register, and the risk register.

*The **manage quality** process information is adapted from: PMBOK® Guide – Sixth Edition. Page 288-297*

Congratulations on Completing Section 2!

To evaluate your learning and retention of the Section 2 concepts. After you have completed the review questions and the vocabulary, complete Practice Exam 2 in Appendix B as a closed-book, 90-minute timed exam. Upon completion, record your score and your time-to-complete on your Performance Evaluation sheet on Page 9.

Chapter 8 - Review Questions

Time Limit: 18 Minutes

1. **The project has been underway for six months and the team has made considerable progress. As you move into the phase of deliverable development, your team has discovered a significant quality problem. What should you do next?**
   A. Escalate the situation to the sponsor for notification
   B. Develop an Ishikawa diagram to determine root causes of the quality issue
   C. Refer the issue to the quality team for resolution
   D. Continue with the project to see if the problem continues to appear

2. **One of the fundamental tenets of modern quality management is:**
   A. Quality is planned and inspected in
   B. Quality does not cost
   C. Quality is planned, designed, and built in – not inspected in
   D. Quality requires constant inspection

3. **Precision and accuracy can best be described as:**
   A. Precision means the values of repeated measurements are consistent while accuracy means the values are very close to the true value.
   B. Precision means the values are very close to the true value while accuracy means the values of repeated measurements are consistent.
   C. Precision and accuracy both mean that the values of repeated measurements are consistent.
   D. Precision is the degree to which characteristics fulfill requirements and accuracy is a category assigned to products having the same functional use but different technical characteristics.

4. **You have assumed the management of a large, multi-location project. You are evaluating the quality costs associated with the project. The cost of quality will include all of the following except:**
   A. Training of the project team
   B. Product returns
   C. Inconsistent results
   D. Facilities management

5. **Quality and grade are different in that grade:**
   A. May or may not be an indicator of how well the product fulfills the customer's requirements
   B. Is the measurement of how close the product is to the target value
   C. Is the degree to which the product meets the customer's requirements
   D. Is the category assigned to products that have the same technical characteristics but different functional uses

6. **Your organization has conducted an extensive benchmarking study. Which statement is least accurate regarding benchmarking:**
   A. Can determine what approaches to use
   B. Can determine what product life cycle to use
   C. Can determine what products or services to offer
   D. Can determine what standards to achieve

7. **Inspection:**
   A. Is not a cost-effective way to build quality into a product
   B. Is the best method to create quality products
   C. Is only effective if it is done at random intervals in a production process
   D. Is never an appropriate tactic during quality assurance

8. **A control chart has all of the following characteristics except:**
   A. It illustrates how a process behaves over time
   B. It is used to determine whether or not a process is stable or has predictable performance
   C. It illustrates how various factors might be linked to potential problems or effects
   D. It can be used to monitor any type of output variable

9. **Regarding effective quality management, which statement is least accurate?**
   A. Ideally, QA finds the defects versus QC fixing the process
   B. Ideally, quality is built into the product versus QC finding the defect and fixing it
   C. Ideally, QC finds the defect versus the customer finding the defect
   D. Ideally, a quality culture is implemented versus quality is built into the product

10. **Joseph Juran**
   A. Believed organizations could increase quality and reduce costs by practicing continuous improvement
   B. Developed the principle of DIRFT
   C. Categorized quality into three aspects: quality planning, quality control, and quality improvement
   D. Was considered the father of statistical quality control

11. **The following chart is an example of:**

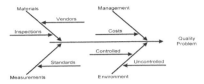

   A. A control chart
   B. A fishbone diagram
   C. A Pareto diagram
   D. A trend analysis

12. **Your development team is producing switch mechanisms for the new product. After each batch is produced it is checked through quality control to validate that the mechanisms function appropriately. This would be considered an example of:**
   A. Variable sampling
   B. Random sampling
   C. Attribute sampling
   D. Common sampling

13. **The PMO in your organization has implemented a policy that all active projects must undergo quality audits. Which statement is least accurate regarding quality audits?**
   A. Quality audits identify inefficient and ineffective policies, processes, and procedures that are in use
   B. Quality audits may confirm the implementation of approved change requests and their effectiveness
   C. Quality audits must be scheduled on a set basis to determine full effectiveness
   D. Quality audits determine whether project activities comply with organizational policies and procedures

14. **Your project team has completed the first deliverables for the project. What do you do next?**
   A. Evaluate the deliverables through quality assurance (QA)
   B. Review the deliverables with the customer in the validate scope process
   C. Provide a report to the sponsor
   D. Evaluate the deliverables through control quality (QC)

15. **Which statement is most accurate regarding project quality management?**
   A. The manage quality process is employed only when the project is producing a product
   B. Work performance information is used in the plan quality management process to evaluate if the quality standards are being met
   C. Continuous process improvement should not be confused with quality assurance
   D. Quality control measurements are used in the manage quality process to evaluate if the results are in alignment with metrics prescribed in the quality management plan

Review Question Answers

1. **Answer: B**

   Evaluating the quality problem proactively for root causes would be the most appropriate next step, versus waiting to see if the problem will recur again. As the PM, you should always evaluate the situation and potential solutions before escalation to the sponsor. You may or may not have a dedicated quality team.

2. **Answer: C**

   One of the primary philosophies of quality management is that quality is planned, designed, and built-in (proactively) versus quality being inspected in (reactive). It is not cost effective to "inspect quality in" to a product.

3. **Answer: A**

   Precision means the value of repeated measurements are consistent (getting the same result each time). Accuracy means the value is close to the true or desired value (like getting a bulls-eye in archery). Results can be precise without being accurate.

4. **Answer: D**

   The cost of quality includes the cost of conformance (money spent to avoid failures) and the cost of non-conformance (money spent because of failures). Training would be considered a cost of conformance. Product returns and inconsistent results would be considered the cost of non-conformance. Facilities management is not considered cost of quality.

5. **Answer: A**

   Just because something is "high" grade, it does not mean it will be high quality. For example, a high-grade egg that is broken is low quality. For answer D, the definition is transposed making it incorrect: grade is a category assigned to products that have the same functional use but different technical characteristics.

6. **Answer: B**

   Benchmarking will not determine what product life cycle to use as there is only one product life cycle, regardless of the product. It is the project life cycle that will vary based on industry, project type, etc.

7. **Answer: A**

   Because inspection is reactive, not proactive, it is not a cost-effective way to build quality into a product. Quality is built-in through accurate design and development.

8. **Answer: C**

   A control chart does not illustrate how various factors might be linked to potential problems or effects. A cause-and-effect diagram would be more appropriate to illustrate the linkage.

9. **Answer: A**

   Effective quality management progression, from least optimal to most optimal is: customer finds the defect, QC finds the defect and fixes it, QA fixes the process, quality is built into the product, and a quality culture is implemented. Ideally QA fixes the process versus QC finding the defect.

10. **Answer: C**

    Juran categorized quality into three aspects: quality planning, quality control, and quality improvement. It was Deming who believed organizations could increase quality and reduce costs by practicing continuous improvement. Crosby developed the principle of DIRFT. Shewhart was considered the father of statistical quality control.

11. **Answer: B**

    The diagram is a fishbone diagram. It is also known as a cause-and-effect or Ishikawa diagram.

12. **Answer: C**

    Because they are testing for one feature or function, and it is pass/fail, this would be considered attribute sampling.

13. **Answer: C**

    Quality audits may be scheduled or random. That do not have to be scheduled to be effective.

14. Answer: D

As the deliverables are being completed, they will be evaluated through the control quality (QC) process to ensure they are correct and conform to requirements. QA does not evaluate deliverables, but rather QC measurements. The deliverables must be reviewed through QC before given to the customer in the validate scope process for review and approval.

15. Answer: D

The QC measurements, an output from the control quality process, are used in manage quality (quality assurance) to evaluate if the results are in alignment with the QC measurements. This allows the team to look for process improvement opportunities. QA is appropriate on all projects. Work performance information is not considered, typically for planning quality management, because it is quality data that has already been analyzed. QA is considered the umbrella over continuous process improvement.

Chapter 8 - Vocabulary Review

* Accuracy	Design for X	* Quality control
* Affinity diagrams	* Flowchart	* Quality control measurements
* Alternative analysis	* Grade	* Quality management plan
* Attribute sampling	* Histogram	* Quality metrics
Audit	Inspection	* Quality report
* Benchmarking	* Interviews	* Questionnaires
Brainstorming	Juran	* Root cause analysis
* Cause-and-effect diagram	Logical data model	* Scatter diagram
Checklist	* Matrix diagram	Shewhart
* Checksheets	* Mind mapping	Special cause
Common cause	* Multicriteria decision analysis	* Statistical sampling
* Control chart	* Performance reviews	* Test and evaluation documents
* Control limits	* Precision	* Tolerance
* Cost of quality	* Quality	Variable sampling
Crosby	* Quality assurance	*Verified deliverables
Deming		

1. _____ The values of repeated measurements are consistent

2. _____ The measured value is very close to the true or desired value

3. _____ A formal or informal approach to elicit information from stakeholders by talking to them directly

4. _____ A category or rank used to distinguish items that have the same functional use but different technical characteristics

5. _____ Project documents that describe the activities used to determine if the product meets the quality objectives stated in the quality management plan

6. _____ Method of measuring quality that consists of noting the presence (or absence) of some characteristic (attribute) in each of the units under consideration

7. _____ A component of the project or program management plan that describes how an organization's quality policies will be implemented

8. _____ Cause of variance that is predictable and expected, also known a random variance

9. _____ The quantified description of acceptable variation for a quality requirement

10. _____ A testing process that measures results on a scale or range to determine conformity

11. _____ Completed project deliverables that have been check and confirmed for correctness through the control quality process

12. _____ A technique that allows large numbers of ideas to be classified into groups for review and analysis

13. _____ The degree to which a set of characteristics fulfills requirements

14. _____ Theorist that focused on the principle of DIRFT: doing it right the first time

15. _____ A graphic display of process data over time and against established control limits

16. _____ A visual representation of an organization's data, described in business language versus specific technical jargon, used to identify where quality issues or data integrity issues can arise

17. _____ Used to verify that a set of required steps has been performed

18. _____ A validation process, conducted in-house or with an external party, to ensure the project is employing the appropriate quality processes

19. _____ The process of monitoring and recording the results of executing the quality activities to assess performance and recommend necessary changes

20. _____ The process of auditing of the quality requirements and the results from quality control measurements to ensure appropriate quality standards and operational definitions are used

21. _____ The process of comparing cost, cycle time, productivity, or quality to another that is considered industry standard or best practice

22. _____ An operational definition that describes what something is and how the quality control process measures it

23. _____ Theorist that believed organizations can increase quality and reduce costs by practicing continuous process improvement and thinking of manufacturing as a system versus bits and pieces

24. _____ A method of determining the costs incurred to ensure quality

25. _____ Free, structured, or semi-structured process for capturing ideas

26. _____ A technique used to evaluate identified options in order to select the options or approaches to use to execute and perform the work of the project

27. _____ A technical guideline that may be applied during the product design to optimize a specific aspect, such as assembly, manufacturing, cost, usability, safety, quality, customer satisfaction, etc.

28. _____ The depiction in a diagram format of the inputs, process actions, and outputs of one or more processes within a system

29. _____ A correlation chart that uses a regression line to explain or to predict how the change in an independent variable will change a dependent variable

30. _____ Statistician that developed the plan-do-check-act (PDCA) cycle

31.	A decomposition technique that helps trace an undesirable effect back to its root cause
32.	A tally sheet that can be used as a checklist when gathering data
33.	A special form of bar chart used to describe the central tendency, dispersion, and shape of a statistical distribution
34.	Th area composed of three standard deviations on either side of the centerline or mean of a normal distribution of data plotted on a control chart, which reflects the expected variance in the data
35.	Checking or validating a product, deliverable or other output
36.	Theorist that applied the Pareto principle to quality issues
37.	A technique used to consolidate ideas crated through individual brainstorming sessions into a single map to reflect commonality and differences in understanding and to generate new ideas
38.	A project document that includes quality management issues, recommendations for corrective actions, and a summary of findings from quality control activities and may include recommendations for process, project, and product improvements
39.	Written sets of questions designed to quickly accumulate information from a large number of respondents
40.	A tool used to perform data analysis within the organizational structure created in the matrix, showing the strength of relationships between factors, causes, and objectives that exist between the rows and columns that form the matrix
41.	A cause of variance that is unusual and difficult to predict
42.	A technique that is used to measure, compare, and analyze actual performance of work in progress on the project against the baseline
43.	Choosing part of a population of interest for inspection
44.	A technique that utilizes a decision matrix to provide a systematic analytical approach for establishing criteria, such as risk levels, uncertainty, and valuation, to evaluate and rank many ideas
45.	The documented results of control quality activities
46.	An analytical technique used to determine the basic underlying reason that causes a variance or a defect or a risk

* These definitions are taken from the Glossary of *PMBOK® Guide - Sixth Edition*

Vocabulary Review Answers

1. Precision
2. Accuracy
3. Interviews
4. Grade
5. Test and evaluation documents
6. Attribute sampling
7. Quality management plan
8. Common cause
9. Tolerance
10. Variable sampling
11. Verified deliverables
12. Affinity diagrams
13. Quality
14. Crosby
15. Control chart
16. Logical data model
17. Checklists
18. Audit
19. Quality control
20. Quality assurance
21. Benchmarking
22. Quality metrics
23. Deming
24. Cost of quality
25. Brainstorming
26. Alternative analysis
27. Design for X
28. Flowchart
29. Scatter diagram
30. Shewhart
31. Cause-and-effect diagram
32. Checksheet
33. Histogram
34. Control limits
35. Inspection
36. Juran
37. Mind mapping
38. Quality reports
39. Questionnaires
40. Matrix diagram
41. Special cause
42. Performance reviews
43. Statistical sampling
44. Multicriteria decision analysis
45. Quality control measurements
46. Root cause analysis

Section 2 - Process/Output Match

Match each process to its key output(s). Please note that some processes may have more than one key output and some may have no key output.

Control Quality	Estimate Activity Durations	Plan Quality Management
Define Activities	Estimate Costs	Plan Schedule Management
Determine Budget	Manage Quality	Sequence Activities
Develop Schedule	Plan Cost Management	

Process	Key Output
1.	Activity attributes
2.	Cost estimates
3.	Duration estimates
4.	Activity list
5.	Basis of estimates
6.	Basis of estimates
7.	Cost baseline
8.	Cost management plan
9.	Milestone list
10.	Project calendars
11.	Project funding requirements
12.	Project schedule
13.	Project schedule network diagrams
14.	Quality control measurements
15.	Quality management plan
16.	Quality metrics
17.	Quality reports
18.	Schedule baseline

19.	Schedule data
20.	Schedule management plan
21.	Test and evaluation documents
22.	Verified deliverables

These definitions are taken from the Glossary of *PMBOK® Guide – Sixth Edition*

Process/Output Match Answers

1. Define Activities
2. Estimate Costs
3. Estimate Activity Durations
4. Define Activities
5. Estimate Costs
6. Estimate Activity Durations
7. Determine Budget
8. Plan Cost Management
9. Define Activities
10. Develop Schedule
11. Determine Budget
12. Develop Schedule
13. Sequence Activities
14. Control Quality
15. Plan Quality Management
16. Plan Quality Management
17. Manage Quality
18. Develop Schedule
19. Develop Schedule
20. Plan Schedule Management
21. Manage Quality
22. Control Quality

Chapter 9

Project Resource Management

What's in This Chapter

- Project Resource Management
- Estimate Activity Resources
- Acquire Resources
- Develop Team
- Manage Team
- Control Resources

Project Resource Management

Project resource management involves both the management of human resources (the project team) and physical resources (material, equipment, facilities, infrastructure, and supplies). The human resources are the project personnel and they may be assigned full-time or part-time to the team and will have varied skill sets. As we review the resource processes and the stakeholder processes, you will notice that there are some distinct overlaps. The

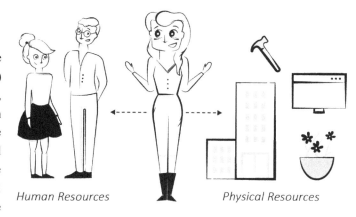

Human Resources　　　*Physical Resources*

processes that are included in this chapter are specific to the subset of the stakeholder population that is assigned as a team member to the project.

Physical resource management allocates and utilizes the physical resources required for the efficient and effective completion of the project. Failing to manage and control resources efficiently may lead to failing to secure critical equipment or infrastructure leading to delays, ordering low-quality materials, or keeping too much or too little inventory which may reduce the organization's profit.

The tactical management of the project team is just one facet of the responsibilities of the project manager. The overall leadership, motivation, and development of the project team are also key to ensuring an active and effective team structure. Ideally, your team members are involved in planning the project work and activities to be engaged in the project approach and the project goals, while having an opportunity to offer their insight and expertise.

As the team leader, there are many aspects that can influence the team members that the project manager should be aware of and manage. This can include the geographical locations of the team members, communication styles, organizational change management, politics – internal and external, and cultural issues.

How do you feel when you are giving a list of tasks to complete, told how to complete those tasks, and continually monitored while you complete those tasks? Probably not very good, right? As an adult, we certainly do not want to be micromanaged. This form of management is considered command-and-control and was the management approach of the past. Current trends in management are servant leadership or a collaborative approach to achieving the work objectives. This is just one aspect that has made agile approaches very productive and therefore very popular.

Many agile approaches leverage what is considered to be self-organizing teams. The team functions without centralized control and with a leader who provides support and trust, allowing the team to get their work done. Versus subject matter experts, generalized specialists adapt to a changing environment and utilize constructive feedback.

Because the reality of today's project environments is that resources are scarce, many organizations are applying resource management methods and approaches. These methods include lean management, just-in-time (JIT) manufacturing, Kaizen, total productive maintenance (TPM), and the theory of constraints (TOC).

Lean management. Lean management, an aspect of lean manufacturing, focuses on minimizing waste within a system without sacrificing productivity. This includes taking into consideration waste created through overburden and unevenness in workloads.

Just-in-time (JIT) manufacturing. Just-in-time manufacturing is a model in which products are produced to meet demand, versus in surplus or in advance of the need. The goal is to avoid waste associated with overproduction and excess inventory.

Kaizen. Kaizen refers to activities that improve functions and involve all employees from an organization, top-down. The plan-do-check-act (PDCA) cycle is an example of Kaizen.

Total productive maintenance (TPM). Total productive maintenance is a system to maintain and improve the integrity of production and quality systems. This includes equipment, human resources, processes, etc. that add value to an organization. The focus is keeping the resources in optimal working condition.

Theory of constraints (TOC). A management philosophy originated by Eliyahu Goldratt, TOC views any manageable system as being limited in achieving more of its goals by a small number of constraints. There is always at least one constraint that is identified, and work is structured around it. Follows the saying of "only as good as the weakest link." Goldratt's philosophy applied to project management is known as critical chain.

Project Resource Management Processes

There are six processes in the project resource management knowledge area involved in assigning, managing, and leading the project team and resources that will be discussed in this Chapter:

Plan Resource Management. This process in the planning process group defines how the project will estimate, acquire, manage, and control both physical and team resources.

Estimate Activity Resources. This process in the planning process group estimates the team resources and the types of material, equipment, and supplies that will be needed for the project.

Acquire Resources. This process in the executing process group obtains the team members and the physical resources required for the project.

Develop Team. This process in the executing process group focuses on improving the project team's competencies and interactions.

Manage Team. This process in the executing process group tracks team member performance, provides feedback, resolves issues and manages changes to optimize performance.

Control Resources. This process in the monitoring and controlling process group ensures that the physical resources assigned to the project are available as plan, monitoring the planned versus actual use of resources, and performing any needed corrective actions.

Plan Resource Management

resource knowledge area | planning process group

Defining how the physical resources and the project team members will be estimated, acquired, managed, and utilized is the primary objective of planning resource management. This process may be performed just once or at defined points within the project. Ultimately resource planning is conducted to ensure that there are enough resources for the project, specifically in situations or environments where resources are scarce. These resources may come from internal organizational sources or via the procurement processes.

Plan Resource Management: ITTOs

Inputs	Tools & Techniques	Outputs
1. Project charter	1. Expert judgment	1. Resource management plan
2. Project management plan	2. Data representation	2. Team charter
• Quality management plan	• Hierarchical charts	3. Project documents updates
• Scope baseline	• Responsibility assignment matrix	• Assumption log
3. Project documents	• Text-oriented formats	• Risk register
• Project schedule	3. Organizational theory	
• Requirements documentation	4. Meetings	
• Risk register		
• Stakeholder register		
4. Enterprise environmental factors		
5. Organizational process assets		

PMBOK® Guide – Sixth Edition. Page 312

Plan Resource Management: Inputs

Common Inputs:

- **Project charter** - The project charter will provide a high-level description of the project and the requirements, along with the key stakeholder list, summary milestones, and financial resources that will impact resource management and allocation.
- **Project management plan** - As this process is conducted and revisited throughout the project, components of the project management plan may be leveraged such as the quality management plan and the scope baseline.
- **Project documents** - Project documents leveraged for this process include the project schedule, the requirements documentation, and the risk and stakeholder registers.
- **Enterprise environmental factors** - Internal and external influences that may be considered include the organizational culture and structure, the geographic distribution of resources, existing resources and capabilities and the marketplace conditions.

- **Organizational process assets** - Templates, human resource policies and procedures, safety policies, and historical information can be leveraged to plan resource management.

Plan Resource Management: Tools and Techniques

Organizational Theory

In determining the training, staffing, and rewards and recognition needs, it can be helpful for a project manager to consider various organizational and motivational theories.

Organizational Theorists

Abraham Maslow

Abraham Maslow (1908-1970). Hierarchy of Needs – lower level needs must be met before higher level needs are considered. Typically depicted as a pyramid with five levels: physiological, safety, social, self-esteem, self-actualization.

Frederick Herzberg

Frederick Herzberg (1923-2000). Two-Factor Theory or Dual-Factor Theory – motivating factors give positive satisfaction arising from intrinsic conditions of the job itself: recognition, challenging work, achievement, personal growth. Hygiene factors, extrinsic to the job itself, do not give positive satisfaction although dissatisfaction results from their absence: salary, status, job security.

Victor Vroom

Victor Vroom (1932-). Expectancy Theory – Employees will be motivated when they believe that putting in more effort will yield better job performance. Better job performance will, in turn, yield organizational rewards.

Douglas McGregor

Douglas McGregor (1906-1964). X & Y Theories of Management – "X" theory states that people are generally lazy, do not want to work, and thus need to be micromanaged. "Y" theory states that people are self-led and motivated and accomplish things on their own with little intervention.

William Ouchi

William Ouchi (1943 -). Theory Z – Organizations can increase employee loyalty by providing a job for life with a strong focus on the well-being of the employees.

David McClelland

David McClelland (1917-1998). Need for Achievement Theory – Refers to an individual's desire for significant accomplishment, mastering of skills, control, or high standards. Employees with a low N-Ach may choose very easy tasks, in order to minimize risk of failure, or highly difficult tasks, such that a failure would not be embarrassing.

Belinda's Hint

Here are my silly (I warned you) hints for the organizational/HR theorists:

Maslow – Mas<u>low</u> / High – hierarchy of needs

Herzberg – <u>H</u>erzberg = <u>h</u>ygiene. Also, salary is a hygiene factor. I remember that because when my salary is good, I can buy my expensive shampoo (hygiene!)

Vroom – Expectancy – when we're expecting a baby, we need to vroom-vroom to the hospital

McGregor – X and Y theory – X them out, we don't want them on the team. Y is open arms, we welcome them to the team. McGregor also reminds me of Scotch and I picture men and women (X's and Y's) at a bar drinking Scotch.

Ouchi – Z theory, a job for their entire life, like Z is the last letter of the entire alphabet and it will hurt (ouchi) if they leave

McClelland – McClella<u>nd</u> = <u>n</u>ee<u>d</u> (for achievement)

Common Tools and Techniques:

Expert Judgment

Expert judgment may come from a variety of individuals with expertise regarding resource negotiation, talent management, market conditions, resource risks, managing sellers and suppliers, working within government and union regulations, or determining the effort level needed in order to meet the project objectives.

Meetings

The project team and appropriate parties may hold meetings to determine the best approach for acquiring, managing, and utilizing physical and human resources for the project.

Data Representation Techniques

There are three data representation techniques that may be used during resource planning:

Hierarchical charts may be used to visualize relationships between the resources needed and the organizational reporting structure. These may include:

- Work breakdown structure (WBS) – a graphical representation of the work to be completed on the project, decomposed to the work package level.
- Organizational breakdown structure (OBS) – a graphical representation of the organization's departments, units, or teams with the work activities or work packages listed under each department.
- Resource breakdown structure (RBS) – a graphical representation of the types and categories of resources that are required for the project, depicted in descending detailed descriptions.

A *responsibility assignment matrix* shows the allocation of resources to each work package, showing the connection between the work that needs to be done and the individuals that are responsible for completing that work. In a RACI (responsible | accountable | consult | inform) responsibility assignment matrix (RAM), individuals are classified and assigned based on their role with that work increment. Ultimately, there will only be one person accountable for any one task to avoid confusion. The RACI RAM ensures role clarity with both internal and external resources.

Task	Sue	Tom	Jason	Sandy	Bob
Develop Course Outline	A	R	I	C	I
Select Images		A	C		R
Develop Content	A	C	R	I	I
Design Participant Activities		A	R	I	
Develop Assessment	I	A	R		
Schedule Pilot	A	R	I		

R = Responsible   A = Accountable   C = Consult   I = Inform

Text-oriented formats may include written detailed descriptions of team member responsibilities, authority, competencies, and qualifications. These can include position descriptions and role-responsibility-authority forms.

Plan Resource Management: Outputs

Resource Management Plan

The resource management plan, a subsidiary plan, encompasses information on how physical and human resources will be defined, allocated, managed, and released. Components of the resource management include:

Resource identification and acquisition. How the human and physical resources will be identified and acquired.

Roles and responsibilities. Documenting roles and responsibilities provides clarity and prevents confusion as it relates to the project work.

- Role – the function of the individual
- Authority – the right to apply resources, make decisions, sign approvals, accept deliverables, and influence others to carry out the work of the project
- Responsibility – the assigned duties and work that a project team member is expected to perform
- Competency – the skill and capacity required to complete assigned activities within the project constraints

Project team resource management, training, development, and recognition. Guidance on how the resources will be defined, staffed, managed, and released; training strategies, how the team will be developed, and plans and approaches for rewards and recognition.

Resource control. What methods the team will use to ensure adequate physical resources are available; while optimizing those resources.

Project organization charts. A project organization chart should depict all the team members and their reporting relationships within the team and to the broader organization.

Team Charter

The team charter captures the team values, agreements, and operating guidelines. Developing a team charter with your team members allows them to engage in setting the appropriate boundaries while learning about each other. The charter may include information such as communication guidelines within the team, the approach to conflict management, meeting guidelines, and other team agreements.

Common Output:

- **Project document updates** - Project documents that are updated through resource planning may include the assumption log and the risk register.

*The **plan resource management** process information is adapted from: PMBOK® Guide – Sixth Edition. Page 312-320*

Estimate Activity Resources

resource knowledge area | planning process group

The **estimate activity resources** process determines the types and quantities of resources required for the project, including people, materials, and equipment. Performed periodically throughout the project, resource estimating is closely linked with estimating the project costs, as the biggest expense on a project is typically the resource cost.

Estimate Activity Resources: ITTOs

Inputs	Tools & Techniques	Outputs
1. Project management plan	1. Expert judgment	1. Resource requirements
• Resource management plan	2. Bottom-up estimating	2. Basis of estimates
• Scope baseline	3. Analogous estimating	3. Resource breakdown structure
2. Project documents	4. Parametric estimating	4. Project documents updates
• Activity attributes	5. Data analysis	• Activity attributes
• Activity list	• Alternatives analysis	• Assumption log
• Assumption log	6. Project management information system	• Lessons learned register
• Cost estimates	7. Meetings	
• Resource calendars		
• Risk register		
3. Enterprise environmental factors		
4. Organizational process assets		

PMBOK® Guide – Sixth Edition. Page 321

Estimate Activity Resources: Inputs

Common Inputs:

- **Project management plan** - As this process is conducted and revisited throughout the project, components of the project management plan may be leveraged such as the resource management plan and the scope baseline.
- **Project documents** - Project documents leveraged for this process include the activity attributes and activity list, the assumption log, the cost estimates, the resource calendars, and the risk register.
- **Enterprise environmental factors** - Internal and external influences to be considered may include resource location and availability, team skills, organizational culture, and marketplace conditions.
- **Organizational process assets** - Templates, policies and procedures, and historical information can be leveraged to estimate the project resources.

Estimate Activity Resources: Tools and Techniques

Bottom-Up Estimating

A bottom-up estimate may be used when the project resources cannot be estimated with a reasonable degree of confidence. The resources that are needed for each activity or work package are estimated and then totaled across the project or phase.

Analogous Estimating

A combination of historical information and expert judgment, analogous estimating uses a similar, past project as the basis for estimating the project resources. Analogous estimating, also known as top-down estimating, is frequently used when there is minimal information on the current project. It is quick and easy to perform but will not be as accurate as other techniques. For example, on last year's course re-write project, it involved five subject matter experts, two illustrators, and an editor, I can use that as a basis for this year's course re-write project that is similar in nature.

Parametric Estimating

Parametric estimating also leverages historical information and considers a statistical relationship between variables to determine the quantity of resources required. To leverage parametric estimating, it is important that the underlying data sources are accurate and scalable. For example, for my one-month project, if there are 300 pages to edit and it takes one person a month to edit, I will need three editors to get the work completed on time.

Common Tools and Techniques:

Expert Judgment

Expertise may be leveraged from individuals with knowledge and experience with resource estimating.

Data Analysis Techniques

Data analysis for estimating project resources includes an *alternatives analysis* which evaluates the various options and approaches for resourcing the project. This can include conducting a make-or-buy analysis.

Project Management Information System (PMIS)

The PMIS includes resource allocation tools and software, resource calendars, and other systems.

Meetings

Meetings for estimating the project resources can determine the resources required for the project activities. This can include evaluating the level of effort (LoE) needed, the skills required, and the quantity of materials that are needed.

Estimate Activity Resources: Outputs

There are three key outputs from the activity resource estimating process:

Resource Requirements

The activity resource requirements are a description of the types and quantities of resources required for each activity in a work package. The resource requirements should include any assumptions that were made while developing the estimates.

Basis of Estimates

For the resource estimates, the project manager should provide supporting detail and documentation regarding those estimates. This can include documenting how the estimates were developed, the resources that were leveraged, assumptions and constraints, the range and confidence levels of the estimates, and any associated risks that were documented in association with the estimates.

Resource Breakdown Structure (RBS)

Like any "breakdown structure," the RBS gives a graphical representation of the types of resources required by resource category and resource type. The RBS may be useful in organizing and communicating the schedule along with information on resource utilization.

Example: Resource Breakdown Structure

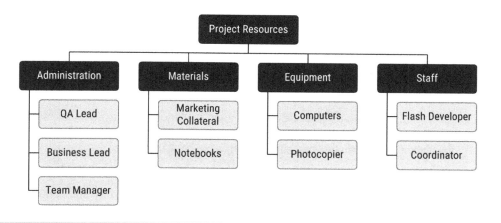

Belinda's Hint

Do not confuse the RBS with the project organization chart that we developed in the **plan resource management** process. The RBS shows the types of resources needed, not actual people / names.

Common Output:

- **Project document updates** - Project documents that are updated through activity resource estimating include the activity attributes, the assumption log, and the lessons learned register.

*The **estimate activity resources** process information is adapted from: PMBOK® Guide – Sixth Edition. Page 320-327*

Acquire Resources

resource knowledge area | executing process group

There are three resource processes within the executing process group:

- **Acquire resources** – securing the resources (human and physical) by validating availability and skill alignment.
- **Develop team** – enhancing the team dynamic and effectiveness through training and team-building (this is the fun stuff!)
- **Manage team** – ongoing management, handling of team issues, and conflict resolution (this is the not-so-fun stuff!)

Belinda's Hint

To remember the differences between these three resource management processes, we compared them to courtship.

When looking for a partner, the first thing we want to do is find people that meet our needs, while also confirming that they are "available" for a relationship.

A = Ask | A = Acquire

Once we confirm availability and we've entered a relationship, we are in our "dating" phase. During dating, we are falling in love and "training" each other as to our likes and dislikes. Think of dating as the "fun stuff" – team-building and training.

D = Date | D = Develop

And then we move on to marriage. Sometimes this may include the "un-fun stuff" when we are no longer necessarily on our best behavior. We must manage issues, resolve conflicts, and work through problems.

M = Marriage | M = Manage

The **acquire resources** process confirms both human and physical resource availability and acquires the necessary resources to complete the work of the project. This process is ongoing throughout the project, as new work begins, or changes are introduced. The resources that are acquired may be internal or external the project organization. If external resources are needed, they would be obtained through the procurement processes, whereas internal resources are typically assigned by functional or resource managers.

Typically, the project manager will not have the direct authority to acquire the necessary resources for the project. As such, securing the resources may involve negotiation with the functional managers, PMO, or other project managers. If the project manager is unable to get the appropriate resources for the project, the schedule, budget, customer satisfaction, and quality will all be affected, and the project manager needs to be prepared to communicate those impacts. The project manager may need to assign alternative resources to the project and should anticipate any knowledge or skill gaps and identify a training plan to bring up their competency level. Any training or development that is required may impact the schedule and the budget. Ultimately, the inability to get the resources could decrease the probability of success and result in project cancellation.

Acquire Resources: ITTOs

Inputs	Tools & Techniques	Outputs
1. Project management plan	1. Decision making	1. Physical resource assignments
• Resource management plan	• Multicriteria decision analysis	2. Project team assignments
• Procurement management plan	2. Interpersonal and team skills	3. Resource calendars
• Cost baseline	• Negotiation	4. Change requests
2. Project documents	3. Pre-assignment	5. Project management plan updates
• Project schedule	4. Virtual teams	• Resource management plan
• Resource calendars		• Cost baseline
• Resource requirements		6. Project documents updates
• Stakeholder register		• Lessons learned register
3. Enterprise Environmental Factors		• Project schedule
4. Organizational Process Assets		• Resource breakdown structure
		• Resource requirements
		• Risk register
		• Stakeholder register
		7. Enterprise environmental factors updates
		8. Organizational process assets updates

PMBOK® Guide – Sixth Edition. Page 328

Acquire Resources: Inputs

Common Inputs:

- **Project management plan** - As this process is conducted and revisited throughout the project, components of the project management plan may be leveraged such as the resource and procurement management plans and the cost baseline.

- **Project documents** - Project documents leveraged for this process include the project schedule, the resource calendars and requirements, and the stakeholder register.

- **Enterprise environmental factors** - Internal and external influences to be considered when acquiring resources may include the organizational structure, the geographic locations involved in the project, and pertinent information on the existing organizational resources.

- **Organizational process assets** - Templates, policies and procedures, and historical information may be leveraged to acquire the resources.

Acquire Resources: Tools and Techniques

Pre-assignment

If project team members are known in advance, they are pre-assigned to the project. Pre-assignment may occur when the project is awarded because of a competitive proposal or if the project is dependent upon the specialized knowledge or skill-set of an individual.

Virtual teams

Virtual teams are groups with a shared goal that are not located geographically in the same area and have minimal, if any, face-to-face time. The project manager will be responsible for ensuring that communications are consistent and available to provide as much electronic "face time" as possible, such as:

- Video conferences
- Web-based meetings
- Conference calls

Project management is not a one-size-fits-all approach, and when faced with managing a virtual project team versus a co-located project team, the management approach needs to be adapted. One of the biggest impacts will be on the project schedule, ensuring there is enough time allocated for effective communication within the team.

Pros	Cons
Add teams of people in different geographic locations	Increased possibilities for misunderstandings
Add special expertise to the team without regards to location	Feelings of isolation
Form teams of people with different shifts and hours	Difficulties sharing knowledge and experience
Include people with mobility limitations or disabilities	Increased cost of technology
Virtual work locations may reduce costs	Additional time needed for setting expectations, communications, etc.
Projects that may have been cancelled due to travel restrictions may be pursued	Increased chance of time zone and language barrier issues

Belinda's Hint

Just from a numbers perspective, it is very likely that you will get a high number of questions on the exam regarding your management of the project team (as three of the ten executing processes are in the resource management knowledge area and 31% of the exam questions come from the executing process group).

Because the use of virtual teams is more likely than not in a PM's career, anticipate questions on the management of a virtual team and how it differs from a co-located team. Specifically, recognizing the need for increased communication and team-building.

Common Tools and Techniques:

Decision-making techniques

A common decision-making technique for acquiring resources is a *multicriteria decision analysis*. The criteria for selecting both physical and human resources can be developed, and a weighting applied to assist in the selection decisions. Criteria may include resource availability, cost, ability, experience, knowledge, skills, attitude, and international factors.

Interpersonal and team skills

Negotiation is the act of engaging in dialogue to achieve a mutually agreeable solution. When acquiring resources, the project manager must work with functional and resource managers, PMO members, other project managers, and potential suppliers while trying to obtain the needed resources. The project manager needs to be prepared to present a solid case as to why the resources are needed and why it is beneficial for the other party to participate.

Acquire Resources: Outputs

There are three key outputs from resource acquisition:

Physical Resource Assignments

Physical resources include the materials, equipment, supplies, and other resources needed for the project work. The physical resource assignments are the written documentation of the physical resources that will be used for the project.

Project Team Assignments

The project team assignments are documented assignments of appropriate people that will be doing the project work. Team assignments may include a project team directory and project organization charts.

Resource Calendars

Resource calendars document the time periods that each project team member can work on the project, while also including any vacation time and commitments to other work activities or projects. These resource calendars may be at the project or activity level and may include consideration of other attributes needed.

Common Outputs:

- **Change requests** - Change requests may be generated based on the resource acquisition activities. These changes will become an input to the **perform integrated change control** process.
- **Project management plan updates** - The project management plan may be updated, including the resource management plan and the cost baseline.
- **Project document updates** - Project documents that may be updated through resource acquisition include the lessons learned register, the project schedule, the resource breakdown structure and resource requirements, and the risk and the stakeholder registers.
- **Enterprise environmental factors updates** - Environmental factors that may be updated through resource acquisition would include the resource availability and the amount of the organization's resources that have been used.
- **Organizational process assets updates** - Organizational assets that may be updated through resource acquisition include any processes and procedures related to resource acquisition, assignment, and allocation.

*The **acquire resources** process information is adapted from: PMBOK® Guide – Sixth Edition. Page 328-335*

Develop Team

resource knowledge area | executing process group

The **develop team** process improves the competencies of team members through training and enhances the interactions of team members through team-building. As a project manager, developing an effective project team is one of the primary responsibilities. Motivation of team members comes through providing challenges and opportunities, providing timely feedback, and recognizing and rewarding good performance. A component of developing the project team is to consider any cultural implications and a culturally diverse project team – capitalizing on those cultural differences and promoting working together, interdependently, with mutual trust.

Team-building is an ongoing process and is crucial to project success and may move teams through the stages of team development quicker. The Tuckman Ladder describes the stages of team development:

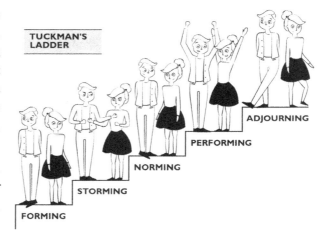

Stage	Description	Manager's Role
Forming	Begins when the team meets and learns about the project, their roles and responsibilities. At this point, the team members are functioning in isolation and are not as open with each other.	Allowing team members to get to know each other and trust one another
Storming	The environment can become destructive and counterproductive if the team members are not working collaboratively or are not open to differing ideas and perspectives. Team members are often defensive in this stage.	Resolving conflict and achieving consensus
Norming	Team members begin to work together and adjust work habits and behaviors to support the team, increasing their trust. Work may be occurring independently with each team member contributing "their piece."	Less structured and more informal focusing on maintaining momentum
Performing	For teams that reach the performing stage, they are a well-organized team and are interdependent, working through issues smoothly and effectively. This illustrates the concept of synergy where the sum is greater than the individual parts.	Less structured and more informal focusing on sustaining momentum
Adjourning	The team completes the work and moves on to other activities	

PMBOK® Guide – Sixth Edition. Page 338

Belinda's Hint

Know the stages of team development! You will have questions asking about the stages and/or describing a team and wanting you to identify what stage they are in. Some key words:

Forming = isolation

Storming = defensive, counterproductive

Norming = progressing independently

Performing = maximizing by working interdependently

Develop Team: ITTOs

Inputs	Tools & Techniques	Outputs
1. Project management plan	1. Colocation	1. Team performance assessments
• Resource management plan	2. Virtual teams	2. Change requests
2. Project documents	3. Communication technology	3. Project management plan updates
• Lessons learned register	4. Interpersonal and team skills	• Resource management plan
• Project schedule	• Conflict management	4. Project documents updates
• Project team assignments	• Influencing	• Lessons learned register
• Resource calendars	• Motivation	• Project schedule
• Team charter	• Negotiation	• Project team assignments
3. Enterprise environmental factors	• Team building	• Resource calendars
4. Organizational process assets	5. Recognition and rewards	• Team charter
	6. Training	5. Enterprise environmental factors updates
	7. Individual and team assessments	6. Organizational process assets updates
	8. Meetings	

PMBOK® Guide – Sixth Edition. Page 336

Develop Team: Inputs

Common Inputs:

- **Project management plan** - As this process is conducted and revisited throughout the project, components of the project management plan may be leveraged including the resource management plan.
- **Project documents** - Project documents leveraged for this process include the lessons learned register, the project schedule, the project team assignments, the resource calendars, and the team charter.
- **Enterprise environmental factors** - Internal and external influences to be considered when developing the team may include policies on human resource policies, team member skills and competencies and the geographic locations of the employees.
- **Organizational process assets** - Templates, policies and procedures, and historical information can be leveraged to develop the project team.

Develop Team: Tools and Techniques

Colocation

Team colocation is when the team physically sits in one location. This potentially increases communication and a shared sense of team identity. While it's a good strategy, the use of virtual teams is sometimes unavoidable. A co-located team is also known as a tight matrix. Colocation strategies can include having a dedicated team meeting room, known as a war room, or a centralized location to post schedules or team communications.

Virtual Teams

As discussed previously in this Chapter, there are benefits to using a virtual team, including the ability to find resources with the skills needed for the project, reduced costs, less travel, and potentially the ability to have resources located in close proximity to client locations. With virtual teams, however, there is also the consideration of increased communications needs.

Communication Technology

For both co-located and virtual teams benefit from leveraging various communication technology options for team development but is especially important for virtual teams. Communication technology could be a shared repository for information sharing (such as SharePoint, an intranet, Slack), video conference (such as Zoom or GoToMeeting), audio conferencing, and email/chat.

Recognition and Rewards

Team recognition and rewards should be documented in the human resource planning process, identifying options to recognize contributions and the performance of team members. This can increase commitment to the project and the organization

Some key considerations on recognition and rewards:

- It needs to be based on performance
- Consider leveraging and/or complimenting the organization's existing recognition program(s)
- Be aware of any cultural considerations
- Make it meaningful to the person
- Recognition does not necessarily have to cost money

Training

Training includes all activities that are designed to enhance the competencies of the project team members and may take the form of mentoring, classroom activities, online or virtual learning, checklists and job-aids, and self-study. Any training activities need to be considered in terms of impact on the budget and the schedule.

Individual and Team Assessments

Individual and team assessments provide the project manager and the team with insight into the strengths and weaknesses of the project team. Attitudinal surveys, structured interviews, ability tests, and focus groups may reveal helpful information regarding the project team, improving understanding, trust, commitment, and communications among team members. For example, personality profiles such as DISC or Myers-Briggs (MBTI) can provide insight into the communication and work styles of the project team members, allowing for better interactions and communication.

Common Tools and Techniques:

Interpersonal and Team Skills

Developing the project team involves leveraging a number of different of interpersonal and team skills. Five common techniques include:

Conflict management involves actively working with the team members to resolve differences in opinion in a constructive manner.

Influencing is a skill needed to gather relevant information, address issues, and reach agreements while maintaining mutual trust.

Motivation is providing reason for someone to act. The project manager needs to create a compelling vision for the project to encourage the action and the participation on the project.

Negotiation is used to reach consensus on the project needs and the project approach. By addressing situations through a mutual agreement ensures that there are collaboration and trust within the team.

Team building is conducting activities to enhance the relationships within the team, building a cooperative and collaborative environment. As mentioned previously, teams may progress through the stages of team development known as Tuckman's Ladder. The project manager should be aware of the stage of development the team members are in and work to move them through the stages. There are several activities that can be used with a project team, ranging from no-cost to more extensive activities. Any activities designed to allow the team members to get to know each other personally can prove beneficial. I recommend simple things like using photos on the project organization chart or asking team members about their weekend can create a more personal environment.

Meetings

As a team, there will be many meetings that may be leveraged, including team status and development meetings, kick-off meetings, team-building meetings and project orientation meetings.

Develop Team: Outputs

Team Performance Assessments

The team performance assessment is a formal or informal assessment of the project team's effectiveness, including indicators such as:

- Improvements in skills
- Improvements in competencies and sentiments
- Reduced staff turnover rate

While it is important that the team has a good working relationship and enjoys their job, it is also important that they are delivering on the technical requirements of the project. They may be measured in terms of technical success, according to the agreed-upon:

- Project objectives
- Performance on project schedule
- Performance on budget

This information may be used by the project management team to identify specific training, coaching, or mentoring opportunities that would be helpful in improving the team's performance.

Common Outputs:

- **Change requests** - Change requests may be generated based on developing the project team. These changes will become an input to the **perform integrated change control** process.
- **Project management plan updates** - The project management plan may be updated, including the resource management plan.
- **Project document updates** - Project documents that are updated because of developing the team may include the lessons learned register, the project schedule, the project team assignments, the resource calendars, and the team charter.
- **Enterprise environmental factors updates** - Environmental factors that may be updated include the employee development plan records and the skill assessments.

- **Organizational process updates** - Organizational assets that may be updated include the training requirements and the personnel assessments.

*The **develop team** process information is adapted from: PMBOK® Guide – Sixth Edition. Page 336-344*

Manage Team

resource knowledge area | executing process group

An ongoing process, managing the team tracks team member performance and provides feedback to the team members. The project manager and project management team will be resolving issues, managing changes to optimize project performance, and this may also involve disciplinary escalations to the functional manager or to the HR department. Specialized skills for the project manager that may be leveraged during team management include conflict management, communication, negotiation, and leadership. These skills are especially pertinent during challenging situations involving team member performance, conflict, or behavior.

Conflict Management

The reality of any work setting, or situation, is that there is bound to be differences of opinions that can lead to conflict. Conflict, when managed effectively can be productive and healthy. Conflict arises on almost every project, and when managed properly, the differences of opinion are healthy, and can lead to increased creativity and better decision-making. However, when the differences become a negative factor, project team members are initially responsible for resolving their own conflicts. If unable to resolve, the project manager may need to help facilitate resolution through a number of tactics.

Technique	Description	Utilization
Collaborating | Problem-Solving	Incorporates multiple viewpoints and insights from different perspectives, leading to consensus and commitment Is the best way to manage conflict from the *PMBOK® Guide* perspective	When the team is working well together, has a cooperative attitude and open dialogue
Compromising | Reconciling	Implies that one or both parties give up on some of their interests to come to an agreement May be seen as a "lose-lose"	When the individuals are not able to reach consensus
Forcing | Direct	When one person forces a solution on another	When the scenarios involve legal, safety, or ethical concerns
Smoothing | Accommodating	A temporary way to solve a problem, focusing on common ground between the individuals, neutralizing the emotion	When the individuals are in a state of heightened emotion that is preventing them from reaching agreement
Withdrawing | Avoiding	Implies removing yourself from the conflict	When the conflict does not impact the project objectives and is not a legal, safety or ethical issue

PMBOK® Guide – Sixth Edition. Page 349

Emotional Intelligence

Emotional intelligence is the ability to recognize and manage your own emotions while also identifying and managing the emotions of others. Early research into the competencies associated with emotional intelligence or EQ is attributed to psychological researchers Stanley Greenspan, followed by Peter Salovey and John Mayer. It was, however, Daniel Goleman's layman's approach to EQ that popularized the competency in the mainstream community when he published his book in 1995. The five elements of emotional intelligence are:

- Self-awareness – knowing how you feel and how your emotions and actions affect others
- Self-regulation – the ability to stay in-control of your emotions and actions
- Motivation – working consistently towards goals and having high standards for your work
- Empathy – the ability to put yourself in someone else's situation
- Social skills – having strong communication skills, the ability to manage conflict diplomatically, and the ability to manage change effectively

As a project manager, higher emotional intelligence has been correlated with increased project success. It certainly makes sense that as a project manager, you are responsible for leading people without authority, influencing the stakeholders and the organization, leading and implementing change, and dealing with various personalities, deadlines, limited budgets, and project risks.

Decision-Making

Effective decision-making involves the ability to negotiate and influence the organization and the project management team. When approaching decision-making situations focusing on the goals and following a decision-making process is beneficial. Emotional intelligence and an understanding of the organizational and environmental considerations, as well as risk factors surrounding the decision, are all important components of an effective approach.

Manage Team: ITTOs

Inputs	Tools & Techniques	Outputs
1. Project management plan	1. Interpersonal and team skills	1. Change requests
• Resource management plan	• Conflict management	2. Project management plan updates
2. Project documents	• Decision making	• Resource management plan
• Issue log	• Emotional intelligence	• Schedule baseline
• Lessons learned register	• Influencing	• Cost baseline
• Project team assignments	• Leadership	3. Project documents updates
• Team charter	2. Project management information system	• Issue log
3. Work performance reports		• Lessons learned register
4. Team performance assessments		• Project team assignments
5. Enterprise environmental factors		4. Enterprise environmental factors updates
6. Organizational process assets		

PMBOK® Guide   Sixth Edition. Page 345

Manage Team: Inputs

Work Performance Reports

Work performance reports, also considered status reports or situation reports (sit reps), are an output of the **monitor and control project work** process. As addressed previously, work performance data once analyzed through the monitoring and controlling processes becomes work performance information. The work performance information is used to create the work performance reports. Leveraging the work performance reports, the project manager can identify and address issues within the project team.

Team Performance Assessments

The team performance assessment may be a formal or informal assessment of the project team's performance. Based on these assessments, actions can be taken, or issues addressed as a component of managing the project team.

Common Inputs:

- **Project management plan** - As this process is conducted throughout the project, components of the project management plan may be leveraged such as the resource management plan.
- **Project documents** - Project documents leveraged for this process include the issue log, the lessons learned register, the project team assignments, and the team charter.
- **Enterprise environmental factors** - Internal and external influences that are considered while managing the project team may include the human resource management policies.
- **Organizational process assets** - Templates, policies and procedures, and historical information may be leveraged to manage the project team.

Manage Team: Tools and Techniques

Common Tools and Techniques:

Interpersonal and Team Skills

There are five interpersonal and team skills that may be leveraged when managing the project team:

Conflict management is the effective facilitation of a resolution when there is a difference of opinion, an issue, or concerns amongst the team members or other stakeholders. A number of techniques were discussed earlier in this process.

Decision-making is the ability to negotiate and influence the organization and the project management team towards a resolution.

Emotional intelligence is the ability to identify and manage your emotions and identify and manage the emotions of others.

Influencing is a skillset that enables the project manager to motivate individuals towards a certain path, action, or outcome by being persuasive, clearly articulating points and positions, having effective listening skills, possessing situational awareness, and gathering relevant information.

Leadership is the ability to lead the team and inspire them to do their jobs well.

Project Management Information System (PMIS)

The PMIS can include resource management or scheduling software that may be used for managing and coordinating project team members.

Manage Team: Outputs

Common Outputs:

- **Change requests** - Change requests may be generated based on managing the project team. These changes will become an input to the **perform integrated change control** process.
- **Project management plan updates** - The project management plan may be updated, including the resource management plan and the cost and schedule baselines.
- **Project document updates** - Project documents that are updated may include the issue log, the lessons learned register, and the project team assignments.
- **Enterprise environmental factors updates** - Environmental factors that may be updated include the personnel skill levels and the inputs to the performance appraisals.

*The **manage team** process information is adapted from: PMBOK® Guide – Sixth Edition. Page 345-351*

Control Resources

resource knowledge area | monitoring and controlling process group

Concerned with the physical resources of the project, the **control resources** process is conducted throughout the project to ensure that the resources assigned and allocated are available as planned. In addition, the utilization of those resources will be monitored against the plan to ensure that the assigned resources are available when needed and then released in a timely manner.

Controlling project resources involves monitoring resource expenditures and identifying and addressing resource shortages or surpluses in a timely manner; validating that the resources are being utilized and released in a timely manner; communicating with stakeholders regarding any resource concerns or issues; and managing any changes associated with the resources.

Control Resources: ITTOs

Inputs	Tools & Techniques	Outputs
1. Project management plan	1. Data analysis	1. Work performance information
• Resource management plan	• Alternatives analysis	2. Change requests
2. Project documents	• Cost-benefit analysis	3. Project management plan updates
• Issue log	• Performance reviews	• Resource management plan
• Lessons learned register	• Trend analysis	• Schedule baseline
• Physical resource assignments	2. Problem-solving	• Cost baseline
• Project schedule	3. Interpersonal and team skills	4. Project document updates
• Resource breakdown structure	• Negotiation	• Assumption log
• Resource requirements	• Influencing	• Issue log
• Risk register	4. Project management information system	• Lessons learned register
3. Work performance data		• Physical resource assignments
4. Agreements		• Resource breakdown structure
5. Organizational Process Assets		• Risk register

PMBOK® Guide – Sixth Edition. Page 352

Control Resources: Inputs

Agreements

All resources acquired externally will be associated with an agreement. The agreements will provide details as to how to handle various resource situations, including any changes or issues.

Common Inputs:

- **Project management plan** - As this process is conducted and revisited throughout the project, components of the project management plan may be leveraged such as the resource management plan.
- **Project documents** - Project documents leveraged for this process include the issue log, the lessons learned register, the physical resource assignments, the project schedule, the resource breakdown structure and resource requirements, and the risk register.
- **Work performance data** - Work performance data is the raw measurements and information coming from the execution of the project activities. This data will be used to validate the resource utilization.
- **Organizational process assets** - Templates, policies and procedures, and historical information can be leveraged to control the project resources.

Control Resources: Tools and Techniques

Problem-Solving

As problems arise related to resource control, internally or externally, the project manager will need to take steps to resolve the situation. The typical steps involved in problem-solving include: identifying the problem, defining the problem in smaller pieces, collecting information and data, analyzing to find the root cause of the problem, solving the problem with the best solution, and then validating to ensure that the problem has been fixed.

Common Tools and Techniques:

Data Analysis Techniques

Data analysis for controlling the project resources includes four techniques:

An *alternatives analysis* is used to consider the best resolution for correcting variances with resource utilization by evaluating multiple options.

A *cost-benefit analysis* helps to determine the best corrective action in terms of cost in case of project deviations.

Performance reviews measure, compare, and analyze planned resource utilization to actual utilization to identify issues and concerns.

A *trend analysis* evaluates data points over time to determine if the resource utilization is appropriate, improving, or deteriorating.

Interpersonal and Team Skills

There are two interpersonal and team skill techniques that may be used resource control:

Negotiation involves having active discussions, seeking a mutually agreeable resolution.

Influencing allows the project manager to engage and convince the organization and other parties toward a desired action related to resource allocation and management.

Project Management Information System (PMIS)

The PMIS includes resource management and scheduling systems that can be used to monitor resource utilization.

Control Resources: Outputs

Common Outputs:

- **Work performance information** - Work performance information, analyzed work performance data, will provide insight into the actual resource utilization as compared to the planned utilization.
- **Change requests** - Change requests may be generated based on the controlling of the resources. These changes will become an input to the **perform integrated change control** process.
- **Project management plan updates** - The project management plan may be updated, including updating the resource management plan and the schedule and cost baseline.
- **Project document updates** - Project documents that may be updated include the assumption and issue logs, the lessons learned register, the physical resource assignments, the resource breakdown structure, and the risk register.

*The **control resources** process information is adapted from: PMBOK® Guide   Sixth Edition. Page 352-358*

Chapter 9 - Review Questions

1. **The responsibility assignment matrix (RAM)**
   A. Is used for development of the project budget
   B. Is developed at the activity level and used to closely link project roles and responsibilities to project network activities
   C. Is used to show the connections between work that needs to be done and project team members. It can show responsibilities at various levels of detail.
   D. Is used to identify accountabilities in individual performance appraisals

2. **The five stages of team development are:**
   A. Forming, storming, norming, conforming, and adjourning
   B. Forming, storming, norming, performing, and adjourning
   C. Meeting, assignments, work progression, reporting, and disbanding
   D. Acquisition, assignment, status reporting, results, and re-assignment

3. **An OBS:**
   A. Is a graphical, hierarchical depiction of the client's organizational departments
   B. Depicts all of the obstructions anticipated by the performing organization
   C. Is arranged according to an organization's existing departments, units, or teams, with the project activities or work packages listed under each department.
   D. Is a mandatory component of the requirements documentation

4. **Which of the following is a true statement about team-building activities:**
   A. They should only be conducted when the project is nearing completion
   B. Only top performers should participate
   C. They must be facilitated by the project manager
   D. They can range from brief agenda items to extended off-site activities

5. **Allison has recently assumed the project management of the office relocation project, which has been underway for a number of months. As Allison becomes familiar with the existing team members on the project, she observes their interactions and notices that they seem to be working independently and not collaboratively. When Jimmy offered a suggestion to streamline the tear-down of the cubical walls, Esmeralda, the facilities manager, became very defensive and shut the idea down quickly. In what stage of team development is the office relocation project team?**
   A. Storming
   B. Norming
   C. Forming
   D. Performing

6. **Which of the following is not an objective of developing the project team?**
   A. Improve knowledge and skills of team members in order to increase their ability to complete project deliverables, while lowering costs, reducing schedules, and improving quality
   B. Develop a permanent team structure that can stay in place and perform well despite organizational changes
   C. Improve feelings of trust and agreement among team members in order to raise morale
   D. Create a dynamic and cohesive team culture to improve both individual and team productivity

7. **As project manager, you witness two of your team members having a heated discussion in the break room. When you approach them, you realize that they are discussing the results of last night's reality TV show. How can you best handle this situation?**
   A. Confront them, as disputes can interrupt project work
   B. Advise them to have personal discussions outside of work hours
   C. Smooth the conversation by pointing out that we all have different opinions
   D. Withdraw from the situation as it does not impact the project

8. **Why is observation and conversation a recommended technique for managing the project team?**
   A. By observing and talking with the team, the project manager may become aware of issues and concerns that are not evident through non-interactive communication
   B. It is mandatory for a project manager to have interactive communication with all team members
   C. Interaction with the team will improve their trust in the project manager
   D. The project manager will be able to more quickly identify quality control issues

9. **Tools and techniques to acquire the resources include all of the following except:**
   A. Pre-assignment
   B. Multicriteria decision analysis
   C. Staffing management plan
   D. Negotiation

10. **Questions that may arise when planning the acquisition of project team members generally include all of the following except:**
    A. Whether the human resources come from within the organization or from external, contracted sources
    B. The costs associated with each level of expertise needed for the project
    C. Senior executive compensation
    D. The extent of assistance that the organization's human resource department can provide to the project management team

11. **You have a female team member that has met all of the requirements for promotion to a team leadership position. However, she is from a country where women are forbidden from holding leadership roles. How do you best handle this?**
    A. Offer her the role
    B. Provide her with the financial compensation without the title
    C. Offer the role to the next person in line
    D. Provide her with the role but do not change her title

12. **The company you work for has experienced significant growth over the last few years. You have been a project manager for a number of years and have led multiple successful projects. All of your projects have leveraged co-located teams. Your manager has now assigned you a project that will leverage the use of a virtual team. What is the first thing you should do?**
    A. Refuse the project as you do not have experience managing a virtual team
    B. Identify the virtual team structure as a risk and document it on your risk register
    C. Modify your previous communication approach to ensure optimal and increased communication with the team members
    D. Leverage your plans from the previous successful projects as the basis for the current project

13. **The project has been underway for a short period of time and two of your team members are having difficulty working together. When you approach them regarding the situation, one team member starts crying and the other team member is escalating and is now shouting. What is the best way to handle this situation?**
    A. Allow the team members to work the issue out themselves with a problem-solving approach
    B. Using a compromising approach, ask each team member to come to a resolution they can both agree upon
    C. Using a forcing approach, directly resolve the conflict
    D. Using a smoothing approach, try to diffuse the emotion in the situation

14. **The new project you have been assigned has a very aggressive schedule and strict quality requirements as it is regulatory in nature. Upon evaluating the assigned team members, you realize that the team does not have the necessary skills to deliver upon their assignments. What is the best thing to do?**
    A. Advise the sponsor that the project needs to be cancelled
    B. Place the project on-hold until appropriate resources are identified
    C. Document the skill gap and identify a plan to increase their knowledge
    D. Document the unskilled team as a risk

15. **To ensure the best outcome for your project with the small team, you will be relocating the team members to a war room set-up so that they are co-located. This is also known as:**
    A. Risk avoidance
    B. A tight matrix
    C. Peer-to-peer work
    D. Agile project management

Review Question Answers

1. **Answer: C**

   The RAM shows the work that needs to be done and the team members that will be responsible for that work. It can be done at various levels: activity, work package, deliverable.

2. **Answer: B**

   The stages of team development (also known as Tuckman's ladder) are forming, storming, norming, performing, and adjourning.

3. **Answer: C**

   An organizational breakdown structure (OBS) is arranged according to an organization's existing departments, units, or teams, with the project activities or work packages listed under each department.

4. **Answer: D**

   Teambuilding activities can range from brief agenda items to more extensive activities. They should be conducted throughout the project, with all team members, and they need not be facilitated by the project manager to be effective.

5. **Answer: A**

   Upon reading the description of the project team, it at first appears to be that the project team is in norming. The key word in the question, is the word "defensive". Defensiveness tends to occur in teams that are storming.

6. **Answer: B**

   Projects are temporary endeavors; therefore, an objective would not be to develop a permanent team structure.

7. **Answer: D**

   While the question states that the discussion is "heated", there is no indication that their discussion is disrupting the work of the project or the work of the organization. As such, the most appropriate response would be to withdraw from the situation.

8. **Answer: A**

   Project managers that rely solely on emailed status reports may miss important details about their team members. It is important to interact with your team members to ensure that you are picking up on any issues that may not be conveyed within printed or emailed status reports.

9. **Answer: C**

   The staffing management plan is a component of the resources management plan and is not a tool/technique that is used to acquire the project team. Plans are either inputs or outputs, they are never tools/techniques. Pre-assignment, acquisition, negotiation, virtual teams, and multi-criteria decision analysis are the tools/techniques used to acquire the project team.

10. **Answer: C**

    Senior executive compensation is typically not a question that would arise when planning the acquisition of your project team members.

11. **Answer: A**

    Because she has met the criteria for promotion, you would still offer her the position. She has the right to refuse the position if she feels that it is inappropriate for her.

12. **Answer: C**

    The first thing to evaluate would be your communication approach. What was successful on co-located teams may need to be modified for virtual teams. You do not have to refuse the project, but it would be appropriate to let your manager know that it will be your first virtual project team. A virtual team, itself, will not necessary be a risk, but there could be risks that arise as a result of the virtual team. Leveraging your plans from other projects would not incorporate the change needed for a virtual team.

13. **Answer: D**

    Because the team members are in a state of heightened emotion, it is unlikely they will respond well to any type of collaborative approach. The first thing to do would be to try and diffuse the emotion of the situation.

14. **Answer: C**

The best thing to do is to document the skill gap and put together a plan to increase their knowledge, ensuring to determine the cost and schedule implications of doing so. At that point, the information can be used to evaluate the project for feasibility.

15. **Answer: B**

This is describing a tight matrix

Chapter 9 - Vocabulary Review

Adjourning	McGregor	* Resource management plan
* Alternatives analysis	Motivation	* Resource requirements
* Analogous estimating	* Multicriteria decision analysis	* Responsibility assignment matrix
* Bottom-up estimating	Negotiation	* Self-organizing team
* Colocation	Norming	Storming
Conflict management	* Organizational breakdown structure	Team building
* Cost-benefit analysis	Ouchi	* Team charter
* Emotional intelligence	* Parametric estimating	Team performance assessments
Forming	* Performance reviews	Theory of constraints
Herzberg	Performing	Tight matrix
Influencing	Physical resource assignments	Total productive maintenance
Just-in-time manufacturing	Pre-assignment	* Trend analysis
Kaizen	Project team assignments	Tuckman's ladder
Lean management	* Resource breakdown structure	* Virtual teams
Maslow	* Resource calendars	Vroom
McClelland		

1.	Actively engaging in discussion in an attempt to come to a mutually agreeable resolution
2.	An estimating technique in which an algorithm is used to calculate quantity, duration, or cost of an item based on historical data and project parameters
3.	The ability to identify, assess, and manage the personal emotions of oneself and other people, as well as the collective emotions of groups of people
4.	A grid that shows the project resources assigned to each work package
5.	Theorist that identified two theories of management: theory x and theory y
6.	The first stage of Tuckman's Ladder where team members are learning about their role on the project
7.	An evaluation of the team's progress, performance, and effectiveness
8.	The written description of the physical resources required for the project
9.	A technique for estimating the duration or cost of an activity or a project using historical data from a similar activity or project
10.	The third stage of Tuckman's Ladder when employees are settling in to the work environment and relationships, working independently

11.	A management philosophy originated by Eliyahu Goldratt, that views any manageable system as being limited in achieving more of its goals by a small number of constraints
12.	Theorist that developed the dual-factor theory regarding motivators and hygiene factors
13.	Activities intended to enhance the relationships and cohesiveness of the team members
14.	The fourth stage of Tuckman's Ladder where team members are working interdependently
15.	The ability to motivate a group of people to take an action or make a decision based on different types of power.
16.	The ability to resolve differences of opinions and disputes leveraging a number of different techniques
17.	An analytical technique that uses mathematical models to forecast future outcomes based on historical results
18.	A model in which products are produced to meet demand, versus in surplus or in advance of the need
19.	A financial analysis tool used to determine the benefits of an action versus the costs of that action
20.	Theorist who developed the expectancy theory
21.	Theorist who created the hierarchy of needs, depicted as a pyramid
22.	A team formation where the team functions with an absence of centralized control
23.	An individual's impetus to take action
24.	The last stage of Tuckman's ladder where team members leave the project
25.	A model that describes group relationship development as a series of stages
26.	A technique that is used to measure, compare, and analyze actual performance of work in progress on the project against the baseline
27.	Theorist that developed Theory Z, focusing on the well-being of the employee
28.	The types and quantities of resources required for each activity in aa work package
29.	When a team member has been allocated to the project prior to the project beginning
30.	An organizational placement strategy where the project team members are physically located close to one another in order to improve communication, working relationships, and productivity

31.	A document that records the team values, agreements, and operating guidelines, as well as establishing clear expectations regarding acceptable behavior by project team members
32.	The written descriptions of the team members assigned to the project
33.	Groups of people with a shared goal who fulfill their role with little or no time spent meeting face to face
34.	An approach that focuses on minimizing waste within a system without sacrificing productivity, including taking into consideration waste created through overburden and unevenness in workloads
35.	The second stage of Tuckman's Ladder where team members may be confrontational and defensive
36.	Theorist that developed the need for achievement theory
37.	System to maintain and improve integrity of production and quality systems, including equipment, human resources, processes, etc. that add value to an organization with the focus on keeping the resources in optimal working condition.
38.	A technique used to evaluate identified options in order to select the options or approaches to use to execute and perform the work of the project
39.	Another name for a collocated team
40.	A hierarchical representation of resources by category and type
41.	A technique that utilizes a decision matrix to provide a systematic analytical approach for establishing criteria, such as risk levels, uncertainty, and valuation, to evaluate and rank many ideas
42.	A component of the project management plan that describes how project resources are acquired, allocated, monitored, and controlled
43.	Calendars that identify the working days and shifts upon which each specific resource is available
44.	A hierarchical representation of the project organization, which illustrates the relationship between project activities and the organizational units that will perform those activities
45.	Activities that improve functions and involve all employees from an organization, top-down
46.	A method of estimating by aggregating the estimates of the lower-level components

* These definitions are taken from the Glossary of *PMBOK® Guide – Sixth Edition*

Vocabulary Review Answers

1. Negotiation
2. Parametric estimating
3. Emotional intelligence
4. Responsibility assignment matrix
5. McGregor
6. Forming
7. Team performance assessments
8. Physical resource assignments
9. Analogous estimating
10. Norming
11. Theory of constraints
12. Herzberg
13. Team building
14. Performing
15. Influencing
16. Conflict management
17. Trend analysis
18. Just-in-time manufacturing
19. Cost-benefit analysis
20. Vroom
21. Maslow
22. Self-organizing team
23. Motivation
24. Adjourning
25. Tuckman's Ladder
26. Performance reviews
27. Ouchi
28. Resource requirements
29. Pre-assignment
30. Colocation
31. Team charter
32. Project team assignments
33. Virtual teams
34. Lean management
35. Storming
36. McClelland
37. Total productive maintenance
38. Alternatives analysis
39. Tight matrix
40. Resource breakdown structure
41. Multicriteria decision analysis
42. Resource management plan
43. Resource calendars
44. Organizational breakdown structure
45. Kaizen
46. Bottom-up estimating

Chapter 10

Project Risk Management

What's in This Chapter

- Project Risk Management
- Plan Risk Management
- Identify Risks
- Perform Qualitative Risk Analysis
- Perform Quantitative Risk Analysis
- Plan Risk Responses
- Implement Risk Responses
- Monitor Risks

Project Risk Management

Project risk management is directly related to project success. All projects have an inherent amount of risk, and that amount of risk can vary greatly depending on the environment, complexity, and approach that is being used to pursue the project objectives. Project risk needs to be managed in relation to the project constraints and assumptions, while also taking into consideration stakeholder attitudes and expectations. Ongoing risk management is a balance between organizational risk and reward.

Risk, or uncertainty, exists at the individual risk level as well as the overall project risk level. The overall risk of the project is a combination of the individual project risks and other sources of uncertainty. Project risk management needs to address both individual and overall project risk.

A project risk is an uncertain event that has an impact on the project. That impact may be positive or negative. The goal of project risk management to decrease the probability and/or impact of negative risks while increasing the probability and/or impact of positive risk. Project risk management is ongoing throughout the project as new risks will emerge continuously. Managing the risk effectively means that the project manager and the project team must understand the acceptable level of risk exposure for the organization and the stakeholders by clearly identifying risk thresholds.

Key Concepts and Definitions

Risk management must be fully integrated with project management and must be addressed at the project, program, and portfolio level. A coordinated and consistent approach to risk management organizationally is ideal and effective. Building risk efficiency into the structure of programs and portfolios will provide the greatest overall value.

Agile projects. For adaptive or agile environments, risk is managed through frequent reviews of the incremental work products. Cross-functional teams also accelerate knowledge sharing and ensure that the risk is understood and managed. Risk is also considered as each iteration is planned. Because the requirements in an agile project are kept as a fluid document, those requirements may be adjusted at any time to respond to risk. For significant risks, the agile team may use *risk-based spikes* to allocate time and money to addressing the risk.

Event versus non-event risk. Risks may be event risks or non-event risks. Historically, project risk management focused on event risk, meaning uncertain future events that may or may not occur (such as losing a key resource to another company). However, there is momentum around the recognition of non-event risk.

Non-event risk may be variability risk or ambiguity risk. Variability risk refers to uncertainty related to key characteristics of a planned activity or decision (such as an increase in errors discovered during QC). A method of addressing variability risk is by using a Monte Carlo analysis. This technique will be discussed in further detail in the **perform quantitative risk analysis** process. Ambiguity risk refers to uncertainty about what may happen in the future (such as system complexity or regulatory changes). Ambiguity risk can be managed by defining areas where there are knowledge deficits or gaps and by seeking out expert feedback or information. Ambiguity risk may also be addressed through incremental development, prototypes, and simulation.

Emergent risk. Emergent risks are considered "unknowable-unknowns." These risks can only be recognized once they have occurred. To deal with emergent risk effectively, the project will need to have contingency reserve specifically allocated for emergent risks, flexible processes for dealing with the emergent risks, an empowered project team, reviews of early warning signs, and clear input from stakeholders as to where the scope or strategy may be adjusted in response to these risks.

Black swan risks. Black swan risks are those thought to be impossible. If the probability scale is 0 – 1, a black swan risk would have a probability score of 0. The name black swan comes from early European settlements when the only swans that had ever been seen were white. They believed, 100%, that swans could only be white. However, when traveling to Australia, a European explorer discovered black swans, shattering the previous belief.

As in the quality knowledge area, there is a heavy emphasis on risk vocabulary on the PMP exam. While we typically focus on negative risks (threats) in practice, PMI expects the project manager to consider positive risks (opportunities), as well. Challenge yourself to consider risk as possibly positive, not just negative risk. Some of the terms may be used differently in your organization, so it is critical to align the terminology as applied within the *PMBOK*® *Guide*.

Term	Description	Example
Risk Appetite	Degree of uncertainty an organization is willing to take on in anticipation of a reward	A speculative firm will be willing to invest in exchange for a large potential payout
Risk Tolerance	Degree of risk the stakeholders will withstand – this can vary and change throughout the project	The vice president that is contributing budget to the project will have minimal tolerance towards cost risk
Risk Threshold	The level of uncertainty or impact at which a stakeholder may have a specific interest	A risk that represents greater than a $50,000 impact may result in project cancellation
Project Risk	An uncertain event that if it occurs will have an impact on the project. The impact may be positive or negative.	There is a risk of a tropical storm causing a disruption to operations in the southeast states
Cause	A given or potential requirement, assumption, constraint, or condition that creates the possibility of negative or positive outcomes	The project requires expertise that is not currently handled in-house and therefore, must be out-sourced
Effect	Impact on one or more of the project objectives	Utilizing an outside vendor will potentially increase costs
Threat	A negative project risk	There is a risk the project will not deliver within the required timeline
Opportunity	A positive project risk	There is a risk the project will deliver early allowing us to be first to market
Issue	A realized negative risk	The vendor increased costs exceeding the allocated budget
Benefit	A realized positive risk	The product was first to market and gained market share

PMBOK® Guide – Sixth Edition, Glossary

There are seven processes within the project risk management knowledge area that will be discussed in this Chapter:

Plan Risk Management. This process in the planning process group defines the project's approach to project risk management.

Identify Risks. This process in the planning process group seeks to identify all knowable project risks and sources of overall project risk.

Perform Qualitative Risk Analysis. This process in the planning process group analyzes the project risks in terms of probability and impact in order to prioritize the risks for further action.

Perform Quantitative Risk Analysis. This process in the planning process group analyzes the risks in terms of cost and schedule impact in order to further prioritize the risks for action or escalation.

Plan Risk Responses. This process in the planning process group identifies the most appropriate responses based on the risk rating.

Implement Risk Responses. This process in the executing process group implements the agreed-upon risk responses.

Monitor Risks. This process in the monitoring and controlling process group monitors the implementation of the agreed-upon risk response plans, tracking identified risk, identifying and analyzing new risks, and evaluating risk process effectiveness throughout the project.

Plan Risk Management

risk knowledge area | planning process group

Thorough risk planning is the essential first step in ensuring that effective strategies are in place for managing risk throughout the life of the project. Having a plan in place ensures that the approach to risk management is proportionate to the impact and importance of risk to the project and to the stakeholders. Risk management planning should begin very early in the project to determine if the project is even feasible based on the identified uncertainty. Throughout the project, however, the risk management plan will be revisited periodically to ensure that it is still timely, effective, and appropriate.

Of the subsidiary plans developed, the risk management plan is one of the more critical plans. Without a documented approach to risk management, the other risk processes will be difficult, if not impossible to conduct. Personally, regardless of the project size, type, or complexity, I always want a risk management plan in place so that my team members and my stakeholders understand how we will be responding to uncertainty. There has never been a project with no risk. Plan for it!

Plan Risk Management: ITTOs

Inputs	Tools & Techniques	Outputs
1. Project charter	1. Expert judgment	1. Risk management plan
2. Project management plan	2. Data analysis	
• All components	• Stakeholder analysis	
3. Project documents	3. Meetings	
• Stakeholder register		
4. Enterprise environmental factors		
5. Organizational process assets		

PMBOK® Guide – Sixth Edition. Page 401

Plan Risk Management: Inputs

Common Inputs:

- **Project charter** - The project provides the team with information related to the high-level project description, requirements, and risks.
- **Project management plan** - The project management plan and the subsidiary plans will influence the development of the risk management plan.
- **Project documents** - Project documents leveraged for this process include the stakeholder register. Key stakeholders may play a role in developing or consulting on the approach to project risk management for the project.
- **Enterprise environmental factors** - The overall risk context and risk thresholds set by the organization or the key stakeholders will influence the development of the risk management plan.

- **Organizational process assets** - Templates, policies and procedures, and historical information can be leveraged to plan the approach to risk management and the risk management activities. Ideally, risk management for your project is consistent with the organizational approach.

Plan Risk Management: Tools and Techniques

Common Tools and Techniques:

Expert Judgment

Expertise may be leveraged from individuals with knowledge and experience with project risk management, types of risks that may be encountered, and the best approach to dealing with those risks.

Data Analysis Technique

Data analysis for planning risk management may include conducting a *stakeholder analysis* in order to determine the stakeholders' risk tolerances.

Meetings

These meetings will be attended by key stakeholders, the sponsor, the project manager, and perhaps individuals with organizational risk responsibilities. This will not be a meeting with the entire project team, but rather those with an interest in how risk will be managed on the project.

Plan Risk Management: Outputs

There is one key output from the **plan risk management** process:

Risk Management Plan

Of the subsidiary plans in the *PMBOK® Guide,* this is the most detailed plan and you may receive questions over the components of the risk management plan. The risk management plan includes:

Risk methodology and strategy. The risk methodology documents the approach and tools that will be used to manage risks on the project. The risk strategy is the general approach to project risk management that will be employed on the project.

Roles and responsibilities. It is critical that the project manager understands that they cannot possibly manage risk for the project on their own. To ensure that people understand their specific roles and responsibilities related to risk, it should be called out within the risk management plan, including who will be in a lead role, support role, and other team members responsible for managing risk. This prevents confusion or disruption later in the project. Note: anticipate a question on this! You, and even you and your team, are not sufficient for identifying risk; you must involve other parties and experts.

Budgeting. At the start of the project, the project manager along with the key stakeholders and sponsor should determine the amount of funding that will be allocated to project risk management. This can include funding for risk responses, contingency, management reserve, and allocations to cover responses to emergent risks.

Timing. To manage expectations, the timing of risk activities will be documented in the project management plan. This includes identifying when and how risks management activities will be performed during the project, including how contingency reserve will be managed.

Risk categories. Risk categorization is an identification of the defined and standard risk categories for the project. Risk categorization is a best practice as it allows for more effective and efficient risk responses. In addition, it may help the team identify certain areas or aspects of the project that have increased risk exposure. Categorization may be:

- Source-based – all the sources of risk on the project, such as people, technology, environment
- Effect-based – the areas affected by risk, such as budget, schedule, quality

A component of risk categorization is developing a risk breakdown structure (RBS). As another best practice, a risk breakdown structure (RBS), a hierarchical depiction of the risks by category and subcategory, may be used to identify the various areas and causes of potential risks. The RBS may be depicted graphically or in a text format, such as in a spreadsheet.

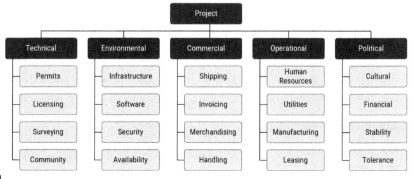

The top layer of the RBS is often a prompt list. In this graphic, it is a TECOP prompt list. Prompt lists will be discussed in more detail later.

Definition of risk probability and impact. To assess and prioritize the project risks, the risk management plan should include the definitions of risk probability and risk impact. These scales will be applied in qualitative risk analysis. Those standard definitions of risk probability and impact should be defined and agreed-upon by the key team members.

Risk probability is the likelihood a risk event will occur and it is commonly defined on a scale of zero to one, where one represents a 100% chance that the risk event will occur (as risks are always "uncertain", a risk would never have a probability score of "1," in this example).

Risk impact is usually communicated on a scale determined by the organization, and it may be a high-medium-low scale or a numerical scale, such as one to five. To gain more effective prioritization, a numerical scale is preferred in order to calculate a true risk score. A risk score is determined by multiplying the impact by the probability. For example, a risk that has an impact of 5 and a probability of 0.3 (30%), would have a risk score of 1.5.

Ideally, the definitions and scales of risk probability and impact will align with the organizational definitions. This allows for project risk comparisons that are apple-to-apple, which improves the analysis, allocation of resources, and team and stakeholder understanding. If one project has a one-to-five scale for impact and another project uses high-medium-low and another project uses a one-to-100 scale, you can see how there would be confusion project-to-project.

Definitions should be provided that correlate with the probability and impact scales in order for the risk scoring to be understood and applied consistently. For example, a risk impact of five may correspond to "> six-month delay" whereas a risk impact of two may correspond to "one to four-week delay." Adding the criteria helps to minimize the bias in the assessment process.

Probability and impact matrix. The probability and impact matrix provides a visual representation of the risk probability and impact ratings. As mentioned previously, probability is commonly ranked on a zero to one scale (for example, .3 would represent a 30% probability of occurring) whereas the scale used for impact is defined organizationally (for example, a 1-10 scale or 1-5 scale). The risk rating rules, or the "zones" of the matrix, are organizationally defined, but also may be modified to be project-specific and noted within the risk management plan. Threats and opportunities may be plotted on a shared matrix as demonstrated below:

	Threats						**Opportunities**				
.80	.80	1.60	2.40	3.20	4.00	4.00	3.20	2.40	1.60	.80	**.80**
.60	.60	1.20	1.80	2.40	3.00	3.00	2.40	1.80	1.20	.60	**.60**
.40	.40	.80	1.20	1.60	2.00	2.00	1.60	1.20	.80	.40	**.40**
.20	.20	.40	.60	.80	1.00	1.00	.80	.60	.40	.20	**.20**
	1	2	3	4	5	5	4	3	2	1	

Probability (left axis) / Probability (right axis)

Negative Impact — **Positive Impact**

PMBOK® Guide – Sixth Edition. Page 408

The "zones" can be used to guide risk responses. For example, those risks with ratings falling in the highest scoring zone may warrant proactive risk response strategies; those risks within the middle zone may warrant a contingent response strategy; and those in the lowest zone will be placed on the watchlist. Both threats and opportunities can be displayed on the same probability and impact matrix, but it is important they are separated into two sections.

Reporting formats. The reporting formats will determine how information regarding the management of risks will be documented and communicated during the project, including the format of the risk register and risk reports. Again, consistency with organizational templates and reporting is important so that the recipients are familiar with the format and how to interpret the data.

Belinda's Hint

Never "force" risk reporting based on a field-size limitation. For example, many organizations create risk reporting templates and restrict reporting to the "top 5" or "top 10" list of risks. What you report should be based on what is needed-to-know for that particular reporting period. That may be three risks one week and 15 risks the following week. This is a tricky, and common, exam question!

Tracking. Risk analysis is dependent upon consistent tracking of the risks. Risk tracking will outline how risk activities will be captured and recorded for the project and for use in future projects. Tracking risk data will yield trending information that can be very important to managing risk, contingency, and corrective and preventive actions. Risk tracking may also include information about how the risk management activities will be audited during and after the project.

Stakeholder risk tolerances. The stakeholder risk tolerances should be identified and documented, recognizing that the tolerances may change as it relates to the particular project as the project or environment changes. I have personally found that the best way to assess risk tolerance with my stakeholders is to ask them "regarding this project, what keeps you awake at night or are you most concerned with?" Their answer helps me understand not only their risk tolerance, but also their risk attitude.

It is helpful to be aware of the stakeholder risk attitudes that may exist within your organization. Understanding your stakeholders' risk attitudes allows you to be proactive in your approach to risk management. The risk attitudes are risk-averse, risk-tolerant, risk-neutral, and risk-seeking.

Term	Definition
Risk-averse	The risk-averse person feels uncomfortable with uncertainty and ambiguity, seeking security and resolution in the face of risk. This stakeholder will tend to over-react to threats and under-react to opportunities. As the project manager, it is important that you provide information to them as to how you are responding to threats, while also highlighting the potential opportunities of the project.
Risk-tolerant	The risk-tolerant person is reasonably comfortable with most uncertainty. The laissez-faire approach fails to result in proactive action and missed opportunities and as such, may be the most dangerous of the risk attitudes. Typically, when I see someone exhibiting a risk tolerant approach they are "checked-out". Oftentimes they are getting ready to quit, to retire, to go on sabbatical, or they just don't believe the project impacts them. Be on the lookout for these stakeholders as their lack of engagement can be very detrimental to risk management.
Risk-neutral	The risk-neutral person sees present risk-taking as a price worth paying for future pay-offs, seeking strategies and tactics that have high future pay-offs. For both threats and opportunities, this attitude is mature, focusing on the longer term. Ideally, your project sponsor falls into this category!
Risk-seeking	The risk-seeking person tends to be adaptable, resourceful, and they are not afraid to take action. They are likely to identify few threats as they see them as part of normal business but may overestimate the importance of possible opportunities. As the project manager, you may need to level-set their optimistic expectations and making them aware of the project threats.

Risk Attitudes

Risk Averse

- Does not like uncertainty
- Overestimates threats and underestimates opportunities
- Glass-half-empty personality

Risk Tolerant

- Has a laissez-faire approach to risk
- May not take proactive action
- Most dangerous risk attitude

Risk Neutral

- Views risk management from a long-term perspective, weighing the risks with the rewards
- Healthiest attitude

Risk Seeking

- Ready to jump in to anything
- Underestimates threats and overestimates opportunities
- Glass-half-full personality

*The **plan risk management** process information is adapted from: PMBOK® Guide – Sixth Edition. Page 401-408*

Identify Risks

risk knowledge area | planning process group

An ongoing process, risk identification begins early in the project, with an assumption that preliminary risk identification occurred before the project was chartered. Risk identification involves multiple participants, including the project manager, the project team, subject matter experts, and anyone else with knowledge of potential risks. Essentially, you should be leveraging anyone and everyone who may have insight into the uncertainty faced by the project. It is especially important that the project team members are involved in risk identification to instill awareness and collective ownership.

Risk identification is an on-going process throughout the life of the project and project managers should always be identifying risk until the moment the project is officially and administratively closed. Risk identification is going to be used for individual project risks as well as sources of overall project risk. Recording the risks should occur in a consistent and standard manner, using the appropriate risk meta-language to minimize confusion and ambiguity in the statements. During risk identification, the risk owners may be nominated. Those risk owners will be confirmed when the risk responses are planned.

Example: Risk Identification

While Kim has an excellent team, a well-defined scope, and organizational support, she recognizes that there is risk to her project. During the kick-off meeting with her team, Kim provided all of the team members with an introduction to project risk management and conducted a brainstorming session to identify risks on the project.

To ensure comprehensive risk identification, Kim also arranges to meet with the key stakeholders, the project sponsor, her contact from the PMO, and other subject matter experts. Kim is able to capture a comprehensive list of risks that includes not only negative risks (threats) but she has also been able to identify some significant positive risks (opportunities). Her evaluation and discussion with the sponsor have also highlighted some overall project risk.

Identify Risks: ITTOs

Inputs	Tools & Techniques	Outputs
1. Project management plan	1. Expert judgment	1. Risk register
• Requirements management plan	2. Data gathering	2. Risk report
• Schedule management plan	• Brainstorming	3. Project documents
• Cost management plan	• Checklists	updates
• Quality management plan	• Interviews	• Assumption log
• Resource management plan	3. Data analysis	• Issue log
• Risk management plan	• Root cause analysis	• Lessons learned register
• Scope baseline	• Assumption and constraint analysis	
• Schedule baseline	• SWOT analysis	
• Cost baseline	• Document analysis	
2. Project documents	4. Interpersonal and team skills	
• Assumption log	• Facilitation	
• Cost estimates	5. Prompt lists	
• Duration estimates	6. Meetings	
• Issue log		
• Lessons learned register		
• Requirements documentation		
• Resource requirements		
• Stakeholder register		
3. Agreements		
4. Procurement documentation		
5. Enterprise Environmental Factors		
6. Organizational Process Assets		

PMBOK® Guide — Sixth Edition. Page 409

Identify Risks: Inputs

Agreements

When using external vendors or suppliers, the agreements should be consulted to determine any associated risks or uncertainty. The agreements will provide details regarding the contractual relationship such as milestone dates, contract types, acceptance criteria, etc. In addition, many agreements with vendors will also dictate the agreed-upon approach to risk management.

Procurement documentation

Along with the agreements with the vendors or suppliers, the procurement documentation may also provide insight into risk and exposure. This will include the ongoing documentation related to the work and progress of the vendors, including their performance reports, information on any inspections, and the approved change requests.

Common Inputs:

- **Project management plan** - As this process is conducted and revisited throughout the project, components of the project management plan may be leveraged such as the requirements, schedule, cost, quality, resource, and risk management plans. In addition, the scope, schedule, and cost baselines will be leveraged.

- **Project documents** - Project documents leveraged for this process include the assumption and the issue log, the lessons learned register, the cost and duration estimates, the resource requirements, the requirements documentation, and the stakeholder register.
- **Enterprise environmental factors** - Internal and external influences that will be considered include the organizational culture and structure, results of studies and benchmarking, published material including risk databases or checklists or studies, and the volatility of the environment.
- **Organizational process assets** - Templates, policies and procedures, and historical information can be leveraged to control the project resources. Specifically, for risk identification, the project manager and the team should leverage risk statement formats and checklists from previous similar projects. They say lightning does not strike twice in the same location. That is actually a false statement: it does! If I risk was identified on a previous project, there is a strong likelihood that it will be a risk to your current project. Use the past to predict the future!

Identify Risks: Tools and Techniques

Prompt Lists

A prompt list is a predetermined set of risk categories and the list can serve as a framework for identifying for project risk through the other identified techniques. As mentioned in **plan risk management**, the prompt list can serve as the top level of the risk breakdown structure (RBS). They are called *prompt lists* as they prompt you to think of common categories, ensuring entire categories are not missed. Examples of common prompt lists include:

- PESTLE – political, economic, social, technological, legal, environmental
- TECOP – technical, environmental, commercial, operational, political
- SPECTRUM – socio-cultural, political, economic, competitive, technology, regulatory/legal, uncertainty, market
- VUCA – volatility, uncertainty, complexity, ambiguity

Common Tools and Techniques:

Expert Judgment

Expertise may be leveraged from anyone and everyone with insight into risk exposure and uncertainty related to the project, the product, and the environment. The project manager cannot identify risks in isolation! You must leverage other people.

Data Gathering Techniques

There are three common data gathering techniques:

Brainstorming is the generation of ideas, under the guidance of a facilitator. These sessions may be free-form or more structured, depending on the environment and situation. The ultimate goal of the sessions is to create a comprehensive list of risks. The facilitator will need to ensure that the risks that are identified are specific and not too generic or high-level.

Checklists are a list of items, actions or points to be considered and serve as a prompt for considering or remembering all aspects of project risk management. Often developed from past experience and historical information, they provide great insight into what has happened previously and therefore what may occur again. While leveraging a checklist is a best practice to ensure no aspects of the project are overlooked, it is unlikely that the checklist will be comprehensive. All projects have unique risk exposure and opportunities.

The checklist should be reviewed during project closure to add any new lessons learned and improve the checklists for use on future projects. This includes pruning the checklist to remove redundant entries. According to PMI, the checklist can be the lowest level of the risk breakdown structure (RBS), however, I typically that to be far too detailed for the RBS.

Belinda's Hint

The term "checklist" may be a little misleading. One way to visualize this checklist is to think of it as a "master list of risks" that has been documented over time by the organization.

Interviews involve dialogue, either one-on-one, or with a group to uncover and discuss risks for the project. As the facilitator, it is important that the participants can speak openly and honestly, and therefore respect and trust is critical.

Data Analysis Techniques

There are four data analysis techniques commonly used to identify project risks:

A *root cause analysis* determines the underlying cause that leads to the problem in order to develop preventive actions to minimize the occurrence of that problem or risk. This technique can be used for both threats and opportunities.

An *assumption and constraint analysis* evaluates the basis for the project approval and structure, including the limitations placed upon the project and the factors that are considered to be real, true, and factual. This analysis explores the validity of assumptions as they apply to the project and identifies any risk from inaccuracy, inconsistency, or incompleteness of assumptions. These assumptions are tested: should the assumption prove to be false, would it have an impact on the project? If so, the assumption could be a project risk. Constraints are also evaluated to determine if there could be opportunities should one or more of the constraints be relaxed or removed, or on the other hand, if the constraint was tightened, would there be a threat to the project success?

A *SWOT analysis* ensures examination of the project from each perspective: What are the strengths of organization and the project team? What are the opportunities available to the organization and the project team? What are the weaknesses of the organization and project team? What are the threats against the organization and the project team? Commonly, an organization's strengths give way to opportunities and weaknesses give rise to threats. Using this analysis as a structure for brainstorming encourages consideration for both threats and opportunities.

Belinda's Hint

While you may have heard of a SWOT analysis before, many people associate it with marketing or even the up-front analysis of a project. From an exam perspective, be sure to associate a SWOT analysis with the **identify risks** process. It is a good way to ensure that your team is also considering opportunities given the common tendency to focus strictly on threats.

A *document analysis* is the ongoing review of project documentation to identify any indications of uncertainty or risk.

Interpersonal and Team Skills

In identifying project risk, the project manager and the team will be working with several individuals, perhaps both internally and externally. Interpersonal and team skills will be involved to elicit beneficial information.

Facilitation is the effective management, coordination, and oversight of meetings.

Meetings

Risk identification meetings will occur throughout the project with various participants. A risk workshop is a specialized meeting that involves brainstorming on risk topics. A risk workshop may be used to gather information for each of the risk processes. Participants in risk workshops can vary depending on the goals and objectives.

Identify Risks: Outputs

There are two key outputs from the risk identification process:

Risk Register

The risk register documents each identified risk with a unique risk identifier, the associated root causes of the risks, and the potential risk owners and risk responses. Risks may be documented with risk statements or risk metalanguage, such as:

- EVENT may occur causing IMPACT
- If CAUSE exists, EVENT may occur leading to EFFECT

Depending on the risk register format described in the risk management plan, additional information added to the risk register may include the risk category, risk status, risk triggers, WBS reference, and timing information. The risk register will be updated in the remaining risk processes with additional information related to responses and prioritization.

Risk Report

The risk report details information on the sources of overall project risk and a summary of the individual project risks. Like the risk register, the risk report will be expanded and modified throughout the risk processes.

Common Output:

- **Project document updates** - Project documents that may be updated include the assumption and issue logs, and the lessons learned register.

*The **identify risks** process information is adapted from: PMBOK® Guide — Sixth Edition. Page 409-418*

Perform Qualitative Risk Analysis

risk knowledge area | planning process group

The **perform qualitative risk analysis** process prioritizes the identified risks for further action by assessing and combining the probability of the risk occurring and the impact on the project objectives if the risk does occur. The definitions of risk probability and impact defined within the project risk management plan will be leveraged to reduce the influence of biases. Qualitative risk analysis is usually a quick and cost-effective way to establish priorities for risk response planning and performing a quantitative risk analysis, if needed.

A qualitative risk analysis is considered subjective and it is based on the positions and opinions of the individuals participating in the analysis and review of the risks. Identifying and addressing biases in the process will be important to validate the integrity of the assessments. Performed on both opportunities and threats, the qualitative analysis of the identified risks will occur periodically throughout the project to capture trending data on the risk exposure of the project.

Perform Qualitative Risk Analysis: ITTOs

Inputs	Tools & Techniques	Outputs

1. Project management plan
  • Risk management plan
2. Project documents
  • Assumption log
  • Risk register
  • Stakeholder register
3. Enterprise environmental factors
4. Organizational process assets
	1. Expert judgment
	2. Data gathering
	  • Interviews
	3. Data analysis
	  • Risk data quality assessment
	  • Risk probability and impact assessment
	  • Assessment of other risk parameters
	4. Interpersonal and Team Skills
	  • Facilitation
	5. Risk categorization
	6. Data Representation
	  • Probability and impact matrix
	  • Hierarchical charts
	7. Meetings
		1. Project documents updates
		  • Assumption log
		  • Issue log
		  • Risk register
		  • Risk report

PMBOK® Guide – Sixth Edition. Page 419

Perform Qualitative Risk Analysis: Inputs

Common Inputs:

- **Project management plan** - As this process is conducted and revisited throughout the project, components of the project management plan may be leveraged, specifically the risk management plan.
- **Project documents** - Project documents leveraged for this process include the assumption log, the risk register, and the stakeholder register.
- **Enterprise environmental factors** - Internal and external influences will be considered when qualitatively assessing the project risks, including, but not limited to, industry studies of similar projects and available published materials.
- **Organizational process assets** - Templates, policies and procedures, and historical information may be leveraged to perform a qualitative risk analysis.

Perform Qualitative Risk Analysis: Tools and Techniques

Risk Categorization

Risks may be categorized by the sources of project risk (for example, using the RBS), the area of the project affected by the risk (scope, time, cost, quality, etc.), or other useful categories (for example, project phase). Grouping risks by common root causes can allow for effective response strategies.

Common Tools and Techniques:

Expert Judgment

Expertise may be leveraged from individuals with knowledge and experience of the specific risks that are being evaluated, including your team members and work package owners.

Data Gathering Techniques

Data will be gathered for the qualitative risk analysis primarily through *interviews*, which may be structured or semi-structured. Information will be gathered in a facilitated manner and it is important that the interviewer creates an environment of trust and confidentiality to get accurate assessments.

Data Analysis Techniques

There are three data analysis techniques that may be used during a qualitative risk analysis process:

A *risk data quality assessment* evaluates the degree to which the data about individual project risks is accurate and reliable. Essentially, it is the consideration of "garbage-in = garbage-out." How good is our data that we are using to assess and evaluate our risks? Is it up-to-date and comprehensive?

A *risk probability and impact assessment* evaluates the identified risks in terms of the probability of the risk event occurring as well as the impact on the project objectives if it does occur. The scales and the criteria defined with the risk management plan will be leveraged during this analysis.

An *assessment of other risk parameters* is an evaluation of other characteristics that may have an impact on the prioritization of the project risks. Additional characteristics may include:

Urgency. The period in which action needs to be taken. A short period would be a high urgency.

Proximity. The period of time before the risk might have an impact. A short period would be high proximity.

Dormancy. The period of time that may elapse after a risk has occurred before it is discovered. A short period would be low dormancy.

Manageability. The relative ease of managing the risk. If the management is easy, the manageability would be high.

Controllability. The ability to control the impact of the risk. If the outcome can be easily controlled, the controllability would be high.

Detectability. The ease of detecting that the risk is about to or has occurred. If it is easily detected, the detectability would be high.

Connectivity. The extent to which the risk is related to other risks. If the risk is connected to multiple other risks, the connectivity is high.

Strategic impact. The potential for the risk to influence the organization's strategic objectives. If the risk has a significant effect, the strategic impact is high (and can be either positively or negatively impacting the objectives).

Propinquity. The degree to which the risk is perceived in importance to one or more stakeholders. If the risk is perceived as very significant, the propinquity is high.

PMBOK® Guide – Sixth Edition. Page 424

Interpersonal and Team Skills

Facilitation is used to guide, coordinate, and manage the risk analysis meetings effectively, while minimizing conflict and discourse.

Data Representation

There are two techniques for representing the data captured during a qualitative risk analysis:

A *probability and impact matrix* is a grid for mapping the probability of the risk event occurring and the impact on project objectives should it occur. Using this data, decisions can be made as to the most appropriate response based on the risk rating. The project team may use the matrix for all project risks or may have separate matrices representing the impact on each of the project objectives. Both threats and opportunities can be depicted.

Hierarchical charts are used to characterize risks when there are more than two factors or parameters being considered in the evaluation. An example would be a bubble chart, where the risks are represented as bubbles: the bubble size represents one parameter, the x-axis and the y-axis represent other parameters.

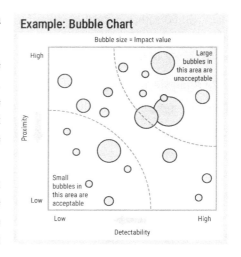

Example: Bubble Chart

Meetings

Risk workshops are a specific risk meeting dedicated to discussing and evaluating the identified individual project risks. In the risk workshop, the assessment scales are presented and discussed, and the risks will be assessed against the scales.

Perform Qualitative Risk Analysis: Outputs

Common Output:

- **Project document updates** - Project documents that may be updated through this process include the assumption and issue logs, along with the risk register and risk report. The risk register will be updated with the assessments of probability and impact for each risk, its priority level or risk score, the nominated risk owner, risk urgency, risk categorization, and a watchlist of low-priority risks. The risk report will be updated to reflect the highest priority risks based on the qualitative analysis, a prioritized list of risk, and a summary conclusion. As the project progresses, the qualitative risk analysis will be repeated. This will yield information as to the increasing or decreasing risk on the project, which in turn will be used to conduct the reserve analysis.

*The **perform qualitative risk analysis** process information is adapted from: PMBOK® Guide – Sixth Edition. Page 419-427*

Perform Quantitative Risk Analysis

risk knowledge area | planning process group

While all risks will go through the qualitative analysis in order to be prioritized, not all risks will be evaluated quantitatively. Once the risks have been prioritized through a qualitative risk analysis, a quantitative risk analysis will evaluate the effect of the subset of prioritized risks and assign a numerical, or quantitative, rating in terms of cost and schedule impact. In a qualitative risk analysis, an impact may be a "3". However, a quantitative analysis may assess the risk as a $3,000 cost impact or a 4-month delay impact.

A number of techniques, such as a Monte Carlo simulation or a decision tree analysis can be used to quantify the possible outcomes of the project and their probabilities while assessing the probability of achieving specific project objectives.

As a result of performing a quantitative risk analysis, an additional level of prioritization may occur, identifying those risks needing the most attention. This will allow the project team to determine project management decisions when conditions or outcomes are uncertain and is used to evaluate the aggregate effect of risk on the project objectives.

A quantitative risk analysis is dependent upon high-quality data and in some instances, robust tools and methodologies. Because of this, not all projects and not all organizations will use quantitative analysis techniques for project risk management. It is more likely to be appropriate for large, complex projects that have resources with specialized risk analysis experience.

As with a qualitative analysis, a quantitative risk analysis may be revisited throughout the project to assess effectiveness of risk responses and any changes in the project risk environment. Risk trending data will be used to monitor and control the project work and the project contingency.

Perform Quantitative Analysis: ITTOs

Inputs	Tools & Techniques	Outputs
1. Project management plan	1. Expert judgment	1. Project documents updates
• Risk management plan	2. Data gathering	• Risk report
• Scope baseline	• Interviews	
• Schedule baseline	3. Interpersonal and team skills	
• Cost baseline	• Facilitation	
2. Project documents	4. Representation of uncertainty	
• Assumption log	5. Data analysis	
• Basis of estimates	• Simulations	
• Cost estimates	• Sensitivity analysis	
• Cost forecasts	• Decision tree analysis	
• Duration estimates	• Influence diagrams	
• Milestone list		
• Resource requirements		
• Risk register		
• Risk report		
• Schedule forecasts		
3. Enterprise environmental factors		
4. Organizational process assets		

PMBOK® Guide – Sixth Edition. Page 428

Perform Quantitative Risk Analysis: Inputs

Common Inputs:

- **Project management plan** - As this process is conducted and revisited throughout the project, components of the project management plan may be leveraged such as the risk management plan and the scope, schedule, and cost baselines.
- **Project documents** - Project documents leveraged for a quantitative risk analysis include the assumption log, the cost and duration estimates and the basis of those estimates, the cost and schedule forecasts, the milestone list, the resource requirements, and the risk register and report.
- **Enterprise environmental factors** - Internal and external influences to be considered include any industry studies and published material such as commercial risk databases or checklists.

- **Organizational process assets** - Templates, policies and procedures, and historical information may be leveraged to conduct a quantitative risk analysis.

Perform Quantitative Risk Analysis: Tools and Techniques

Representation of Uncertainty

One of the most common outputs from a quantitative analysis is a probability distribution. Probability distributions represent the uncertainty impacting the budget and the schedule. There are many types of probability distributions that can depict the uncertainty in a data set: triangular, normal, lognormal, beta, uniform, or discrete. While you should understand that this is the way the uncertainty is displayed, do not expect detailed statistical questions on the exam. (Thank goodness, right?)

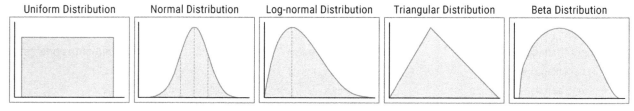

| Uniform Distribution | Normal Distribution | Log-normal Distribution | Triangular Distribution | Beta Distribution |

Common Tools and Techniques:

Expert Judgment

Expertise may be leveraged from individuals with knowledge and experience with quantitative risk analysis techniques.

Data Gathering Techniques

Interviews may be conducted one-on-one or with a group and are the main source of quantitative risk data. Consider your environment. When you ask your team members "worst-case scenario", you are essentially interviewing them to quantify the risk of their component of work.

Interpersonal and Team Skills

Facilitation is the effective coordination, management, and oversight of meetings. Facilitated workshops are an example of structured meeting sessions to elicit quantitative assessments of the project risks.

Data Analysis Techniques

There are four data analysis techniques that may be used during a quantitative risk analysis:

Simulations evaluate the project model through multiple iterations to determine the probability of achieving the project's cost and schedule objectives. The most commonly used simulation tool is a Monte Carlo analysis. A Monte Carlo analysis involves robust software and extensive, quality data.

A Monte Carlo analysis can be conducted on both the schedule and budget objectives. To evaluate the impact of risk on the schedule, the schedule network diagram is used, along with the duration estimates. To evaluate the impact of risk on the budget, the project cost estimates are leveraged. In a Monte Carlo analysis, the project model is iterated thousands of times with risk and risk impacts selected at random to predict an overall cumulative sensitivity to the risks. The output may be a histogram or a cumulative probability distribution (S-curve).

Let's walk through the difference in applying a Monte Carlo simulation versus using a three-point estimate in the following example. Interviewing relevant stakeholders helps to determine three-point estimates for each WBS element. These estimates are provided as:

WBS Element	Low	Most Likely	High
Design	$8,000	$14,000	$20,000
Build	$32,000	$40,000	$70,000
Test	$22,000	$32,000	$46,000
Total Project	$62,000	$86,000	$136,000

If we were to use this information as provided by the stakeholders or work package owners, we could say that our most likely cost estimate for the project is $86,000. Applying a triangular 3-point (computing the mean), the estimate would be $94.67k.

Now, we will take all the cost data and risk and probability data and run a Monte Carlo simulation through software. The project model is iterated thousands of times, pulling in random risk events and impacts. The output is the following continuous distribution:

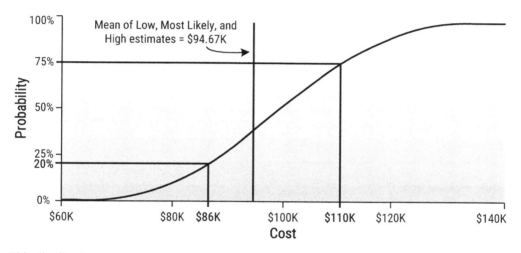

This distribution shows that the project is only 20% likely to be completed at or below the $86k "most likely" estimate. That is often referred to as a P20 confidence level where P represents probability of coming in at that amount or less. Considering the triangular 3-point of $94.67k would only result in about a P40 confidence level. If a conservative organization wants a 75% likelihood of success, a budget of $110k is required. That is a contingency of nearly 28% (($110k - $86k)/$86k)

A Monte Carlo simulation can also be used to evaluate schedule implications. In evaluating the schedule risk, a criticality analysis determines which risks or risk elements will have the greatest impact on the critical path, calculating a "criticality index." This information can be used to focus the team's response planning efforts on those activities with the highest potential impact on the overall schedule performance.

The next technique used in a quantitative risk analysis is a *sensitivity analysis.* A *sensitivity analysis* determines which individual risks or sources of risk have the most impact on the project outcomes. The most common example of a sensitivity analysis to appear on the PMP exam is a tornado diagram, which is used to display the potential "spread" from the base value of the risk impact, both from a positive and negative perspective. The risks are then displayed top-down by broadest spread or range of impact. Tornado diagrams only display cost risk data, not schedule risk data. This is due to the fact that not all schedule risk will have the same impact. For example, a schedule delay due to a realized risk may not impact the schedule as the impacted activities may have float. However, a cost impact is a cost impact!

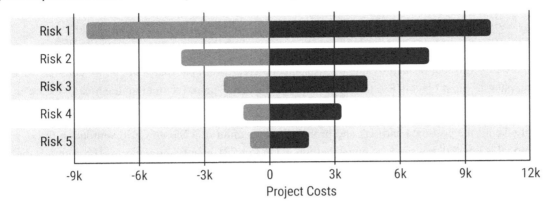

There are three questions you may see on the PMP exam related to the tornado diagram. The first one is "what is this diagram". Hopefully you would not get that wrong given that it looks like a tornado! The second question is "what type of data is displayed in a tornado diagram?" and the answer is cost risk data. The third question may be something like "you and your team are developing a tornado diagram. What process are you doing?" and because you will know that a tornado diagram represents cost risk, it must be **quantitative risk analysis**.

Decision tree analyses are used to evaluate alternate courses of actions or anticipated events in order to calculate a probability or make an appropriate decision based on the relative uncertainty of the different options or outcomes. Decision trees can be used for both schedule and cost uncertainty.

We will work through schedule decision trees first:

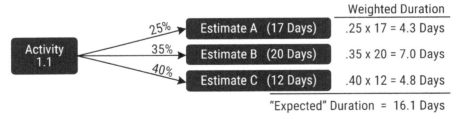

Based on the information in the diagram above, you see they are telling us that there are three potential durations for activity 1.1 and they have provided us with the probabilities of each estimate. To calculate an "estimated" or "expected" or "blended" duration, simply multiply probability times impact and sum the results. In this example, based on the probabilities provided the estimated duration is 16.1 days. Now how you will use that information would depend on how risk averse your environment is. A very risk averse environment may go with the 20-day estimate, for example.

Belinda's Hint

A couple of things to keep in mind when evaluating questions on decision trees on the exam:

The first thing to notice is that the sum of the probabilities is 100% - meaning that one of those estimates will happen. It is possible on the exam that they may not give you one of the probabilities. For example, in the previous graphic, they may give you 25% for Estimate A and 35% for Estimate B, and you will need to calculate the probability for Estimate C. A and B only equal 60%, therefore C must be 40%.

If provided this data in a word problem and it happens to have three options, be careful that you do not assume they are asking you to do a PERT (3-Point) calculation. We would only do PERT if we didn't have the probabilities and as such, we "force" the probabilities. If they provide the probabilities, use them!

Let's check your understanding of using a decision tree for schedule risk. The answer to Exercise 10.1 is on page 289.

Exercise 10.1 – Decision Tree for Schedule Risk

You have been working with your work package owners to determine potential schedule risk associated with their components. You received the following information from one of your team members:

There are four potential teams that may complete the component. Based on skill level and past experience, team A would be able to complete the component in 10 days, team B would be able to complete the component in 15 days, team C would be able to complete the component in 6 days, and team D would be able to complete the component in 18 days. There is a 30% probability the work will be assigned to team B, 10% probability it will be assigned to team A, and a 40% probability it will be assigned to team C.

What is the estimated duration based on this information?

Expected monetary value analysis. The same concept and process that was used to calculate duration, when applied to costs is called an expected monetary value (EMV) analysis. EMV analysis is a statistical concept that calculates the average financial outcome when the future includes scenarios that may or may not happen. EMV is calculated by multiplying the value of each possible outcome by its probability of occurrence and adding them together. Just like with durations, the sum of the probability percentages must equal 100%.

The EMV represents the potential cost risk of the scenario based on all of the outcomes and their probabilities. The EMV will be added back to the original estimate to determine the "total value" of the scenario.

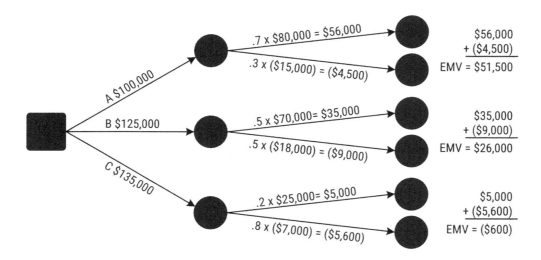

Let's look at this example:

Vendor A provided a bid of $100,000, Vendor B provided a bid of $125,000, and Vendor C provided a bid of $135,000. According to the diagram:

Vendor A has a 70% probability of delivering late at an additional cost of $80,000 and a 30% probability of delivering early at a savings of $15,000.

Vendor B has a 50% probability of delivering late at an additional cost of $70,000 and a 50% probability of delivering early at a savings of $18,000.

Vendor C has a 20% probability of delivering late at an additional cost of $25,000 and an 80% probability of delivering early at a savings of $7,000.

To determine the expected monetary value (EMV) of the risk of working with each vendor, multiple the probability by the financial impact and sum the results. To determine the total value of each bid, the EMV would be added to the original bid amount.

Vendor A EMV = $51,500 + Bid $100,000 = Total Value: $151,500

Vendor B EMV = $26,000 + Bid $125,000 = Total Value: $151,000

Vendor C EMV = ($600) + Bid $135,000 = Total Value: $134,400

Based on the analysis, you select Vendor C as the total value including the risk scenario for Vendor C is $134,400, lower than the other two vendors.

Belinda's Hint

Read the question carefully!

Is this money the organization or project is spending? If so, lower and/or negative numbers will be better, meaning we are possibly spending less than anticipated.

Is this money the organization or project will be making? If so, higher numbers will be better, meaning that we are possibly earning more than anticipated.

Always double-check your positive and negative numbers to ensure they align with the scenario.

Remember if they are asking for EMV, that is simply the sum of the risk scenario branches. However, if they ask for total value, the EMV must be added back to the original estimate.

Let's check your understanding of using a decision tree for an EMV analysis. The answers to Exercise 10.2 are on page 289.

Exercise 10.2: Decision Tree for EMV Analysis

You are evaluating two potential profit scenarios for a new product launch. Product A is estimated to make $30,000 profit, and Product B is estimated to make a $50,000 profit.

For Product A: There is a 20% chance that it will be poorly received by the market at a loss of $10,000, a 50% chance that it will be well-received by the market at an increased profit of $20,000, and a ___ chance that it will exceed market expectations at an increased profit of $50,000.

What is the EMV of the risk scenario? What is the total value?

For Product B:

There is a 40% chance that it will be poorly received by the market at a loss of $20,000, a ___ chance that it will be well-received by the market at an increased profit of $30,000, and a 30% chance that it will exceed market expectations at an increased profit of $40,000.

What is the EMV of the risk scenario? What is the total value?

Influence diagrams are graphical aids for decision making when there is uncertainty, depicting entities, outcomes, and influences and the relationships between them. Elements that are uncertain can be depicted with ranges or probability distributions.

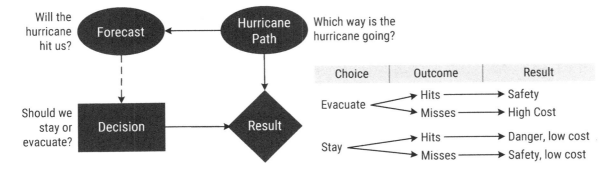

Perform Quantitative Risk Analysis: Outputs

Common Output:

- **Project document updates** - Project documents that may be updated as a result of a quantitative risk analysis include the risk register and the risk report. The risk report will be updated with a number of key items:
  - An assessment of the overall project risk exposure, including the chance for project success given the uncertainty and the degree of inherent variability remaining within the project when the analysis was conducted
  - A probabilistic analysis of the project with data from S-curves, tornado diagrams, and criticality analyses, that can determine the amount of contingency needed, which risks have the greatest impact on the crucial path, and the major drivers of overall project risk
  - A prioritized list of individual project risks
  - Trends in quantitative analysis as it is repeated throughout the project
  - Recommended risk responses

*The **perform quantitative risk analysis** process information is adapted from: PMBOK® Guide – Sixth Edition. Page 428-436*

Plan Risk Responses

risk knowledge area | planning process group

During risk response planning, the prioritized risks are evaluated for an appropriate response. A response strategy will be identified, a risk owner will be assigned to the risk, and funding will be allocated, if needed. Any planned risk responses should be appropriate to the level and priority of the risk, while being cost-effective and realistic within the context of the project. We do not want to spend more preventing a risk than it would cost us if the risk event occurred.

Be strong in your risk vocabulary for this exam! Here are some risk response definitions:

Term	Definition
Risk strategy	A response to a project risk that may be implemented prior to the risk event occurring. These would be typically used for the highest rated risks (red risks). For threats, strategies include: avoidance, mitigation, and transferring For opportunities, strategies include: sharing, enhancement, and exploitation
Contingent response strategy	A response that is planned in advance of a risk event that will be implemented based on a trigger or the actual event occurring. This presents an "if…then" scenario. If XXXX happens, then we'll XXXX. A contingent response strategy is considered active risk acceptance. This would be typically used for moderate risks (yellow).
Trigger	A pre-cursor event that indicates that a risk has occurred or is about to occur
Fallback Plan	Used when the primary response (whether a proactive strategy or a contingent response strategy) is inadequate. This is one of the terms that many people confuse. Do not consider a fallback plan as synonymous with a contingency plan. A fallback plan is always a secondary response after an original response is not effective. Contingency plans are primary responses. Think of a fallback plan as a plan "B." B = Back.
Residual Risks	Those that remain after planned responses have been taken. If mitigation is the chosen strategy, there will always be residual risk as mitigation only serves to reduce or decrease the probability and/or impact of the identified risk.
Secondary Risks	Arise as an outcome of implementing a risk response. A secondary risk would not exist had we not taken a certain response.
Workaround	A response to a negative risk that has occurred. Workarounds are not planned in advance. NOTE: The need for workarounds would be identified in monitoring and controlling (the **monitor risks** process), as they are not "planned" in advance.

PMBOK® Guide Sixth Edition, Glossary

To help illustrate these definitions, let's consider a couple of different scenarios for this grand opening celebration. In scenario one, our grand opening celebration is being held in my beautiful home state of Maine, in the month of May. Probability of rain is high, and the impact would be high; therefore, a red risk. As such, we will take a proactive mitigation strategy to the risk by putting the tent up. Rain or shine, there will be a tent. Now, I have a secondary risk that someone could trip over the tent pole. Because I have mitigated (reduced) the risk, not eliminated it, there is some residual risk that the attendees may get wet walking from the parking lot to the tent. In the event the rain or the weather gets crazy, we may have a fallback plan that we will move the event to a local restaurant if the tent is not enough.

Because it may rain during the grand opening celebration, there is a risk that the guests could get wet and not enjoy the event.

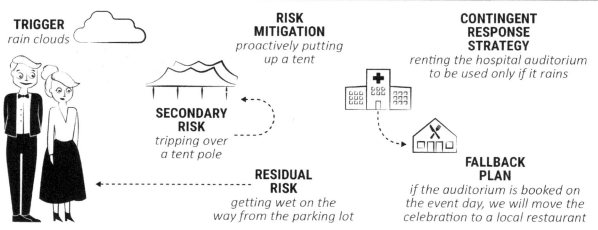

TRIGGER
rain clouds

RISK MITIGATION
proactively putting up a tent

CONTINGENT RESPONSE STRATEGY
renting the hospital auditorium to be used only if it rains

SECONDARY RISK
tripping over a tent pole

RESIDUAL RISK
getting wet on the way from the parking lot

FALLBACK PLAN
if the auditorium is booked on the event day, we will move the celebration to a local restaurant

Now let's consider this same situation, but our celebration is in Arizona in May. The probability of rain is low, but the impact would still be high. We can consider this a yellow risk. As such, we will take active risk acceptance by identifying a contingent response strategy. If it rains on the morning of the event, or we see the rain clouds (our trigger), we will go to the hospital auditorium. As with our proactive strategy, we may have a fallback plan, a plan "B", that if the auditorium is booked, we will go to a local restaurant.

Plan Risk Responses: ITTOs

Inputs	Tools & Techniques	Outputs
1. Project management plan	1. Expert judgment	1. Change requests
• Resource management plan	2. Data gathering	2. Project management plan updates
• Risk management plan	• Interviews	• Schedule management plan
• Cost baseline	3. Interpersonal and team skills	• Cost management plan
2. Project documents	• Facilitation	• Quality management plan
• Lessons learned register	4. Strategies for threats	• Resource management plan
• Project schedule	5. Strategies for opportunities	• Procurement management plan
• Project team assignments	6. Contingent response strategies	• Scope baseline
• Resource calendars	7. Strategies for overall project risk	• Schedule baseline
• Risk register	8. Data analysis	• Cost baseline
• Risk report	• Alternatives analysis	3. Project documents updates
• Stakeholder register	• Cost-benefit analysis	• Assumption log
3. Enterprise environmental factors	9. Decision making	• Cost forecasts
	• Multicriteria decision analysis	• Lessons learned register
4. Organizational process assets		• Project schedule
		• Project team assignments
		• Risk register
		• Risk report

PMBOK® Guide – Sixth Edition. Page 437

Plan Risk Responses: Inputs

Common Inputs:

- **Project management plan** - As this process is conducted and revisited throughout the project, components of the project management plan may be leveraged including the resource and risk management plans and the cost baseline.
- **Project documents** - Project documents leveraged for this process include the lessons learned register, the project schedule, the project team assignments and resource calendars, the stakeholder register, and the risk register and report.
- **Enterprise environmental factors** - Influences to be considered when planning the risk responses include the risk appetite and risk thresholds of the stakeholders, as well as other environmental and situational factors.
- **Organizational process assets** - Templates, policies and procedures, and historical information can be leveraged to plan the risk responses.

Plan Risk Responses: Tools and Techniques

Strategies for Threats

There are five strategies for risks that potentially have a negative impact on project objectives: escalate, avoid, transfer, mitigate, and accept.

Escalate. Escalation may be appropriate when the threat is outside of the scope of the project, or any response would exceed the project manager's level of authority. Those escalated risks may be managed at the program or portfolio level or within another area of the organization. The turnover or hand over of the escalated risk is very important to ensure that the new owner accepts that ownership. Once a threat has been successfully escalated it is no longer monitored or managed by the project team.

Avoid. Risk avoidance implies changing the project management plan to eliminate the threat posed by an adverse risk. Key-words to look for in the questions: eliminate, obsolete, removed. This is the related response to opportunity exploitation – both eliminate the uncertainty. I have a risk that someone could walk on the wet concrete, so I use crushed rock instead of concrete. The risk has been avoided.

This is the related response to opportunity exploitation – eliminating the uncertainty.

Transfer. Risk transference involves shifting the negative impact to a third party. The probability of the event occurring has not decreased. This can involve purchasing an insurance policy or adding a penalty, or risk clause, to a contract or agreement. This includes non-disclosure agreements, etc. It is important to note that the act of transferring the risk may also mitigate the risk. For example, adding a penalty clause is transference, but may also serve to reduce the probability that the vendor will deliver late. From an exam-perspective, if the risk response involves a contractual agreement, transfer is the first option that should be selected.

This is the related response to opportunity sharing – both involve agreements with external parties.

Mitigate. Risk mitigation reduces the probability and/or impact of an adverse risk event to an acceptable level. Key words to look for: reduce or decrease. Because mitigation only reduces the probability and/or impact, there is always residual risk associated with mitigation.

This is the related response to opportunity enhancement – mitigation decreases whereas enhancement increases probability.

Accept. Risk acceptance acknowledges the risk without changing the project plan. This could be because there is not a suitable response or because it is deemed low priority. Acceptance of threats may be passive or active: passive acceptance requires no action (green risks) whereas active risk acceptance would be establishing a contingency reserve and/or a contingent response strategy (yellow risks).

Because one of the modalities offered will be animal therapy, there is a risk the animals may behave inappropriately for the health setting. Kim has evaluated the potential responses:

ESCALATE
Kim could escalate the situation to the sponsor

TRANSFER
Kim could purchase some type of liability insurance on the animals

ACTIVE ACCEPTANCE
Kim could identify a contingency plan that would be invoked in the event the animals start misbehaving

AVOID
Kim could eliminate the pet therapy from the treatment options

MITIGATE
Kim could verify that all animals have been through the appropriate training and certification program

PASSIVE ACCEPTANCE
Kim could note the risk, but not take any action

Strategies for Opportunities

There are five strategies for risks that have a positive impact on project objectives: escalate, exploit, share, enhance, or accept.

Escalate. Opportunity escalation may occur when the team feels that the opportunity is not within the scope of the project or the response would exceed the project manager's authority. Escalation would be to the program or portfolio level or to another organization. Once the opportunity is escalated, it will no longer be monitored by the project team.

Exploit. Risk exploitation implies ensuring the opportunity will happen through identifying strategies to eliminate the uncertainty. Do not overthink this one! If the question advises that they are able to capture the opportunity, it is exploitation.

This is the related response to threat avoidance – both eliminate the uncertainty.

Share. Risk sharing allocates ownership to a third party who is best able to capture the opportunity for the benefit of the project. Risk sharing involves some type of contract or agreement. Look for joint ventures and partnerships as examples of risk sharing. If the question mentions a contractual relationship due to risk, you will need to read the context of the question: if it is a positive risk, it will be risk sharing; if it is a negative risk, it will be risk transference.

This is the related response to threat transferring – both involve agreements with external parties.

Enhance. Risk enhancement modifies the size of the opportunity by increasing the probability and/or positive impacts.

This is the related response to threat mitigation – enhancement increases whereas mitigation decreases probability.

Accept. Risk acceptance means that the project team is willing to take advantage of the opportunity if it comes along, but they are not changing the plan to actively pursue it. Opportunity acceptance does not come in active and passive form as there is no such thing as a contingency plan for an opportunity!

While there are other hospitals evaluating the possibility of offering a holistic health center, Bingham Hospital has the opportunity to be the first regional hospital to actually open a specialized wellness center

---

ESCALATE
Kim could escalate to the sponsor to determine the appropriate action

ENHANCE
Kim could increase the chances of delivering early and prior to other hospitals by adding the most experienced team to the project

ACCEPT
Kim could accept the opportunity without changing the plan

SHARE
Kim could share this opportunity by partnering with another organization that has experience in developing holistic wellness centers that would allow them to deliver quickly

EXPLOIT
Kim could exploit the opportunity by ensuring that Bingham Hospital will be the first to open a wellness center by accelerating the timeline with schedule compression techniques

Belinda's Hint

The risk responses for threats mirror the responses for opportunities:

Avoidance is to threats as exploitation is to opportunities: both involve modifying the plan to eliminate the uncertainty

Transference is to threats as sharing is to opportunities: both involve a contractual relationship with an external party

Mitigation is to threats as enhancement is to opportunities: both involve modifying the plan to minimize the uncertainty

Acceptance is used for both; however, acceptance may be passive or active for threats

Contingent Response Strategies

As previously mentioned, contingent response strategies include documented contingency plans and/or contingency reserves for time or money. They are designed for use only if certain events occur, typically for yellow risks. This is considered active risk acceptance.

Strategies for Overall Project Risk

There are five strategies for risks that address overall project risk: avoid, exploit, transfer/share, mitigate/enhance, and accept. You will notice that these align with the strategies for the individual risks.

Avoid. If there is significant negative overall project risk beyond the risk thresholds for the project, the team or sponsor may pursue an avoidance strategy to bring the project back within the threshold. If the response or responses are not effective enough, the project may be cancelled.

Exploit. If there is significant positive overall project risk, action may be taken to capture the positive effect of the uncertainty. An example would be adding high-benefit elements to the scope of the project to add value to the stakeholders.

Transfer/share. If the level of overall project risk is high, but the organization is unable to address it effectively, a third party may be involved to manage the risk on behalf of the organization. Risk transference involves shifting the negative impact to a third party. Risk sharing involves partnering with a third party, such as through a joint venture, in order to achieve the project objectives.

Mitigate/enhance. If the overall project risk is negative, mitigation actions may be employed. For positive risks, enhancement actions would be used. This could involve changing the scope and boundaries of the project, adjusting launch dates, etc.

Accept. When there is no acceptable option for addressing overall project risk, or if the risk is deemed to be within the acceptable limits, risk acceptance may be used. Passive acceptance implies that there is no action taken whereas active risk acceptance would involve developing a contingent response strategy and/or allocating contingency time or money.

Common Tools and Techniques:

Expert Judgment

Expertise may be leveraged from individuals with knowledge and experience in risk response planning.

Data Gathering Technique

Interviews may be structured, semi-structured, one-on-one, or with a group with risk owners in order to determine the best response for the identified risks.

Interpersonal and Team Skills

Facilitation improves the effectiveness of risk response planning meetings, guiding the participants to evaluate various options and determine the best solution or outcomes.

Data Analysis Techniques

There are two data analysis techniques that may be used to plan risk responses:

An *alternatives analysis* considers the various options and approaches for responding to the risks.

A *cost-benefit analysis* evaluates the risk responses in terms of the amount of money that would be needed to respond to the risk versus the financial or other impact if the risk occurred.

Decision-Making Techniques

A *multi-criteria decision analysis* can be used to evaluate risk response strategies against pre-determined and weighted criteria to make decisions. This technique may be revisited periodically depending on the effectiveness of the implemented response strategies.

Plan Risk Responses: Outputs

Common Outputs:

- **Change reques**ts - Change requests may be generated based on the planned risk responses. Change requests will be reviewed and approved through the **perform integrated change control** process.
- **Project management plan updates** - Based on the planned risk responses, the project management plan will be updated. Responses imply action, action is work, work is scope! Any changes to the project scope must be included in the scope baseline. Components of the project management plan that may be updated include: the schedule, cost, quality resource, and procurement management plans and the scope, schedule, and cost baselines.
- **Project document updates** - Project documents that may be updated because of planning the risk responses include the assumption log, the cost forecasts, the lessons learned register, the project schedule, the project team assignments, and the risk report. The risk register will now be updated with: the details of the chosen risk response strategies, the actions to implement the chosen strategies, the identified risk owners and their assigned responsibilities, the low priority risks that may be included on a "watch list" for ongoing monitoring, the triggers, residual risks and secondary risks, the fallback plans, and the contingency reserves.

*The **plan risk responses** process information is adapted from: PMBOK® Guide - Sixth Edition. Page 437-448*

Let's check your understanding of the risk responses. The answers to Exercise 10.3 are on page 289.

Exercise 10.3: Risk Responses

Match each action with the type of response it reflects. Each response will only be used once.

Avoid	Active Acceptance	Sharing
Transference	Exploitation	Acceptance
Mitigation	Enhancement	

1.	Acme Corp has entered into a joint venture partnership with XYZ Limited
2.	The high-risk project is cancelled
3.	The best-performing team has been assigned to the project
4.	The product being produced by the project may exceed the sales projections
5.	J&J Partners has requested a confidentiality/non-disclosure agreement with their vendor
6.	The project schedule has been compressed to ensure it will launch before the holiday season
7.	In the event the course materials do not reach the customer within the delivery window, the instructor will hand-carry the materials
8.	The project team lead has provided training to her back-up for her impending maternity leave

Implement Risk Responses

risk knowledge area | executing process group

This process is concerned with implementing the agreed-upon risk response plans to address overall risk exposure while minimizing threats and maximizing opportunities. Comprehensive risk management involves not only planning for and identifying risk, but also invoking responses to those risks.

While there is not a lot of detail in this process, you will be receiving questions on the implementation of the risk responses that were presented in the **plan risk responses** process. Again, 31% of your PMP exam questions are coming from the executing process group!

Implement Risk Responses: ITTOs

Inputs	Tools & Techniques	Outputs

1. Project management plan
  • Risk management plan
2. Project documents
  • Lessons learned register
  • Risk register
  • Risk report
3. Organizational process assets
	1. Expert judgment
	2. Interpersonal and team skills
	  • Influencing
	3. Project management information systems
		1. Change requests
		2. Project documents updates
		  • Issue log
		  • Lessons learned register
		  • Project team assignments
		  • Risk register
		  • Risk report

PMBOK® Guide   Sixth Edition. Page 449

Implement Risk Responses: Inputs

Common Inputs:

- **Project management plan** - As this process is conducted and revisited throughout the project, components of the project management plan may be leveraged such as the risk management plan.
- **Project documents** - Project documents leveraged for this process include the issue log, the risk register, and the risk report.
- **Organizational process assets** - Templates, policies and procedures, and historical information may be leveraged during risk response implementation.

Implement Risk Responses: Tools and Techniques

Common Tools and Techniques:

Expert Judgment

Expertise may be leveraged from individuals with knowledge and experience with the risk responses, specifically including the risk owners.

Interpersonal and Team Skills

One of the key interpersonal and team skills to be used during risk response implementation is *influencing*: motivating and compelling individuals to act when required. Because this process is concerned with implementing the previously identified risk responses, as the project manager, you will need to influence the team and the stakeholders regarding the implementation of those responses, the justification for the responses, and any associated actions that they may be responsible for taking.

Project Management Information System (PMIS)

The PMIS includes schedule, resource, and cost software that will be used during the implementation of the risk response plans.

Implement Risk Responses: Outputs

Common Outputs:

- **Change requests** - Change requests may be generated based on implementing the risk response plans. These changes will become an input to the **perform integrated change control** process.
- **Project document updates** - Project documents that may be updated include the issue log, the lessons learned register, the project team assignments, and the risk register and report.

*The **implement risk responses** process information is adapted from: PMBOK® Guide – Sixth Edition, Page 449-452*

Monitor Risks

risk knowledge area | monitoring and controlling process group

The **monitor risks** process will continuously identify and analyze risks and reanalyze the previously identified risks. This is the process where the team will determine the need for workarounds. As previously mentioned in this chapter, workarounds are responses to negative risk events that have occurred. Workarounds are completely reactive, not planned in advance. In addition, during this process, the team will:

- Monitor the trigger conditions
- Evaluate the effectiveness of the risk response strategies
- Evaluate the project assumptions to determine if they are still valid
- Analyze any risk trends
- Evaluate the risk management policies and procedures
- Modify the contingency reserves to correspond with the level of risk of the project

Monitor Risks: ITTOs

Inputs	Tools & Techniques	Outputs
1. Project management plan	1. Data analysis	1. Work performance information
• Risk management plan	• Technical performance analysis	2. Change requests
2. Project documents	• Reserve analysis	3. Project management plan updates
• Issue log	2. Audits	• Any component
• Lessons learned register	3. Meetings	4. Project documents updates
• Risk register		• Assumption log
• Risk report		• Issue log
3. Work performance data		• Lessons learned register
4. Work performance reports		• Risk register
		• Risk report
		5. Organizational process assets updates

PMBOK® Guide – Sixth Edition. Page 453

Monitor Risks: Inputs

Work Performance Reports

Work performance reports, also known as status reports or sit reps, provide detailed information as to the current status of the project. The work performance reports detail information such as variance analysis, earned value data, and forecasting data.

Common Inputs:

- **Project management plan** - This ongoing process will leverage the project management plan and specifically, the risk management plan.

- **Project documents** - Project documents used to monitor risks include the issue log, the lessons learned register, and the risk register and report.

- **Work performance data** - Work performance data is the raw measurements and information coming from the execution of the project activities. This data will be used to monitor the effectiveness of the risk processes.

Monitor Risks: Tools and Techniques

Audits

Risk audits examine and document the effectiveness of risk responses in dealing with identified risks and their root causes and the effectiveness of the risk management processes. The risk audits may be included during routine project review meetings or separate risk audit meetings may be held. Ultimately, it is the responsibility of the project manager to ensure the audits happen. They may be conducted by the project team or by an external party.

Common Tools and Techniques:

Data Analysis Techniques

There are two data analysis techniques that may be used to monitor the risks:

A *technical performance analysis* compares technical accomplishments during project execution to the project management plan's schedule of technical achievement. Trends in the project's execution are reviewed using performance data and earned value analysis. Any deviations from the baseline plan may indicate the potential impact of threats or opportunities and can help to forecast the degree of success in achieving the project's scope. Variance and trend analysis may expose the degree of technical risk faced by the project.

A *reserve analysis* compares the amount of the contingency reserves to the amount of risk remaining to determine if the remaining reserve is adequate. If the project has become more defined with less risk, the contingency should be reduced, and any remaining funds should be allocated back to the organization. In some situations of increased risk, the project manager may need to request additional contingency funding.

Meetings

Common meetings during risk monitoring include risk reviews. These risk review meetings are scheduled on a regular basis and evaluate and document the effectiveness of the project's risk management activities, reassess existing risks, close risks that are obsolete, review issues from realized risk, and identify lessons learned. These meetings may give rise to new risks, which would then be evaluated and responded to through the previous risk processes. The risk review meeting may be a component of the project status meeting or held as a stand-alone meeting.

Having risk as a standing agenda item at your team meeting is the best way to monitor the project risk landscape.

Monitor Risks: Outputs

Common Outputs:

- **Work performance information** - Work performance information, analyzed work performance data, will provide insight into the effectiveness of risk responses and current deviations because of realized risks.
- **Change requests** - Change requests may be generated based on monitoring the project risks. These changes will become an input to the **perform integrated change control** process.
- **Project management plan updates** - As project risks are monitored throughout the project life cycle, any component of the project management plan may need to be updated.
- **Project document updates** - Project documents that may be updated include the assumption and issue logs, the lessons learned register, and the risk register and report.
- **Organizational process assets updates** - Organizational assets that may be updated include the risk breakdown structure and any templates for the risk management plan, risk register, and risk report.

*The **monitor risks** process information is adapted from: PMBOK® Guide - Sixth Edition. Page 453-458*

Chapter 10 – Answer Key

Exercise 10.1: Decision Tree for Schedule Risk

The estimated or expected duration is 11.5 days

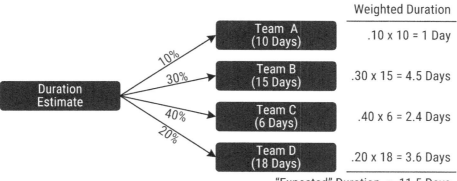

Exercise 10.2: Decision Tree for EMV Analysis

For Product A: There is a 20% chance that it will be poorly received by the market at a loss of $10,000, a 50% chance that it will be well-received by the market at an increased profit of $20,000, and a __30%__ chance that it will exceed market expectations at an increased profit of $50,000.

.2 x ($10,000) = ($2,000)

.5 x $20,000 = $10,000

.3 x $50,000 = $15,000

EMV = $23,000

What is the total value? **$23,000 EMV + $30,000 initial estimate = $53,000 total value**

For Product B: There is a 40% chance that it will be poorly received by the market at a loss of $20,000, a __30%__ chance that it will be well-received by the market at an increased profit of $30,000, and a 30% chance that it will exceed market expectations at an increased profit of $40,000.

.4 x ($20,000) = ($8,000)

.3 x $30,000 = $9,000

.3 x $40,000 = $12,000

EMV = $13,000

What is the total value? **$13,000 EMV + $50,000 initial estimate = $63,000 total value**

Exercise 10.3: Risk Responses

1. Sharing
2. Avoid
3. Enhancement
4. Acceptance

5. Transference
6. Exploitation
7. Active Acceptance
8. Mitigation

Chapter 10 - Review Questions

1. Along with your sponsor, you are working with your key stakeholders regarding the approach to risk management on the construction project. After extended discussion, one of your key stakeholders approaches you to discuss their concerns. She states that renovating the work area of her team will be extremely disruptive and she is concerned that if the work is not completed on time, it will have a negative impact on her team during the busy holiday season. What should you do next?

   A. Escalate the situation to the project sponsor to determine if the project can be rescheduled
   B. Provide the stakeholder with a copy of the risk register
   C. Communicate to the other key stakeholders that the risk threshold is any schedule delay
   D. Document that the stakeholder has minimal risk tolerance for any schedule delays

2. The risk management plan has been completed and approved by the key stakeholders. You are working with your team to identify risks to the project and are performing a qualitative risk analysis. The objective of the qualitative risk analysis is to:

   A. Assess the impact and likelihood of the identified risks
   B. Prioritize the identified risks for further analysis or for response
   C. Determine if the risk responses have been implemented as planned
   D. Select alternative strategies for dealing with risks

3. You were assigned the strategic development project which is your first large project for your new organization. You carefully documented the risk management plan, identified the project risks, analyzed the risks both qualitatively and quantitatively, and planned your risk responses. What did you do wrong?

   A. You did not engage your team, stakeholders, and other potential information sources in your risk processes
   B. Nothing, all processes were completed per the *PMBOK® Guide* recommendations
   C. Quantitative risk analysis was not necessary
   D. You did not work with your sponsor to identify the risks

4. There was a software risk associated with the infrastructure project. To mitigate the risk, you leveraged a software provider that has been known to be compatible with your organization's systems. However, upon install, you realize that the new software is causing a major problem. What is the next thing you do?

   A. Implement the contingent response strategy
   B. Implement the residual risk plan
   C. Implement the risk mitigation strategy
   D. Implement the fallback plan

5. You are the Project Manager of ABC project. The project is being executed in an earthquake-prone area. To take care of this you buy insurance for earthquakes. This is an example of:

   A. Risk mitigation
   B. Transfer of risk
   C. Risk contingency planning
   D. Accepting the consequences passively

6. You are the project manager of ABC project. One of the risks that have been identified is attrition of team members. Mid-way through the project you notice that the morale and motivation of the team members is going down. You think that this is a precursor to people leaving the organization. For this risk, low motivation is an example of a:

   A. Work-around
   B. Trigger
   C. Risk monitoring
   D. Risk planning

7. You are managing the project of planning a party for your company employees. There is a risk that the employees will not come to the party. You decide to not take any action against this as the likelihood of this is low. Which risk response strategy are you following?

   A. Acceptance
   B. Avoidance
   C. Mitigation
   D. Transference

8. **Which of the following is a true statement about risks?**

    A. If a risk is identified in a risk response plan, then that means that risk has already happened
    B. Once a risk has happened, you refer to the risk management plan to determine what action needs to be taken
    C. A risk that was not planned but has happened is called a trigger
    D. Risk identification happens in all phases of the project

9. **The organization is very sensitive to any risk impacting the project budget or schedule. You are working with your team and subject matter experts to conduct a quantitative risk analysis on the identified risks. Which statement is least accurate?**

    A. The output of quantitative risk analysis techniques are typically probability distributions
    B. A Monte Carlo simulation takes into consideration both cost and schedule risks
    C. A tornado diagram only represents schedule risk data
    D. Decisions trees are used for both schedule and cost risks

10. **This is the process of analyzing the effect of identified risks on overall project objectives, assigning a numerical rating to those risks individually or evaluating the aggregate effect of all risks affecting the project, and presents an approach to making decisions in the presence of uncertainty.**

    A. Perform qualitative risk analysis
    B. Perform quantitative risk analysis
    C. Control quality
    D. Perform quality management

11. **There is a meeting in Europe for the organization's senior leadership team. To reduce the risk associated with having the executives all on one plane, you send no more than two executives on the same flight. What risk strategy are you using?**

    A. Risk avoidance
    B. Risk transference
    C. Active risk acceptance
    D. Risk mitigation

12. **There is a potential opportunity if your product is first to market. You decide to team up with another business in order to increase the chances that you will make it to market first. What risk strategy are you using?**

    A. Enhancement
    B. Sharing
    C. Exploitation
    D. Teaming agreement

13. **Mitigation is to threats as _____ is to opportunities.**

    A. Enhancement
    B. Exploitation
    C. Acceptance
    D. Tolerance

14. **Upon discussion with the work package owner you learn that based on the vendor used, there are four potential durations for the work. There is a 20% chance of using a local vendor, with a duration of 12 days; a 30% chance of using a domestic vendor, with a duration of 18 days; a 10% chance of using an international vendor, with a duration of 27 days; the remaining possibility is to do the work in-house, with a duration of 15 days. What is the best estimate to use?**

    A. 16 days
    B. 17 days
    C. 10.5 days
    D. 11 days

15. You have been presented with three options for purchasing materials for your project. Option A will cost $40,000. With Option A, there is a 30% probability additional support will cost $12,000 and 70% probability additional support will cost $18,000. Option B will cost $38,000. With Option B, there is a 60% probability additional support will cost $15,000 and a 40% probability additional support will cost $30,000. Option C will cost $25,000. With Option C, there is a 75% probability additional support will cost $18,000 and a 25% probability additional support will cost $40,000. There is a 30% probability the organization will pursue Option A and a 40% probability the organization will pursue Option C. Based on the probability of the selection process, what is the value of Option B?

    A. $21,000
    B. $11,400
    C. $59,000
    D. $17,700

Review Question Answers

1. **Answer: D**

   The most appropriate response would be to document the risk tolerance. Escalating to the sponsor for rescheduling would not be appropriate because the schedule has been developed and based on the existing schedule the project will launch before the holiday season. Providing the stakeholder with a copy of the risk register will not have an effect on the situation. Communicating that any schedule delay is the risk threshold would also not be appropriate, as there could be situations of schedule delay that are able to be managed.

2. **Answer: B**

   While the identified risks will be evaluated for impact and likelihood during qualitative risk analysis, the objective of doing so is to prioritize the risks. Qualitative analysis does not evaluate if risk responses have been implemented as planned.

3. **Answer: A**

   It would be impossible for the project manager to be able to fully and accurately identify and assess all risks impacting the project and it is important that other individuals are leveraged for their knowledge and experience.

4. **Answer: D**

   Because you already took a proactive response, the next step would be to implement the fallback plan. Fallback plans are used when the original response is not effective. Contingent response strategies are used only if the risk event occurs. In this scenario, if the risk was deemed to be a lower impact, a contingent response strategy would have been utilized instead of a proactive mitigation approach. Residual risk plan is not a recognized term. The mitigation strategy was already used.

5. **Answer: B**

   Shifting the negative impact to a third party is considered risk transference.

6. **Answer: B**

   The low motivation is a pre-cursor event to people leaving the organization. As such, it is considered a trigger.

7. **Answer: A**

   Because you are taking no action, this is considered risk acceptance. Avoidance would have meant eliminating the risk – such as cancelling your company party. Mitigation would have meant decreasing the risk – such as providing transportation or other incentives. Transference would have meant shifting the negative impact – such as some type of cancellation policy on the party venue.

8. **Answer: D**

   Risk identification is not a "one-and-done" type of activity. Risk identification is occurring throughout all phases of your project. Risks are identified in the risk register, not the response plan. The risk register will detail the actions to be taken if the risk occurs, not the risk management plan. The risk management plan is focused on how risk management will be approached overall. A trigger is a pre-cursor event that means a risk is about to or has occurred.

9. **Answer: C**

   Tornado diagrams only display cost risk data, not schedule risk data. Monte Carlo simulations and decision trees can evaluate both cost and schedule implications. A probability distribution, showing the uncertainties in the identified variables, is a common way to display data from these quantitative risk analysis techniques.

10. **Answer: B**

    This is describing the perform quantitative risk analysis process. Quantitative risk analysis assigns a numerical rating (cost and/or schedule) and then aggregates the values in order to assess the potential cost and schedule risk impact. Quantitative analysis can also aid in decision making, such as by using decisions trees and expected monetary value.

11. **Answer: D**

    Because they are "reducing" the risk, this would be risk mitigation. Mitigation reduces the probability and/or the impact.

12. **Answer: B**

The act of partnering with a vendor to pursue an opportunity (a positive risk) would be risk sharing. This can also serve to enhance the opportunity, but because they mention a relationship with a vendor, it is considered risk sharing.

13. **Answer: A**

Mitigation decreases the probability and/or impact of a negative risk while enhancement increases the probability and/or impact of a positive risk.

14. **Answer: B**

.2 x 12 = 2.4

.3 x 18 = 5.4

.1 x 27 = 2.7

.4 x 15 = 6 (Because the sum of the probabilities of the prior three options only equals 60%, there must be a 40% probability for the fourth option. The sum of the probabilities always adds up to 100%).

2.4 + 5.4 + 2.7 + 6 = 16.5 (rounded up to 17 for the best answer)

15. **Answer: D**

Because of the length of this question, it is important to skip to the end of the question to see what they are asking about. This is especially important prior to doing extensive mathematical problems.

The question only asks about the value of Option B.

The first step would be to determine the probability Option B will occur:

Option A = 30% probability

Option C = 40% probability

Option B must be a 30% probability

The next step would be to determine the expected monetary value and the total value based on the information provided:

For Option B:

Original estimate = $38,000

(.6 x $15,000 = $9,000) + (.4 x $30,000 = $12,000) = $21,000 (EMV)

$38,000 + $21,000 = $59,000 (Total Value)

The last step would be to multiply the total value by the probability of Option B occurring:

.3 x $59,000 = $17,700

Chapter 10 - Vocabulary Review

* Contingent response strategy	* Residual risk	* Risk register
* Decision tree	* Risk acceptance	+ Risk sharing
* Expected monetary value analysis	* Risk avoidance	* Risk transference
* Fallback plan	* Risk breakdown structure	* Root cause analysis
* Monte Carlo simulation	+ Risk enhancement	* Secondary risk
* Opportunity	+ Risk exploitation	* SWOT analysis
+ Probability distribution	+ Risk impact	* Threat
* Probability / impact matrix	* Risk mitigation	* Tornado diagram
* Project risk	+ Risk probability	* Trigger

1. _____ A diagram to compare available alternatives and their implications

2. _____ Analysis of strengths, weaknesses, opportunities, and threats of an organization, project, or option

3. _____ A documented plan of action to be used when the primary risk response is inadequate

4. _____ A risk that remains after risk responses have been implemented

5. _____ An uncertain event that, if it occurs, will have a positive impact on project objectives

6. _____ An uncertain event that, if it occurs, has a positive or negative effect on a project's objectives

7. _____ A risk response planning technique that shifts the impact of a threat to a third party, together with ownership of the response

8. _____ A risk response planning technique that involves partnering with another team or organization to improve the probability of realizing an opportunity

9. _____ A risk response planning technique that involves changing the project plan to improve the probability of an opportunity occurring

10. _____ A risk response planning technique that indicates that the project team has decided not to change the project management plan to proactively address a risk

11. _____ A table or an equation that links each outcome of a statistical experiment with its probability of occurrence.

12. _____ An analytical technique used to determine the basic underlying reason that causes a variance or a defect or a risk

13.		A special type of bar chart used in a sensitivity analysis for comparing the relative cost impact of risks
14.		A grid for mapping the probability of each risk occurrence and its impact on project objectives if that risk occurs
15.		The likelihood that a specific risk will occur
16.		A statistical technique that calculates the average outcome when the future includes scenarios that may or may not happen
17.		The potential effect a risk might have on a project objective
18.		A risk response planning technique for a threat that creates changes to the project management plan that are meant to either eliminate the risk or to protect the project objectives from its impact
19.		A risk that arises as a direct result of implementing a risk response
20.		A risk response planning technique, associated with threats, that seeks to reduce the probability of occurrence or impact of a risk to below an acceptable threshold
21.		A computerized mathematical technique that computes or iterates the project cost or project schedule numerous times using input values to calculate a distribution of possible total project cost or completion dates
22.		A hierarchically organized depiction of the identified project risks arranged by risk category and subcategory that identifies the various areas and causes of potential risks
23.		A risk response strategy that is planned in advance and only executed under certain predefined conditions
24.		An indication that a risk has occurred or is about to occur
25.		A risk response planning technique that involves changing the project plan to ensure realization of an opportunity
26.		An uncertain event that, if it occurs, will have a negative effect on the project objectives
27.		The document containing details of all the identified project risks

* These definitions are taken from the Glossary of *PMBOK® Guide – Sixth Edition*

+ These definitions are taken from: Project Management Institute, *A Guide to the Project Management Body of Knowledge, (PMBOK® Guide) – Sixth Edition*, Project Management Institute Inc., 2017, 317, 337, 345, 346.

Vocabulary Review Answers

1. Decision tree
2. SWOT analysis
3. Fallback plan
4. Residual risk
5. Opportunity
6. Project risk
7. Risk transference
8. Risk sharing
9. Risk enhancement
10. Risk acceptance
11. Probability distribution
12. Root cause analysis
13. Tornado diagram
14. Probability/impact matrix
15. Risk probability
16. Expected monetary value analysis
17. Risk impact
18. Risk avoidance
19. Secondary risk
20. Risk mitigation
21. Monte Carlo simulation
22. Risk breakdown structure
23. Contingent response strategy
24. Trigger
25. Risk exploitation
26. Threat
27. Risk register

Chapter 11

Project Communication Management

What's in This Chapter

- Project Communication Management
- Plan Communications Management
- Manage Communications
- Monitor Communications

Project Communication Management

An often-quoted statistic is that approximately 90% of a project manager's job is communication. Depending on your business, your industry, and your project, that can easily hold true for many project managers. Project managers ultimately manage change and oftentimes are not the person making the technical change, but rather preparing the organization, the users, and the clients for that change. That preparation comes through effective communication.

In this chapter, we will present the communication processes which on the surface will appear very simple and straight-forward. However, do not slip into the comfort zone when studying them! Truly take the time to understand these processes and the underlying impact of them. When considering project communication for the exam, always know the PMI-perspective and the preferred approach. In some situations, this may feel a bit uncomfortable, especially if you work in a very hierarchical/title-conscious organization or in an environment that tends to be passive-aggressive. Remember: direct communication is always best.

In project management, there are several communication dimensions. These dimensions include:

- An internal focus on stakeholders within the project and the organization
- An external focus on external stakeholders
- Formal communications such as reports, agendas, and briefings
- Informal communications such as emails, social media, and ad hoc communications
- A hierarchical focus, including upward to senior management, downward to the team, and horizontal to peers
- Official communications such as annual reports and reports to regulators or government agencies

- Unofficial communications such as those communications that establish and build the profile and recognition of the project, between the team and the stakeholders
- Written and oral communication

Communication refers to the exchange of information. That exchange may be intended, or it may be involuntary. For example, I had a student in class who was distracted, not punctual, and on her phone through much of the lecture. She was communicating to me that she was not engaged nor interested in the material and perhaps that she did not take her exam preparation seriously.

After further discussions with her, I learned that her mother had become very ill and she was attempting to facilitate her care. She did, in fact, want to succeed on her exam as the PMP credential was a condition of employment. Intended versus involuntary communication speaks volumes. Her involuntary communication gave me the message she did not care. Consider yourself: what involuntary communications do you transmit?

As a project manager, not only do you need to seek out clues as to the feelings, perspectives, and opinions of others, you must be very cautious as to what you are communicating, especially involuntarily.

Information exchange can occur through various channels:

- Physical or electronic writing
- Face-to-face or remote speaking
- Formal or informal methods, such as research papers or social media
- Body language, including tone of voice, posture, eye contact, expressions
- Media such as pictures, videos, or memes
- Word choice, which can be very important in cross-cultural or global teams

For communication to be successful, the appropriate communication strategy needs to be employed, and the appropriate messages need to be conveyed. The project communications, the messages, are supported by efforts to prevent misunderstandings and miscommunication. This means that the methods, messengers, and messages must be mindful and deliberate.

There are some practices that can be used to improve your communication, including to the 5Cs of written communication partnered with effective communication skills. For traditional written or spoken messages (not tweeting or other social media channels), here are the 5Cs:

1. Correct grammar and spelling – poor grammar and spelling are not only distracting it sends a message that you are uneducated, sloppy, or lazy. Today's word processing systems have spell-check and grammar-check. Use them!

2. Concise expression and elimination of excess words – do not use 100 words for what you can say in three. Keep your messages concise and to-the-point. Small bites of information resonate best.

3. Clear purpose and expression directed to the needs of the reader – what are you trying to convey and why does the recipient need the information? Make it clear.

4. Coherent, logical flow of ideas – do not meander through your message. Use clear statements in an order that allows the recipient to understand what is being conveyed.

5. Controlling flow of words and ideas – what will convey your message the best? Maybe it is a picture. Maybe it's a chart. Maybe it's a few bullet points.

And when all else fails, remember KISS: keep it simple, sweetheart. Flowery language, technical jargon, and unrecognizable vocabulary does not convey your message well.

Trends in Communication

One of the most disruptive trends in communication is advancing technology; whether it's real-time video meetings such as a Zoom call or emojis in a text message, we are inundated with communication 24 hours a day. These advances allow us better insight into the intentions of the message that we could not as easily discern with a written memo or even an email. Emojis, although debatable from a professional perspective, convey messages and feelings with an image. And the human brain likes images! As a project manager, having attendees in your meetings that were on their phone was considered rude and distracting. Now, your attendees may be taking notes on your message or tweeting about your awesome presentation. Project managers need to learn to work with communication technology versus working against it.

With agile and adaptive techniques going more mainstream and expanding beyond software development, we are seeing that stakeholders are getting more and more entrenched in project work and project activities. The days of the "us-them" mentality are waning. It used to be that requirements were thrown over the fence and an attempt to fulfill the requirements was thrown back. Inclusive collaboration with stakeholders is being found to improve the processes and the likelihood of project success and acceptance.

A key consideration in project communication management is ensuring that all entitled parties receive updated and transparent communication regarding the status of the project, any changes, and any trends. Bad news is better than no news, especially when it comes to managing expectations. Be cautious of scenario questions where the sponsor or another key stakeholder is advising you against distributing project information. You cannot withhold information from entitled parties.

There are three processes associated with project communication management that will be discussed in this chapter:

Plan Communications Management. This process in the planning process group documents the approach to project communications, creating the communications management plan.

Manage Communications. This process in the executing process group ensures the timely creation, distribution, management, and disposition of project information.

Monitor Communications. This process in the monitoring and controlling process groups ensure that the communication is effective and the stakeholders' communication needs are met.

Plan Communications Management

communication knowledge area | planning process group

The **plan communications management** process is usually completed early in the project, however, as the project changes the need for communication may change, and the project manager must be monitoring communication effectiveness throughout the project.

Communications planning determines:

- Who needs information?
- What exactly do they need?
- When and at what frequency do they need it?
- Why do they need it?
- What will it be used for?
- Who will be providing it?

Other considerations when planning communications include time zone differences, language barriers, cross-cultural considerations. As project manager, there are several communication skills common to general business management and project management:

- Listening actively and effectively
- Questioning and probing ideas and situations to ensure better understanding
- Educating to increase the team's knowledge so they can be more effective
- Fact-finding to identify or confirm information
- Setting and managing expectations
- Persuading a person, a team, or an organization to perform an action
- Motivating to provide encouragement or reassurance
- Coaching to improve performance and achieve desired results
- Negotiating to achieve mutually acceptable agreements between parties
- Resolving conflict to prevent disruptive impacts
- Summarizing, recapping, and identifying next steps

Plan Communications Management: ITTOs

Inputs	Tools & Techniques	Outputs
1. Project charter	1. Expert judgment	1. Communications management plan
2. Project management plan	2. Communication requirements analysis	2. Project management plan updates
• Resource management plan	3. Communication technology	• Stakeholder engagement plan
• Stakeholder engagement plan	4. Communication models	3. Project documents updates
3. Project documents	5. Communication methods	• Project schedule
• Requirements documentation	6. Interpersonal and team skills	• Stakeholder register
• Stakeholder register	• Communication styles assessment	
4. Enterprise environmental factors	• Political awareness	
5. Organizational process assets	• Cultural awareness	
	7. Data representation	
	• Stakeholder engagement assessment matrix	
	8. Meetings	

PMBOK® Guide – Sixth Edition. Page 366

Plan Communications Management: Inputs

Common Inputs:

- **Project management plan** - As this process is conducted and revisited throughout the project, the project management plan, including the resource and stakeholder engagement plans, will be leveraged.
- **Project documents** - Project documents used to plan communications for the project include the requirements documentation and the stakeholder register.
- **Enterprise environmental factors** - Internal and external influences that may be considered include the organizational culture, political climate, personnel policies, stakeholder risk thresholds, established communication channels and systems, and the location of resources and facilities.
- **Organizational process assets** - Templates, policies and procedures, and historical information will be leveraged to plan the project communications.

Plan Communications Management: Tools and Techniques

Communication Requirements Analysis

Based on the stakeholder analysis and management strategy, the project manager and project team can conduct an analysis of the communication needs of the stakeholders. Some things to evaluate when analyzing the communication requirements:

- Organization charts
- Stakeholder responsibilities and relationships
- Departments and specialties involved in the project
- Logistics of project personnel
- Internal and external information needs
- Pertinent stakeholder information
- Legal requirements

In previous versions of the PMP exam, candidates would be asked periodically to calculate communication channels. However, I have not received any evidence that the candidates are being tested on the channel calculation for 6th edition. But to err on the side of caution, the communication channels formula is $n(n-1)/2$, where "n" represents the number of stakeholders, including yourself as the project manager. The communication channels formula simply illustrates the number of paths or channels that your messages will travel on. Needless to say, the higher the number of channels, the higher the risk for misunderstanding.

Communication Technology

Communication technology encompasses the modes and methods used to transfer information among stakeholders. As I discussed at the start of this chapter, there is a large array of communication technology options! As the project manager, you will need to evaluate your team and your environment to determine what is most appropriate. For some groups, robust communication suites will be ideal, whereas other teams may function better with a whiteboard in a job area.

Technology factors that can affect the selection of technology include:

- Urgency of the need for information
- Availability and reliability of technology
- Ease of use
- The project environment
- Sensitivity and confidentiality of the information

Communication Models

The general communication model includes the following components:

- Sender – the individual that needs to convey a message
- Receiver – the intended recipient of that message
- The message – what the sender intends to convey
- Encoding and decoding – the interpretation of the message
- The medium – the method in which the message is conveyed
- Noise – biases, perspectives, and conditions that may impact the receiver's decoding of the message
- Acknowledge – upon receipt of the message, the receiver may signal (acknowledge) receipt of the message, but this does not necessarily mean agreement with or comprehension of the message

- Feedback / response – when the received message has been decoded and understood, the receiver encodes thoughts and ideas into a message and then transmits this message to the original sender

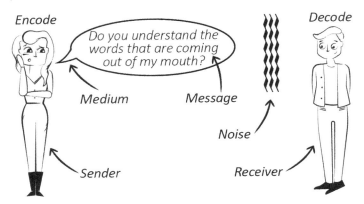

It's not just about relaying the appropriate information but confirming that the information was received appropriately and as intended.

Communication Methods

There are several communication methods that can be used to share project information. Generally, those methods fall into three categories: interactive, push, and pull.

Interactive communication. Interactive communication is the most efficient method of communication to ensure a common understanding as it is real time. Interactive communication should be used when an immediate response is required and/or when the communication is sensitive. Interactive communication methods include meetings, phone calls, and video conferences.

Push communication. Push communication is communication delivered by the sender to the recipients. While the communication can be confirmed that it was sent, it does not necessarily mean it was received and understood. Push communication should be used when the recipients need the information, but it does not require an immediate response, and/or the communication is non-urgent or not sensitive in nature. It is primarily used for the reporting of status through work performance reports. Push communication methods include email and voice-mail.

Pull communication. Pull communication is a communication method that provides access to the information however the receiver must proactively retrieve the information. Pull communication should be used when the communication is informational only and/or when there are very large volumes of information or very large audiences. Pull communication methods include posting information to a website, a knowledge repository, or a bulletin board.

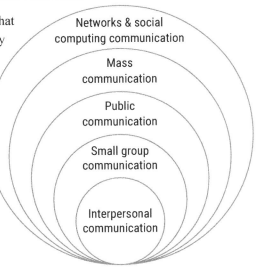

Communication, like project management, is not a one-size-fits-all approach. The communication content and delivery should be adjusted to reflect the needs of the major communication audiences.

Common Tools and Techniques:

Expert Judgment

Expert judgment from individuals with specialized knowledge or expertise may be used to assist in developing the communication management plan.

Interpersonal and Team Skills

A *communication styles assessment* is used to assess communication styles in order to identify the most appropriate communication method, format and content. This assessment may be appropriate if the project manager has unsupportive stakeholders and there is a need to increase their engagement.

Political awareness concerns the recognition of both formal and informal power relations. By understanding the structures, who wields power, and the strategies of the organization, the project manager can more effectively plan project communications.

Cultural awareness is an understanding of the differences between individuals, groups, and organizations. The project manager will need to tailor communications appropriately with this awareness and to reflect these differences. This is true for global projects but can also come into play with regional differences.

Data Representation Techniques

A *stakeholder engagement assessment matrix* is used to evaluate the stakeholders and the difference or gap between their current level of engagement and their desired level of engagement. With this understanding, the project manager can adapt their communications to influence the engagement of the stakeholders.

Meetings

Meetings, in-person or virtual, may be used to discuss and determine the best approach to project communication management for the project.

Plan Communications Management: Outputs

Communications Management Plan

The key output from the **plan communications management** process is the communications management plan. The communication plan is one of your most valuable tools as a project manager. This allows you to manage the expectations of your stakeholder audience and your team, allowing you to keep them engaged and increase trust. A subsidiary plan, the communications management plan includes:

- Stakeholder communications requirements
- Format, content, and level of detail of information to be communicated
- Person responsible for communicating the information
- Person or groups who will receive the information
- Methods or technologies used to convey the information
- Frequency of communication
- Escalation process
- Glossary of common terminology and acronyms

Common Outputs:

- **Project management plan updates** - The project management plan may be updated, including the resource management plan and the cost baseline.
- **Project document updates** - Project documents that may be updated through communication planning include the lessons learned register, the project schedule, the resource breakdown structure and resource requirements, and the risk and the stakeholder registers.

*The **plan communications management** process information is adapted from: PMBOK® Guide – Sixth Edition. Page 366-378*

Manage Communications

communication knowledge area | executing process group

The **manage communications** process creates, collects, distributes, stores, and retrieves project information and disseminates the information to the stakeholders based on the communication plan. This also may include the distribution of information under unplanned circumstances. While managing project communications, the project manager will leverage a number of different techniques that we have previously discussed, including:

- sender-receiver models
- choice of media
- writing style
- meeting management techniques and presentations
- facilitation techniques
- active listening

Manage Communications: ITTOs

Inputs	Tools & Techniques	Outputs
1. Project management plan	1. Communication technology	1. Project communications
• Resource management plan	2. Communication methods	2. Project management plan updates
• Communications management plan	3. Communication skills	• Communications management plan
• Stakeholder engagement plan	• Communication competence	• Stakeholder engagement plan
2. Project documents	• Feedback	3. Project documents updates
• Change log	• Nonverbal	• Issue log
• Issue log	• Presentations	• Lessons learned register
• Lessons learned register	4. Project management information system	• Project schedule
• Quality report	5. Project reporting	• Risk register
• Risk report	6. Interpersonal and team skills	• Stakeholder register
• Stakeholder register	• Active listening	4. Organizational process assets updates
3. Work performance reports	• Conflict management	
4. Enterprise environmental factors	• Cultural awareness	
5. Organizational process assets	• Meeting management	
	• Networking	
	• Political awareness	
	7. Meetings	

PMBOK® Guide – Sixth Edition, Page 379

Manage Communications: Inputs

Work Performance Reports

Work performance reports are distributed to the project stakeholders as a component of managing the communications. The work performance reports detail the current status of the project, earned value calculations and variance analyses, and risk summaries. These work performance reports can take many forms, depending on the organization and the industry. Report formats include dashboards, stop light charts, and heat reports. The objective is to increase awareness and generate decisions.

Common Inputs:

- **Project management plan** - As this process is conducted and revisited throughout the project, components of the project management plan may be leveraged such as the resource management plan, the communications management plan, and the stakeholder engagement plan.
- **Project documents** - Project documents leveraged while managing communications include change and issue logs, the lessons learned register, the quality and risk reports, and the stakeholder register.
- **Enterprise environmental factors** - Internal and external influences to be considered may include the organizational culture, personnel policies, stakeholder risk thresholds, global, regional, or local trends, and the geographic distribution of resources.
- **Organizational process assets** - Templates, policies and procedures, and historical information may be leveraged to manage the project communications.

Manage Communications: Tools and Techniques

Communication Technology

There are many communication technology options available to project managers. Size, location, project length, and human factors should be considered when selecting the most appropriate technology to employ.

Communication Methods

Communication methods generally include interactive, push, and pull. These can include meetings, video conferences, email, and other communication methods.

Communication Skills

There are several communication skills that the project manager can use to ensure accurate and effective communication with the project team and the project stakeholders. These can include communication competence, receiving and providing feedback openly and honestly, nonverbal communication methods, and the use of presentations. A presentation is a technique of providing formal information to the stakeholders regarding the project's progress, background information, general information on the project, or specific information that needs to be delivered to raise awareness. To be successful, presentations need to meet the needs and expectations of the audience and the needs and objectives of the project and the project team.

Belinda's Hint

How effective are your presentations? Have your attendees suffered Death by PowerPoint? How about Death by Meeting?

Confidence, clarity, and brevity are key skills. A great book on the topic is "Death by Meeting" by Pat Lencioni.

If you are nervous presenting in front of groups, try and get involved with a speaking group such as Toastmasters or check out your local National Speakers Association (NSA) Chapter.

Project Reporting

Project reporting provides information to the project stakeholders at an appropriate level for each audience. The format and detail may vary depending on the project, industry, and stakeholder needs.

Common Tools and Techniques:

Interpersonal and Team Skills

There are several interpersonal and team skills that will be used to manage the project communications:

Active listening involves acknowledging, clarifying and confirming, understanding, and removing barriers that adversely affect comprehensive communication. Listening to understand versus listening to respond!

Conflict management is the effective facilitation and resolution of disputes and differences of opinions using various techniques. Remember conflict in and of itself is not bad, it is how we handle conflict that can become disruptive and damaging.

Cultural awareness is an understanding of the differences between individuals, groups, and organizations. This includes company cultures, regional differences, generational differences, and other factors.

Meeting management is the facilitation of effective meetings. Typically, this should include: preparing and distributing the agenda prior to the meeting, ensuring that the meeting starts and finishes on time, ensure the right participants are invited and attend, stay on-topic during the meeting, manage issues and expectations during the meeting, and recording all action items and follow-ups.

Networking is interacting with others to exchange information and develop contacts.

Political awareness assists the project manager in engaging stakeholders appropriately to maintain their support throughout the project.

Project Management Information System (PMIS)

The PMIS includes any standard tools for the project manager to capture and share information with the stakeholders regarding the project's progress in a consolidated or standard manner.

Meetings

Meetings are used throughout the project and are a key component of managing project communication.

Manage Communications: Outputs

Project Communications

The project communications may include performance reports, deliverable status, schedule progress, and cost incurred to-date on the project. The communications may vary based on the audience needs, urgency and impact, method of delivery, and level of confidentiality.

Belinda's Hint

Some of the questions on the PMP exam will ask, "what is the next thing" or "what is the best thing" a project manager should do in the scenario. Oftentimes, the best answer is to "check the plan first."

For example, if the PM is asked to modify the performance report, the PM should check the plan first to see how that request should be handled. The communication plan may advise that the organization's standard performance report template must be used, with no modifications allowed. Check the plan first before taking action or making changes!

Common Outputs:

- **Project management plan updates** - The project management plan may be updated, including the communications management and stakeholder engagement plans.
- **Project document updates** - Project documents that may be updated through communication management include the issue log, the lessons learned, risk, and stakeholder registers, and the project schedule.
- **OPA updates** - Organizational assets that may be updated while managing communications include the project records, meeting minutes, planned and ad hoc project reports and presentations.

*The **manage communications** process information is adapted from: PMBOK® Guide – Sixth Edition. Page 379-388*

Monitor Communications

communications knowledge area | monitoring and controlling process group

The **monitor communications** process monitors communications throughout the entire project life cycle in order to ensure the information needs of the stakeholders are met and to ensure an optimal flow of communication among all participants. If the current communication process is not effective, it may be necessary to revisit the previous communication processes of **plan communication management** and **manage communications**.

Monitor Communications: ITTOs

Inputs	Tools & Techniques	Outputs

1. Project management plan
  • Resource management plan
  • Communications management plan
  • Stakeholder engagement plan
2. Project documents
  • Issue log
  • Lessons learned register
  • Project communications
3. Work performance data
4. Enterprise environmental factors
5. Organizational process assets
	1. Expert judgment
	  • Communication technology
	2. Project management information system
	3. Data analysis
	  • Stakeholder engagement assessment matrix
	4. Interpersonal and team skills
	  • Observation/ conversation
	5. Meetings
		1. Work performance information
		2. Change requests
		3. Project management plan updates
		  • Communications management plan
		  • Stakeholder engagement plan
		4. Project documents updates
		  • Issue log
		  • Lessons learned register
		  • Stakeholder register

Monitor Communications: Inputs

Common Inputs:

- **Project management plan** - As communications are monitored throughout the project, the project management plan, including the resource management, communications management, and the stakeholder engagement plans may be referenced.
- **Project documents** - Project documents leveraged for monitoring communications includes the issue log, the lessons learned register, and the project communications.
- **Work performance data** - Work performance data is the raw data from the project executing that will be analyzed against the project baselines.
- **Enterprise environmental factors** - Internal and external influences considered may include the organizational culture, political climate, established communication channels, tools, and systems, global or regional trends, and the geographic distribution of resources and facilities.
- **Organizational process assets** - Templates, policies and procedures, and historical information may be leveraged to monitor communications.

Monitor Communications: Tools and Techniques

Common Tools and Techniques:

Expert Judgment

Expertise in communication monitoring may come from individuals or groups with specialized knowledge of communications and communication systems.

Data Representation Techniques

A *stakeholder engagement assessment matrix* is used to evaluate the stakeholders and the difference or gap between their current level of engagement and their desired level of engagement. With this understanding, the project manager can adapt their communications to influence the engagement of the stakeholders.

Interpersonal and Team Skills

Observation and conversation involves having discussion and dialogue with the project team, allowing the project manager to identify issues, conflicts, or individual performance issues. In today's environment, it is very easy to rely on electronic communication. However, to truly understand and engage with your team and other stakeholders, a project manager needs to purposely take the time to engage in conversations and observations. Oftentimes, issues do not become readily apparent in electronic formats, but a discussion with someone can provide significant context and clues.

Meetings

Meetings are used for decision-making while monitoring communications.

Project Management Information System (PMIS)

The PMIS encompasses any tools or systems for managing the project information and may be used for information distribution to both internal and external stakeholders. Information in the PMIS is monitoring to assess its validity and effectiveness.

Monitor Communications: Outputs

Common Outputs:

- **Work performance information** - Work performance information includes information on the effectiveness of the project communications as compared to the communication plan. Surveys and feedback on communication effectiveness would also be considered work performance information.
- **Change requests** - Change requests may be generated based on the communication monitoring activities. These changes will become an input to the **perform integrated change control** process.
- **Project management plan updates** - The project management plan may be updated, including the communication management plan and the stakeholder engagement plan.
- **Project document updates** - Project documents that may be updated through communication monitoring include the issue log and the lessons learned and stakeholder registers.

*The **monitor communications** process information is adapted from: PMBOK® Guide – Sixth Edition. Page 388-393*

Congratulations on Completing Section 3!

To evaluate your learning and retention of the Section 3 concepts. After you have completed the review questions and the vocabulary, complete Practice Exam 3 in Appendix C as a closed-book, 90-minute timed exam. Upon completion, record your score and your time-to-complete on your Performance Evaluation sheet on Page 9.

Chapter 11 - Review Questions

1. **A new key stakeholder has been identified for your project. A week after joining the team, the stakeholder has requested significant changes to the project performance report. What is the first thing you should do?**
   A. Because it is a key stakeholder, make the requested changes
   B. Consult the communications management plan
   C. Refuse the changes given that the format was already determined
   D. Evaluate the requested changes and determine how to incorporate them

2. **Despite some changes in the sponsorship of your project, the team is progressing well against the project objectives. You have some new stakeholders and you are finding that they are reaching out to you frequently for clarification on the project and the project status. What is the best thing you should do regarding this situation?**
   A. Evaluate the communication needs and revisit the communication planning process
   B. Provide the new stakeholders with a copy of the communication plan
   C. Do nothing as you are following the agreed-upon communication plan
   D. Refer the new stakeholders to the new sponsor for a discussion on project communications

3. **The project manager is providing information to the stakeholders based on the communication management plan. At a recent meeting, he overheard two key stakeholders discussing the fact that they felt they were not accurately informed or up-to-date on the project status. What is the best thing for the project manager to do?**
   A. Provide all of the stakeholders with a copy of the communications management plan
   B. Nothing, because he is following the communications management plan
   C. Discuss project communication and the communications management plan at the next stakeholder meeting
   D. Increase the frequency and detail of the project communications

4. **The components of the communication model include all of the following, except:**
   A. Sender and receiver
   B. Encode and recode
   C. Noise
   D. Message and medium

5. **You have updated the knowledge repository that contains general information for the stakeholders. What communication method was used?**
   A. Pull
   B. Push
   C. Interactive
   D. Meeting

6. **You have a number of time-sensitive issues on which you need information from your stakeholders. What would be the most appropriate communication method?**
   A. Push
   B. Pull
   C. Interactive
   D. On-line meeting

7. **Project intranets and home pages are examples of _____ communication:**
   A. Open access
   B. Free will
   C. Pull
   D. Push

8. Although your project has been progressing very well and has been relatively stable against the project baselines, there have recently been some unexpected costs that are causing the project to trend over-budget. Upon review with your sponsor, she advises you to not send out the monthly performance report or discuss the situation with the other key stakeholders as she fears it will cause unnecessary concern. What is the best thing for you to do?

   A. Document that the sponsor requested the performance report not be distributed
   B. Meet with the key stakeholders off-line to advise them of the situation
   C. Distribute the performance report per the terms of the communication plan
   D. Wait to distribute the performance report until the next reporting cycle

9. Your project has kicked off and you are evaluating different communication technology options as proposed by the PMO. Your team is mainly a virtual team, spanning five different countries. You are expecting the project to last at least a year. Which of the following would be the least likely factor to consider when selecting the appropriate communication technology?

   A. Your previous organization's communication tools
   B. The length of the project
   C. The team members desire and willingness to engage with or learn a new technology
   D. The availability of technology within the organization

10. The biases and perspectives that may interfere with the communication's receiver's interpretation of the message

    A. Noise
    B. Static
    C. Conditions
    D. Interference

11. Which of the following is not a focus direction for communication?

    A. Upward
    B. Horizontal
    C. Lateral
    D. Downward

12. A fundamental attribute of effective communication activities and artifacts:

    A. Creating a centralized website
    B. Defining the purpose of the communication
    C. Ensuring that everyone in the organization receives identical communications
    D. Validating all communications with the sponsor

13. An understanding of the differences between individuals, groups and organizations and adapting the communication strategy in the context of these differences is known as:

    A. Political awareness
    B. Horizontal communication
    C. Environmental factor influences
    D. Cultural awareness

14. One of your team members has approached you regarding her concerns with some of her team members. The majority of the team members for her particular piece of the project are located out of the country. She feels that based on their emails to her they are not understanding the project constraints. What technique would you recommend that she use to address the situation?

    A. A stakeholder engagement assessment matrix
    B. Observation and conversation
    C. The project management information system
    D. Co-location

15. Presentations

    A. Will be successful when the content and delivery meets the audiences' expectations and needs and the needs and objectives of the project and project team
    B. Are best handled by the project sponsor
    C. Are not used in adaptive environments as the team is working on sprints
    D. Should be scheduled once per month to provide project status updates

Review Question Answers

1. **Answer: B**

   The first thing you should do is consult the communication management plan, as it may indicate that no changes can be made to the performance report. It may also provide the process by which changes can be made. Just because it is a key stakeholder, it doesn't mean you simply implement the change to something that has been agreed-upon by the rest of the team. Refusing the changes may or may not be appropriate, depending on what is documented in the communication management plan. If changes are allowed, then the changes would be evaluated, and the change request submitted through the change control board.

2. **Answer: A**

   Given that there is apparently an issue with the communication of the project status, the best thing to do would be to evaluate the communication needs and revisit the communication planning process to ensure that the new stakeholders are getting the information they need. Providing them with a copy of the plan won't necessarily address the situation and it would not be appropriate to escalate the situation to the sponsor. As PM, it is your responsibility to ensure project communications are timely and effective.

3. **Answer: C**

   Because there is the potential that the communications are not effective, it will be appropriate to discuss the project communications and the communications management plan at the next meeting. Providing the stakeholders with a copy of the plan will not change the situation if something is wrong – theoretically they have all received a copy of the plan. It would not be acceptable to do nothing, as any communication issue must be addressed. Increasing the frequency and detail of the communications would be scope creep – outside of the initial scope definition. Do not let the fact that it states the "next stakeholder meeting" discourage you from the correct answer. The next meeting may be in a few hours.

4. **Answer: B**

   Recode is not a component of the communication model. It should encode and decode.

5. **Answer: A**

   Putting communication into a central location or repository is considered pull communication.

6. **Answer: C**

   Because it is time-sensitive, interactive communication should be used.

7. **Answer: C**

   Intranets and home pages are an example of pull communication.

8. **Answer: C**

   As part of your professional responsibility, you are still bound to provide transparent and timely information and follow the approved communication plan. Therefore, the performance report should still be distributed based on the communication plan.

9. **Answer: A**

   When evaluating the appropriate communication technology for your team, your previous organization's choice would not be a factor to consider. However, the length of the project, the team members "will", and the availability of technology are all factors to consider.

10. **Answer: A**

    The components of a communication model are: sender, receiver, encode, decode, message, medium, and noise. The noise is the biases, perspectives, conditions of the receiver that can interfere with them decoding the message as intended.

11. **Answer: C**

    Lateral is not a communication focus direction. The three directions are upward, downward, and horizontal.

12. **Answer: B**

    One of the fundamental attributes of effective communication activities and communication artifacts is that there needs to be a purpose for the communication.

13. **Answer: D**

    Cultural awareness is an understanding of the differences between individuals, groups and organizations and adapting the communication strategy in the context of these differences.

14. **Answer: B**

    Because your team member is basing her opinion on email communication only, she should talk with the team members and possibly schedule a video conference: observation and conversation. Co-location is not necessarily feasible based on location.

15. **Answer: A**

    Presentations will be successful when the content and delivery meets the audiences' expectations and needs and the needs and objectives of the project and project team.

Chapter 11 - Vocabulary Review

+ Acknowledge

+ Active listening

* Communications management plan

  Conflict management

+ Cultural awareness

+ Decode

+ Encode

+ Feedback

+ Interactive communication

+ Medium

  Meeting management

+ Message

  Networking

+ Noise

+ Political awareness

+ Pull communication

+ Push communication

+ Receiver

+ Sender

1. _____ The individual providing the message

2. _____ Thoughts or ideas are translated into language by the sender

3. _____ Communication sent to specific recipients who need to receive the information. Ensures the information is distributed but does not ensure that it actually reached or was understood by the intended audience.

4. _____ The information that needs to be conveyed

5. _____ The chosen communication channel

6. _____ The intended recipient of the information

7. _____ Message translation back into meaningful thoughts or ideas

8. _____ Used for very large volumes of information, or for very large audiences, and requires the recipients to access the communication at their own discretion

9. _____ Response from another party to provide information, guidance, or other information

10. _____ Actively seeking to resolve issues, concerns or disagreements within a group of people using various techniques

11. _____ Administration and handling of all tasks and requirements related to a successful meeting

12. _____ Demonstrating empathy with the sender, listening to understand.

13. _____ Biases, perspectives, and past experiences that may interfere or impact the understanding of communication or the communication process

14. _____ An understanding of the power structure and roles within an organization

15.	Establishing connections and relationships with other people from the same or other organizations
16.	Real-time communication
17.	A component of the project management plan that describes how, when, and by whom information about the project will be administered and disseminated
18.	An understanding of the differences between individuals, groups and organizations and adapting the communication strategy in the context of these differences
19.	When the receiver confirms the message was received to the sender

* These definitions are taken from the Glossary of *PMBOK® Guide – Sixth Edition*

Vocabulary Review Answers

1. Sender
2. Encode
3. Push communication
4. Message
5. Medium
6. Receiver
7. Decode
8. Pull communication
9. Feedback
10. Conflict management
11. Meeting management
12. Active listening
13. Noise
14. Political awareness
15. Networking
16. Interactive communication
17. Communications management plan
18. Cultural awareness
19. Acknowledge

Section 3 - Process/Output Match

Match each process to its key output(s). Please note that some processes may have more than one key output, and some may have no key output.

Acquire Resources   Manage Communications   Perform Quantitative Risk Analysis

Develop Team   Manage Team   Plan Communications Management

Estimate Activity Resources   Monitor Communications   Plan Resource Management

Identify Risks   Monitor Risks   Plan Risk Management

Implement Risk Responses   Perform Qualitative Risk Analysis   Plan Risk Responses

Process	Key Output
1.	Basis of estimates
2.	Communication management plan
3.	Physical resource assignments
4.	Project communications
5.	Project team assignments
6.	Resource breakdown structure
7.	Resource calendars
8.	Resource management plan
9.	Resource requirements
10.	Risk management plan
11.	Risk register
12.	Risk report
13.	Team charter
14.	Team performance assessments

These definitions are taken from the Glossary of Project Management Institute, *A Guide to the Project Management Body of Knowledge, (PMBOK® Guide)* – Sixth Edition, Project Management Institute Inc., 2017.

Process/Output Match Answers

1. Estimate Activity Resources
2. Plan Communications Management
3. Acquire Resources
4. Manage Communications
5. Acquire Resources
6. Estimate Activity Resources
7. Acquire Resources

8. Plan Resource Management
9. Estimate Activity Resources
10. Plan Risk Management
11. Identify Risks
12. Identify Risks
13. Plan Resource Management
14. Develop Team

Chapter 12

Project Procurement Management

What's in This Chapter

- Project Procurement Management
- Contract Types
- Plan Procurement Management
- Conduct Procurements
- Control Procurements

Project Procurement Management

If your project is purchasing or acquiring products or services from an external vendor or supplier, the procurement processes will apply. Given the legal nature and risks associated with procurements, procurement management can be a complex and somewhat challenging topic. Ultimately, if the project manager is involved in any type of procurement relationship for their project, it is essential that all legal and organizational procedures are followed and that the project manager understands the terms and conditions of any agreements. Agreements may take many forms, including purchase orders, contracts, memoranda of agreement (MoA), memoranda of understanding (MoU), or even internal service level agreements (SLAs).

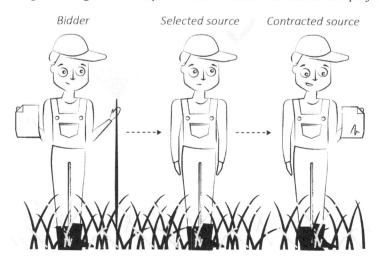

Bidder   Selected source   Contracted source

Procurement Roles

The organization or the project manager are the "buyer" and the contracted vendor is the "seller." The seller may also be called a contractor, subcontractor, vendor, service provider or supplier. During the contract life cycle, the seller is first a bidder, then the selected source, and finally the contracted supplier or vendor.

The assumption you can make on the exam is that you, as the project manager, do not have procurement authority (the authority to contractually bind the organization). Although there is no procurement authority, the project manager should have a strong understanding of any contractual requirements and implications, as it is the responsibility of the project manager to ensure that all contractual obligations are fulfilled as it relates to the project. The individual or group that is authorized to procure the resources may be part of the team, the project management office, or a part of the organization's purchasing department.

Procurement procedures vary by company, so be sure to understand those procedures for your specific organization. Some organizations have very specific policies and procedures regarding procurements, including the approved contract types, qualified sellers' lists with approved vendors, and bid requests and selections.

Depending on the type of project and the seller's role, the work that the vendor is responsible for completing may be considered, in and of itself, a project. Upon entering into an agreement, the project manager and team become a "key stakeholder" for that seller's project. The vendor would leverage the terms and conditions of the contract and the procurement statement of work (SOW) as their key inputs to chartering their project. The procurement statement of work is also known as the technical statement of work. The vendor, in turn, may purchase or acquire goods or services from a sub-contractor to fulfill the contract obligations, which makes them a buyer as well as a seller.

Current Trends

In the market today, there have been advances in procurement management. As with most every aspect of business, technology has enabled significant advancements in procurement tools, including many web-based and automated systems. One example of this in construction, engineering, and infrastructure projects is the use of the building information model (BIM). Shown to significantly reduce time and money on the projects that use it, BIM has started to become mandated for large projects by many companies and governments globally.

Risk management for procurements is also a hot topic. While all risk cannot be eliminated, taking steps to ensure that the contracts are written accurately is critical. A vendor will not be able to manage all the possible major project risks, so the buyer will need to accept the risks that the vendor has no control over, such as external, uncontrollable risks like a change in the regulatory requirements. Some contracts will specify that risk management is to be performed under the terms and conditions of the contract.

If you watch the Discovery Channel on cable television, you may have caught an episode of Extreme Engineering. The mega-projects featured on that show are another trend. Multi-billion-dollar projects have become more common and involve working with multiple contractors. This has added significant complexity to the contracting process and the handling of claims. Many of these mega-projects leverage internationally recognized standard contract forms to minimize problems. With the mega-projects, logistics and supply chain management is also a critical topic, with more projects identifying primary suppliers, secondary suppliers, and other back-up sources.

Live streaming is not only a social media phenomenon. Many publicly funded projects are using webcams to broadcast the construction project publicly live. The recordings of the broadcast are useful for any disputes or concerns. Another trend is trial engagements, where the vendor will be engaged for some initial work. If the work is satisfactory, the vendor's contract will be renewed. In agile or adaptive environments, there may be an overarching or governing master services agreement (MSA), with the adaptive work being in an appendix or supplement. The changes can occur to the adaptive scope without impacting the overall contract.

Contract Types

A contract legally binds the buyer and seller, and as such, must go through a more intense and rigorous review process than many of the other project documents. The contract must state the deliverables and results expected in very clear terms with minimal, if any, room for interpretation. Any agreements that are made that are not in the executed contract, cannot be legally enforced.

The project manager must include any verbal or informal agreements with a vendor in the contract terms and conditions. Despite having a clearly documented contract, there can be issues interpreting and enforcing contract terms in the case of international relationships. Local laws and culture may vary and cause problems if there is a performance issue.

There are multiple contract types available, but they generally fall into three categories:

- Fixed price (also known as lump sum)
- Cost reimbursable
- Time and material

Fixed Price Contracts

Fixed price contracts involve a fixed total price for the product. Because the buyer is paying one set price for the product or service, the risk is on the seller: should the product or service cost more to deliver than anticipated, the seller would have to absorb those costs. In a fixed price contract, the profit is typically not known by the buyer.

As the buyer, we prefer fixed price contracts, due to the lower risk, however, if the scope of the work is not clearly defined, a cost-reimbursable contract may be the only option. A vendor would not agree to enter into a fixed priced contract if they did not have an adequate scope definition.

Fixed price contracts may also include incentives for meeting or exceeding selected project objectives.

The simplest form of a fixed-price contract is a purchase order. There are three common types of fixed priced contracts: firm fixed price (FFP), fixed price incentive fee (FPIF), and fixed price with economic price adjustment (FPEPA).

Firm Fixed Price (FFP)

A firm fixed price contract is the most commonly used contract type, and it is favored by most organizations because the price is set and is not subject to change unless the scope of work changes. Any cost increases due to adverse performance would be the responsibility of the seller.

Example: Firm Fixed Price (FFP)

The contract states that the website developer will be paid $5,000 for the completed website. The website will have three static pages and a contact form.

Fixed Price Incentive Fee (FPIF)

A fixed price incentive fee gives the buyer and seller flexibility in that it allows for deviation from performance, with a financial incentive for achieving certain metrics. Generally, the incentives are related to cost, schedule, or the technical performance of the seller. A price ceiling is set and any costs above that ceiling are the responsibility of the seller.

Example: Fixed Price Incentive Fee (FPIF)

The contract states that the instructor will receive $2,000 to facilitate the course. In addition, the company will pay the instructor an extra $500 for each student that successfully completes their PMP® exam.

Fixed Price With Economic Price Adjustment (FPEPA)

FPEPA contracts are used for long-term contractual relationships. This contract type allows for pre-defined adjustments to the contract price due to changed conditions, such as inflation changes or increased or decreased costs for specific commodities. The contract is intended to protect both the buyer and seller from external conditions over which they have no control. Two common situations that employ FPEPA contracts include projects that are heavily reliant on oil / gas and those that may have international currency concerns. Oil and exchange rates are volatile, and the FPEPA contract protects both the buyer and seller during times of that volatility.

Example: Fixed Price with Economic Price Adjustment (FPEPA)

The contract states that the trucking company will be paid $1,000 per week. If the price of fuel increases or decreases by more than 10%, the weekly pay will increase or decrease by 5% accordingly.

Cost-Reimbursable Contracts

Cost-reimbursable contracts involve payment to the seller for seller's approved, actual costs, plus a fee that typically represents the seller's profit. Cost-reimbursable contracts place more risk on the buyer, as the buyer will not know the final amount until the work is completed. As the buyer, we prefer the low-risk fixed price contracts. However, as mentioned previously, if the scope is not clearly defined, we will not be able to use a fixed price contract. With cost-reimbursable contracts, there will be invoices to validate and approve throughout the contracted work, leading to more oversight and management by the project team.

There are three common types of cost-reimbursable contracts: cost plus fixed fee (CPFF), cost plus incentive fee (CPIF), and cost plus award fee (CPAF)

Cost Plus Fixed Fee (CPFF)

In a CPFF contract, the seller is reimbursed for allowable costs for performing the work and receives a fixed fee payment that is calculated as a percentage of the initial estimated project costs.

Notice that that the fixed fee is based on estimated project costs, not actual project costs. The fee is fixed (does not change regardless of final costs), and as such, it must be based on the estimated costs. If the fee was based on actual costs, that could not be fixed, as we would not know what those costs will be. The fee amount would only change if there was a change to the project scope, such as an approved work order.

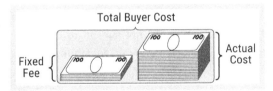

The contract value of a CPFF contract = actual costs + fixed fee

Example: Cost Plus Fixed Fee (CPFF)

The contract states that the builder will be reimbursed for the costs associated with the construction of the shed, estimated at $10,000. In addition, the builder will receive a fixed fee equal to 50% of the estimated costs ($10,000 x 50% = $5,000)

If the final costs are $18,000, the builder will receive:

$18,000 Cost (100% of actual costs)

+ $5,000 Fixed Fee (50% of the $10,000 estimate)

= $23,000

Cost Plus Incentive Fee (CPIF)

In a CPIF contract, the seller is reimbursed for allowable costs. In addition, the seller receives an incentive fee based on achieving certain performance objectives. However, if the final costs are less or greater than the original estimated costs, then both the buyer and seller share costs based upon a pre-negotiated formula such as 80/20, 50/50, or 20/80.

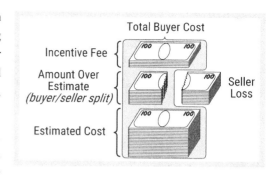

The first number in the split refers to the buyer's portion that they will be responsible for paying and the second number refers to the seller's portion that they will have to absorb. Buyer / seller – just remember B/S ☺!

The contract value for a CPIF contract = estimated costs ± percentage of difference between the estimate and actual costs + incentive fee.

Example: Cost Plus Incentive Fee (CPIF)

The contract states that the artist will have all costs reimbursed for the new sign, estimated at $5,000 and in addition, for each day that the sign is completed early, the artist will receive $200. If final costs are higher than $5,000, the difference will be split 50/50.

If the final costs are $6,000 and the artist delivers the sign three days early, the artist will receive:

$5,000 Cost (100% of estimated costs)

+ $500 Cost (50/50 split of the $1000 over the estimate)

+ <u>$600</u> Incentive Fee ($200 x 3 days early)

= $6,100

Cost Plus Award Fee (CPAF)

In a CPAF contract, the seller is reimbursed for allowable costs while much of the fee is only earned based on the satisfaction of identified broad subjective performance criteria. The performance criteria are defined and included in the contract and the fee determination is based solely on the determination of seller performance by the buyer and is usually not subject to appeals. This contract type is very rarely used as most sellers would not want to risk not making a profit on their work.

The contract value for a CPAF contract = actual costs + buyer-defined performance fee

Example: Cost Plus Award Fee (CPAF)

The contract states that the performer will be reimbursed for their costs and in addition, will receive an award fee based on the reaction of the audience.

If the final costs are $10,000, anything above the $10,000 would be paid at the discretion of the buyer.

Belinda's Hint

When you go out to dinner at a sit-down restaurant, you enter into an implied CPAF contract. You must pay for any food or drinks you order. However, anything above and beyond the food and drinks would be paid at your discretion, such as tipping your server.

If you feel the service was not good, you can choose not to add a gratuity to the bill. The server cannot sue you for not leaving a tip!

Time and Material Contracts (T&M)

T&M contracts are a hybrid type of contractual agreement that has both cost-reimbursable and fixed-price type arrangements. A T&M contract places moderate risk on the buyer: not as much as risk as a cost-reimbursable contract but more than a fixed price contract.

T&M contracts are usually used for staff augmentation, acquisition of experts and any outside support. The contracts can increase in contract value as if they were cost-reimbursable contracts and as such, the organization may add a "not-to-exceed" value to prevent unlimited cost growth.

Example: T&M Contract

Your project will be using a contract resource to complete the website redesign. The flash developer will be $25/hour. In addition, the developer will have his travel expenses reimbursed. The contract has a $40,000 not-to-exceed limit. Should additional work be required above and beyond the $40,000, the limit will need to be increased through the designated approval process.

Let's check your understanding of the contract types. The answers to Exercise 12.1 are on page 345.

Exercise 12.1: Contract Types

1. The contract states that the painter will be reimbursed for their costs and will also receive an additional $1,000 per day for each day they finish the job early. The painter estimates their costs to be $12,000. If the final costs are lower or higher than the $12,000, they will split the difference 50/50. Contract value if the final costs are $18,000 and the painter completed the job two days early:
   A. CPFF, $20,000
   B. CPIF, $18,000
   C. CPFF, $17,000
   D. CPIF, $17,000

2. The contract states that the company will pay the staffing agency $50 per hour for the contract manager, with a not-to-exceed value of $10,000. Contract type:
   A. T&M
   B. FFP
   C. FPIF
   D. CPFF

3. The contract states that the pet-sitter will receive $500 for the duration of the pet care and will receive an additional $20 per trick that the dog has learned while in the pet-sitter's care. Contract type:
   A. T&M
   B. CPIF
   C. FPIF
   D. FFP

4. The contract states that the delivery company will be paid $800 per month regardless of the number of deliveries. If the price of gas increases by more than 20%, the amount will increase to $900 or if the price of gas decreases by more than 20%, the amount will decrease to $700 per month. Contract type:
   A. FFP
   B. FPIF
   C. CPIF
   D. FPEPA

5. The contract states that the sub-contractor will be paid for costs associated with digging the trenches, estimated at approximately $15,000. In addition, the sub-contractor will receive an additional payment of $7,500 (50% of the estimated costs). Contract type and value if the final costs are $20,000:
   A. CPFF, $27,500
   B. CPFF, $22,500
   C. CPIF, $27,500
   D. CPIF, $22,500

6. The buyer issues a purchase order for 100 books at $200 each. Contract type:
   A. FPIF
   B. FFP
   C. CPFF
   D. FPEPA

7. The contract states that the magician will be reimbursed for his costs associated with the performance. In addition, the magician will receive a "gratuity" based on the reaction, participation, and enjoyment of the guests at the performance.
   A. CPAF
   B. FFP
   C. CPFF
   D. FPEPA

There are three processes associated with project procurement management that will be discussed in this chapter:

Plan Procurement Management. This process in the planning process group documents the project procurement decisions, including the approach and the potential sellers.

Conduct Procurements. This process in the executing process group obtains the seller responses, selects the sellers, and awards the contracts.

Control Procurements. This process in the monitoring and controlling process group manages the procurement relationships, monitoring contract performance, making changes and corrections, and closing out the contracts.

Plan Procurement Management

procurement knowledge area | planning process group

The **plan procurement management** process identifies the project needs that will best be met or must be met by acquisition external to the organization. During this process, the team will determine what to acquire, how to acquire it, how much is needed, and when to acquire it and will then document the project's purchasing decisions and the purchasing approach. Planning procurement management also identifies potential sellers and determines the type of contracts to use.

When planning the procurement approach, the project team must consider the risks involved in the procurements – which may be positive (opportunities) or negative (threats). For example, by using a vendor, the project can be delivered sooner (positive risk) however, the costs may be increased (negative risk). The decision to enter into a contract with a vendor may be based on a business case or a documented make-or-buy analysis.

According to the *PMBOK® Guide, 6th Edition*, roles and responsibilities for procurement activities should be documented early in procurement planning. The steps and responsibilities involved in procurements include:

- Prepare the procurement statement of work (SOW) or terms of reference (TOR)
- Prepare a high-level cost estimate
- Advertise the job or opportunity
- Identify a short list of qualified sellers
- Prepare and submit proposals or bids by the seller
- Evaluate the proposals, including quantifying the estimated costs and considering the quality
- Using the quality and cost evaluation, select the winning proposal
- Finalize negotiations and execute the contract

PMBOK® Guide – Sixth Edition, Page 468

Plan Procurement Management: ITTOs

Inputs	Tools & Techniques	Outputs
1. Project charter	1. Expert judgment	1. Procurement management plan
2. Business documents	2. Data gathering	2. Procurement strategy
• Business case	• Market research	3. Bid documents
• Benefits management plan	3. Data analysis	4. Procurement statement of work
3. Project management plan	• Make-or-buy analysis	5. Source selection criteria
• Scope management plan	4. Source selection analysis	6. Make-or-buy decisions
• Quality management plan	5. Meetings	7. Independent cost estimates
• Resource management plan		8. Change requests
• Scope baseline		9. Project documents updates
4. Project documents		• Lessons learned register
• Milestone list		• Milestone list
• Project team assignments		• Requirements documentation
• Requirements documentation		• Requirements traceability matrix
• Requirements traceability matrix		• Risk register
• Resource requirements		• Stakeholder register
• Risk register		10. Organizational process assets updates
• Stakeholder register		
5. Enterprise environmental factors		
6. Organizational process assets		

PMBOK® Guide – Sixth Edition. Page 466

Plan Procurement Management: Inputs

Business Documents

The project's business case and the benefits management plan will be considered when planning the procurement approach to ensure that any proposed procurements do not impact the validity of their project assessment and proposed benefits.

Common Inputs

- **Project charter** - The project charter provides the high-level project description, summary milestones, and the pre-approved financial resources

- **Project management plan** - The project management plan will be consulted during procurement planning, specifically leveraging the scope, quality, and resource management plans and the scope baseline.

- **Project documents** - Project documents that may be evaluated during procurement planning include the milestone list, the project team assignments, the requirements documentation and traceability matrix, the resource requirements, and the risk and stakeholder registers.

- **Enterprise environmental factors** - Environmental factors considered during procurement planning include, but are not limited to, market conditions, legal procurement advice, contract management systems, financial account and contract payments systems, and the seller's past performance.

- **Organizational process assets** - There are several policies, procedures, guidelines, and templates that will be leveraged for procurement planning including pre-approved seller lists and contract procedures.

Plan Procurement Management: Tools and Techniques

Source Selection Analysis

As the team considers the vendor selection process, source selection criteria are defined in advance to ensure the integrity and accuracy of the bid or proposal review process, while also ensuring the vendors understand how they will be evaluated. Selection methods include:

Least cost. Selecting a vendor based on the lowest cost. This may be appropriate for procurements that are standard or routine.

Qualifications only. If the procurement is relatively small and it is not worth it to do a full vendor evaluation, a quick consideration of qualifications may be appropriate. Factors that may be used could include the vendor's credibility, qualifications, experience or references.

Quality-based / highest technical proposal score. For vendors that are being evaluated through the request for proposal (RFP) process, a weighted scoring method is applied to the proposal responses. Using that weighted scorecard, the vendors are placed in rank-order by the highest scoring result. The vendor with the highest technical score will be invited to enter into financial negotiations for the contract price.

Quality and cost-based. An evaluation technique that includes the proposed cost in the proposal evaluation, as well as the technical evaluation.

Sole source. Without competition, a selected vendor is asked to prepare a technical and financial proposal. Because this can be considered preferential treatment, it is not a frequent or necessarily recommended procedure.

Fixed budget. The buyer sets the fixed budget and invites the vendor to submit technical proposals describing what they are willing to deliver within that budget. This method is appropriate when the SOW is very well defined, and no changes are anticipated.

Common Tools and Techniques:

Expert Judgment

Expert judgment will come from individuals and groups with procurement, regulatory, and compliance experience and knowledge.

Data Gathering Techniques

Market research is the examination of industry and specific seller capabilities. Information may come from conferences, online reviews, testimonials, etc.

Data Analysis Techniques

A *make-or-buy analysis* is an analysis to determine whether the product or service can be produced by the project team or can be purchased within the project constraints, with an understanding of the risks involved. This analysis may involve various financial calculations, such return on investment (ROI), internal rate of return (IRR), net present value (NPV), or a benefit/cost analysis (BCA).

Meetings

Meetings are used to determine the most appropriate approach to procurement management on the project.

Plan Procurement Management: Outputs

Procurement Management Plan

The procurement management plan describes how the procurement processes will be managed from developing procurement documentation through contract closure. The procurement management plan may be formal or informal, high-level or detailed, and may include information on the sources of funding for the procurements. In addition, the procurement management plan will give guidance on:

- The types of contracts to be used
- Ownership of independent estimates
- Standardized procurement documents
- Coordinating procurement with other project aspects
- Constraints and assumptions
- Handling of make-or-buy decisions
- Form and format of the contract statement of work
- Procurement metrics to be used
- Risk management issues
- Prequalified sellers

Procurement Strategy

The procurement strategy is the documented approach to procurements for the project. The strategy will include:

Delivery methods. For professional services, the delivery methods could be: buyer/services provider with no subcontracting, buyer/services provider with subcontracting allowed, joint venture between buyer and services provider, and buyer/services provider acts as the representative. For industrial or commercial construction, delivery methods may include: turnkey, design build (DB), design bid build (DBB), design build operate (DBO), build own operate transfer (BOOT), etc.

Contract payment types. Defining the contract payment types such as fixed-price contracts, cost-plus contracts, time-and-material contracts, and any incentives and awards that may be used.

Procurement phases. Procurement phase information will include the sequencing or phasing of the procurement with a description of each phase and the related objectives, performance indicators and milestones, criteria for moving from one phase to the next, progress tracking, and how knowledge will be transferred in subsequent phases.

Bid Documents

The procurement documents are used to solicit the responses from prospective sellers. If the seller selection will be based on price, the terms used will be bid, tender, or quotation:

- Request for quotation (RFQ)
- Invitation for bid (IFB)
- Tender notice

If the selection is based on technical capability, management approach, etc., the term proposal is generally used, such as the request for proposal (RFP). A request for information (RFI) is used when the organization is trying to gather more information about the goods and services to be acquired. An RFI will typically be followed by an RFQ or an RFP.

Procurement documents should be structured in such a way as to facilitate accurate and complete responses from prospective sellers and to allow for easy evaluation of the responses. The complexity and level of detail should be consistent with the value of, and risks associated with, the planned procurements.

Procurement Statement of Work (SOW)

The procurement statement of work is developed from the project scope baseline, reflecting the portion of the project scope that will be included with the related contract. The SOW should include sufficient detail to allow prospective sellers to determine if they can provide the product or service and must be written in a clear and concise manner. The SOW includes a description of any collateral services required, such as training, help-desk support, on-site implementation support, etc.

Each individual procurement item requires a SOW; however, multiple products or services can be grouped as one procurement item within a single SOW.

When contracting services, the phrase terms of reference (TOR) may be used which is similar to an SOW. A TOR includes the tasks the contractor is required to perform, standards they will fulfill, data that needs to be submitted for approval, a detailed list of all data and services that will be provided to the contractor by the buyer, and a definition of the schedule for initial submission and the review/approval time required.

Source Selection Criteria

If the vendor selection is going to be completed through a proposal process, the source selection criteria are developed to rate or score all the seller proposals that are received and is included as part of the RFP documentation. The criteria may include:

- Understanding of the procurement need
- Overall or life-cycle cost
- Technical capability
- Risk management approach
- Technical approach
- Warranty
- Financial capacity
- Business size and type
- Past performance of sellers
- Intellectual property rights

Make-or-Buy Decisions

The make-or-buy decisions are the documented decisions from the make-or-buy analysis. These decisions determine which products or services will be acquired and which will be developed by the project team. Along with the make-or-buy decision, the project team should also include the justification and supporting documentation for the decisions.

Independent Cost Estimates

For large procurements, many organizations will prepare, or have prepared by an outside estimator, an independent estimate to use as a benchmark for the bids that are received. If there is a significant difference between the independent estimate and the bids, it could indicate that the vendors did not fully understand the procurement SOW or that the SOW was ambiguous.

Common Outputs

- **Change requests** - Change requests may be generated based on planning the approach to procurement management. These changes will become an input to the **perform integrated change control** process.
- **Project document updates** - Project documents that may be updated through procurement planning include the stakeholder, risk and lessons learned registers, the milestone list, and the requirements documentation and traceability matrix.
- **Organizational process assets updates** - Organizational assets that may be updated through procurement planning include information on qualified sellers.

*The **plan procurement management** process information is adapted from: PMBOK® Guide – Sixth Edition. Page 466-481*

Conduct Procurements

procurement knowledge area | executing process group

Conducting procurements, which may be ongoing throughout the project, obtains the seller responses, selects the seller, and awards the contract. The project team will receive bids or proposals and will apply previously defined selection criteria to select one or more sellers who are qualified to perform the work needed by the project.

The procurement processes may involve a screening system and a weighting system: A screening system provides a pass/fail mechanism on potential sellers. Sellers who have been successfully screened are added to the qualified sellers list. A weighting system is an easy and objective process for selecting the best seller for the procurement and allows the proposals to be ranked by the weighted evaluation scores.

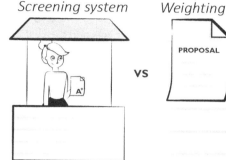
Screening system   *Weighting system*

Conduct Procurements: ITTOs

Inputs	Tools & Techniques	Outputs
1. Project management plan • Scope management plan • Resource management plan • Communications management plan • Risk management plan • Procurement management plan • Configuration management plan • Cost baseline 2. Project documents • Lessons learned register • Project schedule • Requirements documentation • Risk register • Stakeholder register 3. Procurement documentation 4. Seller proposals 5. Enterprise environmental factors 6. Organizational process assets	1. Expert judgment 2. Advertising 3. Bidder conferences 4. Data analysis • Proposal evaluation 5. Interpersonal and team skills • Negotiation	1. Selected sellers 2. Agreements 3. Change requests 4. Project management plan updates • Requirements management plan • Quality management plan • Communications management plan • Risk management plan • Procurement management plan • Scope baseline • Schedule baseline • Cost baseline 5. Project documents updates • Lessons learned register • Requirements documentation • Requirements traceability matrix • Resource calendars • Risk register • Stakeholder register 6. Organizational process assets updates

PMBOK® Guide – Sixth Edition. Page 482

Conduct Procurements: Inputs

Procurement Documentation

Procurement documentation can include bid documents, the procurement statement of work (SOW), independent cost estimates, and the source selection criteria.

Seller Proposals

The seller proposals are developed by the sellers and describe the seller's ability and willingness to provide the requested products, services, or results described in the procurement documentation. Proposals constitute a formal and legal offer in response to a buyer's request. A price proposal is often submitted separately from the technical proposal.

Common Inputs:

- Project management plan - There are many components of the project management plan that may be leveraged when conducting procurements, including: the scope, requirements, communications, risk, procurement, and configuration management plans and the cost baseline.
- Project documents - Project documents that may be leveraged when conducting procurements include the lessons learned, risk, and stakeholder registers, the project schedule, and the requirements documentation.
- Enterprise environmental factors - Internal and external factors to be considered while conducting procurements include local laws and regulations, economic environment, contract management systems, prior agreements already in place, and market conditions.
- Organizational process assets - Organizational assets that can be used to conduct procurements include the list of prequalified sellers, seller selection policies, templates or guidelines, and financial policies and procedures.

Conduct Procurements: Tools and Techniques

Advertising

Advertising the procurement may be used to increase the list of potential sellers and may be required by some government contracts. Advertising can be in industry journals, or local print or web-based news mediums.

Bidder conference

A bidder conference is a meeting with prospective sellers prior to preparation of a bid or proposal that allows prospective sellers to have a clear, common understanding of the procurement and ensuring no sellers have preferential treatment. The bidder conference allows the buyers to gain valuable information based on who attends and the questions asked. Bidder conferences are also called contractor conferences, vendor conferences, and pre-bid conferences.

Common Tools and Techniques:

Expert Judgment

Expert judgment can be applied to conducting procurements from individuals with experience and knowledge of the proposal review process, laws, regulation, negotiation, or technical or subject matter expertise.

Data Analysis Techniques

A *proposal evaluation* is used to evaluate the proposals, ensuring that they are complete and that they respond to the bid documents, the procurement SOW, the source selection criteria, and any other components distributed in the bid package.

Interpersonal and Team Skills

Negotiation is a discussion aimed at reaching an agreement. The structure, requirements and terms of the purchases may be negotiated to reach agreement prior to signing the contract.

If the procurement is complex, contract negotiation may be an independent process. For simple procurement items, the terms and conditions of the contract can be previously set and non-negotiable, only needing to be accepted by the seller.

The negotiations may or may not be led by the project manager, although the project team may be present during negotiations to provide assistance and clarify the project's technical, quality, and management requirements.

Conduct Procurements: Outputs

There are two key outputs from conducting the procurements:

Selected Sellers

Selected sellers are those judged to be in a competitive range based on the outcome of the proposal or bid evaluation and have negotiated a draft contract.

Agreements

The procurement contract is awarded to each of the selected sellers and may be a complex document or a simple purchase order.

The major components will vary, but usually include the following:

- Statement of work or deliverables
- Schedule baseline
- Performance reporting
- Period of performance
- Roles and responsibilities
- Seller's place of performance
- Pricing
- Payment terms
- Place of delivery
- Inspection and acceptance criteria
- Warranty
- Limitation of liability
- Incentives
- Insurance and performance bonds
- Change request handling

Common Outputs:

- **Change requests** - Change requests may be generated based conducting the procurements. These changes will become an input to the **perform integrated change control** process.
- **Project management plan updates** - The project management plan may be updated, including the requirements, quality, communications, risk, and procurement management plans, and the scope, schedule, and cost baselines.
- **Project document updates** - Project documents that may be updated through conducting the procurements, include the risk, stakeholder, and lessons learned registers, the requirements documentation and traceability matrix, and the resource calendars.
- **Organizational process assets updates** - Organizational assets that may be updated through conducting the procurements include the listings of prospective and prequalified sellers, and information on the team's positive or negative experience with the sellers.

*The **conduct procurements** process information is adapted from: PMBOK® Guide Sixth Edition. Pages 467-491*

Exercise 12.2: Weighted Scorecard Evaluation

Three potential sellers have submitted a proposal in response to your RFP: Acme Corp, Jones & Son, and Lane Associates. You and your team have evaluated each seller based on the categories identified in the RFP. Determine the 1st choice, 2nd choice, and 3rd choice sellers. The answer to exercise 12.2 is on page 345.

Acme Corp

Categories	Weighting		Seller Score		Total
Experience	10	x	4	=	
Location	5	x	3	=	
Technology	5	x	2	=	
Availability	10	x	5	=	
			Total Score:		
			Possible Score:		150
			Percent Score:		

Jones & Son

Categories	Weighting		Seller Score		Total
Experience	10	x	3	=	
Location	5	x	5	=	
Technology	5	x	5	=	
Availability	10	x	4	=	
			Total Score:		
			Possible Score:		150
			Percent Score:		

Lane Associates

Categories	Weighting		Seller Score		Total
Experience	10	x	2	=	
Location	5	x	5	=	
Technology	5	x	4	=	
Availability	10	x	5	=	
			Total Score:		
			Possible Score:		150
			Percent Score:		

Control Procurements

procurement knowledge area | monitoring and controlling process group

Controlling the procurements involves managing the relationship with the various sellers, ensuring that the seller's performance is in alignment with what they are scheduled to deliver within the contract. This process will document and review how well a seller is performing or has performed based on the contract and may establish corrective actions, if needed. This will generate information that may be used to determine if the seller could or should be used on future procurements. In addition, this process manages any early terminations of the contracted work in accordance with the termination clause of the contract.

Contract administration, because of the legal aspect, may be an organizational function versus being managed at the project level, although there may be a procurement administrator on the team that reports up to a supervisor. There are a number of administrative activities associated with procurements which can include collecting data and managing project records, refining procurement plans and schedules, monitoring the procurement environment, and the payment of invoices.

A key aspect of this process is ensuring that the contract requirements are being met and invoices are approved in a timely manner. Seller compensation should be linked to the seller's progress as defined within the contract. Ideally, payments made to the seller should be for work accomplished and deliverables versus labor hours.

Belinda's Hint

Be on the lookout for questions regarding payment to a vendor. As project manager, you cannot withhold payment to a vendor because you "suspect" the project is being over-charged. Any disputes would need to be escalated per the terms and conditions of the contract. Simply withholding payment creates a potential contract breach situation.

Control Procurements: ITTOs

Inputs	Tools & Techniques	Outputs
1. Project management plan	1. Expert judgment	1. Closed procurements
• Requirements management plan	2. Claims administration	2. Work performance information
• Risk management plan	3. Data analysis	3. Procurement documentation updates
• Procurement management plan	• Performance reviews	
• Change management plan	• Earned value analysis	4. Change requests
• Schedule baseline	• Trend analysis	5. Project management plan updates
2. Project documents	4. Inspections	• Risk management plan
• Assumption log	5. Audits	• Procurement management plan
• Lessons learned register		• Schedule baseline
• Milestone list		• Cost baseline
• Quality reports		6. Project documents updates
• Requirements documentation		• Lessons learned register
• Requirements traceability matrix		• Resource requirements
• Risk register		• Requirements traceability matrix
• Stakeholder register		• Risk register
3. Agreements		• Stakeholder register
4. Procurement documentation		7. Organizational process assets updates
5. Approved change requests		
6. Work performance data		
7. Enterprise environmental factors		
8. Organizational process assets		

PMBOK® Guide – Sixth Edition. Page 492

Control Procurements: Inputs

Agreements

Agreements are the legal, binding documents between parties. The agreements will be reviewed to ensure that the terms and conditions are being met by both parties.

Procurement documentation

Procurement documentation includes the supporting records to administer the procurement processes and can include the statement of work, payment information, work performance information, plans, memos and other relative documentation.

Approved change requests

Change requests that have been approved through the **perform integrated change control** process can include modifications to the terms and conditions of the contract. All changes to the agreements must be documented and approved through the appropriate procedures.

Common Inputs:

- **Project management plan** - The project management plan will be consulted as the procurements are controlled. This may include using the requirements, risk, procurement, and change management plans, and the schedule baseline.
- **Project documents** - Project documents that may be evaluated during the controlling of the procurements include the assumption log, the lessons learned, risk, and stakeholder registers, the milestone list, the quality reports, and the requirements documentation and traceability matrix.
- **Work performance data** - The work performance data includes information on the seller data, project status, activities status, cost status, and seller invoices that have been paid.
- **Enterprise environmental factors** - Internal and external factors to be considered include the contract change control system, marketplace conditions, the accounts payable system, and the organization's code of ethics.
- **Organizational process assets** - Procurement procedures, guidelines, and templates will be used to control the procurements.

Control Procurements: Tools and Techniques

Claims Administration

Claims are also called disputes or appeals and are documented, processed, monitored, and managed throughout the contract life cycle in accordance with the terms of the contract. Contested changes and potentially constructive changes are those requested changes where the buyer and seller cannot agree on compensation for the change or cannot agree that a change has even occurred.

Inspections

An inspection is a review of the work being performed by the contractor, and it may be a simple review of the deliverables or an actual physical review of the work itself. Inspections may be walkthroughs of a job site, for example.

Audits

Audits are a structured review of the procurement process and the rights and obligations are described in the procurement contract. The results of the procurement audit would be shared with both the buyer's and the seller's project managers in order for them to make an adjustment, as necessary.

Common Tools and Techniques:

Expert Judgment

Expert judgment may come from individuals with knowledge of the functional areas, laws, regulations, and compliance requirements, and claims administration.

Data Analysis Techniques

There are three data analysis techniques that may be used while controlling the procurements on the project:

Performance reviews are a structured review of the seller's progress to deliver project scope and quality, within cost and on schedule, as compared to the contract. The objective is to identify performance successes or failures, progress with respect to the contract statement of work, and contract non-compliance.

An *earned value analysis* is an evaluation of the schedule and cost variances and the schedule and cost performance indexes. These measurements show the degree of variance from the baseline which will be helpful in controlling the procurements.

A *trend analysis* involves tracking data points over time to determine if the performance is improving or deteriorating.

Control Procurements: Outputs

There are two key outputs from controlling the procurements:

Closed Procurements

When the vendor has completed the contracted work, they will provide the buyer with formal written notice that the contract has been completed. The procedures for completing and closing out any procurements will be documented in the terms and conditions of the contract as well as the procurement management plan. To officially close the procurement, all the work of the contract must have been completed per the SOW, there should be no outstanding claims, and all final payments have been made. All deliverables from the vendor would be approved by the project team prior to contract closure.

Procurement Documentation Updates

All the procurement documentation may be updated throughout this process, including approved change requests, requested but unapproved change requests, the contract and supporting schedules, technical documentation and work performance information.

In addition to the key outputs, the following commonly applied outputs may also be created:

Common Outputs:

- **Work performance information** - Work performance information includes information on how a seller is performing by comparing their work, deliverables, and progress to the contract and project baselines.
- **Change requests** - Change requests may be generated based on controlling the procurements. Change requests are reviewed through the **perform integrated change control** process. Requested but unresolved changes may be considered constructive changes. These constructive changes may be disputed by one party and lead to a claim against the other party. As such, these changes will be uniquely identified and documented.
- **Project management plan updates** - The project management plan may be updated, including the risk and procurement management plans, and the schedule and cost baselines.
- **Project document updates** - Project documents that may be updated include the lessons learned, the risk, and the stakeholder registers, the resource requirements, and the requirements traceability matrix.
- **Organizational process assets updates** - Several organizational assets that may be updated include the payment schedules and requests, the seller performance evaluation documentation, the prequalified seller lists, the lessons learned repository, and the procurement file.

*The **control procurements** process information is adapted from: PMBOK® Guide – Sixth Edition. Pages 492-501*

Chapter 12 – Answer Key

Exercise 12.1: Contract Types

1. D. CPIF, $17,000
2. A. T&M
3. C. FPIF
4. D. FPEPA
5. A. CPFF, $27,500
6. B. FFP
7. D. FPEPA

Exercise 12.2: Weighted Scorecard Evaluation

1st choice: Jones & Son (80% score)

2nd choice: Acme Corp (77% overall score, which is the same as Lane, but Acme has a higher score in "Experience" which has a heavier weighting)

3rd choice: Lane (77% score)

Chapter 12 - Review Questions

Time Limit: 18 Minutes

1. **Requested but unresolved changes within a contractual relationship:**
   A. Must be added to the risk register
   B. Can only be resolved through mediation
   C. Do not involve the project manager, only senior leadership of the organization
   D. Could be considered a constructive change to the contract that may be disputed by one party and lead to a claim against the other party

2. **The contract change control system:**
   A. Is a component of the integrated change control system
   B. Is administered by an individual with procurement authority
   C. Manages changes to the contract with the end-user
   D. Is separate from the integrated change control system

3. **Your sponsor over the very complex project has requested that if a vendor will be necessary, the lowest risk contract that would allow the vendor to deliver on all of the terms and conditions must be used. As such, you know you will need to use:**
   A. Firm fixed price
   B. No vendor
   C. Time and material
   D. Cost plus fixed fee

4. **The buyer structures procurement documents to accomplish all of the following except:**
   A. Facilitate an accurate and complete response from each prospective seller
   B. Include the relevant contract statement of work and any required contractual provisions
   C. Include a description of the desired form of the response
   D. Provide a list of potential bidders to each prospective seller

5. **Which of the following is false about advertising as a tool and technique of the conduct procurements process?**
   A. It is sometimes required on government projects
   B. It can often be used to expand the existing lists of potential sellers
   C. It can cause public pressure resulting in bid disputes
   D. It can be placed in general circulation publications, such as newspapers, or in specialty publications, such as professional journals

6. **Evaluation criteria are developed and used to rate or score proposals. These criteria have all of the following characteristics except:**
   A. They generally require specification of the name of the transportation organization responsible for delivery of procured items
   B. They can be limited to purchase price if the procurement item is readily available from a number of acceptable sellers
   C. They can be subjective, such as, "The proposed project manager needs to have documented previous experience with similar projects"
   D. They can be objective, such as, "The proposed project manager needs to be a certified Project Management Professional (PMP)"

7. **The primary goal of a bidder's conference is:**
   A. To ensure that all prospective sellers have a clear and common understanding of the procurement
   B. To allow certain bidders to receive preferential treatment
   C. To determine if certain information in the procurement request was missing
   D. To determine which sellers will be responding to the procurement request

8. **What contract type has lowest risk for the buyer yet allows flexibility in the form of an incentive for achieving defined performance objectives?**
   A. CPIF
   B. FFP
   C. FPEPA
   D. FPIF

9. **If someone in the organization has been delegated procurement authority it means that the individual is:**
   A. Authorized to maintain an intellectual property database containing information concerning the performance of sellers on prior projects
   B. Authorized to initiate and conduct negotiations with prospective sellers
   C. Authorized to contractually bind the organization
   D. Authorized to review and approve payment on billings submitted by sellers

10. **You are developing the SOW that will be provided to the selected vendor. Which statement is least accurate regarding the procurement SOW?**
   A. It defines the portion of the project scope that will be included with the related contract
   B. It will include a description of any collateral services required
   C. It will be used to solicit proposals from prospective sellers
   D. It will include sufficient detail to allow prospective sellers to determine if they are capable of providing the product or service

11. **Generally, a bid differs from a proposal in that the term:**
   A. Proposal is used when source selection will be based on price
   B. Proposal is used when the project time frame is limited
   C. Bid is used when source selection will be based on price
   D. Proposal disregards price considerations

12. **A cost-plus-fixed-fee (CPFF) contract has all of the following characteristics except:**
   A. Seller is reimbursed for allowable costs for performing the contract work
   B. Seller receives a fixed fee payment calculated as a percentage of the actual project costs
   C. Seller receives a fixed fee payment calculated as a percentage of the estimated project costs
   D. The fixed fee does not vary with actual costs unless the project scope changes

13. **Jansen Bros. Construction has been selected as a contractor for the downtown construction project. The costs for equipment rental, manpower, and other supplies will be included in the contract price. If the final costs are higher or lower than anticipated, Jansen Bros will split the difference with the buyer 50/50. In addition, Jansen Bros will receive $30,000 for each day they complete their job prior to the scheduled delivery date. What type of contract are they working under?**
   A. CPFF
   B. FPIF
   C. CPAF
   D. CPIF

14. **The seller is working under a cost reimbursable contract with a 70/30 split. As an incentive from the buyer, the vendor will receive $1,500 for each day they deliver the final product early. The original cost estimate on the project was $750,000. The vendor delivered the product six days early at a final invoice price of $810,000. What is the contract value?**
   A. $810,000
   B. $801,000
   C. $852,000
   D. $783,000

15. **You have assumed the management of a project that was well underway. One of your team members lets you know that the primary vendor working on the project was hired based upon being a solo source. You know that this means:**
   A. The vendor was the least expensive vendor
   B. The vendor had the highest technical proposal score
   C. The vendor is on the qualified sellers list
   D. The vendor submitted a proposal without competition

Review Question Answers

1. **Answer: D**

   Requested but unresolved changes could be considered a constructive change to the contract and may cause a dispute. Unresolved changes are not a risk, but rather an issue. The situation may be resolved through negotiation or other options outside of mediation. As the PM is the individual involved directly in the management of the project, it is possible that they would be involved in a contract dispute, representing the project.

2. **Answer: A**

   The contract change control system is a component of the overall integrated change control system. It may or may not be administered by an individual with procurement authority.

3. **Answer: A**

   The lowest risk contract type for the buyer is a firm fixed price (FFP) contract.

4. **Answer: D**

   The procurement documents are not structured to provide a list of potential bidders to each prospective seller.

5. **Answer: C**

   Advertising procurement opportunities is sometimes required based on the type of procurement, especially in government projects. Advertising may expand the response pool and the procurement can be advertised in general and/or specialty publications. Advertising the procurement does not cause public pressure resulting in bid disputes.

6. **Answer: A**

   All statements are true and accurate other than the answer that states they specify the name of the transportation organization responsible for delivery. It is not a given that all procurements will require delivery via a transportation organization.

7. **Answer: A**

   The objective of the bidder's conference is to provide open access to information for all prospective bidders. This prevents any preferential treatment. As a benefit of doing a bidder's conference, it may help alert the buyer to missing information and also provide a preview of what sellers may be bidding on the initiative.

8. **Answer: D**

   Fixed price contracts place the lowest risk on the buyer. A fixed price incentive fee (FPIF) contract allows flexibility to incent the buyer based on predefined performance objectives – for example, delivering early.

9. **Answer: C**

   Procurement authority means that the individual has the ability to contractually bind the organization (sign contracts on behalf of the organization). The assumption on the exam is that you, as a project manager, do not have procurement authority, even if in real practice you do.

10. **Answer: C**

    The procurement statement of work (SOW) does not solicit proposals, as it is the request for proposal (RFP) that would do so. However, while the procurement statement of work (SOW) does not solicit the proposals it is typically included as part of the RFP.

11. **Answer: C**

    The terms bid, tender, and quotation will be used when the vendor selection will be based on price: invitation for bid (IFB), tender notice, request for quotation (RFQ). Proposal will be used when vendor selection will be based on other factors beyond just price.

12. **Answer: B**

    The fixed fee in the CPFF contract is calculated as a percentage of estimated costs, not actual costs. The fact that it is based on estimated costs is what makes it a "fixed" fee. If it were based on actual costs, it would be variable and would therefore not be fixed.

13. **Answer: D**

    The vendor is being reimbursed for their allowable costs and is being offered an incentive, representing a cost plus incent fee contract. Another hint on this one would be the fact that there is also a buyer/seller split. From an exam perspective, buyer/seller splits will be only on CPIF contracts.

14. **Answer: B**

Using the estimate of $750,000, the buyer is only responsible for 70% of any costs that exceed that $750,000. The seller exceeded the estimate by $60,000. As such, the buyer will pay:

100% of the estimate: $750,000

70% of the $60k overage: $42,000

Six x $1,500 incentive: $9,000

Total Value: $801,000

15. **Answer: D**

A solo source vendor means that the selected vendor was asked to prepare a technical and financial proposal but did not have any competing proposals going against them.

Chapter 12 - Vocabulary Review

* Bidder conference
* Buyer
* Cost plus award fee contract
* Cost plus fixed fee contract
* Cost plus incentive fee contract
* Cost reimbursable contract

* Firm fixed price contract
* Fixed price contract
* Fixed price incentive fee contract
* Fixed price with economic price adjustment contract
* Procurement management plan

* Procurement statement of work
* Qualified seller list
  Screening system
* Seller
* Time and material contract
  Weighting system

1. _____ Allows proposals to be ranked by the weighted evaluation scores

2. _____ A type of contract involving payment to the seller for the seller's costs plus a fee typically representing seller's profit

3. _____ Provides a pass/fail mechanism on potential sellers

4. _____ Meetings with prospective sellers prior to the preparation of a bid or proposal

5. _____ The buyer pays the seller a set amount and the seller can earn an additional amount if the seller meets pre-defined performance criteria

6. _____ A listing of sellers who have been pre-screened for their qualifications and past experience, so that procurements are directed to only those sellers who can perform on any resulting contracts

7. _____ The acquirer of products, services, or results for an organization

8. _____ A component of the project or program management plan that describes how a project team will acquire goods and services from outside the performing organization

9. _____ A provider or supplier of products, services, or results to an organization

10. _____ The buyer reimburses the seller for the seller's costs and the seller earns profit for meeting pre-defined performance criteria

11. _____ A general contract type where the buyer pays the seller a set amount regardless of the seller's costs

12. _____ A narrative description of products, services, or results to be supplied by the seller

13. _____ The seller is reimbursed for all costs, but the majority of the fee is only earned based on the satisfaction of identified broad subjective performance criteria

14. _____ A type of contract that is a hybrid contractual arrangement containing aspects of both cost-reimbursable and fixed-price contracts

15.	A contract with a defined set price for the product
16.	A type of contract used for longer term projects that allows for pre-defined adjustments to the contract price due to changed conditions
17.	The buyer reimburses the seller for the seller's allowable costs plus a fixed fee usually calculated as a percentage of the estimated costs

* These definitions are taken from the Glossary of *PMBOK® Guide - Sixth Edition*

Vocabulary Review Answers

1. Weighting system
2. Cost reimbursable contract
3. Screening system
4. Bidder conference
5. Fixed price incentive fee contract
6. Qualified seller list
7. Buyer
8. Procurement management plan
9. Seller
10. Cost plus incentive fee contract
11. Qualified seller list
12. Buyer
13. Procurement management plan
14. Time and material contract
15. Firm fixed price contract
16. Fixed price with economic price adjustment contract
17. Cost plus fixed fee contract

Chapter 13

Project Execution

What's in This Chapter

- Project Execution
- Direct and Manage Project Work
- Manage Project Knowledge
- Perform Integrated Change Control
- Manage Stakeholder Engagement
- Monitor Stakeholder Engagement

The project manager is responsible for managing the work of the project while also managing the many interfaces that exist. Projects can range from very simple and repetitive initiatives to multi-billion-dollar megaprojects, and project management can be applied vastly different in various environments. The field of project management and the role of the project manager are continually changing, reflecting changes in practices, approaches, and tools.

The high volume of data and information that can be collected, processed, and analyzed has been both augmented and supported by the advancements in automated project management tools. Those tools and systems make up the project management information system (PMIS). While technology has advanced, there has also been a return to simpler approaches for adaptive environments such as using a white-board and sticky notes to visualize tasks and progress.

There is also a generational and transitory consideration to managing the project knowledge. In the late 20th century, many workers that were considered "project managers" were technical experts over their product or process. Employees stayed at a company oftentimes until retirement, so the knowledge of the experts was retained within the organization.

Today's workforce, however, is much more transient and there is increased collaboration with other parties. How then do we capture all that tribal knowledge before it walks out the door? Managing project knowledge is crucial to organizational growth and success. Having a succinct lessons learned process certainly helps when managed in a timely manner, throughout the project versus waiting until the end of the project. Making those lessons learned available and accessible is another challenge. In the *PMBOK*® *Guide, 6th Edition*, there is increased focus on managing this project knowledge.

Activities that previously were owned by the project sponsor or the project management office (PMO) are now becoming the responsibility of the project manager is some environments. This can include business case development and validation and benefits management. Strategically, the project manager is playing a more mature and engaged role versus simply being a task manager for the project team and schedule.

As the role of the project manager has matured and grown, so also has the approach to managing projects. There is increased recognition that there are many different approaches to project management and it does not have to look the same from organization-to-organization or even from project-to-project. The project manager and the project organization need to consider the project objectives and the project environment and adjust their approach accordingly. This is giving rise to a lot of hybrid methodologies, such as a waterfall approach with agile practices built-in.

While completing the work of the project, there are five processes involved in the ongoing management and execution of the project that will be discussed in this lesson:

Direct and Manage Project Work. This process is in the executing process group and the integration knowledge area and is the process of leading and performing the work as defined in the project scope statement.

Manage Project Knowledge. This process is in the executing process group and the integration knowledge area and is the process of using existing knowledge and creating new knowledge to achieve the project's objectives.

Perform Integrated Change Control. This process is in the monitoring and controlling process group and the integration knowledge area and is the process of reviewing all change requests and approving and managing changes.

Manage Stakeholder Engagement. This process is in the executing process group and the stakeholder knowledge area and involves communicating and working with stakeholders to meet their needs and expectations, address issues, and engage the stakeholders.

Monitor Stakeholder Engagement. This process is in the monitoring and controlling process group and the stakeholder knowledge and involves monitoring the stakeholder relationships and tailoring engagement strategies and plans.

Direct and Manage Project Work

integration knowledge area | executing process group

During the **direct and manage project work** process the project manager and project team will perform the work on the project as defined in the project scope statement. The project manager will be responsible for directing the performance of the planned project activities and managing the technical and organizational interfaces that exist within the project. Changes that are approved through the **perform integrated change control** process will be implemented.

The work performance data will be collected and communicated to the appropriate monitoring and controlling processes, where-upon analyzation, it will be considered work performance information. Work performance data will also lend to the development of the lessons learned register.

Project activities can include:

- Performing activities to accomplish project requirements
- Creating project deliverables
- Staffing, training, and managing team members that are assigned to the project
- Obtaining, managing and using resources, such as materials, tools, and equipment
- Establishing and managing project communication channels
- Issuing change requests
- Managing risks and implementing risk responses
- Managing sellers and suppliers

Belinda's Hint

Think of this process as the "big dog" process – an integration/umbrella process bringing together all of the work that is being performed on the project. A typical integration process, it is light on ITTOs but heavy on importance.

Direct and Manage Project Work: ITTOs

Inputs	Tools & Techniques	Outputs
1. Project management plan • Any component 2. Project documents • Change log • Lessons learned register • Milestone list • Project communications • Project schedule • Requirements traceability matrix • Risk register • Risk report 3. Approved change requests 4. Enterprise environmental factors 5. Organizational process assets	1. Expert judgment 2. Project management information system 3. Meetings	1. Deliverables 2. Work performance data 3. Issue log 4. Change requests 5. Project management plan updates • Any component 6. Project documents updates • Activity list • Assumption log • Lessons learned register • Requirements documentation • Risk register • Stakeholder register 7. Organizational process assets updates

PMBOK® Guide – Sixth Edition. Page 490

Direct and Manage Project Work: Inputs

Approved Change Requests

Once the change requests are approved by the change control board (CCB) through the **perform integrated change control** process, they will be implemented in this process. Change requests may include updates, scope changes, corrective actions, preventive actions, and defect repairs.

Common Inputs:

- **Project management plan** - All components of the project management plan will be consulted throughout the **direct and manage project work** process.
- **Project documents** - Project documents that may be used to direct and manage the project work include the change log, the lessons learned and risk registers, the milestone list, the project communications, the project schedule, the risk report, and the requirements traceability matrix.
- **Enterprise environmental factors** - Influences on directing and managing the project work include the organizational structure and culture, the infrastructure of the organization, and the stakeholder risk thresholds.
- **Organizational process assets** - Multiple organizational assets will be leveraged for directing and managing the project work, includes processes, templates, guidelines, and historical project files.

Direct and Manage Project Work: Tools and Techniques

Common Tools and Techniques:

Expert Judgment

Expertise may come from any individuals or groups with specialized knowledge or experience that could benefit the project.

Meetings

Meetings are the primary source of project information and communication. There are many types of meetings, including: kick-off, technical, sprint or iteration planning, scrum daily standups, steering committee, problem-solving, progress update, and retrospective meetings. The scrum standup meeting is a daily meeting that is exactly what the name implies. The core members of the team stand-up and share the following information:

- What they accomplished the previous day

- What they plan to accomplish today

- What they might need assistance with in order to accomplish their work goals

The idea of standing is to encourage brevity in the updates. Any action items or extended discussion are handled after the meeting in small group discussions. Anyone is welcome to attend and listen to the daily standup but only the core team members can talk.

Project Management Information System (PMIS)

The PMIS includes automated tools, such as a scheduling tool (for example, Microsoft Project), a configuration management system, information collection and distribution systems, and web interfaces to online automated systems. The PMIS is also considered an enterprise environmental factor, as the availability and limitations of information systems will influence the management of the project. For example, built-in templates may increase the efficiency of project schedule development.

Direct and Manage Project Work: Outputs

There are three key outputs from directing and managing the project work:

Deliverables

The deliverables are unique and verifiable products, results or capabilities to perform a service as identified in the project management plan. The deliverables are an input to the **control quality** (QC) process where they will be checked for correctness against the requirements, and upon verification, will become "verified deliverables" The "verified deliverables" will then become an input to the **validate scope** process where the verified deliverables will be reviewed and accepted by the customer. The "accepted deliverables" will become an input to the **close project or phase** process.

DELIVERABLE
Direct & Manage Project Work

VERIFIED DELIVERABLE
Control Quality

ACCEPTED DELIVERABLE
Validate Scope

Work Performance Data

Work performance data includes the status of project activities being performed and should be considered raw data. Work performance data is a "common" input, as it will be used in the monitoring and controlling processes to analyze the current status and health of the project.

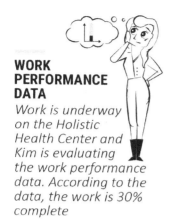

WORK PERFORMANCE DATA

Work is underway on the Holistic Health Center and Kim is evaluating the work performance data. According to the data, the work is 30% complete

WORK PERFORMANCE INFORMATION

Kim works with her work package owners to compare that progress against the baselines. She learns that acording to the schedule baseline, the crews should be closer to 40% complete and as such, is about 10% behind schedule

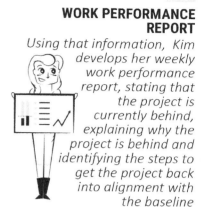

WORK PERFORMANCE REPORT

Using that information, Kim develops her weekly work performance report, stating that the project is currently behind, explaining why the project is behind and identifying the steps to get the project back into alignment with the baseline

---

Belinda's Hint

These two sequences are important to remember for the exam:

Deliverable → Verified deliverable → Accepted deliverable

Work performance data → Work performance information → Work performance reports

It is also important to remember that this process, **direct and manage project work**, creates these two key outputs: deliverables and work performance data. One way to remember is to think of the popular Food Network show: Diners, Drive-Ins and Dives, also called "Triple D." Think of these as "Triple D":

D̲irect and manage project work produces: D̲eliverables and Work Performance D̲ata

---

Issue Log

The issue log captures the problems, gaps, or inconsistencies that need to be addressed to minimize disruption to the project constraints and objectives. The issue log is a critical and highly utilized project management tool. The issue log typically includes: the issue type, who raised the issue, description, priority, the assigned owner, the target resolution date, status, and the final resolution.

Common Outputs:

- **Change requests** - Change requests will be generated while directing and managing the project work. These change requests will become an input to the **perform integrated change control** process.
- **Project management plan updates** - Any component of the project management plan may be updated throughout this process.
- **Project document updates** - Project documents that may be updated include the activity list, the assumption log, the lessons learned, stakeholder, and risk registers, and the requirements documentation.
- **Organizational process assets updates** - Any organizational process asset may be updated as the project work progresses.

*The **direct and manage project work** process information is adapted from: PMBOK® Guide – Sixth Edition. Pages 90-97*

Manage Project Knowledge

integration knowledge area | executing process group

Managing the project knowledge uses existing knowledge and creates new knowledge to achieve the project objectives while also contributing to organizational learning. Knowledge can be considered explicit and tacit. Explicit knowledge can be easily conveyed and understood using words, pictures or numbers. Tacit knowledge is not easily conveyed or expressed because it is personal. Tacit knowledge includes beliefs, insights, and experiences. As a project manager, you will need to manage and leverage both explicit and tacit knowledge for reusing existing knowledge and creating new knowledge.

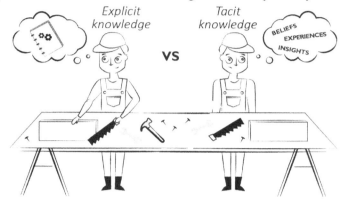

When lessons learned are documented and shared, this is considered codified learning and is leveraging explicit knowledge only, not tacit knowledge. Tacit knowledge is in the minds of the individuals and can be considered tribal knowledge: not easily documented so sharing occurs through discussion, conversations, and interactions. To leverage tacit knowledge, the project manager needs to focus on creating an environment of trust and collaboration.

Manage Project Knowledge: ITTOs

Inputs

1. Project management plan
   - All components
2. Project documents
   - Lessons learned register
   - Project team assignments
   - Resource breakdown structure
   - Source selection criteria
   - Stakeholder register
3. Deliverables
4. Enterprise environmental factors
5. Organizational process assets

Tools & Techniques

1. Expert judgement
2. Knowledge management
3. Information management
4. Interpersonal and team skills
   - Active listening
   - Facilitation
   - Leadership
   - Networking
   - Political awareness

Outputs

1. Lessons learned register
2. Project management plan updates
   - Any component
3. Organizational process assets updates

PMBOK® Guide – Sixth Edition, Page 98

Manage Project Knowledge: Inputs

Deliverables

Deliverables, outputs of the **direct and manage project work** process, are any type of unique, verifiable product, result or capability to perform a service. Deliverables are typically tangible items that are defined within the project scope statement.

Common Inputs:

- **Project management plan** - All components of the project management plan may be used to manage project knowledge.
- **Project documents** - Project documents that may be leveraged include the lessons learned and stakeholder registers, the project team assignments, and the resource breakdown structure.
- **Enterprise environmental factors** - Internal and external influences include, but are not limited to, the organizational, stakeholder, and customer culture, the geographic distribution of facilities and resources, and organizational knowledge experts.
- **Organizational process assets** - Procedures, guidelines, and templates will be used to manage project knowledge.

Manage Project Knowledge: Tools and Techniques

Knowledge Management

Knowledge management is a collection of tools and techniques that facilitate the sharing of both explicit and tacit knowledge. The approach to knowledge management is dependent upon the environment, the complexity of the project, the degree of innovation, and the diversity of the teams. Techniques include networking, communities of practice, meetings, job shadowing, focus groups, seminars or conferences, workshops, storytelling, knowledge fairs, and training.

While face-to-face communications and interactions typically improve the learning process, advances in technology have also created ways for people to connect virtually to enable learning and the sharing of knowledge. Using real-time video conferencing tools, such as Zoom or Skype, allow the individuals to connect in a way that mimics in-person networking or information sharing.

Information Management

Information management tools and techniques allow the people to connect to the information, specifically unambiguous, codified, and simple knowledge components. These could include the lessons learned register, web searches, articles, and the project management information system (PMIS).

Common Tools and Techniques:

Expert Judgment

Expertise in managing the project knowledge can come from any individual or group with specialized expertise.

Interpersonal and Team Skills

There are five interpersonal and team skills that may be used to manage the project knowledge:

Active listening helps reduce misunderstandings and improves communication and knowledge sharing. Listening to understand versus listening to respond.

Facilitation is effectively guiding a group to a successful decision, solution, or conclusion.

Leadership is used to communicate the vision and inspire the project team to focus on the appropriate knowledge and knowledge objectives.

Networking allows informal connections and relations among project stakeholders to be established, creating conditions to share tacit and explicit knowledge.

Political awareness is an understanding of the project and the organization's culture and environment.

Manage Project Knowledge: Outputs

There is one key output from managing project knowledge:

Lessons Learned Register

The lessons learned register includes details about the situation, including: category and description, the impact, recommendations, challenges, problems, realized risks and opportunities, etc. All team members should be contributing lessons learned throughout the project. At the end of the project, the information contained within the lessons learned register is transferred to the lessons learned repository.

Belinda's Hint

As the project manager, you set the tone and environment for harvesting lessons learned. Encourage your team to share what they are learning throughout the project, not just at the end. I have instituted friendly competitions or challenges where people get points for contributing their lessons.

Another trick is to give your team members special notebooks for jotting down the lessons as they occur and then sharing anything particularly insightful during the weekly team meeting. I make sure that the notebooks I give my team are unique and standout and are perhaps a little silly – like a Trolls notebook. This helps the notebook to stay present and not get lost amidst other books and documents.

Common Outputs:

- **Project management plan updates** - Any component of the project management plan may be updated because of managing the project knowledge.
- **Organizational process assets updates** - Any organizational process assets may be updated as the knowledge is embedded and codified into the deliverables or outputs.

*The **manage project knowledge** process information is adapted from: PMBOK® Guide – Sixth Edition. Pages 98-105*

Perform Integrated Change Control

integration knowledge area | monitoring and controlling process group

The **perform integrated change control** process is performed from project inception all the way through project completion and is critical to the management of the project scope statement, project management plan, and other key deliverables. Before the baselines are established, changes are not required to be formally controlled, but once the project is baselined, the changes need to go through integrated change control.

A designated committee or board (often called a change control board (CCB)), made up of key stakeholders, will review change requests and either approve or reject the request based on the impact to the project objectives. Approved change requests may require new or revised constraint considerations such as cost estimates, schedule dates, resource requirements, and activity sequences. It is possible that after CCB approval, the change would need additional customer or sponsor approval.

Belinda's Hint

While the project manager is typically not a member of the CCB, they may be the facilitator of the CCB. The project manager would document the change requests, the potential impact of the change requests, and then present those requests to the CCB for approval or rejection.

A comprehensive change control process will:

- Identify that a change has occurred or needs to occur
  - If a change occurs outside of the change control process, the project manager should still evaluate the change through the CCB to determine the impact of the change and if the change needs to be reversed
- Ensure only approved change requests are implemented
- Manage approved changes when and as they occur
- Maintain the integrity of the baselines
- Control and update the scope, cost, schedule, and quality requirements
- Document the impact of requested changes
- Control project quality to standards

A component of the **perform integrated change control** process is configuration management: the management of proposed changes that specifically affect project scope and the technical specifications of the deliverables. A configuration management plan will define which project artifacts are under configuration control.

Example: Scope Change vs Configuration Management

SCOPE CHANGE vs CONFIGURATION MANAGEMENT

After a preliminary walkthrough of the waiting room design and set-up, Kim requests a couple of changes. Upon sponsor approval, Kim requests to add a music system to the waiting room to play peaceful, soothing music. Adding the music system will be a scope change as it is adding work to the project.

The original chairs that were picked out for the waiting room were a hard plastic. Kim has submitted a change to replace the plastic with soft, imitation leather. Because this is changing the technical specifications of the chairs, this change would fall under configuration management.

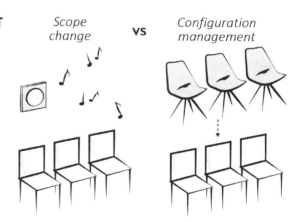

Scope change **vs** *Configuration management*

Perform Integrated Change Control: ITTOs

Inputs	Tools & Techniques	Outputs
1. Project management plan	1. Expert judgment	1. Approved change requests
• Change management plan	2. Change control tools	2. Project management plan updates
• Configuration management plan	3. Data analysis	• Any component
• Scope baseline	• Alternatives analysis	3. Project documents updates
• Schedule baseline	• Cost-benefit analysis	• Change log
• Cost baseline	4. Decision making	
2. Project documents	• Voting	
• Basis of estimates	• Autocratic decision making	
• Requirements traceability matrix	• Multicriteria decision analysis	
• Risk report	5. Meetings	
3. Work performance reports		
4. Change requests		
5. Enterprise environmental factors		
6. Organizational process assets		

PMBOK® Guide – Sixth Edition, Page 113

Perform Integrated Change Control: Inputs

Work Performance Reports

The work performance reports provide information to the project manager and the change control board as to the status of the project. This needs to be considered when evaluating change requests and may include information such as resource availability, schedule and cost data, earned value reports, and burnup or burndown charts.

Change Requests

Change requests include updates, scope changes, corrective actions, preventive actions, and defect repairs. If the change is going to impact a project baseline, the impacts and implications of the change need to be documented and presented. These changes would need to be approved by both the CCB and the customer or sponsor, unless they are part of the CCB.

Common Inputs:

- **Project management plan** - The project management plan will be leveraged through change control, including the change and configuration management plans, and the scope, schedule, and cost baselines.
- **Project documents** - Project documents that may be leveraged for change control include the basis of the estimates, the requirements traceability matrix, and the risk report.
- **Enterprise environmental factors** - Internal and external influences include, but are not limited to legal restrictions, government or industry standards, legal and regulatory requirements, organizational governance framework, and contracting and purchasing constraints.
- **Organizational process assets** - Policies, procedures, guidelines, and templates along with past project information will be used to perform integrated change control.

Perform Integrated Change Control: Tools and Techniques

Change Control Tools

There are manual and automated change control tools that may be used to manage the configuration management and change management process and the resulting decisions. Change control tools are a component of the PMIS.

For configuration management, tools should support: identifying the configuration items, recording and reporting about the configuration items, and verifying and auditing the items under consideration to ensure that the composition of the configuration items is correct. For change management, tools should support: change identification, change documentation, change decisions, and the tracking of changes.

Common Tools and Techniques:

Expert Judgment

Expert judgment is provided by individuals or organizations with specialized knowledge and experience. This includes knowledge from the change control board (CCB).

Data Analysis Techniques

There are two data analysis techniques that may be used while performing integrated change control:

An *alternatives analysis* is used to consider the various change requests to determine which will be accepted, rejected, or modified.

A *cost-benefit analysis* is used to determine if the change request is worth its related cost.

Decision-Making Techniques

Voting uses unanimity, majority, or plurality to decide whether to accept or reject the change requests.

Autocratic decision-making implies that one individual is making the decision for the entire group.

A *multicriteria decision analysis* uses a decision matrix to provide a systematic analytical approach to evaluate the changes based on predefined criteria.

Meetings

The most prevalent meeting for performing integrated change control is the change control board meetings to evaluate the submitted change requests. Once the changes have been assessed, alternatives to the change may be reviewed and discussed, and then the decision is communicated to the requestor.

Perform Integrated Change Control: Outputs

Approved Change Requests

If approved, the changes will be implemented as part of the **direct and manage project work** process. If the changes are rejected, the reason for the rejection is documented and communicated to the requestor. The status and disposition of the change requests will be updated in the change log.

Common Outputs:

- **Project management plan updates** - Any formally controlled component of the project management plan may be changed through this process. The integrity of the baselines is protected by ensuring that when a baseline change is needed, it is only from this point forward and not a complete re-baselining.

- **Project document updates** - All formally controlled documents may be updated as a result of change control. In addition, the change log will be updated with the documented changes that have occurred.

*The **perform integrated change control** process information is adapted from: PMBOK® Guide   Sixth Edition. Pages 113-120*

Manage Stakeholder Engagement

stakeholder knowledge area | executing process group

The **manage stakeholder engagement** process involves managing communications and interactions to satisfy the needs of, and resolve issues with, project stakeholders and foster their involvement in the project. In addition, this process addresses concerns that have not become issues yet, usually related to the anticipation of future problems, and clarifies and resolves issues that have been identified. A key objective is to actively manage the expectations of stakeholders through negotiation and communication, to increase the likelihood of project acceptance.

Belinda's Hint

While it will be virtually impossible to deliver everything your stakeholders want, it is critical to deliver what they expect. That relies on you, as the project manager, actively managing their expectations throughout the project.

For example, if I'm looking for a quick, cheap, some-what warm and some-what edible meal that I can purchase without leaving my car, a fast food drive-through restaurant will meet my expectations. However, if that fast food restaurant has advertised a 5-star dining experience with a perfectly prepared meal and a nice glass of wine, they would fail to meet my expectations. Failure to manage stakeholder expectations is an often-cited reason for project failure, according to PMI.

Manage Stakeholder Engagement: ITTOs

Inputs	Tools & Techniques	Outputs
1. Project management plan	1. Expert judgment	1. Change requests
• Communications management plan	2. Communication skills	2. Project management plan updates
• Risk management plan	• Feedback	• Communications management plan
• Stakeholder engagement plan	3. Interpersonal and team skills	• Stakeholder engagement plan
• Change management plan	• Conflict management	3. Project documents updates
2. Project documents	• Cultural awareness	• Change log
• Change log	• Negotiation	• Issue log
• Issue log	• Observation / conversation	• Lessons learned register
• Lessons learned register	• Political awareness	• Stakeholder register
• Stakeholder register	4. Ground rules	
3. Enterprise environmental factors	5. Meetings	
4. Organizational process assets		

PMBOK® Guide   Sixth Edition. Page 523

Manage Stakeholder Engagement: Inputs

Common Inputs:

- **Project management plan** - The project management plan will be consulted while managing stakeholder engagement, specifically the communications, risk and change management plans, and the stakeholder engagement plan.
- **Project documents** - Project documents that may be used to manage stakeholder engagement include the change and issue logs and the lessons learned and stakeholder registers.
- **Enterprise environmental factors** - Internal and external influences include, but are not limited to, the organization's culture, stakeholder risk thresholds, communication channels, trends and habits, and geographic distribution of resources and facilities.
- **Organizational process assets** - Procedures, guidelines, templates, and past project files may be used to manage the stakeholder engagement.

Manage Stakeholder Engagement: Tools and Techniques

Communication Skills

Communication throughout the project will be based on the communications management plan but will also encompass informal or ad hoc communications. A key communication technique to be leveraged is the gathering of feedback. Feedback can be collected through surveys, progress reporting, meetings, formal and informal conversations, and issue identification and discussion.

Ground Rules

Created by the team members themselves, ground rules are included in the team charter and set expectations as to interactions, behaviors, and relationships.

Common Tools and Techniques:

Expert Judgment

Expertise will be leveraged from individuals or groups with specialized knowledge, experience, or training.

Interpersonal and Team Skills

There are five interpersonal and team skills that may be used to manage stakeholder engagement:

Conflict management involves working with the appropriate parties to resolve disputes and differences of opinion.

Cultural awareness is used to help the project manager and team communicate effectively by understanding the differences in the audiences.

Negotiation is used to achieve support or agreement by discussing solutions that all parties can agree to pursue.

Observation and conversation involves engaging with the team and the stakeholders in an interactive manner, allowing the project manager to stay in touch with attitudes and progress of the team.

Political awareness is achieved through understanding the power relationships within and around the project.

Meetings

There are several meetings that are used to manage stakeholder engagement, including decision-making, issue resolution, lessons learned and retrospectives, project kick-off, sprint planning, and status update meetings.

Manage Stakeholder Engagement: Outputs

Common Outputs:

- **Change requests** - Change requests may be generated based on managing stakeholder engagement. These changes will become an input to the **perform integrated change control** process.
- **Project management plan updates** - The project management plan may be updated, including the communications management plan and the stakeholder engagement plan.
- **Project document updates** - Project documents that may be updated include the change and issue logs and the lessons learned and stakeholder registers.

*The **manage stakeholder engagement** process information is adapted from: PMBOK® Guide – Sixth Edition. Pages 523-529*

Monitor Stakeholder Engagement

stakeholder knowledge area | monitoring and controlling process group

The **monitor stakeholder engagement** process monitors the project stakeholder relationships, adjusting the strategies to engage stakeholders, and increasing the effectiveness of stakeholder engagement activities as the project evolves.

Monitor Stakeholder Engagement: ITTOs

Inputs	Tools & Techniques	Outputs

1. Project management plan
  • Resource management plan
  • Communications management plan
  • Stakeholder engagement plan
2. Project documents
  • Issue log
  • Lessons learned register
  • Project communications
  • Risk register
  • Stakeholder register
3. Work performance data
4. Enterprise environmental factors
5. Organizational process assets
	1. Data analysis
	  • Alternatives analysis
	  • Root cause analysis
	  • Stakeholder analysis
	2. Decision making
	  • Multicriteria decision analysis
	  • Voting
	3. Data representation
	  • Stakeholder engagement assessment matrix
	4. Communication skills
	  • Feedback
	  • Presentations
	5. Interpersonal and team skills
	  • Active listening
	  • Cultural awareness
	  • Leadership
	  • Networking
	  • Political awareness
	6. Meetings
		1. Work performance information
		2. Change requests
		3. Project management plan updates
		  • Resource management plan
		  • Communications management plan
		  • Stakeholder engagement plan
		4. Project documents updates
		  • Issue log
		  • Lessons learned register
		  • Risk register
		  • Stakeholder register

PMBOK® Guide – Sixth Edition. Page 530

Monitor Stakeholder Engagement: Inputs

Common Inputs:

- **Project management plan** - The project management plan will be consulted to monitor stakeholder engagement, including the resource and communications management plans, and the stakeholder engagement plan.
- **Project documents** - Project documents that may be evaluated include the issue log, the project communications, and the lessons learned, risk, and stakeholder registers.
- **Work performance data** - Work performance data includes the raw data from the project work, including which stakeholders are supportive of the project and the level and type of engagement they are demonstrating.
- **Enterprise environmental factors** - Internal and external influences include, but are not limited to, the organizational culture and policies, personnel administration policies, stakeholder risk thresholds, global or local trends, and the geographic distribution of resources and facilities.
- **Organizational process assets** - Policies, procedures, guidelines, and templates may be levered to monitor the stakeholder engagement.

Monitor Stakeholder Engagement: Tools and Techniques

Communication skills

Communication skills include capturing and using feedback from the stakeholders and presenting clear information to the stakeholders to increase engagement.

Common Tools and Techniques:

Data Analysis Techniques

There are three data analysis techniques that may be used to monitor stakeholder engagement:

An *alternatives analysis* is used to evaluate options to respond to variances in the desired results of the stakeholder engagement.

A *root cause analysis* is used to find the underlying reasons for stakeholder engagement issues.

A *stakeholder analysis* determines the position of stakeholder groups and individuals at any particular time in the project.

Decision-Making Techniques

There are two decision-making techniques that may be used:

A *multicriteria decision analysis* prioritizes and weights the criteria for successful stakeholder engagement in order to make decisions.

Voting is used to select the best response for a variance in stakeholder engagement.

Data Representation

A *stakeholder engagement assessment matrix* monitors the stakeholder engagement through tracking changes in the level of engagement for each stakeholder.

Interpersonal and Team Skills

There are five interpersonal and team skills that may be used:

Active listening is used to reduce misunderstandings and miscommunications.

Cultural awareness helps the project manager and the project team work and engage with stakeholders with different locations, beliefs, perspectives, backgrounds, and experiences.

Leadership is used to communicate the vision and inspire stakeholders to support the work and outcomes of the project.

Networking involves connecting interactively with other people to develop relationships and further understandings.

Political awareness is used to understand the strategies of the organization, understand who wields power and influence, and to develop an ability to communicate effectively.

Meetings

There are several meetings that are used to manage stakeholder engagement, including decision-making, issue resolution, lessons learned and retrospectives, project kick-off, sprint planning, and status update meetings.

Monitor Stakeholder Engagement: Outputs

Common Outputs:

- **Work performance information** - Work performance information includes information on the status of the stakeholder engagement as compared to the desired level of engagement defined within the stakeholder engagement assessment matrix, stakeholder cube, or other tools.
- **Change requests** - Change requests may be generated based on monitoring the stakeholder engagement. These changes will become an input to the **perform integrated change control** process.
- **Project management plan updates** - The project management plan may be updated, including the resource and communications management plans and the stakeholder engagement plan.
- **Project document updates** - Project documents that may be updated include the issue log, and the lessons learned, risk, and stakeholder registers.

*The **monitor stakeholder engagement** process information is adapted from: PMBOK® Guide – Sixth Edition. Pages 530-536*

Chapter 13 - Review Questions

Time Limit: 18 Minutes

1. **Creeping scope is a major concern of any project. The person responsible for safe-guarding customer change requests is the:**
   A. Functional manager
   B. Project manager
   C. Project sponsor
   D. President

2. **An approved change request impacting project scope is:**
   A. Any modification to the agreed-upon project scope baseline, as defined by the approved project scope statement, WBS, and WBS dictionary
   B. Any change in project personnel
   C. Any change in project authorization
   D. Any modification in technical specifications as defined in the WBS

3. **A Change Control Board (CCB) is:**
   A. Charged with making sure no changes are made to project baselines
   B. A group of experts external to the project
   C. Designated by a steering committee
   D. A group of stakeholders who are capable of evaluating change requests and are responsible for approving or rejecting change requests

4. **Change requests:**
   A. Can come from anyone
   B. Must be documented
   C. Must be subjected to an integrated change control process
   D. All of the above are correct

5. **Which is an acceptable cause for "re-baselining" a $10 million project?**
   A. The client has authorized a $100,000 addition to the scope of the project
   B. The contractor's company has instituted a quality program in which it has pledged to spend one million dollars during the next year
   C. The productivity in the drafting department is lower than anticipated, which has resulted in 1,000 additional hours over what was budgeted
   D. The engineering department has converted to a new $200,000 CAD system

6. **This process is performed from project inception through completion and includes multiple change management activities.**
   A. Perform integrated change control
   B. Manage project execution
   C. Monitor and control project work
   D. Manage configuration

7. **Which statement is most accurate?**
   A. Tacit knowledge includes beliefs and insights whereas explicit knowledge can be easily codified and conveyed
   B. Tacit knowledge involves tactile driven activities whereas explicit knowledge follows a checklist
   C. Tacit knowledge can be codified and taught whereas explicit knowledge is only learned through training
   D. Tacit knowledge is easy to transfer to another person whereas explicit knowledge cannot be shared or transferred

8. **The perform integrated change control process includes all of the following change management activities except:**
   A. Reviewing and approving requested changes
   B. Resource leveling
   C. Maintaining the integrity of baselines by releasing only approved changes for incorporation into project products or services, and maintaining their related configuration and planning documentation
   D. Controlling and updating the scope, cost, budget, schedule, and quality requirements based upon approved changes, by coordinating changes across the entire project

9. **Which of the following best describes configuration management?**
   A. Management and control of the physical and functional characteristics of the product, service, result, or component
   B. Management and control of the project requirements
   C. The description of the product to be developed
   D. The management of quality as it relates to the project scope

10. **Which of the following change requests would most likely change the project baselines?**
    A. A request to add additional resources to critical path activities on a project that is late
    B. A request to change a project team member
    C. A request to change the functionality of the product
    D. A request to change communication methods

11. **What is the most appropriate approach to handling an unapproved change request that's already been implemented?**
    A. Identify the individual responsible for implementing the unapproved change request and provide feedback
    B. Reverse the change
    C. Do nothing as the change has already been implemented
    D. Evaluate the change through the integrated change control process

12. **A team member made a change to the design of the deliverable based on verbal feedback received from one of the customers. The completed deliverable was rejected by the customer as it did not meet the documented requirements. What type of a change request would be needed to modify the completed deliverable?**
    A. Scope change
    B. Defect repair
    C. Corrective action
    D. No change request required

13. **This is the process of communicating and working with stakeholders to meet their needs and address issues as they occur:**
    A. Manage Stakeholder Engagement
    B. Distribute Information
    C. Identify Stakeholders
    D. Conduct Stakeholder Analysis

14. **Throughout the project, you have consistently provided the stakeholders with an updated status report on the progress of the project in order to manage their expectations. This includes providing updates on any changes that have been approved. As a result of actively managing stakeholders' expectations:**
    A. The project is more likely to come in on time and on budget
    B. The project is more likely to have increased acceptance
    C. The project is more likely to have improved communication
    D. The project is more likely to have lower attrition

15. **How is the stakeholder engagement strategy used in the manage stakeholder engagement process?**
    A. It shows which stakeholders are involved in the project
    B. It details the product acceptance criteria
    C. It documents the stakeholders' roles and responsibilities
    D. It provides the evaluation of the stakeholders' needs based on factors such as power and interest

Review Question Answers

1. **Answer: B**

   As the project manager, one of your primary responsibilities will be to guard the project against scope creep – ensuring that all changes go through the appropriate change control process.

2. **Answer: A**

   Change requests impacting to the project scope would be defined as changes to the scope baseline (scope statement, WBS, and WBS dictionary). Changes in personnel, changes in authorization, and modification of technical specifications would not necessarily be a project scope change.

3. **Answer: D**

   The change control board (CCB) is made up of stakeholders with enough authority to accept/reject changes and enough knowledge of the project to understand and evaluate the change requests.

4. **Answer: D**

   Change requests can come from anyone, must be documented, and must be subjected to an integrated change control process.

5. **Answer: A**

   A $100,000 addition of scope would be a scope change and would therefore impact the project baselines. The quality program and the new CAD system do not necessarily impact your project. The lower productivity would be a reason to preserve the baseline, as it is important to track that variance and any type of corrective actions that are taken to fix the problem.

6. **Answer: A**

   This is describing the perform integrated change control process.

7. **Answer: A**

   Tacit knowledge includes beliefs and insights whereas explicit knowledge can be easily codified and conveyed.

8. **Answer: B**

   Resource leveling is done during the develop schedule and the control schedule processes but would not be considered part of integrated change control.

9. **Answer: A**

   Configuration management encompasses any changes to the technical specifications, the physical and functional characteristics, of the product, service, or result.

10. **Answer: C**

    The change that would most likely change the baselines would be changes to the functionality of a product. Adding resources (crashing), changing a team member, or changing communication methods, would not be a change to the scope.

11. **Answer: D**

    Even though it has already been implemented, it is important for the change to be evaluated through the change control process. This will identify the impact of the change and make the determination if the change will stay or potentially be reversed.

12. **Answer: B**

    Because there was not a documented and accepted change request, and despite the verbal request, this would be considered a quality issue and the fault of the project team. As such, the change request would be a defect repair.

13. **Answer: A**

    The manage stakeholder engagement process is the process responsible for communicating and working with stakeholders to meet their needs and address issues. The only other *PMBOK® Guide* process listed in the answers is the identify stakeholders process, but this question is not describing that process.

14. **Answer: B**

    By actively managing the stakeholders' expectations, it increases the chances of project acceptance. PMI cites one of the most common reasons for project failure is due to failing to manage expectations. It's not about giving your customer everything they want but you must give them what they expect. It is up to the project manager and the team to manage those expectations.

15. **Answer: D**

The stakeholder engagement strategy considers the stakeholders' power and interest which allows the project team to prioritize their interactions with those stakeholders with the potentially biggest impact.

Chapter 13 - Vocabulary Review

Active listening

* Alternatives analysis

Autocratic decision-making

* Change control tools

Conflict management

* Cost-benefit analysis

Cultural awareness

* Deliverables

Facilitation

* Ground rules

Implicit knowledge

Information management

* Issue log

Knowledge management

Leadership

* Lessons learned register

* Multicriteria decision analysis

Negotiation

* Networking

Observation/conversation

Political awareness

* Root cause analysis

* Stakeholder analysis

* Stakeholder engagement assessment matrix

Stand-up meetings

* Tacit knowledge

Voting

* Work performance data

1.	Knowledge that is easily codified and transferred
2.	An understanding of the differences between individuals, groups and organizations and adapting the communication strategy in the context of these differences
3.	The ability to influence and convey a motivating vision to a group of people over whom you may, or may not, have authority
4.	Engaging in active dialogue in order to reach a mutually agreeable conclusion
5.	Manual or automated tools to assist with change and/or configuration management
6.	Engaging in interactive dialogue and face-to-face or virtual evaluation
7.	A collection of tools and techniques that facilitate the sharing of both explicit and tacit knowledge
8.	A matrix that compares current and desired stakeholder engagement levels
9.	Actively seeking to resolve disputes or differences of opinion within a group
10.	Members of the group provide their choice in a decision-making process
11.	Effective oversight and management of a group activity
12.	Personal knowledge that can be difficult to articulate and share such as beliefs, experience, and insights
13.	Demonstrating empathy with the speaker and listening to understand

14.	An agile technique where immediate team members provide their status updates each day in a relatively quick format
15.	The use of tools and techniques to allow people to connect to information, specifically unambiguous, codified, and simple knowledge components
16.	A technique of systematically gathering and analyzing quantitative and qualitative information to determine whose interests should be taken into account throughout the project
17.	A financial analysis tool used to determine the benefits provided by an action against the costs of that action
18.	An analytical technique used to determine the basic underlying reason that causes a variance or a defect or a risk
19.	Any unique and verifiable product, result, or capability to perform a service that is required to be produced to complete a process, phase, or project
20.	A project document used to record knowledge gained during a project so that it can be used in the current project and entered into the lessons learned repository
21.	An understanding of the power structure and the individual power roles within the organization
22.	A technique used to evaluate identified options in order to select the options or approaches to use to execute and perform the work of the project
23.	Establishing connections and relationships with other people from the same or other organizations
24.	Expectations regarding acceptable behavior by project team members
25.	Utilizes a decision matrix to provide a systematic analytical approach for establishing criteria, such as risk levels, uncertainty, and valuation, to evaluate and rank many ideas
26.	A project document where information about issues is recorded and monitored
27.	Implies that one person is making the decision for the group
28.	The raw observations and measurements identified during activities being performed to carry out the project work

* These definitions are taken from the Glossary of *PMBOK® Guide – Sixth Edition*

Vocabulary Review Answers

1. Implicit knowledge
2. Cultural awareness
3. Leadership
4. Negotiation
5. Change control tools
6. Observation/conversation
7. Knowledge management
8. Stakeholder engagement assessment matrix
9. Conflict management
10. Voting
11. Facilitation
12. Tacit knowledge
13. Active listening
14. Stand-up meetings
15. Information management
16. Stakeholder analysis
17. Cost-benefit analysis
18. Root cause analysis
19. Deliverables
20. Lessons learned register
21. Political awareness
22. Alternatives analysis
23. Networking
24. Ground rules
25. Multicriteria decision analysis
26. Issue log
27. Autocratic decision-making
28. Work performance data

Chapter 14

Controlling the Project

What's in This Chapter

- Monitoring and Controlling the Project
- Monitor and Control Project Work
- Control Scope
- Control Schedule
- Control Costs
- Earned Value, Forecasting, and TCPI

Mature project management comes through the ability to not only manage the work of the project but to understand, predict, and control the impact of project variances and realized risks. There is risk associated with all projects, and it is up to the project manager to control and respond to that risk as early as possible.

In this chapter, I will discuss controlling the project to the defined constraints and the scope, schedule, and cost baselines. Effective project monitoring and controlling is a product of understanding the project baselines, identifying and analyzing the variances from the baselines, predicting the impact of those variances, communicating about the variances and the handling of those variances. This is why the baselines are so important for any project. If you do not have a baseline, you have no way of gauging your progress and discovering any trends.

There are four processes in the monitoring and controlling process group that will be discussed in this chapter:

Monitor and Control Project Work. This integration process tracks, reviews, and reports overall progress to meet the performance objectives defined in the project management plan.

Control Scope. This scope management process monitors the status of the project and product scope and manages changes to the scope baseline.

Control Schedule. This schedule management process monitors the status of the project schedule and manages changes to the schedule baseline.

Control Costs. This cost management process monitors the status of the project budget and manages changes to the cost baseline.

Lastly, this chapter will conclude with an in-depth review and practice section for earned value, forecasting, and the to-complete performance index formulas.

Monitor and Control Project Work

integration knowledge area | monitoring and controlling process group

The **monitor and control project work** process monitors the project processes within the initiating, planning, executing, and closing process groups, comparing the actual project performance to the planned performance. This process determines the need for any corrective or preventive actions, analyzes, tracks, and monitors project risks, and monitors the implementation of any approved changes.

Monitor and Control Project Work: ITTOs

Inputs	Tools & Techniques	Outputs
1. Project management plan	1. Expert judgment	1. Work performance reports
• Any component	2. Data analysis	2. Change requests
2. Project documents	• Alternatives analysis	3. Project management plan updates
• Assumption log	• Cost-benefit analysis	• Any components
• Basis of estimates	• Earned value analysis	4. Project documents updates
• Cost forecasts	• Root cause analysis	• Cost forecasts
• Issue log	• Trend analysis	• Issue log
• Lessons learned register	• Variance analysis	• Lessons learned register
• Milestone list	3. Decision making	• Risk register
• Quality reports	• Voting	• Stakeholder register
• Risk register	4. Meetings	
• Risk report		
• Schedule forecasts		
3. Work performance information		
4. Agreements		
5. Enterprise environmental factors		
6. Organizational process assets		

PMBOK® Guide – Sixth Edition, Page 105

Monitor and Control Project Work: Inputs

Work Performance Information

Work performance information is the result of comparing the work performance data to the project baselines and analyzing any variances that exist. The work performance information will be used during this process to create the work performance reports.

Agreements

Procurement agreements document the terms and conditions associated with the project procurements. This information is used in this process to ensure that those terms and conditions are being met by both the buyer and the seller.

Common Inputs:

* **Project management plan** - All components of the project management plan may be leveraged while monitoring and controlling the project work.

- **Project documents** - Project documents that may be used include the assumption log, the cost and schedule forecasts, the risk and lessons learned registers, the milestone list, and the quality and risk reports.
- **Enterprise environmental factors** - Internal and external influences should be considered, including, but not limited to the organizational culture and infrastructure, the administration of personnel, and marketplace conditions.
- **Organizational process assets** - Policies, procedures, guidelines, templates, and past project files may be used to monitor and control the project work.

Monitor and Control Project Work: Tools and Techniques

Common Tools and Techniques:

Expert Judgment

Expertise may come from individuals or organizations with specialized knowledge or experience that would pertain to this process.

Data Analysis Techniques

There are six data analysis techniques that may be used during the monitoring and controlling of the project work:

An *alternatives analysis* is used to select the corrective actions or a combination of corrective and preventive actions to implement when there is a deviation from the baseline.

A *cost-benefit analysis* helps to determine the best corrective action in terms of cost compared to the anticipated results.

An *earned value analysis* is used to analyze the amount of value earned by the project compared to the planned value and/or the actual costs. This allows the project manager and the team to assess if the project is potentially over-budget and/or behind schedule.

A *root cause analysis* is used to evaluate the root causes for quality problems, project issues, or risks, allowing the responses to be more targeted and efficient.

A *trend analysis* evaluates trending data on the project progress to proactively identify the need for preventive actions.

A *variance analysis* is used to evaluate the progress of the project against the project baselines to identify any variances and appropriate actions needed.

Decision-Making Techniques

Voting is used to make decisions and may involve unanimity, majority, or plurality agreements.

Meetings

Meetings may be formal or informal, face-to-face or virtual, and may involve various individuals. Common meetings for monitoring and controlling the project work include user group and review meetings.

Monitor and Control Project Work: Outputs

There is one key output from monitoring and controlling the project work:

Work Performance Reports

Work performance reports are the compilation of work performance information into an electronic or physical representation, such as status reports, memos, justifications, information notes, recommendations, etc.

Common Outputs:

- **Change requests** - Change requests may be generated based on monitoring and controlling the project work, and they will become an input to the **perform integrated change control** process.
- **Project management plan updates** - Any component of the project management plan may be updated based on this process.
- **Project document updates** - Project documents that may be updated include the cost and schedule forecasts, the issue log, and the risk and lessons learned register.

*The **monitor and control project work** process information is adapted from: PMBOK® Guide – Sixth Edition. Pages 105-113*

Control Scope

scope knowledge area | monitoring and controlling process group

The **control scope** process monitors the status of the project and the product scope, manages changes to the scope baseline, and ensures the project scope is controlled by confirming that all requested changes are processed through the **perform integrated change control** process.

Although change is inevitable, a clearly defined and communicated change control process will limit the impact of changes and minimize the occurrence of scope creep.

Control Scope: ITTOs

Inputs	Tools & Techniques	Outputs
1. Project management plan	1. Data analysis	1. Work performance information
• Scope management plan	• Variance analysis	2. Change requests
• Requirements management plan	• Trend analysis	3. Project management plan updates
• Change management plan		• Scope management plan
• Configuration management plan		• Scope baseline
• Scope baseline		• Schedule baseline
• Performance measurement baseline		• Cost baseline
2. Project documents		• Performance measurement baseline
• Lessons learned register		4. Project documents updates
• Requirements documentation		• Lessons learned register
• Requirements traceability matrix		• Requirements documentation
3. Work performance data		• Requirements traceability matrix
4. Organizational process assets		

PMBOK® Guide – Sixth Edition. Page 167

Control Scope: Inputs

Common Inputs:

- **Project management plan** - The project management plan will be consulted while controlling the project scope, including the scope, requirements, change, and configuration management plans, and the scope and performance measurement baselines.

- **Project documents** - Project documents that may be evaluated include the lessons learned register, and the requirements documentation and traceability matrix.
- **Work performance data** - Work performance data can include the number of change requests received, the number of requests accepted, and the number of deliverables that have been verified, validated, and completed.
- **Organizational process assets** - Policies, procedures, guidelines, and templates may be used to control the project scope.

Control Scope: Tools and Techniques

Common Tools and Techniques:

Data Analysis Techniques

A *variance analysis* is used to compare the baseline to the actual results and determine if any variance is within the threshold amount of if corrective or preventive action is appropriate.

A *trend analysis* is used to examine project performance over time to determine if the project is improving or deteriorating.

Control Scope: Outputs

Common Outputs:

- **Work performance information** - Work performance information includes information on how the actual scope progress compares to the scope baseline and plan for technical accomplishments. This can include categorizing the scope changes, scope variances, and schedule or cost impacts.
- **Change requests** - Change requests may be generated and will become an input to the **perform integrated change control** process.
- **Project management plan updates** - The project management plan may be updated, including the scope management plan, and the scope, schedule, cost, and performance measurement baselines.
- **Project document updates** - Project documents that may be updated include the lessons learned register, the requirements documentation, and the requirements traceability matrix.

*The **control scope** process information is adapted from: PMBOK® Guide – Sixth Edition. Pages 167-171*

Control Schedule

The **control schedule** process evaluates the current status of the project schedule, considers the influencing factors, reconsiders the schedule reserves, determines if the schedule has changed, and manages changes to the schedule when and as they occur.

For agile projects, schedule control is slightly different than for waterfall projects. The status of the project is determined by comparing the total amount of work delivered and accepted against the estimates of what should have been completed at this point. Retrospectives are used to correct and improve processes, and the remaining work is prioritized from the backlog. Another element of agile schedule control is calculating velocity.

Velocity is the average amount of work a scrum team completes during a sprint, measured in either story points or hours. The product owner can use velocity to predict how quickly a team can work through the backlog, because the report tracks the forecasted and completed work over several iterations–the more iterations, the more accurate the forecast.

For example: the product owner wants to complete 500 story points in the backlog. The development team generally completes 50 story points per iteration. The product owner can reasonably assume the team will need ten iterations (give or take) to complete the required work.

As a component of schedule control, it is important to monitor how velocity evolves over time. New teams can expect to see an increase in velocity as the team optimizes relationships and the work process. Existing teams can track their velocity to ensure consistent performance over time and can confirm that a particular process change made improvements or not. A decrease in average velocity is usually a sign that some part of the team's development process has become inefficient and should be discussed at the next retrospective.

Let's check your understanding of velocity. The answers to Exercise 14.1 are on page 407.

Exercise 14.1: Velocity

Consider the following:

Remaining backlog is 700 story points

Sprint duration is 1 month

Team velocity averages 35 story points per Sprint

Today is January 1, 2018

Team cost is $40,000 per month

Calculate the approximate delivery month and cost of the project:

What happens if the team increases its' velocity to 50 story points per sprint?

How about 70?

During the **control schedule** process, the earned value technique (EVT) will be used for variance management, including identifying the schedule variance (SV) and the schedule performance index (SPI). The earned value technique will be discussed in more detail later in this chapter.

Control Schedule: ITTOs

Inputs	Tools & Techniques	Outputs

1. Project management plan
  • Schedule management plan
  • Schedule baseline
  • Scope baseline
  • Performance measurement baseline
2. Project documents
  • Lessons learned register
  • Project calendars
  • Project schedule
  • Resource calendars
  • Schedule data
3. Work performance data
4. Organizational process assets
	1. Data analysis
	  • Earned value analysis
	  • Iteration burndown chart
	  • Performance reviews
	  • Trend analysis
	  • Variance analysis
	  • What-if scenario analysis
	2. Critical path method
	3. Project management information system
	4. Resource optimization
	5. Leads and lags
	6. Schedule compression
		1. Work performance information
		2. Schedule forecasts
		3. Change requests
		4. Project management plan updates
		  • Schedule management plan
		  • Schedule baseline
		  • Cost baseline
		  • Performance measurement baseline
		5. Project documents updates
		  • Assumption log
		  • Basis of estimates
		  • Lessons learned register
		  • Project schedule
		  • Resource calendars
		  • Risk register
		  • Schedule data

PMBOK® Guide — Sixth Edition. Page 222

Control Schedule: Inputs

Common Inputs:

- **Project management plan** - The project management plan will be used in controlling the schedule, including the schedule management plan, and the schedule, scope, and performance measurement baseline.
- **Project documents** - Project documents that may be leveraged include the lessons learned register, project calendars, project schedule, resource calendars, and the schedule data.
- **Work performance data** - Work performance data will supply data on the project status, including which activities have started, their progress, and which activities have completed.
- **Organizational process assets** - Policies, procedures, guidelines, templates, and past project files may be used to control the project schedule.

Control Schedule: Tools & Techniques

Critical Path Method

Critical path method, presented in Chapter Six, presents the schedule model based on the activity dependencies. Any variance on the critical path will impact the completion date of the project. The team will also want to monitor the risk associated with near-critical activities.

Resource Optimization Techniques

Presented in Chapter Six, there are two resource optimization techniques that can be performed. The first technique is resource leveling. Resource leveling is used to optimize the distribution of work among resources and includes moving resources to critical activities. Resource leveling may alter the critical path.

After resource leveling, the team may pursue resource smoothing which adjusts the activities so that the requirements for resources do not exceed certain predefined limits. This is accomplished by leveraging the available float, and as such, smoothing may not be able to optimize all resources. Resource leveling does not alter the critical path.

Example: Resource Optimization Techniques

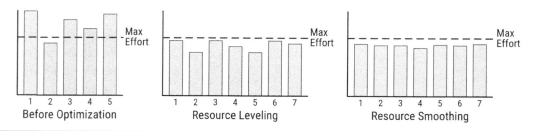

Before Optimization | Resource Leveling | Resource Smoothing

Leads and Lags

Let's check your memory of leads and lags. The answers to Exercise 14.2 are on page 407.

Exercise 14.2: Leads and Lags

Test your memory by filling in the blanks as to what the statement is describing (lead, lag, or both?):

1. _____ Represents a delay in the start of the successor activity

2. _____ Only used in FS discretionary relationships

3. _____ Reflected as a negative number above the arrow in a PDM

4. _____ Represents an acceleration in the start of a successor activity

5. _____ Reflected as a positive number above the arrow in a PDM

6. _____ May be used in FS, SS, FF, SF relationships

7. _____ Represents time we are saving

8. _____ Represents time we are adding

Schedule Compression

If the project is running behind schedule, schedule compression techniques may be used. Let's check your memory of the schedule compression techniques. The answers to Exercise 14.3 are on page 407.

Exercise 14.3: Schedule Compression Techniques

Test your memory by filling in the blanks as to what the statement is describing (fast-tracking, crashing or both?):

1. _____ Adds resources/money to activities on the critical path

2. _____ Performs sequential activities concurrently

3. _____ Focuses on activities on the critical path first

4. _____ Of the two techniques, typically performed first

Common Tools and Techniques:

Data Analysis Techniques

There are six data analysis techniques that may be used while controlling the project schedule:

An *earned value analysis* is a comparison of value earned in the project to the planned value to determine the schedule status. This technique will be discussed in more detail later in this chapter.

An *iteration burndown chart* is a chart used on agile projects to track the work that remains to be completed in the iteration backlog. Actual remaining work is compared to ideal remaining work and variances are noted and addressed. A forecast trend line can be used to predict the likely variance at the completion of the sprint.

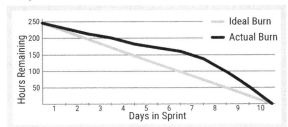

Performance reviews measure, compare, and analyze schedule performance against the schedule baseline.

A *trend analysis* examines project performance over time to determine whether performance is improving or deteriorating.

A *variance analysis* looks at variances in planned versus actual start and finish dates, planned versus actual durations, and variances in float. The cause and degree of the variance is also investigated to estimate the implications of the variance. This will allow the team to determine if a corrective or preventive action is required. Not all schedule variance will have an impact on the project, such as when the variance can be absorbed with existing float that is available.

A *what-if scenario analysis* is used to assess the various scenarios guided by the output from the project risk management processes to bring the schedule model into alignment with the project management plan and approved baseline.

Project Management Information System

The PMIS includes scheduling software that provides the ability to track the schedule progress and to forecast the effects of changes to the project schedule model.

Control Schedule: Outputs

Schedule Forecasts

The schedule forecasts are an estimate or prediction of the project schedule activities and completion. Forecasts are updated and reissued based on the work performance information that is generated. Schedule forecasts can include earned value performance indicators, as well as schedule reserve information.

Common Outputs:

- **Work performance information** - Work performance information includes information on how the project is progressing, including any variance calculations and other performance measurements.
- **Change requests** - Change requests may be generated and will become an input to the **perform integrated change control** process.
- **Project management plan updates** - The project management plan may be updated, including the schedule management plan, and the schedule, cost, and performance measurement baselines.
- **Project document updates** - Project documents that may be updated include the assumption log, the basis of the estimates, the lessons learned and risk registers, the project schedule and schedule data, and the resource calendars.

*The **control schedule** process information is adapted from: PMBOK® Guide – Sixth Edition. Pages 222-230*

Control Costs

cost knowledge area | monitoring and controlling process group

The **control costs** process ensures that requested changes to the budget are agreed upon and manages the actual changes when and as they occur. This process ensures that potential cost overruns do not exceed the authorized funding limits and acts to bring any expected cost overruns within acceptable limits. Controlling the costs on the project involves ensuring that change requests are acted on in a timely manner, monitoring cost performance to isolate and understand variances from the approved baseline, informing appropriate stakeholders of any approved changes and their associated costs, and monitoring the work performance against the money that has spent on that work.

Control Costs: ITTOs

Inputs	Tools & Techniques	Outputs
1. Project management plan	1. Expert judgement	1. Work performance information
• Cost management plan	2. Data analysis	2. Cost forecasts
• Cost baseline	• Earned value analysis	3. Change requests
• Performance measurement baseline	• Variance analysis	4. Project management plan updates
2. Project documents	• Trend analysis	• Cost management plan
• Lessons learned register	• Reserve analysis	• Cost baseline
3. Project funding requirements	3. To-complete performance index	• Performance measurement baseline
4. Work performance data	4. Project management information system	5. Project documents updates
5. Organizational process assets		• Assumption log
		• Basis of estimates
		• Cost estimates
		• Lessons learned register
		• Risk register

PMBOK® Guide – Sixth Edition. Page 257

Control Costs: Inputs

Project Funding Requirements

The project funding requirements, an output of the **determine budget** process, document the project expenditures and anticipated liabilities.

Common Inputs:

- **Project management plan** - The project management plan will be used in controlling the costs of the project, including the cost management plan, and the cost and performance measurement baseline.
- **Project documents** - Project documents that may be leveraged include the lessons learned register.
- **Work performance data** - Work performance data contains data on the project status such as which costs have been authorized, incurred, invoiced, and paid.
- **Organizational process assets** - Policies, procedures, guidelines, templates, and past project files may be used in controlling the project costs.

Control Costs: Tools & Techniques

To-Complete Performance Index (TCPI)

TCPI is a measure of the cost performance that must be achieved with the remaining resources in order to meet a specified management goal. TCPI is expressed as a ratio, comparing work remaining to funds remaining. TCPI will be discussed in detail in the next section.

Common Tools and Techniques:

Expert Judgment

Expertise can be provided by an individuals or groups with specialized knowledge and experience, such as with earned value analyses and forecasting.

Data Analysis Techniques

There are four data analysis techniques that may be used while controlling the costs of the project:

An *earned value analysis* compares the performance measurement baseline to the actual schedule and cost performance of the project, integrating the scope baseline with the cost and schedule baselines to form the performance measurement baseline. This analysis will be discussed later in this chapter.

A *variance analysis* is used to determine the amount of variance between the planned and actual progress. In the next section, the calculations will be discussed including cost variance (CV), cost performance index (CPI), schedule variance (SV), schedule performance index (SPI), and variance at completion (VAC).

A *trend analysis* examines project performance over time to determine if the project is improving or deteriorating. This analysis is going to encompass forecasting, which will be discussed in the next section. Forecasting includes calculating the estimate to complete (ETC) and the estimate at completion (EAC).

A *reserve analysis* is used to evaluate the amount of contingency reserve as compared to the amount of risk or uncertainty on the project. Contingency reserve is determined based on known-unknowns: risks that have been identified and are known, it is just unknown if the risk event is going to happen (thus it being a risk). As the project progresses and the work is defined with increasing confidence, the contingency reserve should be reduced or perhaps eliminated. Cost contingency reserve is included in the schedule baseline.

The assumption on the exam is that as a project manager, a reserve analysis is part of your professional responsibilities. As the project progresses, the estimates should become more and more accurate, minimizing the use of the contingency. In addition, it is assumed that you, as project manager, control the identification and the use of the contingency.

Project Management Information System (PMIS)

The PMIS provides tools and systems used to support the analysis of the project budget and any identified variances.

Control Costs: Outputs

There is one key output from controlling the project costs:

Cost Forecasts

The cost forecasts include the estimate to complete (ETC) and the estimate at completion (EAC). These forecasts are documented and communicated to the stakeholders.

Common Outputs:

- **Work performance information** - Work performance information includes information on how the project is performing compared to the baselines.
- **Change requests** - Change requests may be generated and will become an input to the **perform integrated change control** process.
- **Project management plan updates** - The project management plan may be updated, including the cost management plan and the cost and performance measurement baselines.
- **Project document updates** - Project documents that may be updated include the assumption log, the cost estimates and the basis of those estimates, and the lessons learned and the risk registers.

*The **control costs** process information is adapted from: PMBOK® Guide – Sixth Edition. Page 257-270*

Earned Value, Forecasting, & To-Complete Performance Index

monitoring and controlling process group

The concepts of earned value and forecasting are not applied in all environments, although there are some industries that have high utilization of these techniques and formulas. Outside of the exam environment, if you wanted to know how to calculate a variance or a forecast, you can simply ask Google or Alexa. However, for the PMP exam, you will need to have these formulas memorized. There is a relatively low percentage of "math" questions on the exam, however, there is a large pool of questions that could be asked. This section is dedicated to the equations and the interpretations.

During the **control schedule** process, the earned value technique (EVT) or earned value management (EVM) will be used for variance management. There is one set of calculations:

- Earned value to determine schedule variance (SV) and schedule performance index (SPI)

Controlling costs will potentially involve three sets of calculations:

- Earned value to determine cost variance (CV) and cost performance index (CPI)
- Estimate to complete (ETC) and estimate at completion (EAC) – forecasting the remaining estimated spend (ETC) and the overall estimated spend (EAC)
- To-complete performance index (TCPI) - determining efficiency required based on a comparison of work remaining to money remaining (either in the budget or the forecast)

Earned Value Management: Schedule

An earned value analysis measures, compares, and analyzes schedule performance, such as actual start and finish dates, percent complete, and the remaining duration of any work that is in process. Earned value may be calculated at the project, work package, or activity level. The earned value technique (EVT) determines the schedule variance (SV) and the schedule performance index (SPI).

- Schedule variance (SV) = earned value (EV) – planned value (PV)
- Schedule performance index (SPI) = earned value (EV) / planned value (PV)

Earned Value (EV)

Earned value is the "theoretical" value we have earned in the project based on what percentage complete we are with the budgeted work. For example, if we are 50% complete with $90,000 worth of work, we have earned $45,000 in value.

Earned value (EV) = budget at completion (BAC) x percent complete

Percentage complete can be determined based on the percentage of time that has been completed or based on the percentage of effort that has been completed. For example, if we are three months into a 6-month project, we are 50% complete from a time perspective.

However, just because we are 50% complete from a time perspective, it does not necessarily mean that 50% of the work has been completed. As such, an effort-based percent complete is more accurate. On the exam, if they provide you with the effort-based percent complete, use that. If not, you will need to use the time-based percent complete.

Planned Value (PV)

Planned value is the dollar value of the work we planned to have completed by this point in the project. PV will be cumulative from the start date through the status date. To determine PV, we use our cost baseline (and/or the s-curve graph) to calculate the budgeted planned spend as of the status date. (You may remember that we learned about PV during the **determine budget** process).

HINT: On the exam, PV may be provided to you as either periodic values or cumulative values. If periodic, be sure to add up the values to arrive at a cumulative PV.

For example, using the following table, the PV for period 3 would be $42,000 (the cumulative of the first three periods).

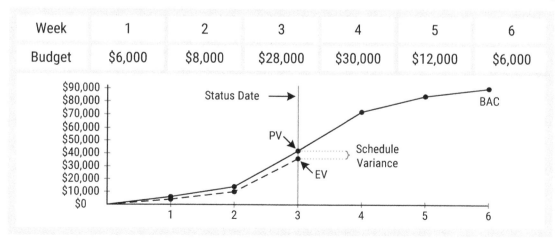

Week	1	2	3	4	5	6
Budget	$6,000	$8,000	$28,000	$30,000	$12,000	$6,000

The schedule variance (SV) is equal to the earned value (EV) minus the planned value (PV)

SV = EV – PV --- how much we've earned versus how much we planned to have earned at this point.

- An SV of zero indicates the component is exactly on schedule

- A negative SV indicates the component is behind schedule
- A positive SV indicates the component is ahead of schedule

The schedule performance index (SPI) is equal to the earned value (EV) divided by the planned value (PV)

$$SPI = EV \div PV$$

- An SPI of one indicates the component is on schedule
- An SPI less than one indicates the component is behind schedule
- An SPI greater than one indicates the component is ahead of schedule

---

Belinda's Hint

In the earned value equations, we always want the value that we have earned (EV) to be as much or greater than what we planned. If we have earned less than we planned, it indicates we are behind schedule.

If the exam is asking you about the status of the schedule, we compare earned value to planned value. It may help you to correlate the two by thinking about your schedule as your "plan".

Because SV and SPI are using the same variables, they will always align:

if the SV is positive, the SPI will be greater than 1

If the SV is negative, the SPI will be less than 1

If the SV is zero, the SPI will be 1

For any of the variance calculations (schedule variance, cost variance, variance at completion), a negative variance is BAD. One way to remember that is to think of your bank account:

If you log in to your bank account and there is a negative balance, it is a bad situation. In the case of SV, a negative variance indicates we are behind schedule.

Keep in mind that earned value equations are considered "point-in-time." As such, they can change at any time. This is why the trending of earned value data is more helpful than just a single value.

Example: Earned Value - Schedule

To open the new restaurant, the kitchen layout must be designed, equipment ordered, and plumbing and electrical renovations completed. The kitchen build-out has been underway for a period of three weeks and is estimated to take six weeks from start to finish.

The kitchen build-out has a budget of $90,000 and is 40% complete. The earned value of the work completed is $36,000 (the budget at completion (BAC) multiplied by the percentage of work completed). The budget for the work has been allocated as follows:

Week	1	2	3	4	5	6
Budget	$6,000	$8,000	$28,000	$30,000	$12,000	$6,000

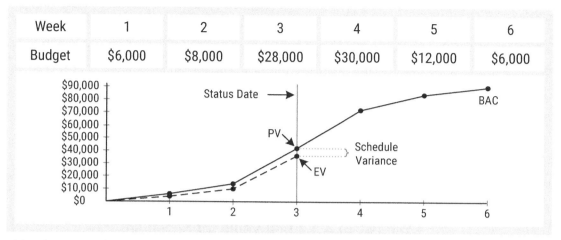

Using this information, the planned value (PV) of the work to be done by the end of week three is $42,000 ($6,000 + $8,000 + $28,000).

The team has earned value of $36,000 but had planned to have $42,000 worth of work completed. This results in a negative schedule variance (SV) indicating that the work is progressing behind schedule.

SV = earned value (EV) − planned value (PV) = $36,000 - $42,000 = ($6,000)

To determine how far behind schedule the component is, the schedule performance index (SPI) can be calculated by dividing the earned value by the planned value.

SPI = earned value (EV) ÷ planned value (PV) = $36,000 ÷ $42,000
= .86

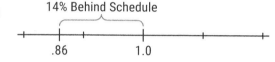

An SPI of .86 indicates that the project is 14% behind schedule

Variable	Acronym	Description
Planned Value	PV	The amount of money budgeted for a component between its start date and the status date.
Budget at Completion	BAC	The total amount of money allocated to the component. Equal to the total PV at the end of the component.
Earned Value	EV	Estimated value of the work completed. EV = BAC x percent complete
Schedule Variance	SV	The difference between the earned value and the planned value. SV = EV - PV
Schedule Performance Index	SPI	The ratio of earned value to planned value. SPI = EV ÷ PV

PMBOK® Guide – Sixth Edition, Glossary

Let's check your understanding of using earned value to assess the schedule. The answers to Exercise 14.4 are on page 407.

Exercise 14.4: Earned Value for Schedule

Your 10-month project has a budget of $20,000. You are evaluating the progress of your project after two months. According to your team, the project is 30% complete. Based on your project budget, you planned to spend $8,000 by this date.

Budget at completion (BAC) =

Percentage complete =

Earned value (EV) =

Planned value (PV) =

Schedule variance (SV) =

Schedule performance index (SPI) =

Status of the schedule?

Earned Value Management: Cost

Cost performance measurements are used to assess the magnitude of variance from the original cost performance baseline. In earned value management for the schedule, we learned that earned value (EV) is the "theoretical" value we have earned in the project based on what percentage complete we are with the budgeted work. For example, if we are 60% complete with $90,000 worth of work, we have earned $54,000 in value.

Earned value (EV) = budget at completion (BAC) x percent complete

We are going to use that same calculation of EV but are now going to compare it to actual costs (AC) to determine the status of our budget.

Actual Costs (AC)

AC is the actual money spent on the project or the component from the start date to the status date. They may use phrases such as "invoiced-to-date," "paid-to-date," "billed," etc. AC will be cumulative from the start date through the status date. To determine AC, the information would be provided within the question as AC is not planned in advance.

HINT: On the exam, AC may be provided to you as either periodic values or cumulative values. If periodic, be sure to add up the values to arrive at a cumulative AC.

For example, using the following table, the AC for period three would be $38,000 (the cumulative of the first three periods).

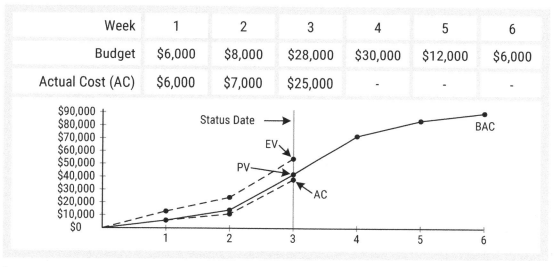

Week	1	2	3	4	5	6
Budget	$6,000	$8,000	$28,000	$30,000	$12,000	$6,000
Actual Cost (AC)	$6,000	$7,000	$25,000	-	-	-

Cost variance (CV) is equal to the earned value (EV) minus the actual costs (AC)

CV = EV – AC

- A variance of zero indicates the component is exactly on budget
- A negative variance indicates the component is over-budget
- A positive variance indicates the component is under-budget

Cost performance index (CPI) is equal to the earned value (EV) divided by the actual cost (AC)

CPI = EV ÷ AC

- A CPI of one indicates the component is on budget
- A CPI less than one indicates the component is over-budget
- A CPI greater than one indicates the component is under-budget

Belinda's Hint

In the earned value equations, we always want the value that we have earned (EV) to be as much or greater than what we spent (AC). If we have earned less than we spent, it indicates we are over budget.

If the exam is asking you about the status of the budget, we compare earned value to actual costs (AC). It may help you to correlate the two by thinking cost = cost.

Because CV and CPI are using the same variables, they will always align:

If the CV is positive, the CPI will be greater than 1

If the CV is negative, the CPI will be less than 1

If the CV is zero, the CPI will be 1

For any of the variance calculations (schedule variance, cost variance, variance at completion), a negative variance is BAD. Again, as mentioned previously, one way to remember that is to think of your bank account: If you log in to your bank account and there is a negative balance, it is a bad situation. In the case of CV, a negative variance indicates we are over budget.

Example: Earned Value - Cost

The kitchen build-out is a component of the new restaurant opening project. The kitchen build-out has been underway for a period of three weeks and is estimated to take six weeks from start to finish.

The kitchen build-out has a budget of $90,000 and is 60% complete. The earned value of the work completed is $54,000 (the budget at completion (BAC) multiplied by the percentage of work completed).

Invoices paid-to-date (actual costs) have been:

Week	1	2	3	4	5	6
Budget	$6,000	$8,000	$28,000	$30,000	$12,000	$6,000
Actual Cost (AC)	$6,000	$7,000	$25,000	-	-	-

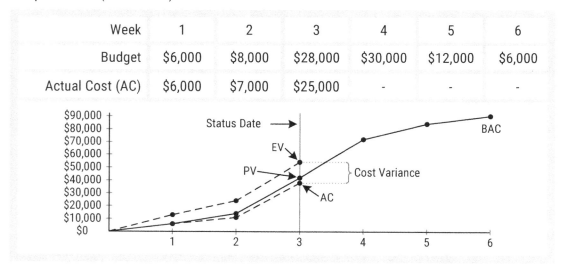

Using this information, the actual cost (AC) of the work completed is $38,000, and the team has earned value of $54,000 to complete this portion of the work. This results in a positive cost variance (CV) indicating that the work is progressing under budget.

CV = Earned Value (EV) − Actual Cost (AC) = $54,000 - $38,000 = $16,000

To determine how far under or over budget the component is, the cost performance index (CPI) can be calculated by dividing the earned value by the actual cost.

CPI = Earned Value (EV) ÷ Actual Cost (AC) = $54,000 ÷ $38,000 = 1.42

A CPI of 1.42 indicates that the project is 42% under budget

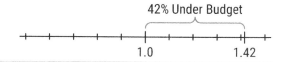

Variable	Acronym	Description
Actual Cost	AC	The actual cost of the component to date.
Cost Variance	CV	The difference between the earned value and the actual cost. CV = EV - AC
Cost Performance Index	CPI	The ratio of earned value to actual cost. CPI = EV ÷ AC

PMBOK® Guide – Sixth Edition, Glossary

Example: EVM Graph

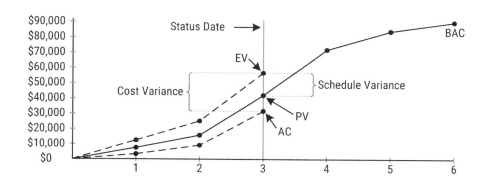

Belinda's Hint

On the exam, they may provide you with an EVM graph, as above, and ask you the status of the project. Remember that for the status of the schedule, you will evaluate EV as it relates to PV. For the status of the budget, you will compare EV to AC.

Do not try to compare PV to AC (what we planned to spend versus what we actually spent) as it does not provide us with a true analysis because it does not incorporate the amount of work that has been completed.

Let's check your understanding of using earned value for the cost status of the project. The answers to Exercise 14.5 are on page 407.

Exercise 14.5: Earned Value for Cost

You are the project manager for a six-month, $120,000 project. According to the work performance information, your team is about 40% complete with their work.

According to the project budget, estimated costs to-date should be $50,000. Costs billed to-date are $40,000.

Budget at completion (BAC) =

Percentage complete =

Earned value (EV) =

Actual cost (AC) =

Cost variance (CV) =

Cost performance index (CPI) =

Status of the budget?

Forecasting

Project forecasting predicts the remaining and total project spending based on information and knowledge available at the time of the forecast. Estimate to complete (ETC) is the anticipated remaining project spending to complete the project from this point forward. ETC does not include what has been already spent, the actual costs (AC).

Estimate at completion (EAC) is the total anticipated spending upon completion of the project. EAC includes what has already been spent (AC) and the estimate to complete the remaining project work. The difference between the ETC and the EAC is always the actual cost (AC). Estimate to complete does not include the actual costs but estimate at completion does include it.

For example, if the estimate to complete the project is $70,000 and I have already spent $40,000 to-date, the estimate at completion would be $110,000.

Variance at completion (VAC) compares the budget at completion to the estimate at completion (the forecast). VAC = BAC – EAC. For example, if the budget $100,000 and the forecast (EAC) is $110,000, there will be ($10,000) variance at completion, as we will exceed the budget by $10,000.

Belinda's Hint

The difference between estimate to complete (ETC) and estimate at completion (EAC), is simply actual costs (AC). Because the ETC is just what is the estimated remaining spend, it would not include AC. However, because EAC is a forecast of the overall spend on the project, it would include AC.

If you start with the EAC, subtract the AC to determine the ETC

If you start with the ETC, add the AC to determine the EAC

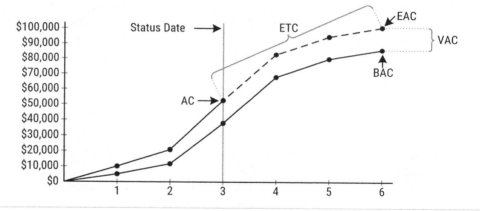

Unfortunately, there are a number of different formulas that may be used to calculate the estimate at completion. Determining which formula to use is based on the situation or scenario: no variance noted, an atypical variance noted, a typical variance noted, or a variance related to both cost and schedule.

Here are the scenarios and the associated formulas:

Situation	Description	EAC Formula
No variance noted	Used when there have been no major variances noted. Also referred to as a bottom-up estimate.	EAC = AC + ETC

Example: Your vendor has informed you that the remaining costs are estimated to be $15,000. You have already paid the vendor $10,000.
ETC = $15,000 (new estimate)
EAC = AC + ETC = $10,000 + $15,000 =$25,000

Situation	Description	EAC Formula
Atypical variance	Used when variances are not expected to continue to impact the project	EAC = AC + BAC − EV

Example: During your $20,000 project, you unexpectedly needed to pay a consultant for a complex piece of work. The work was isolated and will not continue to impact the project. To-date the project has cost $12,000 and has an EV of $9,000.
EAC = AC + BAC − EV = $12,000 + $20,000 - $9,000 = $23,000
ETC = EAC − AC = $23,000 - $12,000 = $11,000

Situation	Description	EAC Formula
Typical variance	Used when variances are expected to continue to impact the project	EAC = BAC ÷ CPI

Example: Your original estimates for the outsourced portion of the work of the $70,000 project did not account for a higher hourly fee for the resources. This will continue to impact the work of the project. The current CPI is 0.82 and the AC is $53,000.
EAC = BAC / CPI = $70,000 / 0.82 = $85,366
ETC = EAC − AC = $85,366 - $53,000 = $32,366

Situation	Description	EAC Formula
Consideration of both SPI and CPI	Used when the project schedule is a factor impacting the effort.	EAC =AC + [(BAC − EV) ÷ (CPI X SPI)]

Example: The $250,000 project is 30% complete. The CPI is 0.85 and the SPI is 0.7. Actual costs are $90,000.
EAC = [(BAC − EV) ÷ (CPI X SPI)] = $90,000 + [($250,000 - $75,000) / (0.85 x 0.7)] = $90,000 + $294,118 = $384,118
ETC = EAC − AC = $384,118 - $90,000 = $294,118

Belinda's Hint

For forecasting (ETC / EAC) questions on the exam, it is best to use a decision-tree approach:

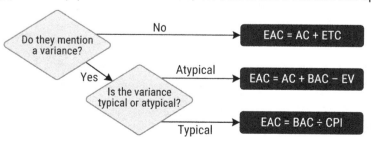

Do not get distracted by extra numbers and information in the questions − stick to the formulas! Disregard any productive rates, fees, costs, etc.

Example: Forecasting

The kitchen build-out is a component of the new restaurant opening project. The kitchen build-out has been underway for a period of three weeks and is estimated to take six weeks from start to finish. The earned value (EV) of the project is $34,000. The CPI is .71. The SPI is 0.65. Actual costs (AC) to-date have been $48,000. The project has a budget (BAC) of $85,000.

Bottom-Up Forecast

The contractor advises you that the remaining work will cost $33,000. The $33,000 represents the estimate to complete (ETC) the project. Adding the ETC to the AC of $48,000 results in an estimate at completion (EAC) of $81,000. The variance at completion (VAC) would be the BAC of $85,000 minus the EAC of $81,000 = $4,000. This indicates that the project is forecasted to come in $4,000 under budget.

Atypical Variance Forecast

While the kitchen build-out was in-progress, the builders found mold under the existing sheetrock. The removal of the mold added costs to the project. These costs were a one-time cost. Instead of using the new estimate, the EAC will be calculated:

$$EAC = AC + BAC - EV$$

$EAC = \$48,000 + \$85,000 - \$34,000 = \$99,000$ | The total forecasted spend is $99,000

$ETC = EAC - AC = \$99,000 - \$48,000 = \$51,000$ | The remaining spend is $51,000

$VAC = BAC - EAC = \$85,000 - \$99,000 = (\$14,000)$

This indicates the project is forecasted to exceed the budget by $14,000.

Typical Variance Forecast

The primary material used for the kitchen build-out is 10% more expensive than anticipated. This material will be used throughout the project and, as such, will continue to impact the project. Instead of using the new estimate, the EAC will be calculated:

$EAC = BAC \div CPI = \$85,000 \div .71 = \$119,718$

$ETC = EAC - AC = \$119,718 - \$48,000 = \$71,718$

$VAC = BAC - EAC = \$85,000 - \$119,718 = (\$34,718)$

Because the variance will continue to recur, the EAC and ETC is greater for a typical variance versus an atypical variance.

EAC Factoring in SPI and CPI

Your team lead has advised you that issues with the schedule are having an impact on the project costs. To factor in both the SPI and the CPI, the EAC will be calculated:

$EAC = AC + [(BAC-EV) \div (CPIxSPI)] = \$48,000 + [(\$85,000 - \$34,000) \div (0.71x0.65)] = \$306,696$

$ETC = EAC - AC = \$306,696 - \$48,000 = \$258,696$

$VAC = BAC - EAC = \$85,000 - \$306,696 = (\$221,696)$

Let's check your understanding of the forecasting formulas. You will use each EAC formula one time only. The answers to Exercise 14.6 are on page 408.

Exercise 14.6: Forecasting EAC, ETC, and VAC

You are the project manager for the two-year, $400,000 renovation project. After one year, your team reports that they are 60% complete with the project work. Invoices received total $250,000. Planned value of the work to be completed by the status date is $260,000.

Budget at completion (BAC) =

Percentage complete =

Earned value (EV) =

Actual cost (AC) =

Planned value (PV) =

Cost performance index (CPI) =

Schedule performance index (SPI) =

1. Your contractor informs you that remaining costs will be $180,000.

   Estimate to complete (ETC) =

   Estimate at completion (EAC) =

   Variance at completion (VAC) =

2. Your contractor informs you that there was an unexpected cost variance during month three that is not anticipated to recur.

   Estimate at completion (EAC) =

   Estimate to complete (ETC) =

   Variance at completion (VAC) =

3. Your contractor informs you that the primary material being used for the project is 15% more expensive than originally planned. This will continue to affect the project.

   Estimate at completion (EAC) =

   Estimate to complete (ETC) =

   Variance at completion (VAC) =

4. Calculate the forecasts factoring in both the cost and schedule performance indexes.

   Estimate at completion (EAC) =

   Estimate to complete (ETC) =

   Variance at completion (VAC) =

To-Complete Performance Index (TCPI)

The to-complete performance index (TCPI) is a calculation of the cost performance that must be achieved to meet the specified budget objective. TCPI is a ratio of the work remaining to the funds remaining and is calculated by taking the work remaining (BAC – EV) divided by the funds remaining (BAC – AC or EAC – AC). (BAC – AC) will be used when the original budget (BAC) is the target. (EAC – AC) will be used when the forecast (EAC) is the revised target.

Work Remaining

To determine our work remaining on the project, we will subtract the earned value (EV) from our budget at completion (BAC). For example, if the $20,000 project is 20% complete, the earned value is $4,000 ←the value we've earned in the project today. The value of the remaining work would be: $20,000 - $4,000 = $16,000 worth of work remaining.

Money Remaining

There will be two ways to determine the money remaining, based on whether the team is managing to the original budget or if they are managing to the current forecast. To manage to budget, money remaining would be calculated as the BAC – AC. For example, if my BAC is $20,000 and I've already spent $12,000, I would have $8,000 remaining.

To manage to the forecast, money remaining would be calculated as the EAC – AC. If you notice, this is the same formula for arriving at our estimate to complete (ETC). For example, if my EAC is $26,000 and I've already spent $12,000, my ETC would be $14,000.

When the work remaining is divided by the money remaining, it lets us know how efficient we must be with the remaining work. In this situation, we prefer that the work remaining is less than or equal to our money remaining.

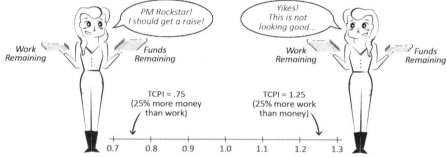

- A TCPI of one indicates that there is the same amount of work remaining as there are funds remaining
- A TCPI greater than one indicates that there is <u>more</u> work than funds remaining
- A TCPI less than one indicates that there is <u>less</u> work than funds remaining

---

Belinda's Hint

Sometimes those crazy mnemonics help while trying to learn equations. So here is a silly mnemonic for TCPI.

Not everyone likes bats or cats, but both serve a purpose: they hunt insects, pests, etc.

Bats And Cats – Eat Vermin / Bats And Cats – Are Cool (BAC-EV)/(BAC-AC)

Or

Bats And Cats – Eat Vermin / Eagles And Cats – Are Cool (BAC-EV)/(EAC-AC)

Remember they must eat the vermin before they can be cool. And if they eat more than one vermin (a TCPI > 1), they will get sick.

Variable	Acronym	Description
To-Complete Performance Index	TCPI	The ratio of work remaining to funds remaining. TCPI = (BAC - EV) ÷ (BAC − AC) [budget] TCPI = (BAC − EV) ÷ (EAC − AC) [forecast] For example, if the BAC is $800, the EV is $400 and the AC is $500, the TCPI would be equal to: 400 ÷300 = 1.3 meaning that there is 30% more work than budget remaining.

PMBOK® *Guide – Sixth Edition. Glossary*

Belinda's Hint

While trying to memorize all the formulas that you will need for your dump sheet, it may be helpful to keep the following in mind:

Variance calculations are always subtraction (SV, CV, VAC).

A negative variance is always bad.

Performance index calculations are always division (SPI, CPI, TCPI).

A PI less than one is bad for SPI and CPI but is good for TCPI.

Let's check your understanding of calculating TCPI. The answers to Exercise 14.7 are on page 408.

Exercise 14.7: TCPI

You are the project manager for the one-year, $100,000 website project. After three months, your team reports that they are 20% complete with the project work. Invoices received total $30,000.

Budget at completion (BAC) =

Percentage complete =

Earned value (EV) =

Actual cost (AC) =

TCPI to budget (TCPI) =

Your manager instructs you to manage to the new estimate at complete (EAC) of $140,000.

TCPI to EAC (TCPI) =

Calculation Review

Term	Formula	Description
Budget at Completion	BAC = Total project budget	Estimated project budget
Earned Value	EV = BAC x % complete	Estimated value of the work completed
Planned Value	PV = Planned value of the work	Estimated value of the work planned to be completed
Schedule Variance	SV = EV - PV	Behind schedule ←→ Ahead of schedule · 0
Schedule Performance Index	SPI = EV ÷ PV	Behind schedule ←→ Ahead of schedule · 1
Actual Cost	AC = What has actually been spent	Actual cost of the work completed
Cost Variance	CV = EV - AC	Over budget ←→ Under budget · 0
Cost Performance Index	CPI = EV ÷ AC	Over budget ←→ Under budget · 1
To-Complete Performance Index	TCPI = (BAC-EV) ÷ (BAC-AC) TCPI = (BAC-EV) ÷ (EAC-AC)	Comparison of the work remaining to the funds remaining. May be based on the original budget (BAC) or the forecast (EAC)
Estimate At Completion	EAC = AC + ETC (no variance) EAC = AC + BAC − EV (atypical variance) EAC = BAC ÷ CPI (typical variance) EAC = AC + [(BAC − EV) / (CPI X SPI)]	Estimated total project spend at completion
Estimate To Complete	ETC = New Estimate ETC = EAC − AC	Estimated cost remaining to complete the project
Variance At Completion	VAC = BAC - EAC	Difference between the budget and the forecast

PMBOK® Guide   Sixth Edition. Page 267

Exam Dump Sheet

As you can see by this section, there are a lot of formulas that you need to remember for the exam. While you will not use all of them on the exam, it is impossible to determine which of the formulas you may need to know based on your pull of exam questions. In order to be best prepared, I recommend memorizing a "dump sheet" for use in your exam.

Practice writing out the formulas, using the acronyms to save time. It may also be helpful to note the interpretation of the calculations, such as "negative variance is bad". The new exam guidelines state that you cannot start writing your dump sheet on your scratch paper until after your actual exam clock starts. Previously, candidates were able to write their dump sheet during the 15-minute system tutorial window. Be aware that any time you are taking writing your dump sheet is reducing your time to complete the exam, so be prudent with what you include.

Here is a suggested format for your dump sheet:

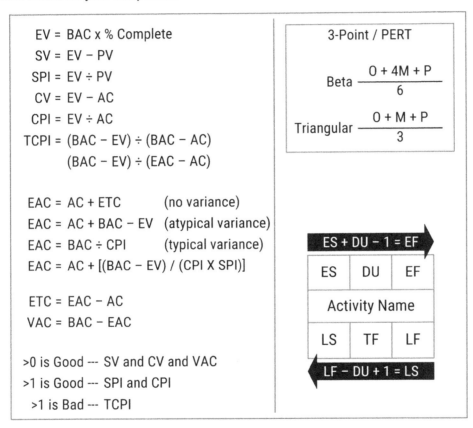

Chapter 14 – Answer Key

Exercise 14.1: Velocity

With the initial velocity the approximate delivery would be the end of August, 2019, at a cost of $800,000. Increasing the velocity to 50 story points changes the approximate delivery to the end of February 2019 at a cost of $560,000. Increasing the velocity to 70 story points changes the approximate delivery to the end of October 2018 at a cost of $400,000.

Exercise 14.2: Leads and Lags

1. Lag
2. Lead
3. Lead
4. Lead
5. Lag
6. Lag
7. Lead
8. Lag

Exercise 14.3: Schedule Compression Techniques

1. Crashing
2. Fast-tracking
3. Both
4. Fast-tracking

Exercise 14.4: Earned Value for Schedule

Budget at completion (BAC) = $20,000

Percentage complete = 30%

Earned value (EV) = $6,000

Planned value (PV) = $8,000

Schedule variance (SV) = ($2,000)

Schedule performance index (SPI) = .75

Status of the schedule? 25% behind schedule

Exercise 14.5: Earned Value for Cost

Budget at completion (BAC) = $120,000

Percentage complete = 40%

Earned value (EV) = $48,000

Actual cost (AC) = $40,000

Cost variance (CV) = $8,000

Cost performance index (CPI) = 1.2

Status of the budget? 20% under budget

Exercise 14.6: Forecasting EAC, ETC, and VAC

Budget at completion (BAC) = $400,000

Percentage complete = 60%

Earned value (EV) = $240,000

Actual cost (AC) = $250,000

Planned value (PV) = $260,000

Cost performance index (CPI) = .96

Schedule performance index (SPI) = .92

1. Your contractor informs you that remaining costs will be $180,000.

Estimate to complete (ETC) = $180,000

Estimate at completion (EAC) = $430,000

Variance at completion (VAC) = ($30,000)

2. Your contractor informs you that there was an unexpected cost variance during month three that is not anticipated to recur.

Estimate at completion (EAC) = $410,000

Estimate to complete (ETC) = $160,000

Variance at completion (VAC) = ($10,000)

3. Your contractor informs you that the primary material being used for the project is 15% more expensive than originally planned. This will continue to affect the project.

Estimate at completion (EAC) = $416,667

Estimate to complete (ETC) = $166,667

Variance at completion (VAC) = ($16,667)

4. Calculate the forecasts factoring in both the cost and schedule performance indexes.

Estimate at completion (EAC) = $431,818

Estimate to complete (ETC) = $181,818

Variance at completion (VAC) = ($31,818)

Exercise 14.7: TCPI

Budget at completion (BAC) = $100,000

Percentage complete = 20%

Earned value (EV) = $20,000

Actual cost (AC) = $30,000

TCPI to budget (TCPI) = 1.14

TCPI to EAC (TCPI) = .73

Chapter 14 - Review Questions

Time Limit: 18 Minutes

1. Which of the following is a tool and technique in the control scope process?
   A. Variance analysis
   B. Replanning
   C. Inspection
   D. Configuration management system

2. A schedule performance index (SPI) of 0.8 suggests that the project is:
   A. Ahead of schedule to date
   B. Behind schedule to date
   C. On schedule
   D. None of the above are correct

3. A project that has a negative cost variance and an SPI less than 1.0 means that the project is:
   A. Over-budget and ahead of schedule
   B. Under-budget and behind schedule
   C. Over-budget and behind schedule
   D. Under-budget and ahead of schedule

4. Based on the performance measures indicated in the following table, what is the schedule variance (SV) for case 3?

Case	PV	AC	EV
1	$10,000	$8,000	$10,000
2	$12,000	$10,000	$11,000
3	$10,000	$8,000	$9,000
4	$10,000	$8,000	$8,000

   A. -1,000
   B. 1,000
   C. 2,000
   D. -2,000

5. A cost performance index (CPI) of 0.8 suggests the project is:
   A. Under-budget to date
   B. Over-budget to date
   C. On budget
   D. None of the above are correct

6. Which formula is used to calculate EAC
   A. AC + BAC - EV
   B. AC ÷ EV
   C. ETC - AC
   D. BAC - CPI

7. The $450,000 project is 75% complete as of month six. The budget was allocated at $50,000 per month for nine months and the invoices paid-to-date are $325,000. What is the TCPI of this project?
   A. 0.9
   B. 1.11
   C. ($12,500)
   D. $12,500

8. The cost performance index (CPI) is calculated as follows:
   A. Divide the earned value (EV) by the actual cost (AC)
   B. Divide the earned value (EV) by the planned value (PV)
   C. Subtract the actual cost (AC) from the earned value (EV)
   D. Subtract the planned value (PV) from the earned value (EV)

9. If the planned value (PV) is $275,000 and the earned value (EV) is $300,000, the schedule variance (SV) is:

A. $25,000
B. -$25,000
C. $125,000
D. $575,000

10. The kitchen remodel project for the Jones family appears to be running behind. As the project manager, you evaluate the construction team's work performance information. Based on the information you received, the $30,000 project appears to be about 40% complete. Work billed to date was $10,000 although the project budget indicates that anticipated costs were to be $12,000 by this date. When you follow-up with the construction team lead, he estimates that there will be approximately $15,000 in remaining costs. The EAC for this project is:

A. $28,000
B. $37,000
C. $25,000
D. $22,500

11. The kitchen remodel project for the Jones family appears to be running behind. As the project manager, you evaluate the construction team's work performance information. Based on the information you received, the $30,000 project appears to be about 40% complete. Work billed to date was $10,000 although the project budget indicates that anticipated costs were to be $12,000 by this date. When you follow-up with the construction team lead, he estimates that there will be approximately $15,000 in remaining costs. The status of the project is:

A. Ahead of schedule and under budget
B. On schedule and under budget
C. Behind schedule and over budget
D. Behind schedule and on budget

12. The process redesign project has been underway for six months and appears to be making good progress. However, to complete your quarterly review, you conduct an earned value analysis. This is a 12 month project with a budget of $50,000. The budget is allocated at $12,500 each quarter. Based on the status reports received the project is 60% complete and billed costs are $40,000. It appears that the project is over budget so you talk to the lead analyst. She tells you that there was an unexpected software cost during the 2nd month of the project of $7,000 (included in the 40,000 above). A good portion of the project costs that will be billed will be resource costs (approximately 300 hours at a loaded resource rate of $80/hr). The SV and SPI for this project are:

A. (10,000) and .75
B. .75 and (10,000)
C. 5,000 and 1.2
D. (5,000) and 1.2

13. The process redesign project has been underway for six months and appears to be making good progress. However, to complete your quarterly review, you conduct an earned value analysis. This is a 12 month project with a budget of $50,000. The budget is allocated at $12,500 each quarter. Based on the status reports received the project is 60% complete and billed costs are $40,000. It appears that the project is over budget so you talk to the lead analyst. She tells you that there was an unexpected software cost during the 2nd month of the project of $7,000 (included in the 40,000 above). A good portion of the project costs that will be billed will be resource costs (approximately 300 hours at a loaded resource rate of $80/hr). The CV and CPI for this project are:

A. (10,000) and .75
B. .75 and (10,000)
C. 5,000 and 1.2
D. (5,000) and 1.2

14. You have just started in your new role in the PMO and one of your first assignments is to evaluate a technical development project to determine if the project is on time and within budget. Upon review of relevant project documentation, you find that the costs to date have been $180,000, the project is a 16-month project, and that after six months of work they are 25% complete. The overall budget for the project is $300,000, with the following allocation:

Month	2	4	6	8	10	12	14	16
Periodic Budget	10K	15K	45K	60K	40K	50K	70K	10K

When you review the project with the project manager, she tells you that they were intending to use an inside resource for all of the programming, but the individual left the company. The programmer they are now using is from a contracting firm and as such, the resource rate for him went from $40/hr to $120/hr. Because programming was the majority of the work needed for the project, this will continue to affect the costs on the project. The SV and SPI for this project are:

A. (5,000) and 1.07
B. (105,000) and .42
C. 1.07 and 5,000
D. 5,000 and 1.07

15. You have just started in your new role in the PMO and one of your first assignments is to evaluate a technical development project to determine if the project is on time and within budget. Upon review of relevant project documentation, you find that the costs to date have been $180,000, the project is a 16-month project, and that after six months of work they are 25% complete. The overall budget for the project is $300,000, with the following allocation:

Month	2	4	6	8	10	12	14	16
Periodic Budget	10K	15K	45K	60K	40K	50K	70K	10K

When you review the project with the project manager, she tells you that they were intending to use an inside resource for all of the programming, but the individual left the company. The programmer they are now using is from a contracting firm and as such, the resource rate for him went from $40/hr to $120/hr. Because programming was the majority of the work needed for the project, this will continue to affect the costs on the project. The ETC for this project is:

A. $275,000
B. $220,000
C. $534,300
D. $500,000

Review Question Answers

1. **Answer: A**

   A variance analysis is a common tool/technique for the monitoring and controlling processes, including the control scope process. A variance analysis evaluates any variance between the project baselines and the actual results.

2. **Answer: B**

   An SPI of one indicates the project is on schedule, greater than 1 and the project is ahead of schedule and less than 1 the project is behind schedule. An SPI of 0.8 indicates the project is 20% behind schedule.

3. **Answer: C**

   An SPI of one indicates the project is on schedule, greater than 1 and the project is ahead of schedule and less than 1 the project is behind schedule. A cost variance of 0 indicates the project is on-budget. A positive cost variance indicates the project is under-budget and a negative cost variance indicates the project is over-budget. As such, this project is over-budget and behind schedule.

4. **Answer: A**

   Schedule variance (SV) = earned value (EV) – planned value (PV)

   $9,000 - $10,000 = ($1,000)

5. **Answer: B**

   A CPI of one indicates the project is right on budget. A CPI less than one indicates the project is over budget and a CPI greater than one indicates the project is under budget. A CPI of 0.8 indicates the project is 20% over budget.

6. **Answer: A**

   There are three formulas to calculate the estimate at completion (EAC):

   EAC = AC + BAC – EV

   EAC = BAC / CPI

   EAC = AC + ETC

7. **Answer: A**

   TCPI = (BAC – EV) / (BAC – AC)

   BAC = $450,000

   EV = $337,500

   AC = $325,000

   TCPI = ($450,000 - $337,500) / ($450,000 - $325,000)

   TCPI = $112,500 / $125,000

   TCPI = 0.9

   This indicates the project has 10% more money than work.

8. **Answer: A**

   CPI = EV / AC

9. **Answer: A**

   SV = EV – PV

   SV = $300,000 - $275,000 = $25,000

10. **Answer: C**

    In reading the scenario, there is no indication of an unexpected cost variance. As such the formula for EAC will be EAC = AC + ETC.

    AC = $10,000

    ETC = $15,000 (the remaining costs)

    EAC = $10,000 + $15,000 = $25,000

11. **Answer: B**

BAC = $30,000

EV = $12,000

AC = $10,000

PV = $12,000

CV = EV – AC = $12,000 - $10,000 = $2,000 (the project is under budget)

SV = EV – PV = $12,000 - $12,000 = 0 (the project is on schedule)

12. **Answer: C**

BAC = $50,000

EV = $30,000

PV = $25,000 ($12,500 x two quarters/6 months)

SV = EV – PV = $30,000 - $25,000 = $5,000

SPI = EV / PV = $30,000 / $25,000 = 1.2

13. **Answer: A**

BAC = $50,000

EV = $30,000

AC = $40,000

CV = EV – AC = $30,000 - $40,000 = ($10,000)

CV = EV / AC = $30,000 / $40,000 = 0.75

14. **Answer: D**

BAC = $300,000

EV = $75,000

PV = $70,000 (cumulative PV through period 6)

SV = EV – PV = $75,000 – 70,000 = $5,000

SPI = EV / PV = $75,000 / 70,000 = 1.07

15. **Answer: C**

Based on the scenario, there is a typical variance. To calculate the ETC, start with calculating the EAC and subtract the AC.

BAC = $300,000

EV = $75,000

AC = $180,000

CPI = EV / AC = $75,000 / $180,000 = .42

EAC = BAC / CPI = $300,000 / 0.42 = $714, 285

ETC = EAC – AC = $714,285 - $180,000 = $534,285 (round up to $534,300)

Chapter 14 - Vocabulary Review

Actual cost

Budget at completion

Cost performance index

Cost variance

Earned value

Earned value management

Estimate at completion

Estimate to complete

Planned value

Schedule performance index

Schedule variance

To-complete performance index

Variance analysis

Variance at completion

1. _____ A method of identifying the causes of differences between the baseline and the actual performance

2. _____ The forecasted amount of total project spending

3. _____ The planned project spending upon completion of the project

4. _____ The total costs actually incurred during a given time period

5. _____ A comparison of the work remaining to the funds remaining

6. _____ The authorized budget assigned to the work that will be accomplished as of the status date.

7. _____ A management methodology where performance is measured by determining the planned and actual value of the work and comparing it to the earned value of the work

8. _____ The difference between the earned value (EV) and the planned value (PV) as of the status date

9. _____ The value of the work already performed on the project

10. _____ A comparison of the earned value (EV) and the actual cost (AC)

11. _____ The difference between the earned value (EV) and the actual cost (AC) as of the status date

12. _____ A projection of the amount of budget deficit or surplus, expressed as the difference between the budget at completion and the estimate at completion

13. _____ A comparison of the earned value (EV) and the planned value (PV)

14. _____ The forecasted amount of project spending for the remainder of the project

* These definitions are taken from the Glossary of *PMBOK® Guide – Sixth Edition*

Vocabulary Review Answers

1. Variance analysis
2. Estimate at completion
3. Budget at completion
4. Actual cost
5. To-complete performance index
6. Planned value
7. Earned value management
8. Schedule variance
9. Earned value
10. Cost performance index
11. Cost variance
12. Variance at completion
13. Schedule performance index
14. Estimate to complete

Chapter 15

Project Closure & Exam Preparation

What's in This Chapter

- Project Closure
- Validate Scope
- Close Project or Phase
- Professional and Social Responsibility

As of the release of the *PMBOK® Guide, 6th Edition* there is only one process in the closing process group: **close project or phase**. This process is concerned with completing all the project closure activities, including early termination or cancellation procedures. Although there is only one process from a Framework perspective, in practice, organizations may have multiple activities associated with closing a project.

In adaptive or agile environments, the work is structured to deliver the highest value work first. If an agile project gets cancelled or closed earlier in the project than expected, there is a good chance that there has at least been some functionality of value that has been delivered. Premature closure of an agile project is typically less damaging than in traditional project approaches.

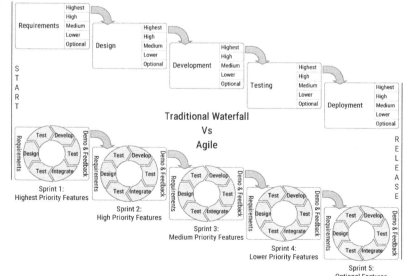

There are two processes associated with closing the project, although one process is in the monitoring and controlling process group and one is in the closing process group. These processes will be discussed in this chapter:

Validate Scope. This process is in the monitoring and controlling process group and the scope knowledge area and is concerned with securing stakeholder, customer, and end-user acceptance of the completed deliverables.

Close Project or Phase. This process is in the closing process group and the integration knowledge area and includes all the steps necessary to satisfy the phase or project exit or completion criteria.

Validate Scope

scope knowledge area | monitoring and controlling process group

The **validate scope** process secures formal acceptance of the completed project deliverables. This includes reviewing the deliverables with the customer to ensure that they are completed satisfactorily. Scope validation will occur periodically throughout the project, with a requirement that all deliverables have been accepted to complete the project.

Do not confuse **validate scope** with **control quality** (QC):

- QC is concerned with ensuring the correctness of the deliverables and meeting the quality requirements
- Scope validation is concerned with the formal acceptance of the deliverables

Validate Scope: ITTOs

Inputs	Tools & Techniques	Outputs
1. Project management plan • Scope management plan • Requirements management plan • Scope baseline 2. Project documents • Lessons learned register • Quality reports • Requirements documentation • Requirements traceability matrix 3. Verified deliverables 4. Work performance data	1. Inspection 2. Decision making • Voting	1. Accepted deliverables 2. Work performance information 3. Change requests 4. Project documents updates • Lessons learned register • Requirements documentation • Requirements traceability matrix

PMBOK® Guide – Sixth Edition. Page 163

Validate Scope: Inputs

Verified Deliverables

The verified deliverables are the project deliverables that are completed and checked for correctness through the **control quality** process.

Common Inputs:

- **Project management plan** - The project management plan will be leveraged to validate the scope, including the scope and requirements management plans, and the scope baseline.
- **Project documents** - Project documents that may be evaluated include the lessons learned register, the quality reports, and the requirements documentation and traceability matrix.
- **Work performance data** - Work performance data can include the degree of compliance with requirements, number of nonconformities, severity of the nonconformities, or the number of validation cycles performed in a period of time.

Validate Scope: Tools & Techniques

Inspection

Inspection involves having the customer, end-user, or requesting party measure, examine or verify the project work and the deliverables to determine whether the work and deliverables meet requirements and product acceptance criteria. Inspection may also be called user acceptance testing (UAT), reviews, product reviews, audits, and walkthroughs.

Common Tools and Techniques:

Decision-Making Techniques

Voting may be used when the customers or end-users are evaluating the deliverables.

Validate Scope: Outputs

Accepted deliverables

Accepted deliverables are the completed deliverables that have been accepted by the individual or group with acceptance responsibilities. The accepted deliverables will include supporting documentation showing acceptance by the customer or stakeholder. If the deliverables have not been accepted, the reasons for non-acceptance are documented, and potentially a change request is generated. If non-acceptance is due to a change in the requirements, the scope change may require updates to the project baselines.

Common Outputs:

- **Work performance information** - Work performance information includes information about project progress, including which deliverables have been accepted and which have not been accepted.
- **Change requests** - Change requests may be generated and will become an input to the **perform integrated change control** process.
- **Project document updates** - Project documents that may be updated include lessons learned register, and the requirements documentation and traceability matrix.

*The **validate scope** process information is adapted from: PMBOK® Guide - Sixth Edition. Page 163-167*

Close Project or Phase

integration knowledge area | closing process group

The **close project or phase** process involves those activities concerned with finalizing all requirements, both for the project and the product. This includes an evaluation by the project manager of the project scope statement to ensure all work has been completed. If the project or phase is terminated prior to completion, the cause will be investigated, and the reasons documented. PMI cites two common reasons for project failure: the project manager failed to manage stakeholder expectations or failed to identify a key stakeholder.

The administrative closure of the project or phase includes the actions and activities necessary to satisfy the completion or exit criteria, fulfill completion of contractual agreements related to the project or phase, transfer the project's products or services to the next phase or to production, collect project or phase records, audit project success or failure and gather lessons learned, and measure stakeholder satisfaction.

Close Project or Phase: ITTOs

Inputs	Tools & Techniques	Outputs
1. Project charter	1. Expert judgment	1. Project documents updates
2. Project management plan	2. Data analysis	• Lessons learned register
• All components	• Document analysis	2. Final product, service, or result transitions
3. Project documents	• Regression analysis	3. Final report
• Assumption log	• Trend analysis	4. Organizational process assets updates
• Basis of estimates	• Variance analysis	
• Change log	3. Meetings	
• Issue log		
• Lessons learned register		
• Milestone list		
• Project communications		
• Quality control measurements		
• Quality reports		
• Requirements documentation		
• Risk register		
• Risk report		
4. Accepted deliverables		
5. Business documents		
• Business case		
• Benefits management plan		
6. Agreements		
7. Procurement documentation		
8. Organizational process assets		

` *PMBOK® Guide – Sixth Edition. Page 121*

Close Project or Phase: Inputs

Accepted Deliverables

The accepted deliverables may include approved product specifications, delivery receipts, and work performance documents. Partial or interim deliverables may also be included for phased or cancelled projects.

Business Documents

The business documents include the business case and the benefits management plan. The business case will be used to determine if the expected outcomes occurred and the benefits management plan is used to measure the benefits and if they were achieved as planned.

Agreements

Formal agreements include the terms and conditions for closing the contract. All contracts will need to be formally closed before the project can be closed.

Procurement Documentation

To close the project, all procurement documentation must be collected, indexed, and filed. This includes all records of changes, information on performance, payment records, and inspection results. This information will be used for capturing lessons learned and as a basis for evaluating future contracts.

Common Inputs:

- **Project charter** - The project charter documents the project success criteria, the approval requirements, and who will sign off on the completed project.
- **Project management plan** - All components of the project management plan will be used in closing the project.
- **Project documents** - Project documents that will be used to close the project include: the assumption, change, and issue logs, the risk register and report, the milestone list, the quality control measurements and reports, the requirements documentation, and the project communications.
- **Organizational process assets** - Policies and procedures to be leveraged include project or phase closure guidelines and requirements.

Close Project or Phase: Tools & Techniques

Common Tools and Techniques:

Expert Judgment

Expertise may be provided by individuals or organization with specialized knowledge, training, or experience with project closures, auditing, and/or legal and procurement processes.

Data Analysis Techniques

There are four data analysis techniques that may be used while closing the project or phase:

A *document analysis* is used to identify lessons learned and knowledge sharing for future projects and organizational assets improvement.

A *regression analysis* is used to analyze the interrelationships between different project variables that contributed to the project outcomes. This information will be used to improve performance on future projects.

A *trend analysis* is an evaluation of data points over time and is used to validate the models used in the organization and to implement adjustments for future projects.

A *variance analysis* compares actual to planned performance to identify variances. This information can be used to improve the metrics of the organization by comparing what was initially planned and the end results.

Meetings

Meetings will be used to facilitate the closure of the phase or the project and to confirm that the deliverables have been accepted. The exit criteria will be validated to ensure that it has been satisfied, contracts will be completed, satisfaction will be evaluated, and lessons learned will be gathered. And we do not want to forget the celebration! A post-project celebration may be a component of project closure.

Types of meetings include close-out reporting meetings, customer wrap-up meetings, lessons learned meetings, and celebration meetings.

Close Project or Phase: Outputs

There are two key outputs from the **close project or phase** process:

Final Product, Service, or Result Transition

The transitioning of the final, product, service or result will include the hand-over or transition of what the project was chartered to deliver. This requires formal handover and acceptance and should also include receipt of a formal statement that the terms and conditions of the contract (for external projects) or the project (for internal projects) have been met.

Final Report

The final report provides a summary of the project performance including a summary description of the project, the scope, schedule, quality, and cost objectives, and a summary of the validation information for the final product, service, or result. The final report should not be a "brag sheet" but rather an honest and objective detail of the project and the project results.

Common Outputs:

- **Project document updates** - All project documents may be updated upon project or phase closure.
- **Organizational process assets updates** - Organizational assets that will be updated include the project documents, the operational and support documents, the project or phase closure documents, and the lessons learned repository.

*The **close project or phase** process information is adapted from: PMBOK® Guide – Sixth Edition. Page 121-128*

Professional and Social Responsibility

To prepare for the exam it is important to familiarize yourself with PMI's Code of Ethics and Professional Conduct (the Code). The Code is available on www.PMI.org. While there is no longer a proficiency score provided for Professional and Social Responsibility, there are still questions on the exam.

Remember to always approach these questions and scenarios from a PMI-perspective!

Ethics in the initiating processes:

Before beginning work on any project, the project manager must validate that the project has been authorized by the organization. Until the project work is authorized through a designated work authorization system, the work cannot begin.

If the project manager is asked to begin work without the formal authorization in place, the project manager is expected to refuse the project.

The ethical and professional responsibilities of a project manager include:

- Ensuring that the project is authorized as demonstrated by the signed project charter
- Validating that the project contributes to the strategic direction of the organization based on information contained within the business case
- Verifying a contract has been signed if the project is being done for an external customer
- Identifying and determining all stakeholders affected by the project

Ethics in the planning processes:

When performing the processes within the planning process group, key ethical considerations include:

- Developing the most accurate estimates based on current information available
- Developing a communication plan that will provide stakeholders with timely, accurate, and appropriate communication regarding the project status
- Ensuring comprehensive plans exist for managing the key aspects of the project:
  - Providing redundancy for the organization should the project manager or key team members not be available for the life of the project
  - Providing direction to the project team members to maximize team member efficiency
  - Documenting a clear change control process
- Obtaining appropriate approvals on the project management plan

Ethics in the executing processes

When performing the processes within the executing process group, key ethical considerations include:

- Auditing the quality requirements and the quality results to ensure that the appropriate processes are being used on the project and making any recommendations for improvements as necessary
- Providing leadership to the project team, including:
  - Addressing any cultural differences
  - Acting in such a way that is free of bias and prejudice
  - Creating an environment where team members feel safe and encouraged to report inappropriate actions by others
  - Providing the appropriate tools and support for team members to deliver on their assignments
  - Administering an appropriate rewards and recognition program that is equally applied and based upon performance

- Escalating any disciplinary issues to the appropriate authorities, including the functional manager or the human resources department
- Communicating project status transparently
- Distributing information to all entitled parties
- Managing stakeholder expectations through consistent and frequent communications
- Ensuring adherence to organizational and legal procurement procedures when purchasing products or services for the project including:
  - Selecting sellers based on legitimate evaluation
  - Using the appropriate contracts to protect the organization

Ethics in the monitoring and controlling processes

The ethical and professional responsibilities of a project manager include:

- Communicating transparently with stakeholders regarding:
  - Approved changes to the project, including corrective actions, preventive actions, defect repairs and scope changes
  - Variances from the project baselines (scope, schedule, and cost performance)
  - The project status and schedule and cost forecasts
- Ensuring that the project deliverables have been checked for quality through the quality control process
- Managing project risks and risk responses to ensure that the responses are appropriate, and the risk impact is appropriately managed

Ethics in the closing process

In closing the project procurements and the project, there are a number of project management ethical considerations:

- Ensuring that deliverables have been completed based on the documented and agreed-upon requirements
- Protecting the organization from any additional costs or charges after completion
- Communicating transparently with stakeholders regarding project successes and failures in the final project report
- Contributing to the development and growth of other project professionals and the organization through the capture of lessons learned
- Evaluating customer and end-user satisfaction to enhance future relationships

---

Belinda's Hint

Here is an exception to the "Check-The-Plan-First Rule":

If asked what you do first if you hear your project is cancelled, the correct answer is that you have your team stop work.

This prevents any billing to your project after cancellation and protects the organization from unnecessary charges.

PMI Code of Ethics and Professional Conduct

PMI's code applies to:

- All PMI members
- Non-members who hold a certification
- Professionals who apply to commence a PMI certification process
- Individuals serve PMI in a volunteer capacity

The PMI code:

- Consists of both aspirational and mandatory standards of conduct
- Aspirational standards describe the conduct we strive to uphold as practitioners
  - Although they may be difficult to measure, these standards are an expectation
- Mandatory standards establish firm requirements
  - Those who do not conduct themselves in accordance will be subject to disciplinary action before the PMI's Ethics Review Committee

Code values

The code encompasses four values:

- Responsibility
- Respect
- Fairness
- Honesty

Responsibility

Our duty to take ownership for the decisions we make or fail to make, the actions we take or fail to take, and the consequences that result.

Respect

Our duty to show high regard for ourselves, others, and the resources entrusted to us. Resources entrusted to us may include people, money, reputation, the safety of others, and natural or environmental resources.

Fairness

Our duty to make decisions and act impartially and objectively. Our conduct must be free from competing self-interest, prejudice, and favoritism.

Honesty

Our duty to understand the truth and act in a truthful manner both in our communications and in our conduct.

In addition, professional and social responsibility encompasses the following categories:

- Maintaining individual integrity
- Contributing to the project management knowledge base
- Enhancing your personal, professional competence
- Promoting interaction and open communication among stakeholders

Maintaining individual integrity

As a project manager, you must maintain individual integrity. This includes:

- Being truthful in project communications
- Protecting confidential company information
- Following PMI's Code of Ethics and Professional Conduct
- Reporting violations of ethics, laws, and business policies
- Not receiving or giving inappropriate gifts or any types of bribes
- Following copyright and other laws

Contributing to the project management knowledge base

Contributing to the knowledge base includes:

- The sharing of lessons learned
- Documenting and writing articles or conducting research on project management practices
- Mentoring other project professionals
- Supporting the ongoing project education of team members and stakeholders

Enhancing your personal professional competence

Continuing professional development includes:

- The identification of your strengths and weaknesses
- Planned professional development activities
- Continued development of their understanding and knowledge of project management theories and principles
- Seeking out new information that will lend to the ongoing maturity of project management within their organization

Promoting interaction and open communication among stakeholders

As a project manager, you are expected to balance stakeholders' interests throughout the life of the project. To balance the stakeholders' interests, it is critical that the project objectives are clearly defined and communicated. By balancing their interests, you will be able to best prioritize the requirements.

PMI reserves the right to amend the Code at any time. For updates to the Code, visit PMI's web-site: www.PMI.org.

Final Thoughts

Congratulations on completing this comprehensive exam preparation self-study book. If you have worked through all of the material and the exercises, you should be feeling confident about completing your exam soon! The PMP exam is challenging but with the proper preparation, there is no doubt that you can be successful.

If you have not yet, submit your application to PMI and comply with all audit requirements, if necessary. It is better to assume you are going to get audited than not. I recommend sending out an email to anyone who would be on-point to verify your experience to give them notice that you may need their signature. This will make the process much smoother in the event you are selected for audit.

To validate your readiness, ensure you are scoring at least 75% on the final mock exam, closed book, within the allocated time limit of four hours. If you have scored 75% or higher, it is very likely you will be successful on your first attempt!

Best of luck on your exam and share your success story on my social media channels. I am passionate about helping project managers achieve their credentials and I am excited to welcome you to the PMP club very soon!

Congratulations on Completing Section 4!

To evaluate your learning and retention of the Section 4 concepts, please complete Practice Exam 4 in Appendix D as a closed-book, 90-minute timed exam. Upon completion, record your score and your time-to-complete on your Performance Evaluation sheet on Page 9.

Chapter 15 - Review Questions

Time Limit: 18 Minutes

1. **The close project or phase process outputs are:**
   A. Final product, service, or result transition, organizational process assets updates, and project management plan updates
   B. Final product, service or result transition and organizational process assets updates
   C. Administrative closure, contract closure, final product, service or result transition
   D. Project management plan, administrative closure, contract closure, final product, work performance information

2. **The foundational values of the PMI Code of Ethics and Professional Responsibility are:**
   A. Integrity, respect, honesty, and fairness
   B. Honesty, fairness, respect, and responsibility
   C. Responsibility, respect, integrity and honesty
   D. Responsibility, respect, truthfulness, and integrity

3. **Actions and activities that are necessary to satisfy completion or exit criteria for the project, and to confirm that the project has met all sponsor, customer, and other stakeholders' requirements, are addressed:**
   A. As part of the administrative closure procedure
   B. Following the plan as outlined in the quality management process
   C. As requested by upper management
   D. As the last step in project management

4. **The project you have been assigned includes team members from multiple countries. What should you do to alleviate any potential cultural differences, so they do not have a negative effect on the project?**
   A. Be very discreet with sensitive project communications
   B. Speak slowly during team meetings to ensure understanding
   C. Focus on developing a comprehensive WBS and WBS dictionary
   D. At each team meeting have a different team member share something unique about their culture

5. **Project files that are archived at the completion of the project include all of the following except:**
   A. Project management plan
   B. Project management information system
   C. Risk register
   D. Change management documentation

6. **As a participant in a PMP® prep course:**
   A. You must adhere to the Code
   B. You are not obligated to adhere to the Code
   C. You are automatically considered a PMI member
   D. Even if you are a member, you will not be obligated to adhere to the Code until you submit your PMP® application

7. **Which of the following would not be the responsibility of the project manager?**
   A. Verify that the company procedures are legal
   B. Protect confidential client information
   C. Be truthful in cost estimates and forecasts
   D. Ensure that the legitimate interest of the customer is not compromised by a conflict of interest

8. **You are offered an assignment to manage a project. However, the project is in an area that you have only minor experience. What should you do?**
   A. Identify a mentor with experience in managing a project of this type
   B. Accept the project and do some research on the area
   C. Refuse the project
   D. Discuss your limited experience with the client and with their approval, develop a strategy to increase your knowledge

9. **You observe a team member taking cable from the discard pile at the client job site. What is the most appropriate action for you to take?**
   A. Do nothing, the cable was in the discard pile
   B. Report the action to the appropriate authorities
   C. Notify the team member's manager
   D. Remove the team member from the project

10. **You heard your project has been cancelled. What is the first thing you should do?**
    A. Check the project management plan
    B. Report the cancellation to your sponsor
    C. Have your team and vendors stop work
    D. Determine the appropriate contingency response

11. **If final procurement negotiations cannot be reached through direct negotiation, what would be the least desirable option:**
    A. Litigation
    B. Mediation
    C. Arbitration
    D. Alternative dispute resolution

12. **All of the following would be considered contributing to the project management knowledge base, except:**
    A. Sharing lessons learned
    B. Conducting research on project management practices
    C. Protecting confidential company information
    D. Mentoring other project professionals

13. **The validate scope process:**
    A. Is the process of obtaining the stakeholders' formal acceptance of the completed project scope and associated deliverables
    B. Refers to the final project report describing the project at completion
    C. Is not necessary if the project completes on time and on budget
    D. Occurs only when revisions or change orders are made to the project

14. **Regarding the project deliverables, which statement is most accurate?**
    A. Scope validation and quality control are synonymous
    B. QC is performed on the deliverables prior to scope validation
    C. Scope validation must occur before the quality can be controlled
    D. Controlling the quality of the product is ongoing whereas scope validation occurs once in planning

15. **User acceptance testing (UAT) is also known as:**
    A. Quality control
    B. Quality assurance
    C. Customer acceptance
    D. Inspection

Review Question Answers

1. **Answer: B**

   The two outputs to the close project or phase process are the final product, service, or result transition and the organizational process assets updates (referencing the archiving of the project files).

2. **Answer: B**

   The four foundational values of the Code are responsibility, respect, fairness, and honesty

3. **Answer: A**

   Administrative closure procedures include the actions and activities necessary to satisfy completion or exit criteria for the project, and to confirm that the project has met all sponsor, customer, and other stakeholders' requirements.

4. **Answer: D**

   To break down any cultural barriers, it may be helpful to have team members share something unique about their culture. Being discreet with communications, speaking slowly, and a comprehensive WBS will not have an impact on potential cultural differences.

5. **Answer: B**

   The project management information system (PMIS) is a collection of tools and systems used to manage project information. As such, the PMIS would not be archived at the end of the project, but the data within it would be.

6. **Answer: B**

   Being a participant in a PMP® course does not obligate you to adhere to the PMI® Code of Ethics and Professional Responsibility. You are obligated to adhere to the Code when you hold a PMI® membership, commence the application process, hold a certification or credential, or volunteer.

7. **Answer: A**

   The project manager is not expected to be an expert in law and as such, would not be able to verify that the company procedures are legal.

8. **Answer: D**

   It is acceptable to be assigned a project where you have minor experience, as long as the knowledge gap is disclosed to the client and a strategy is in place to remedy the gap.

9. **Answer: B**

   Because the individual is removing material from a client site, it could possibly be an issue of theft. The most appropriate action is to report the incident to the appropriate authorities for them to handle as needed. Notifying the team members' manager would not necessarily resolve the situation if it is a legal issue.

10. **Answer: C**

    The first thing you should is have your team and vendors stop work. This will prevent them from billing to the project for any unnecessary additional time. Theoretically, if the project isn't cancelled, they can start working again once the project is confirmed to still be active.

11. **Answer: A**

    The least desirable option for contractual disputes would be litigation. It is both time-consuming and expensive. Any form of alternative dispute resolution (ADR), such as mediation or arbitration, would be preferable.

12. **Answer: C**

    While protecting confidential company information is part of your professional responsibilities as a PMP, it is not considered a method of contributing to the project management knowledge base.

13. **Answer: A**

    The validate scope process is the process of obtaining the stakeholders' formal acceptance of the completed project scope and the associated deliverables.

14. **Answer: B**

    The control quality (QC) process is performed on the deliverables prior to scope validation by the customer or requesting party. QC ensures that the deliverables have been completed and conform to the documented requirements. Both QC and scope validation occur throughout the project.

15. **Answer: D**

   UAT is also known as inspection. Inspection is the primary tool used in scope validation when we seek customer acceptance of the completed deliverables.

Chapter 15 - Vocabulary Review

* Accepted deliverables	Final report	Respect
Administrative closure	Honesty	Responsibility
Aspirational standards	* Inspection	* Trend analysis
Fairness	Mandatory standards	* Variance analysis
Final product, service, or result transition	* Regression analysis	Voting

1.	The formal hand-over or transition of what the project was chartered to deliver
2.	Our duty to understand the truth and act in a truthful manner both in our communications and in our conduct
3.	Standards that establish firm requirements and those who do not conduct themselves in accordance will be subject to disciplinary action before the PMI's Ethics Review Committee
4.	An analytical technique where a series of input variables are examined in relation to their corresponding output results in order to develop a mathematical or statistical relationship
5.	The actions and processes necessary to satisfy the completion criteria for the project or the phase
6.	Our duty to take ownership for the decisions we make or fail to make, the actions we take or fail to take, and the consequences that result
7.	A technique for determining the cause and degree of difference between the baseline and actual performance
8.	Our duty to make decisions and act impartially and objectively
9.	Allowing members of a group to each submit a choice or selection
10.	An analytical technique that uses mathematical models to forecast future outcomes based on historical results
11.	Products, results, or capabilities produced by a project and validated by the project customer or sponsors as meeting their specified acceptance criteria
12.	Examination of a work product to determine whether it conforms to documented standards
13.	Our duty to show high regard for ourselves, others, and the resources entrusted to us
14.	A summary of the project performance including a summary description of the project, the scope, schedule, quality, and cost objectives, and a summary of the validation information for the final product, service, or result
15.	Standards we strive to achieve as professional although they are not easily measured

* These definitions are taken from the Glossary of *PMBOK® Guide — Sixth Edition*

Vocabulary Review Answers

1. Final product, service, or result transition
2. Honesty
3. Mandatory standards
4. Regression analysis
5. Administrative closure
6. Responsibility
7. Variance analysis
8. Fairness
9. Voting
10. Trend analysis
11. Accepted deliverables
12. Inspection
13. Respect
14. Final report
15. Aspirational standards

Section 4 - Process/Output Match

Match each process to its key output(s). Please note that some processes may have more than one key output and some may have no key output.

Close Project or Phase	Control Scope	Monitor Stakeholder Engagement
Conduct Procurements	Direct and Manage Project Work	Perform Integrated Change Control
Control Costs	Manage Project Knowledge	Plan Procurement Management
Control Procurements	Manage Stakeholder Engagement	Validate Scope
Control Schedule	Monitor and Control Project Work	

Process	Key Output
1.	Agreements
2.	Accepted deliverables
3.	Approved change requests
4.	Bid documents
5.	Closed procurements
6.	Cost forecasts
7.	Deliverables
8.	Final product, service, or result transition
9.	Final report
10.	Independent cost estimates
11.	Lessons learned register
12.	Make-or-buy decisions
13.	Procurement management plan
14.	Procurement statement of work
15.	Procurement strategy

16.	Schedule forecasts
17.	Selected sellers
18.	Source selection criteria
19.	Work performance data
20.	Work performance reports

* These definitions are taken from the Glossary of *PMBOK® Guide – Sixth Edition*

Process/Output Match Answers

1. Conduct Procurements
2. Validate Scope
3. Perform Integrated Change Control
4. Plan Procurement Management
5. Control Procurements
6. Control Costs
7. Direct and Manage Project Work
8. Close Project or Phase
9. Close Project or Phase
10. Plan Procurement Management
11. Manage Project Knowledge
12. Plan Procurement Management
13. Plan Procurement Management
14. Plan Procurement Management
15. Plan Procurement Management
16. Control Schedule
17. Conduct Procurements
18. Plan Procurement Management
19. Direct and Manage Project Work
20. Monitor and Control Project Work

Appendix A

Practice Exam 1

What's in This Chapter

- Practice Exam for Chapters 2-5 (75 Questions)
- Answer Key

Start Time:_____

75 Questions   **Time Limit: 90 Minutes**

1. **The develop project charter process**
    A. Develops the project schedule
    B. Develops the document that formally authorizes a project
    C. Creates the project scope statement
    D. Is an optional process

2. **What is the full name of the *PMBOK® Guide*?**
    A. Program Management Body of Knowledge
    B. Project Management Body of Knowledge
    C. A Guide to the Project Management Body of Knowledge
    D. Project Management Book of Knowledge

3. **These are key individuals who play a management role within an administrative or functional area of the business:**
    A. Operations managers
    B. Project team
    C. Project managers
    D. Functional managers

4. **A collection of generally sequential and overlapping project phases is known as the:**
    A. Project life cycle
    B. Phase gates
    C. Product life cycle
    D. Project methodology

5. **If you are a new project manager in an organization, where might you try to find the defined project life cycle for that organization?**
    A. The product life cycle
    B. The organization's project management methodology
    C. *The PMBOK® Guide*
    D. The intranet

6. **How many project life cycles can be contained within one product life cycle?**
    A. 3
    B. 1
    C. There can be no project life cycles within a product life cycle
    D. Multiple

7. **Which statement below is most accurate regarding a PMO?**
    A. The PMO rarely monitors compliance with project management standards, policies, procedures, and templates via project audits
    B. The PMO is managed by the key stakeholders involved in the project
    C. The PMO may be involved in the selection, management, and deployment of shared or dedicated project resources
    D. The PMO usually has budget and procurement authority for projects within the portfolio

8. **Which of the following is a true statement about operations?**
    A. There is not a monitoring and controlling element
    B. Resources are freely available to the operations of an organization
    C. Team members are often temporary and transitional
    D. Work does not terminate when its current objectives are met but instead will follow new directions to support the organization's strategic plans

9. **This process produces the stakeholder register:**
   A. Develop project charter
   B. Collect requirements
   C. Identify stakeholders
   D. Develop project management plan

10. **A project is defined as:**
    A. A strategic initiative that is long-term
    B. The application of skills, knowledge, tools and techniques to project activities
    C. A temporary endeavor undertaken to create a unique product, service, or result
    D. A collection of related programs

11. **You have been assigned to work on the process redesign project. Based on the stakeholder requirements, you have completed your scope statement. What is the next process you should do?**
    A. Distribute scope statement
    B. Create scope baseline
    C. Collect requirements
    D. Create WBS

12. **What would not be an appropriate attribute of a project?**
    A. Temporary
    B. Progressively elaborated
    C. Ongoing management of operations
    D. Creates a unique product, service, or result

13. **This process is part of the initiating process group and the stakeholder knowledge area:**
    A. Identify stakeholders
    B. Develop communication strategy
    C. Develop project charter
    D. Create communication plan

14. **What statement best describes the role of a project manager:**
    A. Project managers monitor the progress of program components to ensure the overall goals, schedules, budget, and benefits of the program will be met
    B. Project managers are not responsible for the management of the project team to meet project objectives
    C. Project managers manage or coordinate the portfolio management staff
    D. Project managers monitor and control the work of producing the products, services or results that the project was undertaken to produce

15. **This is the concept of continuously improving and detailing a plan as more detailed and specific information becomes available:**
    A. Progressive elaboration
    B. Ensuring scope creep is possible
    C. Developing your project management plan
    D. Thinking outside of the box

16. **In project management, if one factor changes it will most likely impact the other factors. What is this concept called?**
    A. Progressive elaboration
    B. Triple constraint
    C. Project reality
    D. Process groups

17. **Which item best describes the difference between a project manager and the PMO?**
    A. Project managers manage major program scope changes while the PMO focuses on specific project objectives
    B. Project managers control assigned project resources while the PMO optimizes the use of shared organizational resources
    C. Project managers optimize the use of shared organizational resources while the PMO controls project resources
    D. Project managers manage methodologies while the PMO manages project constraints

18. **All of the following statements about the project life cycle and the product life cycle are true except:**
    A. The product life cycle generally starts with the business plan, and continues through idea, to product, ongoing operations, and product divestment
    B. The project life cycle also identifies the transitional actions at the end of the project to link the project to ongoing operations of the performing organization
    C. Generally, a product life cycle is contained within the project life cycle
    D. Generally, a project life cycle is contained within the product life cycle

19. **A program is considered to be:**
    A. A strategy for dealing with project risks
    B. Two or more phases of a project
    C. A collection of related projects
    D. A collection of related portfolios

20. **Which project structure is likely to best leverage the parent organization's depth and breadth of technical experts?**
    A. Project-based
    B. Weak matrix
    C. Matrix
    D. Functional

21. **Which statement is most accurate regarding progressive elaboration?**
    A. It is the same as scope creep
    B. It is usually used for longer term projects or projects where there is not clear definition at the start
    C. Long term projects will be defined in detail but short-term projects only have high-level definition
    D. It is a key tool used in the decomposition of work packages

22. **In which organizational structure does the PM function more as an expediter or coordinator of project activities?**
    A. Strong matrix
    B. Weak matrix
    C. Balance matrix
    D. Project-based

23. **All of the following would generally be part of a project life cycle, except:**
    A. Organizing and preparing
    B. Starting the project
    C. Managing the product in operations
    D. Carrying out the project work

24. **The project charter:**
    A. Is an optional document
    B. Is signed by the sponsor and documents the business needs and the current understanding of the customer's needs
    C. Cannot be completed without the project manager assignment
    D. States that the project does not align with the strategic direction of the organization

25. **In a matrix structure:**
    A. Employees are typically assigned 50% of the time to functional tasks and 50% of the time to project tasks
    B. Employees' administrative, development, and performance management are typically focused with their functional manager with proportional performance and developmental input by project managers
    C. Employees are equally answerable to both functional and project managers
    D. Employees are answerable to the project manager, but report both to the functional and project manager

26. **This technique enhances brainstorming with a voting process to rank the ideas.**
    A. Idea/mind mapping
    B. Delphi technique
    C. Affinity diagram
    D. Nominal group technique

27. **The *PMBOK® Guide*'s process groups interact based on what model?**
    - A. Juran's 80/20
    - B. Deming's Continuous Process Improvement
    - C. Maslow's Hierarchy of Needs
    - D. Shewhart's Plan-Do-Check-Act cycle

28. **This process is part of the planning process group and the integration knowledge area:**
    - A. Develop Project Management Plan
    - B. Develop Project Charter
    - C. Identify Stakeholders
    - D. Identify Sponsor

29. **The relationships amongst the triple constraint could best be described as:**
    - A. As project manager, if you change one of the constraints, you must adjust the other factors
    - B. Each are dependent on the others
    - C. The constraints are not related and function independently
    - D. If any one of the constraints is changed or adjusted, most likely at least one other factor is affected

30. **The project manager has the highest authority in this type of an organizational structure:**
    - A. Functional
    - B. Matrix
    - C. Project-based
    - D. Weak matrix

31. **All of the following are examples of organizational structures, except:**
    - A. Dictatorship
    - B. Project-based
    - C. Functional
    - D. Matrix

32. **Why would the project charter be considered a mandatory document on a project?**
    - A. The charter is a contractual requirement
    - B. Because it is signed by the sponsor
    - C. The charter provides authorization for the project to commence
    - D. The charter is the document that assigns the project manager

33. **A chart of accounts:**
    - A. Is not used to monitor project costs by WBS elements
    - B. Is developed as part of the project charter
    - C. Provides a graphical representation of project costs in relation to the project schedule
    - D. Is any numbering system used to monitor project costs by category

34. **While collecting requirements, you want to solicit feedback from a group of experts in a format where they are best enabled to give their individual and honest feedback. What technique would be best in this situation?**
    - A. Interviewing
    - B. Mind mapping
    - C. Affinity diagram
    - D. Nominal group technique

35. **Which of the following is not a characteristic of both projects and operations?**
    - A. Follows the project life cycle
    - B. Limited by constraints
    - C. Performed by individuals
    - D. Planned, executed, monitored and controlled

36. **In general, a project manager's technical skills:**
    - A. Should not be considered when selecting a project manager
    - B. Must be equal to or higher than any other team member's skills
    - C. Must be sufficiently high to understand technical issues and explain technical decisions to others
    - D. Are the most important criterion for selecting a project manager

37. **A project scheduler may typically be found in what type of an organization?**

    A. Strong matrix
    B. Functional
    C. Weak matrix
    D. Project-based

38. **You have been assigned a new project with an aggressive deadline for completion. You learn that you have team members from six countries that speak three different languages and the product is something new for your organization. However, your project has four sponsors. What is of most concern to you?**

    A. Because the product is new for the organization, there will be a learning curve that will delay the project
    B. Communication is going to cause significant issues because the team is not co-located
    C. Having four sponsors is going to most likely cause delays in decision-making and escalations
    D. The aggressive deadline is going to result in a missed constraint

39. **Which of the following is not a true statement about stakeholders?**

    A. The project management team must identify both internal and external stakeholders
    B. Stakeholders may exert influence over the project, its deliverables, and the project team members
    C. Stakeholders are positively affected by the project outcome
    D. The project manager must manage the influence of the various stakeholders in relation to the project requirements

40. **Which of the following is not a knowledge area:**

    A. Integration
    B. Scope
    C. Budget
    D. Schedule

41. **How are the names and numbers of phases on a project determined?**

    A. By determining how long the project is going to take
    B. By following the *PMBOK® Guide* methodology
    C. By the management and control needs of the organization
    D. By the individual project manager

42. **Which statement below is true regarding control accounts?**

    A. A control account is a quality tool that ensure proper authorization is secured
    B. A control account may include one or more work packages, but each work package must be associated with only one control account
    C. A control account may be associated with only one work package, but each work package can be associated with multiple control accounts
    D. Control accounts are only added at the highest level of the WBS

43. **What statement is most accurate regarding scope creep and progressive elaboration?**

    A. Unmanaged progressive elaboration increases the incidence of scope creep
    B. Scope creep is unmanaged changes to the scope while progressive elaboration refines the project details
    C. Progressive elaboration should be managed by the work package owners while the project manager should manage scope creep
    D. Scope creep and progressive elaboration are synonymous

44. **The following may be typically found in the project scope statement, except:**

    A. A description of product deliverables
    B. The project exclusions
    C. The sponsors title and authority
    D. Project constraints and assumptions

45. **The stakeholder engagement plan:**

    A. Identifies the project manager
    B. Is always developed by the customer
    C. Gives authorization for the project to commence
    D. Defines an approach to increase the support and minimize negative impacts of stakeholders

46. **You are a project manager with a technology consulting firm. Your first project is the implementation of an internal resource allocation tool for the home office. You are about to begin work on the project and realize that there is not an executed contract for the project, although there is a signed charter. How should you handle this?**
    A. Escalate the issue to your project sponsor
    B. Begin the project
    C. Report the discrepancy to the customer
    D. Wait for a contract to be executed prior to beginning work

47. **This type of work is ongoing and sustains the organization over time:**
    A. Production
    B. Operations
    C. Projects
    D. Execution

48. **The difference between the scope statement and the project charter could best be described as:**
    A. The scope statement will usually identify the project manager
    B. The project charter will document the project deliverables and product scope description
    C. The scope statement will include the sponsor name and signature
    D. The project charter will capture measurable objectives and success criteria

49. **What is usually the last phase of a product life cycle?**
    A. Transition
    B. Retirement
    C. Death
    D. Closing

50. **You have been assigned the management of a high-priority project. Due to the urgency surrounding the project and conflicting project schedules, the project sponsor has advised you to start the project despite the fact that there is not a project charter. What is the most appropriate response for you to take?**
    A. Proceed with the project
    B. Document the sponsor's information
    C. Seek another position outside of the organization
    D. Escalate the situation

51. **The new project for your organization has been approved and the sponsor has asked you how you will be managing the project. You know that the project is creating a new product for the customer with multiple features. Your organization has not built a similar product in the past and you know that the customer wants to be involved in the testing of the functionality. Which approach would be most appropriate?**
    A. An organic life cycle will allow the project to progress in a natural format
    B. An adaptive life cycle responds to high levels of change and increased stakeholder involvement
    C. A predictive life cycle will be best applied in this situation because of the multiple features that need to be developed
    D. A strong phase gate approach will ensure that work is not progressing until the project team and the customer are ready for the next phase

52. **A new team leader has joined the project organization. She will be managing multiple project resources as part of a large-scale system implementation. In order to increase the probability of delivering the project on time, she has been authorized to provide incentives to the team when they achieve defined milestones early. What type of authority does she have?**
    A. Coercive
    B. Referent
    C. Positional
    D. Reward

53. You are assuming the management of a project that has been underway for six months. You notice that many of the team members are disengaged from the project and not very cooperative. Upon talking with the team, you learn that the previous project manager was very driven to achieve the project objectives in order to be eligible for promotion. He often reminded the team that his promotion was on the line and that they needed to do whatever it takes to get the work done quickly and cheaply. Which statement is most accurate?

   A. The previous project manager was using guilt-based power on the project team which may have caused them to be resentful
   B. As the new project manager, you will need to use positional power given that the team members are disengaged
   C. Because the previous project manager built a case for his promotion, this would be considered persuasive power
   D. Using fear to manage the team, the previous project manager was using punitive power

54. Your landscaping project is nearing completion and your team has begun planting the flowers within the planters. You review the requirements documentation and realize that the flowers should have been yellow and not the pink ones that are being planted. The customer has not yet seen the flowers that were planted. What type of change request would you submit?

   A. Defect repair
   B. Corrective action
   C. Scope change
   D. Preventive action

55. Which statement is most accurate regarding leadership and management?

   A. Leadership and management are both terms to describe the required skills for a project manager
   B. Leadership involves short-term goals whereas management involves long-term goals and strategy
   C. Management involves positional power and focusing on operational issues, while leadership inspires trust and creates a compelling long-range vision
   D. Management is used for the day-to-day management of the team while leadership is used with the key stakeholders

56. You are evaluating the business case for the project you were recently assigned. Upon review of the financial benefits of the project, you find that the project has a projected negative NPV. What statement is most accurate?

   A. If the project has a negative NPV, most likely the business case was not completed correctly
   B. It is likely that the project is being conducted to meet a legal, regulatory, or compliance requirement
   C. The project should be escalated to the sponsor before the project begins
   D. A negative NPV is likely due to a large up-front expenditure in the project

57. Which of the following is not a technique used to define the project scope?

   A. Product analysis
   B. Prototypes
   C. Multicriteria decision analysis
   D. Alternatives analysis

58. This process is part of the initiating process group and the integration knowledge area:

   A. Create charter
   B. Identify stakeholders
   C. Develop project charter
   D. Identify sponsor

59. In collecting requirements from the stakeholders, the difference between affinity diagrams and mind mapping can best be described as:

   A. Affinity diagrams are used during mind mapping to display the relationships between the ideas and the root causes of project problems.
   B. The information generated in an affinity diagram can be used in a sticky note process with mind mapping
   C. Affinity diagrams create a representation of the similarities and differences in opinions and it they are also called a sticky note process.
   D. Affinity diagrams sort a large number of ideas into groups for further review and analysis whereas mind mapping takes ideas that were generated and creates a representation of the similarities and differences in understanding.

60. **Which statement is least accurate regarding the benefits management plan?**
    A. The benefits management plan uses the business case and a needs assessment
    B. The benefits management plan describes how the project will fulfill the business needs related to the strategic direction of the organization
    C. The benefits management plan will identify the accountable person to monitor and report on the benefits
    D. The benefits management plan will be developed by the customer or end-user to justify the project

61. **Your organization established a PMO last year, but the leadership team has not seen an improvement in the project management or project results. The PMO that is in-place provides training and templates to the project managers and is also capturing lessons learned. Which statement is most accurate?**
    A. The existing PMO is a controlling PMO and the leadership should consider moving to a directive PMO
    B. The leadership of the organization should disband the PMO as it is not serving the original intention nor making progress
    C. The existing PMO is a supportive PMO and the leadership should consider moving to a controlling PMO
    D. The leadership should allow an additional 12 months to ensure changes are effective

62. **The development of a project management plan is a PMO requirement for all projects that are over $100,000 or 6 months in length. Which statement is least accurate regarding the project management plan?**
    A. It may be summary level or detailed
    B. Is also known as the project schedule
    C. It includes a description of the processes that will be used on the project
    D. It aides in managing the team member and stakeholder expectations

63. **You are in the process of creating the WBS. Which of the following is the output:**
    A. WBS
    B. Scope statement
    C. Scope baseline
    D. WBS dictionary

64. **The organization has a number of aggressive goals for the year and they have authorized a number of concurrent projects to increase their competitive offerings. Upon assignment of your particular project, you realize that it is part of a much larger program. Which statement is most accurate?**
    A. Your primary concern is the schedule and interface dependencies between your project and the rest of the projects within the program
    B. Your primary concern is that you are not a program manager and you are unsure how to proceed with your project
    C. Your primary concern is that the project is part of a competitive offering and as such, you need to clarify the scope and quality requirements
    D. Your primary concern is the resource constraints given that the organization is doing a number of projects in parallel

65. **Which of the following would not be considered an enterprise environmental factor?**
    A. Financial and market conditions
    B. Organizational culture
    C. Availability of human resources
    D. PMO project templates

66. **You are mentoring a fellow project manager who is new to the organization. She is about to begin a project and would like to know the most appropriate tasks for initiating her project and in what order they would occur. Which statement is most accurate?**
    A. The charter should be approved prior to defining the high-level scope
    B. The SOW should be completed prior to developing the project charter
    C. The contract should be executed prior to developing the SOW
    D. The stakeholder analysis should be completed prior to performing the project assessment

67. **These describe the stakeholder role, the roles that benefit from the feature, what the user needs to accomplish, and the benefit of the functionality to the user or stakeholder.**
    A. User stories
    B. Burndown charts
    C. Stakeholder profiles
    D. Scope statements

68. **The project management plan may include all of the following except:**
    A. Process improvement plan
    B. Scope baseline
    C. Project funding requirements
    D. Risk management plan

69. **During the nominal group technique**
    A. Group members brainstorm on the best option or resolution for a problem or issue
    B. Group members are encouraged to use the fist-to-five approach to voting
    C. Group members respond via survey, anonymously, as to their suggestions for handling the problem or the issue
    D. Group members write down their ideas about the problem, the ideas are shared, and votes are submitted privately on the best ideas

70. **Your project is about to begin, and you have identified 20 core team members. With your team, you are developing your approach to planning the project. You are leveraging the organization's past project files and historical information to provide the foundation for the approach. This would be considered using:**
    A. Enterprise environmental factors
    B. Expert judgment
    C. The project management plan
    D. Organizational process assets

71. **One of your work package owners reports that their component may be delayed due to the absence of a key team member. He asks for a replacement resource. This would be an example of:**
    A. Progressive elaboration
    B. Scope creep
    C. Preventive action
    D. Corrective action

72. **In order to collect requirements, the PMO has suggested that you schedule some facilitated workshops. Which statement is least accurate regarding facilitated workshops?**
    A. They must be conducted in-person to be effective
    B. They are attended by key cross-functional stakeholders
    C. They are a technique to quickly define requirements and reconcile stakeholder differences
    D. They may be called JAD or QFD sessions

73. **Which statement is least accurate regarding the processes within the stakeholder knowledge area:**
    A. They identify the project stakeholders and their influence on the project
    B. They document the roles and responsibilities required for the project
    C. The ensure appropriate generation and distribution of project information to stakeholders
    D. They provide consistent information to manage expectations

74. **Your PMO has issued a policy that all projects must have a project management plan. What is the most likely reason for the policy?**
    A. The project management plan includes the authorization for the project to begin
    B. The project management plan details the scope and requirements of the project
    C. The project management plan minimizes risk to the organization, should the project manager or a key team member leave
    D. The project management plan gives the project manager authority to use organizational resources for the benefit of the project

75. **Interviews, focus groups, observations, prototypes, benchmarking, nominal group technique, affinity diagrams, and mind mapping are tools and techniques for this process:**
    A. Define scope
    B. Create WBS
    C. Collect requirements
    D. Plan stakeholder engagement

End Time:_____

Practice Exam 1   Chapters 2 - 5

Answer Key

1. **Answer: B**

    The output of the Develop Project Charter process is the project charter, which formally authorizes the project.

2. **Answer: C**

    The full name is *A Guide to the Project Management Body of Knowledge*®

3. **Answer: D**

    Functional managers play a management role within an administrative or functional area of the business.

4. **Answer: A**

    A project life cycle is a collection of generally sequential and overlapping project phases.

5. **Answer: B**

    The defined project life cycle for the organization would be found in that organization's project management methodology.

6. **Answer: D**

    A product lifecycle can have multiple project life cycles. It is a one-to-many relationship: one product lifecycle may have multiple project life cycles.

7. **Answer: C**

    The PMO may be involved in the selection, management, and deployment of shared or dedication project resources. The PMO typically monitors compliance with project management standards and policies but they typically do not have budget or procurement authority. The PMO is typically staffed with dedicated PMO resources versus key stakeholders from the various projects.

8. **Answer: D**

    Operations do not terminate, but continue to follow new directions under support of the strategic direction of the organization. Operations are monitored and controlled, team members are typically permanent, and as with projects, resources are constrained or limited.

9. **Answer: C**

    The stakeholder register is an output of the identify stakeholders process.

10. **Answer: C**

    A project is a temporary endeavor undertaken to create a unique product, service, or result.

11. **Answer: D**

    Because you have the requirements and the scope statement, it implies that you have completed the collect requirements and the define scope processes. The next process would be create WBS.

12. **Answer: C**

    Projects are temporary, progressively elaborated, and create a unique product, service, or result. Projects are not the ongoing management of operations.

13. **Answer: A**

    The Identify Stakeholders process is in the initiating process group and the stakeholder knowledge area.

14. **Answer: D**

    Project managers monitor and control the work of producing the project's product, service, or result. Project managers are responsible for the management of the project team. Project managers do not monitor program components, nor do they coordinate portfolio staff.

15. **Answer: A**

    Progressive elaboration continuously improves and details a plan as more information becomes available.

16. **Answer: B**

This is the concept of the triple constraint: scope, time, and cost. When one constraint changes, more than likely (not always), the others will be affected.

17. **Answer: B**

Project managers do not manage program scope changes, optimize the use of shared organizational resources, nor manage methodologies. They do control assigned project resources.

18. **Answer: C**

A product life cycle is not contained within a project life cycle. A product life cycle can have multiple project life cycles.

19. **Answer: C**

A program is a collection of related projects.

20. **Answer: D**

A functional organization is best able to leverage the depth and breadth of the parent's organization's technical experts, as those resources reside within, and work within, their functional areas. Therefore, their knowledge is current and specialized to their area.

21. **Answer: B**

Progressive elaboration is typically used for longer term projects or projects where there is not clear definition at the start of the project. Progressive elaboration will start with a high-level description and then define and refine those details as the project progresses.

22. **Answer: B**

In a weak matrix organization, there is no true project manager. The resource assigned would be more of a coordinator or expeditor of project activities without any real "management" capabilities.

23. **Answer: C**

The project life cycle would not include managing the product once it reaches operations.

24. **Answer: B**

The project charter is signed by the sponsor and documents the business need and current understanding of the customer's needs. The charter may exist prior to the project manager assignment. It is considered mandatory and it commits that the project aligns with the strategic direction of the organization.

25. **Answer: B**

In a matrix structure the functional manager would be responsible for the employees' administrative management, but the project manager would be expected to provide proportional feedback. For example, if the team member is on your project 30% of your time, you should contribute 30% to their performance appraisal. The employee is not equally answerable to both the PM and the functional manager, as the functional manager "owns" the employee and would be the ultimate decision maker on that employee's role and responsibilities.

26. **Answer: D**

Nominal group technique enhances brainstorming by adding a voting process to the ideas that were generated through brainstorming.

27. **Answer: D**

The process groups interact based on Shewhart's Plan-Do-Check-Act cycle.

28. **Answer: A**

The develop project management plan process is in the integration knowledge area and the planning process group.

29. **Answer: D**

The triple constraints are related in that if one changes more than likely the others will be affected. The triple constraint is scope, time, cost.

30. **Answer: C**

A project manager would have the highest authority in a project-based organizational structure.

31. **Answer: A**

The organizational structures include functional, weak matrix, balanced matrix, strong matrix, and project-based.

32. **Answer: C**

The charter is considered mandatory because it provides authorization for the project to commence.

33. **Answer: D**

A chart of accounts, also known as a code of accounts, is any type of unique number system used to monitor project costs by category. The chart of accounts numbering is used on the WBS.

34. **Answer: A**

Interviewing would be the most appropriate technique to capture honest feedback from a group of experts.

35. **Answer: A**

Both projects and operations are limited by constraints, performed by individuals, and are planned, executed, and monitoring and controlled. Only projects follow a project life cycle.

36. **Answer: C**

A project manager's technical skill must be sufficiently high to understand the technical issues of the project and be able to explain technical decisions to others. Technical skills should be considered when selecting a project manager but are not necessarily the most important criterion.

37. **Answer: D**

A project scheduler is a defined project resource. Project schedulers and other defined project support staff would be found in a project-based organizational structure.

38. **Answer: C**

Multiple sponsors is the biggest concern as there will most likely be delays in decision-making. For the other factors, you cannot definitively state they will have the negative impacts as listed in the other answers, although it is not impossible. Multiple sponsors is a "known" issue.

39. **Answer: C**

Stakeholders will not always be positively affected by the project outcome. The assumption on any project is that you will have negative / resistant stakeholders.

40. **Answer: C**

Budget is not a knowledge area: integration, scope, schedule, cost, quality, resources, communication, risk, procurement, and stakeholder

41. **Answer: C**

The names and number of phases on a project determined by the management and control needs of the organization.

42. **Answer: B**

A control account may include one or more work packages, but each work package must be associated with only one control account. Control accounts and work packages have a one-to-many relationship. You cannot split a work package across multiple control accounts.

43. **Answer: B**

Scope creep is any unmanaged changes to the project scope, whereas progressive elaboration is adding detail as more information becomes available on the project.

44. **Answer: C**

The sponsor's title and authority would be found in the project charter, not in the project scope statement.

45. **Answer: D**

The stakeholder engagement plan defines an approach to increase support and minimize negative impacts to the project stakeholders.

46. **Answer: B**

Because the project is being done as an internal project, for your home office, there is no need for a contract. Given that the charter has been executed, the project can begin.

47. **Answer: B**

Operations are ongoing and sustain the organization over time.

48. **Answer: D**

The project charter will capture measurable objectives and success criteria for the project, identify the project manager (if known), and will include the sponsor name, title, and signature. The scope statement will document the project deliverables and the product scope description.

49. **Answer: B**

The last phase of a product life cycle would be product retirement.

50. **Answer: D**

Even though the sponsor has advised you to begin the project, you cannot begin without authorization in place. As such, you would need to escalate the situation.

51. **Answer: B**

An adaptive (or agile) approach would be most appropriate given that there will be some discovery and changes as it is a new product with multiple features. In addition, this would provide the stakeholders with the involvement that they are seeking. There is no organic life cycle. Predictive life cycles are appropriately for projects with minimal change. Because an adaptive approach would be best, phase gates may or may not be leveraged.

52. **Answer: D**

Because she is incenting the team with something they value, this is considered reward authority

53. **Answer: A**

Guilt-based power is used when the project manager was implying that it was their sense of duty or their obligation to perform well so that he would receive his promotion. You may or may not have positional power, depending on the organization. Persuasive power occurs when an individual provides a strong argument or case for behavior, however, that does not appear to be the case in this situation. There was no mention of any type of threat or repercussions if the team did not perform well, so it is not punitive power.

54. **Answer: A**

Because this is a quality issue, it would be considered a defect repair. Corrective actions are typically for cost or schedule problems. Quality issues are defect repairs, regardless of whether the customer has seen the problem or not.

55. **Answer: C**

Leadership and management differ, with leadership focusing on inspiring trust and creating long-range visions and management being a "task-manager" that uses positional power. Leadership should be used with all stakeholders and team members.

56. **Answer: B**

An active project with a negative NPV is most likely being conducted to meet a legal, regulatory, or compliance requirement. You cannot assume the business case was completed incorrectly. The business case is completed by the sponsor, so they would already be aware of the negative NPV. A large up front expenditure wouldn't necessarily cause a negative NPV.

57. **Answer: B**

The tools and techniques used to define the project scope are product analysis, multicriteria decision analysis, and alternatives analysis. Prototypes are a tool/technique for the collect requirements process.

58. **Answer: C**

The process that is in the initiating process group and the integration knowledge area is the develop project charter process.

59. **Answer: D**

Affinity diagrams sort a large number of ideas into groups, which is why they are often referred to as a sticky note process. Mind mapping creates a visual mapping of the similarities and differences in understanding.

60. Answer: D

The benefits management plan is an internal document that provides the information as to how the project will fulfill business needs. It would not be developed by the customer or the end-user.

61. Answer: C

The current PMO is a supportive, or low control PMO, which provides templates and training but does not enforce compliance with policies or procedures. A controlling PMO would provide the same support but would also validate compliance which can help identify the root of the project issues. Twelve months is too specific for a timeline and disbanding the PMO is not necessarily the best option.

62. Answer: B

The project management plan is not the project schedule, but it does include the schedule baseline. The project management plan may be summary level or detailed, includes a description of the processes that will be used on the project and it aides in managing the team member and stakeholder expectations.

63. Answer: C

During the create WBS process, you will be creating the WBS and the WBS dictionary. When you add the WBS and the WBS dictionary to previously developed scope statement, you will have the scope baseline as the output.

64. Answer: A

While it is important to validate the scope and quality requirements for any project, when managing a project that is part of a program, the project manager needs to be concerned with the schedule and interface dependencies. The fact that it is part of a program means that inherently there are going to be schedule and interface constraints. The question does not say that you are a program manager. There is nothing in the question to imply that there are resource issues. The organization may have added more staff, etc.

65. Answer: D

Enterprise environmental factors are things that we "consider", that may have an impact on our project. PMO project templates would be considered organizational process assets – things we use.

66. Answer: B

From a proper sequencing perspective, the first thing needed to launch a project is the project statement of work (SOW). This is the request coming from the requesting party. The sponsor will use the SOW to validate a business case to pursue the project. If the project is being done for an external party, a contract (agreement) will be executed. Once those are in place, the project charter is created.

67. Answer: A

User stories describe the stakeholder role, the roles that benefit from the feature, what the user needs to accomplish, and the benefit of the functionality to the user or stakeholder. Burndown charts show the agile team's progress.

68. Answer: C

The project management plan does not include the project funding requirements. Typically, the high-level funding requirements will be documented in the project charter and the detailed funding requirements will be developed with the budget. All "plans" and all "baselines" are part of the project management plan.

69. Answer: D

Group members write down their ideas, ideas are shared by the facilitator and members vote privately on a scale of 1 to 5. Brainstorming is a component of nominal group technique, but the voting is what makes it the nominal group technique. Fist-to-five is a voting method where votes are not handled privately. Responding to surveys anonymously is describing the Delphi technique.

70. Answer: D

Past project files and historical information are considered part of the organizational process assets.

71. Answer: C

Because the component may be delayed and isn't late yet, the replacement resource would be considered a preventive action.

72. Answer: A

Facilitated workshops can be conducted via virtual team meeting tools and still be effective.

73. **Answer: B**

Specific roles and responsibilities will be documented within the human resources knowledge area, versus in the stakeholder knowledge area. However, on the stakeholder register, it is not uncommon to identify the role that stakeholder is playing in the project (team lead, contributor, sponsor, etc.).

74. **Answer: C**

The project management plan minimizes risk to the organization. Should the project manager or key team members leave or be reassigned, the project management plan will allow them to understand the project quickly. It is the project charter that provides authorization for the project to begin and provides the project manager with authority to use resources. The project scope statement details the project scope.

75. **Answer: C**

These are all tools/techniques for the collect requirements process.

Appendix B

Practice Exam 2

What's in This Chapter

- Practice Exam for Chapters 6 - 8 (75 Questions)
- Answer Key

Start Time:_____

1. Activity A has a duration of 6 days and has 4 days of free float. The ES of the successor activity, Activity B, is day 18. If Activity A is delayed by 7 days, what is the adjusted ES of Activity B?
   A. Day 25
   B. Day 11
   C. Day 21
   D. Day 31

2. Activity A has a duration of 5 days and 0 float, activity B has a duration of 2 days and 3 days float, activity C has a duration of 9 days and 0 float, and activity D has a duration of 8 days and 1 day float. What is the total duration of the activities?
   A. 20 days
   B. 24 days
   C. 14 days
   D. 18 days

3. In shortening the project duration, the first action to take is to:
   A. Change the project scope
   B. Crash as many activities as possible
   C. Fast-track activities on the critical path
   D. Consume the float on the critical path

4. The activity duration estimating technique that uses optimistic, pessimistic, and most likely calculations is:
   A. CPM
   B. GERT
   C. PERT
   D. Gantt

5. A group of related schedule activities that for reporting purposes, is shown as a single aggregate activity:
   A. Hammock activity
   B. PDM
   C. Combination activity
   D. Roll-up activity

6. These dependencies are inherent to the work being done and often involve physical limitations.
   A. Hard logic
   B. Soft logic
   C. External
   D. Discretionary

7. What is the most commonly used formula for a 3-point estimate?
   A. (optimistic time + most likely time + pessimistic time) / 6
   B. (optimistic time + most likely time + pessimistic time) / 3
   C. (optimistic time + 4(most likely time) + pessimistic time) / 6
   D. (optimistic time - pessimistic time) / 2

8. The project completion date will slip if:
   A. Total float = 0
   B. Total float > 0
   C. Total float < 0
   D. Total float > 1

9. You are the project manager of the data backup project. Your team lead has given you a cost estimate that she feels is accurate to within 5% of the actual costs. What type of estimate did she give you?

   A. Budgetary
   B. Rough order of magnitude
   C. Definitive
   D. Phased

10. The cost baseline includes_____ but does not include _____.

    A. Contingency, management reserve
    B. management reserve, contingency
    C. management reserve, basis of the estimates
    D. management reserve, schedule allowances

11. Of the following cost estimate types, which would be the least accurate?

    A. Budgetary
    B. Phased
    C. Progressive elaboration
    D. ROM

12. All of the following statements are true about analogous estimating except:

    A. It is essentially a combination of historical information and parametric estimating
    B. It is frequently used when there is a lack of detailed information about the current project
    C. It is critical that the historical project is as similar as possible to the current project
    D. It is less costly and time-consuming, but also less accurate

13. You are estimating the cost for the website development work package. Most likely the cost will be $1,000. However, there is a chance it can cost as much as $1,800 or as little as $500. What is the best estimate for the work package?

    A. $1,050
    B. $1,100
    C. $3,300
    D. $1,000

14. A cost baseline should not include:

    A. Estimates of the most likely project costs
    B. Contingency cost
    C. Assumptions for the estimates
    D. Management reserve

15. Given the launch of the new system, you also need to take into consideration the cost of associated hardware and software. Your IT team lead anticipates the costs to be approximately $18,000. However, if an upgrade is necessary, it could cost as much as $30,000. There is a chance that existing hardware can be used, which would bring the costs as low as $7,000. What is the best estimate for this portion of the project?

    A. $19,166
    B. $9,166
    C. $36,333
    D. $18,000

16. The project costs have been estimated at $450,000. Because the project has a significant amount of risk, the project manager is adding $50,000 for contingency. In addition, the project sponsor has allocated an additional $75,000 for management reserve. How much is the cost baseline?

    A. $500,000
    B. $450,000
    C. $525,000
    D. $575,000

17. **In what way does free float differ from total float?**

    A. Free float is the amount of total float that does not affect the end date, whereas total float is the accumulated amount of free float
    B. There is no difference - the two terms are functionally equivalent
    C. Free float is the amount of time that a schedule activity can be delayed without delaying the early start of any immediately following schedule activities, whereas total float is concerned with delays that affect the project finish date
    D. An activity's free float is calculated by subtracting the total float from the critical path's total float

18. **All of the following statements are true about three-point estimating except:**

    A. Uses a weighted average to calculate the most appropriate duration
    B. It uses both historical information and analogous estimating
    C. It can be calculated as: $(O + 4(M) + P) \div 6$
    D. It can be used for both cost and duration

19. **Activity A has a finish-to-start relationship with Activity B. Activity A has a duration of 10 days. Activity B has a duration of 6 days with a 3-day lead. What is the duration of the activities?**

    A. 13 days
    B. 16 days
    C. 19 days
    D. 10 days

20. **You have been assigned to work on the process redesign project. Based on the stakeholder requirements, you have completed your scope statement. What is the next thing you should do?**

    A. Collect Requirements
    B. Create WBS
    C. Create Scope Baseline
    D. Distribute Scope Statement

21. **Free float is:**

    A. The amount of time an activity can be delayed without delaying the finish date of the project
    B. The amount of lead time for activities that are not on the critical path
    C. Calculated by subtracting early finish time from late start time (EF-LS)
    D. The amount of time an activity can be delayed without delaying the early start of a subsequent activity

22. **This process produces the stakeholder register:**

    A. Develop project charter
    B. Identify stakeholders
    C. Collect requirements
    D. Develop project management plan

23. **You are three months into a one-year project and are evaluating the project schedule. It appears as though there are only few activities coming up within the next reporting period that have float. The float of an activity is determined by:**

    A. The amount of lag
    B. The amount of time the activity can be delayed before it impacts the critical path
    C. Performing a Monte Carlo analysis to determine the amount of slack
    D. Identifying the free float as compared to the activity durations

24. **Which of the following statements is true about elapsed time versus effort?**

    A. Elapsed time is actual calendar time and effort is the number of hours required to complete the activity
    B. Effort is the amount of calendar time and elapsed time is the total amount of days consumed by the activity
    C. Both are included in the critical path calculation
    D. Effort is used mainly with resource-leveling

25. **These dependencies are also called preferential logic:**

    A. Mandatory
    B. Discretionary
    C. Hard logic
    D. External

26. Your work package owner has submitted the following information: There will be three resources involved in the work, each working five hours per day with no work on the weekends. The start date will be Monday, 1 March and the completion date is Friday, 19 March. Monday, 8 March is a holiday.

    What is the elapsed time of the work?
    A. 14 days
    B. 3 weeks
    C. 15 days
    D. 2.4 weeks

27. Your work package owner has submitted the following information: There will be three resources involved in the work, each working five hours per day with no work on the weekends. The start date will be Monday, 1 March and the completion date is Friday, 19 March. Monday, 8 March is a holiday.

    What is the duration of the work?
    A. 14 days
    B. 3 weeks
    C. 15 days
    D. 2.4 weeks

28. Your work package owner has submitted the following information: There will be three resources involved in the work, each working five hours per day with no work on the weekends. The start date will be Monday, 1 March and the completion date is Friday, 19 March. Monday, 8 March is a holiday.

    What is the effort of the work?
    A. 14 staff-days
    B. 225 staff-hours
    C. 15 staff-days
    D. 210 staff-hours

29. **Total float is:**
    A. The amount of time that an activity can be delayed without delaying the early start of any immediately following activities
    B. The amount of time that an activity can be delayed without delaying the completion date of the project
    C. The amount of float on the critical path
    D. Calculated by subtracting late start from late finish

30. **You have conducted a PERT analysis on a critical work package. Based on the information from your team, you learn that the best-case duration is 4 days and the worst-case duration is 14 days. If the PERT estimate is 7 days, what is the most likely duration?**
    A. 9 days
    B. 7 days
    C. 8 days
    D. 6 days

31. **A preferred dependency is the same as all of the following except:**
    A. Discretionary
    B. Expert
    C. Preferential
    D. Soft logic

32. You have assessed the following critical activities for crashing:

Activity	Original Cost	Crash Cost	Original Duration	Crash Duration
1.1	10K	12k	12d	8d
2.1	8k	15k	20d	13d
3.1	5k	11k	25d	22d
4.1	11k	12k	30d	20d
5.1	3k	4k	10d	6d

What is the best candidate for crashing?

A. 4.1
B. 2.1
C. 5.1
D. 1.1

33. You have assessed the following critical activities for crashing:

Activity	Original Cost	Crash Cost	Original Duration	Crash Duration
1.1	10K	12k	12d	8d
2.1	8k	15k	20d	13d
3.1	5k	11k	25d	22d
4.1	11k	12k	30d	20d
5.1	3k	4k	10d	6d

If you crashed the three best candidates, what would be the adjusted cost and duration?

A. $41,000 / 79 days
B. $43,000 / 80 days
C. $44,000 / 76 days
D. $42,000 / 74 days

34. With your project team, you are identifying any dependencies between the project activities and creating a PDM. What process are you conducting?

A. Activity duration estimating
B. Activity resource estimating
C. Developing the project schedule
D. Sequencing activities

35. Activity A has a duration of 10 days. Activity B has a duration of 9 days with a 3 day lead. Activity A has 4 days of float. Activity A and B have a finish-to-start relationship. What is the total duration?

A. 19 days
B. 22 days
C. 12 days
D. 16 days

36. Which statement is most accurate regarding lag?

A. There are no resources involved
B. It is fundamentally the same as float
C. It is an acceleration of a successor activity
D. It would be represented by a negative number on a PDM

37. You are evaluating the following component of the schedule: activity one has a duration of 4 days, activity two has a duration of 3 days, activity three has a duration of 8 days, activity four has a duration of 5 days (and is dependent upon activities one, two, and three completing), activity five has a duration of 7 days (and is dependent upon activity four completing), and activity six has a duration of 4 days (and is also dependent upon activity four completing).

   If activity two gets delayed by 4 days, what is the impact to the schedule?

   A. There is no impact
   B. The duration gets delayed by 5 days
   C. The amount of free float on the activity decreases to 2 days
   D. There is more than one critical path

38. You are evaluating the following component of the schedule: activity one has a duration of 4 days, activity two has a duration of 3 days, activity three has a duration of 8 days, activity four has a duration of 5 days (and is dependent upon activities one, two, and three completing), activity five has a duration of 7 days (and is dependent upon activity four completing), and activity six has a duration of 4 days (and is also dependent upon activity four completing).

   Which activities are on the critical path?

   A. 2, 3, 4, 5
   B. 1, 2, 3, 4, 5
   C. 3, 4, 5
   D. 3, 4, 5, 6

39. Decomposition is a technique used during what two processes?

   A. Estimate costs and estimate durations
   B. Identify risks and define activities
   C. Define scope and create WBS
   D. Create WBS and define activities

40. You have developed your PDM and estimated the activity durations. What is the next thing you should do?

   A. Secure sponsor sign-off
   B. Estimate your costs
   C. Develop your project schedule
   D. Create the RAM

41. You are the project manager over a large construction project and are about to enter the building phase. There is a dependency on getting the first four lots built out before starting the remaining lots. The lumber is being delivered today for the first four houses.

   Which statement is most accurate?

   A. The lumber delivery is an external dependency
   B. The first four lots being built out illustrate a start-to-start relationship
   C. The development of the first four lots is a mandatory dependency
   D. The lumber delivery is an example of soft logic

42. Which statement is most accurate regarding parametric and analogous estimating?

   A. They both leverage historical information and expert judgment
   B. Analogous is generally more accurate than parametric estimating
   C. Parametric is usually done with costs whereas analogous is more commonly used with durations
   D. The project manager is the most appropriate resource to estimate analogously whereas work package owners would be better suited to estimate parametrically

43. Activity B is 4 days, Activity C is 7 days, Activity D is dependent on B and C and is 9 days. Activity E is dependent on Activity D and is 5 days. Which statement is most accurate?

   A. The duration is 21 days
   B. Activities B, D, and E are the critical path activities
   C. The duration is 25 days
   D. If activity B gets delayed by 3 days, the project will be delayed by 3 days

44. **All of the following are attributes of activities except:**
    A. They have an expected duration
    B. They consume budget and/or resources
    C. They are named in a verb-noun format
    D. They are the lowest level of the WBS

45. **Which of the following is an example of a cost of non-conformance?**
    A. The engineer's time on designing product specifications
    B. Time involved in planning quality activities for the project
    C. The first run of the product does not meet specifications
    D. Training for the project team on the development process

46. **You are planning the approach to your new project and upon approval, will be distributing the cost, schedule, and scope baselines to the project team members and key stakeholders. In order to be complete, the scope baseline:**
    A. Is developed during the define scope process
    B. Is the most critical document within the planning process
    C. Includes the WBS, WBS dictionary, and project scope statement
    D. Is not considered part of the project management plan

47. **All of the following statements are true about analogous estimating except:**
    A. It is frequently used when there is a lack of detailed information about the current project
    B. It is essentially a combination of historical information and parametric estimating
    C. It is critical that the historical project is as similar as possible to the current project
    D. It is less costly and time-consuming, but also less accurate

48. **There are three project documents that are considered required for all projects. What are they?**
    A. Project scope statement, project charter, and project funding authorization
    B. Project charter, project management plan, and sponsor approval
    C. Project scope statement, project statement of work, and contract
    D. Project scope statement, project charter, and project management plan

49. **You are working with your team and the key stakeholders with estimating the durations and costs. You have learned that when estimating the project, the PMO insists that it should be unanimity. This means:**
    A. One person will provide the estimate, thus decreasing the time to determine the estimate
    B. Everyone will need to agree, thus increasing the time to determine the estimate
    C. The estimates will need to be provided to the PMO for sign-off
    D. The project sponsor will be approving the final estimate

50. **This is an organizational body assigned various responsibilities related to the centralized and coordinated management of those projects under its domain.**
    A. Functional managers
    B. Sponsor
    C. Business partners
    D. Project management office

51. **The project manager is managing a large, complex project with 50 stakeholders and more than 18 team members. The project manager may use _____ to ensure that the team clearly knows what work is included in each of their work packages.**
    A. The project schedule
    B. The WBS dictionary
    C. The project scope statement
    D. The product scope description

52. **Activity Z1 is 9 days and activity Z2 is 12 days. The activities have a finish to finish relationship. What is the difference between the best and worst-case durations?**
    A. 12 days
    B. 9 days
    C. 21 days
    D. 3 days

53. **Which of the following is a true statement about the product life cycle:**
    A. There can be multiple product life cycles within a single project life cycle
    B. The product life cycle spans a shorter time duration than a project life cycle
    C. The product life cycle has phases, however they are usually non-overlapping
    D. A project manager manages the entire product life cycle

54. **The performance measurement baseline:**
    A. Typically covers the schedule, and occasionally the cost parameters of a project, but may not include technical and quality parameters
    B. Changes frequently to accommodate current information about the project
    C. Is the evaluation of the team member's performance of the project
    D. Is the approved plan for the project work against which project execution is compared and deviations are measured for management control

55. **The project management plan is considered a mandatory document. Key benefits of having a project management plan include all of the following except:**
    A. The project management plan documents the scope of the project
    B. The project management plan provides protection for the organization should the project manager or key staff no longer be available
    C. The project management plan clarifies the approach and communicates the project approach to the project management team
    D. The project management plan documents the change control process to minimize scope creep

56. **Upon developing your schedule, you realize that your project has multiple critical paths. Because of this:**
    A. You should consider adding in time buffers on the critical paths
    B. You should consider additional management reserve
    C. You should escalate the situation to your project sponsor
    D. You should take an active risk acceptance approach

57. **The project management process groups would best be described as:**
    A. Being defined based on the project's methodology
    B. Sequential and non-overlapping
    C. Representing the phases of a project
    D. Being applied iteratively with many processes repeated during the project

58. **The website redesign project is 50% completed. You are working with your team members on some development activities. You learn that activity 10.17 and activity 10.18 have a start-to-start dependency relationship with a 4-day lag. 10.17 is 12 days and 10.18 is 15 days. What is the best-case duration?**
    A. 19 days
    B. 27 days
    C. 12 days
    D. 15 days

59. **The difference between a process group and a knowledge area could best be described as:**
    A. The knowledge areas align with the project phases, ensuring the project team has the appropriate skills for each phase
    B. The process groups are usually not all utilized on construction projects
    C. The knowledge areas represent specific areas of expertise that could be reasonably expected to be leveraged during a project
    D. The process groups are defined within the project management plan

60. **Of your 35 stakeholders, you have identified four as being key stakeholders. A key stakeholder would be considered:**
    A. Anyone who is participating actively on the project
    B. The individuals who will be funding the project
    C. The sponsor and the project manager
    D. Anyone in a decision-making or management role who is impacted by the project outcome

61. **You are required to estimate the time to paint a large wall. You know it takes two hours to paint one square foot of wall. The wall has an area of 30 square feet. So, you estimate that it will take 60 hours to paint the wall. Which estimation model are you using?**

    A. Bottom-up
    B. Parametric
    C. Analogous
    D. Expert judgment

62. **Which of the following is an example of a FS (finish-to-start) activity relationship?**

    A. Activity B cannot finish until Activity A is completed
    B. Activity B cannot start until Activity A is completed
    C. Activity B cannot finish until Activity A starts
    D. Activity B cannot start until Activity A starts

63. **You have assumed a new role within a large PMO for your technology organization. You are evaluating multiple projects within the portfolio and would like to identify the project managers assigned to each project and their authority level. The best source of this information would be:**

    A. The project management plans
    B. Organizational process assets
    C. The project scope statements
    D. The project charters

64. **Which statement is least accurate regarding management reserve?**

    A. The project manager must obtain approval before spending
    B. It is included in the cost baseline but not in the overall project budget
    C. It is generally not included in earned value measurements
    D. It is budget reserved for unplanned changes to the project scope and cost

65. **You are developing your project schedule with your team leads. A team member has inquired regarding the correct usage of leads, lags, and float. Which statement is most accurate?**

    A. Lead and lag are used in sequential activity relationships, whereas float may occur during concurrent activities
    B. Float is used in sequential activity relationships, whereas lead and lag may be used during concurrent activities
    C. Lag can only be applied to activities with finish-to-start relationships, whereas lead can be found in all relationship types
    D. Float represents the time that can be saved during sequential activities

66. **The project schedule is being developed and upon review of the information submitted from your team members, you see that there are a number of activities that are less than eight hours. In what situation would it be unacceptable to have an activity that is less than eight hours on the schedule?**

    A. The activity cannot be logical combined with any other activity
    B. The activity will be completed by a specialized resource that is doing limited work on the project
    C. The work package owner wants the work to be granular for increased control
    D. The work package owner wants to "call out" the particular activity as important

67. **Activity 7.1.1 is 15 days and Activity 7.1.2 is 18 days, with a start-to-start relationship. What is the best-case duration for these activities?**

    A. 18 days
    B. 33 days
    C. 15 days
    D. 32 days

68. **This diagram find relationships among different factors, causes, and objectives that exist between the rows and the columns. Depending on what is being compared, the diagram may have different shapes: L, T, Y, X, C, or roof-shaped.**

    A. Logical data model
    B. Matrix diagrams
    C. Flowcharts
    D. Control charts

69. **The degree to which characteristics fulfill requirements:**

    A. Quality
    B. Precision
    C. Grade
    D. Accuracy

70. **Which statement is most accurate regarding quality assurance versus quality control?**

    A. Quality control must be completed prior to quality assurance
    B. Quality assurance and quality control are both different than continuous process improvement
    C. Quality control is more concerned with the process while quality assurance is more concerned with the product
    D. Quality assurance must be completed prior to quality control

71. **Which of the following is not part of the SIPOC model?**

    A. Systems
    B. Process
    C. Customer
    D. Outputs

72. **A category assigned to products or services having the same functional use but different technical characteristics:**

    A. Quality
    B. Scoring
    C. Grade
    D. Precision

73. **This technique involves choosing a part of a population for inspection and testing:**

    A. Quality control
    B. Flowcharting
    C. Quality metrics
    D. Statistical sampling

74. **This means the values of repeated measurements are consistent:**

    A. Accuracy
    B. Quality
    C. Satisfaction
    D. Precision

75. **The results of the quality control activities that are fed back to the manage quality / QA process for use in re-evaluating and analyzing the quality standards and processes:**

    A. Quality metrics
    B. Quality results
    C. Quality measurements
    D. QC data

End Time: _____

Practice Exam 2   Chapters 6 - 8

Answer Key

1. **Answer: C**

   Activity A has four days of free float. If it gets delayed by seven days, with only four days of free float, it will cause the successor's early start to be delayed by three days (4 − 7 = -3). This will change the ES of Activity B to day 21.

2. **Answer: C**

   To calculate the total duration of these activities, you can assume a singular critical path. You would only include critical activities in the duration calculation, as activities with float are occurring concurrently with other activities. If you included their duration, it would be "double-counting". Five days plus nine days is 14 days.

3. **Answer: C**

   The first action to take would be to fast-track the activities as it does not reduce the scope and it does not add any costs to the project.

4. **Answer: C**

   A PERT (program evaluation and review technique) estimate uses optimistic, pessimistic and most likely estimates to come up with weighted estimated.

5. **Answer: A**

   A hammock activity (also known as a summary activity) is a group of related schedule activities that are shown as a singular aggregate activity for communication purposes.

6. **Answer: A**

   Hard-logic dependencies, also known as mandatory dependencies, are inherent to the work being done and involve a physical limitation.

7. **Answer: C**

   The most common formula is a beta 3-point: (O +4M + P) / 6. The triangular 3-point is less common: (O + M + P) / 3.

8. **Answer: C**

   If the project has negative float (float <0) the project completion date will slip by the amount that it's negative. Negative float means any float that was available was consumed and there has been an additional delay.

9. **Answer: C**

   An estimate within a 5% confidence range is very accurate from a project management perspective. This would be considered a definitive estimate.

10. **Answer: A**

    The cost baseline includes contingency but does not include management reserve

11. **Answer: D**

    The least accurate estimate type would a rough order of magnitude (ROM), which is essentially an educated guess as to the project costs.

12. **Answer: A**

    Analogous estimating is used when there isn't detailed information about the current project. It is important the historical project be as similar as possible to the current project. Analogous estimating is less time consuming than the other estimating techniques, but it will not be as accurate. Analogous estimating is not the same as parametric estimating. While parametric also uses historical information, it leverages a statistical relationship between variables to calculate the estimate.

13. **Answer: A**

Using a PERT estimate: $(O + 4M + P) / 6$

$(\$500 + 4(\$1,000) + \$1800) / 6$

$(\$500 + \$4000 + \$1800) / 6$

$\$6,300 / 6 = \$1050$

14. **Answer: D**

The cost baseline includes the cost estimates, the contingency, and the assumptions that were made. The cost baseline does not include the management reserve.

15. **Answer: D**

Using a PERT estimate: $(O + 4M + P) / 6$

$(\$7,000 + 4(\$18,000) + \$30,000) / 6$

$(\$7,000 + \$72,000 + \$30,000) / 6$

$\$109,000 / 6 = \$18,166$

The closest answer, using general rules of rounding, would be $18,000

16. **Answer: A**

The cost baseline is the cost estimate and the contingency: $450,000 + $50,000 = $500,000

17. **Answer: C**

Free float is the amount of time an activity can be delayed without delaying the early start (ES) of the successor activity. Total float is the amount of time an activity can be delayed without delaying the project. Total float is also known as float or slack. Free float is only known as free float.

18. **Answer: B**

Three-point estimating is calculated as: $(O + 4M + P) / 6$

Three-point uses a weighted average and can be used for both cost and duration. While it may leverage historical information, it does not use analogous estimating.

19. **Answer: A**

Activity A is 10 days, activity B is six days for a total duration of 16 days. The lead allows you to start B three days early (for a savings of three days). $10 + 6 - 3 = 13$ days.

20. **Answer: B**

You have completed the collect requirements process and the define scope process (as evidenced by the completion of the scope statement), so the next process would be to create WBS.

21. **Answer: D**

Free float is the amount of time an activity can be delayed without delaying the early start of the successor activity. Total float effects the overall project completion date. It is calculated by subtracting the late start (LS) of the activity from the early start (ES) of the successor activity and subtracting one.

22. **Answer: B**

The stakeholder register is an output of the identify stakeholders process.

23. **Answer: B**

The float of an activity is the amount of time that an activity can be delayed before it impacts the critical path. Lag is the delay in the start of a successor activity and is not related to float. A Monte Carlo analysis is a quantitative risk technique.

24. **Answer: A**

Elapsed time is the actual calendar time whereas effort is the number of work units (staff hours, staff days) required to complete the activity.

25. **Answer: B**

Preferential logic is also called soft logic, discretionary, or preferred logic.

26. **Answer: B**

   The work will span three weeks:

   The weeks of 1 March, 8 March, and 15 March

27. **Answer: A**

   The duration will be the work days:

   The week of 1 March: 5 work days

   The week of 8 March: 4 work days

   The week of 15 March: 5 work days

   5 + 4 + 5 = 14 days

28. **Answer: D**

   There are three resources working five hours per day = 15 work hours per day. Multiply the 15 work hours by the 14 day duration = 210 staff-hours.

29. **Answer: B**

   Total float, also known as float or slack, is the amount of time an activity can be delayed without delaying the completion of the project. Free float is the amount of time an activity can be delayed without delaying the early start of the successor activity. There is no float on the critical path (which is what makes it the critical path). Float is calculated as the difference between the early and late starts or the early and late finishes.

30. **Answer: D**

   Using the PERT formula: $(O + 4M + P) / 6$

   $7 = (4 + 4M + 14)/6$

   $42 = 4 + 4M + 14$

   $42 = 18 + 4M$

   $24 = 4M$

   $6 = M$

31. **Answer: B**

   Preferred dependencies are also known as preferential, discretionary, or soft logic

32. **Answer: A**

   The first step would be to calculate incremental crash cost for each activity: (difference in crash cost) / (difference in duration)

   Activity 1.1 = $2,000 / 4 days = $500/day

   Activity 2.1 = $7,000 / 7 days = $1,000/day

   Activity 3.1 = $6,000 / 3 days = $2,000/day

   Activity 4.1 = $1,000 / 10 days = $100/day

   Activity 5.1 = $1000 / 4 days = $250/day

   Activity 4.1 has the lowest incremental crash cost so it would be the best candidate for crashing.

33. **Answer: A**

   The first step would be to calculate incremental crash cost for each activity: (difference in crash cost) / (difference in duration)

   Activity 1.1 = $2,000 / 4 days = $500/day

   Activity 2.1 = $7,000 / 7 days = $1,000/day

   Activity 3.1 = $6,000 / 3 days = $2,000/day

   Activity 4.1 = $1,000 / 10 days = $100/day

   Activity 5.1 = $1000 / 4 days = $250/day

   The best candidates to crash would be Activities 1.1, 4.1, and 5.1.

   The adjusted cost: $12,000 + $8,000 + $5,000 + $12,000 + $4,000 = $41,000

   The adjusted duration: 8 + 20 + 25 + 20 + 6 = 79 days

34. **Answer: D**

    Identifying the dependencies and creating the schedule network diagram (PDM) would be done in the sequence activities process.

35. **Answer: D**

    Activity A is 10 days. Activity B is nine days with a three-day lead. The float is noise in the question.

    $10 + 9 - 3 = 16$ days

36. **Answer: A**

    There are no resources involved in lag – it is just time that has to pass. Lag is a delay in the successor activity, not related to float, and it is a positive number on a schedule network diagram.

37. **Answer: A**

    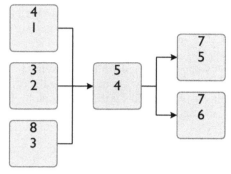

    Based on the diagram, activity two has five days of float. As such, if it gets delayed by four days, there will be no impact.

38. **Answer: C**

    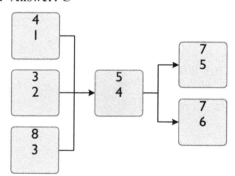

    Based on the diagram, the critical path (the longest path) will be activities three, four, and five

39. **Answer: D**

    Decomposition is used to break down deliverables into work packages in the create WBS process. Decomposition is used to break down the work packages into schedule activities in the define activities process.

40. **Answer: C**

    Having the PDM indicates that you have defined and sequenced your activities. Given that you have your activity durations, the next step would be to develop the schedule.

41. **Answer: A**

    There is no mention of a physical limitation on building the first four lots, so that would be a discretionary dependency. It is not a start-to-start, but rather a finish-to-start, as they are requesting that all four be built out before starting the other lots. The lumber is a physical limitation as the houses cannot be built without the lumber and it is coming from an external source. The best answer is that lumber is an external dependency.

42. **Answer: A**

    Both parametric and analogous estimating leverage historical information and expert judgment.

43. **Answer: A**

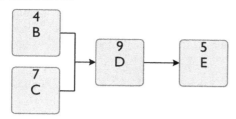

Based on the network diagram the duration would be 21 days, as activities C, D, and E are the critical path: 7 + 9 + 5 = 21 days. Activity B has three days of float and as such, a 3-day delay would not have an impact on the project.

44. **Answer: D**

Activities consume budget and/or resources, have an expected duration, and are named in a verb noun format (hire caterer). The lowest level of a WBS is a work package, not an activity.

45. **Answer: C**

The cost of non-conformance is money spent because of failures. Designing product specifications, planning quality activities, and training the team are all examples of the cost of conformance – money spent to avoid failures. A product that is produced that does not meet specifications would be the cost of non-conformance.

46. **Answer: C**

The scope baseline includes the WBS, the WBS dictionary and the scope statement.

47. **Answer: B**

Analogous estimating is historical information and expert judgment, not parametric estimating.

48. **Answer: D**

According to PMI, the three mandatory project management documents are the project scope statement, the project charter, and the project management plan.

49. **Answer: B**

Unanimity means that all parties must agree on the decision in order to proceed. This will most likely add time to the schedule.

50. **Answer: D**

The PMO is an organizational body assigned various responsibilities related to the centralized and coordinated management of the projects within its domain.

51. **Answer: B**

The WBS dictionary will assist in making sure the team clearly knows what work is included in their work packages.

52. **Answer: B**

In a finish-to-finish relationship, the best-case scenario is that they are happening concurrently, finishing on the same day. The worst-case scenario would be that the activities are completed sequentially with Z1 finishing before starting Z2. Best case would 12 days (concurrent) and worst case would be 21 days (sequential). The difference between best and worst case is the 9 days.

53. **Answer: C**

The product life cycle has sequential, generally non-overlapping phases: ideation, creation, introduction, growth, maturity, decline, and retirement.

54. **Answer: D**

There are three performance measurement baselines: scope, schedule, and cost. The baselines are the approved plan for the project work against which project work will be compared.

55. **Answer: A**

The scope statement documents the scope of the project, not the project management plan.

56. **Answer: A**

Your project having multiple critical paths implies increased risk on your project: if one activity slips, it could impact your overall project. As such, you should consider add duration buffers to account for that risk. This is considered active risk acceptance, but adding the buffers is the most correct (more specific) answer.

57. **Answer: D**

The process groups are applied iteratively with many processes repeated throughout the project. They are not phases.

58. **Answer: A**

The best-case duration is that the activities are happening concurrently, however, the four-day lag must be factored in prior to starting activity 10.18. As such, the best-case duration is 19 days (4 + 15).

59. **Answer: C**

The knowledge areas represent specific areas of expertise that are typically leveraged during a project.

60. **Answer: D**

A key stakeholder is anyone in a decision-making or management role.

61. **Answer: B**

Using the statistical relationship between variables to calculate a productivity rate is a parametric estimate.

62. **Answer: B**

Activity A must finish before Activity B can start in a finish-to-start relationship.

63. **Answer: D**

If known upon project charter development, the charter would document the project manager and the project manager's authority level. These project charters are part of the organizational process assets, but the most specific (correct) answer would be the project charters.

64. **Answer: B**

The management reserve is not part of the cost baseline but is considered to be part of the overall project budget. For management reserve, the project manager must obtain approval to use it, it is not typically included in earned value measurements, and is a budget that is reserved for unplanned changes to the project scope and cost.

65. **Answer: A**

Leads and lags are applied in sequential activity relationships, whereas float occurs when you have concurrent activities of different durations.

66. **Answer: C**

Generally speaking, schedule activities should be between eight and eighty hours for proper management and control. Less than eight hours, and it becomes too granular for the project manager to manage effectively. The exceptions to this would be when the activity cannot be combined with another activity, when it's a specialized resource, or if the activity needs to be called out as specifically important.

67. **Answer: A**

With a start-to-start relationship, the best-case scenario is that the activities happen concurrently and worst-case is that they happen sequentially. Happening concurrently, the best-case duration is 18 days.

68. **Answer: B**

This is describing a matrix diagram.

69. **Answer: A**

Quality is the degree to which characteristics fulfill requirements.

70. **Answer: A**

Quality control (QC) must be completed prior to quality assurance (QA), as the quality control measurements from QC are needed in order to perform the quality audit in QA. QA is the umbrella over continuous process improvement and is concerned with ensuring there are quality processes in place.

71. **Answer: A**

The 'S' in the SIPOC model is for Suppliers not Systems.

72. **Answer: C**

Grade is a category assigned to products that have the same functional use but different technical characteristics. High grade does not necessarily correlate to high quality.

73. **Answer: D**

Selecting a representative population for testing and inspectional is statistical sampling.

74. **Answer: D**

Precision means the value of repeated measurements are consistent, which does not mean that they are accurate. It simply means we are achieving the same result

75. **Answer: C**

The quality measurements are an output of the control quality (QC) process. These are the actual measurements resulting from the QC activities - for example, defect rate, error rate, etc. These measurements are evaluated against the quality metrics that were identified in the plan quality management process, in QA to determine if the right processes and standards are in place.

Appendix C

Practice Exam 3

What's in This Chapter

- Practice Exam for Chapters 9 - 11 (75 Questions)
- Answer Key

Start Time:_____

1. He introduced the quality principle of "doing it right the first time"

   A. Juran
   B. Deming
   C. Maslow
   D. Crosby

2. You are managing a project team with 14 team members. All team members are located on a dangerous construction site. You were notified by one of your team members that a second team member has not been wearing the appropriate safety gear that is required. What is the best conflict management approach to this situation?

   A. Confronting
   B. Problem-solving
   C. Forcing
   D. Collaborating

3. Your project is nearing completion and the final product turnover is scheduled to happen within a few days. Your project has consistently been on-time and on-budget and you have been able to release a good portion of your contingency reserve back to the organization. You are notified that the project is being cancelled because the final product is not acceptable. What is the most likely cause of this?

   A. You did not adequately manage risk
   B. You did not document the appropriate requirements
   C. You did not have a clear WBS
   D. You did not manage the stakeholder expectations

4. Your team members have escalated issues with the QA analyst and despite providing feedback and asking for improvements, the issues are continuing to be a problem for the project team and are disrupting the work that needs to be done. To avoid the risk associated with the QA analyst, you:

   A. Refer the QA analyst to the HR department
   B. Document the disruption as a risk on the risk register
   C. Conduct an off-cycle team meeting to set expectations regarding team behavior
   D. Remove the QA analyst from the project

5. All of these project documents are used to manage stakeholder engagement except:

   A. Communication management plan
   B. Risk breakdown structure
   C. Change log
   D. Stakeholder management plan

6. There are two significant outputs from the directing and managing the project work. They are:

   A. Issue log and change log
   B. Work performance measurements and deliverables
   C. Work performance information and quality metrics
   D. Deliverables and work performance data

7. A document showing the reporting structure within the project, as well as its relationship to the parent organization, is called the:

   A. Organizational chart
   B. Responsibility assignment matrix
   C. Resource staffing histogram
   D. Staffing management plan

8. During this stage of team development, project team members are working independently and achieving project goals:

   A. Performing
   B. Developing
   C. Norming
   D. Collaborating

9. For your project, you will need to hire three vendors to provide services as you do not have the staff internally. During what process would you select the vendors?

   A. Executing
   B. Procurement executing
   C. Conduct procurements
   D. Plan procurements

10. As project manager you are reviewing the resource calendars and staffing assignments to determine an appropriate date for your team building event. Which process are you doing?

    A. Manage team
    B. Develop team
    C. Acquire resources
    D. Improve morale

11. Which conflict management technique incorporates multiple viewpoints and is more likely to lead to consensus and commitment?

    A. Compromising
    B. Smoothing
    C. Confronting
    D. Collaborating

12. You have determined your staffing needs for your 10-month project. You will require resources from three major departments as well as some specialized expertise that may not be available in-house. Which of the following is not a tool or technique used in project team acquisition?

    A. Pre-assignment
    B. Virtual teams
    C. Resource calendars
    D. Negotiation

13. You just completed the initial analysis phase of your project and reported your findings to the sponsor. The project has significant uncontrollable risks and as such, your sponsor decides to cancel the project. Cancelling a troubled project is an example of:

    A. Mitigating project risk
    B. Avoiding the risk
    C. Transferring the risk
    D. Exploiting the project

14. Because there was a risk of rain during the outdoor event, the team decided to put a tent over the main banquet area. A risk has now been identified that the tent may become unsecured with high wind. The tent becoming unsecured is an example of:

    A. A fallback risk
    B. A residual risk
    C. A contingent risk
    D. A secondary risk

15. As the project manager for a relatively small, internal project you had not considered the need for team-building activities when you were developing your cost and schedule estimates. However, the PMO manager has asked you to include some type of estimates in your final project information. What statement is least accurate regarding the project manager's role in project team-building?

    A. The project manager should use appropriate rewards and recognition and create a team identity
    B. Team-building activities can be especially valuable for virtual teams
    C. The project manager must incorporate team-building activities on a set schedule
    D. The project manager should try to move the team through stages of team development

16. Upon evaluation of the project requirements, your product development team lead provides you with the following duration information:

If the product can be developed in-house with existing staff, the estimated duration is 14 days. If the product must be developed by a vendor, the estimated duration is 21 days. If a portion is developed in-house and a portion by the vendor, the estimated duration is 19 days. Based on the information you received, there is a 30% probability that it can be developed fully in-house and a 50% probability that a portion can be developed in-house.

Considering the risk, what is the best duration estimate?

A. 18 days
B. 19 days
C. 15 days
D. 16 days

17. Your project has completed six months of the estimated 18-month duration. You were just notified that a key item you were purchasing for your project is now going to be delayed. What is the best thing you should do?

A. Notify your sponsor
B. Take no action
C. Meet with your project team to identify alternatives
D. Notify your customer and discuss options

18. According to Herzberg, these factors do not give positive satisfaction, although dissatisfaction results from their absence:

A. Motivators
B. Extrinsic
C. Hygiene
D. Y factors

19. Which of the following is a lower consideration in determining the appropriate recognition and rewards for your project team:

A. Making it meaningful to the team member
B. Cultural considerations
C. Leveraging the existing organizational program
D. The length of time participants will be on your project

20. Your project team and key stakeholders have identified over 100 risks for the project. Those risks have been analyzed and prioritized. Risk responses have been validated and approved. For the remaining risks you may:

A. Do something if the risk happens, which will be implementing a fallback plan
B. Do something if the risk happens, which will be implementing the contingency plan
C. Do something if the contingency plans are not effective, which will be implementing the workaround plan
D. Do something if the fallback plans are not effective, which will be implementing the contingency plans

21. All of the following should be included in the project risk management plan except:

A. The timing of risk management activities
B. The reporting format for risks
C. How the risk activities will be tracked, communicated, and escalated
D. The configuration management approach

22. Which statement is least accurate regarding the project management information system (PMIS):

A. It is considered an enterprise environmental factor
B. May also include the configuration management system
C. It should be archived at the completion of the project
D. It provides access to automated tools

23. **You are about 30% complete with your project. Along with your team lead and a PMO representative, you are evaluating the project activities to determine whether they comply with organizational and project policies, processes, and procedures. You are:**
    A. Managing stakeholder expectations
    B. Performing a quality audit
    C. Planning the quality approach for the project
    D. Completing the quality control requirements

24. **Personnel assessment tools are used to:**
    A. Provide feedback to the functional managers
    B. Assess the project team's effectiveness
    C. Provide an evaluation of the project's performance
    D. Engage the PMO or functional managers

25. **Your project team has been making strong progress on the six-month project despite a significant amount of resistance within the organization. You were recently made aware, however, of some conflict between two of your key team members. What is the most appropriate action for you to take?**
    A. Confront the issue as soon as possible
    B. Take a forcing approach as there is already resistance within the organization
    C. Because they are key team members, take an accommodating approach to neutralize the emotion
    D. Allow the team members some time to resolve the issue on their own before intervening

26. **Residual risks are:**
    A. The same as secondary risks
    B. A direct result of implementing a risk response
    C. Those that remain after risk responses have been taken
    D. Those risks that have no impact on the project budget or schedule

27. **An uncertain event that may impact the project in the future, either positively or negatively, is called a(n):**
    A. Risk factor
    B. Risk-opportunity dichotomy
    C. Project risk
    D. Expected value

28. **As you evaluate a vendor bid of $350,000, you take into consideration the probability and impact of any delays. You determine that there is a 65% probability that the vendor will come in behind schedule at a cost of $125,000 and there is a 35% probability that the vendor will come in early for a savings of $50,000. What is the total value of the bid?**
    A. $286,250
    B. $63,750
    C. $448,750
    D. $413,750

29. **Chris is managing the new marketing project in which he is responsible for developing the associated marketing collateral. Chris is using a graphic design company to create the artwork for the new collateral. In order to improve the probability that the graphic designer delivers on time, he inserts a penalty clause for late delivery into the contract. Chris is using which risk response?**
    A. Risk transference
    B. Risk avoidance
    C. Risk mitigation
    D. Risk acceptance

30. **The risk response that can be categorized as either passive or active is:**
    A. Risk avoidance
    B. Risk mitigation
    C. Risk transference
    D. Risk acceptance

31. You are the Project Manager of the construction project. The project is being executed in a hurricane-prone area. Due to the potential risk of storms to the project, you buy insurance for hurricanes and tropical storms. This is an example of:
    A. Transfer of risk
    B. Risk mitigation
    C. Risk avoidance
    D. Risk contingency planning

32. You are conducting a quantitative risk analysis on your project in relation to potential profits earned from a new product. The estimated base profit is $350,000. There is a 20% chance that it will exceed expectations at a value of $180,000, there is a 50% chance it will meet expectations at a value of $40,000, and a 30% chance it will not meet expectations at a value of ($140,000). What is the expected monetary value of the risk?
    A. $364,000
    B. ($364,000)
    C. ($14,000)
    D. $14,000

33. You are evaluating potential outcomes for a new product you are launching. Based on market analysis, there is a projected profit of $125,000. However, depending on the risk of the market segment, the profit may increase or decrease. There is 35% chance that the profit will increase by $30,000, a 40% chance that the profit will increase by $15,000 and a 25% chance that the profit will decrease by $20,000. What is the EMV of this risk scenario?
    A. $21,500
    B. $5,000
    C. $11,500
    D. $136,500

34. This risk response strategy changes the project plan to decrease the probability of an identified threat:
    A. SWOT
    B. Risk response planning
    C. Avoidance
    D. Mitigation

35. Used in modeling and simulation, these represent the uncertainty in values, such as durations of schedule activities and costs of project components:
    A. Sensitivity analysis
    B. Risk analysis
    C. Earned value analysis
    D. Probability distributions

36. This analysis technique is a statistical concept that calculates the average outcome when the future includes scenarios that may or may not happen:
    A. Earned value analysis
    B. Delphi technique
    C. Qualitative risk analysis
    D. Expected monetary value analysis

37. With your team, you are evaluating all of the identified risks to determine the likelihood that those risk events will occur and also assessing the impact if they do occur. What process are you conducting?
    A. Quantitative risk analysis
    B. Monitor and control risks
    C. Qualitative risk analysis
    D. Risk identification

38. You are the project manager for a construction project. A risk has been identified that the installation of the electrical components presents a safety hazard to the workers. You decide to make the area impassable to all workers during the installation. What type of risk response is this?
    A. Risk avoidance
    B. Risk mitigation
    C. Risk acceptance
    D. Risk transference

39. You have completed a risk analysis for your project and assessed the probability and impact for each of the identified risks. Based on the evaluation, your overall risk score is 7.9. As such, this project is considered to be:
    A. Moderate risk
    B. Low risk
    C. Unable to determine
    D. High risk

40. You are the project manager for the development of the new community park. The residents of the community have requested that a portion of the area be used for a dog park. If implemented, the dog park would require the use of a two-gate system in order to reduce the risk of a dog escaping the defined area. What is the most accurate statement regarding the double-gate system?
    A. It is an example of risk avoidance
    B. It is an example of a fallback plan
    C. It is an example of risk mitigation
    D. It is an example of contingent response planning

41. Your product development project is creating a new children's toy. There has been extensive component testing of the parts for the toy. While most of the components tested were satisfactory, piece B has been determined to be a significant choking risk to the target age group. What would be the most appropriate risk response to piece B?
    A. Determine a fallback plan to implement if the beta testing identifies the choking risk as well
    B. Identify a risk avoidance response
    C. Develop a contingent response strategy for dealing with customer complaints
    D. Identify a risk mitigation response

42. Exploitation is to opportunities as _____ is to threats.
    A. Acceptance
    B. Mitigation
    C. Avoidance
    D. Transference

43. All of the following are information gathering techniques for identifying risks, except:
    A. Brainstorming
    B. Delphi technique
    C. Assumptions analysis
    D. Interviewing

44. With your team, you are evaluating the project and project information to determine uncertain events that could affect the project either negatively or positively. This is the process of:
    A. Qualitative risk analysis
    B. Risk identification
    C. Quantitative risk analysis
    D. Monitor and control risks

45. Which statement is most accurate regarding contingency and fallback plans?
    A. The contingency plan is used when the fallback plan is not effective
    B. The fallback plan is another name for the contingency plan
    C. The contingency plan is defined in advance of a risk event whereas the fallback plan is reactive in nature
    D. The fallback plan is used when the contingency plan is not effective

46. **You are evaluating the following information to understand the implications of risk on the estimate. There is 40% chance it will take 12 days, a 25% chance it will take 18 days, and a 35% chance it will take 10 days. What is the best estimate?**
    A. 11.8 days
    B. 13 days
    C. 12.4 days
    D. 14 days

47. **A workaround is considered:**
    A. A contingency plan
    B. Implementation of the contingency plan for a positive risk event
    C. A response to a negative risk that has occurred that was not planned in advance
    D. Using global sourcing to continue project development around the clock

48. **An employee performing consistent with Maslow's self-actualization concept would most likely be McGregor's:**
    A. X people
    B. Y people
    C. High need for achievement
    D. Hygiene driven

49. **One of your team members recently lost their spouse and the performance on the project has suffered as a result. His inability to perform his job is based on his current focus on his social needs according to which theory?**
    A. Vroom's expectancy
    B. Maslow's hierarchy of needs
    C. McClelland's achievement
    D. Herzberg's motivation and hygiene

50. **According to Herzberg's theory of motivation, a base salary is:**
    A. A primary motivator
    B. A secondary motivator
    C. Not a consideration in employee motivation
    D. A hygiene factor

51. **Your new team manager tends to micro-manage his team as he believes that people are generally lazy and don't want to work. How would the team manager classify his team?**
    A. Y people
    B. Low need for achievement
    C. Self-actualized
    D. X people

52. **According to Herzberg, these factors do not give positive satisfaction, although dissatisfaction results from their absence:**
    A. Extrinsic
    B. Motivators
    C. Hygiene
    D. Y factors

53. **He applied the Pareto principle to quality issues and developed the trilogy: quality planning, quality control, and quality improvement.**
    A. Deming
    B. Crosby
    C. Juran
    D. Maslow

54. **Damage to reputation would be considered a:**
    A. Cost of nonconformance
    B. Quality risk
    C. Constraint
    D. Schedule risk

55. **In conducting a stakeholder analysis, there are a number of tools that could be used to rank and rate your stakeholders. The salience model of stakeholder classification, groups stakeholders based on:**
    A. Their power, urgency, and legitimacy
    B. Their level of authority and their level of concern
    C. Their active involvement and their ability to effect changes
    D. Their level of power and influence

56. **The organization is evaluating potential projects to invest in during the upcoming year: project A is a 5-year project with a $30,000 NPV; project B is a 1-year project with a $40,000 NPV; project C is a 1-year project with a ($70,000) NPV. Which statement is most accurate?**
    A. Project A would be the best investment because it will generate $150,000 in profit
    B. Project B would be the worst investment because of the project term
    C. Project C may be selected first if it is a legal or regulatory requirement
    D. Project C would never be selected because it represents the lowest profit

57. **In group decision-making, the use of this method means that the largest block in a group decides, even if a majority is not achieved:**
    A. Unanimity
    B. Majority
    C. Plurality
    D. Dictatorship

58. **With your team, you have generated a large number of potential requirements. You would like to bucket the ideas into groups for further analysis. What technique should you consider using with your team?**
    A. Idea mapping
    B. Affinity diagram
    C. Nominal group technique
    D. JAD session

59. **Risk monitoring and controlling can best be accomplished through:**
    A. A monthly risk monitoring meeting
    B. Assigning specialized risk responsibilities to a team member
    C. Including risk management as an agenda item during periodic status meetings
    D. Evaluation of risks at the beginning of each phase

60. **Your sponsor has scheduled a meeting with you to discuss the project's progress. When you present her with the most current status, she expresses some concern about the project schedule. After evaluating contingency that may be reduced, what would be the next step?**
    A. Add resources and crash the critical path
    B. Determine which activities would be appropriate for schedule compression
    C. Evaluate the project dependencies to determine where there may be flexibility
    D. Ask your team to shorten their activity durations

61. **Which of the following is true about risk audits?**
    A. They must be conducted in-house in order to be effective
    B. They should not be included in routine project review meetings as it requires key stakeholders that may not attend review meetings
    C. Ideally, they should only be conducted at the completion of a project or a phase
    D. The project manager is responsible for ensuring that risk audits are performed at an appropriate frequency

62. **Which statement is least accurate regarding the PDM:**
    A. The PDM is the same thing as the AON
    B. The PDM is an output of sequencing activities
    C. The PDM only displays finish-to-start relationships
    D. The PDM is a type of schedule network diagram

63. **If you have the completed stakeholder register, what process have you completed?**
    A. Plan stakeholder engagement
    B. Manage stakeholders
    C. Identify stakeholders
    D. Develop project charter

64. Financial databases, lessons learned, issue and defect management databases, and previous project files are all considered components of the:

A. Enterprise environmental assets
B. Project management office requirements
C. Change control processes
D. Corporate knowledge base

65. The difference between the project schedule and the schedule baseline could best be described as:

A. The project schedule is updated throughout the project but the schedule baseline is only updated when there's an approved change to scope
B. The terms are synonymous
C. The baseline is created before the schedule
D. The schedule baseline is updated throughout the project and then compared to the project schedule

66. Activity C has a start to start relationship with Activity D. Activity C is 12 days and activity D is 15 days. If the start of activity D gets delayed by six days, what is the best case duration?

A. 27 days
B. 15 days
C. 21 days
D. 33 days

67. A review of the effectiveness of risk responses in dealing with the identified risks and their root causes.

A. Risk audit
B. Risk response review
C. Risk monitoring and controlling
D. Risk evaluation

68. Determining if the remaining reserve is adequate by evaluating the amount of contingency reserves remaining to the amount of risk remaining.

A. Contingency evaluation
B. Monitoring and controlling
C. Reserve analysis
D. Management reserve consideration

69. Identified upper and lower measurements that establish limits that if the repeated results fall within those limits, the process is considered stable:

A. Tolerances
B. Thresholds
C. Control limits
D. Appetite

70. Requirements documentation and the requirements traceability matrix are:

A. Both outputs of the collect requirements process
B. Both outputs of the define scope process
C. Outputs of both plan scope management and plan requirements management
D. Both outputs of create scope baseline

71. The activity attributes are to the activity list as what is to the WBS?

A. WBS dictionary
B. WBS details
C. Work package attributes
D. Work descriptions

72. Which of the following is not a component of the scope baseline?

A. Scope statement
B. Work breakdown structure
C. Scope deliverables
D. Work breakdown structure dictionary

73. **Which output is completed first: the stakeholder register or the stakeholder engagement plan?**

    A. The stakeholder register
    B. The stakeholder management plan
    C. They are both completed simultaneously
    D. There is no relationship between the two

74. **The schedule forecasts will be an output of what process?**

    A. Control schedule
    B. Forecast schedule
    C. Develop schedule
    D. Develop project management plan

75. **You have secured written authorization for your project. What process has been completed?**

    A. Develop project charter
    B. Develop project management plan
    C. Direct and manage project work
    D. Document project authorization

End Time:_____

Practice Exam 3   Chapters 9 - 11

Answer Key

1. **Answer: D**

   Crosby had the principle of "doing it right the first time" - DIRFT

2. **Answer: C**

   Because it is a situation of health/human safety, a forcing approach would be most appropriate. Wearing safety gear is not optional.

3. **Answer: D**

   If the final product is not acceptable it is most likely due to the fact that you did not manage the stakeholder expectations throughout the project.

4. **Answer: D**

   Risk avoidance means making a change to eliminate the risk. The only answer that would eliminate the risk would be to remove the QA analyst from the project.

5. **Answer: B**

   The risk breakdown structure (RBS) is a useful tool for categorizing causes of project risks. However, it does not necessarily lend to better stakeholder engagement.

6. **Answer: D**

   The primary outputs from the direct and manage project work are the deliverables and the work performance data.

7. **Answer: A**

   A document showing reporting structure is known as an organizational chart.

8. **Answer: C**

   When team members are working independently and achieving goals, this would be considered norming. If they are working interdependently and meeting or exceed project goals, it would be the performing stage.

9. **Answer: C**

   The vendors would be selected during the conduct procurements process.

10. **Answer: B**

    Evaluating the availability and staffing for a team-building event would occur during the develop team process. The develop team process focuses on training and team-building.

11. **Answer: D**

    A collaborative (also known as a problem-solving) approach will most likely lead to consensus and commitment as all participants are able to work together towards a resolution.

12. **Answer: C**

    Resource calendars will be an output of the acquire resources process. Resource calendars are either inputs or outputs, not tools/techniques.

13. **Answer: B**

    Cancelling a project is considered risk avoidance – it eliminates the risks associated with the project.

14. **Answer: D**

    The tent being put up was a risk mitigation response. Therefore the risk of the tent becoming unsecured is a secondary risk – a risk that arises directly as a result of implementing a risk response.

15. **Answer: C**

    Team building does not have to be on a set schedule to be effective.

16. **Answer: A**

    There is a 30% probability it will take 14 days. There is a 50% probability it will take 19 days. That only equals 80%, so as such; there must be a 20% probability that it will take 21 days.

    0.3 x 14 = 4.2

    0.5 x 19 = 9.5

    0.2 x 21 = 4.2

    Equals 17.9 days. Rounding up, 18 would be the best estimate.

17. **Answer: C**

    As a project manager, your first action should be to work with the team to identify alternatives and options to make up the time in the schedule. As the project is only 30% complete, there is a chance that the situation can be remedied with minimal to no impact. Escalation to the sponsor and the customer should be limited and only occur if the team is unable to come up with an appropriate response.

18. **Answer: C**

    According to Herzberg hygiene factors do not give positive satisfaction, although dissatisfaction can result from their absence.

19. **Answer: D**

    Regardless of the time your project team will be working together, as project manager, you should be incorporating the appropriate rewards and recognition.

20. **Answer: B**

    For the risks that did not have a proactive response (avoid, transfer, mitigate), one option would be having an active risk acceptance approach, meaning doing some if the risk happens which is implementing the contingency plan. A fallback plan would be used if the original response was not effective. There is no such thing as a workaround plan, as a workaround is not planned in advance. If the contingency plans are not effective, you may implement a fallback plan, but not vice versa.

21. **Answer: D**

    The risk management plan would not include the configuration management approach. Configuration management is a component of change control.

22. **Answer: C**

    The project management information system (PMIS) will not be archived at the completion of the project, as it is the organization's system for managing all project information. The project-specific information within the PMIS will be archived as part of the organizational process assets.

23. **Answer: B**

    Evaluating project activities to ensure they comply with organizational and project policies, processes, and procedures describes a quality audit.

24. **Answer: B**

    Personnel assessment tools are used to assess the project team's effectiveness.

25. **Answer: D**

    Because there is no indication that the conflict is impacting the project work, it would be most appropriate to allow the team members time to resolve the conflict on their own without interference from the project manager.

26. **Answer: C**

    Residual risk is risk that remains after taken a planned response.

27. **Answer: C**

    An uncertain event that may impact the project, positively or negatively, is called a project risk.

28. **Answer: D**

   There is a 65% probability the vendor will come in $125,000 over the estimate and a 35% probability that they will come in $50,000 under the estimate.

   0.65 x $125,000 = $81,250 (positive number as it is a potential additional cost)

   0.35 x ($50,000) = ($17,500) (negative number as it is a potential saving off of the original bid)

   EMV = $81,250 + ($17,500) = $63,750.

   Total Value = $350,000 + $63,750 = $413,750

29. **Answer: A**

   Using a penalty clause in a contractual relationship is considered risk transference.

30. **Answer: D**

   Risk acceptance for threats may be passive or active. Passive risk acceptance means doing nothing about the risk. Active risk acceptance means identifying a contingent response strategy to be used in the event the risk occurs.

31. **Answer: A**

   Purchasing an insurance policy is considered risk transference.

32. **Answer: D**

   There is a 20% probability that the profit will increase by $180,000; a 50% probability it will increase by $40,000, and a 30% probability it will decrease by $140,000.

   0.20 x $180,000 = $36,000

   0.50 x $40,000 = $20,000

   0.30 x ($140,000) = ($42,000) (negative number as it is a loss from the profit)

   EMV: $36,000 + $20,000 + ($42,000) = $14,000

33. **Answer: C**

   There is a 35% probability that the profit will increase by $30,000; a 40% probability it will increase by $15,000, and 25% probability it will decrease by $20,000.

   0.35 x $30,000 = $10,500

   0.40 x $15,000 = $6,000

   0.25 x ($20,000) = ($5,000) (negative number as it is a loss from the profit)

   EMV: $10,500 + $6,000 + ($5,000) = $11,500

34. **Answer: D**

   Changing the plan to decrease the probability and/or impact is considered risk mitigation.

35. **Answer: D**

   Probability distributions represent the uncertainty in values, such as cost or schedule implications. Probability distributions are an output of quantitative risk techniques.

36. **Answer: D**

   Expected monetary value (EMV) analysis calculates the average outcome when the future includes scenarios that may or may not happen.

37. **Answer: C**

   Qualitative risk analysis evaluates the identified risks to determine the probability and the impact of the risk event.

38. **Answer: A**

   Making the area impassable to all workers means that you have eliminated the risk. Therefore this is risk avoidance.

39. **Answer: C**

   There is no scale given, so it is impossible to know what the 7.9 risk score represents. Risk scales are organizationally defined, not prescribed by PMI.

40. **Answer: C**

   Because the double-gate system reduces the risk, it is considered risk mitigation.

41. **Answer: B**

Because it is a choking hazard and is a health/human safety, a risk avoidance response would be most appropriate.

42. **Answer: C**

Both exploitation and avoidance the change the plan to eliminate the uncertainty. Exploitation changes the plan to ensure the opportunity will be realized. Avoidance changes the plan to ensure the threat will not happen.

43. **Answer: C**

An assumptions analysis explores the validity of project assumptions to determine any related risk from invalid assumptions. An assumptions analysis is not considered an information gathering technique.

44. **Answer: B**

Identifying events that could impact the project positively or negatively is the identify risks process.

45. **Answer: D**

The fallback plan will be used when the contingency plan is not effective. Think of the fallback as the "plan B".

46. **Answer: B**

To calculate the best estimate:

0.4 x 12 = 4.8

0.25 x 18 = 4.5

0.35 x 10 = 3.5

The total would be 12.8, rounded up to 13 for the best answer.

47. **Answer: C**

A workaround is a response to a negative risk that has occurred, not planned in advance. A workaround is completely reactive in nature.

48. **Answer: B**

An employee that is high-performing and is self-actualized, would be consistent with McGregor's Y people.

49. **Answer: B**

The idea surrounding the team member's inability to do his job is based on Maslow's hierarchy of needs theory.

50. **Answer: D**

Salary is considered a hygiene factor.

51. **Answer: D**

Team members that are generally lazy and need to be micromanaged are considered to be "x" people.

52. **Answer: C**

Hygiene factors do not give positive satisfaction, but dissatisfaction can result from their absence.

53. **Answer: C**

Juran applied the Pareto principle to quality issues and also had the trilogy: quality planning, quality control, and quality improvement.

54. **Answer: A**

Damage to reputation is considered a cost of non-conformance, money spent because of failure.

55. **Answer: A**

The salience model evaluates stakeholders based on their power, urgency, and legitimacy.

56. **Answer: C**

The term of the project is irrelevant in this question, as it has already been factored into the NPV calculation. Project A will generate $30,000 in profit, Project B is actually the best investment with the highest NPV, and Project C may be selected first if it is legal or regulatory, despite the fact that it will represent a loss.

57. **Answer: C**

Plurality implies the largest subset of the group would decide, even if it's not majority. For example, if you have a group of 12 people and 5 people want option A, 4 people want option B, and 3 people want option C, option A would be the selection.

58. Answer: B

An affinity diagram would be the most appropriate technique to bucket the ideas into groups. Idea mapping will consolidate ideas to reflect commonalities and differences in understanding but would not necessarily group the ideas into buckets. Nominal group technique would simply add a voting process to rank the ideas. A JAD session is a facilitated workshop and helps to work through cross-enterprise requirements.

59. Answer: C

Risk monitoring and controlling can best be accomplished by having risk management as a standing agenda item during the project status meetings. This keeps risk management at the forefront of team discussions and ensures that team members are aware of current risk status.

60. Answer: C

If the project schedule needs to be shortened, once any contingency reduction has occurred, the next step would be to evaluate the dependencies between the activities to determine where there is flexibility. Activities that have discretionary and possibly internal dependencies may be able to be modified. Crashing is not the next option because it costs money. Evaluating for compression is true, but to determine compression-eligible activities, you would first have to evaluate the dependencies.

61. Answer: D

It is the responsibility of the project manager to ensure that risk audits are performed at appropriate frequencies. They can be done in-house or by an external party and should be conducted throughout the project. Having the risk audit as part of the routine project review meetings is effective.

62. Answer: C

PDM is the precedence diagramming method, a way of constructing the project schedule to visually display the relationships between the activities. A PDM can display all types of relationships: finish-to-start, start-to-start, finish-to-finish, start-to-finish. The alternate name for a PDM diagram is an activity-on-node (AON) diagram.

63. Answer: C

The stakeholder register is an output of the identify stakeholders process.

64. Answer: D

Items listed are considered components of the corporate knowledge base, which is part of the organizational process assets (OPA).

65. Answer: A

The project schedule is considered the "living" schedule that is updated throughout the project as needed. The schedule baseline is a "frozen" version of the schedule, part of the project management plan, that should only be updated with there is a significant authorized change to scope.

66. Answer: C

The start-to-start relationship indicates that Activity D can start at the same time, or anytime thereafter, as Activity C, thus implying that they can happen concurrently.

To answer the question, add the time of the six-day delay to the duration of activity D bringing the total duration to 21 days.

67. Answer: A

A risk audit, a tool/technique from the monitor risks process, is a structured review of the effectiveness of the risk responses.

68. Answer: C

A reserve analysis, a fairly common Tool/Technique in the *PMBOK*® *Guide*, refers to an evaluating of the amount of contingency time and money compared to the amount of risk (or uncertainty) remaining on the project. Theoretically, projects are risk-declining and if the amount of risk decreases, the amount of reserve should decrease accordingly, with an extra funding being released back to the organization.

69. Answer: C

A Control limits are represented on a control chart, typically three standard deviations from the mean. If results of any type of output sampling fall outside of those control limits, the process is considered unstable.

70. **Answer: A**

The requirements documentation and requirements traceability matrix are both outputs of the collect requirements process in the project scope management knowledge area/planning process group.

71. **Answer: A**

The activity attributes provide the back-end details related to each of the activities on the activity list. The WBS dictionary provides the back-end details of the work packages contained within the WBS.

72. **Answer: C**

The scope baseline includes the scope statement (an output of the Define Scope process), the work breakdown structure (WBS), and the WBS dictionary.

73. **Answer: A**

In the Initiating process group, the stakeholder register is an output of the identify stakeholders process. Using the information in the stakeholder register, the stakeholder management plan describes how the stakeholders will be involved in the project and how to maintain engagement and increase involvement by those stakeholders.

74. **Answer: A**

In the control schedule process within the Monitoring and Controlling process group, the schedule forecast will be created based upon a variance analysis of actual to planned activities.

75. **Answer: A**

The objective of the develop project charter process is to secure written authorization of the project, as demonstrated by the executed project charter.

Appendix D

Practice Exam 4

What's in This Chapter

- Practice Exam for Chapters 12 - 15 (75 Questions)
- Answer Key

Start Time:_____

1. The deliverables are an output of what process?

   A. Develop project management plan
   B. Monitor and control project work
   C. Perform quality control
   D. Direct and manage project work

2. The project is estimated to have a $12,500 variance at completion. The project budget is $75,000 and the estimate to complete the remaining work is $15,750. What are the actual costs of the project to-date?

   A. Unable to determine
   B. $59,250
   C. $62,500
   D. $46,750

3. You are three months into a 6-month, $195,000 project. Invoices paid to date are $37,500 and the planned costs at three months were $75,000. What is the schedule variance?

   A. $97,500
   B. $22,500
   C. $37,500
   D. $25,000

4. You are three months into a 6-month, $195,000 project. Invoices paid to date are $37,500 and the planned costs at three months were $75,000. What is the cost performance index?

   A. .5
   B. $22,500
   C. 26%
   D. 2.6

5. Procurement documents are an output of what process?

   A. Control procurements
   B. Plan procurement management
   C. Conduct procurements
   D. Define scope

6. You are three months into a 6-month, $195,000 project. Invoices paid to date are $37,500 and the planned costs at three months were $75,000. What is the to-complete performance index?

   A. 1.62
   B. .78
   C. .62
   D. 1.25

7. You have been managing the development project for six months. Upon recent evaluation, you determine that the TCPI is 1.27. Which statement is most accurate?

   A. The project is 27% ahead of schedule
   B. The project needs to be 27% more efficient with resources
   C. The project is 27% over budget
   D. The project is using the resources 27% more efficiently than planned

8. The $75,000 project is 80% complete and has a cost variance of ($12,000). Which statement is most accurate?

   A. The project is over budget
   B. The project is behind schedule
   C. The project is under budget
   D. The project will not meet the project budget objectives

9. The calculated schedule variance on your project is $8,000. Last month it was $10,000, and the month previous it was $18,000. Which statement is most accurate?

   A. The project is trending under-budget
   B. The project is trending behind schedule
   C. The project is trending ahead of schedule
   D. The project is trending over budget

10. The SPI of your project is .8 and your planned value at this point in your project is $125,000. How much value have you earned in your project?

    A. $100,000
    B. $225,000
    C. Unable to determine
    D. $25,000

11. The ratio of earned value to planned value:

    A. Cost variance
    B. Cost performance index
    C. Schedule performance index
    D. To-complete performance index

12. The cost variance on your project is ($18,000) and your earned value is $92,000. What are your actual costs?

    A. $110,000
    B. $74,000
    C. Unable to determine
    D. $98,000

13. The documented start and finish dates of activities, actual costs and durations, percent of work physically completed would all be considered:

    A. Work performance information
    B. Work performance data
    C. Work performance inputs
    D. Work performance reports

14. The validate scope process could best be described as:

    A. Securing customer acceptance of the completed deliverables
    B. Evaluating the requirements for completeness
    C. Reviewing the scope statement with the customer
    D. Performing quality control activities on the completed deliverables

15. A comparison of the earned value and the planned value:

    A. Cost variance
    B. Schedule performance index
    C. Schedule variance
    D. Cost performance index

16. The value of the work already completed on the project:

    A. Earned value
    B. Estimate to complete
    C. Estimate at completion
    D. Planned value

17. **The authorized budget assigned to the work that will be accomplished as of the status date:**
    A. Actual costs
    B. Earned value
    C. Estimate to complete
    D. Planned value

18. **At six months in, your $785,000 project is 35% complete and the TCPI is .74 and you've spent $95,000 to date. What is the earned value of the project?**
    A. $595,000
    B. $580,900
    C. $690,000
    D. $274,750

19. **Which statement is most accurate?**
    A. The define scope process precedes the create work breakdown structure process
    B. The WBS must be complete in order to define scope
    C. The scope baseline is an output of the define scope process
    D. The scope statement is produced after the WBS

20. **You have completed your activity list and activity attributes. What process have you completed:**
    A. Develop schedule
    B. Create WBS
    C. Define activities
    D. Scope decomposition

21. **The project has earned value of $87,750. Costs-to-date have been $110,000, and the budget is $195,000. What percent complete is this project?**
    A. 80%
    B. 45%
    C. Unable to calculate
    D. 56%

22. **Your project has earned value of $300,000 despite invoices totaling $325,000. You've calculated your TCPI as 1.14. What is your budget?**
    A. $500,000
    B. $325,000
    C. $342,000
    D. $370,500

23. **Which statement is most accurate:**
    A. The cost estimates are the project budget
    B. The cost estimates, applied across the schedule, create the budget
    C. The project budget is developed first and then decomposed into cost estimates
    D. The budget may be progressively elaborated whereas the cost estimates must be determined completely at the start of the project.

24. **The scope baseline is an output of what process?**
    A. Plan scope management
    B. Define scope
    C. Collect requirements
    D. Create WBS

25. **The test plan design must be approved by the project engineer prior to implementation. This represents what type of dependency?**
    A. Hard logic
    B. Preferential
    C. External
    D. Mandatory

26. **Based on the information contained in this graphic, what is the status of the project?**

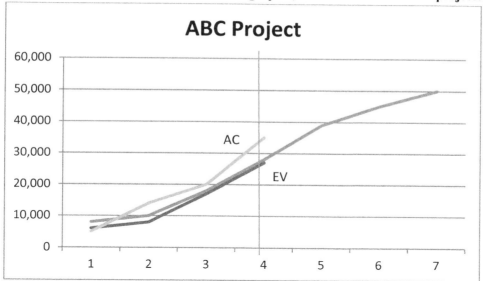

A. Under budget but trending over budget
B. Behind schedule and under budget
C. Ahead of schedule and over budget
D. Over budget and behind schedule

27. **The project has earned value of $87,750. Costs-to-date have been $110,000, and the budget is $195,000. What is the status of the project?**

A. Appears ahead of schedule
B. Appears over budget
C. Appears both over budget and behind schedule
D. Unable to determine based on information provided

28. **Which statement about the deliverables is most accurate?**

A. Deliverables are created through the scope processes
B. Deliverables are evaluated through the validate scope process prior to final review during the control quality process
C. Deliverables are verified once they have gone through the control quality process
D. Accepted deliverables will be provided to the requesting party for verification in the validate scope process.

29. **Which statement is most accurate regarding resource leveling and resource smoothing?**

A. Resource smoothing must occur before resource leveling
B. Resource leveling may alter the critical path whereas resource smoothing will not.
C. Resource smoothing may alter the critical path whereas resource leveling will not.
D. The terms smoothing and leveling are synonymous

30. **Your project has a schedule variance of $2,750 and a cost variance of $7,950. What statement best describes the status of your project?**

A. The project is under budget and behind schedule
B. The project is over budget and behind schedule
C. The project is over budget and ahead of schedule
D. The project is under budget and ahead of schedule

31. **Based on the information in the graphic, what is the current status of the project?**

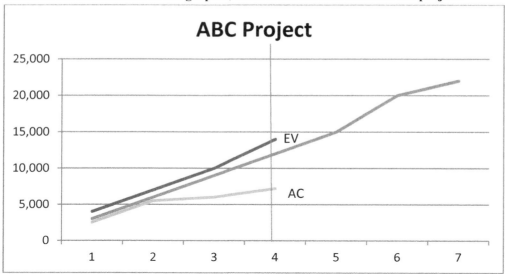

A. The project is ahead of schedule and over budget
B. The project is behind schedule and under budget
C. The project is over budget and behind schedule
D. The project is under budget and ahead of schedule

32. **Based on the graphic, if there's a 35% probability that Option A will occur, what is the value of Option B?**

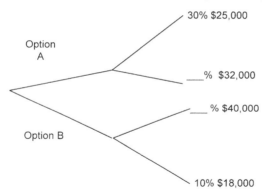

A. $37,800
B. $24,570
C. $37,700
D. $58,000

33. **An efficiency ratio that compares the work remaining on the project to the funds remaining on the project.**

A. Schedule performance index
B. Planned value
C. To-complete performance index
D. Cost performance index

34. **The difference between the estimate to complete and the estimate at completion forecasts can best be described as:**

A. Actual cost
B. Earned value
C. Variance at completion
D. Cost variance

35. **The costs associated with assessing the quality of a product is considered:**
    A. CMMI
    B. Cost of conformance
    C. Cost of nonconformance
    D. Cost benefit analysis

36. **You are evaluating your $89,000 project. The project is estimated to take six months and you have completed month two. After reviewing invoices, you determine that the paid-to-date amount is $27,000. The budget has been allocated as follows:**

    Month 1: $4,000

    Month 2: $12,000

    Month 3: $23,000

    Month 4: $25,000

    Month 5: $15,000

    Month 6: $10,000

    Which statement is most accurate?
    A. The project is ahead of schedule
    B. The project is over-budget
    C. The project is behind schedule
    D. The variance at completion is negative

37. **You are a PMP® and you are having dinner with a friend to celebrate his new job. Over dinner he tells you that the PMP® was a requirement of the job, but that he "fudged" his application knowing that the company didn't verify the information. How do you handle this?**
    A. Do nothing
    B. Report your friend to PMI
    C. Report your friend to his employer
    D. Advise your friend to be honest with his employer

38. **You have completed all of the project deliverables as defined within the project scope statement. As you are working to close the project and distribute the lessons learned and final project report, your manager assigns you to another project. Which statement is most accurate?**
    A. The project is considered closed because of the reassignment and the completed deliverables
    B. The project is open until all requirements are met
    C. The sponsor is able to consider the project closed
    D. The PMO would take over the responsibility of the project

39. **The enhancement project is complete and you are compiling your final performance report. The budget was $72,000 and your actual costs were $68,000. Which statement is most accurate?**
    A. Your variance at completion is positive
    B. You have a positive cost variance
    C. Your estimate at completion is negative
    D. Your variance at completion is negative

40. **The forecasted amount of project spending for the remainder of the project:**
    A. The cost variance
    B. The estimate to complete
    C. The estimate at completion
    D. The variance at completion

41. **The development project was completed in February. In May, you receive notification from one of the vendors that they did not receive the correct payment. What is the most appropriate action for you to take?**
    A. Re-open the project
    B. Nothing, as the project is closed
    C. Refer the project to legal counsel
    D. Escalate to the CEO

42. Your project team has been in place for seven months. Team members are located in six geographical locations. During team meetings, you find that the members tend to be hesitant to speak up or provide information. In what stage of team development would this team most likely be?

   A. Performing
   B. Norming
   C. Forming
   D. Storming

43. You are evaluating four vendors with the following bids:

   Vendor A: $33,000

   Vendor B: $37,000

   Vendor C: $28,000

   Vendor D: $31,000

   Based on historical information, there is a 70% chance that vendor A will have a 20% cost overrun. There is a 48% chance that vendor B will have 25% cost overrun. There is a 55% chance that vendor C will have a 40% cost overrun. There is a 30% chance vendor D will have a 25% cost overrun. Which vendor is the best option?

   A. Vendor B
   B. Vendor C
   C. Vendor A
   D. Vendor D

44. The result is rated on a scale that measures the degree of conformity:

   A. Variable
   B. Attribute
   C. Specific
   D. Acceptance

45. A source of variation that is not inherent in the system and is not predictable.

   A. Common
   B. Random
   C. Special
   D. Conditional

46. Varying in complexity, these tools aid organizations in ensuring consistency in frequently performed tasks:

   A. Quality metrics
   B. Quality diagrams
   C. Quality checklists
   D. Quality measurements

47. The forecasted estimate at completion is $75,000. You have spent $38,000 to date and have earned value of $46,000. The variance at completion is $9,000. What is the budget at completion?

   A. $29,000
   B. $83,000
   C. $84,000
   D. $121,000

48. Which statement is most accurate regarding the control quality process?

   A. It is a successor to scope definition and scope validation
   B. It precedes quality assurance and scope validation
   C. It is a successor to deliverable acceptance
   D. It precedes plan quality management

49. The difference between a quality metric and a quality measurement can best be described as:

   A. A metric describes an attribute whereas a measurement is an actual value
   B. A metric is an actual value whereas a measurement is how it will be calculated
   C. A measurement describes an attribute whereas a metric is an actual value
   D. A measurement is an actual value whereas a metric is how it will be documented

50. You are calculating the CPI for your project and have the following results:

    Month 1: 1.10

    Month 2: 0.98

    Month 3: 0.99

    Month 4: 1.09

    Month 5: 1.12

    Month 6: 1.03

    Month 7: 0.97

    This could best be described as:
    A. Random variance
    B. Special variance
    C. Abnormal variance
    D. Controlled variance

51. **As your project begins producing the XJ9000 component, your QC team is inspecting them to ensure that they each power-on. This is an example of:**
    A. Variance evaluation
    B. Attribute sampling
    C. Variable sampling
    D. Special variance review

52. **Which statement is most accurate regarding tolerances and control limits?**
    A. They are one in the same
    B. Only control limits can be demonstrated in a control chart
    C. Tolerances are typically subjective whereas control limits are typically mathematically defined
    D. Control limits are typically subjective whereas tolerances are typically mathematically defined

53. **The three key outputs from the control quality process include the following except:**
    A. Verified deliverables
    B. Quality control measurements
    C. Validated changes
    D. Quality metrics

54. **Your project has a CPI of .98 and a schedule variance of ($12,000). Which statement is most accurate?**
    A. The project is ahead of schedule and over budget
    B. The project is behind schedule and under budget
    C. The project is over budget and behind schedule
    D. The project is under budget and ahead of schedule

55. **Which of the following is not one of the quality tools?**
    A. Scatter diagram
    B. Histogram
    C. Control chart
    D. Earned value graph

56. **Which statement most accurately describes a verified deliverable?**
    A. The deliverable has been evaluated through quality control
    B. The deliverable has been accepted by the customer
    C. The deliverable has been reviewed through quality assurance
    D. The deliverable has been checked against the scope statement

57. **With your project team, you have identified the need for a workaround. What process are you doing?**
    A. Monitor risks
    B. Plan risk responses
    C. Identify risk
    D. Risk evaluation

58. The schedule variance of your project is ($27,000), your actual costs are $82,000, the budgeted value of the work is $92,000, and the budget at completion is $125,000. What is the earned value of the project?

   A. $55,000
   B. $65,000
   C. $98,000
   D. $43,000

59. An opportunity is also known as a:

   A. Risk response
   B. Project risk
   C. Benefit measure
   D. Project calculation

60. The estimate at completion for your project is $179,000 and the estimate to complete the project is $88,500. Which statement is most accurate?

   A. The cost variance is $90,500
   B. The actual costs are $90,500
   C. The schedule variance is $90,500
   D. The variance at completion is $90,500

61. An easy and objective method for evaluating proposals is a:

   A. Screening system
   B. Weighting system
   C. Team-based evaluation system
   D. Voting system

62. Which of the following allows potential sellers to ask questions about the project and its requirements?

   A. Sellers meeting
   B. Advertised bids
   C. Bidders conference
   D. Annual meeting

63. Why is it important for the project manager to be aware of the contract terms and conditions being used for the project procurements?

   A. The project manager may be responsible for ensuring that the terms and conditions are met
   B. The project manager has procurement authority and will be signing the contract
   C. The project manager will be paying the vendor and will need to leverage the terms and conditions to dictate payment requirements
   D. The project manager will be responsible for the final contract negotiations based on the contract terms

64. You are evaluating the performance of your project, including looking at the status of project risks, the current forecasts, and the status of project activities. The information you are evaluating is an output of:

   A. Quality assurance
   B. Control quality
   C. Manage team
   D. Direct and manage project work

65. The CPFF contract states that the sub-contractor will be paid for costs associated with digging the trenches, estimated at approximately $15,000. In addition, they will receive an additional payment of $7,500 (50% of the estimated costs). What would the contract value be if the final costs associated with the job were $20,000?

   A. $30,000
   B. $22,500
   C. $27,500
   D. $35,000

66. The simplest form of this contract type is a purchase order:

   A. FPIF
   B. FFP
   C. CPIF
   D. CPFF

 © Belinda Goodrich | 888-871-7657 | PMLearningSolutions.com

67. **Which contract type places increased risk on the seller?**
    A. Cost reimbursable
    B. Time and material
    C. Fixed price
    D. Negotiated

68. **In an effort to minimize risk on the project, your sponsor has instructed you to use a fixed price contract with any vendors whenever possible. In a fixed price (FP) contract, the fee or profit is:**
    A. Calculated as a percentage of the estimated costs
    B. Not known by the buyer
    C. Determined by the buyer upon project completion
    D. Will be included as a separate cost during the invoicing process

69. **The contract states that the delivery company will be paid $800 per month regardless of the number of deliveries. If the price of gas increases by more than 20%, the amount will increase to $900 or if the price of gas decreases by more than 20%, the amount will decrease to $700 per month. What type of contract is being used?**
    A. FP-special
    B. FPEPA
    C. CPAF
    D. Commodity-based

70. **Which contract type places increased risk on the buyer?**
    A. Fixed price
    B. Cost-reimbursable
    C. Fixed price with incentive fee
    D. Time and material

71. **Which statement is least accurate regarding procurement documents?**
    A. If the selection will be based upon capability or approach, the term proposal is generally used
    B. They are usually not used to solicit proposals from prospective sellers
    C. If the selection will be based upon price, the term quotation may be used
    D. The complexity and level of detail should be consistent with the value of the planned procurements

72. **This process determines which contract types should be used on the project to procure needed products or services:**
    A. Select Sellers
    B. Plan Procurement Management
    C. Conduct Procurements
    D. Control Procurements

73. **During the development phase of your project, you will be using a vendor for a key component of the product manufacturing. However, prior to development, your team will need to conduct a rigorous analysis to determine the manufacturing needs and requirements. If you needed to enter into a contractual relationship with the vendor prior to completion of the analysis, what contract type would most likely be used?**
    A. CPFF
    B. FPEPA
    C. FFP
    D. CPAF

74. **The contract states that the company will pay the staffing agency $50 per hour for the contract resource, with a not-to-exceed value of $10,000. What type of contract is being used?**
    A. FFP
    B. CPAF
    C. Time and material
    D. CPIF

75. **Your team has been managing the new development project for the past six months. The project is slightly under budget but unfortunately, due to a number of unforeseen issues, the project is running 30% behind schedule. The best action to take would be:**

    A. Submit a corrective action change request asking for additional resources
    B. Submit a defect repair change request as the issues will need to be resolved
    C. Continue normal management and monitoring
    D. Submit a preventive action change request and update the baselines accordingly

End Time:_____

Practice Exam 4

Chapters 12 - 15

Answer Key

1. **Answer: D**

    Deliverables are an output of the direct and manage project work process. They will then become an input to the control quality process where:
    - they will be checked for correctness against the requirements
    - upon verification, the deliverables will become "verified deliverables"

2. **Answer: D**

    A $12,500 VAC tells us that the project is estimated to come in $12,500 under budget (remember that a positive VAC is good (under budget) and a negative VAC is bad (over budget).

    Since the budget is $75,000 and we are estimated to come in $12,500 under budget...The EAC is $75,000 - $12,500 = $62,500

    If the EAC is $62,500 and the ETC is $15,750 (given to you in the question) then $62,500 - $15,750 = $46,750 which is the AC of the project to date

3. **Answer: B**

    To calculate the SV we must use the *PMBOK® Guide* formula SV = EV - PV

    PV is given to us in the question as $75,000

    EV is not given to us so we must calculate the EV by using the *PMBOK® Guide* formula:

    EV = BAC x % Complete

    $195,000 x 50% = $97,500

    (note that the % Complete comes from the question as well...3mo ÷ 6mo = 50% Complete)

    Now that we have calculated the EV, we can use the SV formula above which gives us $97,500 - $75,000 = $22,500

4. **Answer: D**

    To calculate the CPI we must use the *PMBOK® Guide* formula CPI = EV/AC

    AC is given to us in the question as $37,500

    EV is not given to us so we must calculate the EV by using the *PMBOK® Guide* formula:

    EV = BAC x % Complete

    $195,000 x 50% = $97,500

    (note that the % Complete comes from the question as well...3mo ÷ 6mo = 50% Complete)

    Now that we have calculated the EV, we can use the CPI formula above which gives us $97,500 / $37,500 = 2.6

5. **Answer: B**

    The procurement documents are an output of the plan procurement management process. Procurement documents are used to solicit proposals or responses from potential vendors.

    The procurement documents will be updated to include the executed agreement (or contract) in subsequent procurement processes.

    Procurement documents can include:
    - Request for proposal (RFP)
    - Request for quotation (RFQ)
    - Invitation for bid (IFB)
    - Tender notice

6. **Answer: C**

TCPI is calculated as: (Budget at Completion - Earned Value) / (Budget at Completion - Actual Costs)

Budget at completion (BAC) is provided as $195,000

Earned value (EV) is calculated as BAC multiplied by percentage of the project complete which equals $97,500.

Actual costs is provided as $37,500

($195,000 - $97,500) / ($195,000 - $37,500)

$97,500 / $157,500 = 0.62

This indicates that the project has 38% more money than work remaining (a positive situation).

7. **Answer: B**

TCPI is an efficiency ratio. A TCPI greater than one indicates that the project is not operating efficiently. The 1.27 indicates that the project needs to be 27% more efficient with resources in order to achieve the budget and work objectives.

8. **Answer: A**

A negative cost variance indicates that the project is currently over budget. Although it is currently over budget it does not necessarily mean that the project will not meet budget objectives, as corrective actions may be pursued.

9. **Answer: B**

While the project is not yet behind schedule, the consistently decreasing schedule variance indicates that it is trending towards being behind schedule. A positive schedule variance indicates the project is ahead of schedule, a negative schedule variance indicates the project is behind schedule.

10. **Answer: A**

The formula for schedule performance index (SPI) is: SPI = earned value (EV) / planned value (PV).

We are provided with an SPI of 0.8 and a PV of $125,000.

SPI x PV = EV

0.8 x $125,000 = $100,000

11. **Answer: C**

The ratio of earned value (EV) to planned value (PV) is the formula for schedule performance index (SPI).

SPI = EV / PV

12. **Answer: A**

The formula for cost variance (CV):

CV = earned value (EV) - actual costs (AC)

$92,000 + $18,000 = $110,000

The negative cost variance indicates your project is currently over budget.

13. **Answer: B**

The items listed represent work performance data, which is an output of direct and manage project work. Work performance data can be thought of as "raw" data.

Work performance data is an input to multiple Monitoring and Controlling processes where it will be analyzed. The output from those processes will be work performance information. The work performance information will be an input to the monitor and control project work process where the output will be the work performance reports.

Data > Information > Reports

14. **Answer: A**

The validate scope process, in the monitoring and controlling process group, is concerned with getting the customer or requesting party's acceptance of completed deliverables. The control quality process (also known as QC) is performed prior to the validate scope process. Deliverables are checked internally (QC) before being given to the customer for acceptance.

15. **Answer: B**

Schedule performance index (SPI) is a comparison of earned value to planned value. The SPI formula is:

SPI = EV / PV

16. **Answer: A**

    The value of the work already completed on the project is the "earned value". Earned value is calculated as:

    EV = Budget at completion x percentage of project complete

    Percentage complete may be either time-based (i.e. 3 weeks into a 6-week project would be 50% complete) or effort-based (30% complete with the work of the project). Effort-based percent complete is always going to be more accurate and most appropriate to use to calculate EV. If, however, the question does not provide you with an effort-based percent complete, you will use the time-based percent complete.

17. **Answer: D**

    Planned value (PV) is the planned value of the work to be accomplished by the status date. PV at the end of the project is equal to the budget at completion (BAC).

18. **Answer: D**

    To calculate earned value (EV) take the budget at completion (BAC) and multiply it by the percent complete.

    EV = BAC * % Complete = $785,000 * .35 = $274,750

    Please note that the TCPI and the actual costs (AC) were no needed in this problem and were simply noise.

19. **Answer: A**

    There are four processes within the Project Scope Management Knowledge Area / Planning Process Group that are done sequentially: plan scope management, collect requirements, define scope, and create WBS. In order to develop the WBS, the scope statement must be complete. The scope statement is an output of the define scope process and as such, precedes the development of the WBS.

20. **Answer: C**

    The output of the define activities process includes the activity list, the activity attributes, and the milestone list.

21. **Answer: B**

    Earned value (EV) is calculated as:

    EV = Budget at Completion (BAC) * Percent Complete

    As we are solving for Percent Complete, we would divide the EV of $87,750 by the BAC of $195,000.

    $87,750 / $195,000 = .45

22. **Answer: A**

    The formula for TCPI (to-complete performance index) is:

    (Budget at Completion - Earned Value) / (Budget at Completion - Actual Costs)

    (BAC - EV) / (BAC - AC)

    (BAC - $300k) / (BAC - $325k) = 1.14

    ($500k - $300k) / ($500k - $325k) = 1.14

    $200k / $175k = 1.14

23. **Answer: B**

    There are two processes that lead to the cost baseline: estimate costs and determine budget. First costs are estimated across the project, in as much detail as is feasible for the particular stage of the project. Those costs are then applied across the schedule to determine the budget and create the cost baseline.

    Both the project budget and the cost estimates may be progressively elaborated.

24. **Answer: D**

    There are three scope planning processes that lead to the development of the scope baseline:

    Collect requirements - outputs are the requirements documentation and the requirements traceability matrix

    Define scope - output is the scope statement

    Create WBS - output is the scope baseline (consisting of the scope statement, the WBS, and the WBS dictionary)

25. Answer: B

A preferential dependency (also known as a preferred, discretionary, or soft logic dependency) is based on past experience, best practice, industry or organizational standard.

Given that there is no physical dependency on the design being approved prior to being implemented, meaning the design could be physically implemented without the approval, it is considered preferential.

Do not let the word "must" throw you off. On these dependencies, you will be looking for a physical limitation to indicate a mandatory/hard logic dependency.

26. Answer: D

While evaluating a project's status using an Earned Value Management (EVM) chart, you will always compare Actual Cost (AC) to Earned Value (EV) to determine the status of the budget and Planned Value (PV) (the blue line) to Earned Value (EV) to determine the status of the schedule.

Given that the EV is less than the AC (we've earned less than we've spent), the project appears to be over budget.

Given that the EV is also less than the PV (we've earned less than we've planned to have earned at this point), the project appears to be behind schedule.

A project that is progressing well will have an EV the same as, or higher than, the AC and the PV.

27. Answer: B

Using the information provided, you can only determine the status of the budget:

Cost Variance (CV) = Earned Value (EV) - Actual Costs (AC)

$87,750 - $110,000 = ($22,250)

A negative cost variance indicates that the project is currently $22,250 over budget.

28. Answer: C

The deliverables are an output of the direct and manage project work process.

Upon completion, they are first evaluated by the control quality process, where they now become "verified" deliverables.

The verified deliverables are an input to the validate scope process where they now become "accepted" deliverables.

Deliverables > Verified Deliverables > Accepted Deliverables

29. Answer: B

There are two resource optimization techniques: resource leveling and resource smoothing. Resource leveling is always done first and may alter the critical path.

Resource smoothing is done after leveling and uses any float that may be available to "smooth out" the level of effort. As such, you may not be able to optimize all resources when you smooth. Resource smoothing does not alter the critical path.

30. Answer: D

A positive schedule variance (SV) indicates that the earned value (EV) of the project is greater than the planned value (PV), indicating the project is ahead of schedule.

A positive cost variance (CV) indicates that the earned value (EV) of the project is greater than the actual costs (AC), indicating the project is under budget.

31. Answer: D

Using the Earned Value Management (EVM) graphic, and evaluating status compared to the Earned Value (EV) of the project, you can determine:

The project is under budget as the EV is greater than the Actual Costs (AC).

The project is ahead of schedule as the EV is greater than the Planned Value (PV) (the blue line).

32. Answer: B

If there is a 35% probability that Option A will occur, there must be a 65% probability that Option B will occur.

For the expected monetary value (EMV) calculation, if there is a 10% probability of $18,000, there is a 90% probability of $40,000.

0.9 x $40,000 = $36,000

0.1 x $18,000 = $1,800

EMV = $36,000 + $1,800 = $37,800

There is only a 65% probability of Option B, so you multiply the $37,800 by the 65% probability:

0.65 x $37,800 = $24,570

33. Answer: C

To-complete performance index (TCPI) is an efficiency ratio, comparing work remaining to funds remaining:

TCPI = (Budget at completion - earned value) / (Budget at completion - actual cost)

34. Answer: A

Estimate to complete (ETC) is the projection of the remaining costs to complete the project.

Estimate at completion (EAC) is the projection of overall project spending - including both the actual costs and the estimate to complete.

35. Answer: B

The cost of quality encompasses the cost of conformance and the cost of non-conformance.

The cost of conformance is money spent to avoid failures and as such, the costs associated with assessing the quality of a product, would be consider the cost of conformance.

36. Answer: A

For this question, you will calculate the following variables: budget at completion (BAC) = $89,000. At 33% complete, the calculated Earned Value (EV) is $29,370. The actual costs (AC) are $27,000 and the planned value (PV) is $16,000 (the cumulative planned spend of the first two months.

Schedule variance (SV) = EV – PV = $29,370 - $16,000 = $13,370. A positive SV indicates the project is ahead of schedule.

37. Answer: B

Because the PMP® is a professional credential, any known violations are to be reported to PMI. If, as a PMP, you do not report the violation, you can be found in violation.

38. Answer: B

A project is not considered complete until all requirements are met, for both the project and the product. Even if your manager re-assigns you, the project is still considered open and should be identified as such, and escalated as appropriate.

39. Answer: A

Variance at completion (VAC) is calculated as budget at completion (BAC) minus estimate at completion (EAC). In this case, the project is complete so the EAC is the same as the actual costs (AC). A positive VAC indicates that the project delivered under budget.

40. Answer: B

The estimate to complete (ETC) is the estimated remaining spend, from this point forward. ETC does not include actual costs (AC).

41. Answer: A

Because administrative closure activities were not accurately fulfilled, including full and accurate payment of all invoices, the project must be re-opened. Referring the project to legal counsel and escalation to the CEO would be inappropriate first steps.

42. Answer: C

The stages of team development (known as Tuckman's Ladder) are not time-based stages. Given that the team is virtual and they are hesitant to share information openly, this team is most likely in forming, the first stage of team development.

43. **Answer: D**

    To calculate the answer:

    Vendor A: A 20% cost overrun would be $6,600, multiplied by the 70% probability = $4,620, bringing the total value for Vendor A to $37,620 ($33,000 + $4,620 = $37,620).

    Vendor B: A 25% cost overrun would be $9,250, multiplied by the 48% probability = $4,440, bringing the total value for Vendor B to $41,440 ($37,000 + $4,440 = $41,440).

    Vendor C: A 40% cost overrun would be $11,200, multiplied by the 55% probability = $6,160, bringing the total value for Vendor C to $34,160 ($28,000 + $6,160 = $34,160).

    Vendor D: A 25% cost overrun would be $2,325, multiplied by the 30% probability = $2,325, bringing the total cost for Vendor D to $33,325 ($31,000 + $2,325 = $33,325).

    Vendor as the lowest total value, and as this is money we are paying, Vendor D would be the best option.

44. **Answer: A**

    Variable sampling measures the result on a scale to determine the degree of conformity, versus an attribute sampling which measures the result as either pass or fail.

45. **Answer: C**

    Special causes of variance are unusual and difficult to predict. Compare special causes of variance to common causes of variance (also known as random variance), which are predictable variances.

46. **Answer: C**

    Quality checklists, an output of the plan quality management process, are useful when individuals are completing the same set of steps repeatedly. Checklists ensure all individuals are consistent in their completion of the steps.

47. **Answer: C**

    Using the following variables: estimate at completion (EAC) = $75k, actual costs (AC) = $38k, earned value (EV) = $46k, and variance at completion (VAC) = $9k, use the VAC formula to back into the budget at completion (BAC).

    VAC = BAC − EAC

    $9k = BAC - $75k

    Add $75k to the $9k: $84k = BAC

48. **Answer: B**

    The control quality (QC) process precedes both the validate scope process (considered scope verification) and the manage quality (QA) process. QC precedes validate scope as deliverables must be checked for correctness before being provided to the customer for acceptance. QC precedes QA as the QC measurements are required in order to perform the quality audits of QA.

49. **Answer: A**

    A quality metric is the definition of what the team intends to achieve. Quality metrics are an output of the plan quality management process. Quality control measurements are a measurement of the actual results that are being accomplished. Quality control measurements will be an output of the control quality (QC) process.

50. **Answer: A**

    Given that the variance is consistent and stable without extreme outlying values, this would be considered random (or common) variance. Random variance is normal process variation.

51. **Answer: B**

    Because they are testing for a pass/fail result (it either turns on or it doesn't), it would be considered attribute sampling.

52. **Answer: C**

    Both tolerances and control limits can be depicted on a control chart, however, while control limits are typically mathematically defined as three standard deviations from the mean, tolerances are based on preference and are therefore more subjective.

53. **Answer: D**

    Quality metrics are an operational definition of what we intend to achieve, and as such, are an output of the plan quality management process.

54. Answer: C

Because the cost performance index (CPI) is less than one, reflecting that the project has a lower earned value (EV) than actual cost (AC), the project is considered over budget. A negative schedule variance (SV), reflecting that the project has a lower earned value (EV) than planned value (PV), indicates that the project is behind schedule.

55. Answer: D

The seven basic quality tools are: Ishikawa (fishbone or cause and effect) diagram, Pareto chart, control chart, histogram, scatter diagram, checksheet, and flowcharts. Earned value graphs are not considered one of the seven basic quality tools.

56. Answer: A

A verified deliverable is an output of the Perform Quality Control (QC) process, meaning that the deliverable has been checked for correctness and conformance to requirements.

57. Answer: A

Because a workaround is a response to a negative risk event that has occurred, not planned in advance, the need for workarounds would be determined in the monitor risks process.

58. Answer: B

Using the following variables: schedule variance (SV) = ($27,000) and planned value (PV) = $92,000, use the SV formula to back into the earned value (EV).

$SV = EV - PV$

($27,000) = EV - $92,000

Add $92,000 to the ($27,000)

$65,000 = EV

59. Answer: B

An opportunity is considered a project risk. An opportunity is an uncertain event that has a positive impact on the project.

60. Answer: B

The difference between the estimate to complete (ETC) and the estimate at completion (EAC) is the actual costs (AC). EAC includes AC, ETC does not.

$EAC - ETC = AC$

$179,000 - $88,500 = $90,500

61. Answer: B

A weighting system is an easy and objective method of evaluating proposals, as it allows for scoring the criteria based on what is most important to the procurement and the project. A screening system is used to "screen" potential vendors/sellers.

62. Answer: C

A bidder's conference allows potential sellers to ask questions about the project and the requirements. Also known as pre-bid conference, vendor conference, or seller conference.

63. Answer: A

The project manager should be aware of the contract terms and conditions as they may be responsible for ensuring that the terms and conditions of the contract are being met. The PM typically does not have procurement authority and will not be signing the contract, nor will they be paying the vendor or responsible for the final contract negotiations.

64. Answer: D

Status of risks, forecasts, status of activities would all be considered work performance data. Work performance data is an output of direct and manage project work.

65. Answer: C

For a cost plus fixed fee (CPFF) contract, the contract value would be the final costs ($20,000) plus the pre-determined fixed fee ($7,500). Contract value would be $27,500.

66. **Answer: B**

The simplest form of a firm fixed price contract is a purchase order.

67. **Answer: C**

A fixed price contract places the risk on the seller. If there is any type of adverse condition, the seller would have to absorb the additional costs.

68. **Answer: B**

Because the buyer is paying one fixed price, the profit versus the cost is not known by the buyer.

69. **Answer: B**

This is describing the fixed price with economic price adjustment (FPEPA) contract, which protects both the buyer and seller from fluctuations in the price of commodities, scenarios that are outside of the control of both the buyer and seller.

70. **Answer: B**

A cost reimbursable contract places the most risk on the buyer as there is not one set price for the work that will be done.

71. **Answer: B**

Procurement documents are used to solicit proposals from prospective sellers, specifically a request for proposal (RFP).

72. **Answer: B**

The Plan Procurement Management process will determine the contract types that will be used on the project.

73. **Answer: A**

Because the analysis is not complete, it would not be possible to enter into a fixed price contract, as there is not clear definition as to what the seller will be delivering. It is very unlikely that a seller would agree to enter into a cost plus award fee (CPAF) contract as they would not be guaranteed any profit on the job.

74. **Answer: C**

A time and material contract would pay time and expense (T&E) and will also have a not-to-exceed value.

75. **Answer: A**

Because the project is behind schedule, the only appropriate response would be to submit a corrective action. Defect repair would be appropriate if there was a quality issue; preventive action would be appropriate if the project was trending behind schedule but wasn't actually behind yet.

Appendix E

PMP Final Practice Exam

What's in This Chapter

- PMP Final Practice Exam (200 Questions)
- Answer Key

Start Time:_____

PMP Final Practice Exam

200 Questions   **Time Limit: 4 Hours**

1. You are assigned a new project. You learn that the technology department wants the project objective to be a 15% improvement in throughput. The operations department wants no more than 3% of its resources used on the project and senior management is asking the project to reduce tax liability. As PM, the best thing you can do is:
   A. Encourage technology, operations, and management to meet and agree upon one objective
   B. Include only the senior management objective
   C. Include operations and technology objectives but not the management objectives until you have further meetings
   D. Incorporate all objectives into the plan

2. A cost performance index (CPI) of 0.75 suggests the project is:
   A. Under-budget to date
   B. Over-budget to date
   C. On budget
   D. Behind schedule

3. You are the project manager for a $500,000 international project with 20 resources. As project manager you have completed the WBS and WBS dictionary and your project team is working on identifying risks. Your sponsor has asked you to issue the responsibility assignment matrix. This project is very similar to the other projects you have completed for your organization and the risk is minimal. What is the next thing you should do?
   A. Develop the RAM and the risk management plan
   B. Validate the project scope
   C. Understand the sponsor's experience on similar projects
   D. Create an activity list

4. Your sponsor is currently evaluating multiple projects to determine which one would be the best to choose. Project 1 is a 5-year project with a net present value (NPV) of $83,000. Project 2 is a 3-year project with an NPV of $25,000. Project 3 is a 1-year project with an NPV of $67,000. Project 4 is a 2-year project with an NPV of $44,000. Which project should be selected?
   A. Project 4
   B. Project 2
   C. Project 1
   D. Project 3

5. Scope creep is:
   A. A type of residual risk
   B. An activity that needs to be included in the project schedule
   C. Unmanaged changes to the project scope
   D. Allowing team members to make changes

6. The sponsor of the development project has assigned it to you and advised you that the project is on schedule and is 50% complete. Upon conducting an evaluation of the project, you realize that the project is far behind schedule and it will ultimately end up taking twice the time that was originally estimated. What is the best thing for you to do?
   A. Proceed with the original schedule and provide an updated report at the first missed milestone
   B. Refuse the project and turn it back over to the original project manager
   C. Provide your evaluation to the sponsor
   D. Attempt to restructure the schedule to meet the original deadline

7. **You have been assigned a complex new project with a few unknowns that is anticipated to take nine months to complete. The customer has provided you with the statement of work and has stated that they are focused strictly on the end product and only want to see you at the end of the nine months with the completed product. Based on this information, what should you do?**

   A. Verify the scope with the customer occasionally throughout the project, while completing the project as requested
   B. Request that your sponsor check in with the customer
   C. Document that the customer did not want contact
   D. Ensure that you complete the project within the nine months allocated with no contact with the customer until completion

8. **As project manager, you are responsible for publishing the web design project schedule. You have identified the activities, the start and end dates of each activity and the resources have been identified. What is the next thing you should do?**

   A. Based on the communication management plan, distribute the project schedule
   B. Confirm the resource availability
   C. Publish a bar chart
   D. Refine the project management plan to include activity cost information

9. **Consider the following: You are assigned a project that is underway. Activity B is a difficult activity and has an early start of day 10 and a late start of day 15. The SPI on your project is .72 and the CPI is 1.2. You have 15 stakeholders involved in the project. What are you most concerned with?**

   A. Budget
   B. Resources
   C. Float
   D. Schedule

10. **To enhance and improve communications, the sender _____ the receiver.**

    A. Should speak up to
    B. Should demonstrate concern for the perspective of
    C. Should talk slowly to
    D. Should use more physical forms of communication with

11. **Your sponsor wants to discuss with you the most appropriate estimating technique to use on the project. You know that it's important to use a form of expert judgment, but your sponsor feels strongly that analogous estimating should be used. What would be the best option?**

    A. Compromise by suggesting parametric estimating which is a combination of both
    B. Discuss the situation further with the sponsor to understand why they want to use the more time-consuming estimating method
    C. Utilize a 3-point estimate as it would be more accurate
    D. Agree to use analogous as it uses expert judgment

12. **There is a 30% probability that the risk event will happen in a given month. The project is a 12 month project. As such, what is the probability of that risk event occurring during the sixth month of the project?**

    A. 15%
    B. 30%
    C. 5%
    D. 80%

13. **This represents that estimated value of the work actually completed:**

    A. Actual cost (AC)
    B. Planned value (PV)
    C. Earned value (EV)
    D. Actual work (AW)

14. **With the software upgrade project well underway, the project manager is working with the quality assurance department to improve the stakeholder's confidence that the project will meet their desired quality standards. In order to start this process, what must the project team have?**
    A. The quality control measurements
    B. The quality improvement plan
    C. A list of identified quality problems
    D. The rework

15. **Your project has a dependency requiring that the design be completed prior to the beginning of manufacturing. This is what type of dependency?**
    A. Discretionary
    B. Mandatory
    C. External
    D. Preferential

16. **You have recently been assigned a difficult project that requires the use of multiple sub-contractors. You have a major negotiation scheduled with a potential subcontracting firm tomorrow when you are notified that there is a strong probability the project will be cancelled. What should you do?**
    A. Honor the meeting but only negotiate the significant items
    B. Postpone the negotiation meeting
    C. Do not spend a lot of time preparing for the meeting
    D. Meet with the subcontractor but keep the negotiations brief

17. **An effective project management approach would be to break the identified work down into small pieces. All of the following describe how far to break down the work except:**
    A. When it can be realistically estimated
    B. When it cannot be subdivided further
    C. When it can be done by one person
    D. When it has an appropriate conclusion

18. **The values, as defined by the global project management community as most important and that serve as the foundation of the Code of Ethics and Professional Responsibility are:**
    A. Responsibility, honesty, integrity, and knowledge
    B. Responsibility, respect, fairness, and honesty
    C. Respect, honesty, fairness, and integrity
    D. Responsibility, integrity, respect, and fairness

19. **You are managing a complex engineering project with 52 team members. One of your stakeholders is known to make multiple changes on projects. How could you best handle this particular stakeholder?**
    A. Remove the stakeholder from the stakeholder register
    B. As part of your stakeholder management strategy, demonstrate your authority with the stakeholder by rejecting their first few change requests
    C. Ensure that they are involved in the project as early as possible
    D. Work with the stakeholder's manager to identify other options for the stakeholder

20. **You do not have enough resources available on your project to audit invoices. What contract type do you not want to use?**
    A. FPIF
    B. T&M
    C. CPFF
    D. FFP

21. **The project management office is**
    A. The same as the office of the CEO
    B. An organization that may provide project support functions
    C. Another term for the war room
    D. Only used for government projects

22. **You are conducting an analysis of your project budget and schedule using the earned value technique. Based on your forecast, it appears as though the project will have a cost overrun at the end. What should you do?**

    A. Re-estimate upon the elimination of risks in the estimates
    B. Eliminate some of the scope of the project
    C. Remove quality activities
    D. Ask the customer what work can be done sooner

23. **The construction project has been difficult to manage and there is a lot of pressure on the team to complete the project on time. Team meetings have become very tense and there is a lot of shouting and very little progress on project objectives. Because of the shouting, one of your team members has asked to be excused from the meetings as she is too upset and stressed by the tension. The customer is asking for some changes and additions to the scope. Your boss, the sponsor of the construction project, would now like to be involved in the weekly team meetings. How should you handle this situation?**

    A. Conduct a team-building activity and make it mandatory for all team members to attend
    B. Discourage the sponsor from attending the meeting as it could increase tensions
    C. Have the team develop new ground rules and be sure all of the team members understand them
    D. Have a face-to-face meeting with the team member who asked to be excused and show the value of the open communication that is occurring within the team meetings

24. **You and your project management team have identified 73 risks on your project, identified and documented the triggers, plotted the risks on a probability/impact matrix, and evaluated the quality of the data that was used. What did you forget?**

    A. To conduct simulation and modeling
    B. Risk mitigation activities
    C. To involve the other stakeholders
    D. An overall risk rating for the project

25. **Based on past experience, when production is doubled, the unit costs decrease by 15%. Using this information, the company determines that production of 800 units will cost $150,000. This illustrates:**

    A. 80/20 rule
    B. Law of diminishing returns
    C. Evolution learning cycle
    D. Parametric cost estimating

26. **You are the PM for the construction project and your management has promised to provide you with part of the incentive fee from the customer if you are able to complete the project early. Your team informs you that one of the major deliverables is being finalized and although it meets the requirements in the contract, it will not provide the functionality the customer needs. The project will not be able to be completed early if that particular deliverable is late. What would be the best action for you to take?**

    A. Develop a list of delays that were caused by the customer in order to prepare for negotiations
    B. Simply cut out other activities that will be unnoticed in order to provide additional time to fix the deliverable
    C. Provide the deliverable as-is, as it meets the contract requirements
    D. Inform the customer of the situation and determine a mutually agreeable solution

27. **The project manager is estimating the time that will be needed for each activity. Those estimates are then added to the schedule to create the overall project estimate. The project manager provides the timeline to the sponsor, committing to complete the project in the identified timeframe. What did the project manager do wrong?**

    A. A schedule network diagram was not completed, nor was the team involved in creating the estimates
    B. The project estimate should have been created by the sponsor based on the customer's needs
    C. The project manager did too much work as the project estimate is the same as the customer's required completion date
    D. The team should have completed the estimate and the method that was used was too time-consuming

28. **During the contracting process, the best description of the project manager's role is:**

    A. The PM provides instruction to the contract manager regarding the handling of the contract process
    B. The PM functions as the negotiator
    C. The PM has minimal involvement
    D. The PM supplies an understanding of the risks of the project

29. As your project is progressing, one of your team members informs you that one of the work packages does not meet the quality metric and he does not believe it will be possible to meet it. As project manager, you meet with all parties concerned to assess the situation. What quality management process are you involved in?

   A. Plan quality management
   B. Manage quality
   C. Control quality
   D. Perform project control

30. The ABC project has the following activities: Activity A is 30 hours and can be happening at the same time as Activity B, which is 15 hours. Activity C can start after Activity A and is 25 hours. Activity D can start after Activity C and is 10 hours. Activity E, which is 25 hours, can start after both Activity B and Activity C. Activity F can start after Activity D and is 24 hours. Which of the following is true if Activity B actually takes 35 hours?

   A. The critical path has increased by 20 hours
   B. The critical path would shift to include B
   C. The critical path is A, C, D, F
   D. The duration of the critical path is 124 hours

31. As project manager, you have just completed the risk response plan for the multi-million dollar renovation project. What should you do next?

   A. During the next risk meeting conduct a risk reassessment
   B. Update the WBS with the additional work packages
   C. Calculate the overall project risk rating
   D. Conduct a quantitative risk analysis

32. You are the project manager over a high-profile corporate project. One of your team members is conducting an on-site inspection of one of the development areas. Which would be the most important thing to be done on any phone call between you and the team member?

   A. Advise the team member to be alert to change requests
   B. Review the upcoming list of deliverables
   C. Validate the contact information of the stakeholders
   D. Ask that your team member repeat back what you say

33. During risk control, when is additional response development needed?

   A. When the organization is restructuring
   B. When the original risk response is not working as expected
   C. When the project objectives change
   D. When the contingency reserves are used up

34. Mid-way through your project you learn that one of your sellers for your project is having problems with retaining employees due to a labor dispute. You are aware that there are other projects being conducted within your company using this same seller. What action should you take?

   A. Notify the other project managers in your company about the situation with the seller
   B. Take steps to retain the required resources on your project
   C. No longer work with that seller
   D. Provide the seller with notice that you will cancel their work on the project if the labor dispute is not settled.

35. You are a project manager in a matrix organization. Information dissemination is most likely to be effective when:

   A. Information flows both horizontally and vertically
   B. Project and functional managers have social relationships
   C. Communication channels are kept simple
   D. There is an inherent logic in the type of matrix put in place

36. **You are mentoring a fellow project manager. He explains to you that he had a complex problem a few months ago and he took what he thought was the best course of action. However, the problem has resurfaced. What do you ask him?**

    A. Did the project sponsor validate your course of action?
    B. Did you use a fishbone diagram?
    C. Did you confirm that your action solved the problem?
    D. Did you conduct a proper risk analysis?

37. **As project manager for the construction project, you are half way through the project when your senior team manager lets you know that he is concerned that the project will not meet the quality standards set forth. The foundation is complete on the project and the structural reinforcements are being installed. What would be the best thing for you to do in this situation?**

    A. Establish a quality assurance team
    B. Evaluate the results in the last quality management plan
    C. Let the senior team manager know that quality standards were defined up front and the project will meet quality standards
    D. Using parametric estimating, estimate the future results

38. **Your sponsor advises you that there is enough money in the budget to complete the IT project, however, the project is 40% complete and the cost performance index (CPI) is 0.65. Upon reviewing the original cost estimates you learn that the project was analogously estimated. The analogous estimate was then used to determine the activity estimates. What should have been done to reach a more accurate estimate?**

    A. Use SPI instead of CPI
    B. Take into consideration past history
    C. Conduct a bottom-up estimate to ensure that the activity estimates were accurate
    D. Use estimated costs to calculate CPI

39. **An activity has the following: early start (ES) of day 12, late start (LS) of day 17, early finish (EF) of day 18, and late finish (LF) of day 23. Which of the following is a true statement:**

    A. The activity is on the critical path
    B. The activity has six days of total float
    C. The activity has lag
    D. The activity is not on the critical path

40. **In order to use the project management plan to manage your project, it must be realistic. What is the best method for ensuring you have a realistic project management plan?**

    A. As project manager, use input from your project team to create the project management plan
    B. As project manager, leverage input from the senior leadership team to create the project management plan
    C. Allow the project sponsor to create the project management plan, but as project manager, provide input
    D. Allow the functional manager to create the project management plan, but as project manager, provide input

41. **You are the assigned project manager over a new development project. The project is extremely complex and unfortunately neither the customer nor your project team have extensive experience with this type of project. In addition, the schedule for the project is very aggressive. Because of certain contractual conditions, any delay will be expensive for both your company and the customer.**

    Your sponsor has agreed and provided sign-off on the project charter and the project management plan. Throughout the project, you have kept the customer's staff informed of the project's progress in both status reports and progress meetings. Near the end of your project, you are on schedule and within budget. You are notified that the project may be cancelled because the final product developed is completely unacceptable. What could be the most likely cause for this situation?

    A. The project charter and project management plan were not signed off by the customer
    B. Communication was not adequate and information was not provided to interested parties
    C. The project sponsor was not providing the appropriate amount of support
    D. Involvement by a key stakeholder was not adequate

42. **You are the project manager for the renovation project. The project is using a contract landscaping company. Upon auditing the cost plus fixed fee (CPFF) contract, you realize that overcharges are being made. The contract does not specify corrective action, therefore you should:**
    A. Add more frequent audits to the contract
    B. Continue to make the project payments
    C. Do not make any more payments until the problem is fixed
    D. Initiate legal action to recover the overpayments

43. **The scope baseline:**
    A. Is developed during the define scope process
    B. Is the most critical document within the planning process
    C. Includes the WBS, WBS dictionary, and project scope statement
    D. Is not considered part of the project management plan

44. **As project manager, you are evaluating your project schedule. Which of the following risk events would most likely interfere with attaining your project schedule's objective?**
    A. Delays in obtaining approvals required for the project
    B. A delay in the post-implementation review meeting
    C. Significant increases in the cost of materials procured for the project
    D. Contractual disputes that result in claims for increased payments

45. **The project manager is conducting a major construction project in a foreign country. Because the construction is occurring in the downtown area, there is a concern with moving the large equipment through busy streets. The local contact tells the PM that the local police will coordinate traffic for a fee which will ensure that the equipment is delivered successfully. What should the project manager do?**
    A. If the fee is not part of the initial estimate, do not pay it
    B. Pay the fee
    C. Eliminate that portion of the work
    D. The fee is a bribe, so it should not be paid

46. **You learn that a key stakeholder's high interest in the project is due to a sensitive HR issue. How do you handle this?**
    A. Because it's a high interest, document it accordingly on the stakeholder analysis matrix.
    B. Document it on the stakeholder analysis matrix but don't let anyone see it.
    C. Include it in the stakeholder analysis matrix but control the dissemination of the document to carefully identified individuals.
    D. Pretend you never heard about it.

47. **The company intranet project affects over 20 departments and you have 18 team members. The first phase of the project is complete and you have received successful performance reports from three of the departments. To recognize the successful completion of the first phase of the project, you host a luncheon for the key stakeholders, in which those successful department heads can share their success with the other 17 departments.**

    During the luncheon you overhear a manager of one of the departments discussing how he would prefer to see more regular meetings on the project. What is the first thing you should do?
    A. At the soonest date, facilitate a meeting with all stakeholders to discuss their concerns
    B. Review the communications management plan for the information distribution methods being used on the project
    C. Document the effectiveness of the luncheon in the project's lessons learned folder
    D. Send the manager that was overheard a copy of the communications management plan

48. **The project team is developing a new employee training program. The course development team has repeatedly missed their deadlines which has caused the online development team to have to crash the critical path activities multiple times. As the team lead for the online development team you are notified that the course development team will once again be missing the next deadline. You should meet with:**
    A. The project manager alone
    B. The project manager and the management team
    C. The project manager and the team lead of the course development team
    D. The team lead of the online development team

49. **Which of these is not one of the triple constraints of a project?**
    A. Scope
    B. Resources
    C. Time
    D. Cost

50. **The decomposition of deliverables into smaller, more manageable components is complete when:**
    A. Cost and duration estimates can be developed for each work package
    B. Any change requests have been evaluated
    C. Project benefits have been determined
    D. All the work elements are found in the WBS dictionary

51. **Quality audits include all of the following except:**
    A. Validating changes
    B. Confirming the implementation of approved change requests
    C. Determining if there are ineffective or inefficient policies or processes
    D. Determining if project activities comply with the organizational policies

52. **How can you best describe the difference between the cost budget and the cost baseline:**
    A. The difference is the cost account
    B. The difference is the management reserve
    C. The difference is the contingency reserve
    D. The difference is the project cost estimate

53. **The project has 15 team members located in multiple cities. The WBS, estimates for the work packages, and the schedule network diagram is complete. What would be the next thing the project manager should do?**
    A. Evaluate the staffing management plan for the implications of the multiple geographic locations
    B. Create the preliminary schedule and secure the team's approval
    C. Complete the risk management processes
    D. Sequence the activities

54. **You have just taken over an important project for your organization that is in the planning stages and you realize that seven individuals have signed the project charter. What should you be most concerned about?**
    A. Determining the project reporting structure
    B. Identifying a single sponsor
    C. Identifying who will be a member of the change control board (CCB)
    D. Additional time that will need to be spent on configuration management

55. **As PM, you are evaluating the test results for the page load speed on the new website. You learn that more than 30% of the load speeds do not meet your company's quality standards. Despite this result, you feel that the page load speed is fine and does not need to meet the company's quality level. You should:**
    A. Ensure that the future pages on the site meet the standard
    B. Change the quality standards to align with the level achieved
    C. Report the true quality level, even though it's below standards, and try to find a solution
    D. Document in your reports that the page load speed meets "our quality standards"

56. **There are 12 project team members on the website development project. A member of the project team is talking to another team member at lunch and complaining that there are a number of different people asking her to do things. If she works in a functional organization, who has the power to give her direction?**
    A. The team
    B. The sponsor
    C. The project manager
    D. The functional manager

57. **You have just started work at a new company. The company procedures require the creation of a lessons learned document for all projects. What is the best use of lessons learned?**
    A. Historical records that can be used for future projects
    B. A planning record for the current project
    C. Maintaining a record of the project manager's accomplishments
    D. Detailing the progress of the current project

58. **You have assumed the management of a project already underway. The project team has been having some disagreements. What conflict resolution technique would provide the most lasting solution?**

    A. Compromise
    B. Problem solving
    C. Forcing
    D. Smoothing

59. **A new project manager on the team has approached you for assistance with a bid for her project. There is limited scope definition and you want to protect the company from financial risk. What type of contract would you recommend to the project manager?**

    A. CPFF
    B. FFP
    C. T&M
    D. FPEPA

60. **Which of the following is not true about the distribution of project information?**

    A. It is conducted only during the execution phase of the project.
    B. The project manager should consider the appropriate presentation and facilitation techniques to employ.
    C. It is performed throughout the entire project life cycle and in all management processes.
    D. The project manager considers when to communicate face-to-face versus by email.

61. **You are the project manager for a major global network launch. Your customer has more than 90 locations world-wide. You learn that the software company has released a significant upgrade on the equipment that you are implementing. When the project began, the functionality was not available, although the customer did request it. What is the most appropriate action for you to take?**

    A. Proceed with your schedule and continue the implementation
    B. Notify your customer of the upgrade and also the associated impacts to the project's schedule and equipment functionality
    C. Adjust the implementation on the remaining sites to encompass the new upgrade
    D. Honor the original request made by the customer, implement the upgrade and adjust the schedule accordingly

62. **The project manager has been asked to do cost performance measurement as part of the performance report. What is the best way to perform cost performance measurement?**

    A. Use the 80/20 rule and verify that the life cycle cost is less than the project cost
    B. Calculate earned value and use the indexes and other calculations to report past performance and forecast future performance
    C. Focus on the amount spent last month and what will be spent the following month
    D. Ask for a percent complete from all team members and report that in the performance report

63. **You are the project manager for a $1,500,000 software development project that is using multiple international teams. In working with your project team to develop the schedule network diagram, the data architects state that quality could be improved if the data model is approved by the customer prior to starting the other design elements. They cite their source of this information as a recently published article in a leading professional journal. How would you best describe this type of input?**

    A. It is a mandatory dependency
    B. It is an industry dependency
    C. It is a discretionary dependency
    D. It is an external dependency

64. **A stakeholder contacts the project manager of the data integration project to request some additional scope that they would like to add to the project. After asking for the details in writing, the project manager works through the control scope process. When the evaluation of the requested scope change is complete, what should the project manager do next?**

    A. Perform integrated change control
    B. Identify the root cause of why the additional scope was not uncovered during project planning
    C. Ask the stakeholders if there are any additional changes expected
    D. Discuss the impact of the change with the stakeholders to be sure they understand

65. **Your team lead is a few days late with a report that will be discussed in the meeting today. Shortly before the meeting is to start, he provides you with the report and you notice some significant errors. What is the best course of action?**

    A. Cancel the meeting and personally correct the report
    B. Facilitate the meeting as expected but notify the attendees that there are errors in the report
    C. Reschedule the meeting to allow the report to be corrected
    D. Have the team lead present the information and do not voice your concern

66. **Your manager, the vice president, and his boss, the senior vice president, have requested that your assigned project begin immediately. You have created the project charter, but could not get it approved. What is the best thing you should do?**

    A. Discuss with your manager the impact of proceeding without the appropriate approval
    B. Begin work but only on the critical path activities
    C. Establish the change control procedures for the project
    D. Table this project and only focus on projects with completed charters

67. **As project manager, you receive a call from one of your project team members notifying you that there is a variance between the speed of a system on the project and the planned speed. You are surprised as that particular performance measurement was not identified in the planning process. If you evaluate whether the noted variance warrants a response, you are in what project management process group?**

    A. Monitoring and controlling
    B. Executing
    C. Initiating
    D. Closing

68. **You have a 12-month project with a budget of $50,000. The budget is allocated at $12,500 each quarter. Based on the status reports received the project is 60% complete and billed costs are $40,000. It appears that the project is over budget so you talk to the lead analyst. She tells you that there an unexpected software cost during the 2nd month of the project of $7,000 (included in the 40,000 above). The remainder of the project costs that will be billed will be resource costs (290 hours at a loaded resource rate of $80/hr). Which formula would be best to calculate ETC?**

    A. Simply get a new estimate
    B. Cannot be determined from the information provided
    C. (BAC – EV) / CPI
    D. BAC - EV

69. **Your manager has asked that you negotiate the cost with the seller. Your project has a tight budget and the seller has told you that the purchase price is fixed. Your best course of action is:**

    A. Make a good faith effort to find a way to decrease the cost
    B. Cancel the negotiations
    C. Hold off on the negotiations until you convince your manager to change his mind
    D. Continue with the negotiations but only focus on other aspects of the project

70. **You were notified that a key item you were purchasing for your project is now going to be delayed. What is the best thing you should do?**

    A. Notify your sponsor
    B. Take no action
    C. Meet with your project team to identify alternatives
    D. Notify your customer and discuss options

71. **You are conducting a quantitative risk analysis on your project in relation to potential profits earned from a new product. The estimated profit is $350,000. There is a 20% chance that it will exceed expectations at a value of $180,000, there is a 50% chance it will meet expectations at a value of $40,000, and a 30% chance it will not meet expectations at a value of ($140,000). What is the expected monetary value of the risk?**

    A. $364,000
    B. ($364,000)
    C. $14,000
    D. ($14,000)

72. **Steele Construction and the City of Burlington are having complex contract negotiations. The representative from the City of Burlington takes notes for both parties to sign. When the work is being done, Steel Construction claims that they are not required to complete work that was agreed to during negotiations because it was not included in the final contract. What statement is most accurate?**
    A. Both parties must comply with all written and signed materials from the negotiation, so they are incorrect
    B. All agreements must be upheld so they are generally incorrect
    C. There was an offer, so they are correct
    D. Both parties are only required to deliver on the terms of the contract so they are generally correct

73. **When it comes to changes, the project manager's attention is best spent on:**
    A. Making requested changes
    B. Preventing unnecessary changes
    C. Informing the stakeholders of changes
    D. Documenting all changes

74. **As a relatively new project manager in the technology organization, you are struggling to keep the project schedule on track for the new implementation. This is a large, highly visible project with more than 190 team members. The pressing issues have been resolved to your satisfaction, the SPI is 0.59, the CPI is 1.31, and you have 48 activities remaining on critical path. Based on all of this information, your monthly status report should provide the following information:**
    A. Project issues and options
    B. The project is over budget
    C. The project will not meet the target launch
    D. The project is progressing well

75. **As project manager, you are trying to complete the process redesign project but cannot seem to get the appropriate amount of attention for your project. You are finding you have little authority to assign resources and the resources are primarily focused on process-related work. What type of an organization are you working in?**
    A. Matrix
    B. Coordinator
    C. Functional
    D. Project-based

76. **Acceptance criteria is:**
    A. Determined at the end of the project
    B. Always developed by the project manager in response to stakeholder requirements
    C. Never evaluated during project close-out
    D. Performance requirements and essential conditions which must be met before project deliverables are accepted

77. **The performance measurement baseline:**
    A. Typically covers the schedule, and occasionally the cost parameters of a project, but may not include technical and quality parameters
    B. Is the approved plan for the project work against which project execution is compared and deviations are measured for management control
    C. Changes frequently to accommodate current information about the project
    D. Is the evaluation of the team member's performance on the project

78. **The approved project baseline should be changed:**
    A. To reflect approved project scope, cost, schedule, and technical changes
    B. When a sequence of activities has taken longer than originally planned
    C. When the productivity within a certain discipline has been higher than originally planned
    D. When a high-duration activity has been accomplished "out-of-sequence"

79. **The float of an activity is determined by:**
    A. The amount of lag
    B. The amount of time the activity can be delayed before it delays the critical path
    C. Performing a Monte Carlo analysis
    D. The slack time between activities

80. **An engineering project has a schedule performance index (SPI) of 0.72 and a cost performance index (CPI) of 0.89. Generally, what is the best explanation for this?**
    A. A vendor went out of business and a new one needed to be identified
    B. The scope was changed by the customer
    C. Additional material or equipment needed to be purchased
    D. A critical path activity took longer and needed more labor hours to complete

81. **A stakeholder is a(n):**
    A. Project engineer
    B. Individual or agency that controls contingency funds
    C. Person or organization that is actively involved in the project, or whose interest may be positively or negatively affected by execution or completion of the project
    D. Organization's corporate attorney

82. **Your project, Monkey-in-a-Can, has had some unexpected problems. You just learned that the tin can that will be used is actually twice as expensive as originally thought. This is going to continue to impact your overall project budget.**

    What formula would best be used to calculate your EAC?
    A. $BAC \div CPI$
    B. $AC + ETC$
    C. $AC + (BAC - EV)$
    D. $(BAC - EV) \div CPI$

83. **The project manager for a major systems integration project is notified by the quality department that they will be initiating a quality audit of the project. The team objects to the audit as they are under a lot of pressure to complete the project on time. The project manager should explain the purpose of the quality audit to the team as:**
    A. An ISO 9001 requirement
    B. A check-point on the accuracy of the costs submitted on the project
    C. An opportunity to identify ineffective and inefficient policies
    D. A verification that the customer is following the appropriate quality process

84. **In general, a project manager's technical skills:**
    A. Must be equal to or higher than any other team member's skills
    B. Must be sufficiently high to understand technical issues and explain technical decisions to others
    C. Should not be considered when selecting a project manager
    D. Are the most important criterion when selecting a project manager

85. **Jason is the project manager for a highly political organizational project. Jason needs to schedule a meeting with one of the team members but upon review of the team member's calendar, he sees a meeting with a key stakeholder.**

    Jason was not made aware of this meeting. How should Jason approach this situation?
    A. Discuss your concern with the team member's manager
    B. Discuss your concern with the team member
    C. Notify your manager about the situation
    D. Do not address the situation actively but continue to monitor his calendar

86. **The Code of Ethics and Professional Conduct applies to everyone but:**
    A. All PMI Members
    B. Non-members who hold PMI certifications
    C. Non-members who apply to commence a PMI certification process
    D. Non-members who participate in a PMP® exam prep course

87. As part of the weekly project team meeting, the project manager requests that each team member describe the work they are doing, and the project manager assigns new activities to the team members. Because there are many different activities to assign, the length of these meetings has continued to increase. This could be due to all of the following reasons except:

    A. There is no WBS
    B. There is no responsibility assignment matrix
    C. There was no resource leveling
    D. The team was not involved in project planning

88. These standards describe the conduct that we strive to uphold as practitioners. Although not easily measured, conducting ourselves in accordance with these is an expectation that we have for ourselves as professionals – it is not optional.

    A. Aspirational conduct
    B. Mandatory conduct
    C. Inspirational conduct
    D. Expected conduct

89. The new project manager that is leading a large, high-risk project appears to be making some errors. You over-hear team members criticizing the potential mistakes and questioning her credibility, experience, and the fact that she was assigned the project. On what basis would you confront the team members?

    A. Negativity in a team can disrupt project progress
    B. Per the mandatory standards, you can be held responsible for their behavior
    C. You know the new project manager and think they are being too hard on her
    D. Per the aspirational standards of respect, you have a duty to confront them

90. The project management office is considering hiring a project manager from within the organization. Upon review of the project manager's last three projects, the PMO director learns that the project manager's first project finished with a schedule variance of +150, was completed with a significantly compressed schedule and although the sponsor wrote a letter of recommendation, the key product of the project was not used. The second project had 37% more change than expected, had an SPI of 0.89 and 30 open items in the issue log upon completion. The third project had an ending cost variance of -600, used three critical resources, and needed to rework the project charter during project execution.

    Although the project budgets for each of these projects was less than $3,000, they each had 15 – 20% more changes than others of the same size. The PMO director decides against hiring the project manager. What is the best reason why this happened?

    A. Because the project manager used issue logs on projects so small, it indicates he does not have enough knowledge of processes to work in the PMO
    B. The project manager has not managed any high dollar, high priority projects and therefore does not have the necessary experience to work in the PMO
    C. Despite the fact that the project manager had three critical resources on his team, he still needed to rework the project charter, indicating that he does not have the discipline to work in the PMO
    D. The project manager did not effectively involve the stakeholders which is an indication that he does not have the knowledge to work in the PMO

91. The project manager for the systems development project is under a tight schedule. One of her team members is not performing well on the project because he is inexperienced in the type of work required. There is no one else that is available to the project manager with more experience. What is the best thing for the project manager to do?

    A. Work with the functional manager to determine appropriate activity completion incentives for the team member
    B. Arrange for the team member to get the necessary training as it pertains to his responsibilities on the project
    C. Allocate some of the project schedule reserve to backfill the hours
    D. Obtain a more skilled resource for the particular activities

92. Variance that is sporadic, unusual, and difficult to predict is the result of:

    A. Random causes
    B. Common causes
    C. Special causes
    D. External causes

93. **In quality management, a control chart helps the project manager:**
    A. Rank causes of poor quality
    B. Explore a desired future outcome
    C. Determine if a process is functioning within the set limits
    D. Focus on the most critical issues to improve quality

94. **As project manager you are allocating overall cost estimates to the individual activities to establish the cost performance baseline. What process are you doing?**
    A. Cost aggregation
    B. Cost budgeting
    C. Determine budget
    D. Control cost

95. **You have identified three critical paths in your project. How will this affect your project?**
    A. It will make the project more expensive
    B. It will make the project easier to manage
    C. It will increase the project risk
    D. It will increase the need for additional resources

96. **The project manager is managing a large, complex project with 50 stakeholders and more than 18 team members. The project manager may use _____ to ensure that the team clearly knows what work is included in each of their work packages.**
    A. The project schedule
    B. The WBS dictionary
    C. The project scope statement
    D. The product scope description

97. **What is the most commonly used formula for a three-point estimate?**
    A. (Optimistic time + most likely time + pessimistic time) / 6
    B. (Optimistic time + most likely time + pessimistic time) / 3
    C. (Optimistic time – pessimistic time) / 2
    D. (Optimistic time + 4(most likely time) + pessimistic time) / 6

98. **Your customer, LAN Corp, has accepted the completed project scope. Your PMO requires that lessons learned are completed for each project and they have not yet been completed. What is the status of your project?**
    A. Complete as the customer has accepted the deliverable
    B. Complete as the project reached the due date
    C. Incomplete until all project deliverables are complete and accepted
    D. Incomplete due to the need for re-planning

99. **You are a new project manager at the organization. Based on your past experience, you are trying to convince the management of the organization to use more structured project management practices including requiring that a project charter is completed for all projects. Which of the following would be the best reason for an organization and project managers to complete project charters?**
    A. The project charter contains a list of all of the team members
    B. The project charter provides the project history
    C. The project charter describes all of the activities to be completed
    D. The charter gives the project manager authority

100. **If the project's schedule variance (SV) is ($10k) and the planned value is $80k, what is the earned value (EV) of the project?**
    A. Unable to be calculated
    B. $70,000
    C. $90,000
    D. $80,000

101. The seller is most concerned with project scope. As such, which type of contract are they using?

    A. Cost plus fixed fee
    B. Fixed price
    C. Purchase order
    D. Time and material

102. The project manager feels that the project is going well, although there are a number of changes being made. The project manager has abided by the PMO recommendation for the large, international project and is using 18 project management processes. The project manager is not only a technical expert, he has also had training on people management and communication. Based on this information, what is the most likely cause of the project problems?

    A. The amount of project management processes should have increased because it is an international project
    B. Not all stakeholders were identified
    C. The project manager is not receiving the proper oversight from the sponsor
    D. The project manager is not trained in understanding the organization's politics

103. The new project you have been assigned has limited resources. However, the project schedule and the project budget have great flexibility. What would be the best thing to do?

    A. Perform resource leveling
    B. Crash the project
    C. Perform quantitative analysis, such as a Monte Carlo analysis
    D. Escalate your concerns to the project sponsor

104. The project manager is assigned a new retail development project in another state. The project will require the purchase of equipment for the retail store, furniture, and key inventory. The procurement process is centralized for the company and makes use of the new order system. Where would the project manager find the documented procedures for the procurement process?

    A. Enterprise environmental factors
    B. Organizational process assets
    C. Resource management plan
    D. WBS

105. As the project manager, you evaluate the construction team's work performance information for your remodel project. Based on the information you received, the $30,000 project appears to be about 40% complete. Work billed to date was $10,000 although the project budget indicates that anticipated costs were to be $12,000 by this date. When you follow-up with the construction team lead, he estimates that there will be approximately $15,000 in remaining costs. What is the EAC of this project?

    A. $15,000
    B. $25,000
    C. $5,000
    D. $12,000

106. Which of the following is an example of a cost of nonconformance?

    A. Training
    B. Product design
    C. Planning
    D. Rework

107. You are managing an international project and you anticipate there will be some conflict. The most common causes of conflict on any project are project priorities, schedules, and:

    A. Resources
    B. Management
    C. Cost
    D. Politics

108. These standards establish firm requirements, and in some cases, limit or prohibit practitioner behavior. Practitioners who do not conduct themselves in accordance with these standards will be subject to disciplinary procedures before PMI's Ethics Review Committee.
    A. Aspirational conduct
    B. Mandatory conduct
    C. Inspirational conduct
    D. Expected conduct

109. A tool for analyzing and communicating the relationships between process steps is called:
    A. A scatter diagram
    B. A control chart
    C. A trend analysis
    D. A flowchart

110. Cost of quality is used during quality assurance to:
    A. Determine if the cost of the product will meet budget requirements
    B. Persuade management to invest in quality product methods
    C. Assess the cost of implementing quality improvements
    D. Determine the most cost-effective approach when considering prevention, inspection, and repair

111. Based on the performance measures indicated in the following table, what is the cost variance (CV) for case 3?

Case	PV	AC	EV
1	$10,000	$8,000	$10,000
2	$12,000	$10,000	$11,000
3	$10,000	$8,000	$9,000
4	$10,000	$8,000	$8,000

    A. $-1,000
    B. $1,000
    C. $2,000
    D. $-2,000

112. You are the project manager for the large industrial engineering project. All of the project information for the project has been distributed according to the communications management plan. A few of the project deliverables have been changed in accordance with the change management process in the project management plan.

    During the steering committee meeting, one of the stakeholders is surprised to learn that there was a previously published change to a project deliverable. You are certain that all stakeholders received the communication which documented the change. What is the best course of action for you to take?
    A. Address the issue with your sponsor, letting her know that the stakeholder did not understand their responsibility
    B. Let the stakeholder know when the communication was published
    C. In the next steering committee meeting, address the issue in case there are others who missed the published changes
    D. Review the communications management plan and make corrections, as appropriate

113. Workarounds are determined during which risk management process?
    A. Monitor risks
    B. Plan risk responses
    C. Risk identification
    D. Perform qualitative risk analysis

114. In a fixed price (FP) contract, the fee or profit is:
    A. Calculated as a percentage of the estimated costs
    B. Not known by the buyer
    C. Determined by the buyer upon project completion
    D. Will be included as a separate cost during the invoicing process

115. The project sponsor has asked to meet with the project manager to discuss project costs. The sponsor is unhappy with the project estimate, as she feels the price should be lower. She asks the project manager to reduce the estimate by 10%. What should the project manager do?

    A. Identify and add resources that have lower hourly rates
    B. Request all work package owners to cut their estimates by 10%
    C. Provide the sponsor with the activities that will be cut
    D. As the project starts, the project manager should be identifying cost savings

116. You have been working on the development project for the past nine months. The project has consistently been behind schedule and over budget. What statement is most accurate about the completion of the project:

    A. You will end with a negative cost variance
    B. Both cost and schedule variance will be positive
    C. You will have a negative SPI
    D. The SPI of your project will be 1

117. Which of the following provides a pass/fail mechanism for criteria critical to project success?

    A. Weighted scorecard
    B. Expert judgment
    C. Seller rating system
    D. Screening system

118. Which of the following is the higher point on Maslow's hierarchy of needs?

    A. Physiologic
    B. Self esteem
    C. Love and belonging
    D. Security

119. All of the manual or automated tools and techniques used to collect, archive, and distribute project information on a project are known as the:

    A. Project management information system
    B. Communications plan
    C. Project management enterprise software
    D. Communications and feedback system

120. If a risk event has a 30% chance of occurring and the impact of the risk will be $9,000, what does $2,700 represent?

    A. The risk value
    B. The expected monetary value of the risk
    C. The amount of contingency to allocate
    D. The present value

121. The overall process of managing changes that affect the function or characteristics of the deliverable is known as:

    A. Managing by exception
    B. Change control management
    C. Managing by objective
    D. Configuration management

122. Your project team member is very committed to the project being very successful. However, upon review of the project performance report she realizes that the project is currently running behind schedule. She notices that the delay will cause one of her activities to be scheduled while she is out of the office on scheduled vacation and will be unable to work on the activity. How should you handle this situation?

    A. Add the issue to the issue log
    B. Notify the project sponsor
    C. Update the project status report with this information
    D. Recommend corrective action

123. A collection of formal, documented procedures that defines the steps by which the project may be changed is known as:

    A. Managing by exception
    B. Change control system
    C. Configuration management
    D. Managing by objective

124. You are out to dinner with your friend to celebrate his new job. He tells you that the position required a PMP® credential. You know that he does not have his PMP® although you recently received your credential. What is the most appropriate way to handle this?

    A. Report him to PMI
    B. Do nothing as it is after work hours
    C. Advise your friend to pursue his PMP® as it is beneficial for career development
    D. Do nothing as you do not work at that company

125. You are six months into a 12-month, $350,000 project. By this point in your project, you had budgeted to spend $180,000. You have paid $170,000. What statement is most accurate?

    A. The project is approximately 3% ahead of schedule
    B. The project is approximately 3% over budget
    C. If there was a recurring variance, the project will spend approximately $170,000 on the remaining work
    D. The project resources will need to work more efficiently in order to complete the project within the budget allocated

126. The person responsible for ensuring change control is processed through the integrated change control process is the:

    A. Project manager
    B. Functional manager
    C. Project sponsor
    D. President

127. You are the project manager in a matrix organization and you determine that there are additional human resources needed. From whom would you request the additional resources?

    A. The project sponsor
    B. The PMO
    C. The functional manager
    D. The team lead

128. Trend analysis is used to:

    A. Improve variance reporting
    B. Create change requests
    C. Mitigate the harmful effects of scope creep
    D. Forecast future project performance

129. Your team is in the process of defining the project activities. One of the team members feels that an activity should be included however the other team member believes that the activity is not part of the project, based on the scope statement. How should you handle this as the project manager?

    A. Encourage the team to arrive at a consensus
    B. Discuss with the sponsor and seek clarification
    C. Make the decision based on your knowledge of the project
    D. Ask senior management for their perspective

130. You are the project manager and you identify a defect in the deliverable that is due to the customer today. You realize that the customer does not have sufficient technical knowledge to notice the problem. The deliverable meets the contract requirements but not your quality standard. What should you do?

    A. Let the customer know the deliverable will be late
    B. Approach the customer with the issue
    C. Document the problem in lessons learned so that future projects won't repeat the same mistake
    D. Deliver the product and seek formal acceptance from the customer

131. "500 rejected parts" is an example of:

A. Attribute sampling
B. Variable sampling
C. Random sampling
D. Stratified sampling

132. Many quality problems:

A. Originate on the shop floor because of waste and rework
B. Could be eliminated if supervisors monitored their work more closely
C. Originate in the QA organization where the ultimate responsibility for quality rests
D. Could be avoided by management taking action on potential quality improvement ideas

133. Activity A has a duration 3 days, activity B has a duration of 6 days, activity C has a duration of 4 days (and is dependent on both A and B completing), activity D has a duration of 7 days, activity E has a duration of 8 days (and both D and E are dependent on C completing), and activity F is 5 days (and is dependent on activity E).

If activity C is delayed by three days:

A. The duration of the project is 36 days
B. The project is delayed by 3 days
C. There is no effect on the schedule
D. Activity D will now take 7 days

134. Activity A has a duration 3 days, activity B has a duration of 6 days, activity C has a duration of 4 days (and is dependent on both A and B completing), activity D has a duration of 7 days, activity E has a duration of 8 days (and both D and E are dependent on C completing), and activity F is 5 days (and is dependent on activity E).

What is the total duration?

A. Unable to determine
B. 23 days
C. 17 days
D. 33 days

135. Activity A has a duration 3 days, activity B has a duration of 6 days, activity C has a duration of 4 days (and is dependent on both A and B completing), activity D has a duration of 7 days, activity E has a duration of 8 days (and both D and E are dependent on C completing), and activity F is 5 days (and is dependent on activity E).

What is the free float of activity F?

A. 0 days
B. 5 days
C. 6 days
D. (5) days

136. The customer for your IT renovation project has notified you that they want to add another server and five more software packages to your project. What is the most appropriate handling of this?

A. Once approved through the change control process, utilize contingency reserve to cover the costs
B. Once approved through the change control process, utilize management reserve to cover the costs
C. Document the request and update the project management plan
D. Submit a corrective action request to the change control board

137. You are evaluating your project using a tornado diagram. What process are you most likely conducting?

A. Performing integrated change control
B. Performing a qualitative risk analysis
C. Monitoring and controlling the project team
D. Performing a quantitative risk analysis

138. You have been managing a long-term project involving resources in seven different countries. The performance of some of your team members has been exceptional and based on exceeding their target goals, you have been authorized to promote two of your team members.

    The highest performer on your team is a female that lives in a country where women are not permitted in management roles. How should you best handle this?

    A. Because it is against the cultural considerations for that country, it would not be appropriate to promote her
    B. Because she achieved the performance required for promotion, promoting her is appropriate
    C. Because she is only a project team member, not promoting her could be based on her role
    D. Because it is culturally unacceptable, notify her that she would have been promoted but cannot be because of the circumstances

139. You are managing a project to implement a new employee recognition program. This project will include multiple components, such as the development of an intranet web page, an employee survey mechanism, a funding analysis, a role delineation study, and a manager training program. For the manager training program, there will be 80 managers trained at an estimated cost of $65 per manager for the training module. This will be the first time you will be overseeing the development of a web page or conducting a funding analysis. Based on past projects, you have received estimates for the role delineation study ranging from 3 days to 10 days, with the most likely timeframe being 5 days.

    What would be the most appropriate estimating technique to use for the role delineation study?

    A. Parametric estimating because it leverages historical information
    B. Use 3-point estimating because it would be the most reliable technique
    C. Analogous estimating because it would be the most reliable technique
    D. Analogous estimating because it leverages historical information

140. As the third phase of the multi-year project nears completion, your team lead provides the marketing manager with copies of the phase deliverables for her review and sign-off. The team lead is performing:

    A. Scope validation
    B. Quality control
    C. Administrative closure
    D. Quality assurance

141. You have assumed the leadership of a high-exposure project that is approximately 30% complete. The sponsor of the project is the vice president of operations and is under a lot of pressure to deliver the project within the timeframe and budget allocated. He has demonstrated heightened sensitivity to any indications of project problems.

    Upon conducting an analysis, you determine that the project is running behind schedule. Your sponsor has advised you not to include that information in the project performance report due to the implications. What is the best action for you to take?

    A. As the sponsor dictates the communication plan, do not include the schedule information
    B. Because it is early in the project and there is time for correction, do not include the schedule information
    C. Report the schedule information but after detailing the positive progress of the project
    D. Report that the project is behind schedule

142. Which of the following techniques is most likely not used in estimating project durations?

    A. Parametric
    B. Bottom-up
    C. Analogous
    D. PERT

143. The project has experienced a higher number of defects than expected. The team has conducted an analysis of the root causes of the defects and identified more than 15 causes. Upon further research, the team finds that two of the causes account for the majority of the defects.

    Which statement is most accurate about the quality issues?

    A. They were identified through quantitative risk analysis
    B. They are reflective of Juran's quality approach
    C. They would best be illustrated in a control chart
    D. They would be an input to the cost of conformance evaluation

144. Your project is entering the development phase and it is running behind schedule. You have identified a vendor that can produce a key component in less time than your internal team.

    Hiring the vendor is an example:

    A. Risk sharing
    B. The cost of non-conformance
    C. An analogous evaluation
    D. Risk transference

145. You are under contract with a local construction company. The cost-reimbursable contract includes the payment of an incentive for each day the construction firm delivers early: $500 per day. The costs are estimated at $72,000 and there is a 50/50 split on actual costs that are under or over the estimate.

    If the vendor delivers five days early and the total costs are $65,000, what is the final contract value?

    A. $67,500
    B. $78,000
    C. $71,000
    D. $75,000

146. The kitchen renovation project is underway and you have received the first delivery of cabinets. Upon installation, your superintendent informs you that the cabinets do not fit into the space that has been allocated. The change request to modify the cabinets is an example of:

    A. Changing the scope and updating the project baselines
    B. Configuration management
    C. A preventive action
    D. Scope creep

147. Which statement is least accurate regarding a reserve analysis?

    A. A reserve analysis is used during activity duration estimating
    B. A reserve analysis is used during both the cost estimating and budget determination processes
    C. A reserve analysis is conducted during qualitative risk analysis to justify the amount of contingency funding
    D. A reserve analysis is conducted during risk monitoring and controlling to ensure the amount of reserve or contingency is appropriate given the project uncertainty

148. Your project team has provided you with the following information:

Activity	Original Cost Estimate	Revised Cost Estimate	Original Duration	Revised Duration
A	$100	$400	8 days	4 days
B	$300	$500	6 days	5 days
C	$500	$800	10 days	9 days
D	$200	$300	4 days	3 days

    What activity would be the best candidate for crashing?

    A. Activity A
    B. Activity C
    C. Activity B
    D. Activity D

149. Your project team has provided you with the following information:

Activity	Original Cost Estimate	Revised Cost Estimate	Original Duration	Revised Duration
A	$100	$400	8 days	4 days
B	$300	$500	6 days	5 days
C	$500	$800	10 days	9 days
D	$200	$300	4 days	3 days

If activity D has two days of float and is crashed, what is the result?

A. The project duration has been decreased by two days
B. The activity will now have two days of free float
C. The project duration has been decreased by three days
D. The activity will now have three days of float

150. **You are managing the ALEXI project, a multi-year project that involves resources from three geographic locations. In estimating the YZ component's duration, your team leads have provided you with a best case estimate of 12 days and a worst case estimate of 17 days, based on resource availability.**

What is the most likely duration?

A. 14 days
B. Unable to determine
C. 14.5 days
D. 15 days

151. **You have accepted a new role as a PMO project manager. As part of your responsibilities, you are auditing some recent projects. Upon completion, project A, a $750,000 project, was 10% over budget but delivered the project 10% earlier than anticipated. What is the final PV of the project?**

A. $825,000
B. $750,000
C. $675,000
D. Because the project is complete, there is no longer a PV

152. **You are the project manager for an 8-month project. The system development component of the project will cost $10,000 that will be payable at 20% in the first month and the remainder in the third month. The hardware purchase will cost $18,000 that will be payable in the fourth month. The resource fees will be $24,000 billed equally across the life of the project.**

What statement is most accurate if you have a funding limit of $20,000 per month?

A. Because the total project costs do not exceed $160,000 there are no areas of concern
B. The project work in the third month is most at-risk
C. Work may need to be re-planned in the fourth month
D. The funding limit is exceeded in more than one month and should be identified as a risk

153. **You are the project manager for an 8-month project. The system development component of the project will cost $10,000 that will be payable at 20% in the first month and the remainder in the third month. The hardware purchase will cost $18,000 that will be payable in the fourth month. The resource fees will be $24,000 billed equally across the life of the project.**

What is the PV of the project at the end of the sixth month?

A. $49,000
B. $43,000
C. $40,000
D. $46,000

154. You are the project manager for an 8-month project. The system development component of the project will cost $10,000 that will be payable at 20% in the first month and the remainder in the third month. The hardware purchase will cost $18,000 that will be payable in the fourth month. The resource fees will be $24,000 billed equally across the life of the project.

    If the project is 70% complete by the end of the fifth month, what statement is most accurate?

    A. The project will not meet the intended completion date
    B. The project appears to be running behind schedule
    C. The project will be delivered early
    D. The project appears to be running ahead of schedule

155. The project manager is evaluating the cost estimates for the MIAC project. The project has a budget of $150,000. For product launch, the team will be producing 100,000 units at a cost of 0.20 each. For the early project work, the project manager leverages information from a previous project and estimates the costs to be $90,000. In addition, the project manager meets with the web-based interface team assigned to the project and uses their estimate of $20,000 for the interface component.

    What estimating techniques were used?

    A. Bottom-up, PERT, and parametric
    B. PERT, bottom-up, and expert judgment
    C. Expert judgment, parametric, and analogous
    D. Analogous, parametric, and three-point

156. Your project is about 60% complete and has been progressing ahead of schedule and slightly under budget. You hear that your project is going to be terminated. What is the first thing you should do?

    A. Review the project management plan for project closure procedures
    B. Create a lessons learned report
    C. Escalate to the sponsor
    D. Have your team members immediately stop work

157. You are working with the work package owners to develop the project schedule. One of the work package owners provides you with the following information:

    The work will begin on Monday, 12 May and will be complete by Friday, 23 May

    Work days are Monday through Friday, six hours per day

    Monday, 19 May is a holiday

    What statement is most accurate?

    A. The total elapsed time is two weeks
    B. The total effort is 60 staff-hours
    C. The total duration is 12 work-days
    D. The elapsed time and duration is two weeks

158. Risk audits are performed during what process:

    A. Plan risk responses
    B. Plan risk management
    C. Monitor and control project work
    D. Monitor risks

159. You have identified four key stakeholders for your project: the project sponsor, the vice president of marketing, the vice president of operations, and the CIO. The sponsor has been with the company for six years and is well-known throughout the organization. The vice president of marketing is new to the organization but has pledged support and resources for the project. The marketing resources will be the primary project resources. The vice president of operations will be providing a few SMEs to the project, although resources are limited within her teams. This project is not a priority for her. The CIO has a high-level awareness of the project but his level of support is not known.

    Who would you prioritize your time with?

    A. The CIO
    B. The project sponsor
    C. The vice president of marketing
    D. The vice president of operations

160. The construction project for the new high-rise building is running behind schedule and over budget. Upon evaluation of the project performance to-date, you identify that one key reason for the delays is the inexperienced project foreman. You make a recommendation to the change control board to partner the foreman with a more experienced foreman in order to mitigate the risk associated with his inexperience. Once the change is approved, what is the next thing you should do?

A. Archive the change control report
B. Update the WBS and schedule to reflect the additional time and effort needed for the mentoring
C. Update the project baselines
D. Consult with the experienced project foreman and provide him with the background information

161. Because your team is geographically disbursed and will be a virtual team, you are concerned regarding effective communication between the team members. To mitigate the risk, you recommend video teleconferences once per month with the key team members. What statement is most accurate regarding the video teleconferences?

A. Using teleconferences will increase the likelihood of project acceptance by the end-user
B. Allowing for interactive communication will promote team cohesiveness and development
C. Including key individuals will decrease the probability of scheduling activities on the critical path
D. They will only be effective if there is an appropriately structured workaround strategy

162. You are evaluating the vendor invoices against their completed deliverables. You are conducting what process?

A. Planning procurement management
B. Conducting procurements
C. Closing procurements
D. Controlling procurements

163. Your project is not achieving the quality standards that you had previously anticipated. You map out the processes in place in order to determine if and where there is a breakdown in the process. A tool for analyzing and communicating the relationships between process steps is called:

A. A scatter diagram
B. A control chart
C. A trend analysis
D. A flowchart

164. Your team member has completed the weekly performance report for the project. The current earned value measurements were included: schedule performance index 1.3, cost performance index .95, and TCPI 1.5. In association with these measurements, the team member could state:

A. The project is trending under budget and additional funding may be required
B. The project is trending behind schedule and additional time may be required
C. The project appears to have more work remaining than funds remaining
D. The new forecasted time to complete will most likely exceed the original budget at completion

165. For your park development project, you have hired a vendor to install all of the concrete walkways. In the past, your organization has had some quality issues with this particular vendor. You need to mitigate the risks associated with poor quality. What would be the most appropriate response?

A. Insist on the use of a cost-reimbursable contract
B. Assign a team member to visit the job site to monitor the vendor's results on a pre-determined schedule
C. Develop a workaround to be used in the event of quality issues
D. Escalate the issue to the sponsor for resolution

166. The estimated costs for your project are $795,000. Upon evaluation of the project and the associated project risks, you decide to allocate an additional 10% to account for the uncertainty on the project. The sponsor has allocated 15% to account for any major scope changes that may be requested by the customer. What is the project budget?

A. $874,500
B. $795,000
C. $1,005,675
D. $914,250

167. Activity 1.4 has a duration of 5 days and 1 day of FF. Activity 1.11, the successor activity, has a duration of 6 days and an ES of 28. Activity 1.7 has a duration of 15 days and 3 days of total float. If activity 1.4 is delayed by 3 days, what is the impact?

   A. The float on activity 1.7 will be consumed
   B. There will be no effect on the project
   C. The ES of activity 1.11 will be 30
   D. The float on 1.4 will increase to 4 days

168. You are the project manager over the project to upgrade all existing patient systems to comply with electronic record requirements, as determined by the US government. What would be the most appropriate technique to establish a reserve for the schedule duration, budget, estimated cost, or funds for a project based upon the remaining level of project uncertainty:

   A. Risk reassessment
   B. Reserve analysis
   C. Baseline establishment
   D. Risk audit

169. Your project is 70% complete and you are conducting an earned value analysis to include in your project performance report. You are evaluating the team members' performance, work package percent complete, the actual costs that have occurred to date and the overall project budget estimate. What factor represents that estimated value of the work actually completed:

   A. Actual cost (AC)
   B. Planned value (PV
   C. Earned value (EV)
   D. Actual work (AW)

170. You have finalized all of your subsidiary plans. With your approved project management plan, what should you do next?

   A. Execute the tasks as defined in the project plan
   B. Maximize team performance
   C. Conduct a kick-off meeting
   D. Receive authorization to proceed with the project

171. You have taken over the management of a strategy-critical project that is exceptionally time-sensitive. The team members represent the different divisions that will be most impacted by the implementation of the project and have been known to have very strong opinions about the project requirements and the development of the project deliverables. The previous project manager had difficulty managing conflict within the team and this has caused the project to be delayed. You decide to train the team on conflict resolution strategies. This is an example of:

   A. Risk avoidance
   B. Risk exploitation
   C. Risk acceptance
   D. Risk mitigation

172. You are planning the project work and evaluating any schedule dependencies that exist using a PDM. What process are you most likely conducting?

   A. A qualitative risk analysis
   B. Sequencing activities
   C. Determining the budget
   D. A quantitative risk analysis

173. You are updating your project performance report and preparing it for distribution. Your project is progressing well, and the latest milestones were all achieved on schedule. One of your team leads has left the company and a replacement should be identified within the next week. Four of your resources are new to the company. Your CPI measurements for the past three months are: January .9, February .97, March 1.2.

What method of communication would be the most appropriate method of communication given the risks of the project?

A. Because it is a performance report, push communication should be used
B. Because the project is trending over budget, interactive communication should be used
C. Because of the change in the team lead, emergent communication should be used followed up by a pull communication
D. Because the project is performing well, pull communication should be used

174. An activity has the following: early start (ES) of day 12, late start (LS) of day 17, early finish (EF) of day 18, and late finish (LF) of day 23. Which of the following is a true statement?

A. The activity is on the critical path
B. The activity has six days of total float
C. The activity has lag
D. The activity is not on the critical path

175. The Fun-in-a-Can Corporation is hoping to expand their product line. After evaluating multiple project ideas, the Monkey-in-a-Can (MIAC) project was selected by the steering committee as the best product development to pursue. Upon conducting a thorough benefits analysis, the MIAC project has a positive NPV and an IRR that exceeds the company's hurdle rate. In addition, there has been an increased demand for "monkey" products since the recent surge in popularity of these jungle creatures.

An enterprise environmental factor would be:

A. The positive NPV
B. The demand for monkey products
C. The steering committee selection
D. The IRR

176. You are implementing approved changes and risk actions. What process group would these tasks fall under?

A. Monitoring and controlling
B. Integrated change control
C. Closing
D. Executing

177. You have taken over a project that has been rumored to be behind schedule and over budget. Many of the team members are disengaged and are resentful of working on the project. The previous project manager left the company abruptly and provided no turnover documentation. Your first week on the project your primary vendor shuts down. This was not identified as a risk on the risk register. What is the first step you should take?

A. Invoke the contingency plan
B. Mitigate the risk
C. Implement a workaround
D. Evaluate the project management plan for additional change control procedures

178. You have recently assumed the management of a project that has been underway for six months. Upon review of the risk register, you believe that many project risks have not been identified. As such, you decide to interview the key stakeholders and team members to get their input. Which of the following is a weakness of using interviews for risk identification?

A. Used with stakeholders, it can decrease engagement, as they will feel the time is better spent on project activities
B. Specific risks cannot be addressed in detail, only in summary
C. Additional information, such as concerns and alternate perspectives could be surfaced that are non-risk-related
D. The experience and perspectives of others could lead to the identification of opportunities that had not been previously documented

179. Your team has identified risks on the project, performed a qualitative risk analysis and determined the most appropriate responses for the prioritized risks. Which statement is least accurate regarding the updates to, and communication of, the risk register?

   A. The risk register should be written to a level of detail that corresponds with the priority ranking and the planned response
   B. Risks evaluated to low priority should be included on a "watchlist"
   C. The top 20 highest priority risks should be addressed in detail
   D. The risk register should include residual risks and the contingency plans

180. Deliverables are not considered verified until they have completed what process?

   A. Inspection
   B. Quality assurance
   C. Verify scope
   D. Control quality

181. You are nearing the completion of your project. Upon evaluation of the previously identified risks, you realize that 18 of the 35 risks can be closed. What is the appropriate handling of closed risks?

   A. Delete the risks from the risk register
   B. Indicate that the risk is closed on the risk register
   C. Reassign the risk owner to another risk
   D. Perform a quantitative analysis to ensure that the risk can be closed

182. Work performance data and work performance information differ in that:

   A. Work performance data is an output of control schedule
   B. Work performance information represents the data from a variance analysis
   C. Work performance data is developed through the control scope process
   D. Work performance information is an output of direct and manage project execution

183. You are closing your project. Of the following tasks, what must occur first?

   A. Collate lessons learned
   B. Transfer the ownership of the deliverables
   C. Obtain financial, legal, and administrative closure
   D. Obtain final acceptance of the project deliverables

184. You have been working with a vendor to develop an online training module. The project is 60% complete and the vendor has asked that the payment due dates be changed to 5 business days prior to the agreed payment date.

   This is an example of:

   A. A constructive change
   B. A scope change
   C. A preventive action
   D. A corrective action

185. You are delivering the final product to the customer. The product was thoroughly tested through the quality control process and has been validated against the documented product requirements. The project delivered at the cost anticipated and within the requested timeframe. If the client does not accept the deliverable because it is not what they wanted, what statement is most accurate:

   A. The product is high quality because it meets the documented product requirements
   B. The product is high grade because the schedule and budget objectives were met
   C. The product is low quality because it does not meet the customer's requirements
   D. The product is low grade because it does not meet the customer's requirements

186. You assumed the management of a multi-year project that was only 10% complete. Over the last 18 months, the project has been progressing very well, meeting all defined technical performance accomplishments. As the project nears closing, you provide the final deliverables to the customer. Upon review, the customer rejects the deliverables, stating that they do not meet the documented requirements. What statement is most accurate?

   A. Because the project has met the technical performance requirements, any changes to the deliverables would be a scope change
   B. Because the project is in alignment with the objectives, the non-acceptance is not appropriate
   C. Because the deliverable does not meet the customer requirements, any changes would be a defect repair
   D. Because the deliverable is the final project requirement, the customer was at-fault for not providing accurate requirements

187. Your $30,000 project is in the last phase. As project manager, you are evaluating the following information: the project is 60% complete and the billed costs to-date are $17,000.

   Based on this information, you know that:

   A. The project is running behind schedule
   B. The project is over-budget
   C. The project will not meet the target delivery dates
   D. The project has a favorable TCPI

188. Used to collect requirements, this technique consolidates ideas generated through brainstorming into a map to reflect commonalities and differences in understanding:

   A. Affinity diagram
   B. Nominal group mapping
   C. Mind mapping
   D. Delphi technique

189. Which statement regarding leadership and management is the most accurate?

   A. Leadership is about guiding, influencing, and collaborating whereas management is about positional power
   B. Management focuses on operational issues whereas leadership is power-based, relying on control
   C. Leadership and management are synonymous terms and are used to describe the project manager's role
   D. Management challenges the status quo and creates a long-term vision whereas leadership involves acting as a servant leader.

190. To develop the project charter, the project manager and key stakeholders will leverage the business documents, including a business case and the benefits management plan. Which statement most accurately defines how these documents differ?

   A. The benefits management plan is a component of the business case
   B. The benefits management plan is based on the business case and a needs assessment
   C. The benefits management plan will include benefit measurements such as NPV, IRR or ROI
   D. The benefits management plan is created by the project manager whereas the business case is developed by the project sponsor

191. As the newly assigned project manager to the new product development project, you are reviewing the project documentation and meeting with the team leads. In the meetings, the team leads have expressed significant concerns about the project. The project is due to launch near the holidays and there is concern that the holidays will impact the schedule. The technical experts do not feel that they can deliver the infrastructure necessary to support the new product. According to the finance department, the budget for the project will be allocated on a periodic basis, versus being fully funded from the beginning. What is the first thing you address?

   A. The first thing to address is the periodic budget
   B. The first thing to address is the schedule implications
   C. The first thing to address is the technical infrastructure
   D. The first thing to address is the project resourcing

192. Your organization has transitioned to more adaptive projects. You are educating your team regarding release planning for an adaptive project. Which sequence is correct?

   A. The prioritized features drive the iteration plans. The iteration plans create the release plans.
   B. The features drive the user stories which drive the product vision.
   C. The user stories drive the tasks. The tasks drive the product vision and the release plans.
   D. The product vision drives the roadmap which drives the release plans. The release plans establish the iterations and the iteration plans schedule the feature development.

193. It is your first time managing a large project for your new employer. Unlike your previous projects, this project requires the management of a significant budget. You are working with the finance organization liaison on the budget and the contingency. Which statement is least accurate regarding the project budget?

   A. The control accounts include the management reserve and the project budget
   B. The work package estimates include the activity cost estimate and the activity contingency reserve
   C. The project budget includes the control accounts and the management reserve
   D. The cost baseline includes the work package estimates and the contingency reserve

194. The project sponsor has requested a meeting with you to discuss the new product that is under development. The product is being developed for a very important client and it is essential that this customer is very satisfied with the end result. What technique would you leverage?

   A. Nominal group technique
   B. Design for X
   C. Theory of Constraints
   D. Quality assurance

195. This theory is based on the concept that any system is "only as good as the weakest link".

   A. Kaizen
   B. Design for X
   C. Theory of Constraints
   D. Lean management

196. A few of your project team members have approached you regarding the team dynamic on your high-stress infrastructure project. The team members feel that boundaries are not being respected and that the behavior is impacting the work of the project. What could have prevented this disruption?

   A. Developing a resource assignment matrix
   B. Implementing peer-to-peer coaching
   C. Co-locating the team
   D. Creating a team charter

197. Self-awareness, self-regulation, motivation, empathy, and social skills are all elements of:

   A. Emotional intelligence
   B. Servant leadership
   C. Command-and-control management
   D. Group facilitation

198. The risk characteristics of propinquity and proximity can best be described as:

   A. Proximity is the location of the risk event to the project team and propinquity is the extent of property damage expected
   B. Propinquity is the degree to which the risk is perceived in importance and proximity is the period of time before the risk would have an impact
   C. Proximity is the period of time that may elapse after a risk has occurred before it is discovered, and propinquity is the degree to which the risk will have an impact on the project constraints
   D. Propinquity is the appropriateness of the risk management approach to the project and proximity is the relationship of the risk to other projects in the portfolio

199. This data analysis technique is used to analyze the interrelationships between different project variables that contributed to the project outcomes.

   A. Root cause analysis
   B. Nominal group analysis
   C. Regression analysis
   D. Lessons learned analysis

200. **Which of the following is not one of the 5Cs of written communication?**
   A. Clear purpose
   B. Concise expression and elimination of excess words
   C. Coherent flow of ideas
   D. Check for understanding

End Time:_____

PMP Final Practice Exam

Answer Key

1. **Answer: C**

   Referring to project objectives. It is important that objectives are measurable. Only two of the objectives provided in the question are measurable, therefore those would be the two that you would include.

2. **Answer: B**

   A CPI less than 1 indicates the project is over-budget to date.

3. **Answer: D**

   After the WBS is completed, the next step is to decompose the WBS into the activity list. You cannot do the RAM until the activity list is complete.

4. **Answer: C**

   NPV is already discounted for the term or length of the project so the highest NPV is always the best selection.

5. **Answer: C**

   Scope creep is unmanaged changes to the project scope.

6. **Answer: C**

   Because the project is significantly behind schedule, the best option is to provide an evaluation of the project to the sponsor.

7. **Answer: A**

   Although the customer wanted no contact, per your professional responsibility, you need to, at a minimum, check in with them occasionally to verify scope.

8. **Answer: B**

   This question is asking about the time processes. A is wrong because the schedule is not yet complete, C is wrong because again, we don't know if we have resources, and D is wrong because this question isn't talking about the project management plan. There B is the only right answer.

9. **Answer: D**

   Because the SPI is less than 1.0, it indicates the project is behind schedule.

10. **Answer: B**

    The sender should empathize, or show concern for the perspective of the receiver.

11. **Answer: D**

    Remember that analogous estimating is a combination of expert judgment and historical information.

12. **Answer: B**

    The 30% probability is uniform across all 12 months.

13. **Answer: C**

    Earned value is the estimated value of the work actually completed.

14. **Answer: A**

    In order to manage quality, you will need the quality control measurements. These will be compared to the quality metrics from the plan quality process.

15. **Answer: B**

In order to begin manufacturing you must have a design of the product you are building. This is inherent to the work being done and as such, would be considered mandatory.

16. **Answer: B**

Given there is a strong probability the project will be cancelled, you are responsible for protecting resource hours and should postpone the meeting versus wasting your time or their time.

17. **Answer: C**

This is describing decomposing the work within the WBS down to work packages. All of the answers describe a work package accept that it will be done by one person. It will be managed by one person but there might be multiple team members involved in completing the work.

18. **Answer: B**

Code of Ethics values are responsibility, respect, fairness and honesty (integrity is not one of the values).

19. **Answer: C**

Early involvement is critical to preventing late changes (thus more costly changes) in the project. You cannot remove the stakeholder (A), you cannot exert authority to "prove a point" (B), and going above the stakeholder would be inappropriate (D).

20. **Answer: C**

A cost-plus contract would have the most invoices to audit.

21. **Answer: B**

The PMO provides support functions to the project manager.

22. **Answer: A**

Estimates generally include a contingency amount to account for any risk. To be most accurate, that contingency can be removed from the estimate to re-forecast.

23. **Answer: C**

Because there is so much chaos and confusion within the team, one of the best options would be to have the team develop new groups rules which define their values and expectations for the team.

24. **Answer: C**

You always need to involve the other stakeholders in the risk processes, not just your project team.

25. **Answer: D**

Because it is using the number of units and the unit cost, this is parametric estimating.

26. **Answer: D**

As part of the code of ethics, you are required to be transparent with information that affects the customer.

27. **Answer: A**

Before finalizing the schedule, the information needs to be added to a schedule network diagram and have the team involved in the estimating process.

28. **Answer: D**

The project manager does not have procurement authority so is generally not the lead during the negotiations, however, the PM will supply an understanding of the project and the risks the project may be affected by.

29. **Answer: C**

Because you are assessing the work against the quality metric (as defined in the quality management plan), this is QC.

30. **Answer: C**

Because B has 40 days of float, changing the duration by 20 hours does not consume all of the float and as such does not shift the critical path. Activities D and F (combined at 34 hours) are occurring at the same time as activity E (25 hours) and therefore E has 9 hours of float. As such, activities A, C, D, and F are on the critical path.

31. **Answer: B**

    Key word in here is "response" - response means work that has to happen to change the impact or effect of the risk. Any and all work must be reflected in the WBS.

32. **Answer: D**

    The first part of the question is superfluous. The general rule when conversing with someone over the phone is having them repeat back to you what you said.

33. **Answer: B**

    Risk response control is when the risk responses are evaluated for effectiveness. If the original response is not working appropriately, additional response development is required.

34. **Answer: A**

    The only action you can take is to notify the other PMs regarding the situation with the seller.

35. **Answer: A**

    In a matrix organization communication needs to flow both horizontally and vertically (to the project team and to the leadership of the organization).

36. **Answer: C**

    A key step in active problem solving is confirming that the action taken truly did solve the problem.

37. **Answer: A**

    Because you have quality standards, it implies that the Plan Quality process has been done. The manager has data regarding the actual work that's being done (thus QC), so in order to evaluate the QC results against the quality plan, you will need a QA team.

38. **Answer: C**

    An analogous estimate is top-down and therefore not as accurate. To reach a more accurate estimate, you will need to do a bottom-up estimate.

39. **Answer: D**

    Because the activity has float (LS of 17 minus ES of 12 = 5 days of float), the activity is not on the critical path.

40. **Answer: A**

    For the project management plan to be realistic, it's important the project manager seek the feedback of the project team.

41. **Answer: D**

    Most questions that focus on a deliverable being unacceptable is usually due to the fact that a key stakeholder was not involved.

42. **Answer: B**

    Because the contract does not specifically address any corrective actions, you must continue to make the payments. If you did not make the payment, you would now be considered in breach of contract which could result in legal action against your organization.

43. **Answer: C**

    The scope baseline includes: WBS, WBS Dictionary, and the Scope Statement.

44. **Answer: A**

    The correct answer is delays in obtaining approvals that are required. Post-implementation review meeting will be after the project is completed, and the other two answers are referring to cost issues.

45. **Answer: B**

    Because you are paying a government entity (the police), it is ok to pay the fee.

46. **Answer: C**

    You document the reason for their involvement however, the dissemination of the document must be controlled.

47. **Answer: B**

    The first step for resolving many problems is to refer to the plan, in this case the communication management plan.

48. **Answer: C**

Because you're a team lead, not the PM, you should meet with the PM and the team lead of the other group causing the problems.

49. **Answer: B**

The triple constraint is cost, time, and scope.

50. **Answer: A**

Decomposition is complete when cost and duration estimates can be developed for each work package.

51. **Answer: A**

A quality audit does not validate changes.

52. **Answer: B**

The baseline does not include the management reserve.

53. **Answer: B**

The fact that the schedule network diagram is complete would indicate that the activities have already been sequenced. The next step is to create the schedule.

54. **Answer: B**

More than one sponsor will cause significant problems for a project. A project should only have one sponsor.

55. **Answer: C**

To comply with the professional responsibilities of being "transparent" with project information, you should report the true quality level and seek a solution.

56. **Answer: D**

In a functional organization, the functional manager always has ultimate authority.

57. **Answer: A**

The lessons learned become part of the corporate knowledge base and will be used to future projects.

58. **Answer: B**

For the most lasting solution, problem-solving is the most appropriate conflict resolution technique.

59. **Answer: A**

Because there is limited scope definition, it would not be possible to use a fixed price contract. T&M wouldn't be appropriate to protect the company from risk. So the best option is CPFF - Cost reimbursable because the scope is not fully defined, and fixed fee so that those costs can be predicted.

60. **Answer: A**

Information is distributed throughout the project.

61. **Answer: B**

This is a question about professional responsibilities and transparency in communication. It is important to notify your customer.

62. **Answer: B**

Cost performance measurement is done by calculating earned value and other calculations.

63. **Answer: C**

This is a discretionary dependency (based on someone's professional judgment).

64. **Answer: A**

Once the evaluation is complete, the next step is to put the change request through the integrated change control process.

65. **Answer: C**

This speaks to managing resource hours carefully. In this scenario it would be best to reschedule the meeting and allow the report to be corrected.

66. **Answer: A**

You need to discuss the impact of proceeding with your manager.

67. Answer: A

Evaluating a variance would occur within the "monitor and control" process group.

68. Answer: D

Because this is an "atypical variance" scenario, the atypical formula for ETC would be used: BAC - EV

69. Answer: A

You cannot cancel the negotiations and should not hold off on the negotiations to convince the manager. In addition, you cannot focus on only limited aspects of the project. Therefore, the best option is to make a good faith attempt to decrease costs.

70. Answer: C

The next step would be to try to identify alternatives with your project team.

71. Answer: C

The EMV is calculated by: multiplying .2 x $180 = $36K; multiplying .5 x $40k = $20k, and multiplying .3 x ($140k) = ($42k). Add those together $36k+$20k+($42k) = $14,000

72. Answer: D

They are only required to deliver on the terms of the contract, so they are generally correct, however, ethically it would be more appropriate to honor the negotiated terms.

73. Answer: B

As PM, priority is to prevent any unnecessary changes.

74. Answer: A

Although your SPI indicates the project is trending behind schedule, you cannot state definitively that you will not meet the target date. The CPI indicates you are under-budget. So the best option is A.

75. Answer: C

Because the resources are primarily focused on process-related work and you have little authority, this is describing a functional environment.

76. Answer: D

Acceptance criteria is the performance requirements and essential conditions that must be met before project deliverables are accepted.

77. Answer: B

The performance measurement baseline (or "baseline") is the approved plan for the project work that the actual will be compared to.

78. Answer: A

The baseline should be changed to reflect approved project scope, cost, schedule, and technical changes.

79. Answer: B

Float is the amount of time an activity can be delayed before it impacts (or delays) the critical path.

80. Answer: D

The most likely explanation is that a critical path activity took longer and needed more labor hours to complete.

81. Answer: C

A stakeholder is a person or organization involved in or affected by the project.

82. Answer: A

Because the variance is going to continue to occur, this is describing a "typical" variance. As such, the typical EAC formula will be used: BAC ÷ CPI

83. Answer: C

The benefit of a quality audit is that it identifies ineffective or inefficient policies.

84. **Answer: B**

The project manager's technical skills should be sufficiently high to understand technical issues and explain technical decisions to others. The project manager is expected to leverage expert judgment from inside and outside of the team.

85. **Answer: B**

Direct approach - contact the team member.

86. **Answer: D**

The PMI Code of Ethics does not apply to individuals who are taking a prep course, but are not a member nor have they begun their application process.

87. **Answer: C**

The only thing that would not have prevented this from happening is resource leveling, which is done to re-allocate or balance resources.

88. **Answer: A**

Aspirational standards are not easily measured, but are not optional.

89. **Answer: D**

This is part of the aspirational standards.

90. **Answer: D**

Because of the significant amount of change on the projects and the fact that one of the deliverables was not used, indicates the project manager did not effectively involve stakeholders.

91. **Answer: B**

Because this is a training issue, incentives will not be appropriate and it is often not feasible to get a new resource. Therefore, the best option is arrange for the team member to get training.

92. **Answer: C**

Variance that is unusual and difficult to predict is "special". Keep in mind random and common are the same, both indicating normal process variations.

93. **Answer: C**

A control chart will demonstrate if a process is functioning within the set limits. It does not show causes of poor quality, explore desired future outcomes, or focus on the most critical issues to improve quality.

94. **Answer: C**

This is describing the "Determine Budget" process.

95. **Answer: C**

Multiple critical paths increase the project risk.

96. **Answer: B**

The WBS dictionary will provide all of the details on the work packages.

97. **Answer: D**

Three point (PERT) estimates are calculated: $(O + 4(M) + P)/6$

98. **Answer: C**

A project is not considered complete until all deliverables are complete, even those required to satisfy internal requirements.

99. **Answer: D**

The best reason to have a charter is it gives the project manager authority. It does not list the team members, provide the project history, or describe the activities that will be needed.

100. **Answer: B**

$SV = EV - PV$. If the SV is ($10k) and the PV is $80k, the EV must be $70k. $70k - $80k = ($10k).

101. Answer: B

If the seller is most concerned with scope, they are using a fixed price contract. Meaning that the scope is their biggest concerns because they are only being paid one set price for the work.

102. Answer: B

If there is a lot of change on the project, it is generally caused by not identifying all of the stakeholders.

103. Answer: A

Resource leveling will allow the PM to maximize usage of limited resources by ensuring they are applied to the most critical activities.

104. Answer: B

Processes and procedures are part of the organizational process assets.

105. Answer: B

To calculate EAC, add the actual costs (AC) to the estimate to complete (ETC). In this case $10k + $15 = $25k.

106. Answer: D

Non-conformance is money spent because of failures. Rework is the only answer that is conducted because of failures.

107. Answer: A

Resources, such as human, are required in order to conduct any project and operations. Because of this, it is often a source of conflict due to limited resources.

108. Answer: B

There are aspirational and mandatory standards of conduct. The mandatory standards are those that if there was any behavior against those standards, could result in disciplinary actions by the PMI Ethics Review Committee.

109. Answer: D

A flowchart is used to analyze and communicate relationships between process steps.

110. Answer: C

Cost of quality would be used in QA to determine the most cost-effective processes to implement.

111. Answer: B

CV = EV - AC, Therefore the answer is 1,000.

112. Answer: D

First step is always to review the "plan" and make appropriate corrections.

113. Answer: A

Workarounds are not planned in advance. Therefore the only non-proactive risk process is the monitor risks process.

114. Answer: B

For fixed price contracts, the profit is wrapped into the price and is not known by the buyer.

115. Answer: C

Because the cost estimate should already be accurate, the only thing to do would be to provide the sponsor with what activities will need to be cut.

116. Answer: D

SPI = earned value divided by planned value. Earned value is calculated as BAC multiplied by the % complete. At the end of your project, you will be 100% complete and therefore it is equal to the BAC. Planned value at the end of the project is also equal to BAC.

117. Answer: D

Pass/fail mechanism is a screening system.

118. Answer: B

The highest point is self-actualization. However, given that it is not provided, the next highest is esteem.

119.Answer: A

This is describing the project management information system (PMIS).

120.Answer: B

$2,700 is .3 x $9k. This is the expected monetary value (EMV).

121.Answer: D

Deliverable changes fall under configuration management.

122.Answer: D

Because the project is already running behind, it will need corrective action.

123.Answer: B

The formal procedures for defining project change management are the change control system.

124.Answer: A

Because you are credentialed, you have a responsibility to report the individual to PMI.

125.Answer: C

Based on the information provided: the SV is (5k) so it is behind schedule. The CV is 5k so it is under budget. The TCPI is .97 so there is more funds than there is work. Using the typical ETC calculation, the forecast for remaining work is $169,900.

126.Answer: A

The project manager is ultimately responsible for ensuring changes are managed through the change control system.

127.Answer: C

Because it's a matrix organization, resources are "owned" by the functional managers.

128.Answer: D

Trend analysis is used to predict future project performance.

129.Answer: B

Ultimately a scope question would go back to the sponsor.

130.Answer: B

This is part of professional responsibility. You would approach the customer with the issue.

131.Answer: A

Attribute sampling is accept/reject or pass/fail.

132.Answer: D

Many quality problems could be avoided by leveraging the quality improvement ideas from the staff members.

133.Answer: B

Because activity C is on the critical path, a 3-day delay would delay the project by 3 days.

134.Answer: B

The total duration (B + C + E +F) is 23 days.

135.Answer: A

There is no free float on activity F.

136.Answer: B

Because this is an "unknown-unknown" situation, one that had not been previously identified, the most appropriate funding source would be management reserve.

137.Answer: D

Tornado diagrams are used in quantitative risk analysis and are generally an output of a sensitivity analysis.

138.Answer: B

Cultural considerations should not play a factor in promotional or reward programs, when the performance of the individual entitles them to receive a promotion or incentive.

139. Answer: B

Because you have the optimistic, pessimistic, and most likely duration estimates, the most accurate estimate would be a 3-point (PERT) estimate.

140. Answer: A

The team lead is seeking customer or end-user acceptance. As such, this would be considered scope validation.

141. Answer: D

Ethically the PM must report transparently and truthfully on the status of the project, regardless of the direction provided by the sponsor.

142. Answer: B

Bottom-up estimating is not used in duration estimating because adding up all of the activity or work package durations would not provide a true representation of the project duration. This is due to the fact that many of the project's activities may be conducted in parallel or with some type of overlap.

143. Answer: B

Juran applied the Pareto principle to quality activities: 80% of the problems arise from 20% of the causes. If you eliminate or remedy that 20%, a majority of the problems are eliminated.

144. Answer: D

Because your project is behind schedule and the vendor will serve as a corrective action, this is considered risk transference. It would be risk sharing if the partnership would result in the realization or sharing of an opportunity.

145. Answer: C

The vendor will receive the total costs of $65,000 plus 50% of the amount they came in under the original bid ($3,500). In addition, they will receive $2,500 for the incentive. $65,000 + $3,500 + $2,500 = $71,000.

146. Answer: B

Changing the previously defined specifications of the cabinets would be considered a configuration change and would therefore fall under configuration management.

147. Answer: C

A reserve analysis does not justify the amount of contingency funding. A reserve analysis evaluates the amount of uncertainty on the project (risk) and the amount of contingency or reserve that's been allocated to ensure that it is appropriate. It is a tool used in duration estimating, cost estimating, budget determination, and risk monitoring and controlling.

148. Answer: A

Activity A would be the best candidate for crashing as it has the lowest incremental crash cost: $75/day.

149. Answer: D

If Activity D has float, crashing it would gain one additional day of float, for a total of three days.

150. Answer: B

Although you have the best case and worst-case estimate, without the PERT estimate you cannot calculate the most likely duration.

151. Answer: B

Planned value at the end of the project is equal to the budget at completion (BAC). In this case the BAC is $750,000 and would be, therefore, also the PV.

152. Answer: C

Because month four planned spending exceeds the funding limit by $1,000, work may need to be re-planned.

153. Answer: D

Planned value at the end of the sixth month would be $46,000 (the cumulative amount of spending planned for the project through the sixth month).

154. Answer: B

The EV of the project is $36,400. With a PV of $43,000 at the end of the fifth month, the schedule variance (SV) would be negative, indicating the project may be running behind schedule.

155. **Answer: C**

The unit cost calculation was parametric estimating, the early project work was estimated analogously, and leveraging the interface team is using expert judgment.

156. **Answer: D**

As PM, you must protect the organization from any unnecessary costs. As such, you would have your team stop work while the cancellation is investigated.

157. **Answer: A**

Elapsed time includes non-work days, such as weekends and holidays. The total elapsed time is two weeks.

158. **Answer: D**

Risk audits measure the effectiveness of risk responses and are conducted during risk monitoring and controlling.

159. **Answer: C**

Because the marketing resources will be the primary project resources, managing the relationship with the VP of marketing will be critical.

160. **Answer: B**

The risk response strategy that is approved will have implications to the work being done and the time required to complete that work. As such, the WBS and schedule must be updated to reflect the new work and the time needed.

161. **Answer: B**

Interactive communication will promote team cohesiveness and development much faster than push communication.

162. **Answer: D**

Vendor payment is a component of the administer procurements process.

163. **Answer: D**

A flowchart is used to analyze and communicate relationships between process steps.

164. **Answer: C**

The project appears to be ahead of schedule, slightly over budget, and there is more work remaining than there are funds remaining (TCPI).

165. **Answer: B**

Implementing on-site visits will allow for quicker identification and remediation of quality issues.

166. **Answer: C**

The project budget includes contingency and management reserve. $795,000 + $79,500 + $131,175 = $1,005,675.

167. **Answer: C**

Activity 1.4 has 1 day of free float. If it is delayed by three days it will change the ES of the successor (1.11) by 2 days, changing it from 28 to 30.

168. **Answer: B**

A reserve analysis is the technique evaluates the amount of uncertainty remaining on the project and the corresponding amount of contingency or reserve that is allocated.

169. **Answer: C**

Earned value is the estimated value of the work actually completed.

170. **Answer: C**

With the project management plan approved, the next step would be to conduct a kick-off meeting with the team members.

171. **Answer: D**

Training the team on conflict resolution strategies decreases the probability of disruptive conflicts. As such, this would be considered risk mitigation.

172. Answer: B

The PDM, a type of schedule network diagram, is developed during the sequence activities process.

173. Answer: A

Performance reporting is generally conducted through push communication, such as email.

174. Answer: D

Based on the ES/EF/LS/LF, the activity has five days of total float. Because it has float, the activity is not on the critical path.

175. Answer: B

The demand for monkey products would be an enterprise environmental factor - an influencer on the project evaluation.

176. Answer: D

The implementation of approved changes and risk responses occurs during the executing process group.

177. Answer: C

Because this was an unidentified risk, and therefore there is no planned risk response, the first step would be to implement a workaround.

178. Answer: C

While conducting interviews for risk identification, it is possible that additional information could be discussed that is non-risk-related.

179. Answer: C

The number of risks reported on should not be based on a reporting limitation (such as the top 20) but should be based on priority and impact to the project.

180. Answer: D

Deliverables are validated during the quality control process.

181. Answer: B

Closed risks should be identified as "closed" on the risk register but should never be deleted.

182. Answer: B

Work performance measurements are the result of conducting variance analyses on the project costs and schedule.

183. Answer: D

Final acceptance of the deliverables must occur first before the other tasks are completed.

184. Answer: A

Changing the terms and conditions of the contract would be considered a constructive change.

185. Answer: C

Quality is defined as the degree to which the product or result meets the customer's expectations. If the deliverable does not meet their expectations it is considered low quality.

186. Answer: C

If the requirements were documented and the deliverable did not meet those documented requirements, this would be considered a defect repair.

187. Answer: D

The TCPI of the project is .92. This indicates that there is less work remaining than there are funds remaining. This is a favorable TCPI.

188. Answer: C

Mind mapping consolidates ideas generated during brainstorming to reflect commonalities and differences.

189. Answer: A

Leadership is about guiding, influencing, and collaborating, whereas management is about control and positional power.

190. **Answer: B**

The benefits management plan is based on the business case and a needs assessment. The business case and benefits management plan are two unique documents, with the business case including the financial calculations such NPV, IRR, or ROI. The benefits management plan and the business case may be developed by anyone, but they would typically be the responsibility of the sponsor.

191. **Answer: C**

The first thing to address is the technical infrastructure, which is required to deliver the scope of the project. If the project cannot deliver the required scope, the schedule and the budget considerations are of no consequence.

192. **Answer: D**

The product vision drives the roadmap which drives the release plans. The release plans establish the iterations and the iteration plans schedule the feature development. The prioritized features are delivered by user stories and the tasks are created to deliver the user stories.

193. **Answer: A**

The work package estimates include the activity cost estimates and the activity contingency reserve. The control accounts include the work package estimates and the contingency reserve. The project budget includes the management reserve and the cost baseline (control accounts).

194. **Answer: B**

Design for X (DfX) is used during product design to optimize a specific aspect, such as customer satisfaction in this situation. Nominal group technique would not necessarily increase customer satisfaction. Theory of Constraints, while it may be able to be applied, would not necessarily increase customer satisfaction. Quality assurance is concerned with quality improvement and the quality of the processes, not the product.

195. **Answer: C**

The Theory of Constraints (TOC) views any manageable system as being limited in achieving more of its goals by a small number of constraints. There is always at least one constraint that is identified, and the work is structured around it. Follows the saying of "only as good as the weakest link."

196. **Answer: D**

A team charter captures the team values, agreements, and operating guidelines, allowing the team to engage in setting the appropriate boundaries while learning about each other.

197. **Answer: A**

Self-awareness, self-regulation, motivation, empathy, and social skills are all elements of emotional intelligence.

198. **Answer: B**

Propinquity is the degree to which the risk is perceived in importance and proximity is the period of time before the risk would have an impact

199. **Answer: C**

A regression analysis is used to analyze the interrelationships between different project variables that contributed to the project outcomes.

200. **Answer: D**

Check for understanding is not one of the 5Cs of written communication. The 5Cs are: correct grammar and spelling, concise expression and elimination of excess words, clear purpose and expression directed to the needs of the read, coherent, logical flow of ideas, and controlling the flow of words and ideas.

Appendix F

Glossary

Acceptance Criteria. Those criteria, including performance requirements and essential conditions, which must be met before project deliverables are accepted.

Accepted Deliverables. Products, results, or capabilities produced by a project and validated by the project customer or sponsors as meeting their specified acceptance criteria.

Accuracy. Within the quality management system, accuracy is an assessment of correctness.

Acquire Resources. The process of obtaining team members, facilities, equipment, materials, supplies, and other resources necessary to complete project work.

Acquisition. Obtaining human and material resources necessary to perform project activities. Acquisition implies a cost of resources and is not necessarily financial.

Activity. A component of work performed during the course of a project.

Activity Attributes [Output/Input]. Multiple attributes associated with each schedule activity that can be included within the activity list. Activity attributes include activity codes, predecessor activities, successor activities, logical relationships, leads and lags, resource requirements, imposed dates, constraints, and assumptions.

Activity Duration. The time in calendar units between the start and finish of a schedule activity. See also *duration.*

Activity Duration Estimates. The quantitative assessments of the likely number of time periods that are required to complete an activity.

Activity Identifier. A short unique numeric or text identification assigned to each schedule activity to differentiate that project activity from other activities. Typically, unique within any one project schedule network diagram.

Activity List [Output/Input]. A documented tabulation of schedule activities that shows the activity description, activity identifier, and a sufficiently detailed scope of work description so project team members understand what work is to be performed.

Activity-on-Node (AON). See precedence diagramming method (PDM).

Actual Cost (AC). Total costs actually incurred and recorded in accomplishing work performed during a given time period for a schedule activity or work breakdown structure component. Actual cost can sometimes be direct labor hours alone, direct costs alone, or all costs including indirect costs. See also *earned value management and earned value technique.*

Actual Duration. The time in calendar units between the actual start date of the schedule activity and either the data date of the project schedule if the schedule activity is in progress or the actual finish date if the schedule activity is complete.

Adaptive Life Cycle. A project life cycle that is iterative or incremental.

Affinity Diagrams. A technique that allows large numbers of ideas to be classified into groups for review and analysis.

Agreements. Any document or communication that defines the initial intentions of a project. This can take the form of a contract, memorandum of understanding (MOU), letters of agreement, verbal agreements, email, etc.

Alternative Analysis. A technique used to evaluate identified options in order to select the options or approaches to use to execute and perform the work of the project.

Analogous Estimating [Technique]. An estimating technique that uses the values of parameters, such as scope, cost, budget, and duration or measures of scale such as size, weight, and complexity from a previous, similar activity as the basis for estimating the same parameter or measure for a future activity.

Analytical Techniques. Various techniques used to evaluate, analyze, or forecast potential outcomes based on possible variations of project or environmental variables and their relationships with other variables.

Approved Change Request [Output/Input]. A change request that has been processed through the integrated change control process and approved.

Assumptions. Assumptions are factors that, for planning purposes, are considered to be true, real, or certain without proof or demonstration.

Assumptions Log. A project document used to record all assumptions and constraints throughout the project life cycle.

Attribute Sampling. Method of measuring quality that consists of noting the presence (or absence) of some characteristic (attribute) in each of the units under consideration.

Authority. The right to apply project resources, expend funds, make decisions, or give approvals.

Backward Pass. The calculation of late finish dates and late start dates for the uncompleted portions of all schedule activities. Determined by working backwards through the schedule network logic from the project's end date. See also *schedule network analysis.*

Bar Chart. A graphic display of schedule-related information. In the typical bar chart, schedule activities or work breakdown structure components are listed down the left side of the chart, dates are shown across the top, and activity durations are shown as date-placed horizontal bars. See also Gantt chart.

Baseline. An approved plan for a project, plus or minus approved changes. It is compared to actual performance to determine if performance is within acceptable variance thresholds. Generally, refers to the current baseline, but may refer to the original or some other baseline. Usually used with a modifier (e.g., cost performance baseline, schedule baseline, performance measurement baseline, technical baseline).

Basis of Estimates. Supporting documentation outlining the details used in establishing project estimates such as assumptions, constraints, level of detail, ranges, and confidence levels.

Benchmarking. Benchmarking is the comparison of actual or planned products, processes, and practices to those of comparable organizations to identify best practices, generate ideas for improvement, and provide a basis for measuring performance.

Benefit Management Plan. The documented explanation defining the process for creating, maximizing and sustaining the benefits provided by a project or program.

Bid documents. All documents used to solicit information, quotations, or proposals from prospective sellers.

Bidder Conference. The meetings with prospective sellers prior to the preparation of a bid or proposal to ensure all prospective vendors have a clear and common understanding of the procurement, Also known as contractor conferences, vendor conferences, or pre-bid conferences.

Bottom-up Estimating [Technique]. A method of estimating a component of work. The work is decomposed into more detail. An estimate is prepared of what is needed to meet the requirements of each of the lower, more detailed pieces of work, and these estimates are then aggregated into a total quantity for the component of work. The accuracy of bottom-up estimating is driven by the size and complexity of the work identified at the lower levels.

Brainstorming [Technique]. A general data gathering and creativity technique that can be used to identify risks, ideas, or solutions to issues by using a group of team members or subject-matter experts.

Budget. The approved estimate for the project or any work breakdown structure component or any schedule activity.

Budget at Completion (BAC). The sum of all the budgets established for the work to be performed on a project or a work breakdown structure component or a schedule activity. The total planned value for the project.

Buffer. See reserve.

Business Case. A documented economic feasibility study used to establish validity of the benefits of a selected component lacking sufficient definition and that is used as a basis for the authorization of further project management activities.

Business Value. The net quantifiable benefit derived from a business endeavor. The benefit may be tangible, intangible, or both.

Buyer. The acquirer of products, services, or results for an organization.

Calendar Unit. The smallest unit of time used in scheduling a project. Calendar units are generally in hours, days, or weeks, but can also be in quarter years, months, shifts, or even in minutes.

Cause and Effect Diagram. A decomposition technique that helps trace an undesirable effect back to its root cause.

Change. A modification to any formally controlled deliverable, project management plan component, or project document.

Change Control. Identifying, documenting, approving or rejecting, and controlling changes to the project baselines.

Change Control Board (CCB). A formally constituted group of stakeholders responsible for reviewing, evaluating, approving, delaying, or rejecting changes to a project, with all decisions and recommendations being recorded.

Change Control System [Tool]. A collection of formal documented procedures that define how project deliverables and documentation will be controlled, changed, and approved. In most application areas, the change control system is a subset of the configuration management system.

Change Control Tools. Manual or automated tools to assist with change and/or configuration management. At a minimum, the tools should support the activities of the CCB.

Change Log. A comprehensive list of changes submitted during the project and their current status.

Change Management Plan. A component of the project management plan that establishes the change control board, documents the extent of its authority, and describes how the change control system will be implemented.

Change Request. Requests to expand or reduce the project scope, modify policies, processes, plans, or procedures, modify costs or budgets, or revise schedules.

Charter. See project charter.

Checklist Analysis. A technique for systematically reviewing materials using a list for accuracy and completeness.

Checksheets. A tally sheet that can be used as a checklist when gathering data.

Claim. A request, demand, or assertion of rights by a seller against a buyer, or vice versa, for consideration, compensation, or payment under the terms of a legally binding contract, such as for a disputed change.

Claims Administration. The process of processing, adjudicating, and communicating contract claims.

Close Procurements [Process]. The process of completing each project procurement.

Close Project or Phase [Process]. The process of finalizing all activities across all of the Project Management Process Groups to formally complete the project or phase.

Closing Processes [Process Group]. Those processes performed to finalize all activities across all Project Management Process Groups to formally close the project or phase.

Code of Accounts. Any numbering system used to uniquely identify each component of the work breakdown structure.

Collect Requirements [Process]. Collect Requirements is the process of defining and documenting stakeholders' needs to meet the project objectives.

Colocation [Technique]. An organizational placement strategy where the project team members are physically located close to one another in order to improve communication, working relationships, and productivity.

Communication Methods. A systematic procedure, technique, or process used to transfer information among project stakeholders.

Communication Models. A description, analogy, or schematic used to represent how the communication process will be performed for the project.

Communication Management Plan [Output/Input]. The document that describes: the communications needs and expectations for the project; how and in what format information will be communicated; when and where each communication will be made; and who is responsible for providing each type of communication. The communication management plan is contained in, or is a subsidiary plan of, the project management plan.

Communication Styles Assessment. A technique to identify the preferred communication method, format, and content for stakeholders for planned communication activities

Communication Technology. Specific tools, systems, computer programs, etc., used to transfer information among project stakeholders.

Conduct Procurements [Process]. The process of obtaining seller responses, selecting a seller, and awarding a contract.

Configuration Management Plan. A component of the project management plan that describes how to identify and account for project artifacts under configuration control, and how to record and report changes to them.

Configuration Management System [Tool]. A subsystem of the overall project management system. It is a collection of formal documented procedures used to apply technical and administrative direction and surveillance to: identify and document the functional and physical characteristics of a product, result, service, or component; control any changes to such characteristics; record and report each change and its implementation status; and support the audit of the products, results, or components to verify conformance to requirements. It includes the documentation, tracking systems, and defined approval levels necessary for authorizing and controlling changes.

Conformance. Within the quality management system, conformance is a general concept of delivering results that fall within the limits that define acceptable variation for a quality requirement.

Constraint [Input]. The state, quality, or sense of being restricted to a given course of action or inaction. An applicable restriction or limitation, either internal or external to a project, which will affect the performance of the project or a process. For example, a schedule constraint is any limitation or restraint placed on the project schedule that affects when a schedule activity can be scheduled and is usually in the form of fixed imposed dates.

Context Diagrams. A visual depiction of the product scope showing a business system (process, equipment, computer system, etc.) and how people and other systems (actors) interact with it.

Contingency. An event or occurrence that could affect the execution of the project that may be accounted for with a reserve.

Contingency Reserve [Output/Input]. The amount of funds, budget, or time needed above the estimate to reduce the risk of overruns of project objectives to a level acceptable to the organization.

Contingent Response Strategies. Responses provided which may be used in the event that a specific trigger occurs.

Contract [Output/Input]. A contract is a mutually binding agreement that obligates the seller to provide the specified product or service or result and obligates the buyer to pay for it.

Contract. A contract is a mutually binding agreement that obligates the seller to provide the specified product or service or result and obligates the buyer to pay for it.

Contract Change Control System. The system used to collect, track, adjudicate, and communicate changes to a contract.

Control Account [Tool]. A management control point where scope, budget (resource plans), actual cost, and schedule are integrated and compared to earned value for performance measurement. See also *work package*.

Control Chart [Tool]. A graphic display of process data over time and against established control limits, and that has a centerline that assists in detecting a trend of plotted values toward either control limit.

Control Costs [Process]. The process of monitoring the status of the project to update the project budget and managing changes to the cost baseline.

Control Limits. The area composed of three standard deviations on either side of the centerline, or mean, of a normal distribution of data plotted on a control chart that reflects the expected variation in the data. See also *specification limits*.

Control Procurements. The process of managing procurement relationships, monitoring contract performance, making changes and corrections as appropriate, and closing out contracts.

Control Quality. The process of monitoring and recording results of executing the quality management activities to assess performance and ensure the project outputs are complete, correct, and meet customer expectations.

Control Resources. The process of ensuring that the physical resources assigned and allocated to the project are available as planned, as well as monitoring the planned versus actual utilization of resources and performing corrective action as necessary.

Control Schedule [Process]. The process of monitoring the status of the project to update project progress and managing changes to the schedule baseline.

Control Scope [Process]. The process of monitoring the status of the project and product scope and managing changes to the scope baseline.

Corrective Action. Documented direction for executing the project work to bring expected future performance of the project work in line with the project management plan.

Cost Aggregation. Summing the lower-level cost estimates associated with the various work packages for a given level within the project's WBS or for a given cost control account.

Cost Baseline. The approved version of the time-phased project, excluding any management reserves, which can b changed only through formal change control procedures and is used as a basis for comparison to actual results.

Cost-Benefit Analysis. A financial analysis tool used to determine the benefits provided by a project against its costs.

Cost Management Plan [Output/Input]. The document that sets out the format and establishes the activities and criteria for planning, structuring, and controlling the project costs. The cost management plan is contained in, or is a subsidiary plan of, the project management plan.

Cost of Quality (COQ) [Technique]. A method of determining the costs incurred to ensure quality. Prevention and appraisal costs (cost of conformance) include costs for quality planning, quality control (QC), and quality assurance to ensure compliance to requirements (i.e., training, QC systems, etc.). Failure costs (cost of non-conformance) include costs to rework products, components, or processes that are non-compliant, costs of warranty work and waste, and loss of reputation.

Cost Performance Baseline. A specific version of the time-phased budget used to compare actual expenditures to planned expenditures to determine if preventive or corrective action is needed to meet the project objectives.

Cost Performance Index (CPI). A measure of cost efficiency on a project. It is the ratio of earned value (EV) to actual costs (AC). CPI = EV divided by AC.

Cost Plus Award Fee Contract (CPAF). A category of contract that involves payments to the seller for all legitimate actual costs incurred for completed work, plus an award fee representing seller profit.

Cost-Plus-Fixed-Fee (CPFF) Contract. A type of cost-reimbursable contract where the buyer reimburses the seller for the seller's allowable costs (allowable costs are defined by the contract) plus a fixed amount of profit (fee).

Cost-Plus-Incentive-Fee (CPIF) Contract. A type of cost-reimbursable contract where the buyer reimburses the seller for the seller's allowable costs (allowable costs are defined by the contract), and the seller earns its profit if it meets defined performance criteria.

Cost-Reimbursable Contract. A type of contract involving payment to the seller for the seller's actual costs, plus a fee typically representing seller's profit. Cost-reimbursable contracts often include incentive clauses where, if the seller meets or exceeds selected project objectives, such as schedule targets or total cost, then the seller receives from the buyer an incentive or bonus payment.

Cost Variance (CV). A measure of cost performance on a project. It is the difference between earned value (EV) and actual cost (AC). CV = EV minus AC.

Crashing [Technique]. A specific type of project schedule compression technique performed by taking action to decrease the total project schedule duration after analyzing a number of alternatives to determine how to get the maximum schedule duration compression for the least additional cost. Typical approaches for crashing a schedule include reducing schedule activity durations and increasing the assignment of resources on schedule activities. See also *fast tracking* and *schedule compression*.

Create WBS (Work Breakdown Structure) [Process]. The process of subdividing project deliverables and project work into smaller, more manageable components.

Criteria. Standards, rules, or tests on which a judgment or decision can be based or by which a product, service, result, or process can be evaluated.

Critical Activity. Any schedule activity on a critical path in a project schedule. Most commonly determined by using the critical path method. Although some activities are "critical," in the dictionary sense, without being on the critical path, this meaning is seldom used in the project context.

Critical Chain Method [Technique]. A schedule network analysis technique that modifies the project schedule to account for limited resources.

Critical Path. Generally, but not always, the sequence of schedule activities that determines the duration of the project. It is the longest path through the project. See also *critical path methodology.*

Critical Path Method (CPM) [Technique]. A schedule network analysis technique used to determine the amount of scheduling flexibility (the amount of float) on various logical network paths in the project schedule network, and to determine the minimum total project duration. Early start and finish dates are calculated by means of a forward pass, using a specified start date. Late start and finish dates are calculated by means of a backward pass, starting from a specified completion date, which sometimes is the project early finish date determined during the forward pass calculation. See also *critical path.*

Data. Discrete, unorganized, unprocessed measurements or raw observations.

Data Analysis Techniques. Techniques used to organize, assess, and evaluate data and information.

Data Date. A point in time when the status of the project is recorded.

Data Gathering Techniques. Techniques used to organize, assess, and evaluate data and information.

Data Representation Techniques. Graphic representations or other methods used to convey data and information.

Decision-Making Techniques. Techniques used to select a course of action from different alternatives.

Decision Tree Analysis [Technique]. The decision tree is a diagram that describes a decision under consideration and the implications of choosing one or another of the available alternatives. It is used when some future scenarios or outcomes of actions are uncertain. It incorporates probabilities and the costs or rewards of each logical path of events and future decisions and uses expected monetary value analysis to help the organization identify the relative values of alternate actions. See also *expected monetary value analysis.*

Decomposition [Technique]. A planning technique that subdivides the project scope and project deliverables into smaller, more manageable components, until the project work associated with accomplishing the project scope and providing the deliverables is defined in sufficient detail to support executing, monitoring, and controlling the work.

Defect. An imperfection or deficiency in a project component where that component does not meet its requirements or specifications and needs to be either repaired or replaced.

Defect Repair. The formally documented identification of a defect in a project component with a recommendation to either repair the defect or completely replace the component.

Define Activities [Process]. The process of identifying the specific actions to be performed to produce the project deliverables.

Define Scope [Process]. The process of developing a detailed description of the project and product.

Deliverable [Output/Input]. Any unique and verifiable product, result, or capability to perform a service that must be produced to complete a process, phase, or project. Often used more narrowly in reference to an external deliverable, which is a deliverable that is subject to approval by the project sponsor or customer. See also *product and result.*

Delphi Technique [Technique]. An information gathering technique used as a way to reach a consensus of experts on a subject. Experts on the subject participate in this technique anonymously. A facilitator uses a questionnaire to solicit ideas about the important project points related to the subject. The responses are summarized and are then recirculated to the experts for further comment. Consensus may be reached in a few rounds of this process. The Delphi technique helps reduce bias in the data and keeps any one person from having undue influence on the outcome.

Determine Budget [Process]. The process of aggregating the estimated costs of individual activities or work packages to establish an authorized cost baseline.

Development Approach. The method used to create and evolve the product, service, or result during the project life cycle such as predictive, iterative, incremental, agile, or a hybrid method.

Develop Human Resource Plan [Process]. The process of identifying and documenting project roles, responsibilities, and required skills, reporting relationships, and creating a staffing management plan.

Develop Project Charter [Process]. The process of developing a document that formally authorizes a project or a phase and documenting initial requirements that satisfy the stakeholder's needs and expectations.

Develop Project Management Plan [Process]. The process of documenting the actions necessary to define, prepare, integrate, and coordinate all subsidiary plans.

Develop Schedule [Process]. The process of analyzing activity sequences, durations, resource requirements, and schedule constraints to create the project schedule.

Develop Team [Process]. The process of improving the competencies, team interaction, and the overall team environment to enhance project performance.

Diagramming Techniques. Approaches to presenting information with logical linkages that aid in understanding.

Direct and Manage Project Work [Process]. The process of performing the work defined in the project management plan to achieve the project's objectives.

Discrete Effort. An activity that can be planned and measured and that yields a specific output. [Note: Discrete effort is one of three earned value management (EVM) types of activities used to measure work performance.]

Discretionary Dependency. A relationship that is established based on knowledge of best practices within an application area or an aspect of the project where a specific sequence is desired

Documentation Reviews. The process of gathering a corpus of information and reviewing it to determine accuracy and completeness.

Distribute Information [Process]. The process of making relevant information available to project stakeholders as planned.

Duration (DU or DUR). The total number of work periods (not including holidays or other nonworking periods) required to complete a schedule activity or work breakdown structure component. Usually expressed as workdays or workweeks. Sometimes incorrectly equated with elapsed time. Contrast with *effort*.

Early Finish Date (EF). In the critical path method, the earliest possible point in time on which the uncompleted portions of a schedule activity (or the project) can finish, based on the schedule network logic, the data date, and any schedule constraints. Early finish dates can change as the project progresses and as changes are made to the project management plan.

Early Start Date (ES). In the critical path method, the earliest possible point in time on which the uncompleted portions of a schedule activity (or the project) can start, based on the schedule network logic, the data date, and any schedule constraints. Early start dates can change as the project progresses and as changes are made to the project management plan.

Earned Value (EV). The value of work performed expressed in terms of the approved budget assigned to that work for a schedule activity or work breakdown structure component.

Earned Value Management. A methodology that combines scope, schedule, and resource measurements to assess project performance and progress.

Earned Value Technique (EVT) [Technique]. A specific technique for measuring the performance of work and used to establish the performance measurement baseline (PMB).

Effort. The number of labor units required to complete a schedule activity or work breakdown structure component. Usually expressed as staff hours, staff days, or staff weeks. Contrast with *duration*.

Emotional Intelligence. The ability to identify, assess, and manage the personal emotions of oneself and other people, as well as the collective emotions of groups of people.

Enterprise Environmental Factors [Output/Input]. Any or all external environmental factors and internal organizational environmental factors that surround or influence the project's success. These factors are from any or all of the enterprises involved in the project, and include organizational culture and structure, infrastructure, existing resources, commercial databases, market conditions, and project management software.

Estimate [Output/Input]. A quantitative assessment of the likely amount or outcome. Usually applied to project costs, resources, effort, and durations and is usually preceded by a modifier (i.e., preliminary, conceptual, feasibility, order-of-magnitude, definitive). It should always include some indication of accuracy (e.g., ± x percent). See also *budget* and *cost*.

Estimate Activity Durations [Process]. The process of approximating the number of work periods needed to complete individual activities with estimated resources.

Estimate Activity Resources [Process]. The process of estimating the type and quantities of material, people, equipment or supplies required to perform each activity.

Estimate at Completion (EAC) [Output/Input]. The expected total cost of a schedule activity, a work breakdown structure component, or the project when the defined scope of work will be completed. The EAC may be calculated based on performance to date or estimated by the project team based on other factors, in which case it is often referred to as the latest revised estimate. See also *earned value technique* and *estimate to complete*.

Estimate Costs [Process]. The process of developing an approximation of the monetary resources needed to complete project activities.

Estimate to Complete (ETC) [Output/Input]. The expected cost needed to complete all the remaining work for a schedule activity, work breakdown structure component, or the project. See also *earned value technique* and *estimate at completion*.

Execute. Directing, managing, performing, and accomplishing the project work; providing the deliverables; and providing work performance information.

Executing Processes [Process Group]. Those processes performed to complete the work defined in the project management plan to satisfy the project objectives.

Expected Monetary Value (EMV) Analysis. A statistical technique that calculates the average outcome when the future includes scenarios that may or may not happen. A common use of this technique is within decision tree analysis.

Expert Judgment [Technique]. Judgment provided based upon expertise in an application area, knowledge area, discipline, industry, etc. as appropriate for the activity being performed. Such expertise may be provided by any group or person with specialized education, knowledge, skill, experience, or training.

Explicit Knowledge. Knowledge that can be codified using symbols such as words, numbers, and pictures.

External Dependency. A relationship between project activities and non-project activities.

Fallback Plan. Fallback plans include an alternative set of actions and tasks available in the event that the primary plan needs to be abandoned because of issues, risks, or other causes.

Fast Tracking [Technique]. A specific project schedule compression technique that changes network logic to overlap phases that would normally be done in sequence, such as the design phase and construction phase, or to perform schedule activities in parallel. See also *crashing* and *schedule compression*.

Fee. Represents profit as a component of compensation to a seller.

Finish Date. A point in time associated with a schedule activity's completion. Usually qualified by one of the following: actual, planned, estimated, scheduled, early, late, baseline, target, or current.

Finish-to-Finish (FF). The logical relationship where completion of work of the successor activity cannot finish until the completion of work of the predecessor activity. See also *logical relationship*.

Finish-to-Start (FS). The logical relationship where initiation of work of the successor activity depends upon the completion of work of the predecessor activity. See also *logical relationship*.

Firm-Fixed-Price (FFP) Contract. A type of fixed price contract where the buyer pays the seller a set amount (as defined by the contract), regardless of the seller's costs.

Fishbone diagram. See Cause and Effect Diagram.

Fixed-Price Contract. An agreement that sets the fee that will be paid for a defined scope of work regardless of the cost or effort to deliver it.

Fixed-Price-Incentive-Fee (FPIF) Contract. A type of contract where the buyer pays the seller a set amount (as defined by the contract), and the seller can earn an additional amount if the seller meets defined performance criteria.

Fixed Price with Economic Price Adjustment Contract (FPEPA). A fixed-price contract, but with a special provision allowing for predefined final adjustments to the contract price due to changed conditions, such as inflation changes, or cost increases (or decreases) for specific commodities.

Float. Also called slack. See *total float* and *free float*.

Flowcharting [Technique]. The depiction in a diagram format of the inputs, process actions, and outputs of one or more processes within a system.

Focus Groups. An elicitation technique that brings together prequalified stakeholders and subject matter experts to learn about their expectations and attitudes about a proposed product, service, or result.

Forecast. An estimate or prediction of conditions and events in the project's future based on information and knowledge available at the time of the forecast. The information is based on the project's past performance and expected future performance, and includes information that could impact the project in the future, such as estimate at completion and estimate to complete.

Forward Pass. The calculation of the early start and early finish dates for the uncompleted portions of all network activities. See also *schedule network analysis* and *backward pass.*

Free Float. The amount of time that a schedule activity can be delayed without delaying the early start date of any immediately following schedule activities. See also *total float.*

Functional Manager. Someone with management authority over an organizational unit within a functional organization. The manager of any group that actually makes a product or performs a service. Sometimes called a line manager.

Functional Organization. A hierarchical organization where each employee has one clear superior, and staff are grouped by areas of specialization and managed by a person with expertise in that area.

Funding limit Reconciliation. The process of comparing the planned expenditure of project funds against any limits on the commitment of funds for the project to identify any variances between the funding limits and the planned expenditures.

Gantt Chart. A bar chart of schedule information where activities are listed on the vertical axis, dates are shown on the horizontal axis, and activity durations are shown as horizontal bars placed according to start and finish dates.

Grade. A category or rank used to distinguish items that have the same functional use (e.g., "hammer"), but do not share the same requirements for quality (e.g., different hammers may need to withstand different amounts of force).

Ground Rules. Expectations regarding acceptable behavior by project team members.

Histogram. A bar chart that shows the graphical representation of numerical data.

Historical Information. Documents and data on prior projects including project files, records, correspondence, closed contracts, and closed projects.

Human Resource Plan. A document describing how roles and responsibilities, reporting relationships, and staffing management will be addressed and structured for the project. It is contained in or is a subsidiary plan of the project.

Identify Risks [Process]. The process of determining which risks may affect the project and documenting their characteristics.

Identify Stakeholders [Process]. The process of identifying all people or organizations impacted by the project, and documenting relevant information regarding their interests, involvement, and impact on project success.

Implement Risk Responses. The process of implementing agree-upon risk response plans.

Imposed Date. A fixed date imposed on a schedule activity or schedule milestone, usually in the form of a "start no earlier than" and "finish no later than" date.

Incentive Fee. A set of financial incentives related to cost, schedule, or technical performance of the seller.

Incremental Life Cycle. An adaptive project life cycle in which the deliverable is produced through a series of iterations that successively add functionality within a predetermined time frame. The deliverable contains the necessary and sufficient capability to be considered complete only after the final iteration.

Independent Estimates. A process of using a third party to obtain and analyze information to support prediction of cost, schedules or other items,

Influence Diagram. A graphical representation of situations showing casual influences, time ordering of events, and other relationships among variables and outcomes.

Information. Organized or structured data, processed for a specific purpose to make it meaningful, valuable, and useful in specific contexts.

Information Management System. Facilities, processes, and procedures used to collect, store, and distribute information between producers and consumers of information in physical or electronic format.

Initiating Processes [Process Group]. Those processes performed to define a new project or a new phase of an existing project by obtaining authorization to start the project or phase.

Input [Process Input]. Any item, whether internal or external to the project that is required by a process before that process proceeds. May be an output from a predecessor process.

Inspection [Technique]. Examining or measuring to verify whether an activity, component, product, result, or service conforms to specified requirements.

Interpersonal and Team Skills. Skills used to effectively lead and interact with team members and other stakeholders.

Interpersonal Skills. Skills used to establish and maintain relationships with other people.

Interviews. A formal or informal approach to elicit information from stakeholders by talking to them directly.

Invitation for Bid (IFB). Generally, this term is equivalent to request for proposal. However, in some application areas, it may have a narrower or more specific meaning.

Issue. A point or matter in question or in dispute, or a point or matter that is not settled and is under discussion or over which there are opposing views or disagreements.

Issue Log. A project document where information about issues is recorded and monitored.

Iterative Life Cycle. A project life cycle where the project scope is generally determined early in the project life cycle, but time and cost estimates are routinely modified as the project team's understanding of the product increases. Iterations develop the product through a series of repeated cycles, while increments successively add to the functionality of the product.

Knowledge. A mixture of experience, values and beliefs, contextual information, intuition, and insight that people use to make sense of new experiences and information.

Lag [Technique]. A modification of a logical relationship that directs a delay in the successor activity. For example, in a finish-to-start dependency with a ten-day lag, the successor activity cannot start until ten days after the predecessor activity has finished. See also *lead*.

Late Finish Date (LF). In the critical path method, the latest possible point in time that a schedule activity may be completed based upon the schedule network logic, the project completion date, and any constraints assigned to the schedule activities without violating a schedule constraint or delaying the project completion date. The late finish dates are determined during the backward pass calculation of the project schedule network.

Late Start Date (LS). In the critical path method, the latest possible point in time that a schedule activity may begin based upon the schedule network logic, the project completion date, and any constraints assigned to the schedule activities without violating a schedule constraint or delaying the project completion date. The late start dates are determined during the backward pass calculation of the project schedule network.

Lead [Technique]. A modification of a logical relationship that allows an acceleration of the successor activity. For example, in a finish-to-start dependency with a ten-day lead, the successor activity can start ten days before the predecessor activity has finished. A negative lead is equivalent to a positive lag. See also *lag*.

Lessons Learned [Output/Input]. The learning gained from the process of performing the project. Lessons learned may be identified at any point. Also considered a project record, to be included in the lessons learned knowledge base.

Lessons Learned Register. A project document used to record knowledge gained during a project so that it can be used in the current project and entered into the lessons learned repository.

Lessons Learned Repository. A store of historical information about lessons learned in projects.

Level of Effort (LOE). An activity that does not produce definitive end products and is measured by the passage of time.

Log. A document used to record and describe or denote selected items identified during execution of a process or activity. Usually used with a modifier, such as issue, change, issue, or assumption.

Logical Relationship. A dependency between two project schedule activities, or between a project schedule activity and a schedule milestone. The four possible types of logical relationships are: Finish-to-Start; Finish-to-Finish; Start-to-Start; and Start-to-Finish. See also *precedence relationship*.

Make-or-Buy Analysis. The process of gathering and organizing data about product requirements and analyzing them against available alternatives including the purchase or internal manufacture of the project.

Make-or-Buy Decisions. Decisions made regarding the external purchase or internal manufacture of a product.

Manage Communications. Manage Communications is the process of ensuring timely and appropriate collection, creation, distribution, storage, retrieval, management, monitoring, and the ultimate disposition of project information.

Management Reserve. An amount of the project budget or project schedule held outside of the performance measurement baseline (PMB) for management control purposes, that is reserved for unforeseen work that is within scope of the project.

Management Skills. The ability to plan, organize, direct, and control individuals or groups of people to achieve specific goals.

Manage Project Knowledge. The process of using existing knowledge and creating new knowledge to achieve the project's objectives and contribute to organizational learning.

Manage Quality. The process of translating the quality management plan into executable quality activities that incorporate the organization's quality policies into the project.

Manage team [Process]. The process of tracking team member performance, providing feedback, resolving issues, and managing changes to optimize project performance.

Manage Stakeholder Engagement. The process of communicating and working with stakeholders to meet their needs and addressing issues as they occur.

Manage Team. The process of translating the quality management plan into executable quality activities that incorporate the organization's quality policies into the project.

Mandatory Dependency. A relationship that is contractually required or inherent in the nature of the work.

Master Schedule [Tool]. A summary-level project schedule that identifies the major deliverables and work breakdown structure components and key schedule milestones. See also *milestone schedule.*

Matrix Diagrams. A quality management and control tool used to perform data analysis within the organizational structure created in the matrix. The matrix diagram seeks to show the strength of relationships between factors, causes, and objectives that exist between the rows and columns that form the matrix.

Matrix Organization. Any organizational structure in which the project manager shares responsibility with the functional managers for assigning priorities and for directing the work of persons assigned to the project.

Methodology. A system of practices, techniques, procedures, and rules used by those who work in a discipline.

Milestone. A significant point or event in the project.

Milestone Schedule [Tool]. A summary-level schedule that identifies the major schedule milestones. See also *master schedule.*

Mind-Mapping. A technique used to consolidate ideas created through individual brainstorming sessions into a single map to reflect commonality and differences in understanding and to generate new ideas.

Monitor. Collect project performance data, produce performance measures, and report and disseminate performance information.

Monitor and Control Project Work [Process]. The process of tracking, reviewing, and regulating the progress to meet the performance objectives defined in the project management plan.

Monitor Communications. The process of ensuring that the information needs of the project and its stakeholders are met.

Monitoring and Controlling Processes [Process Group]. Those processes required to track, review, and regulate the progress and performance of the project, identify any areas in which changes to the plan are required, and initiate the corresponding changes.

Monte Carlo Simulation. A process which generates hundreds, or thousands of probable performance outcomes based on probability distributions for cost and schedule on individual tasks. The outcomes are then used to generate a probability distribution for the project.

Multicriteria Decision Analysis. This technique utilizes a decision matrix to provide a systematic analytical approach for establishing criteria, such as risk levels, uncertainty, and valuation, to evaluate and rank many ideas.

Network. See project schedule network diagram.

Network Logic. All activity dependencies in a project schedule network diagram.

Network Path. Any continuous series of schedule activities connected with logical relationships in a project schedule network diagram.

Networking. Establishing connections and relationships with other people from the same or other organizations.

Node. One of the defining points of a schedule network; a junction point joined to some or all of the other dependency lines.

Monial Group Technique. A technique that enhances brainstorming with a voting process used to rank the most useful ideas for further brainstorming or for prioritization.

Objective. Something toward which work is to be directed, a strategic position to be attained, or a purpose to be achieved, a result to be obtained, a product to be produced, or a service to be performed.

Opportunity. A condition or situation favorable to the project, a positive set of circumstances, a positive set of events, a risk that will have a positive impact on project objectives, or a possibility for positive changes. Contrast with *threat*.

Organizational Breakdown Structure (OBS). A hierarchical representation of the project organization, which illustrates the relationship between project activities and the organizational units that will perform those activities.

Organizational Learning. A discipline concerned with the way individuals, groups, and organizations develop knowledge.

Organizational Process Assets [Output/Input]. Any or all process related assets, from any or all of the organizations involved in the project that are or can be used to influence the project's success. These process assets include formal and informal plans, policies, procedures, and guidelines. The process assets also include the organizations' knowledge bases such as lessons learned and historical information.

Output [Process Output]. A product, result, or service generated by a process. May be an input to a successor process.

Overall Project Risk. The effect of uncertainty on the project as a whole, arising from all sources of uncertainty including individual risks, representing the exposure of stakeholders to the implications of variations in project outcome, both positive and negative.

Parametric Estimating [Technique]. An estimating technique that uses a statistical relationship between historical data and other variables (e.g., square footage in construction, lines of code in software development) to calculate an estimate for activity parameters, such as scope, cost, budget, and duration. An example for the cost parameter is multiplying the planned quantity of work to be performed by the historical cost per unit to obtain the estimated cost.

Pareto Chart [Tool]. A histogram, ordered by frequency of occurrence, that shows how many results were generated by each identified cause.

Path Convergence. The merging or joining of parallel schedule network paths into the same node in a project schedule network diagram. Path convergence is characterized by a schedule activity with more than one predecessor activity.

Path Divergence. Extending or generating parallel schedule network paths from the same node in a project schedule network diagram. Path divergence is characterized by a schedule activity with more than one successor activity.

Percent Complete. An estimate, expressed as a percent, of the amount of work that has been completed on an activity or a work breakdown structure component.

Perform Integrated Change Control [Process]. The process of reviewing all change requests, approving changes, and managing changes to the deliverables, organizational process assets, project documents, and project management plan.

Performance Measurement Baseline. An approved integrated scope-schedule-cost plan for the project work against which project execution is compared to measure and manage performance. Technical and quality parameters may also be included.

Performance Reports [Output/Input]. Documents and presentations that provide organized and summarized work performance information, earned value management parameters and calculations, and analyses of project work progress and status.

Performance Reviews. A technique that is used to measure, compare, an analyze actual performance of work in progress on the project against the baseline.

Performing Organization. The enterprise whose personnel are most directly involved in doing the work of the project.

Perform Qualitative Risk Analysis [Process]. The process of prioritizing risks for further analysis or action by assessing and combining their probability of occurrence and impact.

Perform Quality Assurance [Process]. The process of auditing the quality requirements and the results from quality control measurements to ensure appropriate quality standards and operational definitions are used.

Perform Quantitative Risk Analysis [Process]. The process of numerically analyzing the effect of identified risks on overall project objectives.

Phase. See project phase.

Phase Gate. A review at the end of a phase in which a decision is made to continue to the next phase, to continue with modification, or to end a project or program.

Plan Communications Management [Process]. The process of determining project stakeholder information needs and defining a communication approach.

Plan Cost Management. The process of defining how the project costs will be estimated, budgeted, managed, monitored, and controlled.

Planned Value (PV). The authorized budget assigned to scheduled work.

Planning Package. A work breakdown structure component below the control account with known work content but without detailed schedule activities. See also control account.

Planning Process Group. Those processes required to establish the scope of the project, refine the objectives, and define the course of action required to attain the objectives that the project was undertaken to achieve.

Plan Procurement Management [Process]. The process of documenting project purchasing decisions, specifying the approach, and identifying potential sellers.

Plan Quality Management [Process]. The process of identifying quality requirements and/or standards for the project and product and documenting how the project will demonstrate compliance.

Plan Resource Management The process of defining how to estimate, acquire, manage, and utilize physical and team resources.

Plan Risk Management [Process]. The process of defining how to conduct risk management activities for a project.

Plan Risk Responses [Process]. The process of developing options and actions to enhance opportunities and to reduce threats to project objectives.

Plan Schedule Management. The process of establishing the policies, procedures, and documentation for planning, developing, managing, executing, and controlling the project schedule.

Plan Scope Management. The process of creating a scope management plan that documents how the project and product scope will be defined, validated, and controlled.

Plan Stakeholder Engagement. The process of developing approaches to involve project stakeholders, based on their needs, expectations, interests, and potential impact on the project.

Plurality. Decisions made by the largest block in a group, even if a majority is not achieved.

Policy. A structured pattern of actions adopted by an organization such that the organization's policy can be explained as a set of basic principles that govern the organization's conduct.

Portfolio. A collection of projects or programs and other work that are grouped together to facilitate effective management of that work to meet strategic business objectives. The projects or programs of the portfolio may not necessarily be interdependent or directly related.

Portfolio Management. The centralized management of one or more portfolios to achieve strategic objectives.

Practice. A specific type of professional or management activity that contributes to the execution of a process and that may employ one or more techniques and tools.

Precedence Diagramming Method (PDM) [Technique]. A schedule network diagramming technique in which schedule activities are represented by boxes (or nodes). Schedule activities are graphically linked by one or more logical relationships to show the sequence in which the activities are to be performed.

Precedence Relationship. The term used in the precedence diagramming method for a logical relationship. In current usage, however, precedence relationship, logical relationship, and dependency are widely used interchangeably, regardless of the diagramming method used. See also *logical relationship*.

Predecessor Activity. The schedule activity that determines when the logical successor activity can begin or end.

Preventive Action. A documented direction to perform an activity that can reduce the probability of negative consequences associated with project risks.

Probability and Impact Matrix [Tool]. A common way to determine whether a risk is considered low, moderate, or high by combining the two dimensions of a risk: its probability of occurrence and its impact on objectives if it occurs.

Procedure. An established method of accomplishing a consistent performance or result, a procedure typically can be described as the sequence of steps that will be used to execute a process.

Process. A systematic series of activities directed towards causing an end result such that one or more inputs will be acted upon to create one or more outputs.

Procurement Audits. The review of contracts and contracting processes for completeness, accuracy, and effectiveness.

Procurement Documents [Output/Input]. The documents utilized in bid and proposal activities, which include the buyer's Invitation for Bid, Invitation for Negotiations, Request for Information, Request for Quotation, Request for Proposal and seller's responses.

Procurement Documentation. All documents used in signing, executing, and closing an agreement. Procurement documentation may include documents predating the project.

Procurement Management Plan [Output/Input]. The document that describes how procurement processes from developing procurement documentation through contract closure will be managed.

Procurement Statement of Work. Describes the procurement item in sufficient detail to allow prospective sellers to determine if they are capable of providing the products, services, or results.

Procurement Strategy. The approach by the buyer to determine the project delivery method and the type of legally binding agreement(s) that should be used to deliver the desired results.

Product. An artifact that is produced, is quantifiable, and can be either an end item in itself or a component item. Additional words for products are material and goods. See also deliverable.

Product Analysis. For projects that have a product as a deliverable, it is a tool to define scope that generally means asking questions about a product and forming answers to describe the use, characteristics, and other relevant aspects of what is going to be manufactured.

Product Life Cycle. A collection of generally sequential, non-overlapping product phases whose name and number are determined by the manufacturing and control needs of the organization. The last product life cycle phase for a product is generally the product's retirement. Generally, a project life cycle is contained within one or more product life cycles.

Product Scope. The features and functions that characterize a product, service, or result.

Product Scope Description. The documented narrative description of the product scope.

Program. A group of related projects managed in a coordinated way to obtain benefits and control not available from managing them individually. Programs may include elements of related work outside of the scope of the discrete projects in the program.

Program Evaluation and Review Technique (PERT). A technique for estimating that applies a weighted average of optimistic, pessimistic, and most likely estimates when there is uncertainty with the individual activity estimates.

Program Management. The centralized coordinated management of a program to achieve the program's strategic objectives and benefits.

Progressive Elaboration [Technique]. Continuously improving and detailing a plan as more detailed and specific information and more accurate estimates become available as the project progresses, and thereby producing more accurate and complete plans that result from the successive iterations of the planning process.

Project. A temporary endeavor undertaken to create a unique product, service, or result.

Project Calendar. A calendar of working days or shifts that establishes those dates on which schedule activities are worked and nonworking days that determine those dates on which schedule activities are idle. Typically defines holidays, weekends, and shift hours. See also *resource calendar.*

Project Charter [Output/Input]. A document issued by the project initiator or sponsor that formally authorizes the existence of a project and provides the project manager with the authority to apply organizational resources to project activities.

Project Communications Management [Knowledge Area]. Project Communications Management includes the processes required to ensure timely and appropriate generation, collection, distribution, storage, retrieval, and ultimate disposition of project information.

Project Cost Management [Knowledge Area]. Project Cost Management includes the processes involved in estimating, budgeting, and controlling costs so that the project can be completed within the approved budget.

Project Funding Requirements. Forecast project costs to be paid that are derived from the cost baseline for total or periodic requirements, including projected expenditures plus anticipated liabilities.

Project Governance. The framework, functions, and processes that guide project management activities in order to create a unique product, service, or result to meet organizational, strategic, and operational goals.

Project Initiation. Launching a process that can result in the authorization of a new project.

Project Integration Management [Knowledge Area]. Project Integration Management includes the processes and activities needed to identify, define, combine, unify, and coordinate the various processes and project management activities within the Project Management Process Groups.

Project Life Cycle. A collection of generally sequential project phases whose name and number are determined by the control needs of the organization or organizations involved in the project. A life cycle can be documented with a methodology.

Project Management. The application of knowledge, skills, tools, and techniques to project activities to meet the project requirements.

Project Management Body of Knowledge. An inclusive term that describes the sum of knowledge within the profession of project management. As with other professions, such as law, medicine, and accounting, the body of knowledge rests with the practitioners and academics that apply and advance it. The complete project management body of knowledge includes proven traditional practices that are widely applied and innovative practices that are emerging in the profession. The body of knowledge includes both published and unpublished materials. This body of knowledge is constantly evolving. PMI's *PMBOK® Guide* identifies that subset of the project management body of knowledge that is generally recognized as good practice.

Project Management Information System (PMIS) [Tool]. An information system consisting of the tools and techniques used to gather, integrate, and disseminate the outputs of project management processes. It is used to support all aspects of the project from initiating through closing, and can include both manual and automated systems.

Project Management Knowledge Area. An identified area of project management defined by its knowledge requirements and described in terms of its component processes, practices, inputs, outputs, tools, and techniques.

Project Management Office (PMO). An organizational body or entity assigned various responsibilities related to the centralized and coordinated management of those projects under its domain. The responsibilities of a PMO can range from providing project management support functions to actually being responsible for the direct management of a project.

Project Management Plan [Output/Input]. A formal, approved document that defines how the project is executed, monitored, and controlled. It may be a summary or detailed and may be composed of one or more subsidiary management plans and other planning documents.

Project Management Process Group. A logical grouping of project management inputs, tools and techniques, and outputs. The Project Management Process Groups include initiating processes, planning processes, executing processes, monitoring and controlling processes, and closing processes. Project Management Process Groups are not project phases.

Project Management System. The aggregation of the processes, tools, techniques, methodologies, resources, and procedures, to manage a project.

Project Management Team. The members of the project team who are directly involved in project management activities. On some smaller projects, the project management team may include virtually all of the project team members.

Project Manager (PM). The person assigned by the performing organization to achieve the project objectives.

Project Organization Chart [Output/Input]. A document that graphically depicts the project team members and their interrelationships for a specific project.

Project Phase. A collection of logically related project activities, usually culminating in the completion of a major deliverable. Project phases are mainly completed sequentially but can overlap in some project situations. A project phase is a component of a project life cycle. A project phase is not a Project Management Process Group.

Project Procurement Management [Knowledge Area]. Project Procurement Management includes the processes to purchase or acquire the products, services, or results needed from outside the project team to perform the work.

Project Quality Management [Knowledge Area]. Project Quality Management includes the processes and activities of the performing organization that determine quality policies, objectives, and responsibilities so that the project will satisfy the needs for which it was undertaken.

Project Resource Management [Knowledge Area]. Project Resource Management includes the processes to identify, acquire, and manage the resources needed for the successful completion of the project.

Project Risk Management [Knowledge Area]. Project Risk Management includes the processes concerned with conducting risk management planning, identification, analysis, responses, and monitoring and control on a project.

Project Schedule [Output/Input]. The planned dates for performing schedule activities and the planned dates for meeting schedule milestones.

Project Schedule Management [Knowledge Area]. Project Schedule Management includes the processes required to manage the timely completion of the project.

Project Schedule Network Diagram [Output/Input]. Any schematic display of the logical relationships among the project schedule activities. Always drawn from left to right to reflect project work chronology.

Project Scope. The work that must be performed to deliver a product, service, or result with the specified features and functions.

Project Scope Management [Knowledge Area]. Project Scope Management includes the processes required to ensure that the project includes all the work required, and only the work required, to complete the project successfully.

Project Scope Statement [Output/Input]. The narrative description of the project scope, including major deliverables, project assumptions, project constraints, and a description of work, that provides a documented basis for making future project decisions and for confirming or developing a common understanding of project scope among the stakeholders.

Project Stakeholder Management [Knowledge Area]. Project Risk Management includes the processes required to identify the people, groups, or organizations that could impact or be impacted by the project, to analyze stakeholder expectations and their impact on the project, and to develop appropriate management strategies for effectively engaging stake holders in project decisions and execution.

Project Team. A set of individuals who support the project manager in performing the work of the project to achieve its objectives. See also Project Management Team.

Project Team Directory. A documented list of project team members, their project roles, and communication information.

Proposal Evaluation Techniques. The process of reviewing proposals provided by suppliers to support contract award decisions.

Prototypes. A method of obtaining early feedback on requirement by providing a working model of the expected product before actually building it.

Quality. The degree to which a set of inherent characteristics fulfills requirements.

Quality Audits. A quality audit is a structured, independent process to determine if project activities comply with organizational and project policies, processes, and procedures.

Quality Checklists. A structured tool used to verify that a set of required steps has been performed.

Quality Control Measurements. The documented results of control quality activities.

Quality Management Plan [Output/Input]. The quality management plan describes how the project management team will implement the performing organization's quality policy. The quality management plan is a component or a subsidiary plan of the project management plan.

Quality Management System. The organizational framework whose structure provides the policies, processes, procedures, and resources required to implement the quality management plan. The typical project quality management plan should be compatible to the organization's quality management system.

Quality Metrics. A description of a project or product attribute and how to measure it.

Quality Policy. A policy specific to the Project Quality Management Knowledge Ares, it establishes the basic principles that should govern the organization's actions as it implements its system for quality management.

Quality Report. A project document that includes quality management issues, recommendations for corrective actions, and a summary of findings from quality control activities and may include recommendations for process, project, and product improvements.

Quality Requirement. A condition or capability that will be used to assess conformance by validating the acceptability of an attribute for the quality of a result.

Questionnaires. Written sets of questions designed to quickly accumulate information from a large number of respondents.

RACI Chart. A common type of responsibility assignment matrix that uses responsible, accountable, consult, and inform statuses to define the involvement of stakeholders in project activities.

Regression Analysis. An analytical technique where a series of input variables ae examined in relation to their corresponding output results in order to develop a mathematical or statistical relationship.

Regulations. Requirements imposed by a governmental body. These requirements can establish product, process, or service characteristics, including applicable administrative provisions that have government-mandated compliance

Request for Information (RFI). A type of procurement document whereby the buyer requests a potential seller to provide various pieces of information related to a product or service or seller capability.

Request for Proposal (RFP). A type of procurement document used to request proposals from prospective sellers of products or services. In some application areas, it may have a narrower or more specific meaning.

Request for Quotation (RFQ). A type of procurement document used to request price quotations from prospective sellers of common or standard products or services. Sometimes used in place of request for proposal and in some application areas, it may have a narrower or more specific meaning.

Requirement. A condition or capability that must be met or possessed by a system, product, service, result, or component to satisfy a contract, standard, specification, or other formally imposed document. Requirements include the quantified and documented needs, wants, and expectations of the sponsor, customer, and other stakeholders.

Requirements Documentation. A description of how individual requirements meet the business need for the project.

Requirements Management Plan. A component of the project or program management plan that describes how requirements will be analyzed, documented, and managed.

Requirements Traceability Matrix. A table that links requirements to their origin and traces them throughout the project life cycle.

Reserve. A provision in the project management plan to mitigate cost and/or schedule risk. Often used with a modifier (e.g., management reserve, contingency reserve) to provide further detail on what types of risk are meant to be mitigated.

Reserve Analysis [Technique]. An analytical technique to determine the essential features and relationships of components in the project management plan to establish a reserve for the schedule duration, budget, estimated cost, or funds for a project.

Residual Risk. A risk that remains after risk responses have been implemented.

Resource. Skilled human resources (specific disciplines either individually or in crews or teams), equipment, services, supplies, commodities, material, budgets, or funds.

Resource Breakdown Structure. A hierarchical structure of resources by resource category and resource type used in resource leveling schedules and to develop resource-limited schedules, and which may be used to identify and analyze project human resource assignments.

Resource Calendar. A calendar of working days and nonworking days that determines those dates on which each specific resource is idle or can be active. Typically defines resource specific holidays and resource availability periods. See also *project calendar.*

Resource Histogram. A bar chart showing the amount of time that a resource is scheduled to work over a series of time periods.

Resource Leveling [Technique]. Any form of schedule network analysis in which scheduling decisions (start and finish dates) are driven by resource constraints (e.g., limited resource availability or difficult-to-manage changes in resource availability levels).

Resource Management Plan. A component of the project management plan that describes how project resources are acquired, allocated, monitored, and controlled.

Resource Manager. An individual with management authority over one or more resources.

Resource Optimization Technique. A technique in which activity start and finish dates are adjusted to balance demand for resources with the available supply. See also resource leveling and resource smoothing.

Resource Requirements. The types and quantities of resources required for each activity in a work package.

Resource Smoothing. A resource optimization technique in which free and total float are used without affecting the critical path. See also resource leveling and resource optimization technique.

Responsibility. An assignment that can be delegated within a project management plan such that the assigned resource incurs a duty to perform the requirements of the assignment.

Responsibility Assignment Matrix (RAM) [Tool]. A structure that relates the project organizational breakdown structure to the work breakdown structure to help ensure that each component of the project's scope of work is assigned to a person or team.

Result. An output from performing project management processes and activities. Results include outcomes (e.g., integrated systems, revised process, restructured organization, tests, trained personnel, etc.) and documents (e.g., policies, plans, studies, procedures, specifications, reports, etc.). See also deliverable.

Rework. Action taken to bring a defective or nonconforming component into compliance with requirements or specifications.

Risk. An uncertain event or condition that, if it occurs, has a positive or negative effect on a project's objectives.

Risk Acceptance [Technique]. A risk response planning technique that indicates that the project team has decided not to change the project management plan to deal with a risk or is unable to identify any other suitable response strategy.

Risk Appetite. The degree of uncertainty of an organization or individual is willing to accept in anticipation of a reward.

Risk Audit. A type of audit used to consider the effectiveness of the risk management process.

Risk Avoidance [Technique]. A risk response planning technique for a threat that creates changes to the project management plan that are meant to either eliminate the risk or to protect the project objectives from its impact.

Risk Breakdown Structure (RBS) [Tool]. A hierarchically organized depiction of the identified project risks arranged by risk category and subcategory that identifies the various areas and causes of potential risks. The risk breakdown structure is often tailored to specific project types.

Risk Categorization. Organization by sources of risk (e.g., using the RBS), the area of the project affected (e.g., using the WBS), or other useful category (e.g., project phase) to determine the areas of the project most exposed to the effects of uncertainty.

Risk Category. A group of potential causes of risk. Risk causes may be grouped into categories such as technical, external, organizational, environmental, or project management. A category may include subcategories such as technical maturity, weather, or aggressive estimating.

Risk Data Quality Assessment. Technique to evaluate the degree to which the data about risks is useful for risk management.

Risk Enhancement. A risk response strategy whereby the project team acts to increase the probability of occurrence or impact of an opportunity.

Risk Escalation. A risk response strategy whereby the team acknowledges that a risk is outside of its sphere of influence and shifts the ownership of the risk to a higher level of the organization where it is more effectively managed.

Risk Exploiting. A risk response strategy whereby the project team acts to ensure that an opportunity occurs.

Risk Exposure. An aggregate measure of the potential impact of all risks at any given point in time in a project, program, or portfolio.

Risk Management Plan [Output/Input]. The document describing how project risk management will be structured and performed on the project. It is contained in or is a subsidiary plan of the project management plan. Information in the risk management plan varies by application area and project size. The risk management plan is different from the risk register that contains the list of project risks, the results of risk analysis, and the risk responses.

Risk Mitigation [Technique]. A risk response planning technique associated with threats that seek to reduce the probability of occurrence or impact of a risk to below an acceptable threshold.

Risk Owner. The person responsible for monitoring the risks and for selecting and implementing an appropriate risk response strategy.

Risk Register [Output/Input]. The document containing the results of the qualitative risk analysis, quantitative risk analysis, and risk response planning. The risk register details all identified risks, including description, category, cause, probability of occurring, impact(s) on objectives, proposed responses, owners, and current status.

Risk Report. A project document developed progressively throughout the Project Risk Management processes, which summarizes information on individual project risks and the level of overall project risks.

Risk Review. A meeting to examine and document the effectiveness of risk responses in dealing with overall project risk and with identified individual project risks.

Risk Sharing. A risk response strategy whereby the project team allocates ownership of an opportunity to a third party who is best able to capture the benefit of that opportunity.

Risk Threshold. The level of risk exposure above which risks re addressed and below which risks may be accepted.

Risk Tolerance. The degree, amount, or volume of risk that an organization or individual will withstand.

Risk Transference [Technique]. A risk response planning technique that shifts the impact of a threat to a third party, together with ownership of the response.

Role. A defined function to be performed by a project team member, such as testing, filing, inspecting, or coding.

Rolling Wave Planning [Technique]. A form of progressive elaboration planning where the work to be accomplished in the near term is planned in detail at a low level of the work breakdown structure, while the work far in the future is planned at a relatively high level of the work breakdown structure, but the detailed planning of the work to be performed within another one or two periods in the near future is done as work is being completed during the current period.

Root Cause Analysis [Technique]. An analytical technique used to determine the basic underlying reason that causes a variance or a defect or a risk. A root cause may underlie more than one variance or defect or risk.

Schedule. See project schedule ad schedule model

Schedule Baseline. A specific version of the schedule model used to compare actual results to the plan to determine if preventive or corrective action is needed to meet the project objectives.

Schedule Compression [Technique]. Shortening the project schedule duration without reducing the project scope. See also *crashing* and *fast tracking.*

Schedule Data. The collection of information for describing and controlling the schedule.

Schedule Forecasts. Estimates or predictions of conditions and events in the project's future based on information and knowledge available at the time the schedule is calculated.

Schedule Management Plan [Output/Input]. The document that establishes criteria and the activities for developing and controlling the project schedule. It is contained in, or is a subsidiary plan of, the project management plan.

Schedule Model [Tool]. A model used in conjunction with manual methods or project management software to perform schedule network analysis to generate the project schedule for use in managing the execution of a project. See also *project schedule.*

Schedule Network Analysis [Technique]. The technique of identifying early and late start dates, as well as early and late finish dates, for the uncompleted portions of project schedule activities. See also *critical path method, critical chain method,* and *resource leveling.*

Schedule Performance Index (SPI). A measure of schedule efficiency on a project. It is the ratio of earned value (EV) to planned value (PV). The SPI = EV divided by PV.

Schedule Variance (SV). A measure of schedule performance on a project. It is the difference between the earned value (EV) and the planned value (PV). SV = EV minus PV.

Scheduling Tool. A tool that provides schedule component names, definitions, structural relationships, and formats that support the application of a scheduling method.

Scope. The sum of the products, services, and results to be provided as a project. See also *project scope* and *product scope.*

Scope Baseline. An approved specific version of the detailed scope statement, work breakdown structure (WBS), and it's associated WBS dictionary.

Scope Change. Any change to the project scope. A scope change almost always requires an adjustment to the project cost or schedule.

Scope Creep. Adding features and functionality (project scope) without addressing the effects on time, costs, and resources, or without customer approval.

Scope Management Plan [Output/Input]. The document that describes how the project scope will be defined, developed, and verified and how the work breakdown structure will be created and defined, and that provides guidance on how the project scope will be managed and controlled by the project management team. It is contained in or is a subsidiary plan of the project management plan.

S-Curve. Graphic display of cumulative costs, labor hours, percentage of work, or other quantities, plotted against time. Used to depict planned value, earned value, and actual cost of project work. The name derives from the S-like shape of the curve (flatter at the beginning and end, steeper in the middle) produced on a project that starts slowly, accelerates, and then tails off. Also, a term used to express the cumulative likelihood distribution that is a result of a simulation, a tool of quantitative risk analysis.

Secondary Risk. A risk that arises as a direct result of implementing a risk response.

Self-Organizing Teams. A team formation where the team functions with an absence of centralized control.

Seller. A provider or supplier of products, services, or results to an organization.

Seller Proposals. Formal responses from sellers to a request for proposal or other procurement document specifying the price, commercial terms of sale, and technical specifications or capabilities the seller will do for the requesting organization that, if accepted, would bind the seller to perform the resulting agreement.

Sensitivity Analysis. A quantitative risk analysis and modeling technique used to help determine which risks have the most potential impact on the project. It examines the extent to which the uncertainty of each project element affects the objective being examined when all other uncertain elements are held at their baseline values. The typical display of results is in the form of a tornado diagram.

Sequence Activities [Process]. The process of identifying and documenting relationships among the project activities.

Service Level Agreement (SLA). A contract between a service provider (either internal or external) and the end user that defines the level of service expected from the service provider.

Simulation. A simulation uses a project model that translates the uncertainties specified at a detailed level into their potential impact on objectives that are expressed at the level of the total project. Project simulations use computer models and estimates of risk, usually expressed as a probability distribution of possible costs or durations at a detailed work level and are typically performed using Monte Carlo analysis.

Source Selection Criteria. A set of attributes desired by the buyer which a seller is required to meet or exceed to be selected for contract.

Specification. A precise statement of the needs to be satisfied and the essential characteristics that are required.

Specification Limits. The area, on either side of the centerline, or mean, of data plotted on a control chart that meets the customer's requirements for a product or service. This area may be greater than or less than the area defined by the control limits. See also control limits.

Sponsor. The person or group that provides the financial resources, in cash or in kind, for the project.

Sponsoring Organization. The entity responsible for providing the project's sponsor and a conduit for project funding or other project resources.

Stakeholder. Person or organization (e.g., customer, sponsor, performing organization, or the public) that is actively involved in the project, or whose interests may be positively or negatively affected by execution or completion of the project. A stakeholder may also exert influence over the project and its deliverables.

Stakeholder Analysis. A technique of systematically gathering and analyzing quantitative and qualitative information to determine whose interests should be taken into account throughout the project.

Stakeholder Engagement Assessment Matrix. A matrix that compares current and desired stakeholder engagement levels.

Stakeholder Engagement Plan. A component of the project management plan that identifies the strategies and actions required to promote productive involvement of stakeholders in project or program decision making and execution.

Stakeholder Register. A project document including the identification, assessment, and classification of project stakeholders.

Standard. A document established by an authority, custom, or general consent as a model or example.

Start Date. A point in time associated with a schedule activity's start, usually qualified by one of the following: actual, planned, estimated, scheduled, early, late, target, baseline, or current.

Start-to-Finish (SF). The logical relationship where completion of the successor schedule activity is dependent upon the initiation of the predecessor schedule activity. See also *logical relationship*.

Start-to-Start (SS). The logical relationship where initiation of the work of the successor schedule activity depends upon the initiation of the work of the predecessor schedule activity. See also *logical relationship*.

Statement of Work (SOW). A narrative description of products, services, or results to be supplied.

Statistical Sampling. Choosing part of a population of interest for inspection.

Successor Activity. A dependent activity that logically comes after another activity in a schedule.

Summary Activity A group of related schedule activities aggregated and displayed as a single activity.

Strengths, Weaknesses, Opportunities, and Threats (SWOT) Analysis. This information gathering technique examines the project from the perspective of each project's strengths, weaknesses, opportunities, and threats to increase the breadth of the risks considered by risk management.

Tacit Knowledge. Personal knowledge that can be difficult to articulate and share such as beliefs, experience, and insights.

Tailoring. Determining the appropriate combination of processes, inputs, tools, techniques, outputs, and life cycle phases to manage a project.

Team Charter. A document that records the team values, agreements, and operating guidelines, as well as establishing clear expectations regarding acceptable behavior by project team members.

Team Management Plan. A component of the resource management plan that describes when and how team members will be acquired and how long they will be needed.

Technique. A defined systematic procedure employed by a human resource to perform an activity to produce a product or result or deliver a service, and that may employ one or more tools.

Template. A partially complete document in a predefined format that provides a defined structure for collecting, organizing, and presenting information and data.

Test and evaluation Documents. Project documents that describe the activities used to determine if the product meets the quality objectives stated in the quality management plan.

Threat. A condition or situation unfavorable to the project, a negative set of circumstances, a negative set of events, a risk that will have a negative impact on a project objective if it occurs, or a possibility for negative changes. Contrast with *opportunity*.

Three-Point Estimate [Technique]. An analytical technique that uses three cost or duration estimates to represent the optimistic, most likely, and pessimistic scenarios. This technique is applied to improve the accuracy of the estimates of cost or duration when the underlying activity or cost component is uncertain.

Threshold. A cost, time, quality, technical, or resource value used as a parameter, and which may be included in product specifications. Crossing the threshold should trigger some action, such as generating an exception report.

Time and Material (T&M) Contract. A type of contract that is a hybrid contractual arrangement containing aspects of both cost-reimbursable and fixed-price contracts. Time and material contracts resemble cost-reimbursable type arrangements in that they have no definitive end, because the full value of the arrangement is not defined at the time of the award. Thus, time and material contracts can grow in contract value as if they were cost-reimbursable-type arrangements. Conversely, time and material arrangements can also resemble fixed-price arrangements. For example, the unit rates are preset by the buyer and seller, when both parties agree on the rates for the category of senior engineers.

To-Complete Performance Index (TCPI). The calculated projection of cost performance that must be achieved on the remaining work to meet a specified management goal, such as the budget at completion (BAC) or the estimate at completion (EAC). It is the ratio of "remaining work" to the "funds remaining."

Tolerance. The quantified description of acceptable variation for a quality requirement.

Tool. Something tangible, such as a template or software program, used in performing an activity to produce a product or result.

Tornado Diagram. A special type of bar chart used in sensitivity analysis for comparing the relative importance of the variables.

Total Float. The total amount of time that a schedule activity may be delayed from its early start date without delaying the project finish date or violating a schedule constraint. Calculated using the critical path method technique and determining the difference between the early finish dates and late finish dates. See also *free float*.

Trend Analysis [Technique]. An analytical technique that uses mathematical models to forecast future outcomes based on historical results. It is a method of determining the variance from a baseline of a budget, cost, schedule, or scope parameter by using prior progress reporting periods' data and projecting how much that parameter's variance from baseline might be at some future point in the project if no changes are made in executing the project.

Trigger Condition. An event or situation that indicates that a risk is about to occur.

Unanimity. Agreement by everyone in the group on a single course of action.

Update. A modification to any deliverable, project management plan component, or project document that is not under formal change control.

Validate Scope. The process of formalizing acceptance of the completed project deliverables.

Validation. The assurance that a product, service, or result meets the needs of the customer and other identified stakeholders, Contrast with verification.

Variance. A quantifiable deviation, departure, or divergence away from a known baseline or expected value.

Variance Analysis [Technique]. A method for resolving the total variance in the set of scope, cost, and schedule variables into specific component variances that are associated with defined factors affecting the scope, cost, and schedule variables.

Variance at Completion (VAC). A projection of the amount of budget deficit or surplus, expressed as the difference between the budget at completion and the estimate at completion.

Variation. An actual condition that is different from the expected condition that is contained in the baseline plan.

Verification. The evaluation of whether or not a product, service, or result complies with a regulation, requirement, specification, or imposed condition. Contrast with validation.

Verified Deliverables. Completed project deliverables that have been checked and confirmed for correctness through the control quality process.

Virtual Team. A group of persons with a shared objective who fulfill their roles with little or no time spent meeting face to face. Various forms of technology are often used to facilitate communication among team members. Virtual teams can be comprised of persons separated by great distances.

Voice of the Customer. A planning technique used to provide products, services, and results that truly reflect customer requirements by translating those customer requirements into the appropriate technical requirements for each phase of project product development.

What-If Scenario Analysis. The process of evaluating scenarios in order to predict their effect on project objectives.

Work Breakdown Structure (WBS) [Output/Input]. A deliverable-oriented hierarchical decomposition of the work to be executed by the project team to accomplish the project objectives and create the required deliverables. It organizes and defines the total scope of the project.

Work Breakdown Structure Component. An entry in the work breakdown structure that can be at any level.

Work Breakdown Structure Dictionary [Output/Input]. A document that describes each component in the work breakdown structure (WBS). For each WBS component, the WBS dictionary includes a brief definition of the scope or statement of work, defined deliverable(s), a list of associated activities, and a list of milestones. Other information may include: responsible organization, start and end dates, resources required, an estimate of cost, charge number, contract information, quality requirements, and technical references to facilitate performance of the work.

Work Package. A deliverable or project work component at the lowest level of each branch of the work breakdown structure. See also *control account*.

Work Performance Data. The raw observations and measurements identified during activities being performed to carry out the project work.

Work Performance Information [Output/Input]. Information and data, on the status of the project schedule activities being performed to accomplish the project work, collected as part of the direct and manage project work processes. Information includes: status of deliverables; implementation status for change requests, corrective actions, preventive actions, and defect repairs; forecasted estimates to complete; reported percent of work physically completed; achieved value of technical performance measures; start and finish dates of schedule activities.

Workaround [Technique]. A response to a negative risk that has occurred. Distinguished from contingency plan in that a workaround is not planned in advance of the occurrence of the risk event.

Work Performance Reports. The physical or electronic representation of work performance information compiled in project documents, intended to generate decisions, actions, or awareness.

These definitions are taken from the Glossary of Project Management Institute, A Guide to the Project Management Body of Knowledge, (PMBOK® Guide) – Sixth Edition, Project Management Institute Inc., 2017.

Appendix G

Index

Additional Resources

PMP Flashcards

The ideal complement to your PMP Exam preparation. These supplemental flashcards are contained in a convenient spiral bound format. Contents include:

- Over 350 concepts and terms organized by process groups
- Project Context
- Initiating
- Planning
- Executing
- Monitoring & Controlling
- Closing
- Professional & Social Responsibility

PMP Pocket Guide

Build your exam preparation confidence with this exceptional PMP quick reference study guide. This supplemental tool is a key weapon in your PMP exam preparation arsenal. The concise summaries of all of the important concepts are essential to passing the PMP exam. Includes:

- The PMBOK® Guide Framework
- Descriptions of all 49 processes
- Full list of the inputs, tools & techniques, and outputs (ITTOs)
- Important "must-know" sequences
- Key topics such as critical path method, estimating techniques, and earned value

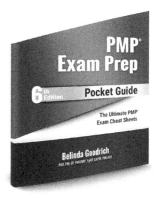

- The ultimate dump sheet
- Application process and timeline
- Summary sheets for all 10 knowledge areas
- Exam tips and exam day experience
- The 7 Deadly Sins of Exam Preparation

PM Learning Solutions, LLC – Exam Prep Boot Camp

PM Learning Solutions, LLC offers PMP Exam Prep Boot Camps that include our exclusive PMP Exam Pass Guarantee! To find your class, visit us on the web at:
https://www.pmlearningsolutions.com/classes/pmp-exam-prep

Made in the USA
Middletown, DE
09 January 2019